Commedia dell' Arte Performance in the Arena at Verona.
Marco Marcola's Oil Painting (1772).

A SOURCE BOOK

in

THEATRICAL HISTORY

(SOURCES OF THEATRICAL HISTORY)

By

A. M. NAGLER

DOVER PUBLICATIONS, INC.
NEW YORK

Published in Canada by General Publishing Company, Ltd., 30 Lesmill Road, Don Mills, Toronto, Ontario.
Published in the United Kingdom by Constable and Company, Ltd., 10 Orange Street, London WC 2.

This Dover edition, first published in 1959, is an unabridged, unaltered republication of the First Edition formerly titled *Sources of Theatrical History*. The publishers are grateful to Miss Blanche Corin of Theater Annual, Inc. for her cooperation.

Standard Book Number: 486-20515-0

Library of Congress Catalog Card Number: 58-59789

Manufactured in the United States of America
Dover Publications, Inc.
31 East 2nd Street
Mineola, N.Y. 11501

To
MY FATHER
and the memory
of
MY MOTHER

ACKNOWLEDGMENTS

The sections by Constantin Stanislavsky on pages 586 to 589 are from *My Life in Art* published by Theatre Arts Books, New York, reprinted by their permission. Copyright 1924 by Little Brown & Co., Copyright 1948 by Elizabeth Reynolds Hapgood, Attorney-in-fact for the Stanislavsky Estate.

The sections by August Strindberg on pages 583 to 586 are from *Plays by August Strindberg:* Miss Julia, The Stronger with the Author's Preface. Translated from the Swedish with an Introduction by Edwin Björkmann. Copyright 1912 by Charles Scribner's Sons; copyright renewal 1940 by Edwin Björkmann. Reprinted by permission of the publisher.

PREFACE

The theater historian is expected to reconstruct, both vividly and accurately, the conditions under which the plays of Sophocles, Corneille, Calderón, Lyly, Goldoni, Hebbel, or Gorky were first performed. And yet the very essence of the theater is absolute transitoriness. Scene designs, if not lost, are preserved only in the artist's original drawings which cannot be accepted as conclusive evidence as to the set's appearance on the stage; if a print of the actual set is preserved, it cannot faithfully convey the ephemeral impression made on contemporary audiences. Theater history deals with costumes that were burnt, with playhouses that have perished, with actors who made their final exits 2,500 years ago, with chandeliers that can be lit no more, and with audiences that have vanished. The theater historian's task approximates most closely that of the archaeologist, but he must also have at his command the methods of the art historian and the sociologist. He has to say something pertinent about a work of art which, being spatial and temporal, existed when he was not around to behold it. He finds himself in the unenviable position of the art historian who plans to evaluate the lost paintings of Polygnotus and Zeuxis.

Evidently, here is the point where the study of the sources of theatrical history comes in, the poring over scholia, letters, archival statistics, eyewitness accounts, prefaces, reviews, drawings, prints, etc. — sources, by the way, of very unequal value. For even today, when a performance is recorded in a dozen daily papers by either raving reviewers or post-mortem examiners, it is extremely difficult to point out enough objective material that will satisfy the ever-questioning scholar who may a hundred years hence attempt an authentic reconstruction of today's stage.

The word "stage" is used advisedly, for the documents crowded into the space of *Sources of Theatrical History* are removed from the drama as a form of literary expression. Here is a purely theatrical anthology, from the Greeks to the end of the nineteenth century (just before, thanks to Appia, Craig, and Reinhardt, things began to look brighter again in the theater), which has been assembled in the hope that a collection of primary sources will be a welcome tool for students of theatrical history. As survey courses have their limits, so this collection has had to be confined to certain climaxes in the development of the various national theaters. Many such volumes would have to be filled if a claim to completeness were to be made.

Here the student of the theater will find documents that are as well known as the Fortune contract or as Hazlitt's pen portraits of Kean's Gloucester, but also such recondite ones as the "Bios Aischylou" or the *Mercure*'s description of Servandoni's sets. Some among the three hundred selections appear in English for the first time. Each excerpt is preceded by an introduction which serves to establish the chronology and to set the scene for the entrance of the source itself.

The playgoer will watch the metamorphoses of Thespis with fascination; under the guidance of an academician, he will participate in a Renaissance revival of *Oedipus Rex* in the Teatro Olimpico, or witness, through the eyes of a Venetian diplomat, a masque performance at the court of James I, or enter, with Washington Irving, the first Park Theater in New York. Wherever he opens the volume, the theater of the past, with its period flavor, will come to life, and he will be bound to concede that the theater historian is not a person who has ceased to feel as a playgoer, but one who is amply rewarded when he can share the transient emotional experiences of former generations of spectators.

With only a few exceptions, the spelling and punctuation of the original sources have been faithfully preserved. Some obvious misprints, however, have been corrected.

It remains for me to express my gratitude to Miss Blanche A. Corin whose imagination turned what was a manuscript into a book, the pages of which make smoother reading thanks to her editorial criticism.

A.M.N.

Yale University

Easter, 1952

TABLE OF CONTENTS

V. TUDOR AND STUART PERIODS

VI. THE AGE OF LOUIS XIV

VII.   THE RESTORATION THEATER

VIII.   VENETIAN COMEDY

IX. EIGHTEENTH-CENTURY FRANCE

X. EIGHTEENTH-CENTURY ENGLAND

XI. WEIMAR CLASSICISM

XII. NINETEENTH-CENTURY ENGLAND

XIII. THE AMERICAN THEATER

XIV.   EUROPEAN NATURALISM

LIST OF ILLUSTRATIONS

INTRODUCTION

The idea of collecting materials for a history of the theater is part of our classical heritage. The earliest attempt dates back to the time of Augustus, when Juba II, King of Mauretania, compiled his seventeen-book *theatriké historia.* The greatest single blow sustained by our field of learning is the loss of Juba's work.

Theatrical history was an avocation for Juba II, on whom his contemporaries bestowed the honorific epithet *historicótatos,* signifying that he was the most historical-minded of all kings. By profession he was a statesman and a politician. Educated in Rome, he evidently learned how to meet influential people, for he accompanied Octavian on his sundry expeditions and married a daughter of Antony. On his return to Africa, he transformed the ancient Carthaginian seaport of Iol into a center of Hellenistic culture, while devoting himself to historical studies ranging from the geography of the Orient to the corruption of language. We may safely assume that he had a complete research staff working for him.

When King Juba was compiling his theatrical history, he had access to the primary sources of Greek and Roman stage practice. He must have had before him all pertinent source mate-- rial, the disappearance of which is responsible for our groping in the dark when we try to investigate the theater of antiquity. Juba must have read Agatharchus' own commentary on the design work he had done for Aeschylus; he must have been familiar with the treatises of Democritus and Anaxagoras on the use of perspective on the Greek stage; he must have abstracted the books on masks which Aristophanes of Byzantium had edited.

The wealth of information contained in Juba's theater history can still be appraised, though indirectly and often despairingly, by an attempt to decipher the few puzzling pages which Pollux, relying on Juba, wrote on the physical aspects and masks of the Greek theater.

In spite of the pioneering done by a king two thousand years ago, theatrical history was late in being recognized as a subject of academic learning. Only within the past fifty years has it been accepted as a branch of university instruction.

It is true that the nineteenth century contributed to our knowledge of earlier stage history, but it is rather obvious that the bulk of the biographies of players and monographs on the theatrical traditions of certain cities were more inspired by personal enthusiasm and local patriotism than guided by scholarship. However, certain books, such as Louis Schneider's history of the Berlin opera and Moritz Fürstenau's work on music and theater in Dresden, are remarkable studies which, based upon a sound knowledge of the sources, tower far above the dilettantism and anecdotism of their coeval pseudo-historians. By 1839, Germany even had two competing theater encyclopedias, which, while granting unjustifiable space to the playwrights, did present a survey of the physical aspects of the theater. Though we have to discard most of the material concerning the past in the encyclopedias of Blum-Herlosssohn-Marggraff and of Düringer-Barthels, we still find them invaluable in relation to the theatrical situation in the first half of the nineteenth century. On the other hand, the older French "theater" handbooks of the De Léris, the *frères* Parfaict, the Chamfort-de Laporte, and the Jal-Harel, with their copious play synopses and actors' anecdotes, can hardly claim to have increased our knowledge of theatrical history. In France, Arthur Pougin in his *Dictionnaire du théâtre* (1885) was the first to exclude the drama as a form of literature from his strictly theatrical encyclopedia. Pougin had discovered the right principle, but weakened the informational value of his tome by insisting that an encyclopedia must be a pleasure to read from A to Z. Here was an opening into which journalism easily slipped. Of course, an attempt at writing an encyclopedia of the theater in 1885 was premature, if not foolhardy. Eight years after Pougin, Germain Bapst published his *Essai sur l' histoire du théâtre,* which exhibited sound scholarship at least in the fields where Bapst had done extensive research of his own.

In 1901, an important event occurred in Germany. Professor Max Herrmann began his lectures and seminars on theater history at the University of Berlin. Till then, any investigation of theatrical history on an academic level had had to be undertaken within the framework of existing university departments, chiefly in the departments of German literature. Professor Herrmann envisaged the possibility of an autonomous department for the study of stage history, outside the older established divisions. The process of liberation was to be a slow one, with literature constantly encroaching upon the purely theatrical. In 1913, Herrmann was still complaining that an assemblage of people primarily interested in theatrical history were forced to listen to oratory on the dramatic structure of a Schiller play. It seems, indeed, that the confusion of theatrical history with dramatic history was already apparent in Juba's work. His articles on theatrical antiquities were interspersed with biographical material on playwrights who could hardly claim admittance into a history of the theater. Well, the confusion is still with us.

The principles formulated by Professor Herrmann have not lost their validity. In opposition to the general dilettantism of the nineteenth century, he called for philological exactitude: the facts must be ascertained before a synthesis can be made or even a pragmatic nexus established. Max Herrmann insisted that a method had to be developed that would allow for a scientific approach to theatrical facts. He himself did not write this methodology, but permitted a deduction of the principles of theatrical scholarship from his *Forschungen zur deutschen Theatergeschichte des Mittelalters und der Renaissance* (Berlin 1914). We are still waiting for a methodology, just as we are waiting for an aesthetics of the pre-naturalistic theater. In default, we can easily feel inclined to pity Molière because he had to put up with spectators on his stage, and regard it as progress if a stage director drags a donkey into the milling *Carmen* crowd.

Max Herrmann must have been highly gratified when, as a result of his stimulation, the Berlin Gesellschaft für Theatergeschichte was founded in 1902. To date the Gesellschaft has published fifty-five volumes dealing with German theater history. In this series students in the field have had an opportunity to see their research work published. Other serial publications, such as the *Theatergeschichtliche Forschungen* and *Die Schaubühne,* both dedicated exclusively to the propagation of knowledge of theater history, have followed.

While the German theater historian has had avenues to the public open to him since the beginning of our century, the French had to wait for an organized effort in this direction till 1932, when August Rondel, the great collector of theatrical materials, founded the Société d'histoire du théâtre in Paris. Between 1893 (Bapst) and 1932, the scholarly investigation of the theater (chiefly of the Middle Ages) had produced some standard French works. But the strongest impetus came, when, in 1933, the Société began to sponsor the *Bibliothèque* for theater historians, a series of theatrical monographs of which some volumes are truly excellent. In 1933, moreover, the Société began to publish the *Bulletin* which, in 1948, was converted into the more ambitious quarterly, *Revue d'histoire du théâtre.*

It is unfortunate that in the English language area there is still nothing comparable to either the German or the French efforts. In England, where during the past thirty years theater history has come into its own, the theatrical researcher must certainly wish that the present slender-sized *Theatre Notebook* could be expanded. In the United States we have no series of monographs set aside for theatrical research. Therefore we have to be the more thankful for the *Theatre Annual,* where students of the field, at least once a year, can find an outlet for their harvest. It is to be hoped that in the future the *Educational Theatre Journal* will allot more space to the historian. At any rate, the list of dissertations, published annually in the *Journal,* very strongly suggests the need for a series, endowed to be sure, of theatrical monographs through which justice could be done to the most distinguished dissertations. And there is the equally urgent need for a society of theater historians which, nationally and internationally, could represent this country's growing exertions in the field.

We do not know what prompted Juba II to delve into the theatrical past, but we have a clear conception of Herrmann's reasoning as he dedicated the major portion of his mature life to the fight for the academic recognition of theatrical history. Many German stage directors and *Dramaturgen* had received their academic training in the purely literary field, chiefly that of German literature. It is no wonder that the academic stage director was at a loss with regard to the production style which, let us say, Molière had given to his own plays, or that he was unaware of Lope de Vega's tortures when the playwright saw how his plays were overproduced after their transplantation from the *corrales* into the court atmosphere. A stage director is doomed when, without knowledge of the historical facts, he is called upon to adapt and produce a classical play for a modern audience. In handling the classics the director must be fully informed of the conditions of the original productions and of the cultural background against which the plays initially came to life. Herrmann fought for the idea that a stage director should have this sort of information, and one of his educational dreams must have been realized when first Copeau and then Jouvet became president of the Société d'histoire du théâtre. A glance into Barrault's production book for *Phèdre* will suffice to show how much the French director owed to the study of historical facts. (In contrast to Stanislavsky who evidently learned nothing from theatrical history, otherwise he could not have mangled *Othello* the way he did.) Herrmann was convinced that the historical-philological approach had to form the basis for the theater historian, but he also insisted that contact had to be maintained with the actual craftsmen of the theater of his day. Hence, he invited professional directors and actors for guest lectures in his Theaterwissenschaftliches Institut (since 1923), which became the pattern for similar institutes connected with the Universities of Munich, Frankfort, Kiel, Cologne, and Vienna. Max Herrmann, to be sure, never lost sight of the fact that his Institut was a part of a larger academic institution and that ultimately only a strictly scholarly path would lead to the goal.

A SOURCE BOOK IN THEATRICAL HISTORY

Chapter I

Antiquity

Oldest Form of the Dionysus Theater in Athens. Reconstruction by Ernst
Fiechter.
(In *Das Dionysus-Theater in Athen,* Stuttgart: W. Kohlhammer, 1936)

1. THESPIS MEETS A CRITIC

GREEK TRAGEDY had its roots in the choric dithyramb. Aristotle tells us this, and we have no reason to disbelieve his testimony; a Greek philosopher, lecturing on tragedy in the 320's B.C., was much closer to the decisive events than the modern scholar.

The genius who accomplished the transition from dithyramb to drama was Thespis of Icaria. Playwright, actor, stage director, and producer, all in one, Thespis is credited with a number of innovations. He is said to have connected the chorus with a plot; he seems to have evolved the protagonist (*hypokrités*, the "answerer"), destined to face a tragic dilemma and forced to answer the ever-questioning chorus; he discarded the cruder dithyrambic make-up by making use of unpainted linen masks; and, if we care to trust Horace, Thespis travelled about with a company of strolling players on a wagon.

Pisistratus, having seized the castle and power of Athens by a *coup d'état* in 560 B.C., decided to enlarge the artistic scope of the City Dionysia by including plays in the official program of the festival. He asked Thespis, the Attic peasant-artist, to participate with his troupe. The date was 534 B.C., though this hardly marks the first appearance of Thespis in Athens as, earlier, he may have participated in the Lenaea Festival.

On one such festive occasion, Solon, the legislator, came to witness one of Thespis' performances and afterward went to see the artist. Plutarch saved this oldest "backstage" scene from oblivion:

Thespis, at this time, beginning to act tragedies, and the thing, because it was new, taking very much with the multitude, though it was not yet made a matter of competition, Solon, being by nature fond of hearing and learning something new, and now, in his old age, living idly, and enjoying himself, indeed, with music and with wine, went to see Thespis himself, as the ancient custom was, act: and after the play was done, he addressed him, and asked him if he was not ashamed to tell so many lies before such a number of people; and Thespis replying that it was no harm to say or do so in play, Solon vehemently struck his staff against the ground: "Ah," said he, "if we honor and commend such play as this, we shall find it some day in our business."

2. AESCHYLUS—MAN OF THE THEATER

AESCHYLUS (525-4 B.C. - 456-5 B.C.) surpassed his predecessors and competitors not only as a dramatic poet but also as a theatrical showman. The following excerpts from an ancient biography record his theatrical accomplishments with enthusiasm. We must be aware, however, that the anonymous biographer compiled his account from rather spurious sources:

In his youth Aeschylus began to compose tragedies; in his poetry, in the brilliant mounting of his plays, in the costuming of his actors, and the magnificence of his choruses, he far surpassed his predecessors. As Aristophanes said in *The Frogs*: "But you, O first of the Greeks, erected noble phrases and embellished tragic trumpery."

A contemporary of Pindar, Aeschylus was born 525 years before our era. Of noble birth, he fought in the Battle of Marathon along with his brother, Cynegirus, and later in the Battle of Salamis with his oldest brother, Aminias. He also is supposed to have served in the Battle of Plataea.

In his writing he always tended toward vigor and loftiness of tone, employing onomatopoeia, epithets, metaphors, and anything that he felt might lend power to his verse. His dramatic structure, however, was quite simple in comparison with that of the younger dramatists since he indulged in fewer peripeties and plot complications. Sublimity meant everything to him. For this reason he concentrated on the grandeur and heroic elevation of his characters, considering it altogether outside the scope of the tragic playwright to portray seemingly ingenious and sententious rogues. Aristophanes made fun of Aeschylus for what he considered the excessive austerity of his characters: in the *Niobe,* even up to the third part, the mother sits by the tomb of her children restraining her feelings and not uttering a sound; likewise, in the *Ransoming of Hector,* Achilles completely suppresses his emotions and, save for a reply or two to Hermes in the beginning, has nothing to say. While one finds many different types of artistic treatment in Aeschylus, one looks in vain for those sentiments which draw tears. He uses his dramatic and scenic devices to evoke the stronger passions.

Aeschylus retired to Sicily, to the court of the tyrant Hieron, because, according to some, he was oppressed by the Athenians and defeated by the young Sophocles at the City Dionysia; according to others, because he was surpassed by Simonides in an elegy on those who fell in the Battle of Marathon. It is said that the elegy of Simonides excelled in subtlety of feeling.

When, at the performance of *The Eumenides,* Aeschylus introduced the chorus in wild disorder into the orchestra, he so terrified the crowd that children died and women suffered miscarriage.

While in Sicily, Aeschylus wrote a tragedy entitled *The Aetnaean Women,* in which he predicted prosperity for the city of Aetna, which had been recently founded by Hieron. He was greatly honored by the tyrant and later by the inhabitants of Gela, on the southwest coast of Sicily, where, being very old, he died. His death, however, was an accident. An eagle having seized a tortoise and not being master of his prey, dropped it against the rocks to crack the shell. It struck the poet and killed him. He had been warned of his fate by an oracle which declared: "A heavenly missile shall slay thee." The citizens of Gela buried him with great pomp in a civic monument, inscribing thereon an epitaph of the poet's own composing: "Here lies Aeschylus of Athens, son of Euphorion, who died in fertile Gela, and whose prowess the long-haired Mede experienced on the celebrated battlefield of Marathon." His tomb became an object of public veneration, while his tragedies as well as a dramatized version of his life were presented there. Indeed, so beloved was the poet that after his death the Athenians voted that anyone wishing to produce his plays should have a chorus. He lived sixty-nine years during which he wrote seventy tragedies and five satyric plays. He won about thirteen victories, and not a few of them after his death.

Aeschylus was the first to advance tragedy by means of a more exalted passion. He introduced scenic decorations — paintings, machinery, altars, tombs, trumpets, spirits, Furies — whose splendor delighted the eyes of the audience. He also supplied the actors with sleeved and full-length robes and heightened the buskins to increase their stature. Cleander was the first actor he employed. Later he added Mynniscus of Chalcis as his second. He was also the instigator of the third actor, though Sophocles is given the credit by Dicaearchus of Messene. If we compare the simplicity of Aeschylus' dramatic compositions with

those of his successors, they might be judged jejune and wanting
in elaborateness. But if we consider those preceding him, we may
well admire our poet for his great talent and inventiveness. Those
who hold that Sophocles was a greater tragic poet are right in
their opinion, but they should keep in mind that it was more
difficult, after Thespis, Phrynichus, and Choerilus, to elevate
tragedy to such heights of greatness than for one who wrote after
Aeschylus to arrive at the perfection of Sophocles.

3. AESCHYLEAN CHOREOGRAPHY

ADDITIONAL INFORMATION with regard to the stage director, Aeschylus,
may be drawn from *Deipnosophistai* (*The Banquet of the Learned*),
which the erudite Athenaeus compiled in the third century of the
Christian Era:

Aeschylus, too, besides inventing that comeliness and dignity
of dress which Hierophants and Torchbearers emulate when
they put on their vestments, also originated many dance-figures
and assigned them to the members of his choruses. For Chamaeleon says that Aeschylus was the first to give poses to his
choruses, employing no dancing-masters, but devising for himself the figures of the dance, and in general taking upon himself
the entire management of the piece. At any rate, it seems that
he acted in his own plays. For Aristophanes, certainly (and
among the comic poets one may find credible information about
the tragedians), makes Aeschylus say of himself: "It was I
who gave new poses to the choruses." And again: "I know about
his Phrygians, for I was in the audience when they came to help
Priam ransom his son who was dead. They made many gestures
and poses, this way and that way and the other." Telesis, also
(or Telestes), teacher of dancing, invented many figures, and
with great art illustrated the sense of what was spoken by
motions of his arms. Phillis, the musician of Delos, says that
the harp-singers of old allowed few movements of the face,
but more with the feet, both in marching and in dance steps.
Aristocles, therefore, says that Telestes, Aeschylus's dancer,
was so artistic that when he danced the *Seven against Thebes*
he made the action clear simply by dancing. They say, too, that

the old poets — Thespis, Pratinas, Cratinus, Phrynichus — were
called "dancers" because they not only relied upon the dancing
of the chorus for the interpretation of their plays, but, quite
apart from their own compositions, they taught dancing to all
who wanted instruction.

4.   SOPHOCLES—MUSICIAN AND DANCER

A GREEK PLAYWRIGHT-DIRECTOR of the fifth century B.C. would have
been lost without a sound training in music and dancing. Another excerpt
from Athenaeus' *Deipnosophistai* establishes Sophocles' (*ca.* 495 B.C. —
406 B.C.) proficiency in both arts:

Sophocles, besides being handsome in his youth, became
proficient in dancing and music, while still a lad, under the
instruction of Lamprus. After the battle of Salamis, at any rate,
he danced to the accompaniment of his lyre round the trophy,
naked and anointed with oil. Others say he danced with his
cloak on. And when he brought out the *Thamyris* he played
the lyre himself. He also played ball with great skill when he
produced the *Nausicaa*.

5.   EURIPIDES REHEARSING

EURIPIDES' (*ca.* 480 B.C. — *ca.* 407 B.C.) struggle with staging problems is suggested in an anecdote which Plutarch preserved:

Euripides the poet one day at a rehearsal instructing the
chorus in a part that was set to a serious air, one of the company
unexpectedly fell out a laughing. "Sir," said Euripides, "unless
you were very stupid and insensible, you could not laugh while
I sing in the grave Mixolydian Mode."

6.   POLLUX ON SCENES, MACHINES, AND MASKS

IN THE SECOND CENTURY of the present era, the Greek sophist and
grammarian, Iulius Pollux, compiled his encyclopedia, *Onomastikon,* excerpts from which have survived, among them the chapter on the

physical aspects of the Greek theater and the catalogue of tragic and comic masks. Pollux' main sources were the scholiasts and the seventeen books of King Juba's *Theatrical History*. No agreement has been reached as to the validity of Pollux' statements, and many of his descriptions have never been satisfactorily explained. We are not always sure whether he speaks of the theater of the Hellenistic or Periclean era, though his reference to the raised stage would indeed indicate that he is discussing the features of the Hellenistic theater:

The Parts of the Theater

The separate parts of the theater are a little gate, arch, apartment, wedges, scene, orchestra, stage, scene-area, scene-avenues, and scene-wings.

The actors occupied the scene, and chorus the orchestra; in which was the *thyméle,* being a sort of eminence, or altar; and in the scene likewise before the doors stood a consecrated altar, and table with seasoned cakes, called *theoris,* or holy table. Whereas the *eleos* was an ancient table, which before Thespis' time they used to get upon and reply to the choristers. Part of the scene-wings [*paraskénia*], that were in sight and joined to the stage-house [*skené*], was ornamented with columns and paintings [*pinakes*?]. Of the three scene-doors likewise the middle opened either into a palace, grotto, hall, or whatever was of first distinction in the play; the right-hand door was a retreat for the next in rank; and the left, which had a very miserable aspect, led to some desolate temple, or had no house.

In tragedy, strangers entered at the right-hand door; and the left was a prison. . . .

At each of the two doors, which stood in the middle, were likewise two others, on each side one, to which were fastened the wheel-machines [triangular prisms called *periaktoi*]; the right showing a prospect into the country, the left a distant view of the city; but chiefly for bringing things forward from the port, seagods, and whatever else was too unwieldy for the vehicle [*ekkyklema*] to bear. By turning the machine the right actually shifts the spot, and both of them change the prospect. Of the avenues too, the right leads from the country, port, or city; but persons, coming on foot from other parts, enter at the left; and crossing the orchestra, go up stairs into the scene; the stair-rows are called steps.

We must also reckon as parts of the theater the vehicle, chariot, machine, watch-tower, wall, turret, light-house, double-roof, lightning-tower, thunder, celestial scaffold, funeral-state-couch, semicircle, Charon's Steps and trap doors. The vehicle [*ekkyklema*] is an high seat, upon wooden steps, adjoining to which is a throne: it brings forth to view secret transactions in the subscenery apartments; and the term for this operation is wheeling out. . . . As for the scaffold [*mechané*] it shows gods and heroes that are in the air (such as Bellerophon and Perseus); and it is fixed at the left avenue aloft above the stage-house. . . .

The watch-tower was on purpose for watchmen or others who kept an observation. The wall and turret were likewise for a distant prospect. As for the light-house, its use is evident from the very name. But the double-roof was, on one occasion, either two separate apartments in a royal palace, such as from whence, in the tragedy, *Phoenissae* [by Euripides], Antigone views the army; and on another, a ridge for pelting with tiles. But the double-roof in comedy was a peeping place for procurers, or for any old or poor woman in the play to look down. The lightning-tower and thunder were, the former an high *periaktos,* and the other backwards under the *skené,* bags full of pebble-stones poured into a brazen vessel. From the celestial scaffold [*theologeion*] which is over the stage-house, appear the gods, Jupiter and those about him, all in deception. The crane [*géranos*] is a kind of *mechané* let down from above for taking up a body, the same which Aurora made use of in seizing the body of Memnon. The ropes which were let down from the upper parts for lifting up heroes or gods, who seemed to be carried in the air, you might call them fly tackles. The representation of scenery on the *periaktoi* was done either by means of tapestries or of painted panels [*pinakes*] with figures on them, adapted to the necessities of the play; and they were let down upon the *periaktoi,* representing either a mountain, the sea, a river, or any such thing. The semicircle is so called from its shape; the situation of it is in the orchestra, and its use to show afar off any particular place of the city or persons swimming in the sea. The funeral-state-couch [*stropheion*], in which were the heroes, shows those who are transformed to divinity or persons who had perished in a tempest or in war. Likewise Charon's Steps, situated at the avenues of the benches, are for the conveyance of ghosts. The *anapiesmata* [evidently trap doors] were partly in the stage-house for the lifting up of a river, or any such appearance, and partly round the stairs by which the furies were raised.

The Tragic Masks

Moreover with respect to masks: the tragic might be a smooth-faced man, a white, grisled, black-haired, flaxen, more flaxen, all of them old: and the smooth-faced oldest of these, having very white locks, and the hairs lying upon the prominence [*onkos*]. By prominence I mean the upper part of the countenance rising above the forehead, in shape of the Greek letter *lambda*. With respect to beard, the smooth-faced should be very closely shaven, and have thin lantern jaws. The white-haired is all hoary with bushy locks about the head, has an ample beard, jutting eyebrows, and the complexion almost white, but the *onkos* short. The grisled denotes the hoary hairs to be a mixture of black and grey. But the black-haired, deriving his name from the color, has a curled beard and hair, rough face and large prominence. The flaxen has yellowish bushy hair, lesser prominence, and is fresh-colored. The more flaxen has a sameness with the other, but is rather more pale to represent sick persons.

The young men's masks are the common, curled, more curled, graceful, horrid, second horrid, pale, less pale.

The common is eldest of the young men, beardless, fresh-colored, swarthy, having locks clustering, and black. The curled is yellow, blustering, with bushy hair encompassing a plump face, has arched eyebrows, and a fierce aspect. The more curled differs in nothing from the former but in being a little younger. The graceful has hyacinthian locks, fair skin, is lively, and of a pleasant countenance, fit for a beautiful Apollo. The horrid is robust, grim-visaged, sullen, deformed, yellow-haired — the yellow-haired attendant. The second horrid is so much more slender than the former, as he is younger; also an attendant. The pale is meager, with disheveled hair, and of such a sickly countenance as is suitable for a ghost or wounded person. The less pale is entirely like the common in every other respect except that it is made pale on purpose to express a sick man or a lover.

The slaves' masks are the leathern, peaked-beard, flat-nose.

The leathern having no *onkos*, has a fillet, and long white hairs, a pale whitish visage, and rough nostrils, an high crown, stern eyes; the beard a little pale, and looks older than his years. But the peaked-beard is in the vigor of life, has an high and broad prominence dented all round, is yellow-haired, rough, ruddy, and suited to a messenger. The flat-nose is bluff, yellow-headed, the locks hang on each side from the forelock; he is beardless, ruddy, and likewise delivers a message.

The women's masks are an hoary disheveled, a freed old woman, an old domestic, a middle-aged, a leathern, a pale disheveled, a pale middle-aged, a shaven virgin, second shaven virgin, girl.

The hoary disheveled, surpassing the rest, both in years and dignity, has white locks, a moderate *onkos*, is inclinable to paleness, and was anciently called the delicate. The freed old woman is of a tawny complexion and hoariness, having a small prominence; the tresses to the shoulders denote misfortune.

The old domestic, instead of prominence has a fillet of lamb's wool, and a wrinkled skin.

But the middle-aged domestic has a short prominence and white skin, is grey-haired, but not quite hoary.

The leathern, younger than her, and has not any prominence.

The pale disheveled has black hair, a dejected countenance, and her name from the color.

But the pale middle-aged is like the disheveled, except where she is shaven out of sight.

But the shaven virgin, instead of *onkos* wears a smooth-combed tate, is shaven almost quite round, and of a color inclinable to paleness.

And the other shaven virgin is perfectly like her, but without the tate and curls, as if she had been often in misfortunes.

The girl is a juvenile mask, such as Danaë might have been, or any other virgin.

The attendant masks are an horned Actaeon, a blind Phineus or Thamyris, one having a blue eye, the other a black; a many-eyed Argus, or Tyro with mottled cheeks, as in Sophocles, which she suffered from the blows of a cruel stepmother; or Euippe, Chiron's daughter, changed into a horse in Euripides; or Achilles disheveled when mourning for Patroclus; an Amymone, a river, mountain, Gorgon, Justice, Death, a fury, Madness, Guilt,

Menander in His Study. Marble Relief, Lateran.

In his left hand the poet is holding the mask of a young lover. On the table before him are the masks of a hetaera and of a choleric father. The woman standing is Glycera, the playwright's mistress.

Injury, centaur, titan, giant, Indian, Triton; perhaps also a
city, Priam, Persuasion, the Muses, Hours, nymphs of Mithaeus,
Pleiades, Deceit, Drunkenness, Idleness, Envy; which latter
might likewise be comic masks.

Satyric Masks

Satyric masks are an hoary satyr, bearded satyr, beardless
satyr, Grandfather Silenus. The other masks are all alike, unless
where the names themselves show a peculiar distinction, as the
Father Silenus has a more savage appearance.

Comic Masks

The comic masks, those especially of the Old Comedy, were
as like as possible to the persons they represented, or made to
appear more ridiculous. But those in the New Comedy were a
first grandfather, a second grandfather, governor, long-bearded,
or shaking old man, Ermoneus, peaked-beard, Lycomodeus, procurer, second Ermoneus, all of them old. The first grandfather
oldest, close-shaven, having very pleasant eyebrows, an ample
beard, lantern jaws, dim sight, white skin, comely face, and
forehead. The other grandfather is more slender, sharper-sighted,
morose, of a pale complexion, has an ample beard, red hair,
cropped ears. The governor, an old man, with a crown of hair
round his head, an ample beard, no elevation of the eyebrows,
dimmer sight. Ermoneus has a bald crown, ample beard, elevated
eyebrows, sharp sight. The procurer resembles Lycomodeus in
other respects, but has distorted lips and contracted eyebrows,
and either a bald crown or pate. The second Ermoneus is shaven
and has a peaked beard. Peaked-beard has a bald crown, elevated
eyebrows, sharp chin, and is morose. Lycomodeus has curled
beard, long chin, and extends one eyebrow representing curiosity.

The young men's masks are a common young man, a black
young man, a curled young man, a delicate, rustic, threatening,
a second flatterer, parasite, a fancied mask, Sicilian. The common is ruddy, athletic, swarthy, having few wrinkles upon his
forehead and a crown of hair, with elevated eyebrows. The black
young man is younger, with depressed eyebrows, like an educated
and accomplished youth. The curled young man is handsome,

young, ruddy, has his name from his hairs, his eyebrows extended, and one wrinkle on his forehead. The delicate young man is haired like the common and youngest of all, fair, educated in the nursery, showing delicacy. The rustic is weather-beaten, broad-lipped, flat-nosed, and has a crown of hair. But the threatening young man, who is a soldier and braggard, of black complexion, and tresses, his hairs shaking like the other threatener, who is more tender and yellow-haired. The flatterer and parasite are black, quite unpolished, cringing, sympathizing. The parasite's ears are more bruised, and he is more pleasant; the flatterer's eyebrows are disagreeably extended.

The fancied mask has cheeks bored and chin shaven, is superbly dressed, and a foreigner. The Sicilian is a third parasite.

The slave's comic masks are a grandfather, upper slave, thin-haired behind, bristly slave, a curled slave, a middle slave, foppish slave, shaking upper slave. The grandfather alone of all the slaves is hoary and shows the freeman. The upper slave wears a crown of red hair, elevates the eyebrows, contracts the forehead, and among slaves is like an aged governor among freedmen. The thin or bristly-haired behind, has a bald crown, red hair, and elevated eyebrows.

The curled slave has curled hairs, but they are red, as is likewise his color; he has a bald crown and distorted face, with two or three black curls, and the same on his chin; the shaking upper slave is like the upper slave, except in the hairs.

The women's masks are a thin old woman or prostitute; a fat old woman, a domestic old woman, either sedentary or active.

The prostitute is tall, with many small wrinkles, fair, palish, and with rolling eyes. The fat old woman has many wrinkles on a plump skin, and a fillet round her hair.

The domestic old woman is flat-faced, and in her upper jaw has two axle teeth, on each side one.

The young women's masks are a talkative, curled virgin, demimondaine, second demimondaine, hoary-talkative, concubine, common whore, beautiful courtesan, golden harlot, lampadion, virgin slave, and slut.

The talkative has full hair smoothed a little, high eyebrows, fair skin. The curled virgin has a distinction of false hair, high eyebrows, and black, and a pale whiteness in her skin. The demimondaine has a whiter skin, and her hair tied behind in a knot; would be thought a bride. The second demimondaine is known by the distinction of her hair only. The hoary-talkative indicates her person by the name; she shows the harlot left off trade. The concubine resembles her, but is full-haired. The common whore is higher colored than the demimondaine and has curls round her ears. The courtesan has least finery, and her head bound with a fillet. The golden harlot has much gold upon her hair. The mitered harlot has her head bound with a variegated miter. Lampadion has her hair platted in the form of a lamp. The virgin slave wears only a short white frock. The slut is distinguished by her hair, and is both squat, and, being dressed in a red gown, waits upon the courtesans.

7. SKEPTICAL VIEW OF TRAGIC CONVENTIONS

WHEN LUCIAN OF SAMOSATA, skeptic, cynic, and blasphemer, looked at Greek tragedy in the second century of the present era, he showed no understanding of the old theatrical conventions which had served the great tragedians of the fifth century B.C.:

In forming our estimate of tragedy, let us first consider its externals — the hideous, appalling spectacle that the actor presents. His high boots raise him up out of all proportion; his head is hidden under an enormous mask; his huge mouth gapes upon the audience as if he would swallow them; to say nothing of the chest-pads and stomach-pads with which he contrives to give himself an artificial corpulence, lest his deficiency in this respect should emphasize his disproportionate height. And in the middle of it all is the actor, shouting away, now high, now low, chanting his iambics as often as not; could anything be more revolting than this sing-song recitation of tragic woes? The actor is a mouthpiece: that is his sole responsibility; the poet has seen to the rest, ages since. From an Andromache or a Hecuba, one can endure recitative: but when Heracles himself comes upon the stage, and so far forgets himself, and the respect due to the lion-skin and club that he carries, as to deliver a solo, no reasonable person can deny that such a performance is in execrable taste.

The Dionysus Theater in Athens Today.

8. EARLY ROMAN THEATRICALS

THE INDIGENOUS ROOTS of the Roman theater are a highly controversial subject. However, we are on rather safe ground when we turn to Book VII, Chapter 2 of Livy's history, where he speaks of the introduction of Etruscan mimetic dances in Rome (364 B.C.) and the beginning of the adaptation work of Livius Andronicus, who, in 240 B.C. on the occasion of the Roman Games (*Ludi Romani*), produced the first Latin translations (*fabulae palliatae*) of Greek plays. The separation of elocution and mimetic action in lyrical monodies was to become a characteristic feature of the later Roman stage:

The pestilence lasted during both this and the following year, the consulship of Gaius Sulpicius Peticus and Gaius Licinius Stolo. In the latter year [364 B. C.] nothing memorable occurred, except that with the object of appeasing the divine displeasure they made a . . . banquet to the gods, being the third in the history of the City; and when neither human wisdom nor the help of Heaven was found to mitigate the scourge, men gave way to superstitious fears, and, amongst other efforts to disarm the wrath of the gods, are said also to have instituted scenic entertainments. This was a new departure for a warlike people, whose only exhibitions had been those of the circus; but indeed it began in a small way, as most things do, and even so was imported from abroad. Without any singing, without imitating the action of singers, players who had been brought in from Etruria danced to the strains of the flautist and performed not ungraceful evolutions in the Tuscan fashion. Next the young Romans began to imitate them, at the same time exchanging jests in uncouth verses [*Versus Fescennini*], and bringing their movements into a certain harmony with the words. And so the amusement was adopted, and frequent use kept it alive. The native professional actors were called *histriones*, from *ister*, the Tuscan word for player; they no longer — as before — alternately threw off rude lines hastily improvised, like the Fescennines, but performed medleys [*saturae*], full of musical measures, to melodies which were now written out to go with the flute, and with appropriate gesticulation.

Livius [Andronicus] was the first, some years later, to abandon *saturae* and compose a play with a plot. Like everyone else in those days, he acted his own pieces; and the story goes that when his voice, owing to the frequent demands made upon it, had lost its freshness, he asked and obtained the indulgence to let a boy stand before the flautist to sing the monody, while he acted it himself, with a vivacity of gesture that gained considerably from his not having to use his voice. From that time on actors began to use singers to accompany their gesticulation, reserving only the dialogue parts for their own delivery. When this type of performance had begun to wean the drama from laughter and informal jest, and the play had gradually developed into art, the young men abandoned the acting of comedies to professionals and revived the ancient practice of fashioning their nonsense into verses and letting fly with them at one another; this was the source of the after-plays which came later to be called *exodia*, and were usually combined with Atellan farces. The Atellan was a species of comedy acquired from the Oscans, and the young men kept it for themselves and would not allow it to be polluted by professional actors; that is why it is a fixed tradition that performers of Atellan plays are not disfranchised, but serve in the army as though they had no connexion with the stage. Amongst the humble origins of other institutions it has seemed worth while to set down the early history of the play, that it might be seen how sober were the beginning of an art that has nowadays reached a point where opulent kingdoms could hardly support its mad extravagance.

9. PROFILES OF TWO ROMAN COMEDIANS

THROUGHOUT the pre-Christian era there was a steady increase of official Roman holidays on which legitimate theatrical performances were given side by side with variety shows and circus productions. In addition to the Roman Games, the Popular, Megalensian, Apollonian, Votive, and Funeral Games gave the playwrights a chance to see their plays produced. At the time of Plautus and Terence, the majority of Roman actors were slaves (legally *infames*, that is, deprived of certain political rights) under the control of a manager (*dominus gregis*). Not until the first century B.C. could a Roman actor gain the social prestige which the great comic star, Quintus Roscius (d. 62 B.C.), attained. Each actor specialized in a certain line, Roscius himself being a specialist in the stock character of parasite. A description of Roman actors in action can be found in Quintilian's handbook of oratory:

We have seen the greatest of comic actors, Demetrius and Stratocles, win their success by entirely different merits. But that is the less surprising owing to the fact that the one was at his best in the roles of gods, young men, good fathers and slaves, matrons and respectable old women, while the other excelled in the portrayal of sharp-tempered old men, cunning slaves, parasites, pimps and all the more lively characters of comedy. For their natural gifts differed. For Demetrius' voice, like his other qualities, had greater charm, while that of Stratocles was the more powerful. But yet more noticeable were the incommunicable peculiarities of their action. Demetrius showed unique gifts in the movements of his hands, in his power to charm his audience by the long-drawn sweetness of his exclamations, the skill with which he would make his dress seem to puff out with wind as he walked, and the expressive movements of the right side which he sometimes introduced with effect, in all of which things he was helped by his stature and personal beauty. On the other hand, Stratocles' *forte* lay in his nimbleness and rapidity of movement, in his laugh (which, though not always in keeping with the character he represented, he deliberately employed to awaken answering laughter in his audience), and finally, even in the way in which he sank his neck into his shoulders. If either of these actors had attempted any of his rival's tricks, he would have produced a most unbecoming effect.

10. A REPRESENTATIVE ROMAN AUDIENCE

The Prologue to the Plautine comedy, *Poenulus*, was addressed to a typical Roman holiday audience that had come to enjoy the Latin adaptation of a Greek comedy some time during the first decade of the second century B.C. For the occasion the crowd had gathered in front of a temporary trestle stage, set up in a market square or in the arena of an amphitheater. The play and the acting had to be first-rate, otherwise the spectators would disperse in search of more exciting entertainment:

I wish to imitate the *Achilles* of Aristarchus; from that tragedy I shall take my opening: "Hush and be silent and pay attention; that you listen is the order of the general" — manager, that both those who have come hungry and those who have come well-filled may cheerfully be seated on the benches; those of you who have eaten have done much more wisely, but you who haven't eaten can have your fill of the play. For it's very stupid of a person who has something to eat to come here for our sake to sit with an empty stomach. "Arise, herald, order the people to be silent." I've been waiting for a long time to see if you know your duty; exercise your voice by which you live and support yourself; for if you don't shout out, starvation will creep upon you in your silence. (*The herald tries to quiet the house.*) Well now, sit down again, that you may get your wages doubled. (*To the audience*) You've done well to obey my commands. Let no worn-out harlot sit in front of the stage, nor the lictor or his rods make a sound, nor the usher roam about in front of people or show anyone to a seat while the actor is on the stage. Those who have had a long leisurely nap at home should now cheerfully stand, or at least refrain from sleeping. Keep slaves from occupying the seats, that there will be room for free men, or let them pay money for their freedom; if they can't do that, let them go home and avoid a double misfortune — being raked with rods here, and with whips at home, if their masters return and find they haven't done their work. And let the nurses keep tiny children at home and not bring them to see the play, lest the nurses themselves get thirsty and the children die of hunger or cry for food like young goats. Let matrons view the play in silence, laugh in silence, refrain from tinkling tones of chatter; they should take home their gossip, so as not to annoy their husbands both here and at home. And now, as to what concerns the directors of the games, no actor should receive the prize unjustly, nor should any be driven out through favoritism so that inferior actors are preferred to the good ones. And there's this point, too, which I had almost forgotten: while the show is going on, lackeys, make an attack on the bakery; rush in now while there is an opportunity, while the tarts are hot. These orders have been given at the command of the manager, and it's a good thing for each man to remember them for himself.

11. A THEATER FOR EIGHTY THOUSAND

BEFORE POMPEY built the first permanent theater in Rome (55 B.C.), Roman theater structures were very ephemeral affairs: they were erected for definite occasions and torn down after having served their purpose.

(Pompey seems to have overcome the hostility of the Grecophobic Senate by crowning his edifice with a temple of Venus Victrix.) The playhouse built by the aedile M. Aemilius Scaurus in 58 B.C. may be cited as an example of a temporary theater. The Elder Pliny gives an amazing report on the oriental splendor of the stage-house wall (*scenae frons*):

> During his aedileship, and just for the temporary use of a few days, Scaurus wrought the greatest work ever achieved by the hands of man, even when intended for permanence: I refer to his theater. The building had three stories, supported on three hundred and sixty columns, and this also in a city which had not given one of its leading citizens permission to erect six pillars of Hymettian marble without some criticism. The lower level was marble; the second, glass — sort of a luxury which since then has been quite unheard of; and the uppermost was made of gilded wood. The lowermost columns . . . were thirty-eight feet high, and placed between them . . . were three thousand bronze statues. The theater could accommodate eighty thousand spectators, even though the Theater of Pompeius, built after the city had been greatly enlarged and its population had increased in vast numbers, was considered large enough when seating only forty thousand.

12. A NOVEL ARCHITECTURAL IDEA

WHEN SHORTLY THEREAFTER another politician, C. Curio, wanted to impress the multitude with a playhouse, he had to think of something entirely new, as he could not dream of surpassing the lavishness of the Scaurus structure. The novelty of his undertaking is stressed in Pliny's *Natural History*:

> C. Curio had two large wooden theaters built close together; each was nicely poised, turning on a pivot. Before noon, a spectacle of games was performed in each, with the theaters back to back so that the noise in each would not interfere with the other's performance. Then, suddenly, toward the latter part of the day, the two theaters would swing around to face each other with their corners interlocking, and, with their outer frames removed, they would form an amphitheater in which gladiatorial combats were presented; combatants whose lives were not much

more endangered than those of the Roman populace that permitted itself to be thus whirled around from side to side. . . . At the funeral games, celebrated at the tomb of Curio's father, no less than the whole Roman populace shared these dangers. When the pivots were overworked and tired, another turn was given to his magnificent display, for, on the final day, the theaters, still in the form of an amphitheater, were cut through the center for an athletic spectacle, and, finally, their stages were suddenly withdrawn on either side to exhibit on the same day combat between those gladiators who had previously been victorious.

13. HOW TO CONSTRUCT A ROMAN PLAYHOUSE

BETWEEN 16 AND 13 B. C. Marcus Vitruvius Pollio completed his ten books entitled *De Architectura* and dedicated them to Emperor Augustus. It is the theoretical work of a professional engineer, who, on the basis of his own experiences and of numerous architectural treatises, deals with city planning. The fifth book is of great interest to the theater historian, as Vitruvius takes up the subject of theater architecture. In the fourth chapter he discusses such subjects as site selection, foundations, and acoustics. The sixth chapter is concerned with the auditorium and the stage building. The sections on scenery and scene shifting by means of triangular prisms (*periaktoi*) had far-reaching consequences when the Renaissance scholars and designers began to study the Latin text upon its publication in 1486:

1. The plan of the theater itself is to be constructed as follows. Having fixed upon the principal center, draw a line of circumference equivalent to what is to be the perimeter at the bottom, and in it inscribe four equilateral triangles, at equal distances apart and touching the boundary line of the circle, as the astrologers do in a figure of the twelve signs of the zodiac, when they are making computations from the musical harmony of the stars. Taking that one of these triangles whose side is nearest to the *scaena*, let the front of the *scaena* be determined by the line where that side cuts off a segment of the circle (A-B), and draw through the center, a parallel line (C-D) set off from that position, to separate the platform of the stage from the space of the orchestra.

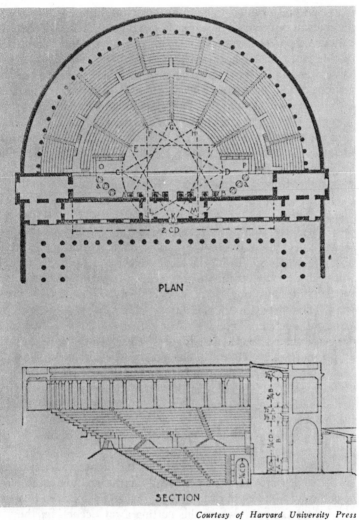

PLAN

SECTION

The Typical Roman Theater According to Vitruvius.
(Drawing in Vitruvius, *The Ten Books of Architecture,* trans. M. H.
Morgan, Cambridge, Mass., 1926)

2. The platform has to be made deeper than that of the Greeks, because all our artists perform on the stage, while the orchestra contains the places reserved for the seats of senators. The height of this platform must be not more than five feet, in order that those who sit in the orchestra may be able to see the performances of all the actors. The sections (*cunei*) for spectators in the theater should be so divided, that the angles of the triangles which run about the circumference of the circle may give the direction for the flights of steps between the sections, as far as up to the first curved cross-aisle. Above this, the upper sections are to be laid out, midway between (the lower sections), with alternating passage-ways.

3. The angles at the bottom, which give the directions for the flights of steps, will be seven in number (C, E, F, G, H, I, D); the other five angles will determine the arrangement of the scene: thus, the angle in the middle ought to have the "royal door" (K) opposite to it; the angles to the right and left (L, M) will designate the position of the doors for guest chambers; and the two outermost angles (A, B) will point to the passages in the wings. The steps for the spectators' places, where the seats are arranged, should be not less than a foot and a palm in height, nor more than a foot and six fingers; their depth should be fixed at not more than two and a half feet, nor less than two feet.

4. The roof of the colonnade to be built at the top of the rows of seats, should lie level with the top of the *scaena*, for the reason that the voice will then rise with equal power until it reaches the highest rows of seats and the roof. If the roof is not so high, in proportion as it is lower, it will check the voice at the point which the sound first reaches.

5. Take one sixth of the diameter of the orchestra between the lowest steps, and let the lower seats at the ends on both sides be cut away to a height of that dimension so as to leave entrances (O, P). At the point where this cutting away occurs, fix the soffits of the passages. Thus their vaulting will be sufficiently high.

6. The length of the *scaena* ought to be double the diameter of the orchestra. The height of the podium, starting from the level of the stage, is, including the corona and cymatium, one twelfth of the diameter of the orchestra. Above the podium, the columns, including their capitals and bases, should have a height of one quarter of the same diameter, and the architraves and

ornaments of the columns should be one fifth of their height. The parapet above, including its cyma and corona, is one half the height of the parapet below. Let the columns above this parapet be one fourth less in height than the columns below, and the architraves and ornaments of these columns one fifth of their height. If the *scaena* is to have three stories, let the uppermost parapet be half the height of the intermediate one, the columns at the top one fourth less high than the intermediate, and the architraves and coronae of these columns one fifth of their height as before.

7. It is not possible, however, that in all theaters these rules of symmetry should answer all conditions and purposes, but the architect ought to consider to what extent he must follow the principle of symmetry, and to what extent it may be modified to suit the nature of the site or the size of the work. There are, of course, some things which, for utility's sake, must be made of the same size in a small theater, and a large one: such as the steps, curved cross-aisles, their parapets, the passages, stairways, stages, tribunals, and any other things which occur that make it necessary to give up symmetry so as not to interfere with utility. Again, if in the course of the work any of the material fall short, such as marble, timber, or anything else that is provided, it will not be amiss to make a slight reduction or addition, provided that it is done without going too far, but with intelligence. This will be possible, if the architect is a man of practical experience and, besides, not destitute of cleverness and skill.

8. The *scaena* itself displays the following scheme. In the center are double doors decorated like those of a royal palace. At the right and left are the doors of the guest chambers. Beyond are spaces provided for decoration — places that the Greeks call *periaktoi*, because in these places are triangular pieces of machinery, which revolve, each having three decorated faces. When the play is to be changed, or when gods enter to the accompaniment of sudden claps of thunder, these may be revolved and present a face differently decorated. Beyond these places are the projecting wings which afford entrances to the stage, one from the forum, the other from abroad.

9. There are three kinds of scenes, one called the tragic, second, the comic, third, the satyric. Their decorations are different and unlike each other in scheme. Tragic scenes are deline-

The Roman Theater in Leptis Magna (Tripolitania).

ated with columns, pediments, statues, and other objects suited to
kings; comic scenes exhibit private dwellings, with balconies
and views representing rows of windows, after the manner of
ordinary dwellings; satyric scenes are decorated with trees, caverns, mountains, and other rustic objects delineated in landscape
style.

14. SHOWMAN POMPEY

THE OFFICIALS in charge of the games hired the acting companies. In
55 B.C., when Pompey's theater — the first Roman stone theater — was
dedicated, Cicero attended the festivities and reported on them to his
friend, M. Marius, who could not be present. When Cicero wrote the
following lines, Roscius was dead, the great tragic actor Aesopus was a
pathetic wreck, and the arenas began to be filled with animals and supernumeraries. Rome was getting ready to receive the emperors:

If you ask me, the games were of course most magnificent;
but they would not have been to your taste; that I infer from my
own feelings. For in the first place those actors had returned to
the stage out of respect for the occasion, who had, as I thought,
quitted it out of self-respect. Indeed your favourite, our friend
Aesop, was such a failure that nobody in the world would have
regretted his leaving off. When he began to swear the oath, his
voice failed him at the crucial point. . . . Why should I tell you
anything more? You know what the rest of the games were like.
Why, they were not even as attractive as games on a middling
scale often are. For any feeling of cheerfulness was extinguished
by the spectacle of such magnificence — a magnificence which, I
am sure, it will not disturb you in the least to have missed
seeing. For what pleasure can there be in the sight of six hundred
mules in the *Clytaemnestra* [of Accius], or of three thousand
bowls in the *Trojan Horse* [of Livius Andronicus] or of the
varied accoutrements of foot and horse in some big battle? All
of which excited the admiration of the people, but would have
given you no pleasure at all. . . .

There remain the wild-beast hunts, two a day for five days—
magnificent; there is no denying it. But what pleasure can it
possibly be to a man of culture, when either a puny human being
is mangled by a most powerful beast, or a splendid beast is trans-

fixed with a hunting-spear? And even if all this is something to be seen, you have seen it more than once; and I, who was a spectator, saw nothing new in it. The last day was that of the elephants, and on that day the mob and crowd were greatly impressed, but manifested no pleasure. Indeed the result was a certain compassion and a kind of feeling that that huge beast has a fellowship with the human race.

15. IN PRAISE OF PANTOMIME

PANTOMIME as a recognized art form made its official Roman debut in 22 B.C. The tragic dancer, Pylades, and the comic dancer, Bathyllus, seem to have been instrumental in giving the new genre its definite style. The comic pantomime, featuring the amorous aspects of Olympic society and outright travesties, was rather short-lived, while tragic pantomime, supported by orchestral music and choral singing and dealing with such subjects as Medea, Phaedra, Pentheus, Hercules, and Oedipus, outlived the Roman Empire. As a true son of his age, Lucian of Samosata (*ca.* 125 — 180) resisted Greek tragedy and its paraphernalia, but promptly succumbed to the sensual charms of pantomime:

And now I come to the pantomime. What must be his qualifications? what his previous training? what his studies? what his subsidiary accomplishments? You will find that his is no easy profession, nor lightly to be undertaken; requiring as it does the highest standard of culture in all its branches, and involving a knowledge not of music only, but of rhythm and metre, and above all of your beloved philosophy, both natural and moral, the subtleties of dialectic alone being rejected as serving no useful purpose. Rhetoric, too, in so far as that art is concerned with the exposition of human character and human passions, claims a share of its attention. Nor can it dispense with the painter's and the sculptor's arts; in its close observation of the harmonious proportions that these teach, it is the equal of an Apelles or a Phidias. But above all Mnemosyne, and her daughter Polyhymnia, must be propitiated by an art that would remember all things. Like Calchas in Homer, the pantomime must know all 'that is, that was, that shall be'; nothing must escape his ever ready memory. Faithfully to represent his subject, adequately to express his own conceptions, to make plain all that might be obscure;

—these are the first essentials for the pantomime, to whom no higher compliment could be paid than Thucydides's tribute to Pericles, who, he says, 'could not only conceive a wise policy, but render it intelligible to his hearers'; the intelligibility, in the present case, depending on clearness of gesticulation.

For his materials, he must draw continually, as I have said, upon his unfailing memory of ancient story; and memory must be backed by taste and judgement. . . .

The pantomime is above all things an actor: that is his first aim, in the pursuit of which (as I have observed) he resembles the orator, and especially the composer of 'declamations,' whose success, as the pantomime knows, depends like his own upon verisimilitude, upon the adaptation of language to character: prince or tyrannicide, pauper or farmer, each must be shown with the peculiarities that belong to him. I must give you the comment of another foreigner on this subject. Seeing five masks laid ready — that being the number of parts in the piece — and only one pantomime, he asked who were going to play the other parts. He was informed that the whole piece would be performed by a single actor. 'Your humble servant, sir,' cries our foreigner to the artist; 'I observe that you have but one body: it had escaped me, that you possessed several souls.'

The term 'pantomime,' which was introduced by the Italian Greeks, is an apt one, and scarcely exaggerates the artist's versatility. . . . It is his profession to show forth human character and passion in all their variety; to depict love and anger, frenzy and grief, each in its due measure. Wondrous art! — on the same day, he is mad Athamas and shrinking Ino; he is Atreus, and again he is Thyestes, and next Aegisthus or Aerope; all one man's work.

Other entertainments of eye or ear are but manifestations of a single art: 'tis flute or lyre or song: 'tis moving tragedy or laughable comedy. The pantomime is all-embracing in the variety of his equipment: flute and pipe, beating foot and clashing cymbal, melodious recitative, choral harmony. Other arts call out only one half of a man's powers — the bodily or the mental: the pantomime combines the two. His performance is as much an intellectual as a physical exercise: there is meaning in his movements; every gesture has its significance; and therein lies his chief excellence. The enlightened Lesbonax of Mytilene called pantomimes 'manual philosophers,' and used to frequent the theatre, in the conviction that he came out of it a better man than he went in. And Timocrates, his teacher, after accidentally witnessing a pantomimic performance, exclaimed: 'How much have I lost by my scrupulous devotion to philosophy!' I know not what truth there may be in Plato's analysis of the soul into the three elements of spirit, appetite, and reason: but each of the three is admirably illustrated by the pantomime; he shows us the angry man, he shows us the lover, and he shows us every passion under the control of reason; this last—like touch among the senses— is all-pervading. Again, in his care for beauty and grace of move- ment, have we not an illustration of the Aristotelian principle, which makes beauty a third part of Good? Nay, I once heard some one hazard a remark, to the effect that the philosophy of Pantomime went still further, and that in the *silence* of the charac- ters a Pythagorean doctrine was shadowed forth.

All professions hold out some object, either of utility or of pleasure: Pantomime is the only one that secures both these ob- jects; now the utility that is combined with pleasure is doubled in value. Who would choose to look on at a couple of young fellows spilling their blood in a boxing match, or wrestling in the dust, when he may see the same subject represented by the pantomime, with the additional advantages of safety and elegance, and with far greater pleasure to the spectator? The vigorous movements of the pantomime — turn and twist, bend and spring —afford at once a gratifying spectacle to the beholder and a wholesome training to the performer; I maintain that no gym- nastic exercise is its equal for beauty and for the uniform de- velopment of the physical powers, — of agility, suppleness, and elasticity, as of solid strength.

Consider then the universality of this art: it sharpens the wits, it exercises the body, it delights the spectator, it instructs him in the history of bygone days, while eye and ear are held beneath the spell of flute and cymbal and of graceful dance. Would you revel in sweet song? Nowhere can you procure that enjoyment in greater variety and perfection. Would you listen to the clear melody of flute and pipe? Again the pantomime sup- plies you. I say nothing of the excellent moral influence of public opinion, as exercised in the theatre, where you will find the evil- doer greeted with execration, and his victim with sympathetic tears. The pantomime's most admirable quality I have yet to mention, — his combination of strength and suppleness of limb; it is as if brawny Heracles and soft Aphrodite were presented to us in one and the same person.

I now propose to sketch out the mental and physical qualifications necessary for a first-rate pantomime. Most of the former, indeed, I have already mentioned: he must have memory, sensibility, shrewdness, rapidity of conception, tact, and judgement; further, he must be a critic of poetry and song, capable of discerning good music and rejecting bad. For his body, I think I may take the Canon of Polycletus as my model. He must be perfectly proportioned: neither immoderately tall nor dwarfishly short; not too fleshy (a most unpromising quality in one of his profession) nor cadaverously thin. Let me quote you certain comments of the people of Antioch, who have a happy knack in expressing their views on such subjects. They are a most intelligent people, and devoted to Pantomime; each individual is all eyes and ears for the performance; not a word, not a gesture escapes them. Well, when a small man came on in the character of Hector, they cried out with one voice: 'Here is Astyanax, and where is Hector?' On another occasion, an exceedingly tall man was taking the part of Capaneus scaling the walls of Thebes; 'Step over' suggested the audience; 'you need no ladder.' The well-meant activity of a fat and heavy dancer was met with earnest entreaties to 'spare the platform'; while a thin performer was recommended to 'take care of his health.' I mention these criticisms, not on account of their humorous character, but as an illustration of the profound interest that whole cities have sometimes taken in Pantomime, and of their ability to discern its merits and demerits.

Another essential for the pantomime is ease of movement. His frame must be at once supple and well-knit, to meet the opposite requirements of agility and firmness. That he is no stranger to the science of the boxing- and the wrestling-ring, that he has his share of the athletic accomplishments of Hermes and Pollux and Heracles, you may convince yourself by observing his rendering of those subjects. The eyes, according to Herodotus, are more credible witnesses than the ears; though the pantomime, by the way, appeals to both kinds of evidence.

Such is the potency of his art, that the amorous spectator is cured of his infirmity by perceiving the evil effects of passion, and he who enters the theater under a load of sorrow departs from it with a serene countenance . . . How natural is his treatment of his subjects, how intelligible to every one of his audience, may be judged from the emotion of the house whenever anything is represented that calls for sorrow or compassion. The Bacchic form of Pantomime, which is particularly popular in Ionia and Pontus, in spite of its being confined to satyric subjects, has taken such possession of those peoples, that, when the Pantomime season comes round in each city, they leave all else and sit for whole days watching Titans and Corybantes, Satyrs and neat-herds. Men of the highest rank and position are not ashamed to take part in these performances: indeed, they pride themselves more on their pantomimic skill than on birth and ancestry and public services.

Now that we know what are the qualities that a good pantomime ought to possess, let us next consider the faults to which he is liable. Deficiencies of person I have already handled; and the following I think is a fair statement of the mental imperfections. Pantomimes cannot all be artists; there are plenty of ignorant performers, who bungle their work terribly. Some cannot adapt themselves to their music; they are literally 'out of tune'; rhythm says one thing, their feet another. Others are free from this fault, but jumble up their chronology. I remember the case of a man who was giving the birth of Zeus, and Cronus eating his own children: seduced by the similarity of subject, he ran off into the tale of Atreus and Thyestes. In another case, Semele was just being struck by the lightning, when she was transformed into Creusa, who was not even born at that time. Still, it seems to me that we have no right to visit the sins of the artist upon the art: let us recognize him for the blunderer that he is, and do justice to the accuracy and skill of competent performers.

The fact is, the pantomime must be completely armed at every point. His work must be one harmonious whole, perfect in balance and proportion, self-consistent, proof against the most minute criticism; there must be no flaws, everything must be of the best; brilliant conception, profound learning, above all human sympathy. When every one of the spectators identifies himself with the scene enacted, when each sees in the pantomime as in a mirror the reflection of his own conduct and feelings, then, and not till then, is his success complete. But let him reach that point, and the enthusiasm of the spectators becomes uncontrollable, every man pouring out his whole soul in admiration of the portraiture that reveals him to himself. Such a spectacle is no less than a fulfilment of the oracular injunction KNOW THYSELF; men depart from it with increased knowledge; they have learnt something that is to be sought after, something that should be eschewed.

But in Pantomime, as in rhetoric, there can be (to use a popular phrase) too much of a good thing; a man may exceed the proper bounds of imitation; what should be great may become monstrous, softness may be exaggerated into effeminacy, and the courage of a man into the ferocity of a beast. I remember seeing this exemplified in the case of an actor of repute. In most respects a capable, nay, an admirable performer, some strange fatality ran him aground upon this reef of overenthusiasm. He was acting the madness of Ajax, just after he has been worsted by Odysseus; and so lost control of himself, that one might have been excused for thinking his madness was something more than feigned. He tore the clothes from the back of one of the iron-shod time-beaters, snatched a flute from the player's hands, and brought it down in such trenchant sort upon the head of Odysseus, who was standing by enjoying his triumph, that, had not his cap held good, and borne the weight of the blow, poor Odysseus must have fallen a victim to histrionic frenzy. The whole house ran mad for company, leaping, yelling, tearing their clothes. For the illiterate riff-raff, who knew not good from bad, and had no idea of decency, regarded it as a supreme piece of acting; and the more intelligent part of the audience, realizing how things stood, concealed their disgust, and instead of reproaching the actor's folly by silence, smothered it under their plaudits; they saw only too clearly that it was not Ajax but the pantomime who was mad. Nor was our spirited friend content till he had distinguished himself yet further: descending from the stage, he seated himself in the senatorial benches between two consulars, who trembled lest he should take one of them for a ram and apply the lash. The spectators were divided between wonder and amusement; and some there were who suspected that his ultrarealism had culminated in reality. However, it seems that when he came to his senses again he bitterly repented of this exploit, and was quite ill from grief, regarding his conduct as that of a veritable madman, as is clear from his own words. For when his partisans begged him to repeat the performance, he recommended another actor for the part of Ajax, saying that 'it was enough for him to have been mad once.' His mortification was increased by the success of his rival, who, though a similar part had been written for him, played it with admirable judgement and discretion, and was complimented on his observance of decorum, and of the proper bounds of his art.

16.   A PANTOMIME PRODUCTION

IN HIS SATIRICAL ROMANCE, *The Metamorphoses*, Apuleius (b. *ca*. 124) has a description of a pantomime on the subject of the Judgment of Paris. We watch the proceedings in the amphitheater of Corinth through the eyes of Lucius, who, transformed into an ass, is earmarked for a role in the carnal afterpiece in the arena. Apuleius' account of the ballet is highly informative with regard to scenery, costume, and music:

There was a mountain of wood, fashioned after the likeness of that famous Mount Ida whereof the poet Homer sang. It was built up into a towering structure, planted with shrubs and living trees, while from its topmost peak it sent forth a running stream that had its source in a fountain wrought by the hands of the artificer. A few goats cropped the young herbage and a youth after the likeness of a Phrygian herdsman, with barbaric mantle streaming from his shoulders, a fair tunic about his body, and a turban of gold on his head, counterfeited the action of those that watch over their flocks. By him was a beauteous boy, naked save for the stripling's cloak that covered his left shoulder, with yellow hair, a mark for all men's eyes, and midst his locks protruding tiny wings of gold, a perfect pair springing from either side his head. The herald's wand showed him to be Mercury. He ran forward with dancing steps and in his right hand held out to the other, who seemed to be Paris, an apple covered with leaf of gold, and signifying by his nod what Jupiter had bidden him deliver, he nimbly withdrew his steps and passed from our sight. Then followed a maiden very noble of countenance in the likeness of the goddess Juno. A shining diadem was about her head, she carried also a scepter. Another burst upon our gaze, whom you would deem to be Minerva, for her head was covered with a shining helmet, and the helmet itself was wreathed with a crown of olive; she raised her buckler and brandished her spear and was as Minerva when she goes forth to battle. After these entered a third, surpassing fair and a joy to behold, in the grace of her ambrosial hue showing forth the likeness of Venus as she was when she was a maid. Her body was naked and uncovered and displayed her perfect beauty, save that it was veiled by a robe of thinnest silk which the wanton wind would blow against her, so that it clung close to her and outlined with all a painter's skill the charms of her fair limbs. The colors wherein the goddess was arrayed were diverse; her body was shining white, in token that she rose from the sea. And each of these maidens, who were deemed to be goddesses, were followed by their several escorts. Juno was followed by Castor and Pollux, whose heads were covered with oval helmets with stars set bright upon their crests. And Castor and Pollux also were no more than youthful actors. This maiden came forward to the rippling music of the Ionian flute, and with quiet and unaffected gesture and stately movement of the head promised the herdsman that if he awarded her the prize of loveliness she would make him king over all Asia. But she whom her array of armor showed to be Minerva was escorted by two boys, the armorbearers that go with the goddess of battle, Terror and Fear, dancing fiercely with naked swords. And behind her a fluteplayer sounded the warlike Dorian mode, mingling deep booming notes with shrill blasts that rang like a trumpet call, and he danced with nimble strength. With restless head and eyes in whose glance were threats, with swift and nervous gesticulation and fiery mien, she showed to Paris that if he accorded her the victory in beauty's battle, he should by her aid be made brave and glorious with the trophies of war.

But lo! Venus, surrounded by a whole host of merry little children, with a sweet smile and charming grace took her stand in the very midst of the stage amid the loud plaudits of all the theater. You would have said that those little boys, so slim and milky white, were true Cupids who had just flown down from heaven or forth from the sea. For they were the very image of Cupids, with their little wings and tiny arrows and their comeliness also, and they lit the path of their mistress with torches as though they were going to honor some nuptial feast. Also there glided on to the stage a lovely troop of unwedded girls, on one side the Graces most full of grace, on the other the Hours exceedingly lovely. These, casting flowers twined in wreaths or free, saluted their goddess and wove a most delicate dance, gladdening the mistress of pleasures with all the petals of spring. And now flutes with many stops breathed forth in sweet accord the airs of Lydia. But though their strains charmed the hearts of the spectators with their sweetness, Venus was sweeter far; and she began to move gently and to advance with slow and lingering step and body gently balanced to and fro and softly bowing head, and with delicate gestures she kept time to the soft sound of the flutes and made signs with eyes now mildly closed, now flashing threats, and sometimes all her dancing was in her glances. And as soon as she came into the presence of the judge, she seemed by the passionate movement of her arms to promise that if she was preferred to the others she would give to Paris for his bride one like herself of surpassing loveliness. Whereat the Phrygian youth with right goodwill gave her the apple that he held, as it were a vote of victory cast with a pebble of gold. . . .

After Paris had given his judgment, Juno and Minerva departed from the stage, downcast and like as though they were angry, and showing by their gestures their indignation at their rebuff. But Venus was full of joy and merriment, and showed her delight by dancing with all the troop of her attendants. Then from the mountain's topmost peak through some hidden pipe there spouted high in air saffron mingled with wine, which being sprinkled abroad fell in odorous rain about the feeding goats until they were dyed to a fairer hue and changed their natural whiteness for yellow. And now, while the whole theater was sweet with the scent, a chasm opened in the ground and swallowed up the mountain of wood.

Chapter II

The Middle Ages

Courtesy of the Stadtarchiv, Cologne

Mansion Stage for Broelmann's Academic *Laurentius-Spiel* (Cologne, 1581).
All the localities shown are within the City of Rome (note the Renaissance
influences), stage left represents the Christian Rome, stage right the pagan
Rome. The illustration shows the following places: Capena Gate, a steep path
leading up to Mt. Caelius, the village Canarius, the house of Faustina, the
dwelling of Pope Sixtus, the prison, the home of the prison warden, the
pedestal for the statue of St. Laurentius, the chair with canopy for the
Praetor, the entrance to the Imperial Palace, the home of the High Priest.
The sacrificial altar of Jupiter and the obelisk are additional set pieces.
Pathways are outlined on the stage floor, which is set upon barrels.

1. THE STAGING OF LITURGIC DRAMA

IN THE TENTH CENTURY, Ethelwold, Bishop of Winchester, drew up the *Concordia Regularis*, a supplement to the *Rule* of St. Benedict. St. Ethelwold gave instructions as to how the third Nocturn at Matins on Easter morning should be performed in Benedictine monasteries. The scriptural core of this Easter morning ceremony is the visit of the three Maries to the sepulchre and their colloquy with the angel who announces the miracle of the Resurrection (*cf.* Matt. 28: 1 - 7 and Mark 16: 1 - 7). In the *Concordia Regularis*, the birth of medieval drama from the spirit of liturgy lies clearly before us, and the *régisseur* Ethelwold has seen to it that no important element of the theater is overlooked:

While the third lesson is being chanted, let four brethren vest themselves. Let one of these, vested in an alb, enter as though to take part in the service, and let him approach the sepulchre without attracting attention and sit there quietly with a palm in his hand. While the third respond is chanted, let the remaining three follow, and let them all, vested in copes, bearing in their hands thuribles with incense, and stepping delicately as those who seek something, approach the sepulchre. These things are done in imitation of the angel sitting in the monument, and the women with spices coming to anoint the body of Jesus. When therefore he who sits there beholds the three approach him like folk lost and seeking something, let him begin in a dulcet voice of medium pitch to sing *Quem quaeritis* [Whom seek ye in the sepulchre, O Christian women?]. And when he has sung it to the end, let the three reply in unison *Ihesum Nazarenum* [Jesus of Nazareth, the crucified, O heavenly one]. So he, *Non est hic, surrexit sicut praedixerat. Ite, nuntiate quia surrexit a mortuis* [He is not here; He is risen, as He foretold. Go and announce that He is risen from the dead]. At the word of his bidding let those three turn to the choir and say *Alleluia! resurrexit Dominus!* [Alleluia! The Lord is risen!] This said, let the one, still sitting there and as if recalling them, say the anthem *Venite et videte locum* [Come and see the place]. And saying this, let him rise, and lift the veil, and show them the place bare of the cross, but only the cloths laid there in which the cross was wrapped. And when they have seen this, let them set down the thuribles which

Courtesy of the Landesmuseum (Welfenmuseum), Hanover

The Three Maries at the Tomb. Anonymous Master of the Lower Rhine
(abt. 1410).

they bore in that same sepulchre, and take the cloth, and hold it up in the face of the clergy, and as if to demonstrate that the Lord has risen and is no longer wrapped therein, let them sing the anthem *Surrexit Dominus de sepulchro* [The Lord is risen from the sepulchre], and lay the cloth upon the altar. When the anthem is done, let the prior, sharing in their gladness at the triumph of our King, in that, having vanquished death, He rose again, begin the hymn *Te Deum laudamus* [We praise Thee, O God]. And this begun, all the bells chime out together.

2. THE MACHINERY FOR THE PARADISE

As LONG AS the medieval religious plays were allowed to stay within the churches, special stages were erected for them. The *sacra rappresentazione*, which Bishop Abraham of Szuszdal saw in 1493 in the Florentine Church of the Annunciation, was presented on a scaffold in the nave, and the audience crowded round to marvel at the hundreds of lights which circled the throne of God, while children, garbed as angels, produced the music of the spheres on cymbals, flutes, and harps. A special contrivance controlled the descent of the Archangel Gabriel. This performance was even surpassed by one that Bishop Szuszdal saw in the Church del Carmine, where the Ascension of Christ was most skilfully staged. To the architect, Filippo Brunelleschi (1377-1446), must go the credit for having contrived the technical apparatus for these performances in, or in front of, the churches in Florence. Due to his efforts, the Florentines learned to look upon their religious theater as a work of art. In his *Vite*, Giorgio Vasari (1511 - 1574) offers a wealth of technical details concerning the secrets of the machines (*ingegni*) in which medieval spectators took a seemingly insatiable delight:

It is said that the apparatus of the Paradise of S. Felice in the piazza of that city [Florence] was invented by Filippo [Brunelleschi] for the representation or feast of the Annunciation according to the time-honoured custom of the Florentines. This thing was truly marvellous, and displayed the ability and industry of the inventor. On high was a Heaven full of living and moving figures, and a quantity of lights which flashed in and out. I will take pains to describe exactly how the apparatus of this machine was devised, seeing that the machine itself is destroyed, and the men are dead who could have spoken of it from experience. . . . For this effect Filippo had arranged a half-globe between two rafters of the roof of the church, like a hollow porringer or a barber's basin turned upside down. It was formed of thin laths secured to an iron star which revolved round a great iron ring upon which it was poised. The whole machine was supported by a strong beam of pine well bound with iron, which was across the timbers of the roof. In this beam was fixed the ring that held the basin in suspense and balance, which from the ground resembled a veritable Heaven. At the base, on the inside edge, were certain wooden brackets just large enough for one to stand on, and at the height of one *braccio* [*ca.* 2 feet] and also inside another iron. On each of the brackets was placed a child of about twelve, making 1½ *braccia* with the iron, and so girt about that they could not fall even if they wanted to. These children, twelve in all, being arranged, as I have said, on pedestals and clad like angels with gilt wings and caps of gold lace, took one another's hands when the time came, and extending their arms they appeared to be dancing, especially as the basin was always turning and moving. Inside this and above the heads of the angels were three circles or garlands of lights arranged with some tiny lanterns which could not turn over. These lights looked like stars from the ground, while the beams being covered with cotton resembled clouds. From the ring issued an immense iron bar furnished with another ring at the side, to which was attached a slender cord which fell to the ground, as we shall see. The bar had eight branches, and revolved in an arc filling the entire space inside the basin. At the end of each branch was a plate as large as a trencher, on which a boy of nine was placed, tied in with an iron fixed at the height of the branch, but so as to allow him to turn in every direction. These eight angels, by means of a crane, descended from the top of the basin to beneath the plane of the beams bearing the roof, a distance of eight *braccia* [*ca.* 16 feet], so that they could be seen and did not interfere with the view of the angels surrounding the inside of the basin. Inside what we may truthfully call the nosegay of eight angels, there was a copper *mandorla* [almond-shaped glory-like machine] filled with small lights placed in many niches, and set upon an iron like cannon, which, upon touching a spring, were all hidden in the hollow of the copper *mandorla,* and when the spring was not pressed all the lights appeared through holes there. When the nosegay had reached its place, the *mandorla* was slowly lowered by another crane to the stage where the performance took place. Above this stage, exactly where the *mandorla* was to rest, was a high throne with four steps, with an opening, through which the iron of the *mandorla* passed. A man was placed below the throne, and when the *mandorla* reached its station he secured it with a bolt. Inside the *mandorla* was a youth of about fifteen, representing an angel, surrounded by an iron and fixed in the *mandorla* so that he could not fall, and to permit him to kneel the iron was in three pieces, so that as he knelt one telescoped into the other. Thus, when the nosegay had descended and the *mandorla* rested on the throne, the man who fastened the *mandorla* unfastened the iron which bore the angel, so that he came out, walked along the stage, and when he came to where the Virgin was saluted her, and made the Annunciation. Then he returned to the *mandorla,* and the lanterns, which had been extinguished when he stepped out, were relighted, and the iron which bore him was newly fastened by the unseen man beneath, whilst the angels of the nosegay sang, and those of the Heaven turned about. It thus appeared a veritable Paradise, the more so as, in addition, a God the Father was placed beside the convex side of the basin, surrounded by angels similar to those above, and fastened with iron in such a manner that the Heaven, the nosegay, the Deity, the *mandorla,* with the numerous lights and sweet music, represented Paradise most realistically. In addition to this, in order that the Heaven might be opened or shut, Filippo added two large doors, five *braccia* [*ca.* 10 feet] high, one on either side, provided with iron or copper rollers running in grooves, so arranged that by drawing a slender cord, the doors opened or closed at will, the two parts of the door coming together or slowly separating. These doors had two properties, one was that, being heavy, they made a noise like thunder, the other was that, when closed, they formed a scaffold for fixing the angels and arranging the other things needed inside. These ingenious things and many others were invented by Filippo, although some assert that they were introduced long before.

3.   THE PARADISE IMPROVED

To THE FLORENTINE carpenter and woodworker, Francesco d'Angelo called La Cecca (1447 - 1488), must go the credit for a number of technical improvements on the fundamental pattern that Brunelleschi had established:

I shall describe the feast of the Ascension. . . . It was very fine. Christ was raised upon a mountain admirably made of wood by a cloud full of angels and carried into heaven, leaving the Apostles on the mountain. This was marvellously done, especially as the heaven was somewhat larger than that of S. Felice in Piazza, though with almost the same apparatus. As the Church of the Carmine, where this was enacted, is considerably broader and loftier than S. Felice, another heaven, besides the one which received Christ, was arranged over the principal tribune, in which large wheels like windlasses moved ten circles representing the ten heavens, from the centre to the circumference, full of lights representing the stars, arranged in copper lanterns and so fixed that when the wheel turned they always remained in position, as some lanterns do which are in common use to-day. From this heaven, which was a truly beautiful thing, issued two large cables connected with the gallery or rood-loft of the church. Each was supplied with a small bronze pulley supporting an iron bar, fixed to a plane upon which stood two angels bound at the waist, counterpoised by a lead weight beneath their feet, and another at the base of the plane on which they stood. The whole was covered with cotton wool, forming a cloud full of cherubim and seraphim, and other angels in divers colours and very well arranged. These being let down by ropes to the top of the screen, announced to Christ His Ascension to heaven, or performed other offices. As the iron to which they were bound by the girdle was fixed in the plane where their feet were set, they could turn round, issuing out and returning, making reverences and turning themselves at need. Thus in mounting upwards they faced the sky, and they were drawn up by the same means by which they had descended. These machines and contrivances were the work of Cecca, who added many things to the devices invented by Filippo Brunelleschi, with great judgment.

4. MEDIEVAL STAGE DIRECTIONS

DUE TO THEIR increasing secularization, the religious plays had to leave
the churches. On their migration from the ecclesiastic into the lay world
they first stopped in front of the church gates. In such an open-air production against the background of a church façade the Anglo-Norman
Jeu d'Adam was played in France in the twelfth century. Its author was
a priest who, in all probability, attended also to the staging. At any rate,
the *mystère* of Adam contains ample stage directions (rubrics) which
enable us to reconstruct the original performance. The anonymous author
gives detailed instructions for the erection and simultaneous placement
of the mansions; he describes at length the costumes to be worn and the
gestures to be used by the amateur actors. Here is the first of the rubrics:

Let Paradise be set up in a somewhat lofty place; let there
be put about it curtains and silken hangings, at such an height
that those persons who shall be in Paradise can be seen from the
shoulders upward; let there be planted sweet-smelling flowers
and foliage; let divers trees be therein, and fruits hanging upon
them, so that it may seem a most delectable place.

Then let the Savior come, clothed in a dalmatic, and let
Adam and Eve be set before him. Let Adam be clothed in a red
tunic; Eve, however, in a woman's garment of white, and a white
silken wimple; and let them both stand before the Figure [*Figura,
i.e.,* God]; but Adam a little nearer, with composed countenance; Eve, however, with countenance a little more subdued.

And let Adam himself be well instructed when he shall make
his answers, lest in answering he be either too swift or too slow.
Let not only Adam, but all the persons, be so instructed that they
shall speak composedly and shall use such gestures as become
the matter whereof they are speaking; and in uttering the verses,
let them neither add a syllable nor take away, but let them pronounce all clearly; and let those things that are to be said be
said in their due order. Whoever shall speak the name of Paradise, let him look back at it and point it out with his hand.

[The stage directions for the temptation scene read as follows:]

Then a serpent, cunningly put together, shall ascend along
the trunk of the forbidden tree, unto which Eve shall approach
her ear, as if hearkening unto its counsel. Thereafter, Eve shall

take the apple, and shall offer it unto Adam. . . . Then shall Adam
eat a part of the apple; and having eaten it, he shall straightway
take knowledge of his sin; and he shall bow himself down so
that he cannot be seen of the people, and shall put off his goodly
garments, and shall put on poor garments of fig-leaves sewn
together; and manifesting exceeding great sorrow, he shall begin his lamentation.

[After the fall of man, Adam and Eve]

. . . shall be clean outside of Paradise, sad and confounded
in appearance, they shall bow themselves to the ground, even
unto their feet, and the Figure shall point to them with his hand,
his face being turned toward Paradise;. and the choir shall begin:
"Behold Adam is become as one [of us]." And when this is
ended, the Figure shall go back unto the church. Then shall Adam
have a spade and Eve a mattock, and they shall begin to till the
ground, and they shall sow wheat therein. After they shall have
finished their sowing, they shall go and sit for a season in a certain place, as if wearied with their toil, and with tearful eyes
shall they look back ofttimes at Paradise, beating their breasts.
Meanwhile shall the Devil come and plant thorns and thistles in
their tillage, and then he shall depart. When Adam and Eve come
to their tillage, and when they shall have beheld the thorns and
thistles that have sprung up, stricken with grievous sorrow, they
shall cast themselves down upon the ground; and remaining there,
they shall beat their breasts and their thighs, manifesting their
grief by their gestures; and Adam shall then begin his lamentation.

[Hellmouth is the ultimate destination of the first sinners:]

Then shall the Devil come, and three or four other devils
with him, bearing in their hands chains and iron shackles, which
they shall place on the necks of Adam and Eve. And certain ones
shall push them on, others shall drag them toward Hell; other
devils, however, shall be close beside Hell, waiting for them as
they come, and these shall make a great dancing and jubilation
over their destruction; and other devils shall, one after another,
point to them as they come; and they shall take them up and

thrust them into Hell; and thereupon they shall cause a great smoke to arise, and they shall shout one to another in Hell, greatly rejoicing; and they shall dash together their pots and kettles, so that they may be heard without. And after some little interval, the devils shall go forth, and shall run to and fro in the square; certain of them, however, shall remain behind in Hell.

5.   THE STAGE MAGIC OF VALENCIENNES

AFTER THE RELIGIOUS PLAYS had freed themselves from the background of the church, they moved into the courtyards of aristocratic mansions (Valenciennes) and invaded the central market squares (Lucerne, Frankfort, Mons); they were produced in earthen arenas (Perranzabuloe, St. Just) and even within the remains of Roman amphitheaters (Bourges). The first chronicler of Valenciennes gave a résumé of the most spectacular aspects of the *Passion* production in 1547:

At Whitsuntide of the year 1547, the leading citizens of the town [of Valenciennes] presented the life, death, and Passion of Our Lord on the stage of the mansion of the Duke of Arschot. The spectacle lasted twenty-five days, and on each day we saw strange and wonderful things. The machines (*secrets*) of the Paradise and of Hell were absolutely prodigious and could be taken by the populace for magic. For we saw Truth, the angels, and other characters descend from very high, sometimes visibly, sometimes invisibly, appearing suddenly. Lucifer was raised from Hell on a dragon without our being able to see how. The rod of Moses, dry and sterile, suddenly put forth flowers and fruits. Devils carried the souls of Herod and Judas through the air. Devils were exorcised, people with dropsy and other invalids cured, all in an admirable way. Here Jesus Christ was carried up by the Devil who scaled a wall forty feet high. There He became invisible. Finally, He was transfigured on Mount Tabor. We saw water changed into wine so mysteriously that we could not believe it, and more than a hundred persons wanted to taste this wine. The five breads and the two fish seemed to be multiplied and were distributed to more than a thousand spectators, and yet there were more than twelve baskets left. The fig tree, cursed by Our Lord, appeared to dry up, its leaves withering in an instant.

The Multiple Stage (*Hourt*) for the *Mystère de la Passion* at Valenciennes (1547).
After a Miniature by Hubert Cailleau and Jacques de Moëlles.
Bibliothèque Nationale, Paris

The places shown are: Paradise, a Hall, the Gate of Nazareth, the Temple, the Gate of Jerusalem, the Palace of Pilate, the Prison under the Palace, the Bishops' House, the Golden Gate, a Lake with Vessel, Limbo, and Hell.

The eclipse, the earthquake, the splitting of the rocks and the other miracles at the death of Our Lord were shown with new marvels.

6. ENGLISH PAGEANT CARS

FOR PROCESSIONAL PLAYS a whole city was turned into a vast auditorium. Mansions on wheels (pageants or carriages in England, *edifizii* in Italy, *carros* in Spain) were moved through the principal streets of a city and brought to a halt at predetermined stations where a scene of the play cycle was performed. The responsibility for these pageant cars rested with the local guilds, whose members had to attend to the building, decorating, and drawing of the floats. The production of religious plays was an undertaking which involved the entire community. Archdeacon Robert Rogers (d. 1595) has left us a description of the pageant cars that were used in the processional presentation of the Chester Whitsun plays:

Every company had his pagiant, or parte, which pagiants weare a high scafolde with two rowmes, a higher and a lower, upon four wheeles. In the lower they apparelled them selves, and in the higher rowme they played, beinge all open on the tope, that all behoulders mighte heare and see them. The places where they played them was in every streete. They begane first at the abay gates, and when the firste pagiante was played it was wheeled to the highe crosse before the mayor, and so to every streete; and soe every streete had a pagiant playinge before them at one time, till all the pagiantes for the daye appoynted weare played: and when one pagiant was neere ended, worde was broughte from streete to streete, that soe they mighte come in place thereof exedinge orderlye, and all the streetes have theire pagiantes afore them all at one time playeinge togeather; to se which playes was greate resorte, and also scafoldes and stages made in the streetes in those places where they determined to playe theire pagiantes.

7. THE MEDIEVAL STAGE DIRECTOR

THE CLERICAL Master of Ceremonies who supervised the execution of the rubrics in the Ordinal was destined to become the interpreter of the stage directions in medieval production books. The first medieval stage directors were ecclesiastics. Later on laymen (city clerks, lawyers, and artists)

English Pageant Car Reconstruction by Thomas Sharp.

(In *A Dissertation on the Pageants or Dramatic Mysteries Anciently Performed at Coventry*, Coventry, 1825)

Multiple Stage for the Passion Play Produced in 1583 in the Central Square (the Present Weinmarkt) of Lucerne. Reconstruction by Albert Köster.

assumed this function The elusive image of the medieval *régisseur* has survived in the sketches of three artists: we see the director among the players in Jean Fouquet's miniature of the *Mystère de Sainte Apolline* (mid-fifteenth century); the director of Jakob Ruf's *Weingartenspiel* (1539) lives on in the sketch of an unkown artist, and Hubert Cailleau has preserved for us at least the costume of the Valenciennes director (1547). In all three sketches the director is holding a promptbook in one hand and a baton (originally the *baculus* of the clerical Master of Ceremonies) in the other. From the Fouquet miniature it becomes clear that the medieval *régisseur*-prompter moved about the stage in full view of the audience. The pictorial evidence for this is supported by the following quaint story from Richard Carew's *Survey of Cornwall*, where he speaks of the popularity of the miracle plays produced in the Cornish "rounds":

The quasy miracle, in English, a miracle play, is a kinde of interlude, compiled in Cornish out of some Scripture history, with that grossenes which accompanied the Romanes *vetus Comedia*. For representing it, they raise an earthen amphitheatre

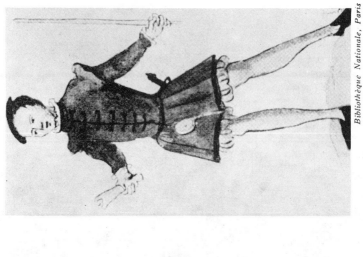

Herald and Stage Director (with Promptbook) of Jakob Ruf's
Von des Herren Weingarten (Zurich, 1539).

The Stage Director of Valenciennes.
Miniature by Hubert Cailleau (1547).

in some open field, having the Diameter of this enclosed playne
some 40 or 50 foot. The country people flock from all sides, many
miles off, to delight as well the eye as the eare; the players conne
not their parts without booke, but are prompted by one called
the Ordinary, who followeth at their back with the book in his
hand, and telleth them softly what they must pronounce aloud.
Which maner once gaue occasion to a pleasant conceyted gentleman of practising a mery pranke; for he vndertaking (perhaps
of set purpose) an actor's roome, was accordingly lessoned (beforehand) by the Ordinary that he must say after him. His turn
came. Quoth the Ordinary, "Goe forth, man, and show thyself."
The Gentleman steps out upon the stage, and like a bad Clarke in
Scripture matters, cleauing more to the letter than the sense, pronounced these words aloud. "Oh" (sayes the fellowe softly in his
eare), "you marre the play." And with this his passion, the Actor
makes the Audience in like sort acquainted. Herein the prompter
falles to flat rayling and cursing in the bitterest terms he could
deuise; which the Gentleman with a set gesture and countenance still soberly related, vntill the Ordinary, driuen at last into
a madde rage, was faine to giue over all. Which trousse, though
it brake off the Enterlude, yet defrauded not the beholders, but
dismissed them with a great deale more sport and laughter than
20 such Guaries could haue affoorded.

Jean Fouquet's Miniature of a Performance of *Le Martyre de Sainte Apolline*
(abt. 1460).
The stage director in clerical garb, with baton and production book, is standing on the *platea* in the midst of the performers. The mansions are arranged in a semicircle.

Chapter III

The Golden Age of Spain

1. STROLLING PLAYERS

In a surprisingly short time the Spanish theater developed from its primitive beginnings to full maturity. The distinct yet overlapping phases of development can still be traced in the *Viage entretenido* of Augustín de Rojas Villandrando (1603). In his treatise, in the form of a conversation between four players, the actor Rojas introduces us to some of the early phases of the Spanish stage, though it must be kept in mind that "The Road" with its rudimentary forms of theatrical enterprise remained intact long after permanent theaters had begun flourishing in the principal cities of the peninsula:

Solano: Well then, know that there are eight kinds of companies of actors, and all quite different; . . . there is the *bululu, ñaque, gangarilla, cambaleo, garnacha, boxiganga, farándula,* and the company. A *bululu* is a player who travels alone and afoot; he enters a village, goes to the curate, and tells him that he knows a comedia and a *loa* or two; he asks him to call the barber and sacristan, and he will recite it to them, so that they may give him something, that he may proceed on his way. These having assembled, he mounts upon a chest, and begins to recite, remarking as he goes on: "Now the lady enters and says so-and-so," and continues his acting while the curate passes around the hat, and having gathered four or five quartos, the curate adds a piece of bread and a bowl of soup, and with this he follows his star and continues his way. A *ñaque* consists of two men; they enact an *entremes* or portions of an *auto*, recite some *octavas* and two or three *loas*; they wear a beard of sheepskin (*zamarro*), play a drum, and charge an ochavo [2 maravedís], or in other kingdoms [parts of Spain] a dinerillo (that is what Rios and I used to do); they live contentedly, sleep in their clothes, go barefoot, are always hungry, rid themselves of their fleas amid the grain in summer and do not feel them on account of the cold in winter. *Gangarilla* is a bigger company; here there are three or four men: one who can play the fool (*que sabe tocar una locura*) and a boy who plays the women's roles. They represent the *auto* "The Lost Sheep," have beards and wigs (*cauellera*), borrow a woman's skirt and bonnet (which they sometimes forget to return),

57

play two comic *entremeses*, charge each spectator a quarto [4 maravedís], and also accept a piece of bread, eggs, sardines, or any kind of odds and ends, which they put into a bag. They eat roast meat, sleep on the ground, drink their draught of wine, travel constantly, show in every farm-yard, and always have their arms crossed. . . . The *cambaleo* consists of a woman who sings and five men who lament; they have a comedia, two *autos*, three or four *entremeses*, a bundle of clothes which a spider could carry, and transport the woman now on their backs, now on a litter or hand-chair (*silla de manos*). They act in the farm-yards for a loaf of bread, a bunch of grapes, a stew of cabbage, and in the villages charge six maravedís, a piece of sausage, a task of flax, and anything else that happens along (not refusing the most worthless gift). They remain in one spot four to six days, hire a bed for the woman, and if any of the men be on good terms with the hostess, he gets a bundle of straw and a cover and sleeps in the kitchen, while in winter the straw-loft is his constant habitation. At noon they eat their beef-stew and each one six bowls of broth, all sitting at a table or sometimes on the bed. The woman distributes the food, shares out the bread and measures the watered wine, and each one wipes his hands wherever he can, for they have but one napkin amongst them, and the table-cloths are so shy that they do not cover the table by a foot. A *garnacha* consists of five or six men, a woman who plays first lady's roles and a boy who plays the second; they carry a chest containing two smock-frocks, a coat, three pelisses, beards, wigs, and a woman's costume of taffeta (*tiritaña*). Their repertory consists of four comedias, three *autos* and as many *entremeses*; they carry the chest on a donkey's back and the woman, grumbling, on his rump, while the rest of the company follow afoot, driving the donkey. They remain eight days in a town, sleep four in a bed, eat a stew of beef and mutton, and some evenings a fricassee well seasoned. They get their wine in drams, their meat in ounces, their bread in pounds, and hunger by quarters [*arroba* = 11.5 kilos]. They give private performances for a fried chicken, a boiled rabbit, four reals in money, two quarts of wine, and may be hired for a festival for twelve reals. In a *boxiganga* there are two women, a boy, and six or seven companions, and not seldom do they meet with vexations, for there is never lacking a fool, a bully, an impatient, an importu-

nate, a sentimental, a jealous or a love-sick fellow, and having
any of these you can never travel with security, live contentedly,
or even have much money. They are provided with six comedias,
three or four *autos*, five *entremeses*, two chests — one containing
the baggage of the company, the other the women's clothes. They
hire four pack-mules — one for the chests, two for the women, and
the other on which the men may alternate every quarter-league.
They generally have two cloaks among the seven players, and
with these they enter two by two, like the friars. Often, however,
the mule-driver makes off with them, leaving the actors cloakless.
Such players dine well; all sleep in four beds, perform by night
and at festivals by day, and sup mostly on hash (*ensalada*), for,
as they finish the comedia late, they always find a cold supper.
While on the road they are fond of sleeping by the fireplaces,
for perchance these may be hung with blood-puddings, chines, or
sausages. These they enjoy with their eyes, touch with their fingers, and invite their friends, wrapping the sausages around their
bodies, the blood-puddings around their thighs, and stowing away
the chines, pigs' feet, chickens, and other trifles in holes in the
yards or stables; and if they happen to be in a country inn, which
is the safest, they mark the spot, so that they may know where
the dead are buried. That sort of a *boxiganga* is dangerous, for
it is more changeable than the moon and more unsafe than the
border-land, unless it has a good head to rule it. The *farándula*
is next to the company: it has three women, eight to ten comedias,
two chests of luggage. The players travel on mules with drivers
and sometimes in carts; visit the more important towns, dine
separately, wear good clothes, perform at Corpus festivals for
200 ducats, and live contentedly (that is, those who are not in
love).... In the companies there is every kind of grub and trumpery; they know something of the seamy side and also of good
manners; there are very clever people among them, men much
esteemed and persons well born, and even very respectable women (for where there are many there must be of all kinds).
They take with them fifty comedias, three hundred quarters of
luggage, sixteen persons who act, thirty who eat, one who takes
the money at the door (and God knows what he steals). Some
want mules, others coaches, some litters, others palfreys, and none
there are who are satisfied with a cart, because they say that they
have weak stomachs. Besides, there are generally many vexations.

Their labor is excessive because of the great amount of study, the continuous rehearsals, and the varied tastes (though of this Rios and Ramirez know only too much), so that it is better to pass this in silence, for, in faith, much could be said on this subject.

2. THE "STEW-PAN"

WITH THE ESTABLISHMENT of permanent theaters in Madrid (in the late 1560's), dramatic art moved into the courtyards (*corrales*) formed by the back walls of houses that were set at right angles to each other. The larger part of the audience viewed the performances in the *patio,* the standing pit behind the seating arrangements (*bancos*) in front of the stage. The most distinguished spectators and their ladies followed the *comedia* from the grated windows (*aposentos*) of the surrounding houses. No women were admitted into the yard; for them a special gallery or balcony in the rear of the *corral* was reserved, the "stew-pan" (*cazuela*). A charming picture of the scenes enacted in such a *cazuela* is given by the playwright, Juan de Zabaleta, in his *Día de fiesta por la tarde* (1666):

On feast-days men go to the play after lunching, but women go *before.* The woman who goes to the comedia on a holiday generally makes it an affair of a whole day. She meets one of her friends, and they take a bite of breakfast, reserving the midday meal for the evening. Then they go to mass, and from the church straight to the *cazuela* to get a good seat. There is no money-taker at the door yet. They enter and find a sprinkling of women as foolish as themselves already in the *cazuela.* They avoid the front seats, for these are for the women who come to see and be seen; so they take a modest seat in the middle. They express their pleasure at having found so comfortable a place and cast their eyes about for some pastime. Finding none, the rest from the hurry of the morning serves as a satisfaction. Other women enter, and some of the more brazen sit by the front railing of the *cazuela,* thus shutting out the light from those in the middle. Now the merry-making is let loose. The money-takers enter. One of our friends draws a handkerchief from beneath the folds of her petticoat, and with her teeth looses a knot tied in the corner of it, and takes out a real (34 maravedís) and asks for the return of ten maravedís. While she is doing this the other takes from her bosom a paper containing ten quartos (40 maravedís), and hands her money to the doorkeeper, who passes on. The one with the ten maravedís in her hand now buys a package of filberts for two quartos, and, like a child, does not know what to do with the remaining ochavo (2 maravedís) which she has received in change; finally she drops it in her bosom, with the remark that it is for the poor. Now the two friends begin to crack the filberts, and you can hear them munching them; but one of the filberts is full of dust, the other contains a dry kernel, while another has an oily taste. . . . Now more women are crowding in. One of those who are in front makes signs to two others who are standing behind our two friends, and without asking permission the newcomers pass between the two, stepping on their skirts and disarranging their cloaks, which provokes the exclamation: "Did you ever see such rudeness!" and they begin to shake and fleck the dust from their skirts. Those in the front seats begin to eat sandwiches, and presently one of the two friends remarks: "Do you see that man down there with grayish hair who is taking a seat on one of the benches on the left?" etc. . . . Here follows some scandal, for which she is reproved by another woman sitting near. . . .

The *cazuela* being now full, the *apretador* enters (he is the doorkeeper, who makes the women sit closer so that they may make more room), accompanied by four women, well dressed and thickly veiled, whom he wants to accommodate, for they have given him eight quartos. He approaches our friends and tells them to sit closer; they protest; he insists, and they reply that the women should have come earlier, when they would have found seats. Finally the newcomers let themselves fall upon those already seated, who, to get away from under them, unconsciously make room. There is grumbling on all sides, but at last quiet is restored. . . . It is now half-past two o'clock, and the friends, who had not dined, begin to get hungry. At length one of the women who had been accommodated by the *apretador* gives to our friends each a handful of prunes and some candied yolks of eggs, with the remark: "Come, let us be friends and eat these sweets which some booby gave me." They begin to eat and want to strike up a conversation, but say nothing, as they cannot stop eating. Presently there is an altercation at the door of the *cazuela* between the doorkeeper and a number of youths who want some women to enter free, and they burst into the *cazuela* quarreling. A great commotion and uproar ensues. The women rise excitedly, and in their anxiety to avoid those who are quarreling they fall over one another. . . . Those who rush up from the *patio* to lend aid or restore order push into the jumbling mass and bowl the women over. All now take to the corners as the best place in the *cazuela,* and some on all fours and others running seek a place of safety. Finally the police expel the men, and every woman takes a seat where she happens to be, none occupying the one she had at first. One of the two friends is now on the last bench, while the other is near the door. The former has lost her gloves and finds that her gown is torn; her friend is bleeding at the nose as the result of the scuffle, and, having lost her handkerchief, makes use of her petticoat. All is lamentation, when the guitar-players enter, and quiet is once more restored.

3.   THE AFTERNOON OF A SPANISH IDLER

JUAN DE ZABALETA also penned a sketch of the Spanish gallant who whiled away his time in the playhouse in very much the same fashion as his idling English and French counterparts:

He must dine hurriedly at noon, who intends to go to the comedia in the afternoon. His anxiety to get a good seat hardly permits him to warm the chair at the dinner-table. He reaches the door of the theater, and the first thing he does is to try to enter without paying. The first misfortune of players is to work much and to have but few persons pay. For twenty persons to enter on three quartos would not do much harm if it were not an occasion for many others to do the same. For if only one has not paid, countless others will also refuse to pay. All wish to enjoy the privilege of free admission in order that others may see that they are worthy of it. This they desire with such intense eagerness that they will fight to obtain it, and by fighting they achieve their object. Rarely does a man who has once quarreled to avoid paying ever pay at any subsequent time. A fine reason to quarrel, in order to profit by the sweat of those who labor to entertain one! And then, because he does not pay, will he be easy to please?

On the contrary, if a player wears a poor costume he insults him or hisses him. I should like to know how this fellow and those who imitate him can expect a player to wear fine clothes, when they refuse to pay him. . . . Our idler moves on into the theater and approaches the person who assigns the seats and benches, and asks for a place. He is met with the reply that there are none, but that a certain seat which has been engaged has not yet been occupied, and that he should wait until the guitar-players appear, and if it be still vacant, he may then occupy it. Our man argues, but to amuse himself, in the meanwhile, he goes to the dressing-room. There he finds women taking off their street clothes and putting on their theatrical costumes. Some are so far disrobed as though they were about to retire to bed. He takes his place in front of a woman who, having come to the theater on foot, is having her shoes and stockings put on by her maid. This cannot be done without some sacrifice of modesty. The poor actress must suffer this and does not dare to protest, for, as her chief object is to win applause, she is afraid to offend any one. A hiss, no matter how unjust, discredits her, since all believe that the judgment of him who accuses is better than their own. The actress continues to dress, enduring his presence with patience. The most indecorous woman on the stage has some modesty in the green-room, for here her immodesty is a vice, while there it is of her profession.

The fellow never takes his eyes off her. . . . He approaches the hangings (*paños*) to see whether the doubtful seat is occupied, and finds it vacant. As it appears that the owner will not come, he goes and takes the seat. Scarcely has he been seated when the owner arrives and defends his claim. The one already seated resists, and a quarrel ensues. Did this fellow not come to amuse himself, when he left his home? And what has quarreling to do with amusement? . . . Finally the quarrel is adjusted, and the one who has paid for the seat yields and takes another place which has been offered him by the peacemakers. The commotion caused by the struggle having subsided, our intruder is also quieted and now turns his eyes to the gallery occupied by the women (*cazuela*), carefully scrutinizing their faces until he finds one who particularly strikes his fancy, and guardedly makes signs to her. . . .

He is looking round in every direction, when he feels some

one pull his cloak from behind. He turns and sees a fruit-seller, who, leaning forward between two men, whispers to him that the woman who is tapping her knee with her fan says that she has much admired the spirit which he has shown in the quarrel and asks him to pay for a dozen oranges for her. The fellow looks again at the *cazuela,* sees that the woman is the one that caught his fancy before, pays the money for the fruit, and sends word that she may have anything else she pleases. As the fruit-seller leaves, the fellow immediately plans that he will wait for the woman at the exit of the theater, and he begins to think that there is an interminable delay in beginning the play. In a loud and peevish manner he signifies his disapproval, exciting the *mosqueteros,* who are standing below, to break forth with insulting shouts, in order to hasten the players.

4. A THEATER RIOT

THE MALE SPECTATORS in the yard were the soul and body of the house, especially if they belonged to the class of the *mosqueteros,* who were standing in the *patio.* They were the supreme arbiters of the play, and there was no appeal from their judgment. A theatrical riot in Spain had all the characteristics of a bullfight. After one of Juan Pérez de Montalván's plays had been whistled off the stage, Francisco de Quevedo Villegas wrote that the play had met with the same reception as a bull in the arena:

Believe me, I took it for a bad omen, when I saw all the planks that had been assembled for the scenic effects, for at once I thought of the barriers in the arena, and it seemed to me that the people might be excused for turning the performance into a bullfight. You should have taken care not to have trumpets sounded in your play, for you must know that in the arena this is the signal for hamstringing the bull. The women were the first to whistle. With this encouragement the *mosqueteros* opened fire, and your comedy died half like a bull amid whistles and hisses, half like a valiant soldier under musketry fire. The whole crowd took part in the revolt. The women were the leaders.

5. SHOEMAKER AND CRITIC

OFTEN ENOUGH such violent audience reaction was perfectly justified, since people, barely able to read and write, had the audacity to work for the stage. The Spanish people's infatuation with the theater brought about a mass production of plays turned out by clerics, noblemen, adventurers, scholars, theater managers, poor licentiates, and by craftsmen, who had the ambition to write plays. We hear of tailors and shoemakers taking an active part in theatrical life. The Countess d'Aulnoy relates that a Madrid shoemaker exercised an outspoken theatrical dictatorship and was fawned on by playwrights who were eager to secure his benevolence:

The finest comedy in the world (I mean those that are acted in the city) very often receives its fate from the weak fancy of some ignorant wretch or other. But there is one in particular, and a shoemaker, who decides the matter, and who hath gained such an absolute authority so to do, that when the poets have written their plays, they go to him, and as it were, sue for his approbation; they read to him their plays, the shoemaker, with grave looks thereupon, utters abundance of nonsense, which neverthe-less the poor poet is obliged to put up with; after all, if he hap-pens to be at the first acting of it, every body has their eyes upon the behavior of this pitiful fellow; the young people, of what quality soever, imitate him. If he yawns, they yawn, if he laughs, so do they. In a word, sometimes he grows angry or weary, and then takes a little whistle and falls a-whistling; at the same time you shall hear a hundred whistles, which makes so shrill a noise, that it is enough to confound the heads of the spectators. By this time our poor poet is quite ruined; all his study and pains having been at the mercy of a blockhead, ac-cording as he was in a good or bad humor.

6. THE CORPUS CHRISTI PROCESSION

IN CONNECTION with the Corpus Christi festival, sacramental plays (*autos sacramentales*) were performed in the streets of Spanish cities, and Corpus Christi became known as the Festival of the Cars because of the pageant cars which moved along with the traditional procession. At predetermined points of the city temporary platform stages were erected on which the *autos* were performed. Madame d'Aulnoy, who visited Madrid in June 1679, has left us a description of the festive atmosphere:

I should now tell you that I have seen the ceremony on Corpus Christi day, which is very solemnly kept here. There is a general procession of all the parishes and monasteries, which are very numerous; the streets through which the holy sacrament is to pass, are hung with the richest tapestry in the world; for I do not only speak of that which belongs to the crown that is there, but also of that which belongs to a thousand particular persons who have most admirable tapestry. All the balconies are then without their lattices, adorned with carpets, rich cushions, and canopies; they hang ticking across the streets to hinder the sun from being troublesome, and they throw water upon it, to make the air cooler. All the streets are spread with sand, well watered, and filled with so great a quantity of flowers, that you can hardly tread upon any thing else. The repositories are extraordinarily large, and adorned with the greatest splendor.

No women go in the procession: the King was there in a black lutestring taffeta suit, a shoulder-belt of blue silk, edged with white, his sleeves were of white taffeta, embroidered with silk and bugles; they were very long and open before: he had small sleeves hanging down to his waist; his cloak was wrapped about his arm, and he had on his collar of gold and precious stones, at which there hung a little sheep in diamonds; he had also diamond buckles at his shoes and garters, and a great hat-band of the same, which shined like the sun; he had likewise a knot which buttoned up his hat, and at the bottom of that a pearl, which they call the peregrine; it is as big as the russet pearl, and of the same shape; it is pretended to be the finest in Europe, and that both its color and kind is in perfection.

The whole court, without exception, followed the holy sacrament, the councils walked after it, without any order or precedency, just as they happened to be, holding white wax candles in their hands; the King had one, and went foremost, next the tabernacle where the sacrament was. It is certainly one of the finest ceremonies that can be seen. I observed that all the gentlemen of the bed-chamber had each a great gold key by his side, which opens the King's chamber, into which they can go when they will; it is as large as a cellar-door key. I there saw several knights of Malta, who wore every one a cross of Malta, made of holland, and embroidered upon their cloaks; it was near two o'clock, and the procession was not yet gone in; when it passed by the palace, they fired several rockets, and other inventions. . . .

As soon as the holy sacrament is gone back to the church, every body goes home to eat, that they may be at the *autos*, which are certain kinds of tragedies upon religious subjects, and are oddly enough contrived and managed: they are acted either in the court or street of each president of a council, to whom it is due. The King goes there, and all the persons of quality receive tickets overnight to go there; so that we were invited, and I was amazed to see them light up abundance of flambeaux, whilst the sun beat full upon the comedians' heads, and melted the wax like butter; they acted the most impertinent piece that ever I saw in my days. This is the subject of it:

The knights of St. James are assembled, and Our Lord comes and desires them to receive him into their order; there are present divers of them that are agreeable to it, but the seniors represent to the others, the wrong they should do themselves, if they should admit into their society a person of ignoble birth; that St. Joseph, his father, was a poor carpenter, and that the Holy Virgin wrought at her needle. Our Lord with great impatience expects their resolution; at last they determine, with some unwillingness, to refuse him; but at the same time propose an expedient, which is to be instituted on purpose for him, the Order of Christ, and with this every body is satisfied.

7. COMMAND PERFORMANCE FOR PHILIP IV

IN 1659, François Bertaut, while on a diplomatic mission in Madrid, had an opportunity to witness a performance in the theater which, in 1632, Philip the Fourth had built in his new summer residence, the palace of Buen Retiro:

The best thing of all, and what I wou'd have you keep as a Secret, is the Comedy that has just now been acted at the Palace by the Light only of six great Wax Flambeaus that stood in Silver Candlesticks of a prodigious Bigness indeed. On the two sides of the great Room there were two Niches, all lattic'd up; in the one were the little Princes, and some People belonging to the Court; and in the other, which was directly against it, was the Mareschal. Along these two sides there were only two large

Benches cover'd with Persian Carpets. The Ladies (to the Number of about ten or twelve) came and sat down on each side upon the Carpets, leaning their backs against Benches. Behind them, on the side where the young Princes were, but far below distinct from the Place where the Actors were, and rather behind them, were some Lords standing; but on the side where the Mareschal was there was but one Grandee. The rest of us French Men stood behind the Bench where the Ladies lean'd. The King, the Queen, and the Infanta came in, following one of these Ladies, who carry'd a Flambeaux. As he enter'd, he put off his Hat to all the Ladies, and then sat him down by a Screen, with the Queen at his Left-Hand, and the Infanta at the Queen's. All the time of the Play (except cne Word that he spoke to the Queen) he neither mov'd Head, Hand or Foot; he only sometimes turn'd his Eyes round him, and had no body near him but a Dwarf. As they went out from the Play the Ladies all rose, and presently after came from each side one by one, and met in the middle like so many Canons leaving their Stalls when Service is done. They took one another by the Hand, made their Honours that lasted about a Quarter of an Hour, and then went out one after another; the King all this while being uncover'd. At last he himself rose, and made a moderate Bow to the Queen; the Queen made a Curtsy to the Infanta, and taking her by the Hand, as I thought, they both went out together.

Chapter IV

Italian Renaissance

1. THE WONDERS OF PERSPECTIVE SCENERY

In 1513, the first performance of Cardinal Bernardo Bibbiena's comedy, *La Calandria*, took place at the court of the Duke of Urbino. Baldassare Castiglione, author of the *Cortegiano*, was one of the directors of the production, for which Girolamo Genga (1476 - 1551) designed the perspective scenery. In a letter to his friend, Lodovico Canossa, Castiglione left us a description of Genga's work:

The stage represented a very beautiful city, with streets, palaces, churches, and towers. The streets looked as if they were real, and everything was done in relief, and made even more striking through the art of painting and well-conceived perspective. Among other things there was an octagonal temple in low relief, so well finished that it seems hardly possible that it could have been built in four months even if one considers all the potential workmanship which the state of Urbino can muster. This temple was done in stucco and decorated with the most beautiful historical pictures. The windows seemed to be made of alabaster, while all the architraves and cornices gave the impression of having been made of fine gold and ultramarine blue. At certain points were pieces of glass used in imitation of jewels, which looked like genuine gems. Round the temple were carved pillars and statues that simulated marble. It would take me too long to describe everything. The temple stood almost in the middle. At one side of the stage there was an arch of triumph at about seven feet distance from the wall, perfectly executed. Between the architrave and the vault the story of the three Horatii had been painted though it looked like a marble frieze. Two Victories, stucco statues holding trophies, were placed in the two niches above the pillars which supported the arch. On the top of the arch stood a very beautiful equestrian statue — a man in armor, with his spear wounding a nude enemy that lay prostrate at his feet. On either side of the horse were two small altars, each of which showed a vessel wherein a bright flame was burning throughout the entire performance.

2.   PERUZZI DESIGNS FOR THE POPE

IN 1514, the *Calandria* was performed in Rome as part of the entertainments which Pope Leo X provided for the visiting Isabella Gonzaga d'Este, Margravine of Mantua. Duke Francesco Maria Rovere, having been in charge of the Urbino première, staged the comedy, while Baldassare Peruzzi (1481 - 1537) designed the scenery, which Vasari regarded as truly epochal:

> When the comedy of *La Calandra*, by Cardinal Bibbiena, was performed for Pope Leo, Baldassare [Peruzzi] designed the scenery, which was not inferior to the other scenery already mentioned [when he designed improvements for St. Peter's in Rome]. He deserved the more praise because comedies had fallen into disuse, and the scenery was consequently neglected. Before the performance of *La Calandra*, which was one of the earliest comedies in the vernacular to be presented, Baldassare did two marvellous scenes in the time of Leo X. which prepared the way for those done afterwards in our own day. It is wonderful how, in the narrow space, he depicted his streets, palaces and curious temples, loggias and cornices, all made to make them appear to be what they represent. He also arranged the lights inside for the perspective, and all the other necessary things. These comedies, in my opinion, when performed with all their accessories, surpass all other spectacular displays in magnificence.

3.   SCENERY FOR THE MEDICEAN COURT

SEBASTIANO, called Aristotile da San Gallo (1482 - 1551), was one of the architects at the Medicean court at Florence. For Duke Alessandro Medici he designed the scenery for G. M. Primerani's religious dramas, *Tamar* and *Joseffo accusato*. The Duke was so pleased with Aristotile's work that he commissioned him to execute the festive decorations for his marriage with Margaret of Parma (1536). Lorenzo Medici's *l'Alidosio* had been chosen as the play for the occasion, and Aristotile designed for it a forum with a great triumphal arch. Alessandro's successor, Cosimo I, retained Aristotile's services, and when the new Duke celebrated his marriage with Eleonora of Toledo in 1539, Aristotile was put in charge of the scenery for the performance of Landi's comedy, *Il commodo*. Giorgio Vasari, at that time an assistant designer at the Medicean court, recalled Aristotile's perspective setting and the features of the magnificent temporary stage, erected in the great courtyard of the palace:

After Lorenzo had slain Duke Alessandro, Duke Cosimo succeeded in 1537, and soon after married the incomparable lady Leonora di Toledo. . . . For the wedding, which took place on 27 June, 1539, Aristotile surpassed himself in a scene representing Pisa, in the great court of the Medici palace containing the fountain. It would be impossible to assemble a greater variety of windows, doors, façades of palaces, streets and receding distances, all in perspective. He also represented the leaning tower, the cupola and round Church of S. Giovanni, with other things of the city. Of the steps and their realism I will say nothing, in order not to repeat myself. It had eight faces with square sides, very artistic in its simplicity, and imparting grace to the perspective above, so that nothing better of its kind could be desired. He next devised an ingenious wooden lantern like an arch behind the buildings, and a sun a *braccio* [*ca.* 2 feet] high made of a crystal ball filled with distilled water, with two lighted torches behind, illuminating the sky of the scenery and the perspective, so that it looked like a veritable sun. It was surrounded by golden rays covering the curtain, and was managed by a windlass, so as to rise to the meridian in the middle of the play, and sink in the west at its end. Antonio Landi, a Florentine noble, wrote the comedy and Giovan-Battista Strozzi, a clever youth, directed the interludes and music.

4. SERLIO'S THREE SCENES

SEBASTIANO SERLIO (1475 - 1554) was a pupil of Peruzzi, from whom he inherited material concerning architectural theory. In 1545, Serlio published in Paris the second book of his *Regole generali di architettura*. This volume, dealing with perspective painting, contains detailed instructions with regard to the construction of a stage and an auditorium. Serlio is thinking in terms of a typical temporary Renaissance theater to be erected in a great banqueting hall or in a courtyard of an Italian prince. Serlio had built such a theater in a courtyard at Vicenza in the 1530's. In true Vitruvian style he raised his playhouse on a circular plan. One half of the circle was designated for the stage, the other half was given to the auditorium. The stage platform cut directly across the center of the circle. It consisted of two sections: the front part, at eye level, was the horizontal acting area (*ca.* 58 ft. wide and 10 ft. deep); behind this was the rear stage, sloping a ninth part of its depth and bearing two-faced anglewings, upon which an illusionistic perspective setting was painted. The scene was closed by a back shutter or screen, two feet distant from the rear wall, for convenient traffic behind the scenes. The vanishing point of Serlio's setting was located beyond the back wall. The angle-wings consisted of wooden frames that were covered with canvas. Following Vitruvius, Serlio distinguished three types of more or less standardized settings for comedies, tragedies, and pastoral plays. He added advice with regard to the artifical lighting of the stage, the use of projectors and reflectors, the appearance of heavenly bodies, and the lightning-and-thunder effects. The following excerpts from the second book, Chapter III, of Serlio's *Architettura* are given in the English translation which was published in London in 1611:

[*The Comic Scene*]

This first [scene] shall be Comicall, whereas the houses must be slight for Citizens, but specially there must not want a brawthell or bawdy house, and a great Inne, and a Church; such things are of necessetie to be therein. How to rayse these houses from the ground is sufficiently expressed, and how you shall place the Horison: neverthelesse, that you may be the better instructed (touching the former of these houses) I have here set down a Figure, for satisfaction of those that take pleasure therein; but because this Figure is so small, therein I could not observe all the measures, but refer them to invention, that thereby you may chuse or make houses which shew well, as an open Gallery, or lodge through the which you may see an other house. The hangings over or shooting out, show well in shortening worke, and some Cornices cut out at the ends; accompanied with some others that are painted, show well in worke: so doe the houses which have great bearing out, like lodgings or Chambers for men, and especially above all things, you must set the smalest houses before, that you may see other houses over or above them, as you see it here above the bawdy house: for if you place the greatest before, and the rest behind still lessen, then the place of the Scene would not be so well filled, and although these things upon the one side be made all upon one floore: Neverthelesse, for that you place great part of the lights in the middle, hanging over the Scene or Scaffold, therefore it would stand better if the floore in the midst were taken away, and all the roundels and Quadrans which you see in the Buildings, they are artificiall lights cutting through, of divers colors.... The windowes which stand before, were good to be made of Glasse or Paper, with light behind them. . . .

Serlio's Design for the Comic Scene (1545).

[*The Tragic Scene*]

Houses for Tragedies, must be made for great personages, for that actions of love, strange adventures, and cruell murthers (as you reade in ancient and moderne Tragedies) happen alwayes in the houses of great Lords, Dukes, Princes, and Kings. Therefore in such cases you must make none but stately houses. . . . I have made all my Scenes of laths, covered with linnen, yet sometime it is necessary to make some things rising or bossing out; which are to bee made of wood, like the houses on the left side, whereof the Pillars, although they shorten, stand all upon one base, with some stayres, all covered over with cloth, the Cornices bearing out, which you must observe to the middle part: But to give place to the Galleries, you must set the other shortening Cloth somewhat backwards, and make a cornice above it, as you

Serlio's Design for the Tragic Scene (1545).

Serlio's Design for the Satyric Scene (1545).

see. . . . All that you make above the Roofe sticking out, as
Chimneyes, Towers, Piramides, Oblisces, and other such like
things or Images; you must make them all of thin bords, cut out
round, and well colloured: But if you make any flat Buildings,
they must stand somewhat farre inward, that you may not see
them on the sides. In these Scenes, although some have painted
personages therein like supporters, as in a Gallery, or doore, as a
Dog, Cat, or any other beasts: I am not of that opinion, for that
standeth too long without stirring or mooving; but if you make
such a thing to lie sleeping, that I hold withall. You may also
make Images, Histories, or Fables of Marble, or other matter
against a wall; but to represent the life, they ought to stirre. . . .

[*The Satyric Scene*]

The Satiricall Scenes are to represent Satirs, wherein you
must place all those things that bee rude and rusticall . . . for
which cause Vitruvius speaking of Scenes, saith, they should be
made with Trees, Rootes, Herbs, Hils and Flowres, and with
some countrey houses. . . . And for that in our dayes these things
were made in Winter, when there were but fewe greene Trees,
Herbs and Flowres to be found; then you must make these things
of Silke, which will be more commendable then the naturall things
themselves: and as in other Scenes for Comedies or Tragedies, the
houses or other artificiall things are painted, so you must make
Trees, Hearbs, and other things in these; the more such things
cost, the more they are esteemed, for they are things which
stately and great persons doe, which are enemies to nigardlinesse.
This have I seene in some Scenes made by Ieronimo Genga, for
the pleasure and delight of his lord and patron Francisco Maria,
Duke of Urbin: wherein I saw so great liberalitie used by the
Prince, and so good a conceit in the workman, and so good Art and
proportion in things therein represented, as ever I saw in all my
life before. Oh good Lord, what magnificence was there to be
seene, for the great number of Trees and Fruits, with sundry
Herbes and Flowres, all made of fine Silke of divers collours. The
water courses being adorned with Frogs, Snailes, Tortuses, Toads,
Adders, Snakes, and other beasts: Rootes of Corrale, mother of
Pearle, and other shels layd and thrust through betweene the
stones, with so many severall and faire things, that if I should

declare them all, I should not have time enough. I speake not of
Satirs, Nimphes, Mer-maids, divers monsters, and other strange
beastes, made so cunningly, that they seemed in shew as if they
went and stirred, according to their manner. And if I were not
desirous to be brief, I would speake of the costly apparel of some
Shepheards made of cloth of gold, and of Silke, cunningly mingled
with Imbrothery: I would also speake of some Fishermen, which
were no lesse richly apparelled then the others, having Nets and
Angling-rods, all gilt: I should speake of some Countrey mayds
and Nimphes carelesly apparelled without pride, but I leave all
these things to the discretion and consideration of the judicious
workmen; which shall make all such things as their pattrons serve
them, which they must worke after their owne devises, and never
take care what it shall cost.

[*Of Artificial Lights of the Scenes*]

I promised in the Treatise of Scenes to set downe the manner how to make these lights shining through, of divers collours,
& first I will speake of a asure collour which is like to a Zaphir,
and yet somewhat fayrer. Take a piece of Salamoniacke, and put
it into a Barbers Basen, or such like thing, and put water into
it: then bruse and crush the Salamoniacke softly therein, till it
be all molten, always putting more water unto it, as you desire
to have it light or sad collour; which done, if you will have it
fayre and cleare, then straine it through a fine cloth into another
vessell, and then it will be a cleare Celestiall blew, whereof you
may make divers kinds of blew with water. Will you make an Em-
erauld collour, then put some Saffron as you will have it pale or
high colloured; for heere it is not necessary to prescribe you any
weight or measure, for that experience will teach you how to doe
it. If you will make a Rubbie collour, if you bee in a place where
you may have red Wine, then you need not use any other thing;
but to make it pall with water, as need requireth: but if you can
get no wine, then take Brazill [red brazil wood] beaten to powder,
& put it into a Kettell of water with Allum, let it seethe, and
skum it well; then strayne it, and use it with water and Vinneger.
If you will counterfeit a Ballayes [rose-colored balas ruby], you
must make it of red and white Wine mingled together; but white
Wine alone will showe like a Topas or a Crisolite: The Conduit

or common water being strayned, will be like a Diamond, and to
doe this well, you must upon a glassie ground frame certaine
points or tablets [lenses to project the light?], and fill them with
water. The manner to set these shining collours in their places,
is thus. Behind the painted house wherein these painted collours
shall stand, you must set a thin board, cut out in the same manner
that these lights shall be placed, whether it be round or square,
cornered or ovale, like an Egge; and behind the same board there
shall be another stronger board layd flat behind them, for the
bottels and other manner of glasses with these waters to stand in,
must be placed against the holes, as it shall necessarily fall out,
but they must be set fast, lest they fall with leaping and
dancing of the Moriscoes. And behind the glasses you must set
great Lampes, that the light may also be stedfast: and if the bottels or other vessels of glasse on the side where the light stands
were flat, or rather hollow, it would show the clearer, and the
collours most excellent and fayre; the like must be done with the
holes on the shortening side [perspective face of the angle-wing]:
But if you need a great light to show more than the rest, then set
a torch behind, and behind the torch a bright Bason; the brightness whereof will shew like the beames of the Sunne. You may
also make glasse of all collours and formes, some four square,
some with crosses, & any other forme with their light behind
them. Now all the lights serving for the collours, shal not be the
same which must light the Scene, for you must have a great
number of torches [a chandelier] before the Scene. You may also
place certaine candlesticks above the Scene with great candles
therein, and above the candlesticks you may place some vessels
with water, wherein you may put a piece of Camphir, which
burning, will show a very good light, and smell well. Sometime
it may chance that you must make some thing or other which
should seeme to burne, which you must wet throughly with excellent good Aquavite; and setting it on fire with a candle it will
burne all over: and although I could speake more of these fires,
yet this shal suffice for this time; & I will speake of some things
that are pleasing to the beholders.

[*Animation of the Inanimate*]

The while that the Scene is emptie of personages, then the
workman must have certaine Figures or formes ready of such

greatnes as the place where they must stand, will afford them to be, which must be made of paste board, cut out round and paynted, signifiing such things as you will, which Figures must leane against a rule or lath of wood, crosse over the Scene where any gate, doore, or way is made, and there some one or other behind the doore must make the Figures passe along, sometime in forme of Musitians with instruments, and some like singers; and behind the Scene some must play on, upon certaine instruments and sing also: sometime you must make a number of footemen and horsemen, going about with Trumpets, Phifes and Drummes, at which time you must play with Drumbes, Trumpets and Phifes, etc. very softly behind, which will keepe the peoples eyes occupied, and content them well.

[*Heavenly Bodies*]

If it be requisite to make a Planet, or any other thing to passe along in the Ayre, it must be framed and cut out of pasteboard; then in the hindermost and backe part of the houses of the Scene, there must be a piece of wire drawne above in the roofe of the house and made fast with certain rings behind to the paste-board painted with a Planet or any other thing that shal be drawne softly by a man with a black threed from one end to the other, but it must be farre from mens sight, that neither of the threeds may bee seene.

[*Thunder and Lightning*]

Sometime you shall have occasion to shew thunder and lightning as the play requireth, then you must make thunder in this manner: commonly all Scenes are made at the end of a great Hall, whereas usually there is a Chamber above it, wherein you must roule a great Bullet of a Cannon or some other great Ordinance, and then counterfeit Thunder. Lightning must be made in this manner, there must be a man placed behind the Scene or Scaffold in a high place with a boxe in his hand, the cover whereof must be full with holes, and in the middle of that place there shall be a burning candle placed, the boxe must be filled with powder of vernis [*i.e.*, varnish, resin] or sulphire, and casting his hand with the boxe upwards the powder flying in the candle, will shew as if it were lightning. But touching the beames of the lightning, you must draw a piece of wyre over the Scene, which must hang downewards, whereon you must put a squib covered over with pure gold or shining lattin [sheet tin] which you will: and while the Bullet is rouling, you must shoote of some piece of Ordinance, and with the same giving fire to the squibs, it will worke the effect which is desired.

5. *KING OEDIPUS* IN THE OLYMPIC THEATER

IN 1556, THE ACCADEMIA OLIMPICA was founded in Vicenza. This literary society was primarily interested in the study of antiquity and in the production of classical and pseudo-classical drama. One of the founders was the architect Andrea Palladio (1508 - 1580), an ardent classicist and student of Vitruvius. For years the Olympic Academy had produced plays in temporary theaters such as the one erected by Palladio in the Basilica of Vicenza. At length Palladio was commissioned to build a permanent theater, the extant Teatro Olimpico. Palladio began its construction in 1580, but died a few months later. The work was completed in 1584 by Vincenzo Scamozzi (1552 - 1616), who added the perspective vistas behind the five doorways in 1585, at the time of the visit of the Empress Maria of Austria. In contrast to the typical Roman theater, Palladio had planned his playhouse on a semi-elliptical rather than semi-circular plan. Around an open orchestra space there are arranged, on an elliptical curve, thirteen tiers of steps (*gradi*) leading up to a colonnade, which in turn is surmounted by a balustrade with statuary. The stage itself is a long and narrow rectangle (82 x 22 feet) after the Roman pattern. It is backed by a permanent scenic façade, richly ornamented with niches, statues, pillars, and reliefs. This *scenae frons*, as the Romans would have called it, was pierced with five apertures: a large central doorway, lesser doorways on either side, and a doorway in each of the side walls. Up to 1584, these five doorways were probably closed with curtains. But since a modern architect in the 1580's could hardly ignore the development of perspective scenery, Scamozzi finally added to Palladio's rigid frame the perspective vistas, built of wood and plaster on the sloping back stage area and representing the streets of an ancient city. One of the first performances at the Teatro Olimpico was a production of *King Oedipus* on March 3, 1585. The following letter written by Filippo Pigafetta to an unknown aristocrat gives a vivid account of this performance and of the pleasures sought and experienced by a cultured late Renaissance society:

Most illustrious Lord and most honored Master!

If my hand would be obedient to my mind, as Michel Agnolo Buonarroti, the eminent painter, sculptor, and architect used to

The Stage of the Teatro Olimpico in Vicenza. Palladio's *scenae frons* (1580) with Scamozzi's perspective vistas (1585).

Courtesy of the Uffizi, Florence

Vincenzo Scamozzi's Sketch for the Perspective Vistas of the Teatro Olimpico.

say, and if the social activities, the flow of wine, and the bustle of the carnival permit me, I would like to please Your Highness and Your friends by describing the theatrical pomp and the magnificence of the tragedy which yesterday was recited in this city. But the aforementioned circumstances will excuse me if I only mention the highlights of this marvellous spectacle, leaving a fuller report to the time when I shall speak to you. Palladio, wanting to leave behind him a perfect work of art, convinced the Academicians of Vicenza, called the Olimpici, that, in view of the fact that their noble institution many times recited eclogues, pastorals, comedies, tragedies, and other such pleasures for the enjoyment of the people, they should build a theater according to the ancient custom of the Greeks and Romans. . . . Little by little they have brought to an end the masterly and admirable work of art. The theater can easily accommodate 3,000 spectators. It is such a charming sight that everybody is usually pleased by it due to the exquisite beauty of its proportions. The eyes of the laymen receive the overall impression of an incredible loveliness, which arises from the friezes, architraves, cornices, festoons, columns with very beautiful capitals, and bases with many

metropes sculptured in low stucco relief. And there are perhaps
eighty stucco statues, made by the best masters, representing the
likenesses of the Academicians, and each one of these statues was
done more than once until it had assumed the proper resemblance.
I leave aside the balustrades, the doors, and the windows, which
it would take too long to enumerate in a brief letter. But I shall
say that even the smallest detail seems to have been executed by
Mercury and adorned by the Graces themselves. The stage perspective is likewise admirable, very well understood and seen,
with its five principal sections, or rather entrances, which represent the seven streets of Thebes. The city is an exhibition of
beautiful houses, palaces, temples, and altars in the style of
antiquity, and of the finest architecture. It is made of strong
wood so that it may last for ages to come. It cost 1,500 ducats.
Just think, Your most illustrious Lordship, a complete building
designed by Palladio in the last years of his life and in the full
mastery of his knowledge. Palladio had asked the Olimpici to
have his name inscribed in it, for he was so proud of his achievement and thought that he would never design anything better.
In this theater, which cost 18,000 ducats with all its appurtenances, the Academicians produced — in tune with the edifice —
the noblest tragedy ever written, *Oedipus the King* . . . by the
Athenian poet Sophocles, exalted above all others by Aristotle.
Thus in the most famous theater of the world, the world's most
excellent tragedy was given. The translation from the Greek
into the vernacular was done by the celebrated Orsato Giustiniani.
Angelo Ingegneri, capable of such things, has directed this tragic
business. The choral music was composed by Andrea Gabrieli,
organist of St. Mark's. The settings were designed by Vincenzo
Scamozzi, architect of Vicenza. The costumes were by [Ales-
sandro?] Maganza. The president of the Academy is the Illustrious Leonardo Valmarana, who has the soul of Caesar and was
born for generous enterprises. This explains why he made the
Empress [Maria of Austria] reside in his house, and in the true
spirit of chivalry he did not overlook any opportunity to please
and invite the strangers who passed through the city, and, for
their delight, to offer his gardens, which can almost stand comparison with the Sallustian Gardens of ancient Rome. The president and the other Academicians were all lavishly dressed, and
all of them did not spare any efforts or money to make this event

perfect in every respect. There were eighty stage costumes. The tragedy has nine speaking parts, and the cast had been doubled by understudies to provide for any emergency. Two of the players, the King and the Queen, were magnificently dressed in gold cloth. Accommodations had been courteously provided for about 2,000 gentlemen from Venice and the State as well as from other countries, not counting the others, so that on the streets of Vicenza one could see nothing but noblemen and noblewomen, carriages, horses, and strangers who had come to attend the performance, and all quartered at the inns, without being known in other ways than that they were strangers. There was an incredible display of kindness on the part of the Academicians toward all the guests, when the latter reached the entrance, where quite a crowd had assembled, and when they were shown their seats inside, receiving, upon request, refreshing wines and fruits; and everything had been personally supervised by the members of the Academy, especially the accommodation of the ladies down in the orchestra, where four hundred chairs had been placed for them, strangers and natives. Among the ladies was the wife of the illustrious French ambassador and one of his nieces. There were more than 3,000 spectators. People came early, that is, between sixteen and twenty o'clock. The performance began at one-thirty at night [*i.e.*, 7:30 P.M.] and was over by five o'clock [11 P.M.]. Some, for instance, I and some of my friends, stayed there perhaps eleven hours, not getting tired at all. Because of seeing one new face after the other, watching the ladies being seated, and the assembly as a whole, the time passed very fast. In different places of the thirteen tiers there were some exits, so that nothing in the way of comfort for the spectators was overlooked. The illustrious Captain and several Senators were present. The Mayor remained outside. For security reasons and as a sort of guard of honor, soldiers were posted at the gates. When the time had come to lower the curtain, a very sweet smell of perfume made itself felt to indicate that in the city of Thebes, according to the ancient legend, incense was burned to placate the wrath of the gods. Then there was a sound of trumpets and drums, and four squibs exploded. In a twinkle of an eye the curtain fell before the stage. I can hardly express in words, nor can it be imagined, how great the joy was, and the infinite pleasure felt by the spectators when they, after a moment of stunned surprise, watched the prologue, and when the sound of harmonized voices and divers instruments could be heard from a distance behind the scenic façade — hymns sung in the city, and prayers and incense offered to the gods to obtain from them health, the alleviation of hunger and pestilence, which harrassed that city for so long. Then began the tragedy proper, and not one point was missed throughout the entire action. The actors are of the best sort, and they are dressed neatly and lavishly according to each one's station. The King had a guard of twenty-four archers dressed in Turkish fashion, pages, and courtiers. The Queen was surrounded by matrons, ladies in waiting, and pages. Her brother, Creon, was likewise accompanied by an appropriate entourage. The chorus consisted of 15 persons, seven on each side, and their leader in the center. The chorus spoke, as is required, in pleasing unison, so that almost all the words could be clearly understood, an effect which is very difficult to achieve in tragedies. The story of Oedipus is full of pity and terror. . . . As it is the task of tragedy, by representing an illustrious and stormy deed, to arouse in the hearts of the spectators pity and terror and to soften the callous souls, purging them, according to Aristotle, or freeing them from such passions as hatred, constant anger, and the desire for revenge, one should think that this tragedy, so perfectly conceived, and composed with so much art, and, above all, so exquisitely performed, should produce its effects and eradicate the afflictions with which part of this our most courteous, courageous, and ingenious city is befallen.

6.   SABBATTINI ON THEATRICAL MACHINERY

NICOLA SABBATTINI (fl. 1636) was a native of Pesaro. He served as an architect, scene designer, and machinist at the court of Urbino under Duke Francesco II Maria. His patron died in 1631, and Sabbattini entered the service of Hieronimo Grimaldi, an art-loving prince of the Church. For Grimaldi, Sabbattini built, or at least equipped, the Teatro del Sol in Pesaro. This theater opened in 1636 with the tragedy *Asmondo*, written by a Pesaro nobleman. The *intermezzi* were, however, the chief attraction of the production. The following year, Sabbattini published the first book of his *Pratica di fabricar scene e machine ne' teatri* (*The Practice of Making Scenes and Machines*), what we would call today a handbook for scene technicians, dealing with the construction of the stage and its scenery. The second book, together with the first, was published in 1638 at Ravenna. Sabbattini asserts that all methods and theories of staging advanced in his treatise had been tested in practice at the Teatro del Sol. Lucrezia d'Este, the widow of the Duke of Urbino, invited Sabbattini to follow her to Modena, where he may have built a theater in 1638. Sabbattini's *Pratica* gives an excellent idea how the Renaissance designers overcame their technical problems. But certain aspects of the stage mechanism described by the author were already outmoded by 1638. The prism (*periaktos*) stage (described in Chapter VII, not to mention the more antiquated methods of changing scenery, explained in Chapters V and VI) had either been discarded by the more advanced designers or developed into a double-prism stage, later — too late to be still fashionable — described by the German architect, Joseph Furttenbach. Flat wings sliding in grooves had been used as early as 1606 by Giovanni Battista Aleotti (1546 - 1632), when he built a stage for the Accademia degl' Intrepidi in Ferrara, and again in the Teatro Farnese in Parma, which he equipped with the flat-wing system in 1618.

When Sabbattini published his treatise, Venice already had a public opera house, and Torelli was about to amaze the Venetians with his unsurpassed mastery of the flat-wing stage. Sabbattini was behind his age, but this hardly lessens the historical value of his *Pratica*. The methods described had been employed by the great designers and machinists of the sixteenth century, and they were still used by architects of smaller stature in the seventeenth. Of the two books of the treatise the second is the more interesting. While the first part is chiefly concerned with theatrical perspective, though such subjects as lighting, the manipulation of the curtain, and the arrangement of the auditorium are also discussed, Sabbattini in his second book takes up the subject of the machinery employed in the staging of the *intermezzi*. The changing of scenery, trap doors, the ways to represent Hell, a conflagration, the sea, boats, clouds, fountains, wind, thunder, lightning, transformations—these were the ever recurrent problems that stimulated the ingenuity of the Renaissance "technical director." With the exception of the chapters on lighting, which are in the first book, all the following chapters have been selected and translated from the second book of the *Pratica*:

Chapter XXXIX: *How to Arrange the Lights on the Stage.*

In arranging the lights on the stage one has to consider a variety of things. They have to be placed in such a manner that they will not interfere with the changes of scenery and the operation of the machines. Nor should they fall down, especially the oil lamps, due to the vibrations caused by the Morisco dances. For this is one of the things that damage the prestige of a stage director. First, then, a number of good oil lamps should be hung behind the festoon and coat-of-arms, which . . . are usually set on top of the front edge of the sky. These proscenium lights, unseen by the spectators, will light up the entire sky and give an excellent effect. Other oil lamps are placed behind the wings, but far enough off stage so that they cannot be seen by the spectators, and so that they do not obstruct the traffic of the stage. But there are other lights necessary, oil lamps and candles (the latter should be given preference). For this, beams of the right thickness should be chosen, and ones long enough to reach from the floor of the hall to the lower edge of the wings. These beams must be securely fastened to the floor of the hall with cement, and they must come up through the stage floor. Here care must be taken that the holes through which the beams run are large enough so that the beams will not touch the stage floor at any point. The upper end of the beams are to be firmly connected with the wall of the stage house by means of crossbeams. The lights must be set on top of the beams. As many lights as are required, and one should not be niggardly in this respect: for they will, if my advice is followed, stand firmly and safely in spite of the stage vibrations caused by dancing and jumping. A light may be placed behind each chimney, but only if there is no change of scenery. It is customary to arrange a great number of oil lamps in a row of footlights. In this case, the lights must be hidden from the spectators by means of a board, which must be higher than the stage floor. But the loss is greater than the gain. The intention is to make the stage brighter, but in reality it becomes darker. I have experienced this on various occasions. The lamps must have strong wicks if they are to give a strong light. But if the strong wicks are chosen, smoke will develop to such density that a sort of haze will interfere with the view of the spectators, who will have difficulty in distinguishing the smaller details on the stage. Add to this the bad smell which emanates from oil lamps, especially when they are placed at a low point. It is to be granted that the costumes of the actors and Morisco dancers appear more striking, but it must also be admitted that their faces appear pale and lean, as if they had just passed through a period of sickness. Besides, the actors and dancers are blinded by these footlights.

Chapter XII: *How to Light the Lamps.*

After all the spectators have been seated and the time has come to begin the performance, the lamps must be lighted, first those in the auditorium, then those on the stage. Care should be taken that this be done as quickly as possible lest the spectators become uneasy and get the impression that the job will never be finished. And yet, the method must be as efficient as safe. For should speed cause some mishap, it would only cause further delay. Hence the various methods should be carefully considered, and the best chosen. There are several possibilities, at least with respect to the house lights. For there is hardly any difficulty with regard to the stage lights, which can be easily reached and quickly lighted because of the numerous stage crew. As for the auditorium lights, there are really only two methods from which to choose. The first is the following. One prepares a tape fuse, made of wire and spun with wick fibers, which has to be saturated with petroleum, distilled spirits, or any other easily inflammable material. This tape fuse must begin at that point of the auditorium wall where the chandelier is hung, and it must lead round the tops of all the candles of the chandelier. Moreover, it should be fastened in three places to the heavy wire which holds up the chandelier. Otherwise that part of the fuse which is immediately above the candles might begin to glow due to the heat of the tapers, and it might fall down on the candles, causing their wax to melt and to drip down on the spectators below. For this reason the tape fuse has to be arranged in such a manner that it will stay all around at the same level. The same should be done with all the other chandeliers, which can be simultaneously lighted by reliable men, who, posted at the various ends of the fuses, set fire to them at a given signal. I must confess, however, that I have never liked this method on account of the disturbances which it is likely to cause. For it happened quite frequently that the flame went out before it had reached the candles, or that some of the wick fiber got loose and fell down still burning. . . . The second method precludes such inconveniences; it is decidedly on the safer side, though the spectator must be more patient. The candles are firmly fixed in the chandeliers, and their wicks are soaked in petroleum. To each chandelier a reliable person is assigned, who is equipped with two poles long enough to reach the candle tops. On one of these poles is a taper for lighting, on the other pole is a sponge soaked in water. The latter is used to extinguish a candle that begins to drip because it is not burning evenly. In this connection I should not fail to mention that a sufficient quantity of water must be held in readiness above the borders or the heavens and below the stage. This can be kept in small tubs, jars, or other containers to meet any emergency. . . . If oil lamps are used in the chandeliers, three persons are needed to light up each chandelier. Poles can be used in this case, too, or the whole chandelier can be lowered, lighted, and hauled up again in position.

Chapter V: How to Change Scenery.

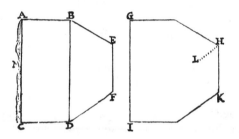

After all the angle-wings (*case*) have been built, one takes cloth, which should not be thick but thin and light. From the cloth, pieces are cut corresponding with the number of angle-wings. Each piece of cloth (GHIK) must be large enough to cover with ease the front (ABCD) and perspective faces (BEDF) of each wing. These pieces of cloth are painted as desired. The painter should be instructed, however, to make the glue or other binders as soft as possible so that the painted cloth can be most easily folded or unfolded to cover or uncover the wings. This done, one takes two poles, two and a half feet long and one and a half inches thick. They must be of very good, hard, and smooth wood. To the upper end (H) of one of these poles (HL) one end of the piece of painted cloth is fastened with nails, *viz.*, the part which is tapering off on the perspective side (HK). Next one takes the other end of the cloth and nails it down in the off-stage corner of the front-face edge (at A). Then the whole cloth is gathered in folds (at M) along the off-stage edge so that it cannot be seen by the spectators. The same should be done with every other wing unit. When the time has come for a change of scenery, at least two men are posted at each piece of cloth. They hold the pole (LH) to which the cloth has been nailed in their hands. Each pole has to be soaped at the end nearest the cloth, as does the ovolo molding at the upper edge (ABE) of the wing. When the scene is to be changed, the men must slide their poles over the ovolo molding to the end of the wing. In this way, the cloth will also slide, and the wings will be covered in an instant. The reverse procedure is followed when the wings are to be uncovered. Should the perspective faces of the wings be too long, then it would be advisable to fasten a second pole to the middle of the cloth, and to use an additional crew so that one group slides the cloth from the middle to the end, the other from the beginning to the middle.

Chapter VI: How to Change Scenery by Another Method.

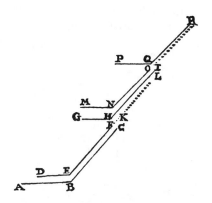

To change the scenes by the second method, the wings are arranged on the stage floor in the following order: the second wing (GHI) should be three inches behind the first (ABC), and the third (PQR) at the same distance from the second, and so forth. This done, a frame (*telaro*, DEF) of the same length, width, and height as the second wing is made. The frame is covered with cloth, and on it the next scene is painted. Moreover, behind the first wing a channel (EL) is made in the floor of the stage. This groove should be two inches wide; its length must equal the combined lengths of the first and second wings, and it must be three inches deep. Similar grooves should be made at the top. The same is done for the other wings, *i.e.*, behind the second there is a frame to cover the third, and behind the third the cover for the fourth, and so on for all the others. When all the frames are finished and painted, the first (DEF) will be placed in the channel behind the first wing, and it should be adjusted so that it will slide easily in the groove until it covers the second wing. The same is done with the others. If the first or second wings have doors or windows to be used in the production, the frame behind them must have incisions facing these doors or windows so that they can be used in the performance. . . . Two trustworthy men should be assigned to each frame, preferably men who know the music, so that, when the cue is given, they will slide the frames in their grooves simultaneously. Prior to this operation the edges of the frames and the channels must be soaped well. In this manner the second and the other wings are changed. As for the first wing, the first method, as described in Chapter V, must be used.

Chapter VII: The Third Method of Changing Scenery.

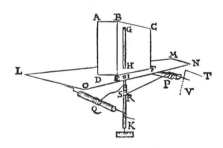

This third method of changing scenery seems to me to be superior to the others mentioned above, but only if it is executed with speed. For otherwise there is great danger that the spectators will have a glimpse behind the scenes, a danger which does not exist in the case of the other methods. To avoid the slightest mishap the operation has to be performed with the greatest possible swiftness. To follow the third method, frames must be made of wooden laths. The bases (DEF) and the tops (ABC) of these frames must be shaped like equilateral triangles. These frames must be the length, height, and width of the houses to be seen on the stage, and their number will likewise correspond to the number of desired houses. The frames must be arranged according to the perspective laws. . . . Yet the bases of the triangles must be in equal distance from the horizon; they must not follow the slope of the stage as they will turn easily only if they are in a perpendicular position. These frames must be covered with painted cloth and placed in their appointed positions. Next, a pivot (GK), running through the middle of the top triangle, is inserted into each frame. This pivot comes down through the base triangle (at H), and, through a hole made in the stage floor (I in LMNO), it is led into a socket (at K) at the very floor of the hall. In this block the pivot will maintain its balance and be turned easily. The same is done for the other triangles. Two winches (Q and P) are put under the stage floor, one near the back shutter, the other toward the stage front. The drums of these winches must have such a large diameter that the ropes that connect with the pivots (QS and PR) can be wound and unwound by a half turn, thereby changing the houses [*i.e., periaktoi*] on the stage. To make the triangle return to its original position, the other winch, the one near the stage front, is given a half turn. This action will unwind the rope from the pivot and will wind it on the winch. At the same time, the other rope will be wound on the pivot and unwound from the first winch. In an instant the triangular house will have returned to its former position. To the same winches and to the other pivots of each triangular house other ropes are attached so that through one half turn, in a single motion of the winches, all the *periaktoi* are revolved and by another half turn brought back to their former positions. When this method is used, great care must be taken to select reliable workers. For it is a tricky op-

eration in view of the many ropes involved, which could easily
become entangled, thereby causing a mishap. To offset this disadvantage I should recommend that reliable men be chosen, men
who know their cues and the music, and that one be stationed at
each triangle. Each one can easily operate his triangle, turning
it back and forth. There will then be no entanglement of the
ropes and winches. I admit that it is quite difficult to co-ordinate
the action of persons stationed at various points . . . but it is
not altogether impossible to accomplish.

*Chapter XXXIV: How to Make Dolphins and Other Sea
Monsters Appear to Spout Water While Swimming.*

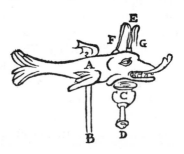

Cut out a dolphin or other animal from a board. After it is
painted, a wooden handle (B), two feet long, is nailed to the
animal's belly (A). This handle must be held by the person who
sets the dolphin in motion. When the moment for the effect has
arrived, the operator walks back and forth below the stage and
between two waves, raising and lowering the dolphin, now its
head and now its tail in imitation of nature. To create the illusion
of water spouting from the head, another man walks up and
down beneath the stage, holding in his hand, behind the dolphin's
head, a cardboard container (C), more than a half foot large
and tapering off to a tube at its bottom. In this container a goodly
quantity of silver foil and ground talc is placed. When the dolphin is to spout, the said container must be brought behind the
dolphin's head, but low enough so that it cannot be seen by the
spectators. Through the tube-shaped bottom (D) of the vessel

air is blown which forces the silver foil out on top (EFG). Due to the reflection of the lights the silver will look like water coming from the dolphin's head. This will be repeated from time to time as there will be a sufficient quantity of silver foil on hand.

Chapter XXXV: How to Produce a Constantly Flowing River.

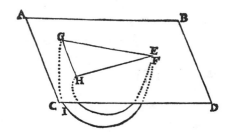

Occasionally the plot demands the showing of one or several rivers with or without statues. If there is a statue, things can be arranged so that water appears to be constantly flowing from an urn to the desired place. To do this, take a piece of thin cloth (EFGH) which is twice as long as the distance from the urn to the end of the river. The cloth must be as wide as the greatest width of the river (at GH). Then the said cloth is painted light blue and sprinkled with silver. This done, one end of the cloth is passed through the mouth of the urn (E), the other end through an opening in the stage floor under the statue (F). An endless belt is formed by leading the cloth from the urn to a slit in the stage floor (GH), and through the slit under the stage back to the opening under the statue. The slit must be as wide as the full width of the cloth. To carry out the effect, only one person is required. He is posted under the stage near the slit (at I), where he sees to it that, while pulling the easily crumpled cloth, it is always stretched. In this manner a continuous flow of water is represented. If there be no statue, things can be arranged so that it will appear that the river originates in the mountains.

Chapter XXXVII: How to Divide the Sky into Sections

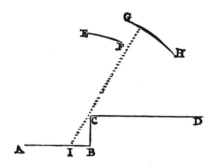

In the *intermezzi* it will frequently be necessary for the machines to rise into the sky or descend onto the stage. In this case the sky has to be divided into sections, both for the sake of operational convenience and for the delight and wonder to be felt by the spectators, who cannot comprehend how the machines, rising from the stage floor (CD), disappear or how those coming from the heavens descend. To accomplish this, a piece of sky must be placed at a convenient height, nearest to the front of the stage and sloping (EF). . . . This sky section must be wide enough to cover the space between the front of the stage and the spot where the machines are to rise. This done, the second section of the sky (GH) must be put parallel to the first, yet so much higher than the lower edge of the first section that the spectators seated in the front rows (at I) cannot see the opening which remains between the edge of the first section and the beginning of the second. Nevertheless, this space between (FG) must be made wide enough so that the machines may emerge and re-enter without hindrance. In the same way the other sky sections can be made as needed. The painter should exercise extreme care in coloring these sections so that the lower edge of the first section blends perfectly with the beginning of the second.

Chapter XXXVIII: How Gradually to Cover Part of the Sky with Clouds.

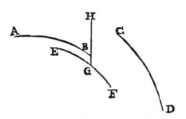

Occasionally it is necessary to cover the heavens little by little with clouds. If this is to be done, the sky must first be divided into several sections (AB, CD), as was described in the preceding chapter. At one side of the stage, behind the wings (*case*), there should be set up one canvas-covered frame (*telaro*, EF) for each opening between the sky sections. This frame is made of thin wooden laths, covered with canvas and painted to resemble clouds. Care should be taken that the clouds in front are stronger colored than the others. . . . After this has been done one or two battens (GH), light in weight but sturdy, must be attached to each cloud frame. These frames will then be placed parallel to the sections of the sky and far enough off stage so that they will be invisible to the spectators. When the effect is to be produced, one or several men, stationed above the sky and with their backs toward the spectators, will hold in their hands the guiding battens (at H), and, when the cue comes, they will let the cloud frames (EF) slide below the sky arc and stop where it is necessary so that it will appear as if the sky is becoming more and more cloudy. Care should be taken that the convex part of the cloud frame (EF) comes as close as possible to the concave surface of the sky arc (AB).

Chapter XLII: How to Cover Part of the Sky, Beginning with Small Cloud That Becomes Larger and Larger and Continually Changes Its Color.

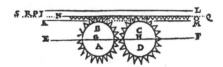

The last method of covering part of the sky with clouds, though it may appear difficult, seems to me the most beautiful and the most marvelous of all. Due to the concavity of the sky, however, it can be done only in the center of the sky. In order to accomplish this, eight or ten cylinders of wooden staves have to be made, each being at least one foot in diameter (AB, CD). Their length must be equal to the opening in the sky where the clouds are to appear. An indented wheel (AB, CD), two inches thick with the same diameter as the cylinder, is placed at the end of each cylinder. The cylinders should be covered with canvas and must be arranged on the floor, the one touching the other, in the same sequence as they are to be placed in the sky, and so that they can be properly painted. A painter of great skill should be employed, for, on the one side (A and D), he has to paint the cylinders so that they will match that part of the sky in which they are to be fitted. On the other side (B and C), the cylinders have to exhibit clouds, starting with a small cloud painted on the first cylinder, which is set toward the rear part of the sky. On the other cylinders the clouds ever increase in size and change in color in a natural way. After the painter has done his work, the cylinders are placed in the opening of the heavens so that they turn easily on their pivots (G, H). The latter may rest on two beams (EF), set on either side above the sky. Lengthwise, above the indented wheels, a wooden groove (IKLM) is set; it should be well polished and firm, somewhat wider than the thickness of the wheels, and hollowed out to at least four inches in depth. In this groove should be set a sliding strip of wood (NO), having indentations which correspond to those of the cylinder wheels. A sliding of the strip will cause the wheels to turn correspondingly. These indented strips of wood must be longer than the groove and a little wider than the cylinder wheels, and so adjusted that by means of their length a certain part of the sky can be covered with clouds and cleared of them again. To carry out the effect, four men should be stationed above the sky (at P and Q), two facing the sky sections, the two others at the opposite side, and let them hold the ends of the aforementioned indented sliding strips. When the clouds are called for, the two men who face the audience (at P, for instance) will slowly draw the sliding strips toward them (toward R, for instance). At the same time those parts of the cylinders will be revealed that have been painted as clouds (B,C). . . . To make the cylinders return to their former state, the men on the opposite side (at Q) will draw the sliding strips in their direction back to their original position. However, if one wishes to create the illusion that the clouds are vanishing while moving forward, the two men, who had drawn the sliding strip first, must continue to draw the strip (toward S) until the cylinders have completed a full revolution.

Chapter XLIII: How to Make a Cloud Descend Perpendicularly with Persons in It.

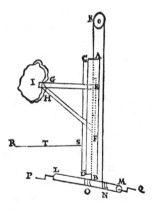

A grooved beam (ABCD) is made of two uprights, which must be rather thick, preferably nine inches, but at least four. This beam must extend from above the sky to below the stage (which is RS). The groove is formed by a dovetailed channel, which must be very smooth, half a foot deep and just as wide. This beam is then brought to a suitable place behind a partition and fastened to the wall in a vertical position to the horizon. A second beam (EF) of the same thickness, or a little less, is fit into the upright so that it can easily slide in the channel. This sliding beam should be six or seven feet long. Once this is done, a crossbeam (EG) is fastened by means of sturdy pegs to the upper end of the sliding beam (at E). This crossbeam is of the same thickness as the sliding beam, and its length will depend on the distance at which the cloud is to be shown. At the point (I), where the cloud is to be affixed, *i.e.*, at a distance of two and a half feet, the supporting beam (HF) is nailed. This diagonal support must be long enough to reach down to the lower end (F) of the sliding beam, to which it is fastened with strong pegs. The three beams form a right-angled triangle (EFG or H). Next, at either end of the sliding beam (at E and F), an iron ring is attached. These rings should be rather thick so that they can support the weight of the cloud as well as that of the persons in it when the cloud is being lowered and when it is made to ascend. To each ring a piece of good rope is fastened. The upper rope (from E) must run over the wheel of a pulley (K), which is firmly secured above the sky and perpendicular to the grooved upright. From the pulley the rope comes down to and is wound round a windlass (LM), which is placed underneath the stage at the end of the grooved upright. The other rope will be tied to the lower ring (at F) and from there run over the windlass in the opposite direction from the first so that when one rope is winding off the other is wound up equally. Next, a cloud (I) of the right size should be made and firmly secured with wooden crossbars so that the persons standing in it will be in comfortable safety. Have the frame covered with canvas, which must be painted in the most natural manner. The cloud should then be nailed down to the extreme end of the crossbeam, made for the purpose. After all this has been done, an opening should be made in the sky above the upright so that the crossbeam holding the cloud can neatly pass through. This cut must be made all the way down to the floor of the stage (RS). To prevent the opening from being noticed, a piece of canvas, as long and as wide as the cut and painted like the sky, should be fastened to the crossbeam so that it will hang down. A second piece of canvas connects the crossbeam with the heavens, and when the cloud descends (to T), the upper canvas will likewise come down and close the opening. At the same time the lower part of the canvas will descend, and no opening is ever visible. Two or four men should be posted at the windlass to lower or raise the cloud.

Chapter XLV: How to Make a Cloud Descend So That It Will Gradually Move from the Extreme End of the Stage to the Middle of the Stage, a Cloud, Moreover, with Persons in It.

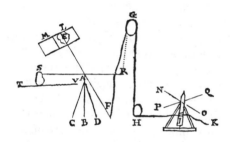

The following method is used provided that there is a space of at least twenty feet behind the scenes. A strong beam (EF), twenty-five feet in length, is used as a lever. In the middle (at A) it is supported on a fulcrum (AB) and well secured by means of an iron brace and stanchions (AC, AD). The fulcrum must consist of a beam that is thicker than the lever. It is to be placed on the floor of the hall (at B) directly under the rear section of the sky. It should come up to a height of four feet above the stage level (TV) and so far back as to be out of sight. Now the lever is fastened on the fulcrum in such a manner that its mobility is not impaired. Next, a pulley (G), preferably of metal, is fastened securely at a height of twenty feet and at a distance of ten feet behind the fulcrum. Directly underneath another pulley (H) of the same size is set three feet above the floor of the auditorium. This second pulley guides the rope to a capstan (I), which is placed in line with the pulley yet so far to one side that its operation will not be obstructed. Next take a good rope . . . and tie it with a knot firmly to the upstage end of the lever (at F).

From there the rope runs up to the upper pulley (G) and comes down to the lower one (H), where it turns to the capstan (I). At the other end of the lever (at E), the one turned toward the spectators, the cloud is built on two pieces of wood with seats to hold securely those persons that have to be in it. When the cloud is finished, its upper end must be set above the end of the lever, and the balance must be achieved by placing the two pieces of wood on the lever in such a way that the cloud and the persons in it remain horizontal regardless whether the lever is raised or lowered. Nor should the lever become visible. This cloud, when lowered, can not come out from the sections of the sky . . . rather must it come through an opening in the sky—a hole large enough to allow easy passage for the cloud on its way out and back again. This opening must be closed again by means of a piece of sky, made of a frame (L to M) of thin wooden strips. This sliding frame must, in color and shape, closely conform to the missing piece of sky. The inner part is painted like the outer so that after the appearance of the cloud through the aperture no difference be discernible. A weight should be placed at the other end of the lever (at F). This weight must be greater than that of the cloud and persons in it combined, so that this part of the lever will be down regardless of the weight of the persons and the cloud. To lower the cloud, four or eight men must be stationed at the capstan. By turning its handles (N, O, P, Q) slowly, they will make the cloud descend in proportion till it reaches the stage level (below S). By turning the handles in the opposite direction, the cloud can be raised to its original position. Make sure that a man be posted behind the capstan, holding the end of the rope (at K) . . . and care should be taken that the men turning the handles be very careful when raising the cloud, since, on account of the counterweight, the cloud would return of itself.

7.   DI SOMI ON STAGECRAFT

LEONE EBREO DI SOMI (1527 - 1592) was in charge of the theatrical productions at the court of Mantua. The Biblioteca Palatina of Parma has a unique manuscript copy of di Somi's *Dialoghi*, a treatise on playwriting and stagecraft. Two courtiers, Massimiano and Santino, visit the workshop of Veridico (di Somi), who, in the course of four dialogues, develops his ideas about dramaturgy and staging, dealing with such subjects as acting, costuming, lighting, and the mounting of pastorals:

[*On Actors and Acting*]

Veridico: I shall say only, generally speaking, that the actor must always be nimble of body, and his limbs must not be inflexible and stiff. He must keep his feet still in a fitting manner while he is speaking, and move them with grace when it is necessary; he must keep his head in a certain natural way, so that it will not appear that it is attached to his neck with nails. And he must let his arms and his hands (when it is not necessary to gesticulate with them) go where nature directs them, and he must not do as so many do, who, wishing to gesticulate too much, do not seem to know what to do with them. For example, if a woman in a certain scene has put her hand on her side, or if a young man has placed his hand on his sword, neither the one nor the other must remain forever, nor very frequently, in that position; but when he has ended the speech which requires such a position, he must abandon that position and find another one more suitable to the speech which follows; and when he does not find another fitting gesture, or when he does not need to assume a posture, he should, as I have said, let his arms and his hands go where nature directs them, loose and relaxed, and not hold them raised or inflexible, as if they were attached with sticks to the body. But he must always maintain in his action greater or lesser dignity, as the situation requires of the person being represented; and likewise with the sound of words, now arrogant and now placid, now spoken with timidity and now with daring, making pauses in their proper place, always imitating and observing the naturalness of the qualities of those persons being represented. And, above all, he must avoid like a curse a certain manner of acting which, for lack of a better term, I shall call pedantic, similar to the recitation of school children before their teacher. He must, I repeat, avoid that mode of delivery which seems a sing-song learned by heart. And he must, above all, make an effort (changing the tone of the voice and accompanying these changes with the proper gestures) to bring it about that what he says be spoken with effectiveness and seem to be nothing more than a familiar discourse which comes about spontaneously.

[*On Stage Costume in General*]

Veridico: I tell you especially that I make efforts to dress the actors always in as noble a fashion as is possible for me, but in such a manner that there is a sense of proportion among them, in view of the fact that the rich costume . . . particularly in these times when pomp is at its highest peak, adds much reputation and beauty to comedies, and even more to tragedies. I would not hestitate to dress a servant in velvet or colored satin, as long as his master's costume were embroidered or decorated with gold, so. rich that there would be maintained the proper proportion between them. But I would not clothe a housemaid with a torn old skirt, or a servant with a torn doublet; on the contrary, I would have her wear a nice skirt and him a showy jacket, and I would add so much nobility to the clothes of their masters as to allow for the beauty of the servants' costumes.

Massimiano: There is no doubt that the sight of the rags which others put on a miser's back, or on a servant's, detracts much from the dignity of a play.

Veridico: One can very well clothe a miser or even a peasant with costumes which have a certain degree of richness about them, without being unnatural.

Santino: It is certainly so, particularly because, as you say, we must follow the ways of our times.

Veridico: I do my utmost to dress the actors very differently from one another, and this is of great help, both in adding beauty and in facilitating the understanding of the plot. And for this reason, more than any other, I believe the ancients had appropriate costumes and assigned colors for each type of actor. If I had, for example, to clothe three or four servants, I would dress one in white, with a hat; another in red, with a small cap on his head; another with a livery of various colors; and another I would adorn, perhaps with a velvet cap and a pair of knitted sleeves, if his position allows it. (I am speaking, of course, of comedies which require Italian costumes.) Thus, if I have to clothe two lovers, I will try, both in the colors and in the style of their costumes, to make them very different, one with a cape, the other with a stately garment; one with plumes on his cap, the other with gold but no feathers, in order that as soon as one sees, not necessarily the face, but the hem of the one's costume or the other's, he will recognize him, without having to wait for him to reveal himself with his words. Bear in mind, however, that in general the manner of wearing a hat is a feature which is more revealing than the costume itself, both in men and women. Therefore, the actors should, with respect to their costumes, be as different as possible in style and color.

Santino: How many times I have been long in doubt in recognizing an actor on the stage, because he was not different enough from another actor, or servant.

Veridico: The variety of colors is very helpful in this connection. The costumes should be of definite colors, light colors; black or any dark color should be used as little as possible. Not only do I try to vary the actors' costumes, but I strive as much as I can to transform each one from his usual appearance, so that he will not readily be recognized by the audience, which sees him daily. I do not, however, want to make the mistake the ancients made, who, in order that their actors should not be recognized, painted their faces with wine sediment or with mud. I find it enough to disguise them, without changing the appearance of their faces, doing my utmost to make them appear new persons, because when the audience recognizes the actor, there is destroyed a part of that sweet illusion in which it should be kept, in order that it may believe as long as possible that everything we present is really happening. But inasmuch as the audience likes novel things especially, a performance is very enjoyable when one sees on the stage costumes that are ancient and remote from our fashions; and for this reason it comes about that comedies in Greek costumes are so appealing.

[*On Costuming Pastoral Plays*]

Veridico: Tomorrow we shall speak about pastoral scenes, along with the other settings. Now, concerning the manner of costuming the actors of pastoral scenes, I say that, if the poet has introduced some divinity or other new invention in them, one should follow his intention in the clothing. But, concerning the costumes of shepherds, one should bear in mind the same thing that was said about the comedies, that is, that one should make them as different from one another as possible. Generally speaking, this should be their costume: their legs and arms should be covered with flesh-colored material, and if the actor should be young and beautiful, it would not be unsuitable for him to have his arms and legs bare, but never his feet. These must always be gracefully covered with buskins or slippers. They should also have a shirt of silk, or of other material of beautiful color, but without sleeves; and over that, two skins (as Homer describes the clothes of a Trojan shepherd), either of leopard or other beautiful animal, one on his chest and another on his back, tied together by the paws over the shepherd's shoulders and below his waist. It is a good idea, for the sake of variety, to have some shepherds wear their skins only over one shoulder. Some of them should have a little flask or wooden bowl hanging from the belt; others should have a knapsack tied to one shoulder and resting on the opposite hip. Each one of them should have in his hand a stick, some stripped of leaves, others bearing leaves. The more they are out of the ordinary, the better. On their heads, natural or false hair. Some will have curly hair, some straight and well-groomed; some will have their foreheads decorated with laurel or ivy, for the sake of variety. In these or similar ways, one can say that they are appropriately dressed. The shepherds will be different from one another in colors, in the quality of the various skins, in their complexion, in the bearing of their heads, and other similar things which cannot be learned except by practice and the exercise of one's judgment. For the nymphs, after one has followed their qualities as described by the poets, ladies' shirts are suitable, embroidered and varied, but with sleeves. I am accustomed to having them starched, so that, fastening them with bracelets or with ribbons of colored silk and gold, they will puff out, making a very beautiful appearance that will satisfy the eye. The nymphs should have, from the waist down, a skirt of some beautifully colored and delicate material, short enough to show the ankle; the foot should be covered with a golden slipper, in the ancient manner, or with elegant footwear of colored leather. The nymphs should have a rich mantle which goes from below one side of the waist to the opposite shoulder, where it is gathered. They should have blond hair in abundance, and it should look natural. And some of them could leave their hair loose on their shoulders and wear a small garland on the head. Others, for the sake of variety, could wear a golden band over the forehead; still others could tie their hair with silk ribbons and cover it with those very flimsy veils, flowing down over the shoulders, which in ordinary life add so much beauty. And this use of the veil, as I say, may be permitted even in these pastoral presentations, for a veil flying in the breeze is generally superior to all other ornaments of a lady's head, and it has that simple, pure quality about it which is required of the costume of an inhabitant of the woods. Some of these nymphs should carry a bow in their hands and a quiver, others only a dart to hurl; some should have both the one and the other. One caution above all others: it is necessary that the one who presents these poems have much experience, because it is more difficult to give a good presentation of one of these plays than it is to present a comedy; and, in truth, it constitutes a much more pleasing and beautiful spectacle.

[On Lighting]

Santino: . . . And inasmuch as here on your scene there are already so many hanging lights that one begins to see it quite clearly, and it presents a very beautiful sight, I wish, Messer Veridico, that first of all you would tell us about the purpose and origin of those many lights which are lighted on the roofs of the houses on the stage. It seems to me that these lights are of no use at all for the needs of perspective; and I see torches in sufficient number to light the stage.

Veridico: I believe that I have told you and repeated to you that comedies are introduced to give pleasure and relief from annoying cares; and for this reason I said to you, and I repeat, that the greatest care an actor must have is to act always in a gay and lively manner. Let us suppose, then, that the poet gives us a delightful and pleasing story, and that the actor presents it in a gay manner. For the part which he has in the comedy, the architect also must represent happiness and joy. And because usage has always been, and still is, that as a sign of joy fires be lighted, and lights placed along the streets, on house roofs and on towers —from this arose the present custom of thus imitating those joyful occasions, for no other need than to give an impression of joy at the first glimpse of the stage.

Santino: Will such lights be out of place, then, in tragedies?

Veridico: Perhaps they will not be entirely out of place,

because in addition to the fact that tragedies, especially in the beginning, are for the most part very cheerful (there are even some which have a happy ending), it will never be unfitting to awaken the spirit to joy as much as possible, even though there may follow in the tragedies some misfortunes or deaths. But I once happened to be presenting a tragedy in which the stage was lighted in a very cheerful manner for the entire time that the events of the story were happy. But when the first sad event, the unexpected death of a queen, occurred, and the chorus thereupon proclaimed its surprise that the sun could bear to witness such a sad event: in that moment I had (as I had already prepared) the greater part of the lights on the stage which did not serve for the purpose of perspective, shaded or put out. This caused very deep horror in the spectators' hearts. All of which, according to universal opinion, achieved remarkable success.

Santino: One could not have judged otherwise.

Massimiano: Please tell us now why these lights of yours are for the most part shaded with transparent glasses and with various colors.

Veridico: This was an invention of those who were acquainted with something which many do not heed; that is, that a light which shines brightly in the eyes is extremely annoying to those who have to look at it continuously. Since the spectator must always fix his glance on the stage, looking now in this direction and now in that, it was made possible by this invention to avoid annoying the spectator, by shading the lights with that grace which you see.

Massimiano: I would buy a meal for ten companions if, of one hundred who use these shades, there are ten who know why they do so.

Veridico: They will tell you, at least, that it is done for greater beauty, and thus they will tell you a part of the whole. Not through book knowledge, but through long practice and experience, I have observed these and many other things. And by my efforts to find the origin of these shades, I have found that the ancients made use of them. And in this connection I wish to tell you also that those little mirrors, which are placed by some in suitable points in the perspective and on the distant sides of the scene, prove very attractive. When those hidden lights, which the architects artfully place behind the columns and along the streets, strike these mirrors, they help, by their reflection, to make the scene appear more brilliant and more joyful. Aside from eliminating a source of eye irritation, the reflector also makes it possible for us to have many lights, without smoke. This is of very great importance, because those who do not attend to having numerous openings made behind the stage so that the smoke from the lights may escape easily, cause great confusion. Because the smoke, gradually increasing and thickening, forms such a heavy cloud (if it has no means of escape) that, before the second act is over the actors seem to us no longer men, but shadows. And the spectators, likewise, seem wrapped in a haze; they feel their vision becoming blurred, and many times they do not know the reason for it. But it is necessary to devote much care to this, for few think about it; and it is the cause of much inconvenience, as experience shows those who consider this matter well.

Massimiano: Now that you have cleared away my doubts, I realize something that I would never have thought about. And yet I realize that it is very true that, toward the end of comedies, we have often found that our eyes ached and that we saw very little as compared to what we saw at the beginning; and I recognize that it was for the reason you state.

Veridico: To avoid the clouding of smoke, I have found it a very useful remedy to have many openings made under the proscenium, and then to have holes made in the stage floor, so that the wind, entering from below, will force all the smoke into the openings above, behind the stage.

Massimiano: I think this should be very helpful.

Veridico: It certainly is.

Santino: I realize, Messer Veridico, that on this scene of yours there are very many lights, some hidden and some in plain view, while here in the hall there are no apparatus to be placed in the back part, other than twelve torches. And I cannot imagine the reason for this, because I have many times counted two hundred and fifty torches in this very large hall.

Veridico: As you know, it is natural that a man in the dark sees an object shining in the distance much better than if he were in a lighted place; because the glance goes more directly to the object, or, according to the Aristotelians, the object is more directly represented to the eye. And for this reason I place only very few lights in the hall, making the stage very bright. I place the very few lights of the hall behind the listeners' backs, so that no interposed lights will interfere with their view; and above them, as you see, I have also made openings, so that they will not cause any harm anywhere by their smoke.

Santino: By placing few lights in the hall, you first check the amount of smoke, and you make the scene appear clearer.

Massimiano: Still another useful thing results from this, namely, that it saves the Duke fifty ducats worth of additional torches which he usually puts in this hall.

Chapter V

Tudor and Stuart Periods

Trees with Palace.
Theatrical Design by Inigo Jones for an Unidentified Masque.

1. MUNICIPAL PREJUDICE AGAINST PLAYS AND PLAYERS

THE TWO RECREATION AREAS of Elizabethan London were Finsbury Field to the north of the city and the Bankside to the south. The playground to the north was a respectable place for family picnics and the practice of various sports, while the Bank had a "naughty" quality due to the long line of brothels along the edge of the river. In view of the antitheatrical attitude of the municipal authorities, the builder of the first London theater structure, James Burbage, wisely selected the reputable territory close to Finsbury Field as the site for "The Theatre" (1576). Not far from the Theatre, London's second playhouse, the Curtain, was erected in 1577. Eventually, however, the Bankside was developed as a region for theatrical entertainment. Players had invaded the territory for some time. The obscure Newington Butts playhouse and the Bear Garden had paved the way for Henslowe's Rose (1587). Burbage and Henslowe seemed to reap profits as theatrical operators. This prompted the goldsmith, Francis Langley, to build a playhouse on his Bankside property. He opened the Swan in 1594. The Lord Mayor had vainly protested against the enterprise. His letter to the Lord High Treasurer summed up the Puritan sentiment of the Common Council toward the stage in general:

My humble duetie remembred to your good L. I vnderstand that one Francis Langley, one of the Alneagers for sealing of cloth, intendeth to erect a niew stage or Theater (as they call it) for thexercising of playes vpon the Banck side. And forasmuch as wee fynd by daily experience the great inconuenience that groweth to this Citie & the government thearof by the sayed playes, I haue embouldened my self to bee an humble suiter to your good L. to bee a means for vs rather to suppresse all such places built for that kynd of exercise, then to erect any more of the same sort. I am not ignorant (my very good L.) what is alleadged by soom for defence of these playes, that the people must haue soom kynd of recreation, & that policie requireth to divert idle heads & other ill disposed from other woorse practize by this kynd of exercize. Whearto may bee answeared (which your good L. for your godly wisedom can far best iudge of) that as honest recreation is a thing very meet for all sorts of men, so no kynd of exercise, beeing of itself corrupt & prophane, can

well stand with the good policie of a Christian Common Wealth.
And that the sayed playes (as they are handled) ar of that sort,
and woork that effect in such as ar present and frequent the
same, may soon bee decerned by all that haue any godly vnder-
standing & that obserue the fruites & effects of the same, con-
teining nothing ells but vnchast fables, lascivious divises, shifts
of cozenage, & matters of lyke sort, which ar so framed & represented by them, that such as resort to see & hear the same, beeing
of the base & refuse sort of people or such yoong gentlemen as
haue small regard of credit or conscience, draue the same into
example of imitation & not of avoyding the sayed lewd offences.
Which may better appear by the qualitie of such as frequent the
sayed playes, beeing the ordinary places of meeting for all vagrant persons & maisterles men that hang about the Citie, theeues,
horsestealers, whoremoongers, coozeners, connycatching per-
sones, practizers of treason, & such other lyke, whear they consort and make their matches to the great displeasure of Almightie God & the hurt and annoyance of hir Maiesties people,
both in this Citie & other places about, which cannot be clensed
of this vngodly sort (which by experience wee fynd to bee the
very sinck & contagion not only of this Citie but of this whole
Realm), so long as these playes & places of resort ar by authoritie
permitted. I omit to trouble your L. with any farther matter how
our apprentices and servants ar by this means corrupted & induced hear by to defraud their Maisters, to maintein their vain
& prodigall expenses occasioned by such evill and riotous compan-
ie, whearinto they fall by these kynd of meetings, to the great
hinderance of the trades & traders inhabiting this Citie, and
how people of all sorts ar withdrawen thearby from their resort
vnto sermons & other Christian exercise, to the great sclaunder
of the ghospell & prophanation of the good & godly religion
established within this Realm. All which disorders hauing observed & found to bee true, I thought it my duetie, beeing now
called to this publique place, to infourm your good L., whome I
know to bee a patrone of religion & lover of virtue & an honourable a friend to the State of this Citie, humbly beeseaching you
to voutchsafe mee your help for the stay & suppressing, not only
of this which is now intended, by directing your lettres to the
Iustices of peace of Middlesex & Surrey, but of all other places,

if possibly it may bee, whear the sayed playes ar shewed & frequented. And thus crauing pardon for this ouer much length I humbly take my leaue. From London the 3. of November. 1594.

2. INDICTING THE THEATER ON FOUR COUNTS

THE OBJECTIONS raised in the Lord Mayor's letter of protest against the Swan project were frequently reiterated by the municipal authorities. One more example must suffice — a letter written by the Lord Mayor and Aldermen to the Privy Council in 1597:

The inconueniences that grow by Stage playes abowt the Citie of London.

1. They are a speaciall cause of corrupting their Youth, conteninge nothinge but vnchast matters, lascivious devices, shiftes of Coozenage, & other lewd & vngodly practizes, being so as that they impresse the very qualitie & corruption of manners which they represent, Contrary to the rules & art prescribed for the makinge of Comedies eauen amonge the Heathen, who vsed them seldom & at certen sett tymes, and not all the year longe as our manner is. Whearby such as frequent them, beinge of the base & refuze sort of people or such young gentlemen as haue small regard of credit or conscience, drawe the same into imitacion and not to the avoidinge the like vices which they represent.

2. They are the ordinary places for vagrant persons, Maisterles men, thieves, horse stealers, whoremongers, Coozeners, Conycatchers, contrivers of treason, and other idele and daungerous persons to meet together & to make theire matches to the great displeasure of Almightie God & the hurt & annoyance of her Maiesties people, which cannot be prevented nor discovered by the Gouernours of the Citie for that they are owt of the Citiees iurisdiction.

3. They maintaine idlenes in such persons as haue no vocation & draw apprentices and other seruantes from theire ordinary workes and all sortes of people from the resort vnto sermons and other Christian exercises, to the great hinderance of traides & prophanation of religion established by her highnes within this Realm.

The Johannes de Witt Sketch of the London Swan Theatre
(abt. 1596), as copied by Arend van Buchell.

4. In the time of sickness it is fownd by experience, that
many hauing sores and yet not hart sicke take occasion hearby
to walk abroad & to recreat themselves by heareinge a play.
Whearby others are infected, and them selves also many things
miscarry.

3. THE INTERIOR OF THE SWAN THEATRE

IN ABOUT 1596, the Dutch traveller, Johannes de Witt, visited London
and attended a performance at the Swan Theatre. He recorded his playhouse impressions and made a pen sketch of the Swan interior, both of
which have survived in a transcription by Arend van Buchell:

There are four amphitheatres in London of notable beauty, which from their diverse signs bear diverse names [the Theatre, Curtain, Rose, and Swan]. In each of them a different play is daily exhibited to the populace. The two more magnificent of these are situated to the southward beyond the Thames, and from the signs suspended before them are called the Rose and the Swan. The two others are outside the city towards the north on the highway which issues through the Episcopal Gate, called in the vernacular Bishopgate. There is also a fifth [the Bear Garden], but of dissimilar structure, devoted to the baiting of beasts, where are maintained in separate cages and enclosures many bears and dogs of stupendous size, which are kept for fighting, furnishing thereby a most delightful spectacle to men. Of all the theatres, however, the largest and the most magnificent is that one of which the sign is a swan, called in the vernacular the Swan Theatre; for it accommodates in its seats three thousand persons, and is built of a mass of flint stones (of which there is a prodigious supply in Britain), and supported by wooden columns painted in such excellent imitation of marble that it is able to deceive even the most cunning. Since its form resembles that of a Roman work, I have made a sketch of it above.

4. THE PRICE OF ADMISSION

IN THE AUTUMN of 1599, Thomas Platter, a visitor from Basel, spent four weeks in England. In his diary he made reference to the scale of admission prices prevailing in Elizabethan theaters:

Every day at two o'clock in the afternoon in the city of London two and sometimes three comedies are performed, at separate places, wherewith folk make merry together, and whichever does best gets the greatest audience. The places are so built, that they play on a raised platform, and every one can well see it all. There are, however, separate galleries and there one stands more comfortably and moreover can sit, but one pays more for it. Thus anyone who remains on the level standing pays only one English penny: but if he wants to sit, he is let in at a further door, and there he gives another penny. If he desires to sit on a cushion in the most comfortable place of all, where he not

only sees everything well, but can also be seen, then he gives yet
another English penny at another door. And in the pauses of the
comedy food and drink are carried round amongst the people,
and one can thus refresh himself at his own cost.

5. THE FORTUNE CONTRACT

SINCE THE GLOBE had become the "glory of the Bank," Henslowe and
Alleyn thought that it would be advantageous to have a new home for
the Admiral's men in another suburban section. The Fortune was therefore erected in convenient proximity to the northwestern limits of the
city. This new playhouse was to surpass the Globe in all respects, though
some of its features were to be patterned after the Globe. Peter Streete,
who had built the Globe, also built the Fortune. The contract between
Henslowe-Alleyn and the carpenter has been preserved. Unfortunately,
the stage plan which was appended to the indenture has not come down
to us, yet the contract is one of the most important theatrical documents:

The frame of the saide howse to be sett square and to conteine ffowerscore foote of lawfull assize everye waie square with-
outt and fiftie fiue foote of like assize square everye waie within,
with a good suer and stronge foundacion of pyles, brick, lyme
and sand bothe without & within, to be wroughte one foote of
assize att the leiste aboue the grounde; And the saide fframe to
conteine three Stories in heighth, the first or lower Storie to
conteine Twelue foote of lawfull assize in heighth, the second
Storie Eleauen foote of lawfull assize in heighth, and the third
or vpper Storie to conteine Nyne foote of lawfull assize in
height; All which Stories shall conteine Twelue foote and a halfe
of lawfull assize in breadth througheoute, besides a juttey for-
wardes in either of the saide twoe vpper Stories of Tenne ynches
of lawfull assize, with ffower convenient divisions for gentlemens
roomes, and other sufficient and convenient divisions for Twoe
pennie roomes, with necessarie seates to be placed and sett, as-
well in those roomes as througheoute all the rest of the galleries
of the saide howse, and with suchelike steares, conveyances &
divisions withoute & within, as are made & contryved in and to
the late erected Plaiehowse on the Banck in the saide parishe of
Ste Saviours called the Globe; With a Stadge and Tyreinge howse
to be made, erected & settupp within the saide fframe, with a

shadowe or cover over the saide Stadge, which Stadge shalbe placed & sett, as alsoe the stearecases of the saide fframe, in such sorte as is prefigured in a plott thereof drawen, and which Stadge shall conteine in length Fortie and Three foote of lawfull assize and in breadth to extende to the middle of the yarde of the saide howse; The same Stadge to be paled in belowe with good, stronge and sufficyent newe oken bourdes, and likewise the lower Storie of the saide fframe withinside, and the same lower storie to be alsoe laide over and fenced with stronge yron pykes; And the saide Stadge to be in all other proporcions contryved and fashioned like vnto the Stadge of the saide Plaie howse called the Globe; With convenient windowes and lightes glazed to the saide Tyreinge howse; And the saide fframe, Stadge and Stearecases to be covered with Tyle, and to haue a sufficient gutter of lead to carrie & convey the water frome the coveringe of the saide Stadge to fall backwardes; And also all the saide fframe and the Stairecases thereof to be sufficyently enclosed withoute with lathe, lyme & haire, and the gentlemens roomes and Twoe pennie roomes to be seeled with lathe, lyme & haire, and all the fflowers of the saide Galleries, Stories and Stadge to be bourded with good & sufficyent newe deale bourdes of the whole thicknes, wheare need shalbe; And the saide howse and other thinges beforemencioned to be made & doen to be in all other contrivitions, conveyances, fashions, thinge and thinges effected, finished and doen accordinge to the manner and fashion of the saide howse called the Globe, saveinge only that all the princypall and maine postes of the saide fframe and Stadge forwarde shalbe square and wroughte palasterwise, with carved proporcions called Satiers to be placed & sett on the topp of every of the same postes, and saveinge alsoe that the said Peeter Streete shall not be chardged with anie manner of pay[ntin]ge in or aboute the saide fframe howse or Stadge or any parte thereof, nor rendringe the walls within, nor seeling anie more or other roomes then the gentlemens roomes, Twoe pennie roomes and Stadge before remembred.

6. A PREMIERE AT THE FORTUNE

SIR ALEXANDER's description of the "fair sweet room" in Act I, Scene 1 of Dekker and Middleton's *The Roaring Girl* constitutes an impressionistic account of the audience jamming the Fortune Theatre:

Goshawk. I like the prospect best.
Laxton.   See how't is furnished!
Sir Davy. A very fair sweet room.
Sir Alex.   Sir Davy Dapper,
The furniture that doth adorn this room
Cost many a fair grey groat ere it came here;
But good things are most cheap when they're most dear.
Nay, when you look into my galleries,
How bravely they're trimm'd up, you all shall swear
You're highly pleas'd to see what's set down there:
Stories of men and women, mix'd together,
Fair ones with foul, like sunshine in wet weather;
Within one square a thousand heads are laid,
So close that all of heads the room seems made;
As many faces there, fill'd with blithe looks
Shew like the promising titles of new books
Writ merrily, the readers being their own eyes,
Which seem to move and to give plaudities;
And here and there, whilst with obsequious ears
Throng'd heaps do listen, a cut-purse thrusts and leers
With hawk's eyes for his prey; I need not shew him;
By a hanging, villainous look youselves may know him,
The face is drawn so rarely: then, sir, below,
The very floor, as 't were, waves to and fro,
And, like a floating island, seems to move
Upon a sea bound in with shores above.
All. These sights are excellent!

7.   THE BURNING OF THE FIRST GLOBE THEATRE

ON JUNE 29, 1613, the roof of the first Globe Theatre caught fire during the fourth scene of the first act of Shakespeare's (and Fletcher's) *Henry VIII*, and within an hour the stately structure was burned to the ground. The following, quoted from Sir Henry Wotton's *Reliquiae Wottonianae,* is a portion of a letter he wrote to his nephew, Sir Edmund Bacon:

I will entertain you at the present with what happened this week at the Bankside. The King's Players had a new play, called

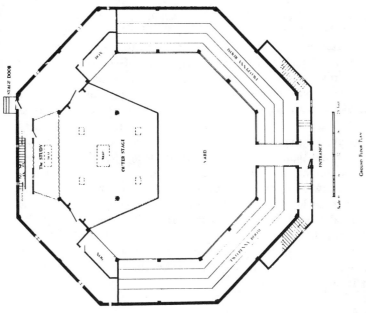

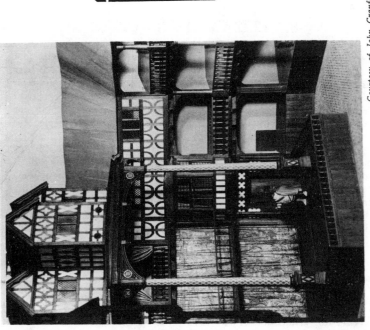

The Stage

Courtesy of John Cranford Adams   Ground Plan

The Globe Theatre. Reconstruction by Dr. John Cranford Adams.

All is True, representing some principal pieces of the reign of Henry the Eighth, which was set forth with many extraordinary circumstances of pomp and majesty, even to the matting of the stage; the Knights of the Order with their Georges and Garter, the guards with their embroidered coats, and the like — sufficient in truth within awhile to make greatness very familiar, if not ridiculous. Now King Henry, making a masque at the Cardinal Wolsey's house, and certain cannons being shot off at his entry, some of the paper or other stuff wherewith one of them was stopped, did light on the thatch, where being thought at first but an idle smoke, and their eyes more attentive to the show, it kindled inwardly, and ran round like a train, consuming within less than an hour the whole house to the very ground. This was the fatal period of that virtuous fabrick; wherein yet nothing did perish but wood and straw, and a few forsaken cloaks; only one man had his breeches set on fire, that would perhaps have broiled him, if he had not, by the benefit of a provident wit, put it out with bottle ale.

8.   ELIZABETHAN ACTING

THE QUESTION whether Elizabethan acting was formal and stylized or realistic in character portrayal is still a topic of debate. Alfred Harbage has made a convincing case for formal acting as against those who prefer to assume that Elizabethan acting anticipated the Moscow Art Theater method. The following pieces of evidence should be examined by anyone intrigued by the subject: Hamlet's advice to the players — a plea for moderation with "the mirror up to nature" thrown in as a cliché of Renaissance criticism (Harbage); two passages from Heywood's *Apology for Actors* (1612); a praise of the actor's social function written, perhaps with Burbage in mind, by John Webster (?, 1615); a description of some Stanislavsky forerunners given by Edmund Gayton, who, in 1654, became nostalgic when he recalled the pre-revolutionary pleasures of playgoing; a few lines from a lengthy epitaph on Burbage; and, finally, Richard Flecknoe's "remembrances" of Burbage, written as late as 1664:

a) [*Hamlet's Advice to the Players*]

Ham. Speak the speech, I pray you, as I pronounc'd it to you, trippingly on the tongue; but if you mouth it, as many of your players do, I had as lief the town-crier spoke my lines. Nor do not saw the air too much with your hand, thus, but use all gently; for in the very torrent, tempest, and, as I may say, the whirlwind of passion, you must acquire and beget a temperance that may give it smoothness. O, it offends me to the soul to see a robustious periwig-pated fellow tear a passion to tatters, to very rags, to split the ears of the groundlings, who for the most part are capable of nothing but inexplicable dumb-shows and noise. I could have such a fellow whipp'd for o'erdoing Termagant. It out-herods Herod. Pray you, avoid it.

1. *Play.* I warrant your honour.

Ham. Be not too tame neither, but let your own discretion be your tutor. Suit the action to the word, the word to the action; with this special observance, that you o'erstep not the modesty of nature. For anything so overdone is from the purpose of playing, whose end, both at the first and now, was and is, to hold, as 'twere, the mirror up to nature; to show virtue her own feature, scorn her own image, and the very age and body of the time his form and pressure. Now this overdone, or come tardy off, though it make the unskilful laugh, cannot but make the judicious grieve; the censure of the which one must, in your allowance, o'erweigh a whole theatre of others. O, there be players that I have seen play, and heard others praise, and that highly, not to speak it profanely, that, neither having the accent of Christians nor the gait of Christian, pagan, nor man, have so strutted and bellowed that I have thought some of Nature's journeymen had made men and not made them well, they imitated humanity so abominably.

1. *Play.* I hope we have reform'd that indifferently with us, sir.

Ham. O, reform it altogether. And let those that play your clowns speak no more than is set down for them; for there be of them that will themselves laugh to set on some quantity of barren spectators to laugh too, though in the mean time some necessary question of the play be then to be considered. That's villanous, and shows a most pitiful ambition in the Fool that uses it. Go, make you ready.

b) [*Cambridge Theatricals*]

In the time of my residence in Cambridge, I have seen tragedyes, comedyes, historyes, pastorals, and shewes, publickly acted, in which the graduates of good place and reputation have bene specially parted. This it held necessary for the emboldening of their junior schollers to arme them with audacity against they come to bee employed in any publicke exercise, as in the reading of the dialecticke, rhetoricke, ethicke, mathematicke, the physicke, or metaphysike lectures. It teacheth audacity to the bashfull grammarian, beeing newly admitted into the private colledge, and, after matriculated and entred as a member of the University, and makes him a bold sophister, to argue *pro et contra* to compose his syllogysmes, cathegoricke, or hypotheticke (simple or compound), to reason and frame a sufficient argument to prove his questions, or to defend any *axioma,* to distinguish of any dilemma, and be able to moderate in any argumentation whatsoever.

To come to rhetoricke: it not onely emboldens a scholler to speake, but instructs him to speake well, and with judgement to observe his commas, colons, and full poynts; his parentheses, his breathing spaces, and distinctions; to keepe a decorum in his countenance, neither to frowne when he should smile, nor to make unseemely and disguised faces in the delivery of his words; not to stare with his eies, draw awry his mouth, confound his voice in the hollow of his throat, or teare his words hastily betwixt his teeth; neither to buffet his deske like a mad man, nor stande in his place like a livelesse image, demurely plodding, and without any smooth and formal motion. It instructs him to fit his phrases to his action, and his action to his phrase, and his pronuntiation to them both.

Tully, in his booke *Ad Caium Herennium,* requires five things in an orator—invention, disposition, eloquution, memory, and pronuntiation; yet all are imperfect without the sixt, which is action, for be his invention never so fluent and exquisite, his disposition and order never so composed and formall, his eloquence and elaborate phrases never so materiall and pithy, his memory never so firme and retentive, his pronuntiation never so musicall and plausive, yet without a comely and elegant gesture, a gratious and a bewitching kinde of action, a naturall and familiar motion of the head, the hand, the body, and a moderate and fit countenance sutable to all the rest, I hold all the rest as nothing. A delivery and sweet action is the glosse and beauty of any discourse that belongs to a scholler. And this is the action behoovefull in

any that professe this quality, not to use any impudent or forced
motion in any part of the body, nor rough or other violent gesture; nor on the contrary to stand like a stiffe starcht man, but
to qualifie every thing according to the nature of the person
personated: for in overacting trickes, and toyling too much in the
anticke habit of humors, men of the ripest desert, greatest opinions, and best reputations, may breake into the most violent
absurdities.

c) [*Qualifications of an Actor*]

Here I must needs remember Tarleton, in his time gratious
with the queene, his soveraigne, and in the people's generall applause, whom succeeded Wil. Kemp, as wel in the favour of her
majesty, as in the opinion and good thoughts of the generall
audience. Gabriel, Singer, Pope, Phillips, Sly, all the right I can
do them is but this, that, though they be dead, their deserts yet
live in the remembrance of many. Among so many dead, let me
not forget one yet alive, in his time the most worthy, famous
Maister Edward Allen. To omit these, as also such as for their
divers imperfections may be thought insufficient for the quality,
actors should be men pick'd out personable, according to the parts
they present: they should be rather schollers, that, though they
cannot speake well, know how to speake, or else to have that
volubility that they can speake well, though they understand
not what, and so both imperfections may by instructions be
helped and amended: but where a good tongue and a good conceit
both faile, there can never be good actor. I also could wish, that
such as are condemned for their licentiousnesse, might by a generall consent bee quite excluded our society; for, as we are men
that stand in the broad eye of the world, so should our manners,
gestures, and behaviours, savour of such government and modesty,
to deserve the good thoughts and reports of all men, and to abide
the sharpest censures even of those that are the greatest opposites
to the quality. Many amongst us I know to be of substance, of
government, of sober lives, and temperate carriages, house-
keepers, and contributory to all duties enjoyned them, equally
with them that are rank't with the most bountifull; and if amongst
so many of sort, there be any few degenerate from the rest in

that good demeanor which is both requisite and expected at their hands, let me entreat you not to censure hardly of all for the misdeeds of some.

d) [*An Excellent Actor*]

Whatsoeuer is commendable in the graue Orator, is most exquisitly perfect in him; for by a full and significant action of body, he charmes our attention: sit in a full Theater, and you will thinke you see so many lines drawne from the circumference of so many eares, whiles the *Actor* is the *Center*. He doth not striue to make nature monstrous, she is often seene in the same Scaene with him, but neither on Stilts nor Crutches; and for his voice tis not lower then the prompter, nor lowder then the Foile and Target. By his action he fortifies morall precepts with example; for what we see him personate, we thinke truely done before vs: a man of a deepe thought might apprehend, the Ghosts of our ancient *Heroes* walk't againe, and take him (at seuerall times) for many of them. Hee is much affected to painting, and tis a question whether that make him an excellent Plaier, or his playing an exquisite painter. Hee addes grace to the Poets labours: for what in the Poet is but ditty, in him is both ditty and musicke. He entertaines vs in the best leasure of our life, that is betweene meales, the most vnfit time, either for study or bodily exercise: the flight of Hawkes and chase of wilde beastes, either of them are delights noble: but some think this sport of men the worthier, despight all *calumny*. All men haue beene of his occupation: and indeed, what hee doth fainedly that doe others essentially: this day one plaies a Monarch, the next a priuate person. Heere one Acts a Tyrant, on the morrow an Exile: A Parasite this man to night, to morow a Precisian, and so of diuers others. I obserue, of all men liuing, a worthy Actor in one kind is the strongest motiue of affection that can be: for when he dies, wee cannot be perswaded any man can doe his parts like him. Therefore the imitating Characterist was extreame idle in calling them Rogues. His Muse it seemes, with all his loud inuocation, could not be wak'd to light him a snuffe to read the Statute: for I would let his malicious ignorance vnderstand, that Rogues are not to be imploide as maine ornaments to his Maiesties Reuels; but the itch of bestriding the Presse, or getting vp on this wodden Pacolet, hath defil'd more innocent paper, than euer did Laxatiue Physicke: yet is their inuention such tyred stuffe, that like Kentish Post-horse they can not go beyond their ordinary stage, should you flea them. But to conclude, I valew a worthy Actor by the corruption of some few of the quality, as I would doe gold in the oare; I should not mind the drosse, but the purity of the metall.

e) [*Subjective Approach*]

Strong passions left too long unsuppress'd, may overthrow the temper of the braine, and totally subvert the rationall parts, and some passions counterfeited long, whether of griefe or joy, have so alter'd the personaters, that players themselves (who are most usually in such employments) have been forc'd to fly to Physick, for cure of the disaffection, which such high penn'd humours, and too passionately and sensibly represented, have occasion'd. I have knowne my selfe, a Tyrant comming from the Scene, not able to reduce himselfe into the knowledge of himselfe till Sack made him (which was his present Physick) forget he was an Emperour, and renew'd all his old acquaintance to him; and it is not out of most mens observation, that one most admirable Mimicke in our late Stage so lively and corporally personated a Changeling, that he could never compose his Face to the figure it had, before he undertook that part.

f) [*Epitaph on Richard Burbage*]

Hee's gone & with him what a world are dead,
Which he reuiud, to be reuiued soe.
No more young Hamlett, ould Heironymoe.
Kind Leer, the greued Moore, and more beside,
That liued in him, haue now for euer dy'de.
Oft haue I seene him leap into the graue,
Suiting the person which he seem'd to haue
Of a sadd louer with soe true an eye,
That theer I would haue sworne, he meant to dye.
Oft haue I seene him play this part in ieast,
Soe liuely, that spectators, and the rest
Of his sad crew, whilst he but seem'd to bleed,
Amazed, thought euen then hee dyed in deed.

g) [*Proteus Burbage*]

It was the happiness of the Actors of those times to have such Poets as these to instruct them, and write for them; and no less of those Poets to have such docile and excellent Actors to Act their Playes, as a Field and Burbidge; of whom we may say, that he was a delightful Proteus, so wholly transforming himself into his Part, and putting off himself with his Cloathes, as he never (not so much as in the Tyring-house) assum'd himself again until the Play was done: there being as much difference between him and one of our common Actors, as between a Ballad-singer who onely mouths it, and an excellent singer, who knows all his Graces, and can artfully vary and modulate his Voice, even to know how much breath he is to give to every syllable. He had all the parts of an excellent Orator (animating his words with speaking, and Speech with Action) his Auditors being never more delighted then when he spoke, nor more sorry then when he held his peace; yet even then, he was an excellent Actor still, never falling in his Part when he had done speaking; but with his looks and gesture, maintaining it still unto the heighth, he imagining Age quod agis, onely spoke to him: so as those who call him a Player do him wrong, no man being less idle then he, whose whole life is nothing else but action; with only this difference from other mens, that as what is but a Play to them, is his Business: so their business is but a play to him.

9. ELIZABETHAN AUDIENCES

An Elizabethan public theater cast its spell over a truly popular audience, representative of all classes of society. Dekker referred to the cross-sectional character of the audience in his *Gull's Hornbook,* quoted below. In the majority of the passages, however, undue emphasis is placed on the undeniable presence of riffraff in the auditorium. As these quotations come from the pens of pamphleteers hostile toward the theater, the testimonies must be taken with a grain of salt:

a) [*"The Fruits of Playes"*]

Do they not maintaine bawdrie, infinit folery, & renue the remembrance of hethen ydolatrie? Do they not induce whordom & vnclennes? nay, are they not rather plaine deuourers of may-

denly virginitie and chastitie? For proofe whereof, but marke the
flocking and running to Theaters & curtens, daylie and hourely,
night and daye, tyme and tyde, to see Playes and Enterludes;
where such wanton gestures, such bawdie speaches, such laughing and fleering, such kissing and bussing, such clipping and cul-
ling, Suche winckinge and glancinge of wanton eyes, and the like,
is vsed, as is wonderfull to behold. Then, these goodly pageants
being done, euery mate sorts to his mate, euery one bringes another homeward of their way verye freendly, and in their secret
conclaues (couertly) they play the *Sodomits,* or worse. And these
be the fruits of Playes or Enterluds for the most part. And
whereas you say there are good Examples to be learned in them,
Trulie so there are: if you will learne falshood; if you will learn
cosenage; if you will learn to deceiue; if you will learn to play the
Hipocrit, to cogge, lye, and falsifie; if you will learne to iest,
laugh, and fleer, to grin, to nodd, and mow; if you will learn
to playe the vice, to swear, teare, and blaspheme both Heauen
and Earth: If you will learn to become a bawde, vncleane,
and to deuerginat Maydes, to deflour honest Wyues: if you will
learne to murther, slaie, kill, picke, steal, robbe, and roue: If you
will learn to rebel against Princes, to commit treasons, to consume treasurs, to practise ydlenes, to sing and talke of bawdie
loue and venery; if you will lerne to deride, scoffe, mock, & flowt,
to flatter & smooth: If you will learn to play the whoremaister, the
glutton, Drunkard, or incestuous person: if you will learn to
become proude, hawtie, & arrogant; and, finally, if you will
learne to Contemne GOD and al his lawes, to care nither for heauen nor hel, and to commit al kinde of sinne and mischeef, you
need to goe to no other schoole, for all these good Examples may
you see painted before your eyes in enterludes and playes: wher-
fore that man who giueth money for the maintenance of them
must needs incurre the damage of *premunire,* that is, eternall
damnation, except they repent.

b) [*"Market of Bawdrie"*]

In our assemblies at playes in London, you shall see suche
heaving and shooving, suche ytching and shouldering to sytte by
women; suche care for their garments that they be not trode
on; such eyes to their lappes that no chippes lighte in them; such

pillowes to their backes that they take no hurte; suche masking in their eares, I know not what; suche geving them pippins to passe the time; such playing at foote saunt without cardes; such ticking, such toying, such smiling, such winking, and such manning them home when the sportes are ended, that it is a right comedie to marke their behaviour, to watch their conceates, as the catte for the mouse, and as good as a course at the game it selfe, to dogge them a little, or follow aloofe by the printe of their feete, and so discover by slotte where the deare taketh soyle.

If this were as well noted as il seene, or as openly punished as secretely practised, I have no doubt but the cause woulde be seared to drye up the effect, and these prettie rabbets verye cunningly ferretted from their borrowes. For they that lacke customers all the weeke, either because their haunt is unknowen, or the constables and officers of their parish watch them so narrowly that they dare not queatche, to celebrate the Sabboth flocke too theaters, and there keepe a generall market of bawdrie. Not that anye filthinesse, in deede, is committed within the compasse of that ground, as was once done in Rome, but that every wanton and [his] paramour, everye man and his mistresse, every John and his Joane, every knave and his queane are there first acquainted, and cheapen the marchandise in that place, which they pay for else where, as they can agree.

c) ["The Fashion of Youthes"]

Theaters are snares vnto faire women. And as I toulde you long ago in my schoole of abuse, our Theaters, and play houses in London, are as full of secrete adulterie as they were in Rome. In Rome it was the fashion of wanton yonge men to place them selues as nigh as they could to the curtesans, to present them pomgranates, to play with their garments, and waite on them home, when the sporte was done. In the playhouses at London, it is the fashion of youthes to go first into the yarde, and to carry theire eye through euery gallery, then like vnto rauens where they spye the carion thither they flye, and presse as nere to the fairest as they can. In stead of pomegranates they giue them pippines, they dally with their garments to passe the time, they minister talke vpon al occasions, & eyther bring them home to theire houses on small acquaintance, or slip into tauerns when

the plaies are done. He thinketh best of his painted sheath, &
taketh himselfe for a iolly fellow, yet is noted of most, to be
busyest with women in all such places. This open corruption
is a pricke in the eyes of them that see it, and a thorne in the
sides of the godly, when they heare it. This is a poyson to beholders, and a nurserie of idelnesse to the Players.

d) [*Rioting*]

In a place so ciuill as this Cittie is esteemed, it is more
than barbarously rude, to see the shamefull disorder and routes
that sometime in such publike meetings are vsed.

The beginners are neither gentlemen, nor citizens, nor any
of both their seruants, but some lewd mates that long for in-
nouation; & when they see aduantage, that either Seruingmen
or Apprentises are most in number, they will be of either side,
though indeed they are of no side, but men beside all honestie,
willing to make boote of cloakes, hats, purses, or what euer they
can lay holde on in a hurley burley. These are the common
causers of discord in publike places. If otherwise it happen (as
it seldome doth) that any quarrell be betweene man and man, it
is far from manhood to make so publike a place their field to
fight in: no men will doe it, but cowardes that would faine be
parted, or haue hope to haue manie partakers.

e) [*More Riots*]

. . . men come not to study at a Play-house, but love such expressions and passages, which with ease insinuate themselves into
their capacities . . . to them bring *Jack Drumm's* entertainment,
Greens tu quoque, the *Devill of Edmunton,* and the like; or if it
be on Holy dayes, when Saylers, Water-men, Shoomakers, Butchers and Apprentices are at leisure, then it is good policy to amaze
those violent spirits, with some tearing Tragaedy full of fights
and skirmishes: as the *Guilphs* and *Guiblins, Greeks* and *Trojans,*
or the three *London Apprentises,* which commonly ends in six
acts, the spectators frequently mounting the stage, and making
a more bloody Catastrophe amongst themselves, then the Players
did. I have known upon one of these *Festivals,* but especially at

Shrove-tide, where the Players have been appointed, notwithstanding their bils to the contrary, to act what the major part of the company had a mind to; sometimes *Tamerlane,* sometimes *Jugurth,* sometimes the *Jew of Malta,* and sometimes parts of all these, and at last, none of the three taking, they were forc'd to undresse and put off their Tragick habits, and conclude the day with the merry milk-maides. And unlesse this were done, and the popular humour satisfied, as sometimes it so fortun'd, that the Players were refractory; the Benches, the tiles, the laths, the stones, Oranges, Apples, Nuts, flew about most liberally, and as there were Mechanicks of all professions, who fell every one to his owne trade, and dissolved a house in an instant, and made a ruine of a stately Fabrick. It was not then the most mimicall nor fighting man, *Fowler,* nor *Andrew Cane* could pacifie; Prologues nor Epilogues would prevaile; the Devill and the fool were quite out of favour. Nothing but noise and tumult fils the house, untill a cogg take 'um, and then to the Bawdy houses, and reforme them; and instantly to the Banks side, where the poor Beares must conclude the riot, and fight twenty dogs at a time beside the Butchers, which sometimes fell into the service; this perform'd, and the Horse and Jack-an-Apes for a jigge, they had sport enough that day for nothing.

10.   "A VERY WINNING DAME"

An Elizabethan production was amply provided with spectacle, pantomime, and music so that foreigners, not familiar with English, would still be rewarded when they visited the theaters, which they never failed to do. With the help of Orazio Busino, Chaplain of the Venetian Embassy, we may mingle with the spectators in the Fortune playhouse one afternoon in 1617. Busino, while having an encounter with a prostitute, is objective enough to notice the presence of respectable women:

Last week I was greatly upset by the sudden death of Sig. Sigismondo Lucchese, his Excellency's butler. To distract me, they took me . . . to one of the numerous theatres here in London where comedies are recited and we saw a tragedy performed there, which moved me very little, especially as I cannot understand a single word of English, though one may derive some little amusement from gazing on the sumptuous dresses of the actors and observing their gestures, and the various interludes of instrumental music, dancing, singing and the like. The best treat was to see and stare at so much nobility in such excellent array that they seemed so many princes, listening as silently and soberly as possible, and many very honourable and handsome ladies come there very freely and take their seats among the men without hesitation. That very evening the secretary was pleased to play off a jest upon me. I was surrounded by a number of young ladies, and after I had been seated awhile a very winning dame in a mask took her seat beside me and spoke to me as if I had been her husband. She asked me for a rendezvous in English and French, and as I turned a deaf ear to both, she showed me some fine diamonds which she wore removing no less than three gloves which she wore one over the other. She was richly dressed from head to foot. I also had from her eyes a few modest glances, perhaps from surprise at seeing an extraordinary and old and ugly phiz. Nevertheless these gallantries have scarcely shaken off my lethargy.

11. THE PLAYHOUSE MANNERS OF A GALLANT

IN 1609 appeared Thomas Dekker's pamphlet, *The Gull's Hornbook*, the sixth chapter of which advises a gallant how he should behave in a playhouse. The section throws light upon the manners some of the Jacobean gallants must have exhibited when they planted themselves "on the very rushes" of the stage:

The Theater is your Poets Royal Exchange, vpon which, their Muses (that are now turnd to Merchants) meeting, barter away that light commodity of words for a lighter ware then words, *Plaudities* and the *Breath* of the great *Beast,* which (like the threatnings of two Cowards) vanish all into aire. *Plaiers* are their *Factors,* who put away the stuffe, and make the best of it they possibly can (as indeed tis their parts so to doe). Your Gallant, your Courtier, and your Capten, had wont to be the soundest paymaisters, and I thinke are still the surest chapmen: and these by meanes that their heades are well stockt, deale vpon this comical freight by the grosse: when your *Groundling,* and *Gallery Commoner* buyes his sport by the penny, and like a *Hagler,* is glad to vtter it againe by retailing.

Sithence then the place is so free in entertainment, allowing a stoole as well to the Farmers sonne as to your Templer: that your Stinkard has the selfe same libertie to be there in his Tobacco-Fumes, which your sweet Courtier hath: and that your Carman and Tinker claime as strong a voice in their suffrage, and sit to giue iudgement on the plaies life and death, as well as the prowdest *Momus* among the tribe of *Critick*: It is fit that hee, whom the most tailors bils do make roome for, when he comes should not be basely (like a vyoll) casd vp in a corner.

Whether therefore the gatherers of the publique or priuate Playhouse stand to receiue the afternoones rent, let our Gallant (hauing paid it) presently aduance himselfe vp to the Throne of the Stage. I meane not into the Lords roome, (which is now but the Stages Suburbs). No, those boxes, by the iniquity of custome, conspiracy of waiting-women and Gentlemen-Ushers, that there sweat together, and the couetousnes of Sharers, are contemptibly thrust into the reare, and much new Satten is there dambd by being smothred to death in darknesse. But on the very Rushes where the Commedy is to daunce, yea and vnder the state of *Cambises* himselfe must our fethered *Estridge,* like a peece of Ordnance be planted valiantly (because impudently) beating down the mewes and hisses of the opposed rascality.

For do but cast vp a reckoning, what large cummings in are pursd vp by sitting on the Stage. First a conspicuous *Eminence* is gotten; by which meanes the best and most essenciall parts of a Gallant (good cloathes, a proportionable legge, white hand, the Persian lock, and a tollerable beard) are perfectly reuealed.

By sitting on the stage, you haue a signd pattent to engrosse the whole commodity of Censure; may lawfully presume to be a Girder: and stand at the helme to steere the passage of *Scaenes* [;] yet no man shall once offer to hinder you from obtaining the title of an insolent, ouer-weening Coxcombe.

By sitting on the stage, you may (without trauelling for it) at the very next doore, aske whose play it is: and, by that *Quest* of *inquiry,* the law warrants you to auoid much mistaking; if you know not the author, you may raile against him: and peraduenture so behaue your selfe, that you may enforce the Author to know you.

By sitting on the stage, if you be a Knight, you may happily get you a Mistresse: if a mere *Fleet street* Gentleman, a wife: but assure yourselfe by continuall residence, you are the first and principall man in election to begin the number of *We three.*

By spreading your body on the stage, and by being a Justice in examining of plaies, you shall put your selfe into such true *Scaenical* authority, that some Poet shall not dare to present his Muse rudely vpon your eyes, without hauing first vnmaskt her, rifled her, and discouered all her bare and most mysticall parts before you at a Tauerne, when you most knightly shal for his paines, pay for both their suppers.

By sitting on the stage, you may (with small cost) purchase the deere acquaintance of the boyes: haue a good stoole for sixpence: at any time know what particular part any of the infants present: get your match lighted, examine the play-suits lace, and perhaps win wagers vpon laying tis copper, &c. And to conclude whether you be a foole or a Justice of peace, a Cuckold or a Capten, a Lord Maiors sonne or a dawcocke, a knaue or an vnder-Sheriffe, of what stamp soeuer you be, currant or counterfet, the Stage, like time, will bring you to most perfect light, and lay you open: neither are you to be hunted from thence though the Scar-crows in the yard, hoot at you, hisse at you, spit at you, yea throw durt euen in your teeth: tis most Gentlemanlike patience to endure all this, and to laugh at the silly Animals: but if the *Rabble* with a full throat, crie away with the foole, you were worse then a mad-man to tarry by it: for the Gentleman and the foole should neuer sit on the Stage together.

Mary let this obseruation go hand in hand with the rest: or rather like a country-seruing-man, some fiue yards before them. Present not your selfe on the Stage (especially at a new play) vntill the quaking prologue hath (by rubbing) got cullor into his cheekes, and is ready to giue the trumpets their Cue that hees vpon point to enter: for then it is time, as though you were one of the *Properties,* or that you dropt out of the *Hangings,* to creepe from behind the Arras, with your *Tripos* or three-footed stoole in one hand, and a teston mounted betweene a forefinger and a thumbe in the other: for if you should bestow your person vpon the vulgar, when the belly of the house is but halfe full, your apparell is quite eaten vp, the fashion lost, and the proportion of your body in more danger to be deuoured, then if it were serued vp in the Counter amongst the Powltry: auoid that as you would the Bastome. It shall crowne you with rich commendation to laugh alowd in the middest of the most serious and saddest scene of the terriblest Tragedy: and to let that clapper (your tongue) be tost so high that all the house may ring of it: your Lords vse it; your Knights are Apes to the Lords, and do so too: your Inne-a-court-man is Zany to the Knights, and (many very scuruily) comes likewise limping after it: bee thou a beagle to them all, and neuer lin snuffing till you haue scented them: for by talking and laughing (like a Plough-man in a Morris) you heap *Pelion* vpon·*Ossa,* glory vpon glory: As first, all the eyes in the galleries will leaue walking after the Players, and onely follow you: the simplest dolt in the house snatches vp your name, and when he meetes you in the streetes, or that you fall into his hands in the middle of a Watch, his word shall be taken for you: heele cry, *Hees such a Gallant,* and you passe. Secondly, you publish your temperance to the world, in that you seeme not to resort thither to taste vaine pleasures with a hungrie appetite: but onely as a Gentleman, to spend a foolish houre or two, because yoe can doe nothing else. Thirdly you mightily disrelish the Audience, and disgrace the Author: mary, you take vp (though it be at the worst hand) a strong opinion of your owne iudgement and inforce the Poet to take pitty of your weakenesse, and, by some dedicated sonnet to bring you into a better paradice, onely to stop your mouth.

If you can (either for loue or money) prouide your selfe a lodging by the water-side: for, aboue the conueniencie it brings, to shun Shoulder-clapping, and to ship away your Cockatrice betimes in the morning, it addes a kind of state vnto you, to be carried from thence to the staires of your Play-house: hate a Sculler (remember that) worse then to be acquainted with one ath' Scullery. No, your Oares are your onely Sea-crabs, boord them, and take heed you neuer go twice together with one paire: often shifting is a great credit to Gentlemen; and that diuiding of your fare wil make the poore watersnaks be ready to pul you in peeces to enioy your custome: No matter whether vpon landing you haue money or no, you may swim in twentie of their boates ouer the riuer upon *Ticket*: mary, when siluer comes in, remember to pay trebble their fare, and it will make your Flounder-catchers to send more thankes after you, when you doe not draw, then when you doe; for they know, It will be their owne another daie.

Before the Play begins, fall to cardes, you may win or loose (as *Fencers* doe in a prize) and beate one another by confederacie, yet share the money when you meete at supper: notwithstanding, to gul the *Ragga-muffins* that stand aloofe gaping at you, throw the cards (hauing first torne foure or fiue of them) round about the Stage, iust vpon the third sound, as though you had lost: it skils not if the foure knaues ly on their backs, and outface the Audience, theres none such fooles as dare take exceptions at them, because ere the play go off, better knaues than they will fall into the company.

Now sir, if the writer be a fellow that hath either epigramd you, or hath had a flirt at your mistris, or hath brought either your feather or your red beard, or your little legs, &c. on the stage, you shall disgrace him worse then by tossing him in a blancket, or giuing him the bastinado in a Tauerne, if, in the middle of his play (bee it Pastoral or Comedy, Morall or Tragedie), you rise with a skreud and discontented face from your stoole to be gone: no matter whether the Scenes be good or no, the better they are the worse do you distast them: and, beeing on your feet, sneake not away like a coward, but salute all your gentle acquaintance, that are spred either on the rushes, or on stooles about you, and draw what troope you can from the stage after you: the *Mimicks* are beholden to you, for allowing them elbow roome: their Poet cries perhaps a pox go with you, but care not you for that, theres no musick without frets.

Mary if either the company, or indisposition of the weather binde you to sit it out, my counsell is then that you turne plaine Ape, take vp a rush and tickle the earnest eares of your fellow gallants, to make other fooles fall a laughing: mewe at passionate speeches, blare at merrie, finde fault with the musicke, whew at the childrens Action, whistle at the songs: and aboue all, curse the sharers, that whereas the same day you had bestowed forty shillings on an embrodered Felt and Feather, (scotch-fashion) for your mistres in the Court, or your punck in the city, within two houres after, you encounter with the very same block on the stage, when the haberdasher swore to you the impression was extant but the morning.

To conclude, hoard vp the finest play-scraps you can get, vpon which your leane wit may most sauourly feede for want of other stuffe, when the *Arcadian* and *Euphuisd* gentlewomen haue their tongues sharpened to set vpon you: that qualitie (next to your shittlecocke) is the onely furniture to a Courtier thats but a new beginner, and is but in his A B C of complement. The next places that are fild, after the Playhouses bee emptied, are (or ought to be) Tauernes, into a Tauerne then let vs next march, where the braines of one Hogshead must be beaten out to make vp another.

12. THE PATRONS OF BLACKFRIARS

THE SOCIETY of the Jacobean era, driving in hackney-coaches to the "private" playhouse in Blackfriars, was interspersed with morbid types. Henry Fitzgeffrey's satiric pen sketched this ghostly merry-go-round in 1620. "To deceiue Time with till the second sound" our London Martial observes strange characters as they enter the playhouse. The first to draw his attention is a bragging captain:

Hee'l tell of Basilisks, Trenches, Retires:
Of Pallizadoes, Parepets, Frontires:
Of Caluerins, and Baricadoes too:
What to bee Harquehazerd: to lye in Perdue:
How many men a Soldier ought to slay
For a Lieutenant-ship: or Twelue month pay. . . .

[The next spectator is Sir Ilaud Hunt, a traveller that will tell]

Of stranger Things then Tatterd Tom ere li't of,
Then Pliny or Herodotus e're writ of:
How he a remnant lately brought with him
Of Iacobs Ladder from Ierusalem:
At the Barmodies how the Fishes fly:
Of Lands inriched by Lottery:
Of Affricke: Aegypt, with strange Monsters fild:
Such as nere Noah's Arke, nere Eden held;
And rare Rarities then all of these.

[The demi-monde sends an attractive representative in the person of]

A Cheapside Dame, by th' Tittle on her head!
Plot (Villain!) plot! Let's lay our heads together!
We may deuise perchance to get her hither.
(If wee to-gether cunnining compact)
Shee'l hold vs dooing till the Latter Act,
And (on my life) Inuite vs Supper home:
Wee'l thrust hard for it, but wee'l finde her rome.
Heer Mis — pox out! she's past, she'l not come ore,
Sure shee's bespoken for a box before.

[Next our attention is turned to the personified "world of fashion"]

In Turkie colours carued to the skin.
Mounted Pelonianly vntill hee reeles,
That scorns (so much) plaine dealing at his heeles,
His Boote speaks Spanish to his Scottish Spurres,
His Sute cut Frenchly, round bestucke with Burres.
Pure Holland is his shirt, which proudly faire,
Seems to out-face his Doublet euery where:
His Haire like to your Moor's or Irish Lockes,
His chiefest Dyet Indian minced Dockes.

[A rather grotesque person now pushes her (or his) way through the crowd]

. . . A Woman of the Masculine Gender.
Looke thou mayst well descry her by her groath,
Out, point not man! Least wee be beaten both.
Eye her a little, marke but were shee'l goe,
Now (by this hand) into the Gallants Roe.
Let her alone! What ere she giues to stand,
Shee'l make herselfe a gayner, By the Hand.

[An effeminate fop is next to arrive]

What think'st thou of yon plumed Dandebrat,
You Ladyes Shittle-cocke, Egyptian Rat:
You Musk-ball Milke-sop: you French Sincopace,
That Vshers in, with a Coranto grace
You Gilded March pane, you All Verdingall:

This is the Puppet, which the Ladyes all
Send for of purpose and solicite so
To daunce with them. Pray (Sir) a step or two
A Galliard or a Iigg: Pox out! cryes hee,
That ere I knew this Toyling faculty.

|Now the Coxcomb makes his entrance|

In you spruse Coxcombe, you Affecting Asse.
That neuer walkes without his Looking-Glasse,
In a Tobacco box, or Diall set,
That he may priuately conferre with it.
How his Band iumpeth with his Peccadilly.
Whether his Band strings ballance equally:
Which way his Feather wagg's: And (to say truth)
What wordes in vtterance best become his mouth.
Oh! Hadst thou yesterday beheld the Valour
I saw him exercising on his Taylor,
How, out of measure, he the Rascall beat,
Not fitting to his minde his Doublet.

[In order that he may look slender]

Hee'l haue an attractiue Lace,
And Whalebone-bodyce, for the better grace.
Admit spare dyet, on no sustnance feed,
But Oatmeale, Milke, and crums of Barly-bread.
Vse Exercise, vntill at last hee fit
(With much adoe) his Body vnto it. . . .
See! euery step an Honor hee doth make:
That Ladyes, may denote him with their Fan,
As he goes by, with a Lo: Hee's the man.

13. "THESE TRANSITORY DEVICES"

Mummings and disguisings have played a role in the entertainment
schedule of English royalty since the days of Henry VII. With the accession of Henry VIII, the courtly revels received a strong impetus. He
is credited with the transplantation of the Italian court masque to England (1512). During the Elizabethan period the Inns of Court served as
nurseries for the budding masque, which reached its artistic apogee during

James I's reign. In the Banqueting House at Whitehall, the Stuart kings and their courts, once or twice a year, "recreated their spirits wasted in grave affairs of state" (Davenant) by participating in the production of sumptuous court masques. Francis Bacon defined these feasts for the eyes and minds of the sophisticated as princely toys, while Samuel Daniel referred to them as "compliments of state." Daniel, who had penned the libretti for two early masques, was quite sensible about the new genre. "In these things," he wrote, "the only life consists in shew; the art and invention of the Architect gives the greatest grace and is of most importance." Ben Jonson, however, about to embark upon a career as a masque librettist, challenged the importance of the architect and, right at the beginning of his work as a court entertainer, stressed the function of the librettist whose poetic imagination was to give permanency to what otherwise would be merely transitory devices. The preface to *Hymenaei* (1606) contains Jonson's policy statement:

It is a noble and just advantage that the things subjected to understanding have of those which are objected to sense; that the one sort are but momentary, and merely taking; the other impressing and lasting: else the glory of all these solemnies had perished like a blaze, and gone out, in the beholders' eyes. So short lived are the bodies of all things, in comparison of their souls. And though bodies ofttimes have the ill-luck to be sensually preferred, they find afterwards the good fortune (when souls live) to be utterly forgotten. . . . And howsoever some may squeamishly cry out, that all endeavour of learning and sharpness in these transitory devises, especially where it steps beyond their little, or (let me not wrong 'em), no brain at all, is superfluous; I am contented these fastidious stomachs should leave my full tables, and enjoy at home their clean empty trenchers, fittest for such airy tastes; where perhaps a few Italian herbs, picked up and made into a sallad, may find sweeter acceptance than all the most nourishing and sound meats of the world. For these men's palates, let not me answer, O Muses. It is not my fault if I fill them out nectar and they run to metheglin.

14. AN EARLY STUART MASQUE

THE FIRST court masque in which Ben Jonson and Inigo Jones collaborated was *The Masque of Blackness*, performed on January 6, 1605 in the old Banqueting House at Whitehall. Inigo Jones, in presenting a concentrated setting, had taken his inspiration from Italian seascape sets. Gone was

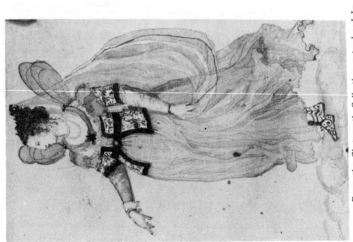

For Iris in *Hymenaei* (1606)

For a Negro Nymph in *The Masque of Blackness* (1605)

Inigo Jones' Costumes.

the older type of dispersed scenery: Jones had finally brought the mounting of English court spectacles up to date, though there was yet little scenic movement on the stage. At least one "engine," the mother-of-pearl shell, was set in motion. It contained the chief masquer, Queen Anne, and her attendants, all made up as Negresses. The Queen had wished to appear with her ladies as blackamoors, and Jonson was sufficiently erudite to think of them as the daughters of Niger. Some of the spectators thought the "leancheeked Moors" a rather loathsome sight. Here is Ben Jonson's description of the production:

PLINY, SOLINVS, PTOLOMEY, and of late LEO the *African,* remember vnto vs a riuer in *Aethiopia,* famous by the name of *Niger*; of which the people were called *Nigritae,* now *Negro's*: and are the blackest nation of the world. This riuer taketh spring out of a certaine *lake,* east-ward; and after a long race, falleth into the westerne *Ocean.* Hence (because it was her Maiesties will, to haue them *Black-mores* at first) the inuention was deriued by me, and presented thus.

First, for the *Scene,* was drawne a LANDTSCHAP, consisting of small woods, and here and there a void place fill'd with huntings; which falling, an artificiall sea was seene to shoote forth, as if it flowed to the land, raysed with waues, which seemed to moue, and in some places the billow to breake, as imitating that orderly disorder, which is common in nature. In front of this sea were placed six *Tritons,* in mouing, and sprightly actions, their vpper parts humane, saue that their haires were blue, as partaking of the sea-colour: their desinent parts, fish, mounted aboue their heads, and all varied in disposition. From their backs were borne out certaine light pieces of taffata, as if carryed by the winde, and their musique made out of wreathed shells. Behind these, a paire of *Sea-maides,* for song, were as conspicuously seated; betweene which, two great *Sea-horses* (as bigge as the life) put forth themselues; the one mounting aloft, and writhing his head from the other, which seemed to sinke forwards; so intended for variation, and that the figure behind, might come off better: vpon their backs, OCEANVS and NIGER were aduanced.

OCEANVS, presented in a humane forme, the colour of his flesh, blue; and shaddowed with a robe of sea-greene; his head grey; and horned; as he is described by the *Ancients*: his beard of the like mixt colour: hee was gyrlonded with *Alga,* or seagrasse; and in his hand a *Trident.*

NIGER, in forme and colour of an *Aethiope*; his haire, and rare beard curled, shaddowed with a blue, and bright mantle: his front, neck, and wrists adorned with pearle, and crowned, with an artificiall wreathe of cane, and paper-rush.

These induced the *Masquers*, which were twelue *Nymphs, Negro's*; and the daughters of NIGER; attended by so many of the OCEAN(I)AE, which were their *light-bearers*.

The *Masquers* were placed in a great concaue shell, like mother of pearle, curiously made to moue on those waters, and rise with the billow; the top thereof was stuck with a *cheu'ron* of lights, which, indented to the proportion of the shell, strooke a glorious beame vpon them, as they were seated, one aboue another: so that they were all seene, but in an extrauagant order.

On sides of the shell, did swim sixe huge *Sea-monsters*, varyed in their shapes, and dispositions, bearing on their backs the twelue *torchbearers*; who were planted there in seuerall greces; so as the backs of some were seene; some in *purfle*, or side; others in face; and all hauing their lights burning out of *whelks*, or *murex* shells.

The attyre of (the) *Masquers* was alike, in all, without difference: the colours, *azure*, and *siluer*; (their hayre thicke, and curled vpright in tresses, lyke *Pyramids*,) but returned on the top with a scroll and antique dressing of feathers, and iewells interlaced with ropes of pearle. And, for the front, eare, neck, and wrists, the ornament was of the most choise and orient pearle; best setting off from the black.

For the *light-bearers, sea-greene,* waued about the skirts with gold and siluer; their haire loose, and flowing, gyrlanded with sea-grasse, and that stuck with branches of corall.

These thus presented, the *Scene* behind, seemed a vast sea (and vnited with this that flowed forth) from the termination, or *horizon* of which (being the leuell of the *State,* which was placed in the vpper end of the hall) was drawne, by the lines of *Prospectiue,* the whole worke shooting downe-wards, from the eye; which *decorum* made it more conspicuous, and caught the eye a farre off with a wandring beauty. To which was added an obscure and cloudy night-piece, that made the whole set of. So much for the bodily part. Which was of Master YNIGO IONES his designe, and act.

15. COSTUMES AND SCENERY BY INIGO JONES

IN 1606, the Twelfth Night masque, Ben Jonson's *Hymenaei,* was presented at Whitehall in honor of the union of the Earl of Essex and Lady
Frances Howard. Inigo Jones attended once more to the "bodily part,"
this time stealing the show with a giant globe, turning round an invisible axle, and a series of cloud effects. The official libretto dwells at length
on the subject of Inigo Jones' costumes:

Such was the exquisit performance, as (beside the *pompe,
splendor,* or what we may call *apparelling* of such *Presentments*)
that alone (had all else beene absent) was of power to surprize
with delight, and steale away the *spectators* from themselues. Nor
was there wanting whatsoeuer might giue to the *furniture,* or
complement; eyther in *riches,* or strangenesse of the *habites,* deli-
cacie of *daunces,* magnificence of the *scene,* or diuine rapture
of *musique.* Onely the enuie was, that it lasted not still, or (now
it is past) cannot by imagination, much lesse description, be
recouered to a part of that *spirit* it had in the gliding by.

Yet, that I may not vtterly defraud the *Reader* of his hope,
I am drawne to giue it those briefe touches, which may leaue
behind some shadow of what it was: And first of the *Attyres.*

That, of the Lords, had part of it (for the fashion) taken
from the *antique Greeke* statue; mixed with some *moderne* additions: which made it both gracefull, and strange. On their
heads they wore *Persick* crownes, that were with scroles of *gold-
plate* turn'd outward, and wreath'd about with a *carnation* and
siluer net-lawne; the one end of which hung carelesly on the left
shoulder; the other was trick'd vp before, in seuerall degrees
of foulds, betweene the plates, and set with rich iewels, and
great pearle. Their bodies were of *carnation* cloth of siluer, richly
wrought, and cut to expresse the *naked,* in manner of the *Greeke
Thorax*; girt vnder the brests with a broad *belt* of cloth of gold,
imbrodered, and fastened before with iewels: Their Labels were
of *white* cloth of siluer, lac'd, and wrought curiously betweene,
sutable to the vpper halfe of their sleeues; whose nether parts,
with their bases, were of *watchet* cloth of siluer, chev'rond all
ouer with lace. Their Mantills were of seuerall-colour'd silkes,
distinguishing their qualities, as they were coupled in payres; the
first, *skie colour*; the second, *pearle colour*; the third, *flame*

colour; the fourth, *tawnie*: and these cut in leaues, which were subtilly tack'd vp, and imbrodered with *Oo's*, and betweene euerie ranke of leaues, a broad siluer lace. They were fastened on the right shoulder, and fell compasse downe the back in gracious folds, and were againe tyed with a round knot, to the fastning of their swords. Vpon their legges they wore *siluer* Greaues, answering in worke to their Labells; and these were their *accoutrements.*

The Ladies *attyre* was wholly new, for the inuention, and full of glorie; as hauing in it the most true impression of a *celestiall* figure: the vpper part of *white* cloth of siluer, wrought with IUNOES *birds* and *fruits*; a loose vndergarment, full gather'd, of *carnation*, strip't with *siluer*, and parted with a golden *Zone*: beneath that, another flowing garment, of *watchet* cloth of siluer, lac'd with gold; through all which, though they were round, and swelling, there yet appeared some touch of their delicate *lineaments*, preseruing the sweetnesse of *proportion*, and expressing it selfe beyond expression. The *attyre* of their heads did answer, if not exceed; their haire being carelesly (but yet with more art, then if more affected) bound vnder the circle of a rare and rich *Coronet*, adorn'd with all varietie, and choise of iewels; from the top of which, flow'd a transparent *veile*, downe to the ground; whose verge, returning vp, was fastened to either side in most sprightly manner. Their shooes were *Azure*, and gold, set with Rubies and Diamonds; so were all their garments; and euerie part abounding in ornament.

No lesse to be admir'd, for the grace, and greatnesse, was the whole *Machine* of the *Spectacle*, from whence they came: the first part of which was a MIKROKOSMOS, or *Globe*, fill'd with *Countreys*, and those gilded; where the *Sea* was exprest heightned with siluer waues. This stood, or rather hung (for no *Axell* was seene to support it) and turning softly, discouered the first *Masque* (as wee haue before, but too runningly declared) which was of the *men*, sitting in faire *composition*, within a *mine* of seuerall metalls: To which, the lights were so placed, as no one was seene; but seemed, as if onely REASON, with the splendor of her crowne, illumin'd the whole Grot.

On the sides of this (which began the other part) were placed two great *Statues*, fayned of gold, one of ATLAS, the other of HERCVLES, in varied postures, bearing vp the Clouds, which were of *Releue*, embossed, and tralucent, as Naturalls: To these, a cortine of painted clouds ioyned, which reach'd to the vpmost roofe of the Hall; and sodainely opening, reueal'd the three *Regions of Ayre*: In the highest of which, sate IVNO, in a glorious throne of gold, circled with *Comets*, and fierie *Meteors*, engendred in that hot and drie *Region*; her feet reaching to the lowest: where, was made a Rainebow, and within it, *Musicians* seated, figuring *airie* spirits, their habits various, and resembling the seuerall colours, caused in that part of the *aire* by reflexion. The midst was all of darke and condensed clouds, as being the proper place, where *Raine, Haile,* and other watrie *Meteors* are made; out of which, two concaue clouds, from the rest, thrust forth themselues (in nature of those *Nimbi,* wherein, by *Homer, Virgil,* &c. the *gods* are fain'd to descend) and these carried the eight *Ladies,* ouer the heads of the two *Termes*; who (as the engine mou'd) seem'd also to bow themselues (by vertue of their shadowes) and discharge their shoulders of their glorious burden: when, hauing set them on the earth, both they and the clouds gathered themselues vp againe, with some rapture of the *beholders*.

But that, which (as aboue in place, so in the beautie) was most taking in the *Spectacle*, was the *sphere* of *fire*, in the top of all, encompassing the ayre, and imitated with such art and industrie, as the *spectators* might discerne the Motion (all the time the *Shewes* lasted) without any Moouer; and that so swift, as no eye could distinguish any colour of the light, but might forme to it selfe fiue hundred seuerall hiewes, out of the tralucent bodie of the *ayre*, obiected betwixt it, and them.

And this was crown'd with a statue of IVPITER, the *Thunderer*.

16. "BEN JONSON TURNED THE GLOBE"

JONSON's description of the *Hymenaei* production is supplemented by the impression of an onlooker, Sir John Pory, in a letter written to Sir Robert Cotton:

But to returne to the maske; both Inigo, Ben, and the actors men and women did their partes with great commendation. The conceite or soule of the mask was Hymen bringing in a bride and Juno pronuba's priest a bridegroom, proclaiming those two should be sacrificed to nuptial vnion, and here the poet made an apostrophe to the vnion of the kingdoms. But before the sacrifice could be performed, Ben Jonson turned the globe of the earth standing behind the altar, and within the concaue sate the 8 men-maskers representing the 4 humours and the fower affections which leapt forth to disturb the sacrifice to vnion; but amidst their fury Reason that sate aboue them all, crowned with burning tapers, came down and silenced them. These eight together with Reason their moderatresse mounted aboue their heades, sate somewhat like the ladies in the scallop shell the last year. Aboue the globe of erth houered a middle region of cloudes in the center wherof stood a grand consort of musicians, and vpon the cantons or hornes sate the ladies 4 at one corner, and 4 at another, who descended vpon the stage, not after the stale downright perpendicular fashion, like a bucket into a well; but came gently sloping down. These eight, after the sacrifice was ended, represented the 8 nuptial powers of Juno pronuba who came downe to confirme the vnion. The men were clad in crimzon and the weomen in white. They had euery one a white plume of the richest herons fethers, and were so rich in jewels vpon their heades as was most glorious. I think they hired and borrowed all the principal jewels and ropes of perle both in court and citty.

17. A COURTLY AUDIENCE

FOR 1618 (January 16), Ben Jonson and Inigo Jones prepared *Pleasure Reconciled to Virtue*. Prince Charles, the future Charles I, made his debut as chief masquer. Although it was not a great masque, the event was a social one of the first magnitude. Orazio Busino's detailed description of the affair allows us to scrutinize the audience which gathered in the Banqueting House to witness the princely capers, an audience probably typical of all Stuart masque audiences:

In London, as the capital of a most flourishing kingdom, theatrical representations without end prevail throughout the year in various parts of the city, and are invariably frequented by crowds of persons devoted to pleasure who, for the most part dress grandly and in colours, so that they all seem, were it possible, more than princes, or rather comedians.

In the king's court, in like manner, after Christmas day there begins a series of sumptuous banquets, well-acted comedies, and most graceful masques of knights and ladies. Of the masques, the most famous of all is performed on the morrow of the feast of the three Wise Men according to an ancient custom of the palace here. A large hall is fitted up like a theatre, with well secured boxes all round. The stage is at one end and his Majesty's chair in front under an ample canopy. Near him are stools for the foreign ambassadors. On the 16th of the current month of January, his Excellency was invited to see a representation and masque, which had been prepared with extraordinary pains, the chief performer being the king's own son and heir, the prince of Wales, now seventeen years old, an agile youth, handsome and very graceful. At the fourth hour of the night we went privately to the Court, through the park. On reaching the royal apartments his Excellency was entertained awhile by one of the leading cavaliers until all was ready, whilst we, his attendants, all perfumed and escorted by the master of the ceremonies, entered the usual box of the Venetian embassy, where, unluckily we were so crowded and ill at ease that had it not been for our curiosity we must certainly have given in or expired. We moreover had the additional infliction of a Spaniard who came into our box by favour of the master of the ceremonies, asking but for two fingers breadth of room, although we ourselves had not space to run about in, and I swear to God that he placed himself more comfortably than any of us. I have no patience with these dons; it was observed that they were scattered about in all the principal places. The ambassador was near the king; others with gold chains round their necks sat among the Lords of the Council; others were in their own box taking care of the ambassadress and then this fellow must needs come into ours. Whilst waiting for the king we amused ourselves by admiring the decorations and beauty of the house with its two orders of columns, one above the other, their distance from the wall equalling the breadth of the passage, that of the second row being upheld by Doric pillars, while above these rise Ionic columns supporting the roof. The whole is of wood, including even the shafts, which are carved and gilt with much skill. From the roof of these hang festoons and angels in relief with two rows of lights. Then such a concourse as there was, for although they profess only to admit the favoured ones who are invited, yet every box was filled notably with most noble and richly arrayed ladies, in number some 600 and more according to the general estimate; the dresses being of such variety in cut and colour as to be indescribable; the most delicate plumes over their heads, springing from their foreheads or in their hands serving as fans; strings of jewels on their necks and bosoms and in their girdles and apparel in such quantity that they looked like so many queens, so that at the beginning, with but little light, such as that of the dawn or of the evening twilight, the splendour of their diamonds and other jewels was so brilliant that they looked like so many stars. During the two hours of waiting we had leisure to examine them again and again. Owing to my short-sightedness I could not form an accurate idea of distant objects, and referred myself in everything to my colleagues. They informed me that they espied some very sweet and handsome faces, and at every moment they kept exclaiming Oh do look at this one! Oh see her! Whose wife is that one on the row and that pretty one near, whose daughter is she? However, they came to the conclusion that amongst much grain there was also a mixture of husk and straw, that is to say shrivelled women and some very devoted to St. Charles, but that the beauties outnumbered them. The dress peculiar to these ladies is very handsome for those who like it, and profits some of them as a blind to nature's defects, for behind it hangs well-nigh from the neck down to the ground, with long, close sleeves and no waist. There are no folds so that any deformity, however monstrous, remains hidden. The farthingale also plays its part. The plump and buxom display their bosoms very liberally, and those who are lean go muffled up to the throat. All wear men's shoes or at least very low slippers. They consider the mask as indispensable for their face as bread at table, but they lay it aside willingly at these public entertainments.

18.   CAPERING CAVALIERS

BUSINO continues his description of the event. Although he has little
to say about Jones' scenery, his report is of interest because of the notes
made of the dances:

At about the 6th hour of the night [about 10 o'clock] the
king appeared with his court, having passed through the apartments where the ambassadors were in waiting. . . . On entering
the house, the cornets and trumpets to the number of fifteen or
twenty began to play very well a sort of recitative, and then
after his Majesty had seated himself under the canopy alone, the
queen not being present on account of a slight indisposition, he
caused the ambassadors to sit below him on two stools, while
the great officers of the crown and courts of law sat upon benches.
The Lord Chamberlain then had the way cleared and in the
middle of the theatre there appeared a fine and spacious area
carpeted all over with green cloth. In an instant a large curtain
dropped, painted to represent a tent of gold with a broad fringe;
the background was of canvas painted blue, powdered all over
with golden stars. This became the front arch of the stage, forming a drop scene, and on its being removed there appeared first
of all Mount Atlas, whose enormous head was alone visible up
aloft under the very roof of the theatre; it rolled up its eyes and
moved itself very cleverly. As a foil to the principal ballet and
masque they had some mummeries performed in the first act;
for instance, a very chubby Bacchus [Comus, "the God of
Cheere"] on a car drawn by four gownsmen, who sang in an
undertone before his Majesty. There was another stout individual on foot, dressed in red in short clothes, who made a speech,
reeling about like a drunkard, tankard in hand, so that he resembled Bacchus's cupbearer. This first scene was very gay and
burlesque. Next followed twelve extravagant masques, one of
whom was in a barrel, all but his extremities, his companions being similarly cased in huge wicker flasks, very well made. They
danced awhile to the sound of the cornets and trumpets, performing various and most extravagant antics. These were followed by a gigantic man representing Hercules with his club,
who strove with Antaeus and performed other feats. Then came
twelve masked boys in the guise of frogs. They danced together,

Inigo Jones' Sketch for the Car of Bacchus (Comus, "the God of Cheere") in *Pleasure Reconciled to Virtue* (1618).

assuming sundry grotesque attitudes. After they had all fallen down, they were driven off by Hercules. Mount Atlas then opened, by means of two doors, which were made to turn, and from behind the hills of a distant landscape the day was seen to dawn, some gilt columns being placed along either side of the scene, so as to aid the perspective and make the distance seem greater. Mercury next appeared before the king and made a speech. After him came a guitar player in a gown, who sang some trills, accompanying himself with his instrument. He announced himself as some deity, and then a number of singers, dressed in long red gowns to represent high priests, came on the stage, wearing gilt mitres. In the midst of them was a goddess in a long white robe and they sang some jigs which we did not understand. It is true that, spoiled as we are by the graceful and harmonious music of Italy, the composition did not strike us as very fine. Finally twelve cavaliers, masked, made their appearance, dressed uniformly, six having the entire hose crimson with plaited doublets of white satin trimmed with gold and silver lace. The other six wore breeches down to the knee, with the half hose also crimson, and white shoes. These matched well their corsets which were cut in the shape of the ancient Roman corslets. On their heads they wore long hair and crowns and very tall white plumes. Their faces were covered with black masks. These twelve descended together from above the scene in the figure of a pyramid, of which the prince formed the apex. When they reached the ground the violins, to the number of twenty-five or thirty began to play their airs. After they had made an obeisance to his Majesty, they began to dance in very good time, preserving for a while the same pyramidical figure, and with a variety of steps. Afterwards they changed places with each other in various ways, but ever ending the jump together. When this was over, each took his lady, the prince pairing with the principal one among those who were ranged in a row ready to dance, and the others doing the like in succession, all making obeisance to his Majesty first and then to each other. They performed every sort of ballet and dance of every country whatsoever such as passamezzi, corants, canaries, Spaniards and a hundred other very fine gestures devised to tickle the fancy. Last of all they danced the Spanish dance. one at a time, each with his lady, and being well nigh tired they began to lag, whereupon the king, who is naturally choleric, got impatient and shouted aloud: "Why don't they dance? What did they make me come here for? Devil take you all, dance." Upon this, the Marquis of Buckingham, his Majesty's favourite, immediately sprang forward, cutting a score of lofty and very minute capers, with so much grace and agility that he not only appeased the ire of his angry lord, but rendered himself the admiration and delight of everybody. The other masquers, thus encouraged, continued to exhibit their prowess one after another, with various ladies, also finishing with capers and lifting their goddesses from the ground. We counted thirty-four capers as cut by one cavalier in succession, but none came up to the exquisite manner of the marquis. The prince, however, excelled them all in bowing, being very formal in making his obeisance both to the king and to the lady with whom he danced, nor was he once seen to do a step out of time when dancing, whereas one cannot perhaps say so much for the others. Owing to his youth he has not yet much breath, nevertheless he cut a few capers very gracefully.

The encounter of these twelve accomplished cavaliers being ended, and after they had valiantly overcome the sloth and debauch of Bacchus, the prince went in triumph to kiss his father's hands. The king embraced and kissed him tenderly and then honoured the marquis with marks of extraordinary affection, patting his face. The king now rose from his chair, took the ambassadors along with him, and after passing through a number of chambers and galleries he reached a hall where the usual collation was spread for the performers, a light being carried before him. After he had glanced all round the table he departed, and forthwith the parties concerned pounced upon the prey like so many harpies. The table was covered almost entirely with seasoned pasties and very few sugar confections. There were some large figures, but they were of painted pasteboard for ornament. The repast was served upon glass plates or dishes and at first assault they upset the table and the crash of glass platters reminded me precisely of a severe hailstorm at Midsummer smashing the window glass. The story ended at half past two in the morning and half disgusted and weary we returned home.

19.   "THE OMNIPOTENT DESIGN"

DURING his long career as a court poet, Ben Jonson, imparting his poetic vision — the "soul" — to the masque, must have had many disputes with Inigo Jones, who was responsible for the "bodily parts" of the court theatricals. The poet's scholarship may often have been irritated by the designer's thinking in terms of lines, colors, and fabrics. In 1631, the two quarrelled again and — parted. Ben Jonson revenged himself on the "omnipotent design" by writing his *Expostulation with Inigo Jones*:

> Master Surveyor, you that first began
> From thirty pounds in pipkins, to the man
> You are: from them leaped forth an architect,
> Able to talk of Euclid, and correct
> Both him and Archimede; damn Archytas,
> The noblest inginer that ever was:
> Control Ctesibius, overbearing us
> With mistook names out of Vitruvius;
> Drawn Aristotle on us, and thence shewn
> How much Architectonice is your own:
> Whether the building of the stage or scene,
> Or making of the properties it mean,
> Vizors or antics; or it comprehend

Something your sur-ship doth not yet intend . . .
What is the cause you pomp it so, I ask?
And all men echo, you have made a masque.
I chime that too, and I have met with those
That do cry up the machine and the shows;
The majesty of Juno in the clouds,
And peering forth of Iris in the shrouds;
The ascent of Lady Fame, which none could spy,
Not they that sided her, Dame Poetry,
Dame History, Dame Architecture too,
And Goody Sculpture, brought with much ado
To hold her up: O shows, shows, mighty shows!
The eloquence of masques! what need of prose,
Or verse, or sense, t'express immortal you?
You are the spectacles of state, 'tis true,
Court-hieroglyphics and all arts afford,
In the mere perspective of an inch-board;
You ask no more than certain politic eyes,
Eyes that can pierce into the mysteries
Of many colours, read them and reveal
Mythology, there painted on slit deal.
Or to make boards to speak! there is a task!
Painting and carpentry are the soul of masque.
Pack with your pedling poetry to the stage,
This is the money-got, mechanic age.
To plant the music where no ear can reach,
Attire the persons as no thought can teach
Sense what they are; which by a specious, fine
Term of [you] architects, is called Design;
But in the practised truth, destruction is
Of any art beside what he calls his.
Whither, O whither will this tireman grow?
His name is *Skenopoios*, we all know,
The maker of the properties; in sum,
The scene, the engine; but he now is come
To be the music-master; tabler too;
He is, or would be, the main *Dominus Do-*
All of the work, and so shall still for Ben . . .
O wise surveyor, wiser architect,
But wisest Inigo; who can reflect

On the new priming of thy old sign-posts,
Reviving with fresh colours the pale ghosts
Of thy dead standards; or with marvel see
Thy twice conceived, thrice paid for imagery;
And not fall down before it, and confess
Almighty Architecture, who no less
A goddess is than painted cloth, deal board,
Vermillion, lake, or crimson can afford
Expression for; with that unbounded line
Aimed at in thy omnipotent design!

An Improvised Stage for the Performance of Drolls.
Frontispiece to Francis Kirkman's *The Wits,* 1672.

20. THE ACTORS GO UNDERGROUND

ON SEPTEMBER 2, 1642, a few days after the military operations of the Great Rebellion had begun, Parliament, where the Puritans had gained the upper hand, acted to close all playhouses by issuing the *First Ordinance against Stage Plays and Interludes.* During the Civil War period, there was a good deal of surreptitious play-acting. The staging of full-length plays, however, had become too risky a venture for the harrassed actors. Short farces, called drolls, and variety acts seemed to be the fare most suitable under the circumstances. Francis Kirkman, introducing his collection of drolls, *The Wits* (1672), had this to say concerning the origin of the genre:

When the publique Theatres were shut up . . . then all that we could divert ourselves with were these humours and pieces of Plays, which passing under the Name of a merry conceited Fellow, called *Bottom the Weaver, Simpleton the Smith, John Swabber,* or some such title, were only allowed us, and that but by stealth too, and under pretence of Rope-dancing, or the like; and these being all that was permitted us, great was the confluence of the Auditors; and these small things were as profitable, and as great getpennies to the Actors as any of our late famed Plays. I have seen the Red Bull Play-House, which was a large one, so full, that as many went back for want of room as had entred; and as meanly as you may think of these Drols, they were then Acted by the best Comedians then and now in being; and I may say, by some that then exceeded all now living, by Name, the incomparable *Robert Cox,* who was not only the principal Actor, but also the Contriver and Author of most of these Farces.

21. RAZING THE "CHAPELS OF SATAN"

MANUSCRIPT additions to a copy of Stowe's *Annales* furnish us with obituary information concerning the final fate of the pre-revolutionary playhouses:

Play Houses. The Globe play house on the Banks side in Southwarke, was burnt downe to the ground, in the yeare 1612. And now built vp againe in the yeare 1613, at the great charge of King Iames, and many Noble men and others. And now pulled downe to the ground, by Sir Matthew Brand, On Munday the 15 of April 1644, to make tenements in the room of it

The Blacke Friers players playhouse in Blacke Friers, London, which had stood many yeares, was pulled downe to the ground on Munday the 6 day of August 1655, and tennements built in the rome.

The play house in Salsbury Court, in Fleetstreete, was pulled downe by a company of souldiers, set on by sectuaries of these sad times, on Saturday the 24 day of March 1649.

The Phenix in Druery Lane, was pulled downe also this day, being Saterday the 24 day of March 1649, by the same souldiers.

The Fortune Playhouse betweene White Crosse streete and Golding Lane was burnd downe to the ground in the yeare 1618. And built againe with brick worke on the outside in the yeare 1622. And now pulled downe on the inside by the souldiers this 1649.

The Hope, on the Banks side in Southwarke, commonly called the Beare Garden, a Play House for Stage Playes on Mundayes, Wedensdayes, Fridayes, and Saterdayes, and for the baiting of the Beares on Tuesdayes and Thursdayes, the stage being made to take vp and downe when they please. It was built in the year 1610, and now pulled downe to make tennementes, by Thomas Walker, a peticoate maker in Cannon Streete, on Tuesday the 25 day of March 1656. Seuen of Mr. Godfries beares, by the command of Thomas Pride, then hie Sheriefe of Surry, were then shot to death, on Saterday the 9 day of February 1655, by a company of souldiers.

22. NOSTALGIA FOR THE PRE-RESTORATION STAGE

LOOKING BACK in 1699, the *Historia Histrionica* is filled with admiration for the pre-Restoration stage. Truman is the spokesman for the traditional dramatic and theatrical values of England, while Lovewit gives him the cues:

Lovew. Honest Old Cavalier! well met, 'faith I'm glad to see thee.

Trum. Have a care what you call me. Old, is a Word of Disgrace among the Ladies; to be Honest is to be Poor and Fool-ish, (as some think) and Cavalier is a Word as much out of Fashion as any of 'em.

Lovew. The more's the pity: But what said the Fortune-Teller in *Ben. Johnson's* Mask of *Gypsies,* to the then *Lord Privy Seal.*

Honest and Old!
In those the Good *Part of a Fortune is told.*

Trum. Ben. *Johnson?* How dare you name *Ben. Johnson* in these times? When we have such a crowd of Poets of a quite different Genius; the least of which thinks himself as well able to correct *Ben. Johnson,* as he could a Country School Mistress that taught to Spell.

Lovew. We have indeed, Poets of a different Genius; so are the Plays: But in my Opinion, they are all of 'em (some few excepted) as much inferior to those of former Times, as the Actors now in being (generally speaking) are, compared to *Hart, Mohun, Burt, Lacy, Clun,* and *Shatterel*; for I can reach no farther backward.

Trum. I can; and dare assure you, if my Fancy and Mem-ory are not partial (for Men of my Age are apt to be over in-dulgent to the thoughts of their youthful Days) I say the Actors that I have seen before the Wars, *Lowin, Tayler, Pollard,* and some others, were almost as far beyond *Hart* and his Company, as those were beyond these now in being.

Lovew. I am willing to believe it, but cannot readily; be-cause I have been told, That those whom I mention'd, were Bred up under the others of your Acquaintance, and follow'd their manner of Action, which is now lost. So far, that when the Question has been askt, Why these Players do not revive the *Silent Woman,* and some other of *Johnson's* Plays, (once of high-est esteem) they have answer'd, truly, Because there are none now Living who can rightly Humour those Parts, for all who related to the *Black-friers* (where they were Acted in perfection) are now Dead, and almost forgotten.

Trum. 'Tis very true, *Hart* and *Clun,* were bred up Boys at the *Blackfriers*; and Acted Women's Parts, *Hart* was *Robinson's* Boy or Apprentice: He Acted the Dutchess in the Tragedy of *the Cardinal,* which was the first Part that gave him Reputation. *Cartwright,* and *Wintershal* belong'd to the private House in *Salisbury-Court, Burt* was a Boy first under *Shank* at the *Blackfriers,* then under *Beeston* at the *Cockpit*; and *Mohun,* and *Shatterel* were in the same Condition with him, at the last Place. There *Burt* used to Play the principal Women's Parts, in particular *Clariana* in, *Love's Cruelty*; and at the same time *Mohun* Acted *Bellamente,* which Part he retain'd after the Restauration.

Lovew. That I have seen, and can well remember. I wish they had Printed in the last Age (so I call the times before the Rebellion) the Actors Names over against the Parts they Acted. as they have done since the Restauration. And thus one might have guest at the Action of the Men, by the Parts which we now Read in the Old Plays.

Trum. It was not the Custome and Usage of those Days, as it hath been since. Yet some few Old Plays there are that have the Names set against the Parts, as, *The Dutchess of Malfy*; *the Picture*; *the Roman Actor*; *the deserving Favourite*; *the Wild Goose Chace,* (at the Black-friers) *the Wedding*; *the Renegado*; *the fair Maid of the West*; *Hannibal and Scipio*; *King John and Matilda*; (at the Cockpit) and *Holland's Leaguer,* (at Salisbury Court.)

Lovew. These are but few indeed: But pray Sir, what Master Parts can you remember the Old *Black-friers* Men to Act, in *Johnson, Shakespear,* and *Fletcher's* Plays.

Trum. What I can at present recollect I'll tell you; *Shakespear,* (who as I have heard, was a much better Poet, than Player) *Burbadge, Hemmings,* and others of the Older sort, were Dead before I knew the Town; but in my time, before the Wars, *Lowin* used to Act, with mighty Applause, *Falstaffe, Morose, Vulpone,* and *Mammon* in the *Alchymist*; *Melancius* in the *Maid's* Tragedy, and at the same time *Amyntor* was Play'd by *Stephen Hammerton,* (who was at first a most noted and beautiful Woman Actor, but afterwards he acted with equal Grace and Applause, a Young Lover's Part) *Tayler* acted *Hamlet* incomparably well, *Jago, Truewit* in the *Silent Woman,* and *Face* in the *Alchymist*; *Swanston* used to play *Othello*: *Pollard,* and *Robinson* were

Comedians, so was *Shank* who used to Act Sir *Roger,* in the
Scornful Lady. These were of the *Blackfriers.* Those of principal
Note at the *Cockpit,* were, *Perkins, Michael Bowyer, Sumner,
William Allen,* and *Bird,* eminent Actors. and *Robins* a Comedian.
Of the other Companies I took little notice.

    Lovew.   Were there so many Companies?

    Trum.   Before the Wars, there were in being all these Play-
houses at the same time. The *Black-friers,* and *Globe* on the
Bankside, a Winter and Summer House, belonging to the same
Company called the King's Servants; the *Cockpit* or *Phaenix,*
in *Drury-lane,* called the Queen's Servants; the private House
in *Salisbury-court,* called the Prince's Servants; the *Fortune* near
White-cross-street, and the *Red Bull* at the upper end of St.
John's-street: The two last were mostly frequented by Citizens,
and the meaner sort of People. All these Companies got Money,
and Liv'd in Reputation, especially those of the *Blackfriers,* who
were Men of grave and sober Behaviour.

    Lovew.   Which I admire at; That the Town much less than
at present, could then maintain Five Companies, and yet now
Two can hardly Subsist.

    Trum.   Do not wonder, but consider, That tho' the Town
was then, perhaps, not much more than half so Populous as now,
yet then the Prices were small (there being no scenes) and better
order kept among the Company that came; which made very
good People think a Play an Innocent Diversion for an idle Hour
or two, the Plays themselves being then, for the most part, more
Instructive and Moral. Whereas of late, the Play-houses are so
extreamly pestered with Vizard-masks and their Trade, (occa-
sioning continual Quarrels and Abuses) that many of the more
Civilized Part of the Town are uneasy in the Company, and
shun the Theater as they would a House of Scandal. It is an
Argument of the worth of the Plays and Actors, of the last Age,
and easily, inferr'd, that they were much beyond ours in this, to
consider that they cou'd support themselves meerly from their
own Merit; the weight of the Matter, and goodness of the Action,
without Scenes and Machines: Whereas the present Plays with all
that shew can hardly draw an Audience, unless there be the
additional Invitation of a *Signior Fideli,* a *Monsier L'abbe,* or
some such Foreign Regale exprest in the bottom of the Bill.

    Lovew.   To wave this Digression, I have Read of one *Ed-*

ward Allin, a Man so famed for excellent Action, that among *Ben. Johnson's* Epigrams, I find one directed to him, full of Encomium, and concluding thus:

> *Wear this Renown, 'tis just that who did give*
> *So many Poets Life, by one should Live.*

Was he one of the *Black-friers?*

Trum.   Never, as I have heard; (for he was Dead before my time.) He was Master of a Company of his own, for whom he Built the *Fortune* Play-house from the Ground, a large, round Brick Building. This is he that grew so Rich that he purchased a great Estate in *Surrey* and elsewhere; and having no Issue, he Built and largely endow'd *Dulwich* College, in the Year 1619, for a Master, a Warden, Four Fellows, Twelve aged poor People, and Twelve poor Boys, &c. A noble Charity.

Lovew.   What kind of Playhouses had they before the Wars?

Trum.   The *Black-friers, Cockpit,* and *Salisbury-court,* were called Private Houses, and were very small to what we see now. The *Cockpit* was standing since the Restauration, and *Rhode's* Company Acted there for some time.

Lovew.   I have seen that.

Trum.   Then you have seen the other two, in effect; for they were all three Built almost exactly alike, for Form and Bigness. Here they had Pits for the Gentry, and Acted by Candlelight. The *Globe, Fortune* and *Bull,* were large Houses, and lay partly open to the Weather, and there they alwaies Acted by Daylight.

Lovew.   But prithee, *Truman,* what became of these Players when the Stage was put down, and the Rebellion raised?

Trum.   Most of 'em except *Lowin, Tayler* and *Pollard,* (who were superannuated) went into the King's Army, and like good Men and true, Serv'd their Old Master, tho' in a different, yet more honourable, Capacity. *Robinson* was Kill'd at the Taking of a Place (I think *Basing House*) by *Harrison,* he that was after Hang'd at *Charing-cross,* who refused him Quarter, and Shot him in the Head when he had laid down his Arms; abusing Scripture at the same time, in saying, *Cursed is he that doth the Work of the Lord negligently. Mohun* was a Captain, (and after the Wars were ended here, served in *Flanders,* where he received

Pay as a Major) *Hart* was a Lieutenant of Horse under Sir *Thomas Dallison,* in *Prince Rupert's,* Regiment, *Burt* was Cornet in the same Troop, and *Shatterel* Quartermaster. *Allen* of the *Cockpit,* was a Major, and Quarter Master General at *Oxford.* I have not heard of one of these Players of any Note that sided with the other Party, but only *Swanston,* and he profest himself a Presbyterian, took up the Trade of a Jeweller, and liv'd in *Aldermanbury,* within the Territory of Father *Calamy.* The rest either Lost, or expos'd their Lives for their King. When the Wars were over, and the Royalists totally Subdued; most of 'em who were left alive gather'd to *London,* and for a Subsistence endeavour'd to revive their Old Trade, privately. They made up one Company out of all the Scatter'd Members of Several; and in the Winter before the King's Murder, 1648, They ventured to Act some Plays with as much caution and privacy as cou'd be, at the *Cockpit.* They continu'd undisturbed for three or four Days; but at last as they were presenting the Tragedy of the *Bloudy Brother,* (in which *Lowin* Acted Aubrey, *Tayler* Rollo, *Pollard* the Cook, *Burt* Latorch, and I think *Hart* Otto) a Party of Foot Souldiers beset the House, surprized 'em about the midle of the Play, and carried 'em away in their habits, not admitting them to Shift, to *Hatton-house* then a Prison, where having detain'd them sometime, they Plunder'd them of their Cloths and let 'em loose again. Afterwards in *Oliver's* time, they used to Act privately, three or four Miles, or more, out of Town, now here, now there, sometimes in Noblemens Houses, in particular *Holland-house* at *Kensington,* where the Nobility and Gentry who met (but in no great Numbers) used to make a Sum for them, each giving a broad Peice, or the like. And *Alexander Goffe,* the Woman Actor at *Blackfriers,* (who had made himself known to Persons of Quality) used to be the Jackal and give notice of Time and Place. At Christmass, and Bartlemew-fair, they used to Bribe the Officer who Commanded the Guard at *Whitehall,* and were thereupon connived at to Act for a few Days, at the *Red Bull*; but were sometimes notwithstanding Disturb'd by Soldiers. Some pickt up a little Money by publishing the Copies of Plays never before Printed, but kept up in Manuscript. For instance, in the Year 1652, *Beaumont* and *Fletcher's Wild Goose Chace* was Printed in Folio, *for the Publick use of all the Ingenious,* (as the Title-page says) *and private Benefit of* John Lowin *and*

Joseph Tayler, *Servants to his late Majesty*; and by them Dedicated *To the Honour'd few Lovers of Dramatick Poesy*: Wherein they modestly intimate their Wants. And that with sufficient Cause; for whatever they were before the Wars, they were, after, reduced to a necessitous Condition. *Lowin* in his latter Days, kept an Inn (the three Pidgions) at *Brentford,* where he Dyed very Old, (for he was an Actor of eminent Note in the Reign of K. *James* the first) and his Poverty was as great as his Age. *Tayler* Dyed at *Richmond* and was there Buried. *Pollard* who Lived Single, and had a Competent Estate; Retired to some Relations he had in the Country, and there ended his Life. *Perkins* and *Sumner* of the *Cockpit,* kept House together at Clerkenwel, and were there Buried. These all Dyed some Years before the Restauration. What follow'd after, I need not tell you: You can easily Remember.

Chapter VI

The Age of Louis XIV

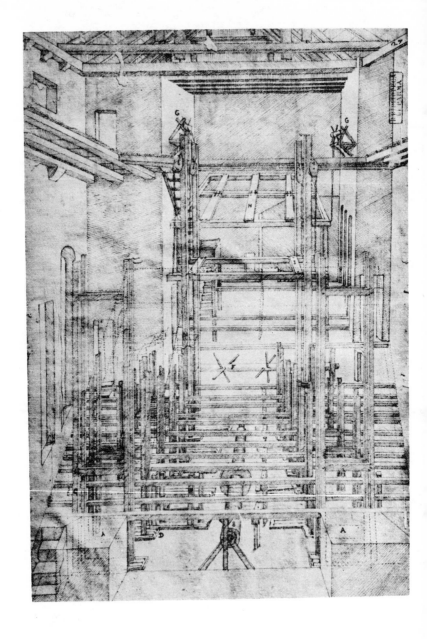

Elaborate Stage Machinery for Operatic Spectacles.
Giacomo Torelli may have been the inventor of the machinery.

1. TORELLI IN PARIS

GIACOMO TORELLI (1608 - 1678), a native of Fano, received his artistic training in the atmosphere of the Medici court in Florence. The novelty of his inventions in the field of stage mechanics caused a stir in Venice (1639), where he created scenery and machines for the public opera houses of SS. Giovanni e Paolo and the Teatro Novissimo. The operatic splendor, which till then had been reserved for Renaissance princes, was made available to the average Venetian in such magnificent productions as *La finta pazza* (1641), *Il Bellerofonte* (1642), *Venere gelosa* (1643), and *Ercole in Lidia* (1644). John Evelyn witnessed a performance of *Ercole* in 1645 and praised the "variety of scenes painted and contrived with no less art of perspective and machines for flying in the air, and other wonderful motions; taken together it is one of the most magnificent and expensive diversions the wit of man can invent . . . the scenes changed thirteen times." Upon the recommendation of the Duke of Parma, Torelli went to Paris, where the designer conquered the court with a repeat production of *La finta pazza* in the great hall of the Petit Bourbon (December 14, 1645). *Orfeo* followed on March 2, 1647 at the Palais Royal. The magic speed of scene shifting in full view of the audience (*a vista*) excited general admiration, and the Parisians began to understand why the Venetians had referred to Torelli as the "Great Sorcerer." Behind this sorcery was an ingenious mechanical system, which Torelli had evolved in Venice: the release of a counterweight would cause the turning of a revolving drum below the stage, and the ropes running over this drum would in turn move the scenic wings and borders. On February 26, 1650, the first performance of Corneille's *Andromède* took place at the Petit Bourbon. The poet had written his operatic libretto with Torelli's perspective scenes and machines in mind. Each act had a new setting, even the Prologue had its special scenery, and there was at least one flying machine in each act. Corneille prided himself on having written a play in which machines were essential elements of the plot rather than mere embellishments. Torelli's settings for *Andromède* have survived in the engravings of F. Chauveau, and the following anonymous account of an eyewitness describes the settings with their scenes in mutation:

Setting of the Prologue

The scene presents to the spectator a vast mountain whose uneven peaks rise one above another, the summit soaring into the clouds. The base of this mountain is cleft open at one point by a deep cave through which the ocean can be seen distantly. The sides of the stage are thick-set with trees, their branches closely interlaced. Melpomene, the tragic Muse, appears on one

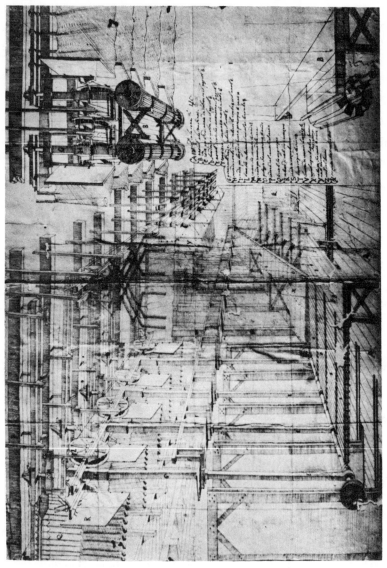

Stage Left of an Unknown Italian Opera House

cf the mountain peaks; and opposite her the Sun rises into the sky, his chariot of flashing fire drawn by the four steeds we read of in Ovid.

Setting of Act I

By a marvelous device, the craggy outlines of the massive mountain range vanish in a twinkling, and in their place appears the capital city of Cepheus' realm, or rather, the public square of this city. Magnificent palaces, each varying in design from the others, surround the square on three sides in such a way that balance and the sense of perspective are admirably maintained. When the eye has had time to feast on their beauty, Queen Cassiopea appears and passes through the public square on her way to the temple. Leading her is Perseus, still incognito, but passing as a gentleman of great worth. She talks with him of the disasters that have beset the kingdom. Then the King rejoins her, and they go together to the Temple.

Setting of Act II

When the Queen and Perseus leave, the public square disappears in an instant, making way for a delectable garden. The great palaces turn into so many white marble vases which alternately spurt jets of water and sprout myrtle and jasmin and similar flowers. From either side, a row of orange trees in other vases breaks away to form a delightful arbor in the center, dividing the stage into three lanes, so that the ingenious use of perspective makes them seem more than a thousand paces long. In this bower Andromeda is seen gathering flowers with her nymphs. They weave the flowers into a garland for her, because she wishes to crown Phineas with it, as a pretty token of her gratitude for the good news he has just brought.

Setting of Act III

When Perseus, before leaving the garden, discovers the monstrous head of Medusa which he will carry everywhere under his shield, there occurs a strange transformation. The myrtle and jasmin change into masses of frightful rocks, and their craggy and uneven shapes seem so exactly a result of Nature's whim, that she would seem to have contributed more than art has, in

Act II

Torelli's Settings for Corneille's *Andromède*. Engravings by Chauveau. Produced at the French Court Theater of Petit-Bourbon.

Act III

ranging them at the sides of the stage. Here the artifice of the design is marvelously effective in hiding the marks of its own handiwork. Sea billows engulf the scene, except for a strip five or six feet wide that serves as a shore. In the gulf formed by the towering cliffs, the waves break continually, and race out its mouth into the first sea. This sea appears so vast that one would swear the vessels, floating near the horizon which bounds the view, are more than six leagues away. No one who sees it can fail to regard this horrible spectacle as the deadly display of the gods' injustice, and of Andromeda's agony. And then she appears in the clouds, whence she is borne off violently by two zephyrs that chain her to the foot of one of the rocks.

Scenery of Act IV

The waves sink beneath the stage, and the hideous masses of rock they buffeted give way to a representation of a magnificent royal palace. The palace is not shown in its entirety; only the vestibule, or rather, the great hall, is visible. Here the nuptials of Perseus and Andromeda are to be held. On either side are two rows of columns, one row being composed of round pillars and the other of square ones. Their bases, cornices and pediments are adorned with white marble statues, splendid in their simplicity. The rear wall has a similar colonnade, and three doors through which the eye travels down three lanes of cypresses that lose themselves in the distance. Perseus enters the hall first, leading Andromeda to his chambers after having received her from the hands of the King and Queen; and, as if their good will did not suffice, he strives still to win her of her own free will, by the homage he pays her and the extraordinary courtesies he bestows on her.

Setting of Act V

The royal palace vanishes, to be succeeded by yet another setting. But the architect has not exhausted the marvels he is capable of executing. The temple which now appears is so much more beautiful than the great hall that it puts to scorn one's previous admiration.

Besides, it is only fitting that the home of the gods should surpass the dwellings of men; and Mr. Torelli's art is here so remarkable that he achieves great diversity between these two settings, although at first they might seem to be alike. Again we are shown two rows of columns flanking the stage, but they prove to be so different from the preceding ones as to bear no resemblance to them whatsoever. These are of porphyry, as are all the supporting pieces. The latter are finished in chiselled bronze, and the carvings represent a quantity of gods and goddesses. The reflection of the lamps on this bronze causes it to give off an extraordinary light. A huge, superbly proportioned dome, likewise enriched with bronze embossings, covers the center of this magnificent temple. And in front of this dome the artisan's skill has erected a gallery glittering with blue and gold. The lower part of this gallery is so constructed that one can see into the temple through three doors of figured silver openwork. Cepheus could be seen there, making sacrifices to Jupiter for the marriage of his daughter, were it not that the spectators, by giving their attention to the sacrifice, would miss what is happening in the outer sanctuary on the forepart of the stage.

2.   ADVICE TO POETS AND MACHINISTS

In 1640, François Hédélin, Abbé d'Aubignac, began his *La Pratique du Théâtre*, which was published in 1657. D'Aubignac's contribution to the dramatic standards of the classical school of French playwriting do not concern us here. On a few pages, however, d'Aubignac dealt with the subject of scenery, and in this connection voiced his opposition to the remnants of medieval simultaneous staging as well as to the machine-play vogue, which had made its way from the Petit Bourbon into the public Marais Theater since Torelli had stimulated the Parisians' interest in this type of spectacle:

'Tis certain that the Ornaments of the Stage with the Scenes, Machines, and Decorations, make the most sensible delight of that ingenious Magick which seems to make Heroes live again in the world after so many Ages; it sets before us a new Heaven, and a new Earth, and many other wonderful appearances of things which we imagine present, though we know at the same time that they are not so, and that we are agreeably deceiv'd: These Ornaments make the Poems themselves more illustrious; the people takes them for Enchantments, and the men of understanding are pleas'd to see the dexterity of the Artists (who deservedly attract admiration) with the concurrence of so many Arts and Professions employed in the Execution of these contrivances, to which all run with joy and delight. It was for this that the People of Greece and Rome . . . did bestow the richest Decorations upon their Theatres. . . .

But for our times, though the Court does not dislike these Ornaments, and that the People crowd to see them, yet I would not advise our Poet to busy himself much in these machine Plays; our Players are neither Rich, nor Generous enough to make the Expence of them, and their Decorators want ability in the performance; I must add that our Authors themselv's have been so negligent in acquiring the knowledge of the Ancients ways in this matter, and in their means of Execution, that we need not wonder if we see so many ill Invented Embellishments of this kind. Yet one would think that our Age, as soon as any might recover the pristine glory of the Theatre, considering the Liberality of our Princes, the Application of our Poets, the Ingenuity of our Workmen, and the Care of our Comedians, and that which we have seen already perform'd in this Kingdom, is, it may be, but a pattern of what we may expect in the plenty of Peace. Therefore that we may not be wanting to any thing that may contribute to the accomplishment of so great a work, I shall here communicate some Observations upon publick Spectacles and Machines, which I hope will be of some use. I consider all publick Spectacles and Decorations of the Scene three ways.

Some are of things; when the Spectacles are permanent and immovable; as a Heaven open, a stormy Sea, a Pallace, or the like Ornaments.

Others are of Actions; when the Spectacle depends principally upon some extraordinary Fact; as that one should throw himself headlong from a Tower, or from a Rock in the Sea.

The Third sort is of those that are mingled with Things and Actions, as a Sea-fight, where at the same time is the Sea and Ships, and Men acting upon it.

These may be all further distinguished into natural, artificial, and marvellous.

The Natural ones are those which represent the most agreeable things in Nature, as a Desert, a Mountain on fire, &c.

The Artificial are those which shew us the most magnificent works of Art, as a Temple, a Pallace.

The Marvellous are those which suppose some Divine Power or Magick Production, as the descent of some God from Heaven, or the rising of some Fury from Hell.

And of all these, the least considerable are the last, because there goes little contrivance to the inventing of them, there being hardly any wit so mean, who by this may not bring in, or carry off a great Intrigue. I saw once a Play, in which the Author having brought on a Rival, and concern'd him so deeply in his Subject, that he did not well know how to bring him off, bethought himself to kill him with a Thunderbolt; the contrivance was pretty sure; but if this sort of Invention be admitted in Dramma's, we need not much trouble our selves to wind up the Plot any other way; therefore all these Machines of Gods and Devils are to be us'd with great discretion, and great care to be taken that in the Execution they play easily, for else the people are apt to laugh, and make Railleries of a God hanging in the Air, or coming down too fast.

I should not likewise advise our Poet to use frequently those, where Actions are to make the greatest Effect, because that all the success depends upon the Exactness of the Comedians, who are often so negligent in the performance, that they will neither study the manner, nor time necessary; or else they are so possessed with an Opinion of their Abilities, that they think it beneath them to be inform'd; so that either their Idleness, or their Vanity, most commonly spoils that which was well invented, and ought to have made the beauty of the Play. That which remains then is the permanent Decorations, of what nature soever they are; and to these I would confine the Poet, but still with many Precautions: For,

First, They are to be necessary, insomuch as the Play cannot be acted without these Ornaments; or else they will not take, though never so ingenious. And in this, I think, our *Andromeda* has not all its Regularity; for in the First and Fourth Act there are two noble Buildings, of different Architecture, and no mention made of them in the Play; since these two Acts might be represented with any of the Decorations of the other three, without offending the Poet, or spoiling any Incident of his Dramma.

Secondly, These Ornaments must be agreeable to the Sight; for 'tis for that, that the People flock to them. Not that I would absolutely forbid the Poet to put in things monstrous or horrible;

Jupiter
in a
Cloud Machine

Frontispiece by
Brissard to *Amphitryon*
in the first complete
edition of
Molière's *Oeuvres,*
1682.

Yale Theatrical Prints Collection

but at least then the Painting must be exquisite, that the Art
may be admir'd.

They must likewise be modest, and not against that Pudour
which the most dissolute love the appearances of. I believe that
the shewing of Mars and Venus supris'd in a Net by Vulcan,
would not be allowed for a fine Decoration.

They must, besides, be easie to put in execution; that is,
that the Machinists do dispose their Machins to play so well,
that there may be no need of great numbers of Hands, but they
do of themselves perform to a Minute; for the People cannot
endure to expect long the Effect of a Machin, and when they do

not hit the Minute, they do not agree with the Motion and Pretence of the Actor upon the stage, and so spoil his Part.

It will likewise be reasonable to consider, whether the Place represented by the Scene, will bear in truth that which is to be shewed in Image; for else it would be a gross Fault against Probability: For example, If the place of the Scene were a Palace, and that close to it were a Prison, or some noisom place; for Princes and Great People do not live near such places.

There must not likewise be any Decorations made which are not agreeable to the Unity of Place; as to suppose the Scene the Palace or Chamber of a Prince, out of which there should be an immediate Passage to a great Forest: For all these Fictions, though pleasing to the Eye, yet are otherwise, to our Reason, which knows them to be false, impossible, and ridiculous.

But particularly, the Poet must so order it, as that out of this Shew and Decorations some notable Event may result in the Body of the Play; that is, something that may contribute either to the perplexing of the Plot, or the easier unweaving of it; for if all this Shew is onely for shew, and not of the Essence of the Piece, the Men of Understanding will value the Decorator for executing, but not the Poet for inventing so useless an Ornament. In the *Rudens* of Plautus, the Shipwrack that is there represented, makes both the Knot and the Unweaving of the Intrigue. The *Frogs* of Aristophanes have a vast Decoration, which serves to all the Acts, and almost to all the Scenes. And we shall find few among the Ancients, but what agree with our Rules.

I cannot omit here to advertise the Poet of two important Considerations: The first that regards himself, which is, That when the Spectacles are of Things, that is, of Permanent Objects, they must, if possible, appear at the first opening of the Stage, to the end that the Surprise and Applause of the People, which generally attends such Sights, may be over, before the Actors begin to speak: or, that if there be any necessity of changing the Decorations, let it be done in the Interval of an Act, that the Workmen may have the time necessary for their Machins moving, and the Actor that is to appear, that of dressing himself at leisure. But if, by the necessity of his Subject, some great Change is to be in the middle of an Act, let him contrive his Actors Part so, as he have but little to say at that time, and those too Words of Admiration, Grief, or Astonishment, to give some time to the

Murmur of the Spectators, which is always rais'd upon some such new Appearance.

The other Consideration regards the Comedians: which is, when the Spectacles consist of Actions: that is, when the Actors are to be in some posture extraordinary: The Actor, I say, must study this Posture with care, before he comes to act it upon the Stage; or else 'tis odds but he performs it very ill and not without danger sometimes to himself: all which does not a little trouble the Beauty of the whole Piece.

3. PRESCRIPTIONS FOR THE AILING FRENCH STAGE

AT THE CONCLUSION of his *Pratique*, d'Aubignac pointed out some of the flaws in the contemporary French theater and proposed a six-point remedial program:

A Project for Re-establishing the French Theater.

The Causes which hinder the French Theater, from continuing the Progress it had made some years ago in Cardinal Richelieu's time may be reduced to six.

1. The common belief that to frequent Plays is a sin against the Rules of Christianity.
2. The Infamy with which the Laws have noted those who make an open profession of being Players.
3. The failings and errours committed in the representation of Plays.
4. The Ill Plays which are indifferently acted with the good.
5. Ill Decorations.
6. Disorders committed by the Spectators. . . .

The fifth Cause about the Decorations is likewise important among the Antients, the Magistrates, and other great Men, who us'd to give publick Spectacles to the people, either by the obligation of their place, or to gain publick favour, us'd to be at the charge of the Decorations, the Players contributing nothing towards it, and by that means those Ornaments were not only magnificent, but perfectly answer'd the Poets Intentions. But now, that our Players, though not very well in their Affairs, nevertheless must undergo all the charge; they cannot be blam'd if they endeavour to do it as cheap as may be; but then the Decorations must be imperfect, and altogether below the dignity of the Poets Invention.

As for the Disorders of the Spectators, we may consider, that nothing was more safe and quiet, than the Antient Theatres, the Magistrates being always present, and every thing done by their orders; but amongst us there is no order at all, but any sorts of people wear Swords in the Pit, and other places, and therewith attack very often many peaceable Spectators, who have no other defence than the Authority of the Laws. Among the Greeks and Romans, the Women were so safe in the publick Theatres, that they often brought their Children with them; but with us a company of young Debauchees come in, and commit a hundred Insolencies, frighting the Women, and often killing those who take their protection.

We may add to that, that the Seats of the Spectators were so conveniently plac'd among the Antients, that every one was plac'd conveniently, and there could be no disorder in changing of place; whereas now the Pit and Boxes are equally inconvenient; the Pit having no rising, nor no Seat, and the Boxes being too far off, and ill situated; so that what with the disorders of the Pit, and inconvenience of the Boxes, the Theatres are much forsaken by the better sort of people.

To remedy all these Disorders, it will be necessary first, that the King be pleas'd to set forth a Declaration, which shall shew on one hand how that Plays being no longer an Act of Religion and Idolatry, as they were formerly, but only a publick diversion; and on the other hand, that the Representations being now perform'd with decency, and the Players themselves living sober, and not of debauch'd lives, (as they were when the Edicts were made, by which they are declared infamous) His Majesty doth upon these considerations make void all those former Laws, forbidding them still nevertheless to do or say any thing upon the Stage against decency or good manners, under such and such penalties, as of being driven from the Stage, and reputed infamous again. And to preserve that Modesty which is necessary, it shall be likewise ordered, that no single Woman shall act, if they have not their Father or Mother in the Company, and that all Widdows shall be oblig'd to marry within six months after their year is out for mourning; and in that year shall not act except they are married again.

And for the Execution of these orders his Majesty may be pleas'd to settle a person of probity and capacity to be as it were an Overseer, Intendant or great Master of the Theatres and other publick Entertainments in France who shall take care that the Stage be free from all Scandal, and shall likewise give an Account of the life and actions of the Players. By this means the two first causes which hinder the Re-establishment of the Stage must cease; for all scandal and obscenities being banished, there will be no scruple of Conscience in assisting at Plays; and the Players will besides be in so good a reputation, as not to fear any reproaches from the sober sort of people. It was by such a declaration as this that the Roman Emperours re-establish'd the Theatre when it was fallen into Corruption.

The third cause must likewise cease, for the profession of Actor being once made reputable, all those who have any Inclination that way will the easilyer take to it; and besides, the Overseer may himself select out of the Schools, and the Companys of Country Players such as shall be fitting, and oblige them to study the representation of spectacles as well as the Recitals and Expressions of the Poet, that so the whole action may be perfect; and to this end none shall be admitted but by the Kings Letters Patents delivered to the Actor by the Intendant General of the Theatres, who shall give a certificate of his capacity and probity, after having tryed him in many ways. By this means there will always be excellent Actors, and the Representations will no longer be defective.

The 4th cause which regards the Poets themselves does require some distinction for those of them who have already the approbation of the publick by the Excellency and number of their works, shall be obliged onely to shew their Plays to the Overseer General to see that there be no Obscenities nor anything against decency in them, all the rest to remain untouched, at the hazard of the reputation they have already acquired.

But as for the new Poets, their plays shall be thoroughly examin'd by the Overseer and reformed according to his orders, by which means the Stage will not be loaded with ill Dramma's, nor the players burdened with rewarding such as afterwards can be of no use to them.

As for the Decorations, they shall be perform'd by the care of the same Overseer, who shall employ understanding and able Workmen at the publick charge, and not at the Players costs, who shall have no Expence to bear but that of their clothes, and the reward they shall give the Authors.

As for the sixth Cause, which concerns the conveniency and safety of the Spectators, the King shall forbid all Pages and Footmen to enter the Play house upon pain of death, and prohibit likewise all other persons, of what quality soever, to wear their Swords there, nor any offensive Arms, upon the same penalty, it being reasonable that that safety which cannot be had here, out of respect of the place, as it is in Churches and Pallaces, be obtain'd by the equality of the Assistants; and for this reason some of the Kings Guards shall be plac'd at the doors of the Play house, to take notice of any that shall go about to contravene this Order.

And for the greater conveniency of the Spectators, the Pit shall be rais'd, and fill'd with Seats, that shall overlook the Stage, which will hinder the quarrelling of the Hectors, there being not room for them to fight.

But to perfect the magnificence of the Stage, the Overseer shall look out a spot of ground, spacious and convenient to build one according to the Model of the Antients, so that it be capable of the noblest Representations, and the Seats so distinguish'd, as that the common people need not mingle with those of the best fashion; and round about which shall be built houses to lodge two Troups or Companies of Players gratis, which I suppose may be enough for the City of Paris.

4.   READING AND CASTING A NEW PLAY

WHILE D'AUBIGNAC was frankly critical of the state of theatrical affairs, Samuel Chappuzeau, at the time of Molière's death (1673), exhibited in his *Théâtre français* a perhaps naïve descriptive enthusiasm concerning all phases of French theatrical life. As a dramatist, Chappuzeau had first-hand knowledge of the mechanics by which a play found its way to the stage:

An author who . . . has not yet gained a high reputation . . . communicates with one of the actors whose intelligence he trusts and whom he regards as most capable to judge his play, so that the player, according to his judgment, submit it to the company or reject it. For the actors insist, and rightly so, that they are able to foretell the success or failure of a play better than all the authors and critics together. Indeed, they have experience and make continual use of it. Moreover, the majority of them are likewise playwrights, and among the Royal Comedians alone are five whose plays have been well received. . . .

If the actor whom the author has given his play for examination finds that it cannot be produced and is only for the closet . . . it would be useless for the playwright to convoke the company and to read the play to them, presuming the actor to have good taste and to have the influence to bring his colleagues around to his opinion easily.

If the actor considers the play good and having a chance of success, the author comes to the theater on the day of a play and informs the players that he has a drama which he wishes to read to them. Sometimes rather than speak for himself, he has one of his friends make this announcement.

After this notification a day and hour are set. The players assemble at the theater or some other place, and the playwright, without introductory remarks (which the players do not like), reads his play with all the emphasis he is capable of giving. . . . It would be difficult to deceive the players in this since they understand this business better than the playwright. At the end of each act, while the reader catches his breath, the players talk about those parts that they find to be boring, or too long, or about some verses that have no zest, or a passion that is badly handled, or some crude verses, or even some joke that is too broad, if it is a comedy. After the entire play has been read, they are in an even better position to judge it. They discuss whether the plot is clever and well-developed, and the dénouement a good one (for that is the reef where most playwrights run aground), whether the scenes are well linked, the lines light or pompous, depending on the nature of the subject, and whether the characters are well sustained without exaggeration, as often happens. . . .

The women, from modesty, let the men judge the plays, and rarely come to the reading, though they have the right to come and certainly are very capable and even able to enlighten the playwright. Those actresses who play the leading roles should always be present in order to get the meaning of the lines from the author and to discuss with him the little difficulties that may arise. There are some of the more celebrated playwrights who deliver their own lines admirably and who give them a good inflection just as they have written them with a beautiful turn. But there are others whose delivery is pitiful and who injure their own works by reading them.

After the play has been read and accepted, it is necessary to make a proper distribution of the parts. Casting often causes minor differences, each player naturally having a good opinion of himself and believing that a leading role will establish him better in the esteem of the spectators. There are, however, some who like to see justice prevail and who content themselves with secondary parts, or who alternate with a colleague when it comes to the leading parts. It is the same way with the actresses, though they are a little harder to manage than the men. The fact remains that their talents differ: one excels in tender passions, another in violent ones; this one acquits herself admirably in a serious part, and that one will do only in a vivacious role. . . . Provincial troupes are more likely to suffer from these petty rivalries, and to prevent that in Paris, when the playwright knows the strength and talent of each player . . . the actors gladly give to him the casting of the roles, in which he often takes the advice of one of the company. But still he is often hampered, and he has to take great pains to satisfy every one. A play well cast succeeds better, and it is in the common interest of the playwright and the company, and even of the spectator, that each player act the part which fits him best.

5.   REHEARSALS

THE ROLES having been distributed, each player memorizes his part:

If there is a lack of time and it is necessary to make an effort, a full-length play can be memorized in eight days. There are some actors who can memorize even a lengthy part in three mornings. But when there is no pressure, the players do not hurry and assemble for the first rehearsal when they are thoroughly familiar with their parts. The first rehearsal serves the purpose of getting a rough idea of the whole, and it is not until the second and third rehearsal that one begins to estimate at all well what success the play is likely to have. They do not risk a performance unless it is well memorized and staged, and the last rehearsal must be just like a regular performance. The author ordinarily assists at these rehearsals and criticizes the actor if he falls into some error, if he does not grasp the meaning, if he becomes unnatural in tone or gesture, or if he uses more or less fire than the situation warrants. Actors of intelligence are permitted to give their suggestions in these rehearsals without their colleagues finding them objectionable, because it is all a question of the common interest.

6. THE FUNCTIONS OF THE ORATOR

THE MOST IMPORTANT function an actor could have in any one of the acting companies was that of *orateur*. Chappuzeau throws light upon the subject, though by 1673, when he finished his treatise, the importance of the orator had somewhat declined:

The orator has two principal functions. It falls to him to address the audience and to compose the poster, and as there is a close connection between the two, nearly the same rules apply to both. At the end of the play he addresses the audience in a speech which has for its aim the gaining of the good will of the spectators. He thanks them for their favorable attention; he announces the play to follow the one that has just been given; he invites the spectators by means of such praises as he showers on them to come to see it. . . . As a rule, his address is a short one and not premeditated. Sometimes, however, he plans his speech, when the King, the King's brother, or some prince of royal blood is present, or when he describes what happens in a machine-play. He also prepares his speech when he announces a new play that needs praising, or when he makes his farewell address in the name of the company on the Friday before Passion Week and at the re-opening of the theater after Easter, when the taste for playgoing has to be rekindled in the people. In his usual announcement the orator gives a preview of new plays to come in order to create anticipation. . . .

The poster follows the lines of the oral announcement. It advises the reader of the crowded house that witnessed the performance the other day, of the merit of the play that follows, and of the necessity for procuring boxes early since the play is new and the members of high society are eager to see it.

In former years, when the orator came to make his announcement, the entire audience fell into silence, and the speaker's address, brief and well-turned, was often listened to with as much pleasure as the preceding play. Each time, the orator invented new traits which roused the spectators and gave proof of his fertility of mind. In both the announcement and the poster the orator showed modesty in the customary praises of the author, the play, and the company that was going to produce it. When the praises are excessive, one feels that the speaker wishes to impose on us, and we are less persuaded by what he wants to impress upon our minds. But as fashions change, all these methods are no longer in use. There is no longer a lengthy discourse in either the speech or the poster. Today the orator simply tells the audience the name of the play to be presented.

Another function of the orator, it seems, is to call the company together on stage or elsewhere, either for the reading of plays or for rehearsals, in short, for all meetings that concern their common interest. It is for him to open the meeting and to propose the agenda.

7.   PROMPTER AND DECORATOR

No PERFORMANCE could be expected to run smoothly without the help of some minor figures such as the candle snuffers, musicians, ushers, lemonade women, the prompter-copyist, and the *décorateurs*. Their various duties are in turn sympathetically outlined by Chappuzeau. What he has to say about the functions of the prompter and the decorator is of considerable interest:

The copyist is the keeper of the library of original play scripts. He has to copy the parts and to distribute them to the players. He is charged with holding the promptbook at one of the wings during the performance. He must keep his eyes open so that he can go to the aid of the actor if the latter should suffer from lack of memory. This is what in the language of the theater is called prompting (*souffler*). This task calls for someone who is prudent and knows the legitimate pauses so as not to suggest a line to an actor when it would disturb him. I have seen in such

cases some actors remonstrate with the prompter and tell him
to keep quiet for they did not need his help or they wanted to
prove that they were masters of their memory. Moreover, it is
advisable to use a prompting voice that can be heard only on
the stage, if possible, and which will not carry down to the pit
so as not to be a subject for laughter for certain spectators who
laugh at everything, and react with a burst of laughter at certain
passages of the play where others would not find material even
for smiles. I have known some actors who never rely on any help
but who depend entirely on their memory and who prefer, at all
events, to jump a line or to make one up on the spot. There are
some actors with very good memories, who know the entire play
by heart simply from having heard it at the reading and stage
rehearsals. If someone on the stage with them happens to lose
his way, they put him back on the right path, and they do it
so skilfully and without anyone else's noticing it. Women, by
the way, have a more reliable memory than men.

The decorators must be people of imagination and must
have skill in embellishing the stage. Ordinarily there are two
decorators, who work in close cooperation when it comes to
important decisions and when they have to concern themselves
with a new production. But for the average performance, there
is only one of them in attendance, and they serve alternately.
Everything related to the decoration of the stage falls to their lot,
and it is necessary for them to check up on the machines used
in the plays, although the machinist has to put them in working
condition. It is the decorators' job to chase from the wings the
little folk who have crept in there and who, apart from obstruct-
ing the players' entrances and exits, give a bad appearance to the
stage and spoil the view of the spectators. . . . It is also the
decorators' task to provide two candle snuffers if they do not
wish to perform that job themselves. Whether it is they or others,
they must perform the task promptly so as not to keep the
audience waiting between the acts, and with skill so as not to
offend the spectator with a bad odor. One does the snuffing at
the front of the stage, the other in the rear, always keeping a
watchful eye that the flats do not catch fire. To prevent such an
accident, they must keep ready barrels filled with water and a
number of pails. . . . The candle remnants form a part of the
small income of the decorators.

8. TYPES OF OPERATIC SETTINGS

In 1681, Claude-François Ménestrier (1631 - 1705) published his treatise, *Des représentations en musique anciennes et modernes*. Father Ménestrier, an expert on heraldry, a student of the dance, and a connoisseur of opera, was familiar with the stage settings designed by Carlo Vigarani for many of Lully's operas, that were produced at the Académie Royale de Musique. In his treatise, Ménestrier pointed out that the operatic settings had become standardized into certain basic types. His tabulation runs as follows:

The celestial scenes are concerned with assemblies of the gods, clouds, the different heavenly bodies, the rainbow, the sky, sunrise and sunset, flashes of lightning, tempests, etc.

The sacred scenes are composed of temples, altars, sacrifices, sacred caves, abodes of priests, prophets, and vestals, etc.

The military scenes represent besieged cities, the ramparts and exterior walls of which are lined with soldiers, artillery, war machines, parade grounds, and tents; a camp, quarters of generals, armories, arsenals, trophies, landscapes strewn with corpses, etc.

The rustic or pastoral scenes are innumerable for they may comprise all sorts of landscapes, mountains, valleys, rocks, fields, secluded spots, forests, prairies, grottoes, villages, hamlets, and rustic festivals. The landscape, according to the season, may be covered with snow, flowers, verdure, fruits, streams, groves, hills, vines, beaches, etc.

The maritime settings represent the sea, vessels, galleys, ports, islands, reefs, tempests, shipwrecks, marine monsters, naval engagements, etc.

The royal scenes are of palaces, thrones, façades of buildings enriched with columns, statues, and other ornaments, balconies, halls, galleries, apartments, closets, gardens, fountains, beds of honor, stables filled with prize horses, wardrobes, treasures, etc.

The civil scenes are of city streets, shops of merchants, studios of painters, sculptors, or artisans; a fair, a storehouse, private dwellings, prisons, houses on fire, buildings under construction, ruins, etc.

Historical scenes are such specific cities as Rome, Athens, Constantinople, Thebes, and certain places in Greece or in

Thessaly, or in Europe, where actions take place in the caves of the sibyl or of Cacus, etc.

The poetic settings are the palaces of the sun, of Thetis, of Eòlus, of Fortune, of Curiosity, and the temples of Death, Honor, and Fame. The places which Homer, Virgil, Ariosto, and Tasso have described.

The magic scenes are the enchanted palaces and islands, the places of witchery, and the horrible abodes of demons, Hell, the court of Pluto, the Elysian Fields, the Styx, Cocytus, Hades, the caverns of sorcerers, where all is dark and filled with phantoms.

The academic scenes are the libraries, studies of the scholars, with books and mathematical instruments, a collection of antiques, a school of painting, etc.

To these one can add hundreds of fanciful settings which can diversify the stage an infinite number of ways.

9. BAROQUE BALLET COSTUMES

BEGINNING IN 1675 with *Thésée*, the great Jean Bérain (*ca.* 1637-1711) designed the costumes for Lully's operas at the Académie Royale de Musique. When, in 1680, Lully and Vigarani dissolved their partnership, Bérain assumed full command of the Opéra's entire scenic department. Upon reading Father Ménestrier's extraordinary treatise on ballet (1682), we realize that his advice to the costume designer anticipates Noverre by almost a century by advocating an historically accurate, yet functional, costume for dancers — the "silent actors." On the other hand, Father Ménestrier, the learned Jesuit, was still perpetuating the allegorical tradition which Bernardo Buontalenti's costumes had established in the *intermezzi* of the Florentine festivals of 1589:

The costumes . . . are not the least part of the decorations. They often enough are essential to the beauty of the stage actions, and sometimes their variety makes up for lack of skill on the part of the dancers. One must show imagination and whimsicality in these ornaments. And since the ballet has only silent actors, it is necessary that their costumes speak for them, as well as their movements.

First of all, a costume should be appropriate to the subject, and if the dancer represents an historical personage, the costume should be, as far as possible, of the period. Undoubtedly, that

Carlo Vigarani's Setting for Lully's Opera *Atys*. Académie royale de musique, Paris, 1676.

Jean Bérain's Setting for Lully's Opera *Armide*. Académie royale de musique. Paris, 1686.

of the ancient Romans is the most impressive of all, while at the same time allowing maximum freedom to the legs. It consists of a cuirass with its scallops, a short cloak reaching to the elbow, and a skirt of pleated silk which serves as a surcoat. A helmet adorned with aigrette and plumes completes this costume, unless the dancers are said to represent victors, in which case they must also wear garlands of laurel.

The same concern for accuracy must prevail with regard to the dress of foreign nations. The Greeks favor circular caps with a quantity of plumes, and the Persians follow almost the same fashion. The Moors are distinguished by their short, curly hair and swarthy complexion; they go hatless, except for fillets embroidered with pearls after the manner of a diadem, and also wear earrings. The Turks and Saracens are clad in dolmans and bright turbans with aigrettes. American Indians sport a multi-colored feathered headdress and loincloths to conceal their nakedness; they also wear feathers about their necks and carry a bouquet of feathers in each hand while dancing. The Japanese bind their hair into large tufts at the back. Calcondyle has pictures of all these oriental costumes, ancient and modern. One also finds in geographical works illustrations of these various oriental peoples clad in accordance with their respective locales.

The second rule is that the costumes must be greatly varied, and, if possible, the same type of dress should never appear twice, or at least the entries should be so arranged that there is a long interval between those that are similar. It is always possible to change the color at least, if no other difference can be made, as will sometimes be the case in historical ballets when all the characters are of the same race and almost of the same station. After an entry of soldiers, it is pleasant to see an entry of shepherds, and after that, an entry of mythological divinities, then of robbers, followed by one of animals, of genii, of Americans, of Persians, of Moors, etc. This diversity always keeps the spectator in suspense.

The third rule is that uniformity must prevail as far as possible in the individual entries, that is to say, all those dancing in them must be costumed in the same color and style if the subject permit.

The fourth rule is that the costume must not be an obstacle, but must leave the body and limbs free to dance. Feminine costumes are the least suitable because they needs must be long.

If the dancers carry any kind of object, it should be functional: a hammer and trowel, for instance, with which to pantomime building, or a sword with which to simulate fighting. Rivers must pour water out of their urns, Zephyrs send forth breezes from their plumed fans, and Cyclopes must strike blows upon their anvils.

The costumes suitable to allegorical persons are the most difficult of all, as well as those for virtues and vices which we represent under human forms. It is precisely here that the talent and ingenuity of the costume designer may be observed. For it is necessary that the costumes express, as well as they can, the nature and properties of the subject.

Cities are garbed in Amazonian costumes whose colors are taken from their coats-of-arms, and a tiara of towers is placed upon their heads. Some make the whole costume from their respective coats-of-arms.

Spring's costume must be of a shadowy green worked with flowers and surmounted by a crown of roses. Winter must make his entrance all in white, with hoary beard, muffled in furs, heavy and sluggish in his gait. Summer's color should be isabelline, which is that of the harvest; ears of ripened grain must serve her for a diadem, while a scythe must be her scepter. Autumn's hue is olive or the color of fallen leaves; she carries a cornucopia full of fruit and vine leaves for a garland.

Winds must be dressed in feathers because of their extraordinary lightness. The Sun must be clothed in gold with gilded tresses, the Moon in cloth of silver; both should wear a mask, one with golden rays, the other with silver.

Time's costume must have four colors to signify the seasons of the year, with a sundial for a headdress, wings on head, shoulders, and feet, an hourglass in one hand and a scythe in the other. Night should be dressed in sable, profusely studded with stars, and a crescent moon must grace her hair. Fortune should have a costume of changing colors, eyes bandaged, and a roulette wheel in her hand. Embroidered upon her costume are scepters, crowns, arms, etc. Destiny should be clad in blue strewn with stars and bits of crystal because it is in the stars and crystal balls that man seeks to know his future. Her crown shall be of stars, and she shall hold a wand in her hand. Cupid should be dressed in rose-hued fabric embroidered with flaming hearts. his eyes bandaged, a bow in his hand, and a quiver on his back. Hate, on the contrary, should wear a fiery robe and carry a dagger in one hand and a vial of poison in the other, or a smoldering torch of black wax. The costume should be somber because this passion is not without sadness. Poverty is recognized by her torn dress and motley rags.

Faith ought to appear in white as a symbol of her sincerity, and with a veil drawn before her eyes to indicate her willingness to submit to religious mysteries. She carries a book in her hand and wears a diadem on her head like that of Constantine. I do not believe that she ought to carry a cross or chalice; it seems to me that we owe respect to sacred things, and that it is not fitting to use those things for stage properties which appear on the altar.

I would clothe Religion in a scarlet tunic embroidered with a golden cross—the symbol of the blood shed by the martyrs. I would crown her with laurel and place in her hand the palm and labarum of Constantine. This costume is modest and less offensive than the one sometimes seen which consists of the pontifical vestments of the synagogue, a tiara for the head and a censer for the hand.

10.   AN ARISTOCRATIC PLAYGOER

AFTER THE PRODUCTION of his *School for Wives*, Molière had to defend himself against charges of indecency and disrespect of religion. His answer was shaped in the form of a playlet, *The Critique of the School for Wives* (1663). Spokesman for the playwright is Dorante, who, in Scene 6, exposes to ridicule the aristocratic fops, such as the Marquis of the *Critique* and his fellow-stoolholders, whose snobbery is contrasted with the sincere and mature judgment of the Parisian pit:

The Marquis. One needs only observe the perpetual loud Laughs set up in the Pit: I want nothing else to prove 'tis good for nothing.

Dorante. Then, Marquis, you are one of those fine Gentlemen who won't allow the Pit to have common Sense, and who wou'd be griev'd to laugh along with that, tho' 'twere at the best thing in the World? I saw t'other Day one of our Friends

upon the Stage, who made himself ridiculous by this. He heard
the whole Piece with the most gloomy Gravity in the World;
and every thing that made others merry, made him frown. At
every loud Laugh he shrugg'd his Shoulders, and look'd with
Pity upon the Pit; and sometimes again looking down with
Vexation, he cry'd out aloud, *Laugh then, Pit, laugh.* Our
Friend's Chagrin was a second Comedy; he shew'd away like a
generous Fellow to the whole Assembly, and every body allow'd
no Man cou'd play his Part better than he did. Learn, Marquis,
you and others with you, that good Sense has no determin'd Place
at a Play; that the difference betwixt Half a Guinea and Half
a Crown makes nothing at all to a good Taste; and whether
one stand, or sit, one may pass a bad Judgment; and that, in
short, to take it in general, I shou'd depend a good deal upon
the Approbation of the Pit, because among those who compose
it, there are many who are capable of judging of a Piece according to Rules, and because others judge by a proper Method of
judging, which is to be guided by Things, and not to have any
blind Prejudice nor affected Complaisance, nor ridiculous Delicacy.

11.   BAD THEATER MANNERS

MOLIÈRE never complained about the custom of having spectators on
the stage, though, occasionally, the stage was so crowded that the audience
could hardly separate the players from the onlooking people of quality.
Molière did not mind the stage spectators — why should he? was not
everyone invited to witness a work of art and not to spy on slices of life?
— as long as they behaved properly. He would lose his temper, however,
when a gallant exhibited such insolent and senseless conduct as the specimen Éraste refers to in the first scene of Molière's *Les fâcheux* (*The
Impertinents*):

I was got upon the Stage in an Humour of hearkening to
the Piece, which I had heard cry'd up by several Persons: The
Actors began, and every body was silent, when, with a blustering Air, and full of Extravagance, in brushes a Man with huge
Pantaloons, crying out, Soho there! a Chair, quickly; and sur-
pris'd the Audience with his great Noise; being interrupted in
one of the most beautiful Passages of the Piece. Heaven defend
us! says I, will our Frenchmen, who are so often corrected,
never behave themselves with an Air of Men of Sense? Must we,

through Excess of Folly, expose ourselves in a public Theatre, and so confirm, by the Noise of Fools, what is every where said of us among our Neighbours? While I was shrugging up my Shoulders at this, the Actors were willing to go on with their Parts: But the Fellow, in seating himself, made a new Disturbance, and crossing the Stage again with large Strides, tho' he might have sat at his Ease on either Side, he planted his Chair in the middle of the Front, and insulting the Spectators with his brawny Back, he hid the Actors from three Fourths of the Pit. There was a Noise set up, that would have 'sham'd another Man; but he, steady and firm, did not at all mind it, and wou'd have continu'd just as he had plac'd himself, had he not, to my Misfortune, spy'd out me. *Ha! Marquis*, says he to me, placing himself by me, *How dost thou do? Let me embrace thee.* I immediately blush'd that People should see I was acquainted with such a Shittle-brain'd Mortal; tho' I was very little so: But it will be seen in those People, who will be hugely great with you from nothing at all, whose Kisses you must endure, as you tender your Happiness, and who are so familiar with you, as even to *thee* and *thou* you. He ask'd me, immediately, a hundred frivolous Questions, exalting his Voice above the Actors. Every body curs'd him, and to stop him, I should be very glad, says I, to hear the Play. *Thou hast not seen this, Marquis, Heh! Rat me, I think it droll enough, and I'm no Ass in these Things; I know by what Rules a Work is to be finish'd, and Corneille reads every Thing he does to me.* Upon this, he gave me a Summary of the whole Piece, telling me, Scene by Scene, what was to be done next, and even the Verses he could say by heart, he repeated aloud to me before the Actors. 'Twas in vain for me to resist, he push'd his Point, and towards the End got up a good while before the Time; for these fine Fellows, to act genteelly, take special care above all things not to hear the Conclusion.

12.   MIDDLE-CLASS CONNOISSEURS

A SPECIAL SECTION of the Parisian middle-class population is repeatedly mentioned as regular patrons of the Marais Theater, the Palais Royal, and the Hôtel de Bourgogne: the merchants of the rue Saint-Denis. The Saint-Denis quarter was the center of the trade in luxury articles, and there tailors, glovemakers, lace dealers, jewelers, and opticians were in fairly constant touch with their aristocratic customers. In his *Zélinde*

(1663), written in reply to Molière's *Critique de l'école des femmes*, Donneau de Visé laid the action of the playlet in the store of the lace merchant Argimont, who portrays his fellow-tradesmen of the rue Saint-Denis as passionate playgoers and the true connoisseurs of the pit. Says Argimont in *Zélinde*:

> Most of the merchants of the Saint-Denis Street are very partial to comedy, and there are forty or fifty of us who usually go to the first performance of all the new plays; and when the plays are something special and cause a great stir, four or five of us get together and rent a box for our wives; but, for ourselves, we are satisfied with the pit. On Sunday, we take four or five of the tradeswomen of this street there, along with the wife of a notary and an attorney's wife. . . . There are fifteen or sixteen merchants in this street who could tell you a good deal about the *Critique de l'école des femmes,* since, for thirty years, they have seen all the comedies that have been played, and all the prominent bourgeois of Paris give deference to their opinion. I must admit a thing which surprises me: I have never seen them condemn a play at its first performance without seeing it fail afterwards, nor heard them say that a play would succeed without seeing it become a hit. And what astonishes me is that they have always been found to be of the same opinion as the people of quality, and that all the plays that succeeded with the pit always succeeded with the people in the boxes and on the stage. There was even one of these merchants who, a few days ago, entered the home of a lady of quality, where he had business while several persons were chatting about a new play. They paid him the compliment of asking him his opinion, which he pronounced in a manner that surprised the whole company and brought forth the admission that people of the Saint-Denis Street are fully qualified to judge a play.

13.   MOLIERE AS STAGE DIRECTOR

IN HIS ONE-ACT *Impromptu of Versailles,* Molière criticized the players of the rival company at the Hôtel de Bourgogne for their declamatory exaggerations, which stood in contrast to the more natural style of delivery practised by Molière's troupe at the Palais Royal. Molière's satire hit the affectations of Montfleury (Prusias in *Nicomède*), Mlle. Beauchâteau (Camille in *Horace*), M. Beauchâteau (Don Rodrigue in the *Cid*), Hauteroche (Pompée in *Sertorius*) and De Villiers (Iphicrate in *Oedipe*). Originally produced at Versailles (October 14, 1663), the playlet takes us to a rehearsal of Molière's company, and we can watch Molière as *régisseur*, directing his company and advising them on stage business and mode of delivery:

Mrs. Du Parc. Nay, as for me, I shall acquit my self very ill of my Character, and I don't know why you gave me this ceremonious Part . . . . for there's no body in the World less ceremonious than I am.

Molière. 'Tis true, and in that you better shew that you are an excellent Comedian, to represent a Character well that is so contrary to your Humour. Endeavour then, all of you, to take the Character of your Parts right, and to imagine that you are what you represent. (*To Du Croisy.*) You play the Poet, and you ought to fill yourself with that Character, to mark the Pedant Air which he preserves even in the Conversation of the *Beau Monde;* that sententious Tone of Voice, and that Exactness of Pronunciation which lays a Stress on all the Syllables, and does not let one Letter escape of the strictest Orthography. (*To Brécourt.*) As for you, you play a Courtier, as you have already done in *The School for Wives Criticis'd*; that is, you must assume a sedate Air, a natural Tone of Voice, and make the fewest Gestures possible. (*To La Grange.*) As for you, I have nothing to say to you. (*To Mrs. Béjart.*) You represent one of those Women who, provided they don't make love, think that every thing else is permitted 'em; those Women who are always fiercely intrench'd in their Prudery, look upon every body with Contempt, and think all the good Qualities that others possess are nothing in comparison of a wretched Honour which no body regards. Have this Character always before your Eyes, that you may make the Grimaces of it right. (*To Mrs. Brie.*) As for you, you play one of those Women who think they are the most virtuous Persons in the World, provided they save Appearances; those Women who think the Crime lies only in the Scandal; who would carry on the Affairs they have quietly on the foot of an honourable Attachment, and call those Friends whom other People call Galants. Enter well into this Character. (*To Mrs. Molière.*) You play the same Character as in the *Critique,* I have nothing to say to you any more than to Mrs. Du Parc. (*To Mrs. Croisy.*) As for you, you represent one of those Persons

Molière as Stage Director.
Brissard's frontispiece to Molière's *Impromptu de Versailles,*
in the 1682 edition of the complete *Oeuvres.*

who are sweetly charitable to all the World, those Women who always give a Lash with their Tongue *en passant,* and would be very sorry if they suffer'd their Neighbour to be well spoke of. I believe you'll not acquit yourself ill of this Part. (*To Mrs. Hervé.*) And for you, you are a conceited Abigail, who's always thrusting her Oar into Conversation, and catching all her Mistress's Terms as much as she can. I tell you all your Characters, that you may imprint them strongly in your Minds. Let us begin to repeat, and see how 'twill do. . . .

First then imagine that the Scene is in the King's Antichamber, for that's a Place where humourous things enough pass every Day. 'Tis easy to bring there all the Persons we have a mind to, and we may even find Reasons to warrant the coming in of the Women which I introduce. The Comedy opens with two Marquisses who meet. (*To La Grange.*) Remember you to come as I told you, there, with that Air which is called the *Bel Air,* combing your Peruke, and humming a Tune between your Teeth. La, la, la, la, la, la, la. Do you range yourselves then, for the two Marquisses must have room, they are not People to be contain'd in a small space. Come speak.

La Grange. Good-morrow, Marquis.

Molière. Lack-a-day! that's not the Tone of a Marquis; you must take it a little higher, the most part of those Gentlemen affect a particular manner of speaking to distinguish themselves from the Vulgar. *Good-morrow, Marquis.* Begin again.

La Grange. Good-morrow, Marquis.

Molière. Hah! Marquis, your Servant.

La Grange. What art thou doing there? . . .

Molière. Go on.

Brécourt. Here's Climena and Eliza.

Molière. (*To Mrs. Du Parc and Mrs. Molière.*) Upon which you two are to come. (*To Mrs. Du Parc.*) Do you take care to make Grimaces as you ought, and to be very ceremonious. This will be a little Constraint upon you, but what can be done? we must sometimes put a Violence on ourselves.

Mrs. Molière. Certainly, Madam, I knew you a great way off, and saw plainly by your Air that it could be no body but you.

Mrs. Du Parc. I am come to wait here, d'ye see, till a Man comes out with whom I have some Business.

Mrs. Molière. And so am I.

Molière. Ladies, these Trunks will serve you for Elbow-Chairs.

Mrs. Du Parc. Come, Madam, pray take your Place.

Mrs. Molière. After you, Madam.

Molière. Good. After these little dumb Ceremonies, let every one take their Place and speak sitting, except the Marquisses, who must sometimes get up and sometimes sit down, according to their natural Restlessness.

Chapter VII

The Restoration Theater

1. DORSET GARDEN

THE DUKE'S COMPANY, under the management of William Davenant, first (November 1660) played at Salisbury Court, a theater that had survived the Puritan wrath. Lisle's Tennis Court, converted into a playhouse by Davenant, housed the company from 1661 - 1671. The transformed tennis court in Portugal Street, near Lincoln's Inn Fields, was too small — Cibber refers to it as "small, and poorly fitted up, within the Walls of a Tennis *Quaree* Court" — so the Duke's theater concern decided to build a commodious playhouse on a plot in Dorset Garden. The Dorset Garden Theatre opened on November 9, 1671. The edifice, said to have cost close to £9,000, had an overall length of 140 feet and a width of 57. Its seating capacity lay between 1,000 and 1,200 persons. The gilded baroque proscenium, lavishly decorated with statuary, carvings, and a heraldic emblem, can still be admired on Dolle's copperplates which adorn the first quarto of Settle's *The Empress of Morocco*. François Brunet, in his *Voyage d'Angleterre* (1676), left us a description of the auditorium. While the Frenchman thought little of the actors' costumes, he liked the arrangements made for the comfort of the spectators:

> The auditorium is infinitely more beautiful and functional than those in the playhouses of our French actors. The pit, arranged in the form of an amphitheater, has seats, and one never hears any noise. There are seven boxes, holding twenty persons each. The same number of boxes form the second tier, and, higher still, there is the paradise.

2. THE FIRST DRURY LANE

THE FIRST Theatre Royal, between Bridges Street and Drury Lane, was the home of the King's Company under the management of Thomas Killigrew. It was opened on May 7, 1663, at the cost of £2,400. Its outside length was 112 feet; width: 58 feet. Pepys, when he first visited the new playhouse on May 8, 1663, noticed some flaws in its design:

> The house is made with extraordinary good contrivance, and yet has some faults, as the narrowness of the passages in and out of the pit, and the distance from the stage to the boxes, which I am confident cannot hear; but for all other things, it is

well, only, above all, the music being below, and most of it sounding under the very stage, there is no hearing of the bases at all, nor very well of the trebles, which sure must be mended.

3.   ALTERATIONS IN PROGRESS

IN THE SPRING of 1666, some alterations were made in the Theatre Royal, and, on March 19, the impatient Pepys walked over to see what progress was being made:

. . . to the King's playhouse, all in dirt, they being altering of the stage to make it wider. But God knows when they will begin to act again; but my business here was to see the inside of the stage and all the tiringrooms and machines; and, indeed, it was a sight worth seeing.

4.   INTERIOR OF THE FIRST DRURY LANE

IN 1669, Prince Cosimo III of Tuscany visited the first Theatre Royal at least twice, and his official diarist, Count Lorenzo Magalotti, recorded the theatrical impressions of the princely party as follows:

. . . to the King's Theatre, to hear the comedy, in his majesty's box. This theatre is nearly of a circular form, surrounded, in the inside, by boxes separated from each other, and divided into several rows of seats, for the greater accommodation of the ladies and gentlemen, who, in conformity with the freedom of the country, sit together indiscriminately; a large space being left on the ground-floor for the rest of the audience. The scenery is very light, capable of a great many changes, and embellished with beautiful landscapes. Before the comedy begins, that the audience may not be tired with waiting, the most delightful symphonies are played; on which account many persons come early to enjoy this agreeable amusement.

The Dorset Garden
Proscenium.

W. Dolle's
engraving in the
first quarto edition
of Elkanah Settle's
*The Empress
of Morocco,*
Act I, Scene ii,
acted at
Dorset Garden
in July, 1673.

Yale Theatrical Prints Collection

5. SECOND THEATRE ROYAL

ON JANUARY 25, 1672, the first Theatre Royal was destroyed by fire, and the King's Company had to take up temporary quarters in Lisle's Tennis Court. Meanwhile, the Theatre Royal in Drury Lane was rebuilt by Christopher Wren at a cost exceeding £4,000. This second Theatre Royal had the same width as the first, but an outside length of 140 feet, 28 feet longer than its predecessor, because a scene-room had been added at the rear. In contrast to the sumptuous Dorset Garden, the second Theatre Royal was simple. Dryden, in his Prologue for the opening of the play-house (March 26, 1674), alluded to this difference:

A Plain built House, after so long a stay,
Will send you half unsatisfy'd away;
When, fall'n from your expected Pomp, you find
A bare convenience only is design'd.
You, who each Day can Theatres behold,
Like *Nero*'s Palace, shining all with Gold,
Our mean ungilded Stage will scorn, we fear,
And for the homely Room, disdain the Chear.

6. "DRONES IN THE THEATRICAL HIVE"

In 1682, while the Duke's Company flourished, the King's Company, which had chronically suffered from mismanagement and internal strife, collapsed. The two companies were merged into the United Company and moved into the Drury Lane house. By 1693, Christopher Rich, "as sly a Tyrant as ever was at the Head of a Theatre," had acquired complete control over the financial affairs of the United Company, and the older actors especially suffered under his crafty management. Colley Cibber, then a beginner under Rich, retained highly unpleasant memories of this period of his apprenticeship:

One only Theatre being now in Possession of the whole Town, the united Patentees imposed their own Terms, upon the Actors; for the Profits of acting were then divided into twenty Shares, ten of which went to the Proprietors, and the other Moiety to the principal Actors, in such Sub-divisions as their different Merit might pretend to. These Shares of the Patentees were promiscuously sold out to Money-making Persons, call'd Adventurers, who, tho' utterly ignorant of Theatrical Affairs, were still admitted to a proportionate Vote in the Menagement of them; all particular Encouragements to Actors were by them, of Consequence, look'd upon as so many Sums deducted from their private Dividends. While therefore the Theatrical Hive had so many Drones in it, the labouring Actors, sure, were under the highest Discouragement, if not a direct State of Oppression. Their Hardship will at least appear in a much stronger Light, when compar'd to our later Situation, who with scarce half their Merit, succeeded to be Sharers under a Patent upon five times easier Conditions: For as they had but half the Profits divided among ten, or more of them; we had three fourths of the whole

Profits, divided only among three of us: And as they might be said to have ten Task-masters over them, we never had but one Assistant Menager (not an Actor) join'd with us; who, by the Crown's Indulgence, was sometimes too of our own chusing. Under this heavy Establishment then groan'd this United Company, when I was first admitted into the lowest Rank of it.

7. LOSS OF INTIMACY

In 1696, Christopher Rich made some alterations in the Drury Lane theater, reducing the apron in order to enlarge the pit. When writing his *Apology* in 1740, Colley Cibber found it necessary to describe the original interior of the second Theatre Royal for the benefit of his readers:

As there are not many Spectators who may remember what Form the *Drury-Lane* Theatre stood in, about forty Years ago, before the old Patentee, to make it hold more Money, took it in his Head to alter it, it were but Justice to lay the original Figure, which Sir *Christopher Wren* first gave it, and the Alterations of it, now standing, in a fair Light; that equal Spectators may see, if they were at their choice, which of the Structures would incline them to a Preference. . . .

It must be observ'd then, that the Area, or Platform of the old Stage, projected about four Foot forwarder, in a Semi-oval Figure, parallel to the Benches of the Pit; and that the former, lower Doors of Entrance for the Actors were brought down between the two foremost (and then only) Pilasters; in the Place of which Doors, now the two Stage-Boxes are fixt. That where the Doors of Entrance now are, there formerly stood two additional Side-Wings, in front to a full Set of Scenes, which had then almost a double Effect, in their Loftiness, and Magnificence.

By this Original Form, the usual Station of the Actors, in almost every Scene, was advanc'd at least ten Foot nearer to the Audience, than they now can be; because, not only from the Stage's being shorten'd, in front, but likewise from the additional Interposition of those Stage-Boxes, the Actors (in respect to the

Spectators, that fill them) are kept so much more backward from the main Audience, than they us'd to be:

But when the Actors were in Possession of that forwarder Space, to advance upon, the Voice was then more in the Centre of the House, so that the most distant Ear had scarce the least Doubt, or Difficulty in hearing what fell from the weakest Utterance: All Objects were thus drawn nearer to the Sense; every painted Scene was stronger, every grand Scene and Dance more extended; every rich, or fine-coloured Habit had a more lively Lustre: Nor was the minutest Motion of a Feature (properly changing with the Passion, or Humour it suited) ever lost, as they frequently must be in the Obscurity of too great a Distance: And how valuable an Advantage the Facility of hearing distinctly, is to every well-acted Scene, every common Spectator is a Judge. A Voice scarce raised above the Tone of a Whisper, either in Tenderness, Resignation, innocent Distress, or Jealousy suppress'd, often have as much concern with the Heart, as the most clamorous Passions; and when on any of these Occasions, such affecting Speeches are plainly heard, or lost, how wide is the Difference, from the great or little Satisfaction received from them?

8.   SOCIAL STRATIFICATION

In 1698, a visitor from France, Henri Misson, described the auditorium of the second Theatre Royal:

The Pit is an Amphitheater, fill'd with Benches without Backboards, and adorn'd and cover'd with green Cloth. Men of Quality, particularly the younger Sort, some Ladies of Reputation and Vertue, and abundance of Damsels that haunt for Prey, sit all together in this Place, Higgledy-piggledy, chatter, toy, play, hear, hear not. Farther up, against the Wall, under the first Gallery, and just opposite to the Stage, rises another Amphitheater, which is taken up by Persons of the best Quality, among whom are generally very few Men. The Galleries, whereof there are only two Rows, are fill'd with none but ordinary People, particularly the Upper one.

9. THE PLAY IS NOT THE THING

RESTORATION SPECTATORS did not sit quietly in the auditorium, as we do today, with more or less unconcerned passivity: they developed among themselves certain dynamics of human relations, which we are still able to study in those precious playhouse minatures which Pepys inserted in his diary. Note the following scene during a *Macbeth* performance in the Duke's house (1668): Charles II is seated in the central royal box with his mistress; above him, in one of the second-tier boxes, is another of his mistresses, the dancer, Moll Davies; Pepys is sitting in the pit directly beneath the royal party, and not far from him is a woman who looks very much like the lady with the King. Pepys' description ties together the participants in this farcical pantomime, and, at the same time, we can feel the presence of the "audience-chorus," which follows this play within the play with intense interest:

The King and Court there; and we sat just under them and my Lady Castlemayne, and close to the woman that comes into the pit a kind of loose gossip, that pretends to be like her, and is so, something. . . . The King and Duke of York minded me, and smiled upon me, at the handsome woman near me: but it vexed me to see Moll Davies, in the box over the King's and my Lady Castlemayne's head, look down upon the King, and he up to her; and so did my Lady Castlemayne once, to see who it was, but when she saw her, she looked fire, which troubled me.

10. MY LADY CASTLEMAYNE AGAIN

ANOTHER SCENE, to which he was not an eyewitness, Pepys heard from an acquaintance, gossip being a seasoning element of the theatrical atmosphere. The *Dramatis personae*: the King, Lady Castlemayne, and a supernumerary — the Duke of York. On this occasion the featured players are not in the same box, and in the audience it is already rumored that Lady Castlemayne has fallen into disfavor. Thereupon the lady does something that makes the audience hold its breath:

Leaning over other ladies awhile to whisper with the King, she rose out of the box and went into the King's right hand, between the King and the Duke of York; which . . . put the King himself, as well as every body else out of countenance. . . . She did it only to show the world that she is not out of favour yet, as was believed.

11. SIR CHARLES STEALS THE SHOW

PEPYS HAD NOT only an eye for feminine beauty and an ear for society
gossip, but also a strongly marked interest in repartee, be it Dryden's
chase of wit on the stage or Sir Charles Sedley's improvisations in one of
the boxes:

To the King's house to *The Mayd's Tragedy*; but vexed all
the while with two talking ladies and Sir Charles Sedley, yet
pleased to hear their discourse, he being a stranger. And one of
the ladies would and did sit with her mask on, all the play, and,
being exceedingly witty as ever I heard woman, did talk most
pleasantly with him; but was, I believe, a virtuous woman and
of quality. He would fain know who she was, but she would
not tell; yet did give him many pleasant hints of her knowledge
of him, by that means setting his brains at work to find out who
she was, and did give him leave to use all means to find out who
she was but pulling off her mask. He was mighty witty, and she
also making sport of him very inoffensively, that a more pleasant
recontre I never heard. By that means lost the pleasure of the
play wholly.

12. THE LADIES IN MASKS

IN JUNE 1663, Pepys had noticed that Lady Mary Cromwell put on
a vizard in the King's house, and that she kept her face hidden behind
the mask during the entire performance, "which of late is become a
great fashion among the ladies which hides her whole face." These vizards
were in evidence till 1704, when Queen Anne forbade their use. Colley
Cibber had his own theory concerning the origin of the custom of mask-
wearing:

But while our Authors took these extraordinary Liberties
with their Wit, I remember the Ladies were then observ'd, to be
decently afraid of venturing bare-fac'd to a new Comedy, 'till
they had been assur'd they might do it, without the Risque of
an Insult, to their Modesty — Or, if their Curiosity were too
strong, for their Patience, they took Care, at least, to save
Appearances, and rarely came upon the first Days of Acting but
in Masks, (then daily worn, and admitted in the Pit, the side

Boxes, and Gallery) which Custom however, had so many ill
Consequences attending it, that it has been abolish'd these many
Years.

13. IMPROMPTU COMEDY IN THE GALLERIES

PROSTITUTES were to be found everywhere in the playhouse. Crowne's
epilogue to *Sir Courtly Nice* described the events caused by the presence
of "Fire-ships" in the twelve- or eighteen-penny galleries:

Our Galleries too, were finely us'd of late,
Where roosting Masques sat cackling for a Mate:
They came not to see Plays but act their own,
And had throng'd Audiences when we had none.
Our Plays it was impossible to hear,
The honest Country Men were forc't to swear:
Confound you, give your bawdy prating o're,
Or Zounds, I'le fling you i' the Pit, you bawling Whore.

14. VIZARD-MASKS

IN HIS *Epilogue on the Union of the Two Companies* (1682), Dryden
refers to the ladies of easy virtue in the middle gallery, and in the Prologue
to Southerne's *The Disappointment* (1684), he gives a more impressionistic account of the presence of vizard-masks:

But stay; methinks some Vizard-Mask I see
Cast out her Lure from the mid Gallery:
About her all the fluttering Sparks are rang'd;
The Noise continues, though the Scene is chang'd:
Now growling, sputt'ring, wauling, such a clutter!
'Tis just like Puss defendant in a Gutter. . . .

Last, some there are, who take their first Degrees
Of Lewdness in our Middle Galleries:
The Doughty Bullies enter Bloody Drunk,
Invade and grubble one another's Punk:
They Caterwaul and make a dismal Rout,
Call Sons of Whores, and strike, but ne're lugg-out:
Thus, while for Paultry Punk they roar and stickle,
They make it Bawdier than a Conventicle.

15. PLAYHOUSE IMPRESSIONS

THE FOURTH ACT of Thomas Shadwell's *A True Widow* (performed at Dorset Garden about March 1678) leads us into the interior of a Restoration playhouse and offers us an opportunity to review some of the male spectators — rowdy sparks and coxcombical practical jokers — on their entrance into the pit. Several men with their ladies force their way into the auditorium, refusing to pay admissions to the doorkeeper:

Doorkeeper. Pray, sir, pay me; my masters will make me pay it.

Third Man. Impudent rascal! Do you ask me for money? Take that, sirrah.

Second Doorkeeper. Will you pay me, sir?

Fourth Man. No; I don't intend to stáy.

Second Doorkeeper. So you say every day, and see two or three acts for nothing.

Fourth Man. I'll break your head, you rascal!

First Doorkeeper. Pray, sir, pay me.

Third Man. Set it down; I have no silver about me, or bid my man to pay you.

Theodosia. What! do gentlemen run on tick for plays?

Carlos. As familiarly as with their tailors.

Second Man. Pox on you, sirrah! Go and bid 'em begin quickly. . . .

Orange-Woman. Oranges! will you have any oranges?

First Bully. What play do they play? Some confounded play or other.

Prigg. A pox on't, madam! What should we do at this damned playhouse? Let's send for some cards and play a langtrillo in the box. Pox on 'em! I ne'er saw a play had anything in't; some of 'em have wit now and then, but what care I for wit?

Selfish. Does my cravat fit well? I take all the care I can it should; I love to appear well. What ladies are here in the boxes? Really, I never come to a play but on account of seeing the ladies. . . .

Stanmore. I cannot find my mistress; but I'll divert myself with a vizard in the meantime.

First Man. What, not a word! All over in disguise! Silence for your folly, and a vizard for your ill face.

Second Man. (*To a Vizard*) Gad! some whore, I warrant you, or chambermaid in her lady's old clothes.

(*He sits down and lolls in the orange-wench's lap*)

Third-Man. She must be a woman of quality; she has right point.

Fourth Man. 'Faith! she earns all the clothes on her back by lying on't; some punk lately turned out of keeping, her livery not quite worn out.

16. MANNERS OF THE RESTORATION GALLANT

SAM VINCENT's *The Young Gallant's Academy*, published in 1674, is an adaptation of Dekker's *The Gull's Hornbook* (1609). Vincent's fifth chapter, "Instructions for a young Gallant how to behave himself in the Play-house," is a modernized version of Dekker's playhouse chapter:

The *Theatre* is your *Poets-Royal Exchange,* upon which their *Muses* (that are now turned to Merchants) meeting, barter away that light Commodity of words, for a lighter ware than words, *Plaudities,* and the breath of the great Beast, which (like the threatnings of two Cowards) vanish into Air.

The *Play-house* is free for entertainment, allowing Room as well to the *Farmers Son* as to a *Templer;* yet it is not fit that he whom the most Taylors bills make room for when he comes, should be basely, like a Viol, cased up in a corner: Therefore, I say, let our Gallant (having paid his *half Crown,* and given the Door-keeper his *Ticket*) presently advance himself into the middle of the Pit, where having made his Honor to the rest of the Company, but especially to the Vizard-Masks, let him pull out his Comb, and manage his flaxen Wig with all the Grace he can. Having so done, the next step is to give a hum to the *China-Orange-wench,* and give her own rate for her Oranges (for 'tis below a *Gentleman* to stand haggling like a *Citizens wife*) and then to present the fairest to the next Vizard-mask. And that I may incourage our Gallant not like the Trades-man to save a shilling, and to sit but in the Middle-Gallery, let him but consider what large comings-in are pursed up sitting in the *Pit.*

1. First, A conspicuous Eminence is gotten, by which means the best and most essential parts of a Gentleman, as his fine Cloaths and Perruke, are perfectly revealed.

2. By sitting in the *Pit,* if you be a Knight, you may happily get you a Mistress. . . . But if you be but a meer *Fleetstreet* Gentleman, a Wife: but assure your self, by your continual residence there, you are the first and principal man in election to begin the number of *We three.*

It shall Crown you with rich Commendation, to laugh aloud in the midst of the most serious and sudden Scene of the terriblest Tragedy, and to let the *Clapper* (your *Tongue*) be tossed so high, that all the House may *ring* of it: for by talking and laughing, you heap *Pelion* upon *Ossa,* Glory upon Glory: as first, all the eyes in the Galleries will leave walking after the Players, and only follow you: the most Pedantick Person in the House snatches up your name; and when he meets you in the Streets, he'l say, *He is Such a Gallant;* and the people admire you.

Secondly, You publish your temperance to the world, in that you seem not to resort thither to taste vain Pleasures with an hungry Appetite; but only as a Gentleman to spend a foolish hour or two, because you can do nothing else.

Now Sir, if the Poet be a fellow that hath *Lampoon'd* or *libelled* you, or hath had a flirt at your Mistress, you shall disgrace him worse than tossing him in a Blanket, or giving him the Bastinado in a Tavern, if in the middle of the Play you arise with a skrew'd and discontented face (as if you had the griping in the Guts) and be gone; and further to vex him, mew at passionate Speeches, blare at merry, find fault with the Musick, whistle at the Songs, and above all, curse the Sharers, that whereas the very same day you had bestowed five pounds for an embroidered Belt, you encounter with the very same on the Stage, when the Belt-maker swore the impression was new but that morning.

To conclude, hoard up the finest Play-scraps you can get, upon which your lean Wit may most savourly feed for want of other stuff; for this is only Furniture for a Courtier that is but a new Beginner, and is but in his A B C of Complement. The next places that are filled after the *Play-houses* be emptied, are *Taverns.*

17. BETTERTON'S ACTING STYLE

THOMAS BETTERTON (1635 - 1710), the leading actor of the Restoration period, appeared first on the London stage in 1660, in a company of players hastily recruited at the end of the Civil War by the bookseller, John Rhodes. Playing in the Cockpit in Drury Lane, neither Betterton nor any one of his young colleagues were experienced actors. There were still some of the older pre-Commonwealth actors left, who, also in 1660, started to give performances at the Red Bull. In the same year, Thomas Killigrew and Sir William Davenant were given a grant "to erect two companies of players, consistinge respectively of such persons as they shall chuse and appoint, and to purchase, builde, and erect, or hire at their charge, as they shall thinke fitt, two houses or theatres." Killigrew chose his players, the King's Company, from the older actors at the Red Bull. Davenant selected the younger actors — Betterton among them — who formed the Duke's Company. For twenty-two years the companies of Davenant and Killigrew continued in rivalry until their competition ended in union in 1682. Prior to this union Betterton played the leading roles in those older plays, assigned to Davenant: he was Macbeth, Henry VIII, Hamlet, Mercutio, King Lear, and Bosola, aside from characters he played in the newer tragedies, notably Otway's. Betterton was also successful in comedy, both Elizabethan and Restoration. With the amalgamation of the two companies, he was given the opportunity of acting the leading parts in plays that had belonged to the King's Company. Thus he was seen as Othello and Brutus. From contemporary accounts, chiefly Aston's *Brief Supplement,* we gather that Betterton's acting was free from rant and exaggeration:

MR. BETTERTON (although a superlative good Actor) labour'd under ill Figure, being clumsily made, having a great Head, a short thick Neck, stoop'd in the Shoulders, and had fat short Arms, which he rarely lifted higher than his Stomach. — His Left Hand frequently lodg'd in his Breast, between his Coat and Waistcoat, while, with his Right, he prepar'd his Speech. — His Actions were few, but just. — He had little Eyes, and a broad Face, a little Pock-fretten, a corpulent Body, and thick Legs, with large Feet. — He was better to meet, than to follow; for his Aspect was serious, venerable, and majestic; in his latter Time a little Paralytic. — His Voice was low and grumbling; yet he could Time it by an artful *Climax,* which enforc'd universal Attention, even from the *Fops* and *Orange-girls.* — He was incapable of dancing, even in a Country-Dance; as was Mrs. BARRY: But their good Qualities were more than equal to their Deficiencies. — While Mrs. BRACEGIRDLE sung very agreeably in the LOVES of *Mars* and *Venus,* and danced in a Country-Dance, as well as Mr. WILKS, though not with so much Art and Foppery, but like a well-bred Gentleman. — Mr. BETTERTON was the most extensive Actor, from *Alexander* to Sir *John Falstaff;* but in that last Character, he wanted the Waggery of ESTCOURT, the Drollery of HARPER, and Sallaciousness of JACK EVANS — But, then, *Estcourt* was too trifling; *Harper* had too much of the *Bartholomew-Fair;* and *Evans* misplac'd his Humour. — Thus, you see what *Flaws* are in *bright Diamonds:* — And I have often wish'd that Mr. *Betterton* would have resign'd the Part of HAMLET to some young Actor, (who might have Personated, though not have Acted, it better) for, when he threw himself at *Ophelia's* Feet, he appear'd a little too grave for a young Student, lately come from the University of *Wirtemberg;* and his *Repartees* seem'd rather as *Apophthegms* from a *sage Philosopher,* than the *sporting Flashes* of a young HAMLET; and no one else could have pleas'd the Town, he was so rooted in their Opinion. His younger Contemporary, (*Betterton* 63, *Powell* 40, Years old) POWELL, attempted several of *Betterton's* Parts, as *Alexander, Jaffier, &c.* but lost his Credit; as, in *Alexander,* he maintain'd not the Dignity of a King, but Out-Heroded HEROD; and in his poison'd mad Scene, *out-rav'd all Probability;* while *Betterton* kept his Passion under, and shew'd it most (as Fume smoaks most, when stifled). *Betterton,* from the Time he was dress'd, to the End of the Play, kept his Mind in the same Temperament and Adaptness, as the present Character required.

18.   BETTERTONIAN ROLES

ASTON's description was meant to be a supplement to Colley Cibber's eulogy of Betterton in the *Apology:*

You have seen a *Hamlet* perhaps, who, on the first Appearance of his Father's Spirit, has thrown himself into all the straining Vociferation requisite to express Rage and Fury, and the House has thunder'd with Applause; tho' the mis-guided Actor was all the while (as *Shakespear* terms it) tearing a Passion into Rags—I am the more bold to offer you this particular

Instance, because of the late Mr. *Addison,* while I sate by him, to see this Scene acted, made the same Observation, asking me with some Surprize, if I thought *Hamlet* should be in so violent a Passion with the Ghost, which tho' it might have astonish'd, it had not provok'd him? for you may observe that in this beautiful Speech, the Passion never rises beyond an almost breathless Astonishment, or an Impatience, limited by filial Reverence, to enquire into the Suspected Wrongs that may have rais'd him from his peaceful Tomb! and a Desire to know what a Spirit so seemingly distrest, might wish or enjoin a sorrowful Son to execute towards his future Quiet in the Grave? This was the Light into which *Betterton* threw this Scene; which he open'd with a Pause of mute Amazement! then rising slowly, to a solemn, trembling Voice, he made the Ghost equally terrible to the Spectator, as to himself! and in the descriptive Part of the natural Emotions which the ghastly Vision gave him, the boldness of his Expostulation was still govern'd by Decency, manly, but not braving; his Voice never rising into that seeming Outrage, or wild Defiance of what he naturally rever'd. But alas! to preserve this medium, between mouthing, and meaning too little, to keep the Attention more pleasingly awake, by a temper'd Spirit, than by meer Vehemence of Voice, is of all the Master-strokes of an Actor the most difficult to reach. In this none yet have equall'd *Betterton.* . . .

A farther Excellence in *Betterton,* was, that he could vary his Spirit to the different Characters he acted. Those wild impatient Starts, that fierce and flashing Fire, which he threw into *Hotspur,* never came from the unruffled Temper of his *Brutus* (for I have, more than once, seen a *Brutus* as warm as *Hotspur*) when the *Betterton Brutus* was provok'd, in his Dispute with *Cassius,* his Spirit flew only to his Eye; his steady Look alone supply'd that Terror, which he disdain'd an Intemperance in his Voice should rise to. Thus, with a settled Dignity of Contempt, like an unheeding Rock, he repelled upon himself the Foam of *Cassius.* . . .

There cannot be a stronger Proof of the Charms of harmonious Elocution, than the many, even unnatural Scenes and Flights of the false Sublime it has lifted into Applause. In what Raptures have I seen an Audience, at the furious Fustian and turgid

Rants in *Nat. Lee's Alexander the Great*! For though I can allow this Play a few great Beauties, yet it is not without its extravagant Blemishes. Every Play of the same Author has more or less of them. . . . When these flowing Numbers came from the Mouth of a *Betterton*, the Multitude no more desired Sense to them, than our musical *Connoisseurs* think it essential in the celebrate Airs of an *Italian* Opera. Does this not prove, that there is very near as much Enchantment in the well-govern'd Voice of an Actor, as in the sweet Pipe of an Eunuch? If I tell you, there was no one Tragedy, for many Years, more in favour with the Town than *Alexander*. . . .

Notwithstanding the extraordinary Power he shew'd in blowing *Alexander* once more into a blaze of Admiration, *Betterton* had so just a sense of what was true, or false Applause, that I have heard him say, he never thought any kind of it equal to an attentive Silence; that there were many ways of deceiving an Audience into a loud one; but to keep them husht and quiet, was an Applause which only Truth and Merit could arrive at: Of which Art, there never was an equal Master to himself. From these various Excellencies, he had so full a Possession of the Esteem and Regard of his Auditors, that upon his Entrance into every Scene, he seem'd to seize upon the Eyes and Ears of the Giddy and Inadvertent! To have talk'd or look'd another way, would then have been thought Insensibility or Ignorance. In all his Soliloquies of moment, the strong Intelligence of his Attitude and Aspect, drew you into such an impatient Gaze, and eager Expectation, that you almost imbib'd the Sentiment with your Eye, before the Ear could reach it.

19.   BETTERTON'S OTHELLO AND HAMLET

OTHER OBSERVERS were impressed by Betterton's acting in specific scenes. Richard Steele, in *The Tatler*, described a few important moments in *Othello*, while *The Laureat*, in 1740, quoted the memories of an old play-goer who remembered Betterton's Hamlet upon meeting the Ghost:

I have hardly a notion that any performer of antiquity could surpass the action of Mr. Betterton on any of the occasions in which he has appeared on our stage. The wonderful agony which he appeared in, when he examined the circumstance of the handkerchief in *Othello*; the mixture of love that intruded upon his mind upon the innocent answers *Desdemona* makes, betrayed in his gesture such a variety and vicissitude of passions, as would admonish a man to be afraid of his own heart, and perfectly convince him, that it is to stab it, to admit that worst of daggers, jealousy. Whoever reads in his closet this admirable scene, will find that he cannot, except he has as warm an imagination as Shakspeare himself, find any but dry, incoherent, and broken sentences; but a reader that has seen Betterton act it, observes there could not be a word added; that longer speech had been unnatural, nay impossible, in *Othello's* circumstances. The charming passage in the same tragedy, where he tells the manner of winning the affection of his mistress, was urged with so moving and graceful an energy, that while I walked in the cloisters, I thought of him with the same concern as if I waited for the remains of a person who had in real life done all that I had seen him represent.

✔   ✔   ✔

I have lately been told by a Gentleman who has frequently seen Mr. *Betterton* perform this part of *Hamlet,* that he has observ'd his Countenance (which was naturally ruddy and sanguin) in this Scene of the fourth Act where his Father's Ghost appears, thro' the violent and sudden Emotions of Amazement and Horror, turn instantly on the Sight of his Father's Spirit, as pale as his Neckcloth, when every Article of his Body seem'd to be affected with a Tremor inexpressible; so that, had his Father's Ghost actually risen before him, he could not have been seized with more real Agonies; and this was felt so strongly by the Audience, that the Blood seemed to shudder in their Veins likewise, and they in some Measure partook of the Astonishment and Horror, with which they saw this excellent Actor affected.

20. A MANUAL FOR ACTORS

IN 1741, *The History of the English Stage* appeared as a work written by Betterton. Its author, however, was either the publisher, Edmund Curll, or William Oldys. Certain sections in which the duties of a player are

Betterton's
Hamlet

in the

Closet Scene.

From
Nicholas Rowe's
Shakespeare,
1709.

Yale Theatrical Prints Collection

enumerated, may have been based upon authentic Bettertonian notes. At any rate, the following paragraphs are of considerable interest to anyone trying to reconstruct the acting style of the period:

We shall . . . begin with the government, order and balance, of the whole body; and thence proceed to the regiment and proper motions of the head, the eyes, the eye-brows, and indeed the whole face; then conclude with the actions of the hands, more copious and various than all the other parts of the body.

The place and posture of the body ought not be be changed every moment, since so fickle an agitation is trifling and light;

nor, on the other hand, should it always keep the same position, fixed like a pillar or marble statue. For this, in the first place, is unnatural, and must therefore be disagreeable, since God has so formed the body with members disposing it to motion, that it must move either as the impulse of the mind directs, or as the necessary occasions of the body require. This heavy stability, or thoughtless fixedness, by losing that variety, which is so becoming of, and agreeable in the change and diversity of speech and discourse, and gives admiration to every thing it adorns, loses likewise that genteelness and grace, which engages the attention by pleasing the eye. Being taught to dance will very much contribute in general to the graceful motion of the whole body, especially in motions, that are not immediately embarrassed with the passions.

That the head has various gestures and signs, intimations and hints, by which it is capable of expressing consent, refusal, confirmation, admiration, anger, &c. is what every one knows, who has ever considered at all. It might therefore be thought superfluous to treat particularly of them. But this rule may be laid down on this head in general; first that it ought not to be lifted up too high, and stretched out extravagantly, which is the mark of arrogance and haughtiness; but an exception to this rule will come in for the player, who is to act a person of that character. Nor on the other side should it be hung down upon the breast, which is both disagreeable to the eye, in rendering the mien clumsy and dull; and would prove extremely prejudicial to the voice, depriving it of its clearness, distinction, and that intelligibility, which it ought to have. Nor should the head always lean towards the shoulders, which is equally rustic and affected, or a great mark of indifference, languidness, and a faint inclination. But the head, in all the calmer speeches at least, ought to be kept in its just natural state and upright position. In the agitation indeed of a passion, the position will naturally follow the several accesses and recesses of the passion, whether grief, anger, &c.

We must farther observe, that the head must not be kept always like that of a statue without motion; nor must it on the contrary be moving perpetually, and always throwing itself about on every different expression. It must therefore shun these ridiculous extremes, turn gently on the neck, as often as occasion requires a motion, according to the nature of the thing, turning now to one side, and then to another, and then return to such a decent position, as your voice may best be heard by all or the generality of the audience. The head ought always to be turned on the same side, to which the *actions* of the rest of the body are directed, except when they are employed to express our aversion to things, we refuse; or on things we detest and abhor; for these things we reject with the *right hand,* at the same time turning the head away to the *left.* . . .

When we are free from passion, and in any discourse which requires no great motion, as our modern Tragedies too frequently suffer their chief parts to be, our aspect should be pleasant, our looks direct, neither severe nor aside, unless we fall into a passion, which requires the contrary. For then nature, if we obey her summons, will alter our looks and gestures. Thus when a man speaks in anger, his imagination is inflamed, and kindles a sort of fire in his eyes, which sparkles from them in such a manner, that a stranger, who understood not a word of the language, or a deaf man, who could not hear the loudest tone of his voice, would not fail of perceiving his fury and indignation. And this fire of their eyes will easily strike those of their audience which are continually fixed on yours; and by a strange sympathetic infection, it will set them on fire too with the very same passion.

I would not be misunderstood, when I say you must wholly place your eyes on the person or persons you are engaged with on the stage; I mean, that at the same time both parties keep such a position in regard of the audience, that even these beauties escape not their observation, though never so justly directed. As in a piece of History Painting, though the figures fix their eyes ever so directly to each other, yet the beholder, by the advantage of their position, has a full view of the expression of the soul in the eyes of the figures.

The looks and just expressions of all the other passions has the same effect, as this we have mentioned of anger. For if the *grief* of another touches you with a real compassion, tears will flow from your eyes, whether you will or not. . . .

You must lift up or cast down, your eyes, according to the

nature of the things you speak of; thus if of heaven, your eyes naturally are lifted up; if of earth, or hell, or any thing terrestrial, they are as naturally cast down. Your eyes must also be directed according to the passions; as to deject them on things of disgrace, and which you are ashamed of; and raise them on things of honor, which you can glory in with confidence and reputation. In swearing, or taking a solemn oath, or attestation of any thing, to the veriety of what you say, you turn your eyes, and in the same action lift up your hand to the thing you swear by, or attest.

Your eye-brows must neither be immoveable, nor always in motion; nor must they both be raised on every thing that is spoken with eagerness and consent; and much less must one be raised, and the other cast down; but generally they must remain in the same posture and equality, which they have by nature, allowing them their due motion when the passions require it; that is, to contract themselves and frown in *sorrow*; to smooth and dilate themselves in *joy*; to hang down in *humility*, &c.

The *mouth* must never be writhed, nor the *lips* bit or licked, which are all ungenteel and unmannerly actions, and yet what some are frequently guilty of; yet in some efforts or starts of passion, the lips have their share of action, but this more on the stage, than in any other public speaking, either in the Pulpit, or at the Bar; because the stage is, or ought to be, an imitation of nature in those actions and discourses, which are produced between man and man by any passion, or on any business, which can afford action; for all other has in reality nothing to do with the scene.

Though to shrug up the shoulders be no gesture in oratory, yet on the stage the character of the person, and the subject of his discourse, may render it proper enough; though I confess, it seems more adapted to Comedy, than Tragedy, where all should be great and solemn. . . .

Others thrust out the belly, and throw back the head, both gestures unbecoming and indecent.

We come now to the hands, which, as they are the chief instruments of action, varying themselves as many ways, as they are capable of expressing things, so is it a difficult matter to give such rules as are without exception. Those natural significations of particular gestures, and what I shall here add, will I hope, be some light to the young actor in this particular. 1st. I would have him regard the *action* of the hands, as to their expression of *accusation, deprecation, threats, desire,* &c. and to weigh well what those actions are, and in what manner expressed; and then considering how large a share those actions have in all manner of discourse, he will find that his hands need never be idle, or employed in an insignificant or unbeautiful gesture.

In the beginning of a solemn speech or oration, as in that of Anthony on the death of Cesar, or of Brutus on the same occasion, there is no gesture, at least of any consideration, unless it begin abruptly, as *O Jupiter, O heavens! is this to be borne? the very ships then in our eyes, which I preserved,* &c. extending here his hands first to heaven, and then to the ships. In all regular gestures of the hands, they ought perfectly to correspond with one another; as in starting in amaze, on a sudden fright, as Hamlet in the scene between him and his mother, on the appearance of his father's Ghost—

> "Save me, and hover o'er me with your wings,
> You heavenly Guards!"

This is spoke with arms and hands extended, and expressing his concern, as well as his *eyes,* and *whole face.* If an action comes to be used by only one hand, that must be by the *right,* it being indecent to make a gesture with the *left* alone; except you should say any such thing as,

> "Rather than be guilty of so foul a deed,
> I'd cut this right hand off, &c.

For here the actions must be expressed by the *left* hand, because the *right* is the member to suffer. When you speak of yourself, the *right* not the *left* hand must be applied to the bosom, declaring your own faculties, and passions; your heart, your soul, or your conscience. But this action, generally speaking, should be only applied or expressed by laying the hand gently on the breast, and not by thumping it as some people do. The gesture must pass from the *left* to the *right,* and there end with gentleness and moderation, at least not stretch to the extremity of violence. You must be sure, as you begin your action with what you say, so you must end it when you have done speaking; for action either before or after utterance is highly ridiculous. The movement or gestures of your hands must always be agreeable to the nature of the words, that you speak; for when you say *come in,* or *approach,* you must not stretch out your hand with a repulsive gesture; nor, on the contrary, when you say, *stand back,* must your gesture be inviting; nor must you join your hands, when you command separation; nor open them, when your order is *closing*; nor hang them down, when you bid *raise such a thing,* or *person*; nor lift them up, when you say *throw them down.* For all these gestures would be so visibly against nature, that you would be laughed at by all that saw or heard you. By these instances of faulty action, you may easily see the right, and gather this rule, that as much as possible every gesture you use should express the nature of the words you utter, which would sufficiently and beautifully employ your hands. . . .

In the lifting up the hands, to preserve the grace, you ought not raise them above the eyes; to stretch them farther might disorder and distort the body; nor must they be very little lower, because that position gives a beauty to the figure; besides, this posture being generally on some surprise, admiration, abhorrence, &c. which proceeds from the object, that affects the eye, nature by a sort of mechanic motion throws the hands out as guards to the eyes on such an occasion.

You must never let either of your hands hang down, as if lame or dead; for that is very disagreeable to the eye, and argues no passion in the imagination. In short, your hands must always be in view of your eyes, and so corresponding with the motions of the head, eyes, and body, that the spectator may see their concurrence, every one in its own to signify the same thing, which will make a more agreeable, and by consequence a deeper impression on their senses, and their understanding.

Your arms you should not stretch out side ways, above half a foot from the trunk of your body; you will otherwise throw your gesture quite out of your sight, unless you turn your head also aside to pursue it, which would be very ridiculous.

In swearing, attestation, or taking any solemn vow or oath, you must raise your hand. An exclamation requires the same action; but so that the gesture may not only answer the pronunciation, or utterance, but both the nature of the thing, and the meaning of the words. In public speeches, orations, and sermons, it is true your hands ought not to be always in motion, a vice which was once called the *babbling of the hands*; and, perhaps, it may reach some characters, and speeches in plays; but I am of opinion, that the hands in acting ought very seldom to be wholly quiescent, and that if we had the art of the Pantomimes, of expressing things so clearly with their hands, as to make the gestures supply words, the joining these significant actions to the words and passions justly drawn by the poet, would be no contemptible grace in the player, and render the diversion infinitely more entertaining, than it is at present. For indeed action is the business of the stage, and an error is more pardonable on the right, than the wrong side.

There are some actions or gestures, which you must never make use of in Tragedy, any more than in pleading, or sermons, they being low, and fitter for Comedy or burlesque entertainments. Thus you must not put yourself into the posture of one bending a bow, presenting a musket, or playing on any musical instrument, as if you had it in your hands.

You must never imitate any lewd, obscene or indecent postures, let your discourse be on the debaucheries of the age, or any thing of that nature, which the description of an Anthony and Verres might require our discourse of.

21.   MRS. BARRY

BETTERTON's leading tragic actress was Mrs. Elizabeth Barry (1658-1713). She celebrated her greatest triumphs as Monimia and Belvidera in Otway's *The Orphan* and *Venice Preserved*, and as Isabella in Southerne's *The Fatal Marriage* — parts in which she "forc'd Tears from the Eyes of her Auditory" (Downes). Her artistic profile emerges from Cibber's and Aston's sketches:

Mrs. *Barry* was then [by the end of the seventeenth century] in possession of almost all the chief Parts in Tragedy: With what Skill she gave Life to them, you will judge from the Words of *Dryden*, in his Preface to *Cleomenes*, where he says,

Mrs. Barry, *always excellent, has in this Tragedy excell'd*

*herself, and gain'd a Reputation, beyond any Woman I have
ever seen on the Theatre. . . .*

Mrs. *Barry,* in Characters of Greatness, had a Presence
of elevated Dignity, her Mien and Motion superb, and gracefully
majestick; her Voice full, clear, and strong, so that no Violence
of Passion could be too much for her: And when Distress, or
Tenderness possess'd her, she subsided into the most affecting
Melody, and Softness. In the Art of exciting Pity, she had a
Power beyond all the Actresses I have yet seen, or what your
Imagination can conceive. Of the former of these two great
excellencies, she gave the most delightful Proofs in almost all
the Heroic Plays of *Dryden* and *Lee;* and of the latter, in the
softer Passions of *Otway's Monimia* and *Belvidera.* In Scenes
of Anger, Defiance, or Resentment, while she was impetuous,
and terrible, she pour'd out the Sentiment with an enchanting
Harmony; and it was this particular Excellence, for which
Dryden made her the above-recited Compliment, upon her acting
Cassandra in his *Cleomenes.* But here, I am apt to think his Partiality for that Character, may have tempted his Judgment to
let it pass for her Master-piece; when he could not but know,
there were several other Characters in which her Action might
have given her a fairer Pretence to the Praise he has bestow'd
on her, for *Cassandra;* for, in no Part of that, is there the least
ground for Compassion, as in *Monimia;* nor equal cause for
Admiration, as in the nobler Love of *Cleopatra,* or the tempestu-
ous Jealousy of *Roxana.* 'Twas in these Lights, I thought Mrs.
Barry shone with a much brighter Excellence than in *Cassandra.*
She was the first Person whose Merit was distinguished, by
the Indulgence of having an annual Benefit-Play, which was
granted to her alone, if I mistake not, first in King *James's*
time, and which became not common to others, 'till the Division
of this Company, after the Death of King *William's* Queen *Mary.*

❧ ❧ ❧

Mrs. *Barry* out-shin'd Mrs. *Bracegirdle* in the Character
of ZARA in the *Mourning Bride,* altho' Mr. *Congreve* design'd
Almeria for that Favour. — And yet, this fine Creature was not
handsome, her Mouth op'ning most on the Right Side, which she
strove to draw t'other Way, and, at Times, composing her Face,
as if sitting to have her Picture drawn. — Mrs. *Barry* was

middle-siz'd, and had darkish Hair, light Eyes, dark Eyebrows and was indifferently plump: — Her Face somewhat preceded her Action, as the latter did her Words, her Face ever expressing the Passions; not like the Actresses of late Times, who are afraid of putting their Faces out of the Form of Non-meaning, lest they should crack the Cerum, White-Wash, or other Cosmetic, trowl'd on. Mrs. *Barry* had a Manner of drawing out her Words, which became her. . . . Neither she, nor any of the Actors of those Times, had any Tone in their speaking, (too much, lately, in Use). — In *Tragedy* she was solemn and august — in *Free Comedy* alert, easy, and genteel — pleasant in her Face and Action; filling the Stage with variety of Gesture. . . . She could neither sing, nor dance, no, not in a Country-Dance.

22.   MRS. BRACEGIRDLE

BETTERTON coached Mrs. Anne Bracegirdle (1663 ? - 1748), who excelled in the high-comedy parts which Congreve had written for her. The first Millimant was overanxious to establish for herself a reputation of chastity, the validity of which was constantly questioned by satirical writers. But Mrs. Bracegirdle's artistic integrity is soundly established by the Messrs. Cibber and Aston:

Mrs. *Bracegirdle* was now, but just blooming to her Maturity; her Reputation, as an Actress, gradually rising with that of her Person; never any Woman was in such general Favour of her Spectators, which, to the last Scene of her Dramatick Life, she maintain'd, by not being unguarded in her private Character. This Discretion contributed, not a little, to make her the *Cara,* the Darling of the Theatre: For it will be no extravagant thing to say, Scarce an Audience saw her, that were less than half of them Lovers, without a suspected Favourite among them: And tho' she might be said to have been the Universal Passion, and under the highest Temptations; her Constancy in resisting them, served but to increase the number of her Admirers: And this perhaps you will more easily believe, when I extend not my Encomiums on her Person, beyond a Sincerity that can be suspected; for she had no greater Claim to Beauty, than what the most desirable *Brunette* might pretend to. But her Youth, and

lively Aspect, threw out such a Glow of Health, and Chearful-
ness, that, on the Stage, few Spectators that were not past it,
could behold her without Desire. It was even a Fashion among
the Gay, and Young, to have a Taste or *Tendre* for Mrs. *Bracegirdle*. She inspired the best Authors to write for her, and two
of them, when they gave her a Lover, in a Play, seem'd palpably
to plead their own Passions, and make their private Court to her,
in fictitious Characters. In all the chief Parts she acted, the
Desirable was so predominant, that no Judge could be cold
enough to consider, from what other particular Excellence, she
became delightful.

To speak critically of an Actress, that was extremely
good, were as hazardous, as to be positive in one's Opinion
of the best Opera Singer. People often judge by Comparison,
where there is no Similitude, in the Performance. So that, in this
case, we have only Taste to appeal to, and of Taste there can be
no disputing. I shall therefore only say of Mrs. *Bracegirdle*,
That the most eminent Authors always chose her for their favourite Character, and shall leave that uncontestable Proof of her
Merit to its own Value. Yet let me say, there were two very
different Characters, in which she acquitted herself with uncommon Applause: If any thing could excuse that desperate Extravagance of Love, that almost frantick Passion of *Lee's Alexander
the Great*, it must have been, when Mrs. *Bracegirdle* was his
Statira: As when she acted *Millamant* [in Congreve's *The Way
of the World*], all the Faults, Follies, and Affectation of that
agreeable Tyrant, were venially melted down into so many
Charms, and Attractions of a conscious Beauty. In other Characters, where Singing was a necessary Part of them, her Voice and
Action gave a Pleasure, which good Sense, in those Days, was
not asham'd to give Praise to.

🖋   🖋   🖋

She was of a lovely Height, with dark-brown Hair and Eyebrows, black sparkling Eyes, and a fresh blushy Complexion;
and, whenever she exerted herself, had an involuntary Flushing
in her Breast, Neck and Face, having continually a chearful
Aspect, and a fine Set of even white Teeth; never making an
Exit, but that she left the Audience in an Imitation of her
pleasant Countenance. Genteel Comedy was her chief Essay, and

that too when in Men's Cloaths, in which she far surmounted all the Actresses of that and this Age. — Yet, she had a Defect scarce perceptible, *viz.*, her right Shoulder a little protended, which, when in Men's Cloaths, was cover'd by a long or Campaign Peruke. — She was finely shap'd, and had very handsome Legs and Feet; and her Gait, or Walk, was free, manlike, and modest, when in Breeches.

23.   RIVAL COMPANIES

IN 1695, the union of the two Restoration companies was broken by a revolt of the older players. In their protest against the cunning practices of Rich, the spokesman for the patentees, they were led by Thomas Betterton. The aging actor obtained a license from the Lord Chamberlain's Office and with Mrs. Barry, Mrs. Bracegirdle, Underhill, Williams, and Dogget — to name but a few of the older players — moved into the reconverted Lisle's Tennis Court in Lincoln's Inn Fields. The new theater was opened on April 30, 1695. The competitive struggle of the two stages, Lincoln's Inn Fields and Drury Lane, and the fluctuations of the taste of the Town, are vividly described in the anonymous *Comparison between the Two Stages* (1702). Of special interest, in this animated dialogue between two gentlemen called Ramble and Sullen, and the critic, Chagrin, is the section on the "Third Day," the net profits of which constituted the problematic income of the playwright:

Sull. . . . Has it not been your wonder *Crit.* as well as mine, That the two Theatres should hold out so long? even against such difficulties as seem'd to be invincible. The Emulation between 'em has now lasted Seven Years, and every body thought the Town wou'd long ago ha' determined in favour of one or the other: But in my Opinion, 'twas strange that the general defection of the old Actors which left *Drury-lane*, and the fondness which the better sort shew'd for 'em at the opening of their *New-house*, and indeed the Novelty itself, had not quite destroy'd those few young ones that remain'd behind. The disproportion was so great at parting, that 'twas almost impossible, in *Drury-lane*, to muster up a sufficient number to take in all the Parts of any Play; and of them so few were tolerable, that a Play must of necessity be damn'd that had not extraordinary favour from the Audience: No fewer than *Sixteen* (most of the old standing) went away; and with them the very beauty and vigour of the

Stage; they who were left behind being for the most part Learn-
ers, Boys and Girls, a very unequal match for them who revolted.

Ramb. 'Tis true, the *Theatre-Royal* was then sunk into a
very despicable Condition: Very little difference appear'd between
that and the Theatre at the Bear Garden.

Sull. If you please, 'twas more like a Bear-Garden before;
for they exercis'd neither Humanity to one another, nor to any
body else that had to do with them.

Cri. As I hear, that matter is not mended yet.

Sull. Truly I hear very little said in its behalf; I hear a great
deal against it, and that there is a very notable Difference between the two Houses, in point of Civility and good Treatment.

Ramb. As how, *Sullen*?

Sull. You must excuse that; the Gentleman gave it me as
a Secret.

Ramb. Pho, prithee Man, we'll be as secret as thou canst
be; come out with it.

Sull. Nay, its no great matter; but if the *Old-house* should
hear of it, they'd swear 'twas a damn'd Lye; but I am satisfy'd
in the truth of it: The thing is this; A Gentleman carry'd a
Play there, a Day was appointed for the reading; a Dinner
was bespoke at a Tavern for half a Score, at least that number
came to judge his Play, tho' not three of 'em cou'd tell the
difference between Comedy and Tragedy; in the reading of it
(that is after Dinner) most of 'em dropt off, but two remain'd
to hear it out, and then they walkt; so that there was but the
Gentleman and his Friend left, and not a Penny all this while
paid towards the Reckoning. The Play was ordered to be
Licenced, so that forty Shillings for the Dinner, and forty more
for the Licence, made just four Pounds, so much it cost him
already. This happened to be in Lent, and the Players having
then the first Day of a Play given 'em, this was bespoke; so the
Author had the Mortification of having it acted in Lent; but the
Devil on't was, he was oblig'd to treat every one of his Players
all the while it was in Rehearsal, to keep 'em in study, and in
that exploit it cost him in Coach hire and Wine near ten Pounds.

Cri. The Devil it did.

Sull. 'Tis certainly true: Well, his Third Day came, and a
good Appearance there was; I sate in the Pit, and I think I

never saw better Boxes; the Play came off pretty well, and the Poet was much exalted with so good an escape, for it was his first; his Friends joy'd him when 'twas over, and he thought he had now the *Indies* to receive: Pay-Day came, and what do you think he received?

Cri. Had he only a third Night?

Sull. No more, it lasted but four.

Cri. I suppose he paid the Charges?

Sull. That you may Swear.

Cri. Then he might receive — the House was full you say?

Sull. Excellent Pit and Boxes, and I believe, full above.

Cri. Why then, He might receive Seventy Pounds; nay, I diminish it as much as I can, because I know their way of bringing in their Bills of Charges.

Sull. He received but fifteen.

Cri. 'Sdeath! How could that be? the Ordinary Charge is about four and thirty Pounds a Day.

Sull. But the extraordinary (when they please to make it so) is very extraordinary, without any Compass. They brought him Bills for Gloves, for Chocolet, for Snuff; this Singer begg'd a Guinea, that Dancer the same; one Actor wished him joy, and ask'd how he lik'd his Performance; Oh very well Mr. — I ought to gratifie — another cries, Oh dear Mr. — I never took so much pains in my Life; that deserves a Kiss and a Present; and the next Morning away flies another Guinea.

Cri. By this account you make him a loser.

Sull. He really prov'd so; but being startled at so great a disappointment, he made it his Business to enquire into the Fraud; and he perceiv'd at last, that he lost one half by the roguery of the Doorkeepers, and others concern'd in the receipt.

Ramb. Then he shou'd ha' put in Doorkeepers of his own.

Sull. He found that too late, for this was his first Play: But whether 'twas owing to his care and his parsimony next time, or that the *other House* did him more Justice, I can't tell, but his next Play brought him in Six times what the first did.

Ramb. 'Twas acted at the *New House*?

Sull. Yes, yes, and Mr. *Betterton* did him (as I have heard him say) greater Justice than he expected.

Ramb. Well, but to go back — you were saying, you

wonder'd that *Drury-lane* House cou'd stand so long, considering all those disadvantages you mention'd; but you must consider too, that they were in possession of the Patent and the Stage, the other had neither; there was an immense charge to go thro' before they cou'd be settled to any purpose; and after that, there must be allowed some time to pay Debts contracted by that Charge.

Sull. 'Tis granted; and I don't wonder more that they both stood, than that either of them stood under such oppressing Hardships; But I must needs think, of the two *Drury-lane* had the hardest time on't; for how can a Stage Subsist without good Actors? As to the other; 'tis true their Charge was great, but we all know what means they found out to make 'em lighter, we know what importuning and dunning the Noblemen there was, what flattering, and what promising there was, till at length, the incouragement they received by liberal Contributions set 'em in a Condition to go on.

Ramb. In the mean time the Mushrooms in *Drury-lane* shoot up from such a desolate Fortune into a considerable Name; and not only grappled with their Rivals, but almost eclipst 'em.

Crit. If the Town had been of my Humour, they shou'd ha' been both supprest; for I think one House too much, unless they gave us better Plays.

Ramb. Don't be too severe *Critick*; you know the New-house opened with an extraordinary good Comedy [*Love for Love*], the like has scarce been heard of.

Cri. I allow that Play contributed not a little to their Reputation and Profit; it was the Work of a popular Author; but that was not all, the Town was ingag'd in its favour, and in favour of the Actors long before the Play was Acted.

Sull. I've heard as much; and I don't grudge 'em that happy beginning, to compensate some part of their Expence and Toil: But the assistance they receiv'd from some Noble Persons did 'em eminent Credit; and their appearance in the Boxes, gave the House as much Advantage as their Contributions.

Ramb. Faith if their Boxes had not been well crowded, their Galleries wou'd ha' fallen down on their Heads.

Sull. The good Humour those Noble Patrons were in, gave that Comedy such infinite Applause; and what the Quality approve, the lower sort take upon trust. But this like other things of that kind, being only nine Days wonder, and the Audiences, being in a little time sated with the Novelty of the *New-house*, return in Shoals to the Old: Some Poets of the first Rank still writ for the latter, and great care being taken to Act every thing as well as they cou'd, they rubb'd on with tolerable Success: After this, they travers'd each other with uncertain Fortune, this sometimes up, and that sometimes down, so that 'twas hard to say which was most like to prevail.

Ramb. And by this time the Town, not being able to furnish out two good Audiences every Day; chang'd their Inclinations for the two Houses, as they found 'emselves inclin'd to Comedy or Tragedy: If they desir'd a Tragedy, they went to *Lincolns-Inn-fields*; if to Comedy, they flockt to *Drury-lane*; which was the reason that several Days but one House Acted; but by this variety of Humour in the Town, they shared pretty equally the Profit.

24.   ANOTHER "THIRD DAY"

THE FOREGOING ACCOUNT, while stressing the financial predicament of a "Third Day" playwright, lacks a description of the proceedings in the auditorium itself. *The Country Gentleman's Vade Mecum* (1699) comes to our aid and supplies the audience background for such a benefit performance:

I must confess, when I look into the Plays that were writ formerly, and compare them with the generality that have been writ here a late, in my poor Judgment, the *Plots* and *Characters*, and (what's more strange) the *Stile* too, is grown so profoundly dull and flat that a Man must have a very good Appetite, that can digest such intolerable trash, without a Surfeit. Well, let it be what it will, provided it be stampt with a New Name, and a strange title, it certainly raises the *Mob*, calls together the *Whores* and *Bawds*, the *Squires, Beaus, Cits, Bullies*, &c. that come all crowding in shoals to hear what this wondrous New Man can say, or do, to please 'em. The third Day, if by the help of a good *Prologue* and *Epilogue*, good *Acting*, good *Dancing*, and *Singing*, good *Scenes*, and the like, the Sickly half-got

Brat can be kept alive so long, is commonly the grand Day; then you may observe the general Humours of the *House*. In one part of it you'll see the *Judges*, and the *Wits*, with abundance of Hangers-on, and *Interlopers*, censuring and mistaking the *Scene*, if there be any, for the *Non-sence*; 't is ten to one if there be any Part above the rest, but some of these pretending *Coxcombs* unluckily pitch upon that, for their Subject to laugh at: the Reason of this is very plain, perhaps they may know a little of the *Merry Andrew* Parts, the dull *Jokes* and *Drolls*, which at best are but the Rubbidge and Lumber of the *Play*; but for the Flights and *Extasies*, and the shining Parts of it, those are utterly out of their Element; and so consequently they are forc'd to damn and censure 'em in course, because they don't understand 'em; the poor Poet must be confounded and maul'd, and, what's worse, if there be e're a *Phanatick* that sets up for a Judge, if there's but a few accidental Expressions, that don't exactly square with his Opinion, and Inclination, the whole *Play*, upon the score of one single Character or Paragraph, must be esteem'd a *Satyr* against the Government, and have an *Embargo* laid upon it and the poor Author be doom'd as an Enemy to the Publick, to be taken into Custody, and whipt, &c. This, within the compass of my own Knowledge, has been the Fate of some of 'em; and indeed I have known One of the best *Tragedies* that ever was writ, stopt upon such a Peque. In another part of the House sit the *Poet's* Friends, which are resolv'd to carry him off, right or wrong; 't is no matter to them, whether the *Play* be well or ill done, they're engag'd either for Friendship, Interest, or else by a Natural Spirit of Contradiction, to oppose the other Faction; and those you'll observe stradling upon the Seats, hollowing, clapping, and flouncing, and making such an impertinent Clatter and Noise, and using so many insolent and indecent Actions, that I advise you as a Friend, to keep as far from 'em as you can. But, what's worse still, perhaps, in the very nick of all, comes in a drunken Lord, with a Party of *Low Country* Warriours; or, what's more common, a Country *Squire*, that has lately taken up the Noble Profession of Scowring and Revelling; and to shew their Parts and their Courage, raise a Quarrel, and put the whole House into a Hurly-burly; then you'll see fine Work, indeed; the *Whores* tumbling over the Seats, and the poor *Squires* and *Beaus* tumbling after 'em in a horrible fright, and disorder; the whole *Pit's* in Arms in a Minute, and every Man's Sword drawn, to defend himself; so that if the Uproar be not instantly supprest, 't is great odds but there's some body murder'd. These Insurrections, I confess, don't often happen, and 't is well they do not; for if they shou'd, they might ev'n play by themselves: for, who but a mad Man would run the risque of being stab'd, or trode to Death, to gratify himself with an empty, insignificant Curiosity? And, indeed, most of our *Novel Farces* have little else, but barely that to recommend 'em.

25. FOREIGN IMPORTATIONS

BOTH COMPANIES developed financial difficulties. Through the importation of foreign singers and dancers, Rich and Betterton tried to attract the fickle multitude, but, as these foreign artists were exorbitantly expensive, they reaped only small profits. A passage from Cibber's *Apology* followed by another from *A Comparison* will illuminate the situation:

But Theatrical Favour, like Publick Commerce, will sometimes deceive the best Judgments, by an unaccountable change of its Channel; the best Commodities are not always known to meet with the best Markets. To this Decline of the Old Company, many Accidents might contribute; as the too distant Situation of their Theatre; or their want of a better, for it was not, then, in the condition it now is; but small, and poorly fitted up, within the Walls of a Tennis *Quaree* Court, which is of the lesser sort. [Barton] Booth, who was then a young Actor, among them, has often told me of the Difficulties *Betterton,* then, labour'd under, and complain'd of: How impracticable he found it, to keep their Body to that common Order, which was necessary for their Support; of their relying too much upon their intrinsick Merit; and though but few of them were young, even when they first became their own Masters, yet they were all now, ten Years older, and consequently more liable to fall into an inactive Negligence, or were only separately diligent, for themselves, in the sole Regard of their Benefit-Plays; which several of their Principals, knew, at worst, would raise them Contributions, that would more than tolerably subsist them, for the current Year. But as these were too precarious

Expedients, to be always depended upon, and brought in nothing to the general Support of the Numbers, who were at Sallaries under them; they were reduc'd to have recourse to foreign Novelties; *L'Abbée*, [Jean] *Balon*, and Mademoiselle *Subligny*, three of the, then, most famous Dancers of the *French* Opera, were, at several times, brought over at extraordinary Rates, to revive that sickly Appetite, which plain Sense, and Nature had satiated. But alas! there was no recovering to a sound Constitution, by those mere costly Cordials; the Novelty of a Dance was but of a short Duration, and perhaps hurtful, in its consequence; for it made a Play, without a Dance, less endur'd, than it had been before, when such Dancing was not to be had. But perhaps, their exhibiting these Novelties, might be owing to the Success we had met with, in our more barbarous introducing of *French* Mimicks, and Tumblers, the Year before. . . .While the Crowd, therefore, so fluctuated, from one House, to another, as their Eyes were more, or less regaled, than their Ears, it could not be a Question much in Debate, which had the better Actors.

✓ ✓ ✓

Crit. . . . I look upon the *Drama* to be in a very wretched condition, when it can't subsist without those absurd and foreign Diversions. . . .

Sull. It has always been the Jest of all the Men of Sense about Town; not that the Fellows perform'd ill, for in their way they did admirably; but that the Stage that had kept it's purity a hundred Years (at least from this Debauchery) shou'd now be prostituted to Vagabonds, to Caperers, Eunuchs, Fidlers, Tumblers and Gipsies.

Crit. Oh what a charming Sight 'twas to see *Madam* — What a pox d'ee call her? — *the high* German *Buttock* — swim it along the Stage between her two Gipsie Daughters: they skated along the Ice so cleaverly, you might ha' sworn they were of right *Dutch* extraction.

Sull. And the *Sieur Allard* —.

Cri. Ay, the *Sieur* with a pox to him — and the two *Monsieurs* his Sons — Rogues that show at *Paris* for a Groat a piece, and here they were an entertainment for the Court and his late Majesty.

Ramb. Oh — *Harlequin* and *Scaramouch.*

Cri. Ay; What a rout here was with a Night piece of *Harlequin* and *Scaramouch?* with the Guittar and the Bladder! What jumping over Tables and Joint-Stools! What ridiculous Postures and Grimaces! and what an exquisite Trick 'twas to straddle before the Audience, making a thousand damn'd *French* Faces, and seeming in labour with a monstrous Birth, at last my counterfeit Male Lady is delivered of her two Puppies *Harlequin* and *Scaramouch.*

Sull. And yet the Town was so fond of this, that these Rascals brought the greatest Houses that ever were known: 'Sdeath I am scandaliz'd at these little things; I am asham'd to own my self of a Country where the Spirit of Poetry is dwindled into vile Farce and Foppery.

Ramb. But what have you to say to *Madame Ragonde* and her *Eight Daughters?* I assure you I think *Nivelong* a very humorous Dancer.

Sull. Not quite so ridiculous as t'other, but altogether as unnecessary: Some things by the courtesie of *England* may be forgiven tho' not justify'd; a Song or a Dance may be introduced into a Play as part of the Play; there ought to be some connexion and affinity between 'em; but when these are lug'd in by the Head and Shoulders without any relation to the Play, I take 'em to be unnatural and monstrous.

Cri. I'll tell you, Gentlemen, what I have known in my time: The late *Duke of Monmouth* was a good judge of dancing, and a good Dancer himself; when he returned from *France,* he brought with him St. *Andre,* then the best Master in *France*: The *Duke* presented him to the Stage, the Stage to gratifie the *Duke* admitted him, and the *Duke* himself thought he wou'd prove a mighty advantage to 'em, tho' he had no body else of his Opinion: A Day was publish'd in the Bills for him to dance, but no one more, besides the *Duke* and his Friends came to see him; the reason was, the Plays were then so good, and *Hart* and *Mohun* acted 'em so well, that the Audience wou'd not be interrupted for so short a time tho' 'twas to see the best Master in *Europe.*

Sull. 'Twas otherwise lately with *Balon*; the Town ran mad to see him, and the prizes were rais'd to an extravagant degree to bear the extravagant rate they allow'd him.

Cri. 'Tis that I lament; 'tis an evident sign of the degeneracy of our Plays.

Ramb. But above all commend me to *Signior Clemente* — he got more by being an *Eunuch* than if he had the best Back in Christendom; the Ladies paid more for his Caponship than they wou'd ha' done for his virility.

Cri. I never knew the Ladies so far out of their Wits; they used to have some regard for a Man's Capacity another way: The Cry used to run, like the Ladies against *Horner* in the *Country Wife, Oh fie upon him filthy Fellow — nasty Fellow — good Sr.* Thomas *don't leave us with this Sign of a Man here, this no Man: An Hermophrodite with two Sexes is better than he, he has no Sex at all.*

Sull. But this Evil increases upon us every Day; there are more of the *Circumcision* come over lately from *Italy.*

Cri. Nay the frolick will go on that's certain: The Women have been hewn down by brawny Soldiers all the War; and for variety they'll now take up with Boys. We are so fond of every thing that comes from *France* or *Italy.*

26. COMEDIANS *VERSUS* TRAGEDIANS

THE MORALE within the "commonwealth" of Betterton's players soon reached a very low level, and the actors at Drury Lane were in constant revolt against the regime of the highhanded Rich. In both houses there were internal dissensions, and Cibber, then an actor under Rich, observed how personal animosities among the players were kindled even by their costumes:

The Tragedians seem'd to think their Rank as much above the Comedians, as in the Characters they severally acted; when the first were in their Finery, the latter were impatient, at the Expence; and look'd upon it, as rather laid out, upon the real, than the fictitious Person of the Actor; nay, I have known, in our own Company, this ridiculous sort of Regret carried so far, that the Tragedian has thought himself injured, when the *Comedian* pretended to wear a fine Coat! I remember *Powel*, upon surveying my first Dress, in the *Relapse*, was out of all temper, and reproach'd our Master in very rude Terms, that he had not so good a Suit to play *Caesar Borgia* in! tho' he knew,

at the same time, my Lord *Foppington* fill'd the House, when
his bouncing *Borgia* would do little more than pay Fiddles, and
Candles to it: And though a Character of Vanity, might be
supposed more expensive in Dress, than possibly one of Ambition; yet the high Heart of this heroical Actor could not bear,
that a Comedian should ever pretend to be as well dress'd as
himself. Thus again on the contrary, when *Betterton* proposed
to set off a Tragedy, the Comedians were sure to murmur at
the Charge of it: And the late Reputation which *Dogget* had
acquired, from acting his *Ben*, in *Love for Love*, made him a
more declared Male-content on such Occasions; he over-valued
Comedy for its being nearer to Nature, than Tragedy; which
is allow'd to say many fine things, that Nature never spoke, in
the same Words; and supposing his Opinion were just, yet he
should have consider'd, that the Publick had a Taste, as well
as himself; which, in Policy, he ought to have complied with.
Dogget however, could not, with Patience, look upon the costly
Trains and Plumes of Tragedy, in which knowing himself to
be useless, he thought were all a vain Extravagance: And when
he found his Singularity could no longer oppose that Expence,
he so obstinately adhered to his own Opinion, that he left the
Society of his old Friends, and came over to us at the *Theatre-
Royal.*

27. NEW COSTUMES

IN MATTERS of stage costume, the Restoration age must be called careless by anyone who chooses to insist on historically accurate costuming.
We are indebted to John Downes, Restoration prompter, for information
on this subject. In his *Roscius Anglicanus*, published in 1708, he recorded the rare occasions when plays were "new cloath'd" and provided
with new scenery. Occasionally, the new costumes were lent or given
by persons of the first rank to their most favored actors:

The Adventures of five Hours, Wrote by the Earl of *Bristol*,
and Sir *Samuel Tuke*: This Play being Cloath'd so Excellently
Fine in proper Habits, and Acted so justly well. . . .
King *Henry* the *8th*, This Play, by Order of Sir *William
Davenant*, was all new Cloath'd in proper Habits: The King's

was new, all the Lords, the Cardinals, the Bishops, the Doctors, Proctors, Lawyers, Tip-staves, new Scenes: The part of the King was so right and justly done by Mr. *Betterton,* he being Instructed in it by Sir *William,* who had it from Old Mr. *Lowen,* that had his Instructions from Mr. *Shakespear* himself. . . .

King *Henry* the 5th, Wrote by the Earl of *Orrery.* . . . This Play was Splendidly Cloath'd: The King, in the Duke of *York*'s Coronation Suit: *Owen Tudor,* in King *Charle*'s: Duke of *Burgundy,* in the Lord of *Oxford*'s and the rest all New. . . .

The Impertinents, or Sullen Lovers, Wrote by Mr. *Shadwell.* . . . This Play had wonderful Success, being Acted 12 Days together, when our Company were Commanded to *Dover,* in *May* 1670. The King with all his Court, meeting his Sister, the Dutchess of *Orleans* there. This Comedy and Sir *Solomon Single* [a comedy by John Caryl], pleas'd Madam the Dutchess, and the whole Court extremely. The *French* Court wearing then Excessive short Lac'd Coats; some Scarlet, some Blew, with Broad wast Belts; Mr. *Nokes* having at that time one shorter than the *French* Fashion, to Act Sir *Arthur Addle* in; the Duke of *Monmouth* gave Mr. *Nokes* his Sword and Belt from his Side, and Buckled it on himself, on purpose to Ape the *French*: That Mr. *Nokes* lookt more like a Drest up Ape, than a Sir *Arthur.* . . .

The Tragedy of *Macbeth,* alter'd by Sir *William Davenant*; being drest in all it's Finery, as new Cloath's, new Scenes, Machines, as flyings for the Witches; with all the Singing and Dancing in it.

28. DISPUTE OVER A VEIL

SUCH LAVISH FINERY, however, was rather exceptional. As a rule, the players, aided by the wardrobe keeper, selected from the available stock of the theater whatever they thought would be becoming to them. One actress might set her heart on a certain veil also desired by another actress. What happened in cases like this only the anonymous author of *The History of the English Stage* can tell:

Once at the acting the last scene of this play [*Alexander the Great*], Miss Barry wounded Miss Boutel (who first played the part of Statira) the occasion of which I shall here recite. Miss Boutel was likewise a very considerable actress; she was low of stature, had very agreeable features, a good complexion, but a childish look. Her voice was weak, though very mellow; she generally acted the young innocent lady whom all the heroes are mad in love with; she was a favourite of the town; and, besides what she saved by playing, the generosity of some happy lovers enabled her to quit the stage before she grew old.

It happened these two persons before they appeared to the audience, unfortunately had some dispute about a *veil* which Miss Boutel by the partiality of the property-man obtained; this offending the haughty Roxana, they had warm disputes behind the scenes, which spirited the Rivals with such a natural resentment to each other, they were so violent in performing their parts, and acted with such vivacity, that Statira on hearing the King was nigh, *begs the Gods to help her for that moment*; on which Roxana hastening the designed blow, struck with such force, that though the point of the dagger was blunted, it made way through Miss Boutel's stays, and entered about a quarter of an inch in the flesh.

This accident made a great bustle in the house, and alarmed the town; many different stories were told; some affirmed, Miss Barry was jealous of Miss Boutel and Lord Rochester, which made them suppose she did it with design to destroy her; but by all that could be discovered on the strictest examination of both parties, it was only the *veil* these two ladies contended for and Miss Barry being warmed with anger, in her part, she struck the dagger with less caution, than at other times.

29. A VISIT TO A RESTORATION DRESSING ROOM

THE CONVENTIONALITY of the heroic costume and the players' make-up may be studied from an anonymous satire, which leads us into the dressing room of Dorset Garden (1699):

> But next the Tiring-Room survey and see
> False Titles, and promiscuous Quality,
> Confus'dly swarm from Heroes and from Queens,
> To those that swing in Clouds, and fill Machines;
> Their various Characters they choose with Art,

The frowning Bully fills the Tyrant's Part:
Swoln Cheeks and swagging Belly make a Host,
Pale Meagre Looks, and Hollow Voice, a Ghost;
From careful Brows, and heavy down-cast Eyes,
Dull Cits, and thick-scull'd Aldermen arise. . . .
    Above the rest the Prince with haughty stalks,
Magnificent in Purple Buskins walks:
The Royal Robes his awfull Shoulders grace
Profuse of *Spangles* and of *Copper-Lace*:
Officious Vassals to his mighty Thigh,
Guiltless of Blood th'unpointed Weapon tye;
Then the Gay Glittring Diadem put on,
Pondrous with Brass, and starr'd with Bristol-Stone.
His Royal Consort next consults her Glass,
And out of Twenty Boxes culls a Face;
The Whit'ning first her Ghastly Looks besmears,
All Pale and Wan th'unfurnisht Form appears;
Till on her Cheeks the blushing Purple glows,
The Prince then enters on the Stage in State,
Behind a Guard of Candle-Snuffers wait:
There swoln with Empire, terrible and fierce,
He shakes the Dome, and tears his Lungs with Verse:
His Subjects tremble, and submissive Pit
Wrapt up with silence and Attention sit;
Till freed at length, he lays aside the Weight
Of Publick Business and Affairs of State,
Forgets his Pomp, dead to Ambitious Fires,
And to some peacefull *Brandy-Shop* retires,
Here in full Gills his anxious Thoughts he drowns,
And quaffs away the Care that waits on Crowns.
And a false *Virgin Modesty* bestows;
Her ruddy Lips, the deep Vermilion dyes;
Length to her Brows the Pencil Touch supplies,
And with black bending Arches shades her Eyes.
Well pleas'd, at last the Picture she beholds,
And spots it o'er with Artificial molds;
Her Countenance compleat, the Beau she warms
With Looks not hers, in spight of Nature's Charms.
    Thus artfully their persons they disguise,
Till the last Flourish bids the Curtain rise.

30.   TRADITIONAL HEROIC COSTUME

THE FIRST eighteenth-century attack on the artificiality of the tragic costume and the conventional handling of supernumeraries came from the pen of Addison in *The Spectator* (1711):

Among all our tragic artifices, I am the most offended at those which are made use of to inspire us with magnificent ideas of the persons that speak. The ordinary method of making an hero is to clap a huge plume of feathers on his head which rises so very high that there is often a greater length from his chin to the top of his head than to the sole of his foot. One would believe that we thought a great man and a tall man the same thing. This very much embarrasses the actor, who is forced to hold his neck extremely stiff and steady all the while he speaks; and not withstanding any anxieties which he pretends for his mistress, his country, or his friends, one may see by his action that his greatest care and concern is to keep the plume of feathers from falling off his head. For my own part, when I see a man uttering his complaints under such a mountain of feathers, I am apt to look upon him rather as an unfortunate lunatic than a distressed hero. As these superfluous ornaments upon the head make a great man, a princess generally receives her grandeur from those additional encumbrances that fall into her tail: I mean the broad sweeping train that follows her in all her motions and finds constant employment for a boy who stands behind her to open and spread it to advantage. I do not know how others are affected at this sight, but I must confess, my eyes are wholly taken up with the page's part; and, as for the queen, I am not so attentive to anything she speaks as to the right adjusting of her train, lest it should chance to trip up her heels or incommode her as she walks to and fro upon the stage. It is, in my opinion, a very odd spectacle to see a queen venting her passion in a disordered motion, and a little boy taking care all the while that they do not ruffle the tail of her gown. The parts that the two persons act on the stage at the same time are very different. The princess is afraid lest she should incur the displeasure of the king her father, or lose the hero her lover, whilst her attendant is only concerned lest she should entangle her feet in her petticoat. . . .

Another mechanical method of making great men, and adding dignity to kings and queens, is to accompany them with halberts and battle-axes. Two or three shifters of scenes, with the two candle-snuffers, make up a complete body of guards upon the English stage; and by the addition of a few porters dressed in red coats, can represent above a dozen legions. I have sometimes seen a couple of armies drawn up together upon the stage, when the poet has been disposed to do honour to his generals. It is impossible for the reader's imagination to multiply twenty men into such prodigious multitudes, or to fancy that two or three hundred thousand soldiers are fighting in a room of forty or fifty yards in compass. . . .

I should therefore, in this particular, recommend to my countrymen the example of the French stage, where the kings and queens always appear unattended, and leave their guards behind the scenes. I should likewise be glad if we imitated the French in banishing from our stage the noise of drums, trumpets, and huzzas; which is sometimes so very great that when there is a battle in the Haymarket Theatre, one may hear it as far as Charing Cross. . . .

The tailor and the painter often contribute to the success of a tragedy more than the poet. Scenes affect ordinary minds as much as speeches; and our actors are very sensible that a well-dressed play has sometimes brought them as full audiences as a well-written one. The Italians have a very good phrase to express this art of imposing upon the spectators by appearances. They call it *fourberia della scena,* the knavery or trickish part of the drama. But however the show and outside of the tragedy may work upon the vulgar, the more understanding part of the audience immediately see through it and despise it.

31. THE HAYMARKET THEATRE

THE BETTERTONIANS were seriously handicapped by the poor location and the smallness of their playhouse. Moreover, Betterton was unable to keep his players in check. When the Drury Lane competition grew too strong, he transferred his manager's license to John Vanbrugh (1704). With the financial help of aristocratic subscribers, Vanbrugh built a new playhouse, the Theatre in the Haymarket, which opened on April 9, 1705. The new building was an acoustic misfit and was ultimately abandoned as a home for legitimate drama. Cibber summarized the critical voices:

These elder Actors . . . having only the fewer, true Judges to admire them, naturally wanted the Support of the Crowd, whose Taste was to be pleased at a cheaper Rate, and with coarser Fare. To recover them therefore, to their due Estimation, a new Project was form'd, of building them a stately Theatre, in the *Hay-Market*, by Sir *John Vanbrugh*, for which he raised a Subscription of thirty Persons of Quality, at one hundred Pounds each, in Consideration whereof every Subscriber, for his own Life, was to be admitted, to whatever Entertainments should be publickly perform'd there, without farther Payment for his Entrance. . . . Almost every proper Quality, and Convenience of a good Theatre had been sacrificed, or neglected, to shew the Spectator a vast, triumphal Piece of Architecture! And that the best Play, for the Reasons I am going to offer, could not but be under great Disadvantages, and be less capable of delighting the Auditor, here, than it could have been in the plain Theatre they came from. For what could their vast Columns, their gilded Cornices, their immoderate high Roofs avail, when scarce one Word in ten, could be distinctly heard in it? Nor had it, then, the Form, it now stands in, which Necessity, two or three Years after, reduced it to: At the first opening it, the flat Ceiling, that is now over the Orchestre, was then a Semi-oval Arch, that sprung fifteen Feet higher from above the Cornice: The Ceiling over the Pit too, was still more raised, being one level Line from the highest back part of the upper Gallery, to the Front of the Stage: The Front-boxes were a continued Semicircle, to the bare Walls of the House on each Side: This extraordinary and superfluous Space occasion'd such an Undulation, from the Voice of every Actor, that generally what they said sounded like the Gabbling of so many People, in the lofty Isles in a Cathedral. The Tone of a Trumpet, or the Swell of an Eunuch's holding Note, 'tis true, might be sweeten'd by it; but the articulate Sounds of a speaking Voice were drown'd, by the hollow Reverberations of one Word upon another. To this Inconvenience, why may we not add that of its Situation; for at that time it had not the Advantage of almost a large City, which has since been built, in its Neighbourhood: Those costly Spaces of *Hanover, Grosvenor,* and *Cavendish* Squares, with the many, and great adjacent Streets about them, were then all but so many green

Fields of Pasture, from whence they could draw little, or no Sustenance, unless it were that of a Milk-Diet. The City, the Inns of Court, and the middle Part of the Town, which were the most constant Support of a Theatre, and chiefly to be relied on, were now too far, out of the Reach of an easy Walk; and Coach-hire is often too hard a Tax, upon the Pit, and Gallery.

32. THE "INCHANTED ISLAND"

TOM BROWN, brilliant hack writer and student of the dregs of London, included, among his *Amusements Serious and Comical, Calculated for the Meridian of London* (1700), a playhouse sketch which is saturated with the backstage atmosphere of a London theater at the end of the seventeenth century:

The *Play-House* is an Inchanted Island, where nothing appears in Reality what it is, nor what it should be. 'Tis frequented by Persons of all Degrees and Qualities whatsoever, that have a great deal of Idle Time lying upon their Hands, and can't tell how to employ it worse. Here *Lords* come to Laugh, and to be Laugh'd at for being there, and seeing their Qualities ridicul'd by every Triobolary Poet. Knights come hither to learn the Amorous Smirk, the *Ala mode* Grin, the Antick Bow, the Newest Fashion'd Cringe, and how to adjust their Phiz, to make themselves as Ridiculous by Art as they are by Nature.

Hither come the Country Gentlemen to shew their Shapes, and trouble the Pit with their Impertinence about Hawking, Hunting, and their Handsome Wives, and their Housewifery.

There sits a *Beau* like a Fool in a Frame, that dares not stir his Head, nor move his Body, for fear of incommoding his Wig, ruffling his Cravat, or putting his Eyes or Mouth out of the Order his *Maitre de Dance* set it in, whilst a *Bully Beau* comes drunk into the Pit, Screaming out, *Damn me,* Jack, *'tis a Confounded Play, let's to a* Whore *and spend our time better.* Here the Ladies come to shew their Cloaths, which are often the only things to be admir'd in or about 'em. Some of them having Scab'd, or Pimpled Faces, wear a thousand Patches to hide them, and those that have none, scandalize their Faces by a Foolish imitation. Here they shew their Courage by being unconcerned

at a *Husband* being *Poison'd*, a *Hero* being *Kill'd*, or a Passion-
ate Lover being Jilted: And discover their Modesties by standing
Buff at a Baudy Song, or a Naked Obscene Figure. By the Signs
that both Sexes hang out, you may know their Qualities or Oc-
cupations, and not mistake in making your Addresses. Men of
Figure and Consideration are known by seldom being there, and
Men of *Wisdom* and Business, by being always absent. The
L— D— is known by his Ribbon, and T— D— or some other
Impertinent Poet, talking Nonsense to him; the L— — by sitting
on the *Kitcat* side, and *Jacob T—* standing Doorkeeper for him;
the rest of the Witty No—ity have their several distinguishing
Characteristicks, and those that are the easiest things to be
understood in the Universe: As for instance, that *Toaster* there,
is it Possible he can give a Judgment of the Beauties of a Play,
while he is wholly taken up in Surveying those of the Ladies?
or that incorrigible Fop know any thing of the Matter, that is
taking such pains not to know himself, as to be carry'd away
with the thoughts that all Eyes were fix'd upon him on account
of his amazing Perfections, when the quite contrary cause diverts
the Audience from what they came to take a view of?

Would you think that little *Lap-dog* in Scarlet there, has
Stomach enough to digest a Guinea's worth of Entertainment at
Pontack's every Dinner-time, or that Odoriferous *Time-server*
there had nothing he so much laid to Heart, as the Disappoint-
ment of not having his Whore brought to him at the Fountain
Tavern, after the Curtain is let down again?

Hey-day! what have we here? A Dutchess, and a Dutchman
together, *Pepper* and *Vinegar* on my Conscience, only 'tis a
difficult time of the Year, and People that lye so close together,
are warm enough without any such matters to heat 'em. But that
Poet there, that shews his Assiduity by following yonder Actress,
is the most entertaining sort of an Animal imaginable. But 'tis
the way of the World, to have an Esteem for the fair Sex, and
She looks to a Miracle when She is acting a Part in one of his
own Plays. Would not any one think it pitty She should not have
an Humble Servant, when that Mrs. *Abigal* there, who is one of
her Attendants can be brought to Bed of a Living Child without
any manner of notice taken of her. Look upon him once more I
say, if She goes to her *Shift,* 'tis Ten to One but he follows her,

not that I would say for never so much to take up her *Smock*;
he Dines with her almost ev'ry day, yet She's a *Maid*, he rides
out with her, and visits her in Publick and Private, yet She's a
Maid; if I had not a particular respect for her, I should go near
to say he lies with her, yet She's a *Maid*. Now I leave the World
to Judge whether it be His or Her Fault that She has so long
kept her *Maidenhead*, since Gentlemen of his Profession have
generally *a greater Respect for the Lady's than that comes to.*

Now for that Majestical *Man* and *Woman* there, stand off,
there is no coming within a Hundred Yards of their High
Mightinesses, they have revolted like the *Dutch* from their once
Lords and Masters and are now set up for Sovereigns themselves. See what a defference is paid 'em by the rest of the
Cringing Fraternity from Fifty down to ten Shillings a week;
and you must needs have a more than Ordinary Opinion of their
Abilities: Should you lye with her all Night, She would not know
you next Morning, unless you had another five Pound at her
Service; or go to desire a piece of Courtesy of him, you must
attend longer than at a Secretary's of State. His Gravity will not
permit him to give you Audience till the Stateliness of his
Countenance is rightly adjusted, and all his high swelling Words
are got in readyness, nor will her Celebrated Modesty suffer her,
almost to speak to an Humble Servant without a Piece or two to
rub her Eyes with, and to conceal her Blushes, while She *Slug-
gishly* goes through a Vacation She might take more *Pains* in,
did she not Grudge a *Pennyworth* for a *Penny*.

There are two setts of these Histrionical Entertainers, and
I should be too partial should I not divide my thoughts equaly
between 'em, both are call'd His *Majesty's Servants*, yet neither
have done any *Service* to their *King* or *Country*: if we may take
Mr. *Collier's* word, or the Affidavits of a multitude of decay'd
Beaux who have been undone and afterwards laught at by 'em.

Do but take notice of that Scornful Piece of Flesh there,
does not She Tread the Stage as Haughtily as if She knew no
such thing as Condescention to the desires of any Man Breathing; yet She was soundly beaten by a Spark of hers, for *opening
her Legs* to *another* humble Servant. I would not for the wealth
of the *Indies* divulge any harm to her, but a Person might say
without the help of a Prophetick *Cassandra*, that it will not be

for want of shewing her endeavours for the Publick Good, that she does not bring his Majesty a New Subject into the World this Year, as she did the last. . . .

That *Beau* there is known by the decent management of his *Sword-knot* and *Snuff-box*; a *Poet*, by his empty Pockets; a *Citizen*, by his Horns and Gold Hatband; a *Whore*, by a Vizor-mask and the multitude of Ribbons about her Breast; and a *Fool*, by talking to her: A *Playhouse Wit* is distinguish'd by wanting Understanding; and a *Judge of Wit*, by nodding and sleeping till the fall of the Curtain, and crowding to get out again awake him.

I have told you already, that the *Playhouse* was the *Land of Enchantment*, the *Country of Metamorphosis*, and perform'd it with the greatest speed imaginable. Here, in the twinkling of an Eye, you shall see Men transform'd into *Demi-gods*, and *Goddesses* made as true Flesh and Blood as our Common Women. Here *Fools* by slight of hand are converted into *Wits*, *Honest Women* into *errand Whores*, and which is most miraculous, *Cowards* into *valiant Heroes*, and rank *Coquets* and *Jilts* into as chaste and virtuous *Mistresses* as a Man would desire to put his *Knife* into.

33. THE AGE OF BUSINESS

In 1698, Jeremy Collier pronounced his anathema against the residue of the Restoration theater spirit. With his ferocious *Short View of the Immorality and Profaneness of the English Stage*, the puritanical reformist "frightened those unwarrantable liberties of wit and humour from the stage which were no longer countenanced at court nor copied in the city" (Hazlitt). Comedy "stooped to conquer" what had become a graver and more businesslike turn of the English mind. In 1702, the critic and playwright, John Dennis, gave an admirable analysis of the change that had taken place in the auditorium since the days of King Charles II. A new generation of playgoers, who lacked the culture and leisure of the typical Restoration spectator, had arisen. Writers were beginning to complain about the sourness of the English temper. The age of William III saw the beginning of a national debt, the founding of the London Stock Exchange, and the birth of the "tired businessman":

In the Reign of *Charles* the Second, a considerable part of an Audience had such an Education as qualified them to judge of Comedy. That Reign was a Reign of Pleasure, even the entertainments of their Closet were all delightful. Poetry and Eloquence were then their Studies, and that human, gay, and sprightly Philosophy, which qualify'd them to relish the only reasonable pleasures which man can have in the World, and those are Conversation and Dramatick Poetry. In their Closets they cultivated at once their Imaginations and Judgments, to make themselves the fitter for conversation, which requires them both. And the Conversation of those times was so different from what it is now, that it let them as much into that particular knowledge of Mankind, which is requisite for the judging of Comedy, as the present Conversation removes us from it. The discourse, which now every where turns upon Interest, rolled then upon the Manners and Humours of Men. For let us take a little view of the state of the Nation, during the Reign of that Prince, from the year Sixty to Eighty. They were overjoy'd to find themselves delivered from the apprehensions of another Civil War, and not only in quiet, but as they thought, in profound security. They were at the same time free from Fears and Taxes, and by reason of that plenty which overflowed among them, they were in the happiest condition in the World, to attain to that knowledge of Mankind, which is requisite for the judging of Comedy. For while some were dissolv'd in the wantonness of ease, and grown careless how they exposed themselves, others were at leisure to observe their frailties, to watch the turns and counterturns of their Humours, and trace the windings of them up to their very springs. All the sheer Originals in Town were known, and in some measure copied. But now the case is vastly different. For all those great and numerous Originals are reduced to one single Coxcomb, and that is the foolish false Politician. For from *Westminster* to *Wapping*, go where you will, the conversation turns upon Politicks. Where-ever you go, you find Atheists and Rakes standing up for the Protestant Religion, Fellows who never saw a Groat in their Lives, vehemently maintaining Property, and People that are in the *Fleet* and the *Kings Bench* upon execution for their Lives, going together by the ears about the Liberty of the Subject. There is not the emptyest Coxcomb in Town, but has got his Politick Shake and his Shrug, and is pretending to wisdom by Gestures, while his Tongue, the surest Index of his Soul, declares him a very

Ass. . . . For all Men are alarmed by the present posture of affairs, because all men believe they are concerned, which universal alarm has reduced those Characters which were so various before, to a dull uniformity. For g⁻eat Fools, like great Wits, require leisure and ease to shew themselves. And as this uniformity of Characters has directly done a great deal of harm to Comedy, because our Poets, for want of Originals are forced to bring Copies, or else to draw after their own Imagination, rather than after the Life, so it has hurt it too indirectly, by the harm which it has done to Playing. . . . And I verily believe, that the want of Originals has been one great cause of the decay of acting. And the decay of this is the cause that when a good Comedy does come to be writ, it can never be lik'd because it can never be Acted, for the better a Play is acted, the better it is sure to succeed. Now an empty trifling Play can better be Acted by ill or indifferent Actors, than one that is strongly writ in Nature, because the last requires Masters.

Besides, there are three sorts of People now in our Audiences, who have had no education at all; and who were unheard of in the Reign of King *Charles* the Second. A great many younger Brothers, Gentlemen born, who have been kept at home, by reason of the pressure of the Taxes. Several People, who made their Fortunes in the late War [the war with France, 1689-1697], and who from a state of obscurity, and perhaps of misery, have risen to a condition of distinction and plenty. I believe that no man will wonder, if these People, who in their original obscurity, could never attain to any higher entertainment than Tumbling and Vaulting and Ladder Dancing, and the delightful diversions of *Jack Pudding,* should still be in Love with their old sports, and encourage these noble Pastimes still upon the Stage. But a 3d sort of People, who may be said to have had no education at all in relation to us and our Plays, is that considerable number of Foreigners, which within these last twenty years have been introduc'd among us; some of whom not being acquainted with our Language, and consequently with the sense of our Plays, and others disgusted with our extravagant, exorbitant Rambles, have been Instrumental in introducing Sound and Show, where the business of the Theatre does not require it, and particularly a sort of a soft and wanton Musick, which has used the People to a delight which is independent of Reason, a delight that has gone a very great way towards the enervating and dissolving their minds.

But thirdly, in the Reign of King *Charles* the Second, a considerable part of an Audience had that due application, which is requisite for the judging of Comedy. They had first of all leisure to attend to it. For that was an age of Pleasure, and not of Business. They were serene enough to receive its impressions: For they were in Ease and Plenty. But in the present Reign, a great part of the Gentlemen have not leisure, because want throws them upon employments, and there are ten times more Gentlemen now in business, than there were in King *Charles* his Reign. Nor have they serenity, by Reason of a War [War of the Spanish Succession, 1701-1714], in which all are concerned, by reason of the Taxes which make them uneasie. By reason that they are attentive to the events of affairs, and too full of great and real events, to receive due impressions from the imaginary ones of the Theatre. They come to a Playhouse full of some business which they have been solliciting, or of some Harrangue which they are to make the next day; so that they meerly come to unbend, and are utterly uncapable of duly attending to the just and harmonious Symetry of a beautiful design. Besides, the Faction which has been so long in their Politicks is got into their Pleasures, and they refuse to be delighted with what some People write, not because they really dislike it, but only because others are pleased with it. . . .

Thus, Sir, I have shewn, that in King *Charles* the Second's time, a considerable part of an Audience were qualified to judge for themselves, and that at present a considerable part of our Audiences are not qualify'd for it. But there is an important thing behind which I have only time to hint at. That they who were not qualified to judge in King *Charles* his Reign, were influenced by the authority of those who were; and that is of the Court, which always in a peculiar manner influences the pleasures of the Gentry. And some of the most eminent young Courtiers had then an admirable taste of Comedy, as it must always happen in a Court where the Prince delights in it. But the Court of *England* at present has other things to mind than to take care of Comedy. 'Tis true, there may be several Gentlemen in it who are capable of setting others right, but neither have they leisure to do it, nor have others time to attend to them.

Chapter VIII

Venetian Comedy

Masked Venetians at the Box Office. Engraving by de Pian.
For Act III, Scene xii of Goldoni's *La putta onorata* in *Opere teatrali,*
Zatta edition, Venice, 1791.

1. IMPROMPTU ACTORS IN REHEARSAL

IN 1699, Andrea Perrucci published his *Dell' arte rappresentativa, premeditata ed all' improvviso,* an important source on all phases of improvised comedy. Perrucci's treatise enables us to reconstruct the typical rehearsal procedure of an average *commedia dell' arte* company. From the following it will become apparent that not all was left to improvisation; that there was, to begin with, a firm plot structure in the scenario (*soggetto*), and a more or less standardized comic business (*lazzi*) as well as premeditated rhetorical material (*concetti*), which, as part of their basic training, had to be mastered by all players regardless of a specialization as Pantalones, Doctors, Captains, Clowns, or Lovers:

The scenario (*soggetto*) is nothing but the tissue of scenes woven from a plot, containing abbreviated hints at an action, divided into acts and scenes, which have to be acted and spoken in an extemporaneous manner by the player. On the margin there are indications where each character has to enter, and a broken line indicates where the actors make their exits. At the top of each scenario is mentioned the place (*e.g.,* Rome, Naples, Genoa, Leghorn, etc.), where the action of the play is supposed to take place. . . .

The manager (*corago*) or most experienced actor of the troupe should rehearse (*concertare*) the scenario before it is acted, so that the players may know the contents of the play and understand where the dialogue should end, and so that they may discover, while rehearsing, where a new bit of comic business (*lazzo*) could be fitted in. The one who conducts the rehearsal, then, will have the task not only of reading the scenario, but of explaining the characters, their names and quality, the subject matter, the place of action, the various stage houses; he will have to plant the *lazzi* and all the necessary details, giving attention to those things which are needed in the play, such as letters, purses, daggers, and other properties mentioned at the end of the scenario.

For instance, he will say: "The play we are going to perform is *La Trappolaria*; the characters are Tartaglia, father of Fedelindo and master of Coviello; Policinella, a slave-dealer, and Turchetta, his slave; the courtezan Isabella with her servants, the parasite Pespice and Pimpinella; the Captain and his servant Pasquariello; Mme. Laura, wife of Tartaglia, who comes from abroad with a servant; a salesman. . . ." Then he will define the stage-houses, assigning to Tartaglia the first house on the right, to Policinella the second on the left, to Isabella the second on the right. Next he will expound the plot.

The actors must, above all, be careful not to make a mistake with regard to the country where the action is going to take place; they should realize whence they come, and for what purpose;' the proper names must be kept well in mind, since it would be a grave error and unpardonable impropriety for one actor to speak of being in Rome and another in Naples; or that the character who comes from Spain should say Germany; or for the father to forget the name of his son or the lover that of his beloved. . . .

Moreover, the actors must pay attention to the distribution of the houses, so that each player may know his own house, for it would be too ridiculous for anyone to knock at or enter into somebody else's house instead of his own: one would regard such a person as a booby or drunkard. . . .

Next, the director explains the *lazzi* and plot complications, saying: "Here such a *lazzo* is needed, there such a metaphor, such a hyperbole, or irony." In this manner he will go through all the *lazzi* and witticisms, giving the actors advice as to how to overcome individual difficulties, trying to avoid, as much as possible, improprieties, though they can sometimes not be prevented. . . .

The characters should take care not to run into each other when they enter, which can more easily happen in improvised than in premeditated plays . . . though to leave the scene upstage and to enter it down-stage is an infallible rule, unless it is changed by some necessity.

Improvised comedy has this advantage over premeditated plays: one can remedy empty and silent scenes, each player being able to continue in the tenor of the preceding scene and to talk until the entrance of the next player marks the signal for the exit of the one who has been on the stage.

After they have been told what they have to do with regard to their entrances, the treatment and termination of scenes, the actors will be able to run through the scenes and among themselves to rehearse a new *lazzo* or new material of their own invention. It will be advisable, however, not to deviate from the plot to such an extent that the actors cannot find their way back into it. It must be avoided that the audience, due to extended and obtrusive comic business, lose the thread of the plot or have difficulty in grasping it again. . . .

All the players should be assembled to listen, and the attitude that they know this comedy by heart or that they have acted it on previous occasions, should be discouraged. For it might very well be that other names and places were chosen when the actors played the same plot under a different director. . . .

After having rehearsed the scenario, the actors ought to think about bringing in something already prepared or something specially designed for the play in question . . . some fact, story, or thing, either applicable to this particular play or some universal things, which they have memorized to be used in any play, such as conceits on first entrances, desperations, dialogues, reproaches, greetings, comparisons. . . . When night is to follow upon some scene, care must be taken to indicate this in the preceding scene by saying: "It's getting dark," . . . and so also when dawn comes and morning approaches.

2. INSIDE THE OLDEST VENETIAN PLAYHOUSE

THE ENGLISHMAN, Thomas Coryat, passed through Venice in 1608, when the craze for opera had not yet reached there. He attended a performance given by *commedia dell' arte* players in an unidentified Venetian playhouse. We can speculate that this may have been the wooden theater which Andrea Palladio had built for the *Compagnia della Calza* back in 1565 and which burnt to the ground in 1630. The inauguration of this theater must have been a spectacle of regal magnificence, as we are told that Federigo Zuccheri di Sant' Angelo had made 12 designs for Montevicentino's neo-classical tragedy, *Antigono*. When Coryat visited Venice, the playhouse was obviously disintegrating, but there were many strange sights to arrest his attention:

I was at one of their Play-houses where I saw a Comedie acted. The house is very beggarly and base in comparison of our stately Play-houses in England: neyther can their Actors compare with us for apparell, shewes and musicke. Here I observed certaine things that I never saw before. For I saw women acte, a thing that I never saw before, though I have heard that it hath beene sometimes used in London, and they performed it with as good a grace, action, gesture, and whatsoever convenient for a Player, as ever I saw any masculine Actor. Also their noble & famous Cortezans came to this Comedy, but so disguised, that a man cannot perceive them. For they wore double maskes upon their faces, to the end they might not be seene: one reaching from the toppe of their forehead to their chinne and under their necke; another with twiskes of downy or woolly stuffe covering their noses. And as for their neckes round about, they were so covered and wrapped with cobweb lawne and other things, that no part of their skin could be discerned. Upon their heads they wore little blacke felt caps very like to those of the Clarissimoes that I will hereafter speake of. Also each of them wore a black short Taffata cloake. They were so graced that they sate on high alone by themselves in the best roome of all the Play-house. If any man should be so resolute to unmaske one of them but in merriment onely to see their faces, it is said that were he never so noble or worthy a personage, he should be cut in pieces before he should come forth of the roome, especially if he were a stranger. I saw some men also in the Play-house, disguised in the same manner with double vizards, those were said to be the favourites of the same Cortezans: they sit not here in galleries as we doe in London. For there is but one or two little galleries in the house, wherein the Cortezans only sit. But all the men doe sit beneath in the yard or court, every man upon his severall stoole, for the which he payeth a gazet.

3.   MOUNTEBANKS

IN THE Piazza of San Marco's Cathedral, Coryat was intrigued by the activities of strolling players on trestle stages who successfully combined variety acts with the practice of quackery:

I hope it will not be esteemed for an impertinencie to my discourse, if I next speake of the Mountebanks of Venice. . . . The principall place where they act, is the first part of Saint Marks street that reacheth betwixt the West front of S. Marks Church, and the opposite front of Saint Geminians Church. In which, twice a day, that is, in the morning and in the afternoone, you may see five or sixe severall stages erected for them: those that act upon the ground, even the foresaid Ciarlatans being of the poorer sort of them, stand most commonly in the second part of S. Marks, not far from the gate of the Dukes Palace. These Mountebanks at one end of their stage place their trunke, which is replenished with a world of new-fangled trumperies. After the whole rabble of them is gotten up to the stage, whereof some weare visards being disguised like fooles in a play, some that are women (for there are divers women also amongst them) are attyred with habits according to that person that they sustaine; after (I say) they are all upon the stage, the musicke begins. Sometimes vocall, sometimes instrumentall, and sometimes both together. This musicke is a preamble and introduction to the ensuing matter: in the meane time while the musicke playes, the principall Mountebanke which is the Captaine and ring-leader of all the rest, opens his truncke, and sets abroach his wares; after the musicke hath ceased, he maketh an oration to the audience of halfe an houre long, or almost an houre. Wherein he doth most hyperbolically extoll the vertue of his drugs and confections. . . . Though many of them are very counterfeit and false. Truely I often wondred at many of these naturall Orators. For they would tell their tales with such admirable volubility and plausible grace, even extempore, and seasoned with that singular variety of elegant jests and witty conceits, that they did often strike great admiration into strangers that never heard them before: and by how much the more eloquent these Naturalists are, by so much the greater audience they draw unto them, and the more ware they sell. After the chiefest Mountebankes first speech is ended, he delivereth out his commodities by little and little, the jester still playing his part, and the musitians singing and playing upon their instruments. The principall things that they sell are oyles, soveraigne waters, amorous songs printed, Apothecary drugs, and a Commonweale of other trifles.

4. THE VENETIAN CARNIVAL

THE ENGLISH traveller of 1608 had to be satisfied with one permanent Venetian theater. But, seven decades later, when Limojon de St. Didier visited Venice, he must have noticed the existence of 10 or 12 playhouses, most of them erected after 1637 when opera seized the imagination of the Venetians. In his report on his visit to Venice the Frenchman set Venetian theatrical life against the colorful background of the famous carnival:

Of the Carnaval

The *Carnaval* of *Venice* is so Famous all over *Europe*, that those of other Countries who are desirous to see *Venice*, wait this Opportunity, at which time this City is usually full of Strangers of all Nations, but the greatest part of them whom Curiosity brings hither find themselves deceiv'd in their Expectations; for the Beauties of the *Carnaval* doe not as they imagine consist in the Magnificence of the many Publick Shows, or in the Pompous Masquerades that are oftentimes seen in several other Parts of *Italy*. Therefore it is something difficult to say precisely, from whence proceeds that esteem which is so generally conceiv'd of the *Carnaval*; yet I am perswaded that an infinity of things concur to the rendering of it Famous; particularly the Custom of assuming any sort of Disguise, the great Liberty which all Masques every where enjoy, the inviolable Respect that is shewn them, and the great number of Diversions which are then at *Venice*.

Nothing can be more singular, than to see in a manner all the City in Masquerade, the Mothers carrying in their Arms their little Children in Disguise: Such of both Sexes as go to the Market, or to the Haberdashers for Six Penny-worth of Tape, are sure to be in Masque. The Place of Saint *Mark* is the great Theater, upon which is to be seen the chief Appearance of the *Carnaval*; for there is scarce a Masque in *Venice* that does not come here about an Hour before Sunset. . . .

The length of the *Carnaval* which begins after *Christ-mass* Holy-days, is one of the things that contribute most to render it agreeable. 'Tis likewise impossible to express what a Consternation there is throughout the whole City, especially of such Persons that wait with impatience the various Advantages of this Season; when One of the Presidents of the Council of Ten, either through Capriciousness or possibly some other Motives, forbids the use of Masquerade or at least restrains the appearance of them to the last Days of *Carnaval* only. As this Order takes away the greatest part of the Pleasures of the Season, so it may be said, That it is very rare notwithstanding the frequent threatnings to accomplish the Execution of it; especially if some Reason of State do not particularly oblige the Council to it. However they are always permitted to go in Masques to the Banque's, the Opera and Comedy.

The *Carnaval* is likewise the principal Season of the Courtisans. They Dress themselves very Neatly in their Disguises, in which they appear upon the Place of Saint *Mark,* where they endeavour to Contract new Familiarities. Yet a great part of them are Hired or retain'd for the whole time of the *Carnaval,* seeing he cannot expect to pass for a Man of Gallantry, that has not such a Companion in this time of Diversion, in which it is accounted Honourable to appear with a Lady at the Opera, Play-House, Ball, and all other Places of Diversion. . . .

Of the Opera

At *Venice* they Act in several Opera's at a time: The Theaters are Large and Stately, the Decorations Noble, and the Alterations of them good: But they are very badly Illuminated; the Machines are sometimes passable and as often ridiculous; the number of Actors is very great, they are all very well in Clothes; but their Actions are most commonly disagreeable. These Opera's are long, yet they would divert the Four Hours which they last, if they were compos'd by better Poets, that were a little more conversant with the Rules of the Theater: For in this matter their present Compositions are very deficient, insomuch they are frequently not worth the Expence that is made upon them. The Ballets or Dancings between the Acts are generally so pittiful, that they would be much better omitted; for one would imagine these Dancers wore Lead in their Shoes, yet the Assembly bestow their Applauses on them, which is meerly for want of having seen better.

The Charms of their Voices do make amends for all imperfections: These Men without Beards have delicate Voices, besides which they are admirably suitable to the greatness of the Theater. They commonly have the best Women-Singers of all *Italy,* for to get a famous Girl from *Rome* or any other Place, they do not scruple at giving Four or Five hundred Pistoles with the Charges of the Journey, and yet their Opera's last no longer than the *Carnaval.* Their Airs are languishing and touching; the whole composition is mingl'd with agreeable Songs, that raise the Attention; the Symphony is mean inspiring rather Melancholy than Gaiety: It is compos'd of Lutes, Theorbos and Harpsicords, yet they keep time to the Voices with the greatest exactness imaginable. . . .

They that compose the Musick of the Opera, endeavour to conclude the Scenes of the Principal Actors with Airs that Charm and Elevate, that so they may acquire the Applause of the Audience, which succeeds so well to their intentions, that one hears nothing but a Thousand *Benissimo*'s together; yet nothing is so remarkable as the pleasant Benedictions and the Ridiculous Wishes of the *Gondoliers* in the Pit to the Women-Singers, who cry aloud to them, *Sias tu benedetta, benedetto el padre che te genero*. But these Acclamations are not always within the bounds of Modesty, for those impudent Fellows say whatever they please; as being assur'd to make the Assembly rather Laugh than Angry.

Some Gentlemen have shewn themselves so Transported and out of all bounds by the charming Voices of these Girls, as to bend themselves out of their Boxes, crying, *Ah cara! mi Butto, mi Butto*, expressing after this manner the Raptures of Pleasure which these divine Voices cause to them. I need not omit the Priests in this Place, for according to the Example of *Rome*, they are no ways scrupulous of appearing upon the Stage in all manner of Parts, and by acquiring the Character of a good Actor they commonly get that of an honest Man. I remember once, that one of the Spectators discerning a Priest in the Disguise of an Old Woman cry'd aloud, *ecco Pre Pierro, che fa'la vecchia*. Nevertheless all things pass with more decency at the Opera than at the Comedy, as being most commonly frequented by the better sort of People. One pays Four Livres at the Door, and Two more for a Chair in the Pitt, which amounts to Three Shillings and Six-Pence *English*, without reckoning the Opera-Book and the Wax-Candle, every one buys; for without them even those of the Country would hardly comprehend any thing of the History, or the subject matter of the Composition.

The *Gentledonna*'s frequent the Opera much more than the Comedy, by reason the Diversions of that place are express'd with more Civility than those of the other: As they are, at this time allowed to dress with their Jewels, so they appear most splendidly by the means of the many lighted Tapers which are in those Boxes. Here their Lovers are employed in the Contemplation of their Charms, and they on their side shew by some Signs that

Courtesy of Presses Universitaires de France

A Venetian Playhouse at the Time of the Carnival.
(From Henry Prunières, *Cavalli et l'opéra vénitien au XVIIe siècle*,
Paris, 1931)

they are pleas'd with the assiduity of their Services: Whenever a
new Girl appears to Sing at the Opera, the principal Nobles esteem
it a point of Honour to be Master of her, and if she Sings well they
spare nothing that may accomplish the Design of getting her. One
of the *Cornaro*'s was upon one of these occasions Rival to the
Duke of *Mantua,* they both endeavour'd to exceed each other in
their Presents, yet the Charms of her Voice were not accompanied
with all those of Beauty: The *Venetian* was successful and got
the better of the Duke.

The Owners of these admirable Female Singers Print a great
many Songs in praise of 'em, which are scatter'd up and down the
Pit and Boxes, when any of 'em acquire the general Applause of
the Audience.

Of the Comedy

The Comedy is only at *Venice* in *Carnaval*-time; however, it
sometimes begins in the end of *October* or beginning of *November,* in which Month one frequently finds here three several Gangs

of *Comedians*, each infinitely worse than the other. The Theaters in which they Act, belong to the Noble *Venetians*, as likewise those of the *Opera's*, from whence they receive very considerable Profits; for they let their Boxes at such a certain Price for the whole *Carnaval*, or else so much a Day. The Profit of the Actors is only what they receive at the Door, which do's not exceed five Pence each Head. The greatest part of the Audience commonly choose the conveniency of being in Masquerade both at the *Comedy* and *Opera*. Their Dress is usually a Champain-Coat or riding Cloak, a sort of a Bonnet of a black Taffeta upon their Heads, which only permits the sight of their Nose and Eyes; over this some add a half Vizour neatly made, and cover'd with fine glaz'd Linnen: Those that wear the *Venetian* Vest with this Disguise are look'd upon for real Nobles, yet the Nobility are rarely in Masques, either at the *Opera* or *Comedy*; unless they are those that dare not approach their Mistresses, nor enjoy the satisfaction of such mutual regards, without creating to the Ladies, both troublesome and dangerous Affairs.

The young Nobility do not go so much to the Comedy to laugh at the Buffoonry of the Actors, as to play their own ridiculous Parts: They commonly bring Courtesans with them to their Boxes, where there is such a confusion and sometimes such surprizing Accidents, so contrary to the Rules of Decency, which are at least due in all Publick Places, that one must indeed see these Transactions before he can believe them. One of their most ordinary Diversions is not only to spit in the Pit, but likewise to pelt them with Snuffs and ends of Candles, and if they perceive any one decently clad, or with a Feather in his Hat, they are sure to ply him with the best of their endeavours, which they may do as being free from all notice or punishment; for the Nobles that are the Protectors of the Theater, have their Bravo's in disguise at the Doors, who are well armed, and ready to obey Orders: Besides the *Comedy* and *Opera* are look'd upon as Privilege-places, where the least Violence would be reckon'd a Crime of State.

The liberty which they in the Pit take, according to the Example of the Nobility, do's finally raise the Confusion to its utmost height. The *Gondoliers* chiefly do give their impertinent Applauses to some certain Actions of the Buffoons, that would be tolerated in no other Place; neither is it seldom that the whole

House makes such terrible Exclamations against the Actors, who are not so happy as to please, that they are forced to retire to be succeeded by others; for the continual cry is, *fuora buffoni*. The Gentlemen find this so agreeable to 'em, that even they themselves are frequently this hissing Party; and if one inquires how it comes to pass, That they are so very prudent and wise at the great *Ridotti* where they Game, and so extravagantly foolish at the *Comedy*; you are answered, That they sit at the former Place to take the hazards of Fortune, but that they come hither to divert themselves only; and as Masters, they are pleas'd to do it according to the method most agreeable to them.

Nothing can equal the Noise which is made when a Play has given satisfaction to the Assembly, or to speak more properly to the *Gondoliers*; for when they come to name the Play to be Acted the next Day, that Mob cries out *questa, questa*, play the same again, which must be of course obey'd.

5. THE SPIRIT OF TRANSFORMATION

LIMOJON de St. Didier published his book on Venice in 1680. Forty years later, an Englishman, Edward Wright, visited Italy and supplied us with colorful *Observations* on the Venetians' fondness for operatic machinery at about the time Goldoni arrived in Venice:

They are very dextrous at managing the Machinery of their Opera's. In one of them [perhaps *Nerone*, music by Orlandini] *Nero* presents *Tiridates* King of *Armenia* with a *Roman* show, of which himself makes a part. The Emperor with the Empress appear in a Triumphal Chariot, drawn by an Elephant. The Head, Trunk, and Eyes of the great Beast move as if alive, and *Tiridates* believes he is so. When, all of a sudden, as soon as the Emperor and Empress are dismounted and have taken their Seats, the Triumphal Chariot is transform'd into an Amphitheatre, and fill'd with Spectators. The Elephant falls all in pieces, and out of his Belly come a great number of Gladiators, arm'd with Bucklers, which were so many parts of the Elephant's Sides, so that he seems in a moment to be tranform'd into a company of arm'd Men, who make a Skirmish, all in time to the Musick.

We saw another Piece of Machinery. In a vast Hall were represented the four Elements, emblematically, in Picture; these opening themselves, form'd two Palaces, those of *Love* and *Hymen,* these again were transform'd into the Palace (or Temple) of *Mars,* all surrounded with Weapons of War. This Scene was so finely imagin'd, and the Lights so well dispos'd, that I think it was the most entertaining Sight I ever saw upon a Stage.

6. VENETIAN AUDITORIA

FOR INFORMATION on some organizational details concerning the Venetian theater we turn to Luigi Riccoboni's *Réflexions historiques et critiques* (1738):

The Italian Theatres are magnificent, they commonly having four Rows of Boxes, besides a lower one, which forms as it were a Partition round the Pit. There is at Venice a Theatre with seven Rows of Boxes; this is distinguished by the Title of Saint Samuel, according to the general Custom of designing their different Theatres by the Name of their respective Parishes where they are built. It is an established Custom all over Italy to sit in the Pit.

In Venice one may see a Comedy for sixteen Sols of Current Money, which is paid at the Door, where they receive a Ticket. But then, if one designs to sit, he must pay ten Sols more; but if the Pit is not full, they are suffered to stand on the Floor, towards the Bottom of the House. As to the Boxes, every Body who is admitted there must pay for a whole one to himself.

The Theatres at Venice commonly contain four and twenty, and sometimes thirty Boxes in a Row; but these Boxes can hold no more than six Persons, so that admitting they were all full, they would contain no more than fourteen hundred Persons in all. The great Theatre in Milan is one of the largest in Italy; but none of them are comparable to that of Parma, which, like those of Ancient Rome, has no Boxes, but Benches arising in form of an Amphitheatre. . . .

The Boxes are hired either for a Year or a Day. But what they call their Year begins, as we have observed before, in the Month of October, and ends on the last Day of the Carnaval. The Price of these Boxes are not fixed, it being regulated according to the Pieces that are represented; the Licencer of the Stage is the Judge how much they shall be enlarged or how much diminished; and that again is commonly regulated by the Merits of the Piece and of the Actors; the Success of a new Piece having sometimes mounted an Upper Gallery to the Price of a Sequin, or ten French Livres; a Front Box to ten Sequins, and the others in Proportion. There are very few Cities in Italy which have not more than one Theatre; they having generally two or three, and the Prices paid at the Door are commonly regulated according to the Rules that obtain at Venice.

7. SCENES AND MACHINES

RICCOBONI greatly admired the Venetian operatic staging methods, though he had to admit that, in 1738, operatic production in Venice was in the midst of a financial crisis:

As to the Decorations and the Machinery it may be safely affirmed, that no Theatre in Europe comes up to the Magnificence of the Venetian Opera; some of them will be handed down to our most distant Posterity; for Instance, the Opera entitled *The Division of the World* [*La divisione del mondo,* music by Legrenzi], which the Marquis Guido Rangoni exhibited in the Year 1675 at his own Expences, upon the Theatre of our Holy Saviour. In *The Shepherd of Amphise* [*Il pastor d'Anfrisio,* music by Pollarolo], which was presented twenty Years after upon the Theatre of St. John Chrysostome, the Palace of Apollo was seen to descend of very fine and grand Architecture, and built of Christals of different Colours which were always playing; the Lights which were placed behind these Christals were disposed in such a Manner, that so great a Flux of Rays played from the Machine that the Eyes of the Spectators could scarcely support its Brightness.

The two Bibienas, these eminent Architects and celebrated Painters now alive, have convinced all Europe, by their grand Decorations, that a Theatre may be adorned without Machinery, not only with as much Magnificence, but with more Propriety. Machines produce a magical, or, if you will, a marvellous Effect; and we are often obliged to call to Mind the Contrivance of the Theatre, and that every thing that we see is moved by Pulleys, Ropes, Springs, and Weights, in order to prevent our Senses from being imposed upon, so as to believe what we see is represented to be real. I shall give one Instance of such an Illusion.

Cato of Utica [*Catone Uticense*, music by Albinoni] is the Subject of an Opera presented upon the Theatre of St. John Chrysostome in the Year 1701. As Caesar with his Army is supposed not to be far from that Scene where the Action is laid, and that the Inhabitants of the Province had prepared an Entertainment for him upon the Banks of the River, the Ground, of the Stage represents a Field, towards the Middle of which there was hung in the Air a Globe, resembling that of the World; this Globe was observed by degrees to advance towards the Front of the Stage, to the Sound of Trumpets and other Instruments, and all this without the Spectators being able to Discern the Pulleys and Machines that directed the whole. In the Moment when it comes opposite to Caesar, it opens into three Parts, representing the then three known Parts of the World. The Inside of the Globe shines all with Gold, Precious Stones, Metals of all Colours, and contains a great Number of Musicians. Thus we see what the Contrivance of a Theatre is capable of effecting, which is artfully to conceal the Pulleys and Springs; for by means of the first Scaffold being built above the Stage, it is easy to sustain and conduct in the Air a Machine of what Weight you please; and in such a Situation a Spectator stands in need of his Reflection, to put him in Mind that all is purely the Effect of the Machinery and Disposition; but in the mean time this is what the Poet and the Musician ought to endeavour to make him forget.

8. THE SPLENDORS OF A VENETIAN OPERA HOUSE

THE SAN GIOVANNI Crisostomo Theater, whose lavish operatic productions were so highly praised by Riccoboni, was built in 1677 by the Grimani family. Opened in 1678, it became the spacious home of grand opera, where Farinelli and the Faustina were to celebrate their greatest triumphs. In 1683, M. de Chassebras de Cramailles, the Venetian correspondent of the *Mercure Galant*, informed the smart set of Paris, that had to enjoy Lully's operas in an inadequate frame, of this latest marvel of Italian theater architecture:

The Interior of the Teatro S. Giovanni Crisostomo, Venice.

The theater of St. John Chrysostome is the largest, most beautiful, and richest in the city. The auditorium is surrounded by five tiers of boxes, one on top of the other, thirty-one in each tier. They are embellished by sculptural ornaments in low and high relief, all gilded, representing various kinds of antique vases, shells, animal heads, roses, rosettes, flowers, foliage, and other types of decoration. Below and between each of these boxes are as many human figures depicted in white marble, also in relief and life-sized, holding up the pillars which form the separations between the loges. These are men with clubs, slaves, terms of both sexes, and groups of little children, all placed in such a way that the heaviest and most massive ones are below and the lightest at the top.

The upper part and the ceiling of the auditorium is painted in the form of a gallery, at one end of which, at the side of the stage, are the arms of the Grimani, and above a glorification of some fabulous divinity, surrounded by a flock of winged children who wind flowers into garlands.

The stage is thirteen *toises* and three feet [*ca.* 85 feet] in depth by ten *toises* and two feet [*ca.* 63 feet] in width, and of proportional height. Its opening is formed by a great proscenium of the height of the auditorium, in the thickness of which are four boxes on each side of the same symmetry as the others, but much more ornate. In the vault of the proscenium two figures of Fame with their trumpets appear suspended in air, and a Venus in the center caresses a little Cupid.

An hour before the opening of the theater, the painting of the Venus is withdrawn, leaving a great opening whence descends a kind of chandelier ornamented with four branches of gold and silver work. The chandelier has a height of from twelve to fourteen feet. Its trunk is a great sculptured cartouche of the Grimani coat-of-arms, with a crown of *fleurs-de-lis* and of rays surmounted with pearls. The chandelier carries four great tapers of white wax, which light the auditorium and remain lighted until the curtain is raised. Then the whole machine vanishes, and the proscenium returns to its first state. As soon as the opera is ended, this machine appears again to light the auditorium and to allow the spectators to leave at their ease and without confusion.

9. SKEPTICAL VIEW OF THE COMMEDIA MASKS

WHEN CARLO GOLDONI (1707 - 1792), after a devious career as a lawyer and diplomat, had finally cast his lot with the comedians, Venice boasted of seven playhouses. The Teatro San Giovanni Crisostomo was then the first in the city. The six other theaters, partly devoted to comedy and partly to comic opera, were: the San Samuele Theater (since 1655), the Teatro SS. Giovanni e Paolo (1638 in wood, 1654 in stone), the San Moisè (since 1639), the Sant' Angelo (1676), the San Cassiano (1637), and the San Luca (originally San Salvatore, 1661).

Theatrical life in Venice was divided into three distinct seasons: the autumn season (*stagione autunnale*), extending from the first Monday in October till December 14, when performances were suspended through Christmas; the carnival season opened on December 26 and continued to Shrove Tuesday; the post-season (*Carnevale della Sensa*), a short season, opened for the fifteen days of the Ascensiontide Fair, and was chiefly devoted to grand opera. When the Venetian theaters were closed, the companies gave performances up and down the peninsula, and it was in Verona that Goldoni joined a company of these strolling players under the management of Giuseppe Imer. As playwright-in-chief of Imer's company, Goldoni returned to his native Venice in 1734.

Goldoni had been with Imer's troupe only a few years when he began to contemplate the theatrical reforms which ultimately resulted in the abolition of *Commedia dell' arte* masks:

I imagine the reader will have no objection to listen for a few minutes to a short account of the origin, employment, and effects of the four masks. Comedy, which in all ages has been the favorite entertainment of polished nations, shared the fate of the arts and sciences, and was buried under the ruins of the empire during the decay of letters. The germ of comedy, however, was never altogether extinguished in the fertile bosom of Italy. Those who first endeavored to bring about its revival, not finding, in an ignorant age, writers of sufficient skill, had the boldness to draw out plans, to distribute them into acts and scenes, and to utter, *extempore,* the subjects, thoughts, and witticisms which they had concerted among themselves. Those who could read (and neither the great nor the rich were of the number) found that in the comedies of Plautus and Terence there were always duped fathers, debauched sons, enamored girls, knavish servants, and mercenary maids; and, running over the different districts of Italy, they took the fathers from Venice and Bologna, the servants from Bergamo, and the lovers and waiting maids from the dominions of Rome and Tuscany. Written proofs are not to be expected of what took place in a time when writing was not in use; but I prove my assertion in this way: Pantaloon has always been a Venetian, the Doctor a Bolognese, and Brighella and Harlequin, Bergamasks; and from these places, therefore, the comic personages called the four masks of the Italian comedy were taken by the players. What I say on this subject is not altogether the creature of my imagination: I possess a manuscript of the fifteenth century, in very good preservation, and bound in parchment, containing a hundred and twenty subjects, or sketches of Italian pieces, called comedies of art, and of which the basis of the comic humor are always Pantaloon, a Venetian merchant; the Doctor, a Bolognese juris-consult; and Brighella and Harlequin, Bergamask valets, the first clever and sprightly, and the other a mere dolt. Their antiquity and their long existence indicate their origin.

With respect to their employment, Pantaloon and the Doctor, called by the Italians the two old men, represent the part of fathers, and the other parts where cloaks are worn. The first is a merchant, because Venice in its ancient times was the richest and most extensively commercial country of Italy. He has always preserved the ancient Venetian costume; the black dress and the woollen bonnet are still worn in Venice; and the red under-waistcoat and breeches, cut out like drawers, with red stockings and slippers, are a most exact representation of the equipment of the first inhabitants of the Adriatic marshes. The beard, which was considered as an ornament in those remote ages, has been caricatured, and rendered ridiculous in subsequent periods.

The second old man, called the Doctor, was taken from among the lawyers, for the sake of opposing a learned man to a merchant; and Bologna was selected, because in that city there existed a university, which, notwithstanding the ignorance of the times, still preserved the offices and emoluments of the professors. In the dress of the Doctor, we observe the ancient costume of the university and bar of Bologna, which is nearly the same at this day; and the idea of the singular mask which covers his face and nose was taken from a wine stain which disfigured the countenance of a juris-consult in those times. This is a tradition still existing among the amateurs of the comedy of art.

Brighella and Harlequin, called in Italy the two Zani, were taken from Bergamo; because, the former being a very sharp fellow, and the other a stupid clown, these two extremes are only to be found among the lower orders of that part of the country. Brighella represents an intriguing, deceitful, and knavish valet. His dress is a species of livery; his swarthy mask is a caricature of the color of the inhabitants of those high mountains, tanned by the heat of the sun. Some comedians, in this character, have taken the name of *Fenocchio, Fiqueto,* and *Scapin*; but they have always represented the same valet and the same Bergamask. The harlequins have also assumed other names; they have been sometimes *Tracagnins, Truffaldins, Gradelins,* and *Mezetins*; but they have always been stupid Bergamasks. Their dress is an exact representation of that of a poor devil who has picked up pieces of stuffs of different colors to patch his dress; his hat corresponds with his mendicity, and the hare's tail with which it is ornamented is still common in the dress of the peasantry of Bergamo.

I have thus, I trust, sufficiently demonstrated the origin and employment of the four masks of the Italian comedy; it now remains for me to mention the effects resulting from them. The mask must always be very prejudicial to the action of the performer either in joy or sorrow; whether he be in love, cross, or good-humored, the same features are always exhibited; and however he may gesticulate and vary the tone, he can never convey by the countenance, which is the interpreter of the heart, the different passions with which he is inwardly agitated. The masks of the Greeks and Romans were a sort of speaking trumpets, invented for the purpose of conveying the sound through the vast extent of their amphitheatres. Passion and sentiment were not, in those times, carried to the pitch of delicacy now actually necessary. The actor must, in our days, possess a soul; and the soul under a mask is like fire under ashes.

These were the reasons which induced me to endeavor the reform of the Italian theatre, and to supply the place of farces with comedies.

But the complaints became louder and louder; I was disgusted with the two parties, and I endeavored to satisfy both; I undertook to produce a few pieces merely sketched, without ceasing to give comedies of character. I employed the masks in the former; and I displayed a more noble and interesting comic humor in the others; each participated in the species of pleasure with which they were most delighted; with time and patience I brought about a reconciliation between them; and I had the satisfaction, at length, to see myself authorized in following my own taste, which became, in a few years, the most general and prevailing in Italy.

10. PANTALONE REJUVENATED

As a theatrical innovator, Goldoni had to proceed rather cautiously because his audiences were not ready for the emergence of the soul from under the mask. But whenever he found a player in whose facial expressiveness he had confidence, Goldoni began to test his theory. He made his first experiment in 1738, when Imer's company was enriched by the engagement of the Pantalone-player, Golinetti, and the famous Harlequino, Antonio Sacchi (1708 - 1788):

Several changes took place in the company during Lent, which brought it as near the point of perfection as possible.

We changed *La Bastona,* the mother, for *La Bastona,* the daughter, an excellent actress, full of intelligence, noble in serious parts, and very agreeable in comic. Vitalba, the principal actor, was succeeded by Simonetti, who was not so brilliant as his predecessor, but more decorous, intelligent, and docile. We made an acquisition of Golinetti for a pantaloon, who was but indifferent with his mask, but admirable in the character of young Venetians without one; and we gained also Lombardi, who both in figure and talents was unrivalled in the part of the doctor. . . .

What rendered the company perfect was the acquisition of Sacchi, the famous harlequin, whose wife was tolerable in the part of secondary lovers, and whose sister, though a little extravagant in her action, performed very well in the character of waiting maid.

"I am now," said I to myself, "perfectly at my ease, and I can give loose to my imagination. Hitherto I have labored on old subjects, but now I must create and invent for myself. I have the advantage of very promising actors; but in order to employ them usefully I must begin with studying them. Every person has his peculiar character from nature; if the author gives him a part to represent in unison with his own, he may lay his account with success. Well then," continued I, "this is perhaps the happy moment to set on foot the reform which I have so long meditated. Yes, I must treat subjects of character: this is the source of good comedy; with this the great Molière began his career, and he carried it to a degree of perfection which the ancients merely indicated to us, and which the moderns have never seen equalled."

Was I wrong in encouraging myself in this manner? No: for my inclinations were fixed on comedy, and good comedy was the proper aim for me. I should have been wrong had I entertained the ambition of equalling the masters of the art; but I merely aspired to reform the abuses of the theatre of my country, and this required no great extent of learning to accomplish. Agreeably with this mode of reasoning, which seemed to me perfectly just, I cast my eyes round the company for the actor best adapted to sustain a new character to advantage. I fixed on Golinetti the pantaloon, not for the purpose of employing him in a mask which conceals the physiognomy and prevents a sensible actor from displaying the passion which he feels in his countenance, but I admired his behavior in the companies where I had seen and sounded him; I believed him possessed of qualifications for an excellent actor, and I was not mistaken.

I composed, therefore, a comedy of character, under the title of *Momolo Cortesan.* Momolo in Venetian is the diminutive of Girolamo (Jerome); but it is impossible to translate the adjective *cortesan* into any other language. This term cortesan is not a corruption of the word courtier (*courtisan*), but is rather derived from courtesy and courteous. The Italians themselves are not generally acquainted with the Venetian cortesan: hence when I committed this piece to the press, I called it *L'Uomo di Mondo,* and were I to translate it into French [Goldoni wrote his *Memoirs* in French], I should be induced to give it the title of *The Accomplished Man.*

Let us see whether I am mistaken. The true Venetian cortesan is serviceable, officious, and possessed of probity. He is generous without profusion; gay without rashness; fond of pleasure without ruining himself; he is prepared to bear a part in everything for the good of society; he prefers tranquillity, but will not allow himself to be duped; he is affable to all, a warm friend and a zealous protector. Is not this an accomplished man?

I shall be asked whether there are many of these cortesans at Venice. Yes; a tolerable number. There are people possessed of these qualities in a greater or less degree; but when we are to exhibit the character to the public, we must always display it in all its perfection.

That any character may be productive of effect on the stage, it has always appeared to me necessary to contrast it with characters of an opposite description. In this piece I introduced a rascally Venetian, who deceives strangers; and my cortesan, without being acquainted with the persons imposed on, secures them from the deceit and unmasks the knave. Harlequin is not a stupid servant in this play; he is an idle fellow who insists on his sister supporting his vices; the cortesan procures an establishment for the girl, and subjects the lazy fellow to the necessity of working for his bread. In short, this accomplished man finishes his brilliant career by marriage, and chooses among the women of his acquaintance the one with the least pretensions and the greatest share of merit.

This piece was wonderfully successful, and I was satisfied. I saw my countrymen renouncing their old relish for farces; I saw the announced reform, but I could not yet boast of it. The piece was not reduced to dialogue; and the only part written out was that of the principal actor. All the rest was outline; I had endeavored to suit the actors; but they were not all equally qualified to fill the void with skill. There was not that equality of style which characterizes the production of one author; I could not reform everything at once without stirring up against me all the admirers of the national comedy, and I waited for a favorable moment to attack them boldly with greater vigor and greater safety.

11.   SACCHI'S HARLEQUIN

AFTER Goldoni's successful trial with Golinetti, it was Sacchi's turn:

In the beginning of the comic year I gave a comedy of intrigue, entitled the Thirty-two Misfortunes of Harlequin. The execution of this fell to Sacchi at Venice; and I was certain of its success.

This actor, known on the Italian stage by the name of Truffaldin, added to the natural graces of his action a thorough acquaintance with the art of comedy and the different European theatres.

Antonio Sacchi possessed a lively and brilliant imagination; he played in comedies of intrigue; but while other harlequins merely repeated themselves, Sacchi, who always adhered to the essence of the play, contrived to give an air of freshness to the piece, by his new sallies and unexpected repartees. It was Sacchi alone whom the people crowded to see.

His comic traits, and his jests, were neither taken from the language of the lower orders nor that of the comedians. He levied contributions on comic authors, on poets, orators, and philosophers; and in his impromptus we could recognize the thoughts of Seneca, Cicero, or Montaigne; but he possessed the art of appropriating the maxims of these great men to himself, and allying them to the simplicity of the blockhead; and the same proposition which was admired in a serious author, became highly ridiculous in the mouth of this excellent actor.

I speak of Sacchi as of a man no longer in existence; for, on account of his great age, there remains only to Italy the regret of having lost him without the hope of ever possessing his equal.

My piece, supported by the actor above-mentioned, was as successful as such a comedy could be. The amateurs of masks and outlines were satisfied with me. They found more propriety and common sense in my Thirty-two Misfortunes, than in the comedies of art.

12. THE WAITING MAID'S TURN

THE waiting maid's turn came next, as Imer had acquired a promising soubrette in Signora Baccherini whom Goldoni describes:

She was a young Florentine, extremely pretty, very gay, and very brilliant, with a plump and round figure, white skin, dark eyes, a great deal of vivacity, and a charming pronunciation. She had not the skill and experience of the actress who preceded her, but she was possessed of a most happy aptitude for improvement, and she required nothing but study and time to arrive at perfection. Madame Baccherini was married as well as myself. We became friends; we were necessary to each other; I contributed to her glory, and she dissipated my chagrin.

It was an established custom amongst the Italian actors, for the waiting maids to give several times every year pieces which were called transformations, as the Hobgoblin, the Female Magician, and others of the same description, in which the actress, appearing under different forms, was obliged to change her dress frequently, to act different characters and speak various languages. Of the forty or fifty waiting maids whom I could name, not two of them were bearable. The characters were false, the costumes caricatured, the languages indistinct, and the whole illusion destroyed. What else was to be expected? for to enable a woman to support in an agreeable manner such a number of changes she must be under the real operation of the charm which is supposed in the piece. My beautiful Florentine was dying of eagerness to display her pretty countenance in different dresses.

I corrected her folly at the same time that I endeavored to gratify it. I invented a comedy, in which, without change of language or dress, she could support different characters; an affair which is not very difficult for a woman, and especially a clever woman. The title of this piece was "La Donna di Garbo" (The Admirable Woman).

13.   CAPRICIOUS AUDIENCE IN ROME

PLAYS that succeeded in Venice were not at all assured of success in other Italian cities, least of all Rome, which had its own theatrical pulse. Here the audience reactions were quite unpredictable, as we can gather from Goldoni's account of the fiasco of his *La vedova spiritosa* in the Teatro Tordinona:

All the theatres are opened in Rome on the same day, the 26th of December. I was tempted not to go, but the count had destined me a place in his box and I could not decently refuse to be present. I went accordingly, and found the house fully lighted and the curtain about to be drawn. There were, at most, not more than a hundred persons in the boxes and thirty in the pit. I had been informed beforehand that the Tordinona Theatre was the resort of coal-heavers and sailors, and that, without Punch, none of the lovers of farce would attend. Still, however, I was inclined to believe that an author sent for expressly from Venice would excite curiosity and attract spectators from the centre of the town; but my actors were sufficiently known in Rome. When the curtain was drawn the actors made their appearance, and played in the same manner as they had rehearsed. The public became impatient and asked for Punch, and the piece went on worse and worse. I could bear it no longer; I began to feel myself growing unwell, and I asked the count's permission to withdraw, which he readily granted me, and even made me an offer of his coach. I quitted the theatre of Tordinona and went to join my wife, who was in that of Aliberti. . . .

The pit of Rome is dreadful; the abbés decide in a vigorous and noisy manner; there are no guards or police; and hisses, cries, laughter, and invectives resound from all quarters of the house. But it must be owned that he who pleases the churchmen may deem himself fortunate. I was at the first representation of an opera by Ciccio di Mayo in the Teatro Aliberti, and the applauses were as violent as the censures had formerly been. A part of the pit went out at the close of the entertainment, to conduct the musician home in triumph, and the remainder of the audience stayed in the theatre, calling out without intermission, *Viva Majo!* till every candle was burnt to the socket. What would have become of me, had I remained at Tordinona till the conclusion of my piece!

Eighteenth-Century France

Inside the Comédie Française in 1726. Engraving by Joullain.
Coypel's frontispiece to his set of Molière drawings.

1. THE AUDITORIUM OF THE COMEDIE-FRANCAISE

ON AUGUST 8, 1680, by order of the King, the two French companies in Paris — the troupe formerly headed by Molière and the rival company at the Hôtel de Bourgogne — were united into one company. After playing at the Guénégaud Theater till 1687, the *Comédiens du Roy* finally moved into a permanent home, the Comédie-Française in the Rue Neuve-des-Fossés-Saint-Germain-des-Prés. The architect of the building was François d'Orbay. The theater was opened on April 18, 1689. The sloping stage, with a depth of 41 feet and a width of 54 feet, had six flat wings on either side. The scene changes — what few there were — were executed by means of the chariot system. The stage projected 12 feet beyond the proscenium line. At the front of this apron were the footlights, to the left and right of the prompter's hood. On either side of the apron, in front of the stage boxes (*balcons*), were five rows of benches for stage spectators. The acting area — not wider than 15 feet at the front and 11 feet at the rear — was railed off against the benches by balustrades. The auditorium (length: 71 feet) had an open U-shape. There was an orchestra pit, whose central section only was reserved for the musicians, as spectators were seated on either side. Bordering on the orchestra was the traditional standing pit, backed by seven rows of benches (the *amphithéâtre*), which gradually led up to the first row of boxes. There were two tiers, each with 19 boxes (5 x 4 feet). The third gallery was open and equipped with benches. D'Orbay's design was severely criticized, especially for the poor sight lines from the boxes. With the guidance of Riccoboni we may enter the Comédie-Française as it appeared in the first half of the eighteenth century:

The Theatres of France are built almost in the same Form with those of Italy, which were the Models of all the rest in Europe, except that beyond the Pit, there is a place a little elevated, called the Amphitheatre. This Amphitheatre has Seats, and is sunk a little lower than the first Row of Boxes, that all the Spectators may have the same free and open View of the Stage. There is also at the Foot of the Theatre a kind of Area, called the Orchestrum, which was formerly designed for the Music, but by contracting their Accommodation, the Spectators may now have Seats there. The Entry to it is below the Theatre, and it accommodates about forty or fifty Persons, who pay the same Price with the Stage; and when the House is thronged, the Wom-

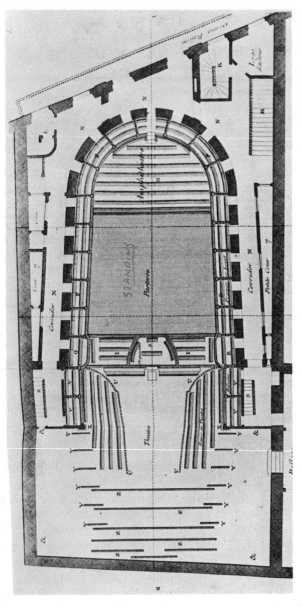

Ground Plan of the Comédie Française.

The plan shows the benches for stage spectators, the standing pit, and the seated *amphithéâtre*. François d'Orbay was the architect of the building in the Rue Neuve-des-Fossés-Saint-Germain-des-Prés (1689).

en sit in it on little Seats without Backs, just as they do in the Amphitheatre. The Theatres here are very small, having only three Ranges of Boxes. There are not here (as in Italy) five or six Rows of Boxes; and the largest Pit in France contains no more than five or six hundred persons standing, and very much crowded. . . .

The Play-house has two Street-doors, one leading to the Pit only, the other to all the other Divisions of the House. On one Side of these Entrances there is a Place with Bars, thro' which the Spectator receives a Ticket that introduces him either to the Pit or the other Places, and the Ticket is commonly marked with the Name of the Seat that is paid for. The Receiver of this, upon delivering it at the Inner-Door of the Play-house, gets another there, marked *Counter-marque,* with the Name of the Place he is entitled to. These Tickets are again delivered to the People who are placed to open the Boxes, to see the Company seated in them, and then to shut them up as soon as they contain eight Persons, that is, four upon the fore and four upon the back Seat. Thus eight may be in one Box, Men and Women, and none of them know one another. But the Truth is, that sometimes it is very troublesome Sitting there on account of the Lady's Hoops; therefore to avoid the Inconvenience, the Ladies commonly send in the Morning, or the Night before, to bespeak a Box for themselves. Each first Box is equivalent to eight Places, and amounts to thirty two Livres, and they who hire it reserve it wholly to themselves. The second Row pays in proportion sixteen Livres, and with regard to the third, as they are upon a level with the Gallery, no Place can be kept there, but by sending a Servant without Livery to keep one, as is done on the Stage and Orchestrum, &c.

The first Front-Box on the right-hand is called the King's Box; and all the Range on that Side to the Bottom of the Playhouse is called the King's Side. The first Front-Box on the lefthand is called the Queen's Box, and all the Range on that Side is called the Queen's Side; and indeed these Boxes are set aside for the King and Queen, whenever their Majesties honour the Play-house with their Presence, which happens very seldom, because there is a Play-house at Court where the Players act as often as they receive Orders.

If the Princes and Princesses of the Blood come to the Playhouse, their Birth entitles them to the principal Boxes, even tho' they may be hired by private People, who are in that Case obliged to take up with inferior Boxes. The Princes of the Blood commonly sit upon the Stage, and then the Players make a Pause in the Action, and all the Spectators rise out of Respect, and the Princes place themselves in the first Seat, which is yielded by whoever possess it; and when the Play is done, the Player who gives out the next Play makes a profound Reverence to them, and with all due respect craves their Permission to give it out.

2. MICHEL BARON

MICHEL BARON (1653 - 1729) was the chief tragedian of the united company. In 1691, however, at the peak of his career, Baron retired from the stage for unknown reasons, and his parts were assumed by Pierre Beaubour (1662 - 1725), who indulged in unrestrained declamatory delivery, while a new tragedienne, Marie-Anne de Chasteauneuf, called Mlle. Duclos (*ca.* 1668 - 1748), surpassed her predecessor, Mlle. Champmeslé, in chanting singsong style. On April 10, 1720, at the age of 67, Baron returned to the stage to resume the parts he had played when a young man. He introduced a new acting style and a type of delivery which, when compared with that of Beaubour and Mlle. Duclos, struck his contemporaries as very natural, but which we might call restrained and subdued in the Bettertonian sense. Charles Collé, who in his youth had seen the aged Baron on the stage, gave a description of him in his *Journal et Mémoires*:

Baron and Mlle. Lecouvreur . . . whom I saw, even though I am not yet very old, have given me an idea of perfection, especially Baron, who sometimes lacked only warmth in order to be the most accomplished actor that ever could have existed. One must even suppose that he had had this essential quality of an actor when he was young. When I saw him, he was already 72 or 75 years old, and at that age he could be forgiven for not entering into a passion as spiritedly as an actor of thirty years could have done. He made up for this deficiency by an intelligence, a nobility, and a dignity such as I have seen only in him. He excelled particularly in the details of a role. He had a naturalness which verged on the familiar, even in tragedy, without thereby detracting from its grandeur. He was no less excellent in comedy; I have seen him play sublimely the roles of the Misanthrope, of Arnolphe, and of Simon in *Andrienne*; there was such great truth in his acting and so much naturalness that invariably he made you forget the actor, and he carried the illusion to the point of making you imagine that the action unfolding before you was real. He never declaimed, not even in the highest tragedy, and he broke the rhythm of the verse in such a way that you did not feel at all the intolerable monotony of the Alexandrine. But then, beautiful verse gained nothing by him, and one was hard put to distinguish from his delivery whether he were speaking lines from Racine or La Chaussée. He never recited verse, but rather conveyed the situation, the feeling. He held pauses so long, and played so slowly that a performance would last half an hour longer when he had a part in it. Upon emerging from the wings, he became animated and spoke in low tones to himself or to the actor with whom he entered upon the stage, and by this means he appeared to live the part from the first verse he spoke. He loved theatrical pomp, and when he played the role of an emperor or a king, he always had himself preceded by eight or ten supernumeraries, dressed as Romans. . . . He was fanatical about his profession, and that is very important to success therein.

3. MLLE. LECOUVREUR

In 1717, the Comédie-Française saw the debut of Adrienne Lecouvreur (1692 - 1730) in the title role of Crébillon's *Électre*. During her short career she was a representative of *"la déclamation simple, noble et naturelle."* As a pupil of Baron she loathed chanting, and there was no greater contrast than between her and Mlle. Duclos. Mlle. Lecouvreur never spoke a line unless she was able to fill it with genuine emotion. But while the actress shunned turgidity, she never fell below heroic grandeur. Once more we turn to Collé:

Mlle. Lecouvreur, having more art than natural talent, nevertheless rendered it into truth. She handled perfectly all the details of a part, and accordingly made one forget the actress. One saw only the character she represented. She excelled more in the passages where subtlety was required than in those that stood in need of power. No one has ever played as she did the first act of *Phèdre* and the role of Monime. She fell far short of being equally good in comedy, though she enacted comic parts with spirit, intelligence, and nobility.

Mlle. Champmeslé in the
Title Role of Racine's
Phèdre.

Michel Baron as Pyrrhus
in Racine's *Andromaque.*

Mlle. Lecouvreur as Cornélie
in Pierre Corneille's
La Mort de Pompée.

Mlle. Dumesnil as
Athalie in Racine's
Athalie.

4. MLLE. DUMESNIL

MARIE-FRANÇOISE Marchand Dumesnil (1713 - 1803), having begun her career as a provincial actress, became a sharing member (*sociétaire*) of the Comédie-Française in 1737. As Phèdre, Cléopatre, Médée, Sémiramis, and, above all, in Voltaire's *Mérope*, she achieved her greatest triumphs. She acted more on the impulse of the moment than by premeditation, and her acting was uneven and capricious, though sublime when inspired. A furious impetuosity was characteristic of her. Even her future rival, Clairon, a by no means objective critic, had to admit that tragic mothers were Mlle. Dumesnil's artistic forte:

Mlle. Dumesnil was neither beautiful nor attractive; her features, her figure, her whole appearance, though without any actual defects, presented to the eye only a middle-class woman devoid of grace and elegance, one often on a level with the lowest class of people. Yet her head was well formed, her eyes expressive, imposing and, when she wished, even awe-inspiring. Her voice, lacking flexibility, was never moving; but it was strong, sonorous and adequate for the greatest bursts of passion. Her pronunciation was pure; nothing impeded the volubility of her delivery. Her gestures were often too vigorous for a woman; they had neither fullness nor mellowness, but she was at least sparing in their use. Full of warmth, of pathos, nothing was ever more winning, more touching than her personification of the distress and despair of a mother. That expression of nature rendered her acting as near the sublime as can be conceived. The passions of love, ambition, or pride were but faintly represented by her. But as she was young, zealous, and ambitious, great hopes were entertained of her emulation and future experience in her profession. Such was Mlle. Dumesnil when I began to work in the theater.

The study to which I pledged myself from the first instant, in enlightening myself on all my faults, taught me after several years of reflection to judge also those of others. I perceived that Mlle. Dumesnil sought to captivate the crowd rather than to please the connoisseurs. Outcries, singular transitions, a mode of utterance more suited to comedy than tragedy, and vulgar gestures often took the place of those terrible and touching beauties of which she had before given such eminent proofs.

5. SPECIALIST IN FURY AND PASSION

COLLÉ compared the acting of Mlle. Dumesnil with that of the Lecouvreur:

Mlle. Dumesnil, who, in tragedy, can today be compared with Mlle. Lecouvreur, plays well only the lively moments of a part, and I confess that in these passages she has more warmth and feeling than had Mlle. Lecouvreur. She goes much farther than that celebrated actress; but what a difference in every other respect! Mlle. Dumesnil plays well only passages of fury and passion. No dignity, no nobility whatsoever! She expresses love badly, pride poorly, and declaims frequently. An ignoble face, a forced bearing, an ugly voice; but in the moments where she is good, she surpasses everyone; she makes one forget all her defects.

6. MLLE. CLAIRON

AFTER THE middle of the century, Mlle. Dumesnil began to be eclipsed by Claire-Joseph Léris, known as Mlle. Clairon (1723 - 1803). Having begun as a provincial soubrette, the Clairon made her debut at the Comédie-Française on September 19, 1743. Observers found in her acting too much display ("*trop déclat*") and not enough sensibility (*sensibilité*). She belonged to the declamatory school, and Collé, in 1750, expressed his disdain:

Mlle. Clairon, who plays leading roles in tragedy, has a large following. I am very far from being one of her fans. . . . Her bombastic declamation, her chanting and frequent sighs — all this reminds me of old Duclos and is unbearable. Nevertheless, she has feeling, and sometimes renders moments of sentiment very well, although she is much inferior in that respect to Mlle. Dumesnil. But she expresses love, above all outraged love, better than the latter. She plays the part of an abandoned princess very well, Ariane, Didon, etc. She is much superior to Mlle. Dumesnil in nobility, in a pride full of intelligence, and in passages which demand little warmth and much dignity. The parts in Corneille's plays suited her well for this reason, and it was for this same reason that she made the most of the role of Fulvie in

Crébillon's *Catilina*. For the rest, a dull voice, good enough nevertheless, but monotonous and full of breathiness and, at times, of disagreeable gasps.

7. CHANGES OF STYLE

DUE TO the influence of Marmontel, Mlle. Clairon is reported to have changed her acting (and dressing) style during 1752 and 1753. Marmontel relates the story of this metamorphosis in his *Mémoires*:

I had long been in the habit of disputing with Mademoiselle Clairon, on the manner of declaiming tragic verses. I found, in her playing, too much violence and impetuosity, not enough suppleness and variety, and above all, a force that, as it was not qualified, was more akin to rant than to sensibility. It was this that I endeavoured discreetly to make her understand. "You have," I used to say to her, "all the means of excelling in your art; and, great as you are, it would be easy for you still to rise above yourself, by managing more carefully the powers of which you are so prodigal. You oppose to me your brilliant successes, and those you have procured me; you oppose to me the opinions and the suffrages of your friends; you oppose to me the authority of M. de Voltaire, who himself recites his verses with emphasis, and who pretends that tragic verses require, in declamation, the same pomp as in the style; and I can only answer I have an irresistible feeling, which tells me that declamation, like style, may be noble, majestic, tragic, with simplicity; that expression, to be lively and profoundly penetrating, requires gradations, shades, unforeseen and sudden traits, which it cannot have when it is stretched and forced." She used to reply, sometimes with impatience, that I should never let her rest, till she had assumed a familiar and comic tone in tragedy. "Ah! no, Mademoiselle," said I, "that you will never have; nature has forbidden it; you even have it not, while you are speaking to me; the sound of your voice, the air of your countenance, your pronunciation, your gestures, your attitudes, are naturally noble. Dare only to confide in this charming native talent, and I dare warrant you will be more tragic."

Other counsels than mine prevailed, and, tired of being importunate without utility, I had yielded, when I saw the actress suddenly and voluntarily come over to my opinion. She came to play Roxane at the little theatre at Versailles. I went to see her at her dressing room, and, for the first time, I found her dressed in the habit of a sultana; without hoop, her arms half-naked, and in the truth of Oriental costume: I congratulated her. "You will presently be delighted with me," said she. "I have just been on a journey to Bourdeaux; I found there but a very small theatre; to which I was obliged to accommodate myself. The thought struck me of reducing my action to it, and of making trial of that simple declamation you have so often required of me. It had the greatest success there: I am going to try it again here, on this little theatre. Go and hear me. If I succeed as well, farewell my old declamation."

The event surpassed her expectation and mine. It was no longer the actress, it was Roxane herself, whom the audience thought they saw and heard. The astonishment, the illusion, the enchantment, was extreme. All inquired, where are we? They had heard nothing like it. I saw her after the play; I would speak to her of the success she had just had. "Ah!" said she to me, "don't you see that it ruins me? In all my characters, the costume must now be observed; the truth of declamation requires that of dress; all my rich stage-wardrobe is from this moment rejected; I lose twelve hundred guineas worth of dresses; but the sacrifice is made. You shall see me here within a week playing Électre to the life, as I have just played Roxane."

It was the *Électre* of Crébillon. Instead of the ridiculous hoop, and the ample mourning robe, in which we had been accustomed to see her in this character, she appeared in the simple habit of a slave, dishevelled, and her arms loaded with long chains. She was admirable in it; and some time afterward, she was still more sublime in the *Électre* of Voltaire. This part, which Voltaire had made her declaim with a continual and monotonous lamentation, acquired, when spoken naturally, a beauty unknown to himself; for on seeing her play it on his theatre at Ferney, where she went to visit him, he exclaimed, bathed in tears and transported with admiration, *"It is not I who wrote that, 'tis she: she has created her part!"* And indeed, by the infinite shades she introduced, by the expression she gave to the passions with which this character is filled, it was perhaps that of all others in which she was most astonishing.

Paris, as well as Versailles, recognised in these changes the true tragic accent, and the new degree of probability that the strict observance of costume gave to theatrical action. Thus, from that time, all the actors were obliged to abandon their fringed gloves, their voluminous wigs, their feathered hats, and all the fantastic apparel that had so long shocked the sight of all men of taste. Lekain himself followed the example of Mademoiselle Clairon; and from that moment their talents thus perfected excited mutual emulation, and were worthy rivals of each other.

8.   VOLTAIRE ON MLLES. DUMESNIL AND CLAIRON

VOLTAIRE was one of Mlle. Dumesnil's admirers. In his *Appel à toutes les nations: des divers changements arrivés à l'art tragique* (1761), he surveyed the progress French theatrical art had made since the days when Mlle. Lecouvreur had emotionalized the Alexandrine:

Declamation, which, till the time of mademoiselle La Couvreur was a measured recitative, a noted song in a manner, obstructed still farther those outbursts of nature which are represented by a word, by an attitude, by silence, by a cry which escapes in the anguish of grief. These strokes were first made known to us by mademoiselle Dumesnil, when, in Merope, with distracted eyes and a broken voice, she, raising her trembling hand, prepared to sacrifice her own son; when Narbas stopped her; when, letting her dagger fall, she was seen to faint away in the arms of her women; when she started from this momentary death with the transports of a mother, and when afterwards, darting forward to Polyfontes and crossing the stage in an instant, she, with tears in her eyes, a face as pale as death, thick sobs and arms extended, cried out, "*Barbare, il est mon fils*;" "Wretch, he is my son." We have seen Baron, his deportment was noble and becoming; but that was his whole excellence. Mademoiselle La Couvreur had grace, just expression, simplicity, truth and dignity, combined with ease; but for the grand pathos of action, we saw the first instance of it in mademoiselle Dumesnil.

Something still superior, if possible, we have seen in mademoiselle Clairon, and the player who acts Tancred in the third act of the piece of that name, and at the end of the fifth; souls were never agitated by such violent emotions, never were tears shed in greater abundance. The perfection of the player's art shewed itself upon those two occasions with a force, of which, till then, we had no idea; and mademoiselle Clairon must be allowed to have surpassed all the painters in the kingdom.

If in the fourth act of Mahomet there had been young players who could form themselves upon this great model, a Seid who could be at once enthusiast and tender, fierce through fanaticism, humane by nature, who knew how to shudder and to weep; a Palmira animated, compassionate, terrified, trembling at the crime she is going to commit; who could feel horror, repentance, and despair at the moment the crime is committed; a father, truly so, who should appear to have the bowels, the voice, and the deportment of a father; a father, who should acknowledge his two children in his two murderers, who should embrace them shedding tears with his blood; who should mix his tears with those of his children, who should rise to clasp them in his arms, who should fall back and throw himself upon them; in fine, if there was every thing that the natural horror of death can furnish a picture with, this situation would even surpass those already mentioned.

It is but a few years since players have ventured to be what they should be, that is, living pictures; before, they declaimed.

9. DIDEROT ON TECHNIQUE *VERSUS* INSPIRATION

GARRICK pronounced Mlle. Clairon a perfect actress, though he hastened to add that when he saw Mlle. Dumesnil he did not think of her as an actress, but only of the character she was playing. While Mlle. Dumesnil played *d'âme* (Diderot), Mlle. Clairon acted *de réflexion*. In his *Paradoxe sur le comédien*, Diderot contrasted the premeditated and self-controlled acting of the one with the inspirational spasms of the other:

What acting was ever more perfect than Clairon's? Think over this, study it; and you will find that at the sixth performance of a given part she has every detail of her acting by heart, just as much as every word of her part. Doubtless she has imagined a type, and to conform to this type has been her first thought; doubtless she has chosen for her purpose the highest,

the greatest, the most perfect type her imagination could compass. This type, however, which she has borrowed from history,
or created as who should create some vast spectre in her own
mind, is not herself. Were it indeed bounded by her own dimensions, how paltry, how feeble would be her playing! When, by
dint of hard work, she has got as near as she can to this idea,
the thing is done; to preserve the same nearness is a mere matter
of memory and practice. . . . Now with Dumesnil it is a different
matter: she is not like Clairon. She comes on the stage without
knowing what she is going to say; half the time she does not know
what she is saying: but she has one sublime moment.

10.   RIVAL ACTRESSES

THE RIVALRY between Mlles. Clairon and Dumesnil caused an occasional
stir even in the highest court circles, as we can gather from the following
account in Fleury's *Mémoires*:

It was whispered that Mademoiselle Clairon intended, on the
occasion of the royal nuptials, to reappear at the Court Theatre,
in compliance with the particular wish of the Duchess de Villeroi,
with whom she was an especial favourite. In the month of April,
1770, *Athalie* had been rehearsed at the Theatre of the Comédie-
Française, in the manner in which it was to be performed at the
grand Court Theatre, on the occasion of the fêtes; that is to say,
with the choruses and all the scenic pageantry appertaining to
the piece. Mademoiselle Clairon took her part in this rehearsal,
and, it was affirmed, acted better than ever, and produced a deep
impression on a numerous and select audience. Confident that I
should have the opportunity of seeing her perform at Versailles,
I neglected to attend the rehearsal at Paris. A few days afterwards it was announced that Mademoiselle Clairon would not
play the part of Athalie, though she had already rehearsed it;
but she would make her reappearance in the part of Aménaïde.
This change was made, it was said, through the influence of Madame Dubarry, who was the patroness of Dumesnil, and who prevailed on the king not to permit Clairon to take a character
which had been appropriated by her no less celebrated rival.
Madame de Villeroi made great exertions to parry the blow
which was thus aimed at her favourite Clairon, to whom she

gave the appellation of Melpomene. This affair made a great sensation at court. Louis XV., influenced by Madame Dubarry, espoused the cause of Dumesnil; and Madame de Villeroi firmly defended Clairon. After a long series of marches and countermarches, solicitations, and intrigues, Madame Dubarry, weary of the conflict, surrendered; and the King of France and Navarre yielded to the Queen of Carthage. The result was, it was solemnly decided Mademoiselle Clairon should play the part of Athalie.

Meanwhile the fêtes of Versailles commenced. No description can convey any adequate idea of their splendour; they attracted an immense concourse of people from different parts of the kingdom and even from foreign countries. The luxury of dress, the splendour of equipages, the beauty of the court ladies, the magnificence of the *grand concert,* presented altogether a perfect scene of enchantment. The gardens of the palace were illuminated by several millions of variegated crystal lamps, which were lighted almost simultaneously, as if by the touch of a magician's wand. Some estimate of the splendour of the illuminations may be formed from the expense of the *bouquet d'artifice* [the final display of fireworks]. In the space of a few moments thirty thousand rockets were let off, each of which cost a crown. (At this time the people were beginning to reflect on the lavish expenditure of the public money. By way of animadversion on the expense of the illuminations, it was a common remark that every lamp in the gardens had been lighted with a bank note.)

At length the performance, which had been so long announced and so anxiously expected, took place at the Court Theatre, and I had the good fortune to witness it. It was a truly royal entertainment; the theatre presented a truly splendid spectacle. Athalie appeared. But no! it was not Athalie: it was not that Queen of the Jews, who is painted in such bold colours by Racine. Mademoiselle Clairon, in that night's performance, fell very far short of her high reputation; she declaimed well, but she was sadly deficient in feeling. Such, at least, was the impression she that evening produced on me, and the majority of the audience was of the same opinion. She failed to maintain her reputation; and her performance was by no means of that great and perfect kind which the occasion demanded. A general disapprobation was felt of the injustice done to Mademoiselle Dumesnil, for the sake of favouring her haughty rival, who had retired from the stage in a fit of ill humour, which gave umbrage to the public.

With respect to the effect produced by the choruses in *Athalie,* opinion was divided; they were greatly admired by some, whilst others thought they enfeebled and impeded the interest of the action: in this latter opinion I must confess I felt very much inclined to concur. However, this is a high question of art, and the experiment made, on the occasion here alluded to, was not calculated to decide it. . . .

But though the choruses generally failed to produce the expected effect, yet the representation, as a whole, was one of indescribable magnificence. The prodigious grandeur of the concluding scene, will never be forgotten by any one who beheld it. When the great temple opened, and the king of the Jews was discovered seated on his throne of gold, and five hundred Levites and warriors marched upon the stage from four different points, ten abreast, the effect was at once grand and terrific. All the ideas I had conceived of the splendour of Jerusalem, seemed realized and visible before me. . . .

The triumph which the proud Clairon gained over her rival, on the occasion above referred to, served only to stimulate the talent of Mademoiselle Dumesnil; I saw the latter play several parts at the Théâtre Français, and I thought that each successive performance increased in sublimity. Her acting was no longer marked by those inequalities which, at the commencement of her career, was perhaps her most prominent defect. She became a distinguished favourite of the public, and her well-deserved popularity soon made her forget the intrigues of Clairon. Madame Dubarry determined that she should have an opportunity of taking her revenge in the presence of the noble personages who were assembled for the dauphin's nuptials. She obtained the royal permission for the performance of *Sémiramis* at the Court Theatre, and she presented to Mademoiselle Dumesnil a superb costume for the part of the Queen of Babylon. I witnessed this performance, and the highest eulogy I can pronounce on it, is to say that it fully convinced me of the truth of an anecdote which I had previously regarded as fictitious. One evening, when Dumesnil had thrown into the character of Cleopatra a more than usual degree of that fiery energy for which she was so distinguished, the persons who occupied the front rows of the pit, instinctively drew back, shrinking, as it were, from her terrific glance. An empty space was thus left between the spectators in the pit and the orchestra.

11. THE DISCARDED PANIER

DIDEROT'S enthusiasm over the discarded panier was great, and he exhorted the actress to advance further in the direction of historic truth:

A courageous actress, Mlle. Clairon, has just discarded her hoops, and no one thinks it wrong. She will go even further, I say. Ah! what if she dared, one day, to appear on the stage in all the nobility and simplicity of dress that her parts demand! In the disorder resulting from an event as terrible as the death of a husband, the loss of a son, or similar catastrophes in a tragic scene — what might become of all these powdered, becurled, tricked-out dolls that surround a disheveled woman? Sooner or later they will have to dress the same way. Nature, Nature! You cannot resist Nature: you must either get rid of it or else obey it. Oh Clairon! I keep coming back to you. Do not let custom and prejudice get the better of you. Trust your taste and your genius. Show us Nature and truth; that is the duty of those we love.

12. COSTUME REFORM

MLLE. CLAIRON had given up the hoop and added a few oriental motifs when she acted Roxana. She had played Crébillon's and Voltaire's Electras without the customary panier, though we can be certain that Marmontel's "mere dress of a slave" was still quite a sumptuous costume. In Voltaire's *Orphelin de la Chine* (1755), the actress wanted to appear with truly Chinese apparel, though, to us, only the trousers would be faintly suggestive of the East. Most of the pseudo-Chinese costumes had been designed by Joseph Vernet whom Voltaire had asked to create costumes, neither too Chinese nor too French, so that they would not excite the audience to laughter. There was no laughter, only enthusiasm for the innovation. In her *Mémoires* Mlle. Clairon summed up her ideas about costume reform:

It is my advice to all women in general to pay the most scrupulous attention to dress: costume contributes much to the spectator's illusion, and the player takes the tone of his role from it more easily; costume exactly copied, however, is not practicable: it would be indecent and ridiculous. Draperies in the antique style set off and reveal too much nudity. (Our actresses, it seems to me, no longer fear costumes which reveal and outline; they dress like statues of antiquity in a way which taxes their shapes, doubtless through love of nature and of truth.) The dresses of antiquity are proper only for statues and paintings. But in making up for this defect, it is necessary to preserve the outlines, to indicate at least our desire to imitate and to follow, as much as possible, the luxury or simplicity of the times and places. Fillets, flowers, pearls, veils, and colored stones, were the only ornaments with which women were acquainted before the establishment of trade with the Indies, and the conquest of the New World.

I wish especially that all chiffons, all current fashions, be avoided with care. The head-dress of French women, at the moment of my writing, the massing and the monstrous arrangement of their hair, give to their whole appearance a shocking disproportion, distort their faces, conceal the movement of the neck, and give them a bold, stiff, and offensive air. The only fashion to follow is the costume of the role one is playing.

One must above all arrange his garments to suit the characters. Age, austerity, and sorrow ill accord with all that suggests youthfulness, the desire to please, and calm of soul. Hermione with flowers would be ridiculous: the violence of her character and the grief that consumes her, allow her neither preoccupation with fashion nor coquetry; she may have a magnificent dress, but an air of utter neglect of everything else must show that she is not in the least concerned about her person. The first appearance of an actress ought to prepare the audience for the character she is going to portray.

13.   CHANGES IN MAKE-UP

WHILE MLLE. CLAIRON modified costume toward ethnographic propriety — fortunately, a very relative propriety — she also paid attention to make-up and abandoned the use of liquid white which converted the

human face into a mask (a legitimate device of stylization and a crime
only on the realistic stage). In her *Mémoires* she has a chapter on this
subject:

The use of white paint is now almost general upon the stage.
This borrowed charm, of which no one is the dupe, and which
all agree in condemning, spoils and discolours the complexion,
weakens and dims the eye-sight, absorbs the whole countenance,
conceals the expressive motion of the muscles, and produces a
kind of contradiction between what we hear and what we see.

I had rather we should have recourse to the custom of using
masks, like those of the ancients. There would be at least this
advantage, that the time thrown away in painting the face might
be employed in improving the delivery.

Is it possible that an actress, whose countenance is enamelled
with paint, and, consequently, incapable of any motion, can give
expression to the passions of rage, terror, despair, love, or anger?

Every motion of the soul is expressed through the medium
of the countenance: the extension of the muscles, the swelling
of the veins, the blush upon the face, all evince those inward
emotions, without which great talents cannot display themselves.
There is no character in which the expression of the countenance is not of the utmost importance. To feel a character, and
to show by the motion of the countenance that the soul is agitated
by what it feels, is a talent of equal consequence in an actress
with any she can possess.

It is by the countenance alone you can distinguish between
irony and jest.

A voice, more or less raised or depressed, or more or less
tremulous, is insufficient to express such or such a sentiment of
terror, or such or such a sentiment of fear. The countenance
alone is enabled to mark its degrees. . . .

I am not against giving every assistance to Nature: I have
often myself borrowed assistance. Generally labouring under an
ill state of health, yet, unremitting in my labours, the paleness of
death was often upon my countenance. I had remarked in others,
that nothing was so injurious to the expression of the features as
having pale lips or pale ears. A little art gave them the appearance of florid health: I darkened the colour of my eyebrows, as
the character I was to perform required; I did the same thing to
my hair, with different coloured powders; but far from concealing,

in the least degree, those features which give animation and expression to the whole countenance. — I have ever made the anatomy of the head my particular study, in order that I might thereby be enabled to dispose it in positions most calculated to display it to advantage.

A white skin is doubtless agreeable: it communicates a charm to the whole figure; it imparts an air of greater sprightliness and animation — the blue veins it discovers are always considered as beauties.

But that whiteness which is acquired by paint covers the countenance with a thick enamel, which conceals and destroys every feature. The pores are filled with the pernicious ingredients of which the paint is composed; and the fear the person who wears it is constantly under, of deranging it by too much action, compels her to keep her face always in one posture: — besides, I know no kind of coquetry more troublesome, humiliating, or useless. Whoever has recourse to it is always afraid of being surprised before her face is made up: she cannot refer to herself any compliment that may be paid her: and I again repeat, that it is a custom of which no one is the dupe.

14.   INNOVATIONS BY MME. FAVART

WHILE MLLE. CLAIRON was carrying out her costume reform at the Comédie-Française, Marie-Justine Favart (1727 - 1772) was moving in the same direction at the Théâtre-Italien. Her husband, Charles-Simon Favart, was the stage director of the Italian Comedy, and in this capacity had insisted on greater truth and more local color in the productions of his own comic operas. In *les Amours de Bastien et Bastienne* (1753), *Ninette à la cour* (1755), *les Chinois* (1756), and *les Trois Sultanes* (1761), Mme. Favart introduced various costume innovations for which she was eulogized by her husband:

It was Madame Favart who first adopted correct costume, and she dared to sacrifice her charming appearance to truth of character. Formerly, actresses representing soubrettes or peasant-women, appeared in wide hoopskirts, gloved to the elbow, their heads weighed down with diamonds. In *les Amours de Bastien et Bastienne,* she dressed her hair plainly and wore a linen dress, such as village women wear, that left her arms bare; a simple gold cross, and wooden shoes. This novelty offended a few critics in the pit. . . .

In the comedy *les Trois Sultanes,* there were seen for the first time authentic dresses of Turkish women; they had been made in Constantinople of native materials. This style of dress, at once modest and voluptuous, encountered opposition too.

When the parody *les Indes galantes* was given at court, Mme. Favart appeared in the fantastically absurd costume that Eastern tradition required. When the opera *Scanderberg* [by Rebel and Francoeur] was given there sometime later [1763], her sultana costume was borrowed, and a dress copied from it [by Louis Boquet]. Mlle. Clairon, who showed similar courage in introducing authentic costumes at the Comédie-Française, had a dress made almost on the same pattern which she used on the stage. In the interlude entitled *les Chinois,* performed at the Théâtre-Italien, Mme. Favart, along with the other players, appeared dressed exactly according to the Chinese fashion: the clothes she had procured had been made in China, as well as the accessories and the decorations. In a word, she neither spared nor neglected anything that would add to the enchantment of the theatrical illusion.

15. SPECTATORS ON THE STAGE

IN HIS *Sémiramis* (1748), Voltaire attempted to introduce spectacle on the hitherto barren stage of the Comédie-Française, notably in the scene where the ghost of Ninus rises out of his tomb to the accompaniment of flashes of lightning and peals of thunder. On the first night this scene suffered, since the stage was so crowded with spectators that the actors were hardly able to move. Marmontel recognized this and attributed the cold reception of the production to the abundance of stage spectators:

He [Voltaire] began by *Sémiramis,* and the grand and tragic manner in which the action of it [was conceived], the sombre, stormy, and terrible colouring he spread over it, the magic style he employed, the religious and fearful majesty with which he filled it, the afflicting scenes and situations he drew from it, in fine, the art with which he contrived to-prepare, establish and sustain the marvellous, were well calculated to annihilate the

Mlle. Clairon as
Aménaïde in Voltaire's
Tancrède.

Yale Theatrical Prints Collection

Lekain as Orosmane
in Voltaire's
Zaïre.

Mme. Favart of the
Comédie Italienne as
Roxelane in Her Husband's
Les trois sultanes
(1761).

Yale Theatrical Prints Collection

Mme. Favart of the
Comédie Italienne in
Bastien et Bastienne
(1753).
Engraving by Daullé after the
painting by Carle Vanloo.

cold and feeble *Sémiramis* of Crébillon. But the theatre was then not susceptible of an action of this kind. The stage was confined by a crowd of spectators, some placed on seats raised one above another, others standing at the bottom of the stage, and along the side scenes; so that the affrightened Sémiramis, and the shade of Ninus coming from his tomb, were obliged to penetrate through a thick line of *petits maîtres*. This impropriety threw ridicule on the gravity of the theatrical action. Without illusion there is no interest, and without probability there is no illusion: thus this piece, the master-piece of Voltaire, as a work of genius, had, in its novelty, so little success, that it might be said to fall. Voltaire shook with grief, but he was not disheartened. He wrote *Oreste* after Sophocles, and he rose above Sophocles himself in the part of Electra, and in the art of saving the indecorum and hardness of the character of Clytemnestra. But, in the fifth act, at the moment of the catastrophe, he had not yet sufficiently enfeebled the horror of parricide; and Crébillon's party being there every thing but benevolent, whatever could give a hold to criticism was caught at with murmurs, and turned into derision. The performance was interrupted at every instant; and this piece, which has since been justly applauded, was hooted.

16.   LEKAIN

HENRI-LOUIS KAIN, known as Lekain (1729 - 1778), a member of the Comédie-Française from 1750, successfully managed to overcome his physical disadvantages and, by taking infinite pains, acquired perfect control of his body and voice. Mlle. Clairon, with whom he shared an interest in propriety of costuming, testified as to her colleague's achievements and limitations:

Lekain, originally a silver-smith, having a displeasing face, a mediocre stature, a harsh voice, and a weak constitution, flung himself from the workshop onto the stage, and, with no other guide than his genius, with no other help than art, developed into the greatest actor, the most handsome, most imposing, and most interesting of men. I discount his first trials and his last efforts: in the former he often lacked self-confidence, went through errors and trials, and that had to be; in the latter, his powers no longer kept pace with his intentions: lacking the means, he was often slow and declamatory. But in his heyday he came the nearest to perfection that has ever been seen.

Without prejudice for or against, I must, however, confess that he did not perform all authors equally well. He did not know how to deliver Corneille, and the roles of Racine were too simple for him. He portrayed the characters of neither of them well, except in some scenes which allowed his soul the great flights which it always needed. His perfection was complete only in the tragedies of Voltaire. To the same degree as the author, Lekain would continually show himself noble, true, sensitive, profound, terrible, or sublime. When evoked by Voltaire, the talents of Lekain were so great that one no longer saw his physical shortcomings. He had studied well, he knew several languages, read much and formed an accurate judgment of what he read. But without recourse to art, he might never have made an actor.

17. TALMA'S TRIBUTE TO LEKAIN

TALMA, in a preface to Lekain's *Mémoires*, paid the highest tribute to the genius of his predecessor:

It must be confessed that Lekain had some faults; but in literature and in the arts of imitation genius is rated in proportion to the beauties it creates. Its imperfections form no part of its fame, and would be forgotten if they were not allied to noble aspirations. Nature had refused to Lekain some of the advantages which the stage demands. His features had nothing noble in them; his physiognomy was common, his figure short. But his exquisite sensibility, the movement of an ardent and impassioned soul, the faculty he possessed of plunging entirely into the situation of the personage he represented, the intelligence, so delicately fine, which enabled him to perceive and produce all the shades of the character he had to paint — these embellisht his irregular features and gave him an inexpressible charm. His voice was naturally heavy, and by no means flexible. It was to some extent what is called a veiled voice, but that very veil imparted to it, defective as it was in some respects, vibrations which went to the bottom of the hearer's soul. However, by dint of application, he contrived to overcome its stiffness, to enrich it with all the accents of passion, and to render it amenable to all the delicate inflexions of sentiment. He had, in fact, studied his voice as one studies an instrument. He knew all its qualities and all its defects. He passed lightly over the harsh to give fuller effect to the vibrations of the harmonious chords. His voice, on which he essayed every accent, became a rich-keyed instrument, from which he could draw forth at pleasure every sound he stood in need of. And such is the power of a voice thus formed by nature attuned by art, that it affects even the foreigner who does not understand the words. Frenchmen who are totally unacquainted with English have been affected even to tears by the accents of the touching voice of Miss O'Neil.

At the commencement of his career, Lekain, like all young actors, gave way to boisterous cries and violent movement, believing that in this way he triumpht over difficulties. In time, however, he felt that of all monotonies that of the lungs was the most unsupportable; that tragedy must be spoken, not howled; that a continual explosion fatigues without appealing; and that only when it is rare and unexpected can it astonish and move. He felt, in fine, that the auditor, shockt by the ranting on the stage, forgets the personage represented, and pities or condemns the actor. Thus Lekain, often fatigued in long and arduous scenes, took care to conceal from the public the violence of his efforts, and at the very moment when his powers were nearly exhausted they seemed to possess all their strength and vigor.

Lekain has been reproacht for having been heavy in his recitation. This defect was natural. He was slow, calm, and reflecting. Besides, Voltaire, whose actor he peculiarly was, would not, perhaps, have readily consented to sacrifice the pomp and harmony of his verse to a more natural tone. He wisht him to be energetic, and as he had deckt out tragedy a little the actor was obliged to follow in the track of the poet. Again, in the days of Lekain, a period so brilliant from the genius of its writers and philosophers, all the arts of imitation had fallen into a false and mannered taste, and Lekain, perhaps, thought himself sufficiently rich in all his gifts and attainments to make a slight concession to the bad taste of his days. Yet, his style, at first slow and cadenced, by degrees became animated, and from the moment he gained the high region of passion he astonisht by his sublimity. . . .

He knew how to regulate all his movements and all his actions. He regarded this as a very essential part of his art. For action is language in another form. If it is violent or hurried, the carriage ceases to be noble. Thus, while other actors were theatrical kings only, in him the dignity did not appear to be the result of effort, but the simple effect of habit. He did not raise his shoulders or swell his voice to give an order. He knew that men in power had no need of such efforts to make themselves obeyed, and that in the sphere they occupy all their words have weight and all their movements authority. Lekain displayed superior intelligence and great ability in the varied styles of his recitation, which was slow or rapid, as circumstances required; and his pauses were always full of deep significance. There are, in fact, certain circumstances in which it is necessary to solicit one's self before we confide to the tongue the emotions of the soul or the calculations of the mind. The actor, therefore, must have the art of thinking before he speaks, and by introducing pauses he appears to meditate upon what he is about to say. But his physiognomy must correspond also with the suspensions of his voice. His attitudes and features must indicate that during these moments of silence his soul is deeply engaged; without this his pauses will seem rather to be the result of defective memory than a secret of his art.

18. APPEAL FOR GREATER SCENIC ILLUSION

COUNT FRANCESCO ALGAROTTI (1712 - 1764), highly educated connoisseur of the fine arts and for nine years adviser to Frederick the Great on operatic problems, wrote his *Saggio sopra l'opera in musica* in 1755. In this treatise he suggested a number of operatic stage reforms which, a few years later, Noverre was to carry out in practice. In Berlin, Algarotti must have met Noverre, who had been in the *corps de ballet* of the new Royal Opera from 1745 to 1747. Algarotti had called for greater illusion in scenery, costume, lighting, and acting. He regarded Ferdinando Galli-Bibiena (1657-1743) as the ideal scene designer since he had done away with the central perspective of the symmetrical Renaissance sets and substituted baroque angular perspective (*"le scene per angolo"*):

It would have been still more necessary for our modern painters to copy after a San Gallo and a Peruzzi, because we

Courtesy of the Oesterreichische Nationalbibliothek, Vienna

Giuseppe Galli-Bibiena: Palatial Hall.

consequently should not see in our theatres the temple of Jupiter or Mars bear a resemblance to the church of Jesus, nor would the architecture of a piazza in Carthage have a gothic complexion; for, in all scene-painting, the costume and propriety must be united. The scenery is the first object in an Opera that powerfully attracts the eye, that determines the place of action, and co-operates chiefly to the illusive enchantment, that makes the spectator imagine himself to be transported either to Egypt, to Greece, to Troy, to Mexico, to the Elysian Fields, or even up to Olympus.

Who does not now perceive of what importance it is that the painter's imagination should be regulated by learning and guided by a correct judgment? To this will greatly contribute the perusal of authors and conversation of learned men well skilled in the customs of antiquity. But the artist should have recourse to no person preferably to the poet, the author of the Opera, who, we are to suppose, has preconceived in his mind every article; and to have omitted nothing that can help to embellish, or make the action he has chosen to exhibit, appear probable.

Although the painters of the fifteenth century are, without doubt, the most excellent, yet the art of scene-painting received considerable improvements in the last age, and the obvious reason is, the many theatres, then erected, gave occasion to that species of painting to become more common; whence it necessarily followed, that a greater number of ingenious persons, applying themselves to it, have brought it nearer to perfection.

The devised contrivances of Girolamo Genga (extolled so much by Serlio) to make, in the theatre of Urbino, trees, &c. of the finest silk, would now-a-days be classed among the childish baubles that adorn the manger, in the shews of Christ's nativity. It is farther my opinion, that Serlio, from whose treatise upon scenery there may nevertheless some good hints be taken, did not sufficiently consider how, without the assistance of relievos in wood, we might conquer all the difficulties of perspective; and how, in very confined situations, we could represent the appearance of extensive space; but to such a pitch the science of deceiving the eye has been improved in our time. The introduction, especially, of accidental points, or rather the invention of viewing scenes by the angle, produces the finest effects imaginable;

but that requires the nicest judgment to bring properly into practice. FERDINANDO BIBIENA was the inventor of those scenes, which, by the novelty of the manner, drew the eyes of all the curious upon him. They soon began to look upon, as unpleasing objects for a stage, those streets, and narrow passages, those galleries that were always made to tend to its center, there at once to limit the spectator's imagination and sight.

He had studied the principles of his art in Vignola under good masters: moreover, being endowed with a picturesque and animating fancy, he came to a resolution of giving a meaning to his scenes, after the same manner as had been done before him, by the painters of the fifteenth century, to the figures of Bellini, Peruzzi, and Mantegna.

Ferdinando Bibiena was the Paul Veronese of the theatre; and, like him, he enjoyed the glory of raising his art to the summit, so far as relates to the magnificent, and to a certain degree of the marvellous. He had the luck too, like Veronese, of not establishing it by the pupils reared up under him. They employed all their pains in imitating the easiest part of his manner which was the whimsical; forgetting the fundamentals of the art, by which means only things are rendered probable: therefore, in professing to follow, they went quite astray from their master.

The most new fangled whims, the most out of the way conceits, that could be imagined, were the objects they delighted to represent; and, not to mention a certain arbitrary perspective of their own creation, they bestowed the name of cabinet on what ought to be called a large saloon or a hall; and the name of prison on what might serve for a portico, or rather for a piazza.

19. SERVANDONI'S ILLUSIONISM

THE GALLI-BIBIENAS, while working for almost all the courts of Europe, never were in the service of the French Bourbons. It was Jean-Nicolas Servandoni (1695 - 1766), a native of Florence and a Pannini student, who introduced the Bibiena principle of angular asymmetrical perspective in Paris. From September 1726 he was the chief designer of the Académie Royale de Musique et de Danse and impressed the spectators with the illusionistic effects of his brush. The *Mercure de France* praised Servandoni's set for the third act of Lacoste's opera *Orion* (1728) in glowing terms:

A Fortified City

The City with the Wall Breached

Giovanni Niccolo Servandoni's Designs for an Unidentified Opera.

The scene shows one of the mouths of the Nile, surrounded by rocks, among which are placed great pyramids and other pieces of architecture supposed to have been destroyed by the Nile, and which form different groups and produce these great effects which the scene demands. These rocks, lighted by the sun, are arranged and painted in a strange and picturesque way, imitating nature so well, however, that they seem real; by means of perspective, the effect of light, and the good taste of the colors, they appear to be one whole entity, and so well that one does not notice any wings. These rocks are so well set off by the hugeness of some and the smallness of others, and so well painted, that they allow a surprising distance to be seen beyond the fall of the Nile, which forms a very natural cascade of ten feet high by sixteen wide. This is ingeniously contrived, above all if one considers the inconveniences found on the stage of the Opera. An empty sky is seen, which goes very well with the whole decoration, of which the angle of sight is from the side. Sir Servandoni is the creator of this fine piece which has received great acclaim. It is entirely painted by his own hand.

20. GRANDEUR OF A TEMPLE SCENE

THE STAGE of the Opera in the Palais-Royal (1673 - 1763) was rather limited in space, but Servandoni succeeded in giving his sets a grandeur and spaciousness which the Parisians had not experienced before. A faint reflection of the overwhelming beauty of Servandoni's Minerva Temple for Lully's *Thésée* (1729) also comes to us from the pages of the *Mercure*:

This temple is of the Ionic order, very richly ornamented. The columns, pilasters, and counterpilasters are of fluted marble the ornamentation of gilded bronze, and the figures and bas-reliefs of white marble.

A great vestibule is formed by four very stilted arcades, two at the right and two at the left, supported by sixteen coupled columns, which allow a considerable passage for the entrance and exit of the actors.

In the space between the arcades there are two columns and counterpilasters with their pedestals and entablatures. Great consoles rest above and uphold spans, which form a vaulted ceiling in the antique mode and which deceive the eyes by the art of

perspective, for it appears true and level to the spectators by
means of the position of the perpendicularly arranged borders.

Between the columns of the vestibule are round pedestals
bearing figures which appear to be really detached from the background on which they are painted. At the back of the vestibule
is a large arcade of thirteen feet wide by twenty-six high, supported by eight columns. The spaces between the columns are
four feet wide, through which one discovers the whole temple;
which, in turn, by the balance of these columns and the manner
of their treatment, and by the daylight which illuminates it (very
much clearer and more brilliant than that of the vestibule), becomes entirely majestic and imposing. Between the columns there
are two isolated figures.

This great arcade serves as the principal entrance to the
temple, which seems to have an actually round shape.

Around the inside of the temple are nine vaulted arcades . . .
the vaults being supported by the columns in the same proportion
as those of the vestibule with which they connect and form but
one body of architecture.

Above these arcades is a gallery or promenade, formed by
five arcades, in whose pilasters there are some columns of the
first order set against the wall. Above their entablature rises a
dome, decorated with mosaics, formed by octagonal shapes in the
antique style with rosettes in their centers. This second order is
Corinthian.

During a scene, this promenade actually appears filled with
a great number of persons, who are the spectators at the ceremonies taking place in the temple. In the middle of this temple is seen a three-dimensional statue of Minerva seated on a
pedestal.

The connoisseurs consider this setting more highly than the
same artist's Palace of Ninus in the opera *Pyrame et Thisbé* [by
François Rebel and François Francoeur]. . . . The perspective
truly seems to have given to this Temple of Minerva an extraordinary elevation, for — despite the limitations of space and
without having put any machine out of place — the set is much
higher at the back of the stage than at the front, an effect which
has not yet been seen at the Opera and which produces an admirable illusion; for beyond the dome, one sees in the background
two architectural orders, the whole being actually 32 feet high,

which appears to the eye to be more than sixty, whereas up to the present no set has been at the most over 18 feet at the rear.

The Ionic order of the vestibule connects completely with the second order of the temple, which is Corinthian. One actually sees 78 columns or pilasters. The largest support the entablature which rests upon the circumference; the smaller, which rise to only two-thirds the height of the large ones, support the vaults and arcades: they make the temple appear to be of still more astonishing size in a space which everyone knows is restricted.

21. CHIAROSCURO LIGHTING

FOR THE SAKE of greater illusion, Algarotti wished to abolish the uniformly brilliant lighting of the scenery in favor of a more dramatic chiaroscuro technique:

There yet remains an article to be mentioned, and of equal importance with the foregoing, though not sufficiently considered, and that erroneously; to wit, the illumination of the scenes. What wonderful things might not be produced by the light, when not dispensed in that equal manner, and by degrees, as is now the custom. Were it to be played off with a masterly artifice, distributing it in a strong mass on some parts of the stage, and by depriving others, as it were, at the same time; it is hardly credible what effects might be produced thereby; for instance, a *chiaro obscuro,* for strength and vivacity, not inferior to that so much admired in the prints of Rembrandt.

22. A PIRANESI PRISON

IN 1760, for the revival of Rameau's *Dardanus,* a Servandoni pupil, Pierre-Antoine de Machy (1723 - 1807), painted for the Parisian Opera a prison set in imitation of the chiaroscuro effects in Piranesi's (1707 - 1778) collection of *Carceri. L'Avant-Coureur* has a precious description of the unusual scene:

The scenery . . . is one of the most beautiful examples of perspective that we have seen on the stage. This prison is taken from the engravings of the celebrated Piranesi, the Venetian architect. . . . At last we see a scene stripped of boring monotony and cold symmetry, but which is ingeniously conceived and tending toward the grandiose, whose ground plan and angular arrangement allows one to catch a glimpse of beautiful vanishing points, and whose effect of light and shade is caused by two lamps.

It is painted freehand and rendered with the intelligence which controls the Piranesi engraving. One can, nevertheless, reproach the painter for not having kept his foregrounds strong enough in order to make the background recede; for having overlighted the lower portion of the ceiling from the fifth wing on, and for having kept the first flat too dull, which naturally ought to be all the more lighted, because it is placed beneath the lamp. Moreover, as it is supposed that the prison is lighted only by two lamps, it was noticed that, in general, the scene was too uniformly lighted. It would have been more appropriate to make total night with the wings, as has been done with the footlights, in order to concentrate all the light on the place where Dardanus is seated, which, if it had not been lighted by an inappropriate light, would have given greater illusion and would have caused the terror which the sight of such objects should naturally inspire. This darkness would have made a still more striking contrast with the brilliant clouds which come down into the prison in order to beautify it with light.

One cannot praise too highly the taste with which the clouds are grouped; their appearance forms a spectacle that is all the more beautiful, as everybody knows the countless difficulties found on the stage of the Opera, where at every turn the artist is forced to restrict his ideas. In general, these clouds are painted with intelligence; but those at the rear hold too closely to the backdrop and do not detach themselves sufficiently.

23.   ORIENTAL STAGE EFFECTS

TURNING FROM the relatively advanced operatic scene to the backward stage of the Comédie-Française, the historian notices that in 1755 Voltaire's *Orphelin de la Chine* was mounted with new scenery. The traditional *palais à volonté* had disappeared, and the spectators beheld what to them was quite suggestive of a Chinese palace. Collé, in his *Journal*, was enchanted by the Far Eastern color of the production:

I forgot to mention that the Comedians went to considerable expense to stage the play Voltaire gave them. They ordered the painting of a setting, that is to say, of a palace designed in the Chinese manner; and they also observed the same style in their costumes. The women wore Chinese robes without hoops or ruffles or covering for their arms. Clairon even assumed exotic gestures to give an oriental effect, often placing one or both hands on her hips, and sometimes facing front with arms akimbo, and so forth. The men, depending on their parts, were dressed as Tartars or as Chinese, to good effect.

24. VOLTAIRE COACHES LEKAIN

THE PART OF Genghis Khan in the *Orphelin* was played by Lekain, but with hardly any success. Late in the fall of 1755, Lekain went to visit Voltaire at Ferney near Geneva and received a lesson in acting from the impetuous playwright. Since then, the role of the savage Tartar has been accepted as one of Lekain's greatest achievements. In a letter, written on January 10, 1756, Lekain reported on his encounter with Voltaire:

Stimulated by the presence of the group that surrounded me, I recited my part with a Tartar's energy, as I had done it with some success in Paris. Nevertheless, I was not so engrossed in the part that I could not observe the discomfort in Voltaire's face: far from discerning the approval I sought there, I detected an expression of indignation, even of a kind of fury, which, too long pent up in him, burst at last with a terrible explosion: "Stop!" he roared at me. "Stop, wretch! He is killing me! He is assassinating me!" At these words, pronounced with that energetic emphasis of his you know so well, the group rose, gathered round him, and sought to calm him. But again he vented all his anger, which the liveliest pleas could not moderate. This was a volcano that nothing could quench. Finally, he fled to his room.

Stunned and confused by such a scene, I was not eager (as you may judge, my friend) to expose myself to a second. So I announced my departure for the next day to Mme. Denis, whose entreaties could not alter my resolve. Before leaving, however, I requested a moment's conversation with M. de Voltaire. "Let him come, if he wishes!" he said. This gentle response was not encouraging. Nevertheless, I entered his room. We were alone.

I told him I was leaving and expressed my regret at not having realized his wishes in the part he had entrusted to me. I added that I would have accepted his advice gratefully. This seemed to mollify him. He took up his manuscript, and from the first scene I realized how wrongly I had interpreted my part.

I would search in vain to give you an idea of the profound impressions M. de Voltaire made on me by the sublime tone, imposing and passionate, with which he painted the diverse shades in the part of Genghis Khan. He finished, and, speechless with admiration, I still listened. After a few moments, he said in a spent, tired voice: "Now, my friend, are you sufficiently impressed by the true character of your part?" — "I believe so, Monsieur," I replied. "And tomorrow you will be able to judge for yourself." — Then I devoted myself to new efforts. They won his approval, and the most flattering praises were the price of my docility. I was proud, I assure you, to be able on my part to move him with the same feelings with which he had tested me. All the passions I expressed were graven in turn on his features. His expressions of affection were as touching as those of his anger had been impetuous, and I left Ferney, enchanted with the new understanding I had just gained of so beautiful and so difficult a part.

25.   VOLTAIRE AS STAGE DIRECTOR

FLEURY left another description of Voltaire as stage director:

Voltaire attended our rehearsals as well as our performances at Ferney. I can fancy I see him now, in his every-day dress, consisting of grey stockings and grey shoes, a large waistcoat of *bazin* descending nearly to his knees, a large wig squeezed into a little black velvet cap, turned up in front; the whole completed by a *robe-de-chambre,* likewise of *bazin,* the corners of which he would sometimes tuck into the waistband of his small-clothes. Arrayed in this costume, any other person would have looked like a caricature; but the appearance of Voltaire, so far from suggesting any idea of the ridiculous, was calculated to command respect and interest. On ordinary occasions, when he happened to enter into conversation with any of the members of our theatrical troop, his manner was marked by good-humoured familiarity. But when he superintended our rehearsals, there was a truce with pleasantry; then he was all in all the dramatic poet; and one too whose correct judgment and refined taste were not to be easily satisfied. He required that every actor should enter heart and soul into his part: this earnestness of feeling he used to call dramatic probity. The observations which I heard from the lips of Voltaire first gave me an idea of the importance which belongs to the accurate conception of a character.

Among the plays which we rehearsed at Ferney was *Zaire*. The actor to whom the part of Lusignan was allotted, conceived that he was giving a faithful portraiture of that character, by representing him old and infirm. "He is," observed he, "a man whose existence is worn out in captivity." "By no means, sir, by no means," exclaimed Voltaire: "say, rather, that he has risen from the tomb — make him pale — make him bend two-fold if you will; but make him energetic. He is a Christian Samuel, an evocation of the Gospel amidst the leaves of the Koran. He is not merely the missionary converting the unbeliever — he is the soldier of Christ converting his own daughter. It is the father who saves the soul of his child. The spirit of the apostle supports and invigorates the old man. Remember, that when Lusignan speaks to Zaire of God, he is inspired by God. Endeavour to imbue yourself with the spirit of fanaticism. Why spare exertion? You die in the fourth act. Let the enthusiasm of Christianity be tempered only by paternal tenderness. The vulgar comparison of the lamp blazing up before it dies out, is quite applicable to Lusignan. The shades and gradations of the character are — apostle, father, old man!" Then, adding example to precept, he repeated some passages of the part. In so doing he divested himself of his ordinary expression of countenance as easily as he would throw aside a mask, and he became Lusignan personified. His attenuated form seemed to derive a sort of supernatural animation from the expression of his eye and the tones of his voice. His meagre hand was tremulously extended, to draw towards him the child whom he wished to save; in short, it is impossible to conceive a more accurate and forcible expression of Christian faith, mingled with paternal affection.

26. AUTHENTIC COSTUMES

IN 1760, Colardeau's *la Caliste* was given at the Comédie-Française, and Favart, in one of his periodic newsletters to Count Durazzo, commented on the actors' efforts to dress themselves in true fifteenth-century Genoese costumes:

> The actors were very well dressed. Here is what their costumes consisted of: the men wore a close-fitting doublet, the short skirt of which was no more than six inches long. The sleeves were wide, slashed in Spanish fashion, with taffeta or satin insets of a different color from the doublet. These sleeves had a little square cuff, which did not hang more than three inches over the arm. The breeches fitted tightly over the thighs. Over the doublet was a short cape (*tabarro*), worn on the left shoulder, falling just to the guard of the sword, which was worn on the hip. The sword was slender and very long, in Spanish style. The boots had no distinguishing feature. The headdress was a blunt cone, brimless and quilted in grooves, with one or two ostrich plumes on the left side. . . . I forgot to mention that the actors had a lace neckerchief with a bunch of ribbons under the chin, and that their long, flowing hair was tied in the nape of the neck by a rosette, which added considerable elegance.

27. CLEARING THE STAGE OF SPECTATORS

ON APRIL 23, 1759, spectators were banned from the stage of the Comédie-Française. The Count of Lauraguais had given 60,000 francs to the actors so that they could afford to abolish stage seats. Collé rejoiced over the event in his *Journal*: "Theatrical illusion is now complete: we no longer behold Caesar about to knock the powder off a fop sitting in the front row." It was a great moment for Voltaire, who for years had waged a struggle against the presence of the *pétits-maîtres* on the stage. A decade earlier, in his *Dissertation sur la tragédie ancienne et moderne* (Preface to *Sémiramis*), Voltaire had pointed out that the scenic deficiencies of French legitimate drama resulted from a stage encumbered by spectators:

> A theatre, built according to the best antient rules, shou'd be very extensive; shou'd represent a part of some public place, the peristyle of a palace, or the entrance to a temple; and shou'd be so contrived, that one person of the drama, though seen by the

spectators, might not be seen by the other actors, if at any time there shou'd be an occasion for concealing him: It shou'd be made so as to deceive the eye, which is the first thing to be consider'd: it shou'd be capable of exhibiting the greatest pomp and splendor imaginable: every spectator shou'd see and hear equally well in whatever part he was seated. But how can this be ever expected upon a narrow stage, in the midst of a croud of young fellows, who will scarce leave the actors ten foot space? Hence it arises, that most of our plays are nothing but long discourses; all theatrical action is lost, or if practis'd, appears ridiculous. This abuse remains, like many others, because it is establish'd; and for the same reason that we do not pull our houses down, though we know them to be badly built. A public nusance is seldom remov'd but at the last extremity. When I speak of theatrical action, I mean dress, ceremony, assemblies of the people, incidents and events necessary to the piece; and not any of those shews frequently exhibited, rather childish than grand, the resources of art to supply the deficiencies of the poet, and amuse the eye when they are incapable of charming the ear, or moving the heart.

28. DIDEROT ON SCENE DESIGN AND STAGE COSTUME

THE PRINTED EDITION of Diderot's *Pére de famille* (1758) included the playwright's essay, *De la poésie dramatique* — the spirited theory of a dull practice. A century later, when the Naturalists began to dismantle the mechanics of the well-made play, they could do no better than Diderot in his fight against the conventionality of French classical tragedy. While the Diderot essay was chiefly concerned with dramatic reforms, the following excerpts (chapters XIX and XX) contain his ideas concerning the staging of domestic drama (*genre sérieux*):

But what shows most of all how far we are from truth and good taste, is the poverty and falseness of the stage settings and the extravagance of the costumes.

You insist that your poet restrict himself to the unity of place, and you leave the setting to the ignorance of a bad scene painter.

But you wish to bring your poets back to the truth in the arrangement and the dialogue of their plays; your actors back to natural acting and true delivery? Then raise your voice, simply demand that the setting be shown to you as it ought to be.

If nature and truth once appear upon your stage, however modestly, you will soon realize how ridiculous and disgusting everything in contrast to them becomes.

The most misunderstood dramatic technique would be that which might be called half false and half true. It is a clumsy illusion in which certain elements disclose to me the impossibility of the rest. I would rather endure a mixture of incongruities; they, at least, are free of falsity. Shakespeare's error is not the greatest a poet can fall into; it merely indicates paucity of taste.

When you have judged his work worthy of being staged by you, let your poet send for the scene painter. Let him read his drama to him. Then let the latter, who is familiar with the locale of the scene, reproduce it faithfully. And above all, let him think that scene painting must be truer and stricter than all other kinds of painting.

Scene design prohibits many things that ordinary painting can allow itself. If an artist has a cottage to represent, he will set the foundation against a broken column, and, near the doorway, he will make a seat of a fallen Corinthian capital. Indeed, it is not impossible that a cottage should stand where there was once a palace. This arrangement will evoke in me a further thought since I shall be moved by the instability of human affairs. But in the stage setting, there can be no question of that. There must be no distraction, no supposition that might create an impression other than the one the poet is intent upon stimulating in me.

Two poets cannot show themselves to full advantage simultaneously. The subordinate talent has to be partly sacrificed to the dominant talent. Taken singly, the former would represent something general, but, subservient to another talent, it can have only the means of a particular case. Just see what a difference in warmth and effect there is between the seacapes Vernet painted from imagination and those he copied from nature! The scene painter is limited by the circumstances which augment the illusion; those which detract from it are forbidden him. He will employ only sparingly those which embellish without spoiling, for they always have the disadvantage of distracting attention.

These are the reasons why the most beautiful setting will never be more than a picture of the second rank. . . .

Ostentation spoils everything. A show of opulence is not beautiful. Wealth has too many caprices: it can dazzle the eye, but not touch the heart. Beneath the garment that is overloaded with gilding, I never see more than a rich man, and it is a *man* I look for. He who is struck by the diamonds that detract from a woman's beauty, is not worthy to see a beautiful woman.

Comedy ought to be played in informal dress. On the stage it is not necessary to be either more or less dressed up than one is at home.

Actors, if you spend too much for costumes for the sake of the spectator, then you have no taste at all, and you forget that the spectator means nothing to you.

The more serious the play, the more austerity there must be in costume.

Is it not contrary to probability that, during a scene of tumult, men should find the time to dress as if for a court affair or a feast day?

What expense were not our actors put to for the production of *l'Orphelin de la Chine*? How much has it not cost them to rob this work of part of its effect? Really, they are nothing more than children — like those one sees stopping in wonder when our streets are motley with banners — to whom luxurious costumes are pleasing. O Athenians, you are children!

Lovely, simple draperies, austere in color — that's what was needed, and not all your tinsel and decorations. Examine again the art of painting on that subject! Is there among us an artist Gothic enough to show you, on canvas, as awkward and as showy as we have seen you on the stage?

Actors, if you wish to learn how to dress properly; if you wish to lose the false taste for ostentation, and to return to the simplicity so strongly suited to great effects, to your fortune, and to your manners, then visit our galleries!

If it ever happened, in fancy, that *le Père de famille* were attempted on the stage, I believe that the title character could not be too simply dressed. As for Cécile, only the boudoir wrap of a wealthy girl is needed. I will concede the Commander, if you wish, some braid and a walking-stick. I should not be too surprised if so capricious a man were to change costume between the first and second acts. But everything is spoiled if Sophie is not dressed in Siam cotton, and Mme. Hébert in a commoner's Sunday best. Saint-Albin is the only one whose age and station will make me, in the second act, accept a certain elegance and luxury. In the first act, however, he needs only a frock-coat of plush over a vest of coarse cloth.

29.   THE PANTOMIME INTERLUDES FOR *EUGENIE*

THE ACT CURTAIN was not used in the French (or English) theater of this period: an empty stage by tradition still marked the end of an act. Beaumarchais, in his *Eugénie* (1767), followed Diderot's suggestion and introduced pantomimic interludes, which linked the acts together while the orchestra played the intermission music. The dumbshow on the stage kept the audience under an illusionistic spell, preventing the spectators from coming to their senses. The following are the stage directions with which Beaumarchais connected the successive acts:

[*Between Acts I and II*]

A servant enters. After having arranged the seats which are round the teatable, he removes the teaset from it and returns the table to its place near the side wall. He takes up some packages which have been left on several chairs, and goes out, having checked whether everything is in good order.

Since theatrical action is never-ceasing, I thought that one could try to join an act to the following by pantomimic action which would sustain the spectators' attention without fatiguing it, and would, during the interlude, indicate what happens "behind the scene." This I described between acts. Everything which tends to give conviction is precious in a *drame sérieux,* and illusion is created by details rather than by big things. The French Comedians, who overlooked nothing in their efforts to make this drama pleasing, feared, however, that the critical eye of the audience might disapprove of so much novelty all at once; they did not dare to risk disfavor with the pantomimic interludes. If these are staged in private performances, it will be seen that what is merely indifferent, so long as the dramatic action is not in full swing, becomes important enough between the last acts.

[Between Acts II and III]

Betsy emerges from Eugénie's chamber, opens a trunk, and removes from it several dresses, one after the other, which she shakes, unfolds, and spreads over the sofa at the back of the drawing room. She then removes from the trunk some garments and her mistress' best bonnet, which she tries on complacently before a mirror, after having made sure that she could not be seen. She kneels before a second trunk and opens it to take out more clothes. While she is engaged in doing this, Drink and Robert enter, arguing: this is the cue for the orchestra to stop playing and for the third act to begin.

[Between Acts III and IV]

A servant enters, puts the drawing room in order, extinguishes the chandelier and the other candles. A bell is heard within. He listens, then indicates by his actions that it was Mme. Murer who had rung. He hurries to her. A moment later, he comes back with a lighted candle and exits by the vestibule door. He re-enters without the candle, followed by several servants to whom he speaks in low tone, and they all cross quietly to Mme. Murer's room, evidently to receive their orders. The servants come back into the drawing room, hurry out through the vestibule, and then return again through the drawing room to Mme. Murer's room. They are now equipped with hunting knives, swords, and unlighted torches. A moment later, Robert enters from the vestibule, a letter in one hand, and night lamp in the other. Since it is the Count of Clarendon's reply that he is bringing, he hurries across to Mme. Murer's chamber to give it to her. There is a short pause during which the stage is empty, and the fourth act begins.

[Between Acts IV and V]

Betsy, very disconsolate, leaves Eugénie's room, carrying a candlestick, for it is the dead of night. She goes to Mme. Murer's room and brings back a cellaret of flacons, which she places on the drawing room table, along with her light. She opens the cellaret and sees that the bottles are the ones wanted. Then, after lighting the candles on the table, she takes the cellaret to her mistress' room. A moment later, the Baron sadly leaves his daughter's room, holding a lighted night lamp with one hand, looking for

a key in his pocket with the other; he goes off through the
vestibule door which leads to his room, and returns promptly with
a bottle of smelling salts which indicates that Eugénie is in a
frightful crisis. He re-enters her room. Upon the ringing of a bell
offstage, a footman appears. Weeping, Betsy leaves her mistress'
room, and tells the footman in whispers to remain in the drawing room within call. She leaves through the vestibule. The footman sits on the couch at the rear, stretches, and yawns with
weariness. Betsy returns with a napkin over her arm, carrying a
covered porcelain bowl. She re-enters Eugénie's room. A moment
later, Sir Charles and Mme. Murer enter; the footman with-
draws, and the fifth act begins. — It would be advisable for the
orchestra, during this interlude, to play only sweet, sad music,
even muted, as if it were not more than faint sounds coming from
a neighboring house; in the house on the stage, everyone is too
concerned with the events so that one can not assume that any
one here is playing music.

30.   NOVERRE'S INNOVATIONS

JEAN GEORGES NOVERRE (1727 - 1810), a Parisian by birth and a student of the celebrated "Dieu de la Danse," Louis Dupré, made his debut as
a dancer in 1743 at the Opéra Comique. He created his first ballet-panto-
mime, les Fêtes Chinoises, at Marseilles (1751). In 1754, he staged the
Chinese ballet again, this time at the Opéra Comique, where he also
mounted la Fontaine de Jouvence and les Rejuissances Flamandes.
Thwarted in his aspirations to become maître de ballet at the Académie
Royale de Musique, Noverre went to Lyons, where, in 1758 - 1759, he
produced some of his most famous ballets d'action (la Toilette de Vénus,
les Jalousies ou les Fêtes du Sérail, les Caprices de Galathée). As chore-
ographer to the Court of Wurttemberg, he staged, between 1760 - 1767,
new pantomimes for the operatic fetes of Duke Karl Eugen (Admète et
Alceste, Amors Sieg, Psyché et l'Amour, la Mort d'Hercule, Médée et
Jason, Orpheus und Eurydice). Vienna, Milan, Turin, and Naples also
had a chance to admire Noverre's art. In 1776, he finally obtained the
post of ballet master to the Grand Opéra in Paris. Three years later, however, he resigned, discouraged by the intrigues that had prevented the
full realization of his artistic ideas expressed earlier in his Lettres sur la
danse et les ballets (1760). His proposed reform of the traditional ballet
sounded so revolutionary that he aroused the antagonism of almost all
other European choreographers. In fighting the mechanical technique of
the geometric-symmetrical Renaissance school of dancing, Noverre de-

manded in his *Lettres* that expression in movement be substituted for timeworn routine. He wanted to rouse the emotions of the spectators, whose souls and hearts were to be affected no less than their eyes by what was not to be a mere spectacle, but a total work of art, brought about by an alliance of all the arts of the theater. Noverre admonished the children of Terpsichore in this manner:

Renounce cabrioles, entrechats and over-complicated steps; abandon grimaces to study sentiments, artless graces and expression; study how to make your gestures noble, never forget that it is the lifeblood of dancing; put judgment and sense into your *pas de deux*; let will-power order their course and good taste preside over all situations; away with those lifeless masks but feeble copies of nature; they hide your features, they stifle, so to speak, your emotions and thus deprive you of your most important means of expression; take off those enormous wigs and those gigantic headdresses which destroy the true proportions of the head with the body; discard the use of those stiff and cumbersome hoops which detract from the beauties of execution, which disfigure the elegance of your attitudes and mar the beauties of contour which the bust should exhibit in its different positions.

Renounce that slavish routine which keeps your art in its infancy; examine everything relative to the development of your talents; be original; form a style for yourselves based on your private studies; if you must copy, imitate nature, it is a noble model and never misleads those who follow it.

As for you young men who aspire to be *maîtres de ballet*. . . . Never undertake great enterprises without first making a careful plan; commit your thoughts to paper; read them a hundred times over; divide your drama into scenes; let each one be interesting and lead in proper sequence, without hindrance or superfluities, to a well-planned climax; carefully eschew all tedious incidents, they hold up the action and spoil its effect. Remember that *tableaux* and groups provide the most delightful moments in a ballet.

Make your *corps de ballet* dance, but, when it does so, let each member of it express an emotion or contribute to form a picture; let them mime while dancing so that the sentiments with which they are imbued may cause their appearance to be changed at every moment. If their gestures and features be constantly in harmony with their feelings, they will be expressive accordingly and give life to the representation. Never go to a rehearsal with

A Ballet Dancer

Bibliothèque de l'Opera, Paris

A Demon

Louis Boquet's Costumes.

a head stuffed with new figures and devoid of sense. Acquire all the knowledge you can of the matter you have in hand. Your imagination filled with the picture you wish to represent, will provide you with the proper figures, steps and gestures. Then your compositions will glow with fire and strength, they cannot but be true to nature if you are full of your subject. Bring love as well as enthusiasm to your art. To be successful in theatrical representations, the heart must be touched, the soul moved and the imagination inflamed.

31. REFORM OF THE BALLET COSTUME

IN A LATER LETTER, Noverre again rejected the dancer's mask and the hoop skirt and gave his ideas concerning costume reform, a task in which he was supported by the designer, Louis Boquet (1717 - 1814). Noverre wrote:

Let us pass to costume; its variety and accuracy are as rare in music, in ballets and in simple dancing. Obstinacy in adhering to out-worn traditions is the same in every part of opera; it is the monarch of all it surveys. Greek, Roman, Shepherd, Hunter, Warrior, Faun, Forester, Games, Pleasures, Laughs, Tritons, Winds, Fires, Dreams, High Priests, Celebrant — all these characters are cut to the same pattern and differ only in colour and in the ornaments with which a desire for ostentatious display rather than good taste has caused them to be bespattered at caprice. Tinsel glitters everywhere: Peasant, Sailor, Hero — all are covered alike. The more a costume is decorated with gewgaws, spangles, gauze and net, the greater the admiration it procures the player and the ignorant spectator.

At the *Opéra*, few things to be encountered are more curious than the sight of a band of warriors who come to do battle, fight and carry off the victory. Do they bring in their wake all the horrors of the carnage? Is their hair dishevelled? No, Sir, nothing of the kind. They are dressed as if going on parade and resemble effeminate men fresh from a perfumed bath rather than survivors of a desperate struggle. What becomes of truth? Where is verisimilitude? How can illusion be suggested? And how can one fail not to be shocked at so false and ill-conceived a spectacle?

I admit that the bound of propriety must not be transgressed, but above all the action must exhibit life and vigour, and an appropriate confusion whenever the theme requires it.

I would do away with those stiff *tonnelets* [short skirts stretched over a frame] which in certain dancing positions transport, as it were, the hip to the shoulder and conceal all the contours of the body. I would banish all uniformity of costume, an indifferent, ungraceful device which owes its origin to lack of taste. I should prefer light and simple draperies of contrasting colours, worn in such a manner as to reveal the dancer's figure. I should like them to be airy, but without stinting the material. I desire beautiful folds, fine masses with the ends fluttering and producing ever-changing forms as the dance becomes more and more animated; everything should convey a sense of filminess. A bound, a lively step, a taking to flight would waft the drapery in different directions and bring us nearer to a painting and consequently to nature; that is what affords charm and elegance to poses, and would give to the dancer that sense of briskness which he cannot attain when clad in the medieval armour ordained by the *Opéra*. I would reduce by three-quarters the ridiculous paniers of our *danseuses,* they are equally opposed to the liberty, speed, prompt and lively action of the dance. Again, they deprive the figure of the elegance and correct proportions which it should have; they lessen the charms of the arms; they disguise, as it were, every grace; they impede and trouble the *danseuse* to such a degree that the movement of her panier generally takes up far more of her attention than that of her arms and legs. Every actor on the stage must be free and unfettered in his movements; he must not be hindered by the manner of costume necessitated by the character he has to represent. If his thoughts be divided, if the style of a ridiculous costume annoy the dancer so that he feels overcome by the weight of his clothes to the extent of forgetting his part and groans under the burden which overwhelms him, how can he act with ease and warmth? From that moment he must escape from a fashion which impoverishes his art and hinders all expression. The inimitable actress, Mlle. Clairon, who seemed born to overthrow habits engendered by custom, discarded paniers and suppressed them reckless of the consequences.

32. THE UNRULY STANDING PIT

AFTER THE MIDDLE of the eighteenth century, guards were posted in all Parisian public theaters to keep the frequently unruly pit in check. L. S. Mercier objected to this restriction on the freedom of public opinion: "We must listen to our good Molière under a grenadier's moustache. Laugh or sob too loudly, the grenadier, who never laughs and never weeps, notices to what degree your sensibility rises." Writing in 1758, Diderot made this regimentation of the parterre responsible for the ennui which had settled over the auditorium:

Fifteen years ago our theaters were tumultuous places. The coldest heads became heated on entering, and sensible men more or less shared the transports of madmen. *Place aux dames!* was heard on one side; *Haut les bras, monsieur l'abbé!* on another; *A bas le chapeau!* elsewhere, and on all sides: *Paix-là, paix la cabale!* There was movement, bustle, and pushing; the soul was beside itself. I know of no frame of mind more favorable to the poet. The play began with difficulties and was often interrupted. But when a fine passage arrived there was an incredible din; encores were demanded unceasingly, the actor and the actress aroused enthusiasm. The infatuation swept from the pit to the amphitheater, and from the amphitheater to the boxes. People had arrived heatedly, they went away in a state of drunkenness. Some went to the brothels, others went into polite society. That is enjoyment! Today, they arrive coldly, they listen coldly, they leave coldly, and I do not know where they go afterward. I am singularly shocked by these insolent fusileers posted to left and to right in order to moderate my transports of admiration, sensibility, and joy, and who turn our theaters into resorts more peaceful and more respectful than our churches.

33. THE PIT SEATED

IN 1782, the new home of the Comédie-Française, erected on the grounds of the Hôtel de Condé, provided the pit with benches. Laharpe had led the group that had clamored for this reform. The players, however, did not care for the innovation, and the progressive Mercier bewailed the passing of the standing pit:

The Parisian theater audience has lost its traditional rights. Since its customs have been challenged and finally taken away, it can no longer exercise its authority vigorously. So it has grown passive.

No sooner was the audience made to sit down during performances, than it fell into a lethargy. The flow of ideas and feelings has been impeded thereby; the electric contact between stage and pit has been broken, and all because the introduction of benches prevents the spectators from rubbing shoulders and putting their heads together.

In former days, an almost incredible enthusiasm stirred the pit, and the general excitement lent to theatrical performances an interest they no longer have. Nowadays, this tumult has given way to calm silence and disapproval.

34.   PARASITICAL BOX-HOLDERS

IF MERCIER had no use for benches in the pit, he was even more critical of the boxes and their occupants — a mixture of parasitical aristocrats and wealthy speculators. Mercier, in anticipation of a People's Theater, considered the box-system the most deep-rooted evil in the theater:

Private boxes are an indecent custom, the result of our present looseness of manners. They sacrifice the public and play to the imperious delicacy of two or three hundred women with nothing to do. And they keep out of the playhouse all honest citizens who might otherwise seek wholesome diversion there, but whose incomes deny them the luxury of similar privacy.

Since box-rents are paid in advance for the entire season, the acting company thrives so well that the actors no longer have to bestir themselves to learn new roles. Their laziness becomes positively arrogant, and their disorderly negligence shockingly debases the art of acting. Even if an actor does not turn a hand for six months out of the year, he receives not less than seventeen or eighteen thousand francs. Yet the Parisian public, which foots the bill, cannot even compel him, in return, to appear on the stage.

The simplest remedy would be to pay the actor so much for each performance. In this way, he would be forced to display his talents; necessity — for Parisian actors the most eloquent of arguments — would breed a healthy rivalry among them.

Another reason for fighting this pernicious practice is that the actors, contrary to all reason and justice, contend that they do not have to account to the playwrights for the proceeds from the box-rents. So the pit gives way to the private boxes, and nobody has a word to say.

If the public protests the arrangement, a fashionable lady retorts: "What! Why should they expect me to sit through an entire play, when I can afford to pay the same for a single act? Oh, what tyranny! Why don't the police stop it? I can't have the actors come to my house, so why shouldn't I be allowed to come to the theater as late as I wish? Is it any business of theirs if I appear *en deshabillé,* as if I have just gotten out of bed; if I choose to bring my pet dog, my own candles, my chamber-pot; or if I want to lounge at my ease in an armchair, receive my admirers, and leave before the play bores me to death? They are simply trying to deprive me of the freedom that comes of having wealth and good taste."

So the lady must have her spaniel at her side; she must have her cushions, her footwarmer, and, above all, some little fop with a spy-glass to keep her posted on people's comings and goings, and to identify the actors. All the while, of course, the lady flutters a fan in which is set a peephole so that she can see, unseen.

In the best interest of art, public, playwrights, and even actors, there should be a second company. All Paris feels the need of one, wants it, and demands it. But what can the mere public do? The gentlemen-in-waiting have the last word. They say to art: "Thus far and no farther!" to the public: "You will take what we choose to give you!" to the playwrights: "As far as you are concerned, we shall do as we see fit." And art, public, and playwrights find themselves in curious bondage to these gentlemen-in-waiting.

Why should these lords assume this strange prerogative? How can they justify such pretensions about works of genius? How dare they impede progress in an art involving both the dignity and pleasure of a nation? What possible connection is there between the obligations of their class and the creation of a play? By what right do they hale a playwright before their tribunal? No one knows. They themselves do not know. But, because they like this strange despotism, they exercise it without legal title, and, because nothing is too small where passions are involved, this regency of princes and princesses of the world backstage becomes for them as burning an issue of partisan feeling as if the loss of their principal functions were at stake.

35. PRE-REVOLUTIONARY PREMIERE

THE COURT and the Town (*la court et la ville*), erstwhile unity of taste, was in the process of disintegration, and amidst convulsions and battles there arose, from the ruins of the old kingdom of taste, the new *empire de l'opinion publique* (de Rulhière). In the pre-revolutionary period the taste of the pit and the predilections of the boxes could no longer be reduced to a common denominator. "The play, greatly applauded in the town, succeeded very ill at court" was a commonplace of contemporary criticism. It happened only on rare occasions that both groups reached an agreement, which, as a rule, was due to a misunderstanding on the part of the subscribers in the loges. The complete success of *le Mariage de Figaro* illustrates the point. Fleury, or his ghost writer, left us a colorful description of the aristocrats who, on April 27, 1784, were driven into the Comédie-Française by their thirst for sensation, expectant of a banquet for jaded nerves to be given by their charming host, Beaumarchais:

Many hours before the opening of the ticket office, I really believe that half the population of Paris was at the doors. Here was a triumph for Beaumarchais! If he sighed for popularity, he had gained it. Persons of the highest rank, even princes of the blood, besieged him with letters, imploring to be favoured with the author's tickets. At eleven o'clock in the forenoon, the Duchess de Bourbon sent her valet to the office to wait until the distribution of the tickets, which was to take place at four o'clock. At two o'clock the Duchess d'Ossun laid aside her accustomed dignity and hauteur, and humbly solicited the crowd to allow her to pass; and Madame de Talleyrand, doing a violence to her parsimonious disposition, paid triple price for a box. *Cordons bleus* were seen elbowing their way through the crowd jostled by Savoyards; the guards were dispersed, the doors forced open, the iron bars broken down, and an inconceivable scene of confusion and danger ensued. One half of the people had not been able to procure tickets, and threw their admission money to the doorkeepers as they passed, or rather, as they were carried along. But whilst all this was happening outside, the disorder which prevailed within the theatre was, if possible, still greater. No less than three hundred persons who had procured tickets at an early period, dined in the boxes. Our theatre seemed transformed into a tavern, and nothing was heard but the clattering of plates and the drawing of corks. Then, when the audience were assembled, what a brilliant picture presented itself. The *élite* of the rank and talent of Paris was congregated there. What a radiant line of beauty was exhibited by the first tier of boxes!

The style in which the comedy was acted, was in all respects worthy of so brilliant an audience. Dazincourt was full of spirit and intelligence; Préville rendered Bridoison a masterly character; Mademoiselle Sainval, in the Countess, evinced a degree of talent which she was not previously supposed to possess; Molé increased his already high reputation, by his personation of the Count Almaviva; Mademoiselle Olivier threw the most enchanting archness and roguishness into the character of the Page. But the gem of the whole performance was Mademoiselle Contat's personation of Suzanne. That actress had heretofore played only the fine ladies of comedy; but it was a happy thought of Beaumarchais to offer her the soubrette. He guessed the versatility of her talent. As soon as the play was over, Préville ran up to her, and embracing her, said, "This is my first infidelity to Mademoiselle Dangeville."

The first twenty performances of this play brought to the treasury of the Comédie-Française one hundred thousand francs; and the attraction continued unabated during seventy-five nights. People flocked from the provinces to see *Figaro*; and, in short, its success was unparalleled in the annals of the French stage.

Chapter X

Eighteenth-Century England

1. TRIUMVIRATE OF ACTOR-MANAGERS

AFTER 1710, Drury Lane was governed by a triumvirate of actors: Colley Cibber, Robert Wilks, and Thomas Dogget, who was later replaced by Barton Booth. The duties of these actor-managers are set forth in Cibber's *Apology*:

Sir, by our Books, it is apparent, that the Menagers have under their Care, no less than One Hundred and Forty Persons, in constant daily Pay: And among such Numbers, it will be no wonder, if a great many of them are unskilful, idle, and sometimes untractable; all which Tempers are to be led, or driven, watch'd, and restrain'd by the continual Skill, Care, and Patience of the Menagers. Every Menager is oblig'd, in his turn, to attend two, or three Hours every Morning, at the Rehearsal of Plays, and other Entertainments for the Stage, or else every Rehearsal would be but a rude Meeting of Mirth and Jollity. The same Attendance is as necessary at every Play, during the time of its publick Action, in which one, or more of us, have constantly been punctual, whether we have had any part, in the Play, then acted, or not. A Menager ought to be at the Reading of every new Play, when it is first offer'd to the Stage, though there are seldom one of those Plays in twenty, which upon hearing, proves to be fit for it; and upon such Occasions the Attendance must be allow'd to be as painfully tedious, as the getting rid of the Authors of such Plays, must be disagreeable, and difficult. Besides this, Sir, a Menager is to order all new Cloaths, to assist in the Fancy, and Propriety of them, to limit the Expence, and to withstand the unreasonable Importunities of some, that are apt to think themselves injur'd, if they are not finer than their Fellows. A Menager, is to direct and oversee the Painters, Machinists, Musicians, Singers, and Dancers; to have an Eye upon the Doorkeepers, Under-Servants, and Officers, that without such Care, are too often apt to defraud us, or neglect their Duty.

2. DISHARMONIES IN THE TRIUMVIRATE

CIBBER seems to have been chiefly responsible for the selection of new plays, while Dogget was in charge of finances. That such a division of labor was by no means conducive to harmony becomes clear in the following passage from the *Apology*:

Dogget, who was naturally on Oeconomist, kept our Expences, and Accounts to the best of his Power, within regulated Bounds, and Moderation. Wilks, who had a stronger Passion, for Glory, than Lucre, was a little apt to be lavish, in what was not always as necessary for the Profit, as the Honour of the Theatre: For example, at the Beginning of almost every Season, he would order two, or three Suits to be made, or refresh'd, for Actors of moderate Consequence, that his having constantly a new one for himself, might seem less particular, tho' he had, as yet, no new Part for it. This expeditious Care of doing us good, without waiting for our Consent to it, Dogget always look'd upon, with the Eye of a Man, in Pain: But I, who hated Pain, (tho' I as little liked the Favour, as Dogget himself) rather chose to laugh at the Circumstance, than complain of what I knew was not to be cured, but by a Remedy, worse than the Evil. Upon these Occasions, therefore, whenever I saw him, and his Followers so prettily dress'd out, for an old Play, I only commended his Fancy; or at most but whisper'd him not to give himself so much trouble, about others, upon whose Performance it would but be thrown away.

3. RICH'S PANTOMIMES

CHRISTOPHER RICH did not live to see the inauguration of his new playhouse in Lincoln's Inn Fields. Upon his death, his sons, Christopher jr. and John, opened the theater on December 18, 1714. Soon John Rich discovered that he could not compete with Drury Lane in the field of legitimate drama and decided to introduce something else that would attract audiences. He created a vogue for pantomime, a genre in which he could not be surpassed by the rival house. Garrick's biographer described the origin of the English harlequinade as follows:

John Rich, the son of Christopher Rich, formerly patentee of Drury Lane theatre, seems to have imbibed, from his very early years, a dislike of the people with whom he was destined to live and converse. We are told, that his father wished rather to acquire wealth by French dancers, Italian singers, and every other exotic exhibition, than by the united skill of the most accomplished comedians. The son inherited the same odd taste; for being left by his father in the joint possession of the patent with his brother Christopher, and after having ineffectually tried his talent for acting in the part of the Earl of Essex, and some other important character, he applied himself to the study of pantomimical representation. In this he was happily very fortunate. He formed a kind of harlequinade, very different from that which is seen at the Opera Comique in Paris, where Harlequin and all the characters speak; and a kind of droll farce, full of ridiculous incidents and bon mots, called naïvetés, keeps the audience in continual laughter. In the first years of his management at Lincoln's Inn Fields theatre, Mr. Rich struggled with a great many difficulties: he was very young and unexperienced; and the governing players, Bullock, Keen, and others, considered him as one very unfit to give laws to them, and manage the business of a theatre. The ill fortune of the new house, which was opened in opposition to the well-established company of Drury Lane, contributed not a little to heighten the usual disgust of the patentee and his actors.

To retrieve the credit of his theatre, Rich created a species of dramatic composition unknown to this, and, I believe, to any other country, which he called a pantomime: it consisted of two parts, one serious, and the other comic. By the help of gay scenes, fine habits, grand dances, appropriate music, and other decorations, he exhibited a story from Ovid's Metamorphoses, or some other fabulous writer. Between the pauses or acts of this serious representation, he interwove a comic fable, consisting chiefly of the courtship of Harlequin and Columbine, with a variety of surprising adventures and tricks, which were produced by the magic wand of Harlequin; such as the sudden transformation of palaces and temples to huts and cottages; of men and women into wheel-barrows and joint-stools; of trees turned to houses; colonnades to beds of tulips; and mechanic shops into

serpents and ostriches. It would be idle to dwell long upon a subject which almost every body is as familiar with as the writer.

It is a very singular circumstance, that of all the pantomimes
which Rich brought on the stage, from Harlequin Sorcerer, in
the year 1717, to the last which was exhibited a year before his
death, which fell out in 1761, there was scarce one which failed
to please the public, who testified their approbation of them forty
or fifty nights successively.

4.   HARLEQUIN RICH

ACTUALLY, the originator of pantomime was John Weaver, dancing
master at Drury Lane. In 1716, he staged *The Loves of Mars and Venus*
and *Perseus and Andromeda* which were "connected Presentations of
Dances in Character" (Cibber). Weaver evidently conceived the idea,
but the credit for its development must go to John Rich, who, under
the stage name of Lun, was his own Harlequin. The genial showman
and mime is eulogized by John Jackson:

He selected from the heathen fables, serious stories, such as
Orpheus and Euridice, Perseus and Andromeda, and the *Rape
of Proserpine,* and mingling with them grotesque and risible
characters, composed that motley kind of entertainment, known
by the name of Pantomime, in which he was eminently successful, having a head to invent, with strength and agility to execute changes and deceptions the most surprising, and almost
incredible to a beholder, especially at first sight. And notwithstanding the absurdities and improbabilities with which they
were made up, they never failed in their attractions; for, however the grave critic might rail at and ridicule them, he would
not fail to renew his visits to *laugh* at their fooleries; and altho'
he contemned the inconsistencies with which he was diverted, he
laughed, he knew not why, but he did laugh, his thoughts were
deluded, and the effects of merriment thus answered. . . .

Mr. *Rich*'s executive faculties were in their wane before I
went to London; I therefore never saw any of his public exhibitions; but I have frequently beheld him go through detatched
scenes in his dining-room, and upon the lawn at Cowley; particularly his catching the butterfly, and the statue scene; and on his
last revival of the *Sorcerer,* I saw him practise the hatching of

Harlequin by the heat of the sun, in order to point out the business to Miles, who, tho' most excellent in the line of dumb significance, found it no easy matter to retain the lesson he had taught him.

This certainly was a master-piece in dumb-shew. From the first chipping of the egg, his receiving motion, his feeling the ground, his standing upright, to his quick Harlequin trip round the empty shell, through the whole progression, every limb had its tongue, and every motion a voice, which "spoke with most miraculous organ," to the understandings and sensations of the observers.

5. THURMOND'S
HARLEQUIN DOCTOR FAUSTUS

THE PANTOMIME FASHIONERS could not overlook the Faustus legend. The dancing master, John Thurmond, staged a *Harlequin Doctor Faustus* at Drury Lane in 1723, and, one month later, John Rich had his version of the Faustus story on the boards of Lincoln's Inn Fields. Here is a description of Thurmond's spectacle, published in 1724, and obviously based on Thurmond's production book:

While the Overture is playing the Curtain rises, and discovers the Study of Faustus; he enters with a paper in his Hand, which he seems to peruse with Concern: He, after some time, pricks his Finger with a Pin, drops the blood into a Pen, and signs the Contract. Immediately, Thunder and Lightning follow, and Mephistophilus flies down upon a Dragon, vomiting Fire: Faustus seems supriz'd, and runs from the Spirit, who lays hold of him and embraces him; and after several Actions of Courtesy from the Spirit, he seems to be pleas'd, and receives a Wand from him, which gives him the conjuring Power. — Immediately two Countrymen their Wives enter. The Doctor seizes the two Women; the Countrymen missing their Wives, immediately turn upon the Doctor, and endeavour to release the Women: The Doctor waves his Wand, it Thunders, several Devils enter, and fright the Husbands, who run into the Porch of the House for Shelter; which on the Instant turns with 'em in, and in their

room, a Table furnish'd with a Collation comes out. Mephistophilus sets himself down to make one at the Table, whose frightful Appearance drives the Women away: Faustus waves his
Wand, and the Spirit is chang'd into a well-dress'd Shepherd,
who dances to entertain 'em, then bows to the Company, and
sinks. The two Husbands, by this time, have found the Windows
up one pair of Stairs on the Inside of the House, which they
open; and perceiving their wives making merry with the Doctor,
threaten 'em out of the Window. The Wives seeing 'em, shew
'em to the Doctor, who waves his Wand, and immediately, upon
both the Countrymen's Foreheads, sprout out a Pair of large
Horns: They still threaten the Doctor, tho' fix'd to the Window,
who goes out with the Women, deriding the Husbands: Faustus
beckons the Table, which runs out after him.

The Scene changes to the Street. An Usurer enters with a
Bag of Money, crosses the Stage, and knocks at the Doctor's
Door; the Servant enters, compliments him, and shews him the
Way in.

The scene changes to the Inside of the House, and discovers
the Doctor writing at a Table: The Usurer enters again with
a Bag of Money, which he puts on the Table before the Doctor;
the Doctor offers him a promissory Note, which he refuses with
Contempt, and points to his right Leg: The Doctor offers him
his Arm, or his Head; but still he insists on his right Leg. At
last he complies, puts it on the Table, the Usurer cuts it off with
a Knife brought for that purpose, and goes out with the Leg,
rejoicing and mocking the Doctor. — The Doctor waves his
Wand, on which enters Mephistophilus, who knowing what he
wants, waves his Wand, and immediately Legs of several Colours,
Sorts and Sizes, both Mens and Womens, flie in; the Doctor
chuses one, which is a Woman's, and it immediately runs from
the rest, and fixes to the Doctor's Leg. He jumps on the Table,
and admires his Leg, then jumps on the Ground, and dances
to a brisk Tune. Immediately after enters a Bawd, with a Courtezan along with her; the Doctor runs to the Bawd, and kisses
her, he afterwards takes hold of the Courtezan, in order to carry
her away, the Bawd interposes, and makes Signs for Money:
the Doctor goes to the Table, and gives her a Bag of Money he
had of the Usurer, with which she seems pleased. The Doctor

hangs his Hat in the Chamber, and makes Signs to her to hold her Apron under it; upon which it pours out large Quantities of Silver, which fall into her Lap; in the mean time the Doctor runs off with the Courtezan. The Bawd comes forward in mighty Joy for the Sum in her Apron, but when she comes to look in it, the Money is vanish'd: She expresses a great Deal of Amazement and Surprize at the Deceit, and runs off after them in a Rage.

Scene changes to the Doctor's Study. — Several Students and Countrymen enter before the Doctor disguis'd, who brings a Statue on a Pedestal, suppos'd to be compos'd of Clockwork; he takes an Engin and winds him in several Postures to please them. One comes to inform the Doctor that he's wanted without, upon which he leaves 'em. One of the Countrymen goes to the Figure, and uses the Engin in the same Manner he observ'd the Doctor, 'till he brings the Figure down distorted on the Pedestal. The Doctor comes on again, and seeing the Condition of the Figure, falls into a Passion. It Thunders aloud, flies a cross, and the Figure is chang'd into a Woman. The Pedestal changes to a Chariot drawn by Dogs, and drives out.

The Scene changes to a Salesman's Shop, the Master discover'd behind the Counter. Enter Harlequin, Scaramouch, Punch, and Pierot. They seem to cheapen some Cloaths, and try 'em on. The Master of the Shop demands his Money of 'em with some Importunity, upon which the Doctor changes him into a Woman. His Wife enters, and seeing a Woman behind the Counter instead of her Husband, supposes her to be her Husband's Whore; she attacks him, pulls off his Headcloaths, and discovers her Husband: They both run out to call for Help, and in the mean time, they rob the Shop, and fly away upon four Spirits in the Shapes of a Cat, a Hog, a Goat, and an Owl.

The Scene changes to the Street, in which is a Tavern-Sign hung out. Enter four Countrymen with Whips in their Hands, they dance a heavy Dance, and then enters to 'em Harlequin, Scaramouch, Punch, and Pierot, who join in another Dance with 'em and go out.

The Scene changes to the Inside of the Tavern. The countrymen, Harlequin, and his Companions enter; Harlequin and his Companions pour Wine out of the Flasks, and as often as the Countrymen offer to pour, nothing comes out; upon which, seeing a Bowl of Punch upon the Table, they go to seize it, and the Liquor flies out of the Bowl. He jumps on the Table which hangs in the Air. The Countrymen take up their Whips, and get upon their Chairs and lash him, he turns himself into the Shape of a Bear, drops thro' the Table, and flies upon the Woman of the House, who is just enter'd; the Countrymen seem surpriz'd, and run away thro' the Windows.

The Scene changes to the Street. Enter the Salesman, Landlord, and a great Mob, they knock at the Door; Harlequin observes 'em, changes himself into a Countryman, and enters with 'em.

The Scene changes to a Justice's Hall, the Justice discover'd at the Table. The Mob enter and intreat the Justice for a Warrant, he grants 'em one; Harlequin seems very busy among 'em, gets hold of the Warrant and tears it, the Mob seize him: He leaves his Countryman's Dress behind him, and flies up thro' the Ceiling. The Mob seem very much surpriz'd and go off.

The Scene changes to the Street. Harlequin and his Companions re-enter very much fatigu'd with the Pursuit; they sit down upon the Ground, he waves his Wand, and immediately a Repast is placed before 'em, which they feed upon; a Porter goes a-cross the Stage with a Hamper of Wine, the Doctor beckons a Flask of Wine, which flies into his Hand. A Man with a Basket of Oranges enters, one comes to purchase some, and while the Man is changing the Money, several of the Oranges fly out of the Basket to the Doctor. When they have sufficiently regaled themselves, they hear the Mob persuing them, they run off, the Mob crosses the Stage: And the Scene changes to a Barn and a Thatch'd-house. Two Threshers are discover'd in the Barn at Work; Harlequin and his Company enter, they intreat for Shelter and Protection, which the Threshers rudely deny 'em; upon which the Doctor, incens'd, changes them into Wisps of Straw, they jump out of the Barn: Harlequin and his Companions enter, and shut the Barn door, the Mob follow them close, and break open the Barn, and go in. The Doctor and his Company run upon the Barn Top, and jump into the Top of the House-chimney, and come down thro' it on the Stage; the Doctor waves his

Wand, and immediately the Barn is set on Fire, the Mob run away. A Tune of Horror is play'd.

The Scene changes to the Doctor's Study. Enter the Doctor in a Fright, when the Music ceases, the Bell strikes One, (which is suppos'd to be the Hour of the Doctor's Death;) Time enters with his Scythe and Hour-Glass, and sings the following Words:

> Mortal, thy dreadful hour is come,
> Thy Days are past, thy Glass is run.

Then Death on the other Side, who sings,

> Tremble while Death strikes the Blow,
> Let thy black Soul prepare to go
> To everlasting Flames below.

When the Songs are ended, it Thunders and Lightens; two Fiends enter and seize the Doctor, and are sinking with him headlong thro' Flames, other Devils run in, and tear him piece-meal, some fly away with the Limbs, and others sink. Time and Death go out.

The Music changes, and the Scene draws, and discovers a poetical Heaven with the Gods and Goddesses rang'd in Order, on both Sides the Stage, who express their Joy for the Enchanter's Death.

6. DEVELOPMENT OF SCENE PAINTING

ALTHOUGH new scenery was a rarity in the legitimate English theater during practically the first three quarters of the eighteenth century, scene painting developed rapidly for pantomime (and Italian opera). Tate Wilkinson, writing his *Memoirs* in the 80's, gives John Rich credit for this:

In the magnificence of theatres, the scenery and lighting are now beyond compare; but it is evident our grannies had an idea of what they did not possess, as may be proved by the orders for scenery in Sir William Davenant's plays, Dryden's Tempest, King Arthur, Lee's Constantine, Cyrus the Great, &c. &c. Except in Mr. Rich's pantomimes, the public then had seldom any scenery that proved of advantage, so as to allure the eye: — But now frequently we have new scenery to almost

every piece. It was very uncommon formerly for new plays to
have more than what we term stock scenery: — There is one
scene at Covent Garden used from 1747 to this day in the Fop's
Fortune, &c. which has wings and flat, of Spanish figures at full
length, and twò folding doors in the middle: — I never see those
wings slide on but I feel as if seeing my very old acquaintance
unexpectedly.

7.   A COVENT GARDEN INVENTORY

ON DECEMBER 7, 1732, John Rich, abandoning the house in Lincoln's
Inn Fields, opened his new Covent Garden theater. A list of theatrical
properties and scenery at Covent Garden in 1743 has been preserved at
the British Museum. From this inventory a conclusion can be drawn
as to the state of scenic affairs during the first half of the eighteenth
century:

A list of Scenes. (*Flats in the Scene Room.*) Cottage and
long village, Medusa's Cave and 3 pieces, Grotto that changes
to Country house. Inside of Merlin's cave, outside of ditto, dairy,
Hermitage, Clock Chamber, Farm Yard, Country House, Church,
town, chimney chamber, fort, Rialto, Harvey's hall, Othello's new
Hall. Hell transparent and 2 peices, Inn Yard, Arch to Waterfall,
Back of Timber Yard, Short Village, Second Hill, front of timber
yard, garden, short wood.
　　(*Flats in the Top Flies*). Shop Flat and Flats in the Shop.
— A large pallace arch, an old low flat of a tower and church,
an open flat with cloudings on one side, and palace on the other.
(*Back flats in Scene room*). Harvey's palace, Bishop's garden,
waterfall, long village, long wood, corn fields, the arch of Har-
veys palace, back Arch of Ariodante's pallace, a canal, a seaport, (*Back Flats in Great Room*). The flat to the Arch and
groves, open country cloth. (*Ditto in the Top Flies*). The Sea
back cloth, the King's Arms, Curtain. (*Wings in the· Scene
Room*). 4 Ariodante's pallace, 12 Harvey's pallace, do. rock, do.
woods, do. Atalanta's garden. . . . Ceres garden, 6 vault, do.
Hill, do. Inn Yard, do. fine chamber, do. plain chamber. (*Wings
in Great Room*), Eight moonlight. (*Do. in Painters Room*), 2 of
Ariodante's pallace, but are rubbed out and not painted. (*Do. in*

the Shop), 2 tapestry, 2 old Rock (*Painted pieces in the Scene Room*), 6 tent pieces, Shakespeare's monument, Macbeth's cave, Oedipus tower, the moon in *emp.* of do. an arbour, 2 pieces transparent Hill, a balcony, old garden wall, a balcony pedestall, front of gallery in Ariodante, a small palace border in do., a frontispiece in do., 2 wings, common canopy in *Richard 2nd.*, a Balustrade, 3 peices open Country, tree, Blind, near garden wall, 2 peices tree in *Margery,* a palmtree in *dragon wantley,* a sign of Rummer with beam, new mount in four peices and 2 brass lines and iron swivells, the two lottery wheels, 6 ground peices to the trees in *Orpheus,* a figure in Harvey's palace, 2 stone figures in Medusa's cave, (*Do. in Great room*), 7 open country peices, 6 peices cornfields, 4 open country peices, 4 orange trees in potts, 6 garden peices, hedge stile and fence 4 peices, a ground peice in two parts, front of garden that changes to house, 4 peices, 6 rock peices with trees, the house at end of melon ground, Balustrade and 2 figures, back part of melon ground and 2 trussells, the burning mountain two peices, the back of machine in *Jupiter and Europa,* the Moon in *Emp.* of do., a blind to the back machine, the back of the back machine, a ground peice of Atalanta's garden, the back cloth, sky border to Arch in *coronation,* cottage in *Margery,* 4 haycocks, eight posts to false stages, the King and Princes box complete. The front of great machine in *Jupiter and Europa.* The water peice to bridge, a pedestall in *Winter's Tale,* a peice ground landskip, (*Do. in Yard*), 2 wings and 1 border to the back machine, 8 wings to great machine in *rape,* four borders to ditto, the falling rock in *Alcina,* four peices, the compass border to Atalanta's garden, the bridge in *The Rehearsal,* 3 peices, the front of a small chariot clouding, 6 gothick chamber borders for false stage, 2 large borders fixed to Battens used in opera, (*Painted peices in first flies*), a gibbet tree in *Apollo and Daphne,* a transparent in *Oedipus, King of Thebes,* a do., a blind in *Theodosius,* a small rock flat, eight peices of old clouding, a marble pedestall, 3 figures on pedestalls, 6 do. with braces, cornfields in 6 peices, a tomb in *Timon,* a garden wall in five pieces, the front of an Altar. (*Do. in the Top Flies*), 6 waves, and 2 shore peices to ditto, a peice of a falling rock in the Operas, 3 old wings, the horses to front of Back machine in *Apollo and Daphne,* (*Do. in painting Room*), a tomb

with figure and lamp, 6 columns to Fame's temple, 2 water peices
out of use, 2 large branches for coronation. (*Do. in Shop*), a
peice of 2 columns and Arches with hinges, arch and balustrade,
part of an old pallace, 2 peices, an arbour, a large border of Ariodante's pallace, and small transparent in *Atalanta*, the front of
a ship, the front of Ceres chariot, the figure of Massinello on a
pedestall, an old rock, two oxen in *Justin*, an old small landskip,
a clouding to a machine, a large frame for scaffold, a border to
frontispiece in *Ariodante*, four furrows in *Justin*, a small old peice
out of use, half an old architect front, two small peices to do.,
a sign of a Harlequin and sign iron, 12 peices of breaking clouds
in *Apollo and Daphne*, an old sky border, 12 pedestalls of different sizes, one of the muses on a pedestall, (*Propertys in Scene
room*), the Spanish table, study of books, a blind used common,
a coffin, a tub, 5 stage ladders . . ., a Gibbet in *Orpheus*, 6
doubters and 8 lighting Sticks, (Properties in Great Room) . . .
a haycock in 2 peices, the mill in *Faustus*, supper table and 2
chairs, . . . 2 scaffolds for *Sorcerer* . . . nine single blinds with
48 tinn candlesticks . . . a red curtain fixt to batten . . . (*Do. in
the Yard*). . . . The stage in the *rape* in four peices, front steps
to do. . . . the great travelling machine made for *Orpheus* . . .
(*Do. in first flies*), 6 battins with red bays for barrs, 12 top
grooves with 6 iron braces and ropes, 2 small borders and 2 iron
rods, large hill hung . . . key and collar to the fly in *Perseus*, the
scroll of 1000 crowns a month . . . 6 handles and 12 brackets
for the sea . . . the statute in the *Rape*, the buck basket, the
tubb, egg, wheelbarrow, dunghill, childs stool, gardner's basket,
a raree show, 3 green banks, a lyon, . . . a turning chair and
screens, Perseus, . . . Rhodope's chair on castors, beaureau, skeleton's case, pidgeon house, skeleton table and leather chair . . .
the great wheel and spindle, a small wheel and barrel to the
circular fly . . . cupids chariot, two rain trunks and frames. . . .
The Stage cloth . . . three canopys to the King and Princes boxes,
a red bench and footstool to ditto, Medusa's couch, . . . The
chariot in *Emp(eror) of Moon*, the dragon in *Faustus*, a Mountebank's stage and tressells . . . 4 barrels, weightes and ropes to the
flies, . . . 41 green benches, the rails that part the pit in 5 peices.
. ., a flying chariot, the great machine *Jupiter and Europa* . . . the
curtain bell and line, a hook to draw off the cloudings, three

lighting sticks. (*Do. in Top flies*), 12 braces and stays to the round fly, a monster, the Calash and wheels in *Emp. of Moon*, 2 barrels, weights, wires and scaffoldings to dragon. (*Do. in Roof*). The barrel to the Stages with ropes, weights, etc., a barrel to figure in *Oedipus*, weight and rope, the barrel to the great machine in *Jupiter and Europa*, now used in *Comus*, with their wires, wts. and ropes, 2 old barrels, 2 old Gibbets. . . . The border bell and 12 candlesticks. (*Properties in Painting Room*). . . . Painters scaffold, wts., ropes and grooves, 2 colour stones and dressers fixt, 2 folding trussels, and 1 fixt for painters use. . . . The fortification chair in *Jupiter and Europa*, the body of a machine in *Apollo and Daphne*, a grindstone handle and trough, a painters easel, and do. with figure of Harlequin, 86 thunder balls, 6 baskets to do. . . . 4 candlesticks for the thunder. (*Do. in the Shop*), 3 hanging scaffolds, ropes and handrails to round fly, 7 waves not covered, the cutt chariot in *Sorcerer*, a large modell of the Stage not finished . . . the thunder bell and line. . . . (*Do., &c., contained in the Cellar*), the lamps in front fixt with barrels, cordage, wts., &c., the grave trap and 3 others with do., the scene barrel fixt with cog wheels, &c., 12 pr. of Scene ladders fixt with ropes, Banquo's trap with barrel and cordage, 6 columns to the dome in *Perseus*, a barrel groove, and wts. to trees in *Orpheus*, 6 trees to do., the post and barrel to pidgeon house, the egg trap and box snaps, flap to grave trap, the Pallisadoes barrel, cordage, &c. . . . an old woman and grooves in *Faustus*, a trophy, a rock and grooves, rope, a cloud, the Shell in *Comus* . . . and 41 sconce candlesticks . . . 5 tin blinds to Stage lamps . . . 115 three corner tinn lamps, 2 long iron braces and screws in *Orpheus*, one long do. in *Merlin*, 3 small do. . . . 6 old iron rings and chains for branches brought from Lincolns Inn. . . . The trap bell and sconce bell, (*Do., &c., on the Stage*), the frontispiece, wings and borders, the curtain and borders, six iron rims and brass chains for branches, 6 borders and 6 pair of cloudings fixt to battens with barrels, wts. and ropes, three hill borders, transparent and blind, do. the melon ground, wts. barrels and ropes, 2 back garden cloths fixt, 24 blinds to scene ladders, 192 tinn candlesticks to do., 12 do. fixt to a post with five canopys, a hanging gibbet fixt with ropes and pulleys, 30 bottom grooves of different sizes, Ceres falling car, 4 large braces to mount in

Perseus, a pyramid in Atlanti's garden, a tree used in a dance, 2 tops to back machine, the serpent and trunk, one large carpet, one throne and 4 other carpets, 4 bell glasses, the bell machine fixt with barrel, wts. &c. . . . (*Stuff in Yard*), 14 lamps posts for stage out of use. (*Do. in Rope Room*), 2 muffle ropes with swivells fit for use. . . . 2 old check ropes with swivells, 19 old ropes of different lengths used in *Rape,* a muffle to fly in *Emp. of Moon.* . . . The weights and their dimensions. The great counterpoize to all the traps and iron hooks 487 lbs. The grave trap, 2 wts. and iron hooks 126 lb., middle trap 67 lb., counterpoize to front lamps 170 lbs., 2 weights in painting room 250 lb., total 1100 lbs.

8. THE "BELLOWER" QUIN

JAMES QUIN (1693 - 1766) began his acting career in Dublin. In London he appeared at Drury Lane in 1715, playing only minor parts under the prevailing seniority system. Two years later, he transferred to Lincoln's Inn Fields under the management of Rich, with whom he remained associated until 1734. After his Falstaff success in 1720, Quin became the leading actor of the period, drawing a salary of £300 a year. In 1734, Fleetwood, patentee of Drury Lane, offered him £500, and he deserted Rich. Quin's forte lay in such declamatory parts as Cato, Brutus, Tamerlane, Bajazet, and Zanga. His exaggerated style was ridiculed by a number of critics, though there were others, not to speak of the playgoers as a whole, who admired Quin's "perfection in speaking the sublime." Tobias Smollett, impatient of grandiloquent gravity, has his Knight of Malta in *Peregrine Pickle* (1751) describe Quin's acting thus:

Yet one of your gratiosos I cannot admire in all the characters he assumes. His utterance is a continual sing-song, like the chanting of vespers; and his action resembles that of heaving ballast into the hold of a ship. In his outward deportment, he seems to have confounded the ideas of dignity and insolence of mien; acts the crafty, cool, designing Crookback, as a loud, shallow, blustering Hector; and in the character of the mild patriot Brutus, loses all temper and decorum; nay, so ridiculous is the behaviour of him and Cassius at their interview, that, setting foot to foot and grinning at each other, with the aspect of two cobblers enraged, they thrust their left sides together with repeated shocks, that the hilts of their swords may clash for the entertainment of the audience; as if they were a couple of merry-andrews, endeavouring to raise the laugh of the vulgar, on some scaffold at Bartholomew Fair. The despair of a great man, who falls a sacrifice to the infernal practices of a subtle traitor that enjoyed his confidence, this English Aesopus represents by beating his own forehead, and bellowing like a bull; and, indeed, in almost all his most interesting scenes, performs such strange shakings of the head, and other antic gesticulations, that when I first saw him act, I imagined the poor man laboured under that paralytical disorder, which is known by the name of St. Vitus's dance. In short, he seems to be a stranger to the more refined sensations of the soul, consequently his expression is of the vulgar kind, and he must often sink under the idea of the poet; so that he has recourse to such violence of affected agitation as imposes upon the undiscerning spectator; but to the eye of taste, evinces him a mere player of that class whom your admired Shakespeare justly compares to nature's journeyman tearing a passion to rags. Yet this man, in spite of all these absurdities, is an admirable Falstaff, exhibits the character of the eighth Henry to the life, is reasonably applauded in the Plain Dealer, excels in the part of Sir John Brute, and would be equal to many humorous situations in low comedy, which his pride will not allow him to undertake. I should not have been so severe upon this actor, had I not seen him extolled by his partisans with the most ridiculous and fulsome manifestation of praise, even in those very circumstances wherein, as I have observed, he chiefly failed.

9. MACKLIN BREAKS THE TONES

THE OPPOSITION to rant and pomposity was led by the Irish Charles Macklin (1697? - 1797), who, during his years of apprenticeship at Drury Lane, had exhibited "low arch comedy." It had been customary to see the part of Shylock entrusted to a first-rate comedian, but, in 1741, Macklin decided to discard the comic conception of the Venetian Jew, though Fleetwood and Quin had advised the "hot-headed conceited Irishman" not to deviate from the established tradition. Macklin's new conception of Shylock was a tremendous success, and Fleetwood, listening to the roar of applause, had to admit: "Macklin, you *was* right at last." *The Dramatic Censor* praised the characterization:

Macklin looks the part as much better than any other person as he plays it. In the level scenes his voice is most happily suited to that sententious gloominess of expression the author intended, which with a sullen solemnity of deportment marks the character strongly. In his malevolence there is a forcible and terrifying ferocity. In the third act scene, where alternate passions reign, he breaks the tones of utterance, and varies his countenance admirably, and in the dumb action of the Trial scene he is amazingly descriptive.

10.   MACKLIN'S SHYLOCK

ONE OF THE FINEST evaluations of Macklin's Shylock was given by the German writer, Georg Christoph Lichtenberg, who, in 1774 - 1775, spent a year in London and saw Macklin in his famous role:

Shylock is not one of those mean, plausible cheats who could expatiate for an hour on the virtues of a gold watch-chain of pinchbeck; he is heavy, and silent in his unfathomable cunning, and, when the law is on his side, just to the point of malice. Imagine a rather stout man with a coarse yellow face and a nose generously fashioned in all three dimensions, a long double chin, and a mouth so carved by nature that the knife appears to have slit him right up to the ears, on one side at least, I thought. He wears a long black gown, long wide trousers, and a red tricorne, after the fashion of Italian Jews, I suppose. The first words he utters, when he comes on to the stage, are slowly and impressively spoken: 'Three thousand ducats.' The double 'th' and the two sibilants, especially the second after the 't', which Macklin lisps as lickerishly as if he were savouring the ducats and all that they would buy, make so deep an impression in the man's favour that nothing can destroy it. Three such words uttered thus at the outset give the keynote of his whole character. In the scene where he first misses his daughter, he comes on hatless, with disordered hair, some locks a finger long standing on end, as if raised by a breath of wind from the gallows, so distracted was his demeanour. Both his hands are clenched, and his movements abrupt and convulsive. To see a deceiver, who is usually calm and resolute, in such a state of agitation, is terrible.

Macklin as Shylock and Mrs. Pope as Portia.
Engraved by W. Nutter from a Painting by J. Boyne.

11. MACKLIN AS A TEACHER

THE REVOLUTIONARY character of Macklin's acting style is admirably summed up by John Hill in *The Actor*, in the first (1750) and second (1755) of his books bearing this title. From Hill we learn that Macklin was active in training students in the new style:

There was a time indeed when everything in tragedy, if it was but the delivering a common message, was spoken in high heroics; but of late years this absurdity has been in a great measure banish'd from the English, as well as from the French stage. The French owe this rational improvement in their tragedy to [Michel] Baron and Madam Cauvreur [Adrienne Lecouvreur], and we to that excellent player Mr. Macklin: the pains he took while entrusted with the care of the actors at Drury-Lane, and the attention which the success of those pains acquir'd him from the now greatest actors of the English theatre, have founded for us a new method of the delivering tragedy from the first rate actors, and banish'd the bombast that us'd to wound our ears continually from the mouths of the subordinate ones, who were eternally aiming to mimic the majesty that the principal performers employ'd on scenes that were of the utmost consequence, in the delivery of the most simple and familiar phrases, adapted to the trivial occasions which were afforded them to speak on.

It is certain that the players ought very carefully to avoid a too lofty and sonorous delivery when a sentiment only, not a passion, is to be express'd: it ought also, as the excellent instructer just mention'd us'd eternally to be inculcating into his pupils, to be always avoided when a simple recital of facts was the substance of what was to be spoken, or when pure and cool reasoning was the sole meaning of the scene; but tho' he banish'd noise and vehemence on these occasions, he allow'd that on many others, the pompous and sounding delivery were just, nay were necessary in this species of playing, and that no other manner of pronouncing the words was fit to accompany the thought the author expressed by them, or able to convey it to the audience in its intended and proper dignity.

𝟭   𝟭   𝟭

There was a time when that extravagance, which has been just recommended for farce, had its place in tragedy, both in action and delivery. The gestures were forced, and beyond all that ever was in nature, and the recitation was a kind of singing. We are at present getting more into nature in playing; and if the violence of gesture be not quite suppressed, we have nothing of the recitative of the old tragedy.

It is to the honor of Mr. Macklin, that he began this great improvement. There was a time when he was excluded [from] the theatres, and supported himself by a company whom he taught to play, and some of whom afterwards made no inconsiderable figure. It was his manner to check all the cant and cadence of tragedy; he would bid his pupil first speak the passage as he would in common life, if he had occasion to pronounce the same words; and then giving them more force, but preserving the same accent, to deliver them on the stage. Where the player was faulty in his stops or accents, he set him right; and with nothing more than this attention to what was natural, he produced out of the most ignorant persons, players that surprized every body.

12. GARRICK'S DEBUT

THE PLAYS in which Macklin's restraint would have been in place were not yet written: he would have done a fine job as Pastor Manders or Gabriel Borkman. Between the singsong of Quin and Macklin's enmity to poetry there was a gap which was successfully bridged by David Garrick (1717 - 1779). He appeared to his contemporaries as a natural actor who never lost sight of the fact that he was playing to an audience and that he was bringing to life a work of art. Where there had been sameness of tone and sweet cadences there were now sudden starts and ominous pauses, though the "studied grace of deportment" was always in evidence. Garrick's electrifying London debut was described by his biographer Davies:

On the 19th of October 1741, David Garrick acted Richard the Third, for the first time, at the playhouse in Goodman's Fields. So many idle persons, under the title of gentlemen acting for their diversion, had exposed their incapacity at that theatre, and had so often disappointed the audiences, that no very large company was brought together to see the new performer. However, several of his own acquaintance, many of them persons of good judgment, were assembled at the usual hour; though we may well believe that the greater part of the audience were stimulated rather by curiosity to see the event, than invited by any hopes of rational entertainment.

An actor, who, in the first display of his talents, undertakes a principal character, has generally, amongst other difficulties, the prejudices of the audience to struggle with, in favour of an established performer. Here, indeed, they were not insurmountable: Cibber, who had been much admired in Richard, had left the stage. Quin was the popular player; but his manner of heaving up his words, and his laboured action, prevented his being a favourite Richard.

Mr. Garrick's easy and familiar, yet forcible style in speaking and acting, at first threw the critics into some hesitation concerning the novelty as well as propriety of his manner. They had been long accustomed to an elevation of the voice, with a sudden mechanical depression of its tones, calculated to excite admiration, and to intrap applause. To the just modulation of the words, and concurring expression of the features from the genuine workings of nature, they had been strangers, at least for some time. But after he had gone through a variety of scenes, in which he gave evident proofs of consummate art, and perfect knowledge of character, their doubts were turned into surprise and astonishment, from which they relieved themselves by loud and reiterated applause. They were more especially charmed when the actor, after having thrown aside the hypocrite and politician, assumed the warrior and the hero. When news was brought to Richard, that the Duke of Buckingham was taken, Garrick's look and action, when he pronounced the words,

> — Off with his head!
> So much for Buckingham!

were so significant and important, from his visible enjoyment of the incident, that several loud shouts of approbation proclaimed the triumph of the actor and satisfaction of the audience. The death of Richard was accompanied with the loudest gratulations of applause.

13. TWO SCHOOLS OF ACTING

REPRESENTATIVES of the old school and of the new were both on the stage when Richard Cumberland first saw Garrick in Rowe's *Fair Penitent*:

For the first time in my life I was treated with the sight of Garrick in the character of Lothario; Quin played Horatio, Ryan Altamont, Mrs. Cibber Calista and Mrs. Pritchard condescended to the humble part of Lavinia. I enjoyed a good view of the stage from the front row of the gallery, and my attention was rivetted to the scene. I have the spectacle even now as it were before my eyes. Quin presented himself upon the rising of the curtain in a green velvet coat embroidered down the seams, an enormous full bottomed periwig, rolled stockings and high-heeled square-toed shoes: with very little variation of cadence, and in a deep full tone, accompanied by a sawing kind of action, which had more of the senate than of the stage in it, he rolled out his heroics with an air of dignified indifference, that seemed to disdain the plaudits, that were bestowed upon him. Mrs. Cibber in a key, high-pitched but sweet withal, sung or rather recitatived Rowe's harmonious strain, something in the manner of the Improvisatories: it was so extremely wanting in contrast, that, though it did not wound the ear, it wearied it; when she had once recited two or three speeches, I could anticipate the manner of every succeeding one; it was like a long old legendary ballad of innumerable stanzas, every one of which is sung to the same tune, eternally chiming in the ear without variation or relief. Mrs. Pritchard was an actress of a different cast, had more nature, and of course more change of tone, and variety both of action and expression: in my opinion the comparison was decidedly in her favour; but when after long and eager expectation I first beheld little Garrick, then young and light and alive in every muscle and in every feature, come bounding on the stage, and pointing at the wittol Altamont and heavy-paced Horatio — heavens, what a transition! — it seemed as if a whole century had been stept over in the transition of a single scene; old things were done away, and a new order at once brought forward, bright and luminous, and clearly destined to dispel the barbarisms and bigotry of a tasteless age, too long attached to the prejudices of custom, and superstitiously devoted to the illusions of imposing declamation. This heaven-born actor was then struggling to emancipate his audience from the slavery they were resigned to, and though at times he succeeded in throwing in some gleams of new born light upon them, yet in general they seemed to *love darkness better than light*, and in the dialogue of altercation between Horatio and Lothario bestowed far the greater *show of hands* upon the master of the old school than upon the founder of the new. I thank my stars, my feelings in those moments led me right; they were those of nature, and therefore could not err.

14. GARRICK'S MOVEMENTS

THE BEST eyewitness accounts of Garrick's acting were written by Georg Christoph Lichtenberg. The following excerpt from one of Lichtenberg's letters analyzes the relationship between the actor's physique and his movements:

There is in Mr. Garrick's whole figure, movements, and propriety of demeanour something which I have met with rarely in the few Frenchmen I have seen and never, except in this instance, among the large number of Englishmen with whom I am acquainted. I mean in this context Frenchmen who have at least reached middle age; and, naturally, those moving in good society. For example, when he turns to some one with a bow, it is not merely that the head, the shoulders, the feet and arms, are engaged in this exercise, but that each member helps with great propriety to produce the demeanour most pleasing and appropriate to the occasion. When he steps on to the boards, even when not expressing fear, hope, suspicion, or any other passion, the eyes of all are immediately drawn to him alone; he moves to and fro among other players like a man among marionettes. From this no one, indeed, will recognize Mr. Garrick's ease of manner, who has never remarked the demeanour of a well-bred Frenchman, but, this being the case, this hint would be the best description. Perhaps the following will make the matter clearer. His stature is rather low than of middle height, and his body thickset. His limbs are in the most pleasing proportion, and the whole man is put together most charmingly. Even the eye of the connoisseur cannot remark any defect either in his limbs, in the manner they are knit, or in his movements. In the latter one is enchanted to observe the fullness of his strength, which, when shown to advantage, is more pleasing than extravagant gestures. With him there is no rampaging, gliding, or slouching, and where other players in the movements of their arms and legs allow themselves six inches or more scope in every direction farther than the canons of beauty would permit, he hits the mark with admirable certainty and firmness. It is therefore refreshing to see his manner of walking, shrugging his shoulders, putting his hands in his pockets, putting on his hat, now pulling it down over his eyes and then pushing it sideways off his forehead, all this with so slight a movement of his limbs as though each were his right hand. It gives one a sense of freedom and well-being to observe the strength and certainty of his movements and what complete command he has over the muscles of his body. I am convinced that his thickset form does much towards producing this effect. His shapely legs become gradually thinner from the powerful thighs downwards, until they end in the neatest foot you can imagine; in the same way his large arms taper into a little hand. How imposing the effect of this must be you can well imagine. But this strength is not merely illusory. He is really strong and amazingly dexterous and nimble. In the scene in *The Alchemist* where he boxes, he runs about and skips from one neat leg to the other with such admirable lightness that one would dare swear that he was floating in the air. In the dance in *Much Ado about Nothing,* also, he excels all the rest by the agility of his springs; when I saw him in this dance, the audience was so much delighted with it that they had the impudence to cry *encore* to their Roscius. In his face all can observe, without any great refinement of feature, the happy intellect in his unruffled brow, and the alert observer and wit in the lively eye, often bright with roguishness. His gestures are so clear and vivacious as to arouse in one similar emotions.

15. GARRICK'S HAMLET MEETS THE GHOST

IN HIS REPORT on how Garrick's Hamlet encountered the Ghost, Lichtenberg described a scene, where the actor combined studied grace with realistic use of the voice ("at the end of a breath"):

Garrick as King Lear in Contemporary Costume with Ermine Cloak.
Mezzotint by B. Wilson, engraved by J. McArdell (1761).
With the King are Kent and Edgar.

Garrick as Richard III.
Engraving by William Hogarth (1746).

"Ah do not kill me, Jaffier"
Garrick (Jaffier) and Mrs. Cibber (Belvidera) in Otway's *Venice Preserved*, Act IV, Scene ii.
Print made by J. McArdell from a painting by Zoffany (1764).

Garrick and Mrs. Bellamy in *Romeo and Juliet.*
Engraving by S. F. Ravenet (1765).

Hamlet appears in a black dress, the only one in the whole court, alas! still worn for his poor father, who has been dead scarce a couple of months. Horatio and Marcellus, in uniform, are with him, and they are awaiting the ghost; Hamlet has folded his arms under his cloak and pulled his hat down over his eyes; it is a cold night and just twelve o'clock; the theatre is darkened, and the whole audience of some thousands are as quiet, and their faces as motionless, as though they were painted on the walls of the theatre; even from the farthest end of the playhouse one could hear a pin drop. Suddenly, as Hamlet moves towards the back of the stage slightly to the left and turns his back on the audience, Horatio starts, and saying: 'Look, my lord, it comes,' points to the right, where the ghost has already appeared and stands motionless, before any one is aware of him. At these words Garrick turns sharply and at the same moment staggers back two or three paces with his knees giving way under him; his hat falls to the ground and both his arms, especially the left, are stretched out nearly to their full length, with the hands as high as his head, the right arm more bent and the hands lower, and the fingers apart; his mouth is open: thus he stands rooted to the spot, with legs apart, but no loss of dignity, supported by his friends, who are better acquainted with the apparition and fear lest he should collapse. His whole demeanour is so expressive of terror that it made my flesh creep even before he began to speak. The almost terror-struck silence of the audience, which preceded this appearance and filled one with a sense of insecurity, probably did much to enhance this effect. At last he speaks, not at the beginning, but at the end of a breath, with a trembling voice: 'Angels and ministers of grace defend us!' words which supply anything this scene may lack and make it one of the greatest and most terrible which will ever be played on any stage. The ghost beckons to him; I wish you could see him, with eyes fixed on the ghost, though he is speaking to his companions, freeing himself from their restraining hands, as they warn him not to follow and hold him back. But at length, when they have tried his patience too far, he turns his face towards them, tears himself with great violence from their grasp, and draws his sword on them with a swiftness that makes one shudder, saying: 'By Heaven! I'll make a ghost

of him that lets me!' That is enough for them. Then he stands
with his sword upon guard against the spectre, saying: 'Go on,
I'll follow thee,' and the ghost goes off the stage. Hamlet still
remains motionless, his sword held out so as to make him keep
his distance, and at length, when the spectator can no longer
see the ghost, he begins slowly to follow him, now standing still
and then going on, with sword still upon guard, eyes fixed on the
ghost, hair disordered, and out of breath, until he too is lost to
sight. You can well imagine what loud applause accompanies this
exit. It begins as soon as the ghost goes off the stage and lasts
until Hamlet also disappears.

16. THE COMEDIAN GARRICK

IN COMEDY, as Archer in Farquhar's *The Beaux' Stratagem* and as Sir
John Brute in Vanbrugh's *The Provok'd Wife*, Garrick was no less
triumphant than in tragedy, and once more Lichtenberg is a sensitive
observer:

Garrick plays Archer, a gentleman of quality disguised as
a servant for reasons which may easily be guessed; and poor
[Thomas] Weston takes the part of Scrub, a tapster in a wretched
inn at which the former is lodging, and where all the wants of
the stomach and the delights of the palate could be had yesterday, will be there on the morrow, but never to-day. Garrick
wears a sky-blue livery, richly trimmed with sparkling silver,
a dazzling beribboned hat with a red feather, displays a pair
of calves gleaming with white silk, and a pair of quite incomparable buckles, and is, indeed, a charming fellow. And Weston,
poor devil, oppressed by the burden of greasy tasks, which call
him in ten different directions at once, forms an absolute contrast, in a miserable wig spoilt by the rain, a grey jacket, which
had been cut perhaps thirty years ago to fit a better-filled paunch,
red woollen stockings, and a green apron. . . . Garrick, sprightly,
roguish, and handsome as an angel, his pretty little hat perched
at a rakish angle over his bright face, walks on with firm and
vigorous step, gaily and agreeably conscious of his fine calves
and new suit, feeling himself head and shoulders taller beside
the miserable Scrub. And Scrub, at the best of times a poor

creature, seems to lose even such powers as he had and quakes in his shoes, being deeply sensible of the marked contrast between the tapster and the valet; with dropped jaw and eyes fixed in a kind of adoration, he follows all of Garrick's movements. Archer, who wishes to make use of Scrub for his own purposes, soon becomes gracious, and they sit down together. An engraving has been made of this part of the scene, and Sayer has included a copy of it among his well-known little pictures. But it is not particularly like either Weston or Garrick, and of the latter, in especial, it is an abominable caricature, although there are in the same collection of pictures such excellent likenesses of him as Abel Drugger and Sir John Brute that they can scarce be surpassed. This scene should be witnessed by any one who wishes to observe the irresistible power of contrast on the stage, when it is brought about by a perfect collaboration on the part of author and player, so that the whole fabric, whose beauty depends entirely on correct balance, be not upset, as usually happens. Garrick throws himself into a chair with his usual ease of demeanour, places his right arm on the back of Weston's chair, and leans towards him for a confidential talk; his magnificent livery is thrown back, and coat and man form one line of perfect beauty. Weston sits, as is fitting, in the middle of his chair, though rather far forward and with a hand on either knee, as motionless as a statue, with his roguish eyes fixed on Garrick. If his face expresses anything, it is an assumption of dignity, at odds with a paralysing sense of the terrible contrast. And here I observed something about Weston which had an excellent effect. While Garrick sits there at his ease with an agreeable carelessness of demeanour, Weston attempts, with back stiff as a poker, to draw himself up to the other's height, partly for the sake of decorum, and partly in order to steal a glance now and then, when Garrick is looking the other way, so as to improve on his imitation of the latter's manner. When Archer at last with an easy gesture crosses his legs, Scrub tries to do the same, in which he eventually succeeds, though not without some help from his hands, and with eyes all the time either gaping or making furtive comparisons. And when Archer begins to stroke his magnificent silken calves, Weston tries to do the same with his miserable red woollen ones, but, thinking better of it, slowly pulls his green apron over them with an abjectness of demeanour, arousing pity in every breast. In this scene Weston almost excels Garrick by means of the foolish expression natural to him, and the simple demeanour that is apparent in all he says and does and which gains not a little from the habitual thickness of his tones. And this is, indeed, saying a great deal.

✦ ✦ ✦

Sir John Brute is not merely a dissolute fellow, but Garrick makes him an old fop also, this being apparent from his costume. On top of a wig, which is more or less suitable for one of his years, he has perched a small, beribboned, modish hat so jauntily that it covers no more of his forehead than was already hidden by his wig. In his hands he holds one of those hooked oaken sticks, with which every young poltroon makes himself look like a devil of a fellow in the Park in the morning (as they call here the hours between 10 and 3). It is in fact a cudgel, showing only faint traces of art and culture, as is generally the case also with the lout who carries it. Sir John makes use of this stick to emphasize his words with bluster, especially when only females are present, or in his passion to rain blows where no one is standing who might take them amiss. . . .

Mr. Garrick plays the drunken Sir John in such a way that I should certainly have known him to be a most remarkable man, even if I had never heard anything of him and had seen him in one scene only in this play. At the beginning his wig is quite straight, so that his face is full and round. Then he comes home excessively drunk, and looks like the moon a few days before its last quarter, almost half his face being covered by his wig; the part that is still visible is, indeed, somewhat bloody and shining with perspiration, but has so extremely amiable an air to compensate for the loss of the other part. His waistcoat is open from top to bottom, his stockings full of wrinkles, with the garters hanging down, and, moreover — which is vastly strange — two kinds of garters; one would hardly be surprised, indeed, if he had picked up odd shoes. In this lamentable condition he enters the room where his wife is, and in answer to her anxious inquiries as to what is the matter with him (and she has good reason for inquiring), he, collecting his wits, answers: 'Wife, as well as a fish in the water'; he does not, however, move away from the doorpost, against which he leans as closely as if he wanted to rub his back. Then he again breaks into coarse talk, and suddenly becomes so wise and merry in his cups that the whole audience bursts into a tumult of applause. I was filled with amazement at the scene where he falls asleep. The way in which, with shut eyes, swimming head, and pallid cheeks, he quarrels with his wife, and, uttering a sound where 'r' and 'l' are blended, now appears to abuse her, and then to enunciate in thick tones moral precepts, to which he himself forms the most horrible contradiction; his manner, also, of moving his lips, so that one cannot tell whether he is chewing, tasting, or speaking: all this, in truth, as far exceeded my expectations as anything I have seen of this man. If you could but hear him articulate the word 'prerogative'; he never reaches the third syllable without two or three attempts.

17. MACKLIN AND GARRICK COMPARED

MACKLIN AND GARRICK are frequently classed together as belonging to the same school of acting. Actually, the two actors were very different, and Boaden's comparison, stressing the dissimilarities, ought to be given due consideration:

As I paid much attention to Macklin's performances, and personally knew him, I shall endeavour to characterise his acting, and discriminate it from that of others. If Macklin really was of the old school, that school taught what was truth and nature. His acting was essentially manly — there was nothing of trick about it. His delivery was more level than modern speaking, but certainly more weighty, direct and emphatic. His features were rigid, his eye cold and colourless; yet the earnestness of his manner, and the sterling sense of his address, produced an effect in Shylock, that has remained to the present hour unrivalled. Macklin, for instance, in the trial scene, "stood like a TOWER," as Milton has it. He was "not bound to please" any body by his pleading; he claimed a right, grounded upon LAW, and thought himself as firm as the Rialto. To this remark it may be said, "You are here describing SHYLOCK:" True; I am describing Macklin. If this perfection be true of him, when speaking the language of Shakespeare, it is equally so, when he gave utterance to his own. Macklin was the author of *Love à la Mode* and the *Man of the World*. His performance of the two *true born Scotsmen* was so perfect, as though he had been created expressly to keep up the prejudice against Scotland. The late George Cooke was a noisy Sir Pertinax compared with Macklin. He talked of *booing*, but it was evident he took a credit for suppleness that was not in him. He was rather Sir Giles than Sir Pertinax. Macklin could inveigle as well as subdue; and modulated his voice, almost to his last year, with amazing skill. . . .

It has been commonly considered that Garrick introduced a mighty change in stage delivery: that actors had never, until his time, been natural. If Macklin at all resembled *his* masters, as it is probable he did, they can certainly not be obnoxious to a censure of this kind. He abhorred all trick, all start and ingenious attitude; and his attacks upon Mr. Garrick were always directed to the restless abundance of his action and his gestures, by which, he said, rather than by the fair business of the character, he caught and detained all attention to himself. . . .

With respect to the alleged unfairness of Garrick in engrossing all attention to himself, a charge often repeated, it may, perhaps, be true, that this great master converged the interest of the whole too much about his particular character; and willingly dispensed with any rival attraction, not because he shunned competition with it as *skill*, but because it might encroach upon, delay or divide that palm for which he laboured — public applause.

18. TWO MANAGERS AT DRURY LANE

In the fall of 1747, David Garrick became joint-patentee of Drury Lane, in association with James Lacy. Davies commented on the division of responsibilities:

Mr. Garrick and Mr. Lacy divided the business of the theatre in such a manner as not to encroach upon each other's province. Mr. Lacy took upon himself the care of the wardrobe, the scenes, and the economy of the household; while Mr. Garrick regulated the more important business of treating with authors, hiring actors, distributing parts in plays, superintending rehearsals, &c. Besides the profits accruing from his half share, he [Garrick] was allowed an income of £500 for his acting, and some particular emoluments for altering plays, farces, &c.

19.   GARRICK'S MANAGEMENT

DAVIES notes that as a manager Garrick introduced certain standards of behavior and discipline among the members of his company:

Order, decency, and decorum, were the first objects which our young manager kept constantly in his eye at the commencement of his administration. He was so accomplished himself in all the external behaviour, as well as in the more valuable talents of his profession, that his example was greatly conducive to that regularity which he laboured to establish.

Punctuality in attendance at rehearsals was exacted and complied with, and as much due attendance paid to the business of the scene as during the time of acting a play. Those players who had fallen into an unlucky habit of imperfection in their parts, and of being obliged to supply that defect by assuming a bold front, and forging matter of their own, Mr. Garrick steadily discouraged, till, by being laid aside for some time, they had learned to pay a proper respect to the audience and the author.

In distributing parts he consulted the genius of the actor; and though he was not without those prejudices which no man can be entirely divested of, yet, in general, the characters were very well suited to those who represented them. In confirmation of this, I need only mention one of the plays he revived; the *Every Man in His Humour*, of Ben Jonson; where all the personages were so exactly fitted to the look, voice, figure, and talents of the actor, that no play which comprehends so many distinct peculiarities of humour, was ever perhaps so completely acted; and to this care of the manager in restoring this obsolete play to the stage, may very justly be attributed its great success.

20. GARRICK AS STAGE DIRECTOR

ELSEWHERE, Davies goes into greater detail on the casting and directing care which Garrick bestowed upon Jonson's *Every Man in His Humour*. Thus we have the rare experience of watching an eighteenth-century director at work. But, while reading the account, we must not lose sight of the fact that this kind of rehearsing was the exception rather than the rule on Garrick's stage:

Towards the beginning of the year 1750, Mr. Garrick was induced, by his own judgement, or the advice of others, to revive this comedy [*Every Man in His Humour*], and to bring it on his stage. He expunged all such passages in it as either retarded the progress of the plot, or, through length of time, were become obsolete or unintelligible; and these were not a few. Of all our old playwrights, Jonson was most apt to allude to local customs and temporary follies. Mr. Garrick likewise added a scene of his own.

Notwithstanding all the care he had bestowed in pruning and dressing this dramatic tree, he was fearful it would not flourish when brought forth to public view. To prevent, therefore, any miscarriage in the acting of the play, he took an accurate survey of his company, and considered their distinct and peculiar faculties. He gave to each comedian a part which he thought was in the compass of his power to hit off with skill. Kitely, the jealous husband, which requires great art in the performer, he took upon himself; to Woodward he assigned Bobadil, which has been thought, by many good judges, to have been his masterpiece in low comedy. Brainworm was played with all the archness and varied pleasantry that could be assumed by Yates: Wellbred and Young Knowell by Ross and Palmer. Shuter entered most naturally into the follies of a young, ignorant, fellow who thinks smoking tobacco fashionable, and swearing a strange kind of oath, the highest proofs of humour and taste. Winstone, who was tolerated in other parts, in Downright was highly applauded. Old Knowell became the age and person of Berry. Mrs. Ward, a pretty woman, and an actress of considerable talents, acted Dame Kitely. Miss Minors, since Mrs. Walker, was the Mrs. Bridget. I must not forget master Matthew, the town gull, which was given, with much propriety, to Harry Vaughan, a brother of Mrs. Pritchard, a man formed by nature for small parts of low humour and busy impertinence; such as Tester in the *Suspicious Husband*, Simple in the *Merry Wives of Windsor*, and Simon in the *Apprentice*.

After all the attention of the acting manager to draw together such a group of original actors as were scarce ever collected before, the antiquated phrase of old Ben appeared so strange, and was so opposite to the taste of the audience, that he found it no easy matter to make them relish the play. However, by obstinate perseverance, and by retrenching every thing that hurt the ear or displeased the judgement, he brought it, at last, to be a favourite dramatic dish, which was often presented to full and brilliant audiences. . . .

The frequent rehearsal of this comedy was a convincing proof of Garrick's great anxiety for its public approbation. As no man more perfectly knew the various characters of the drama than himself, his reading a new or revived piece was a matter of instruction, as well as entertainment, to the players. He generally seasoned the dry part of the lecture with acute remarks, shrewd applications to the company present, or some gay jokes, which the comedians of the theatre, who survive their old master, will recollect with pleasure.

As he took infinite pains to inform, he expected an implicit submission to his instructions. A compliance, after all, which could not be expected from men of great professional abilities, such as Yates and Woodward. All that can be expected from genius is, to take the out-line and to observe a few hints towards the colouring of a character; the heightening, or finishing, must be left to the performer.

During the greatest part of the rehearsals of *Every Man in His Humour*, Woodward seemed very attentive to Garrick's ideas of Bobadil. But, in his absence one morning, he indulged himself in the exhibition of his own intended manner of representation. While the actors were laughing and applauding Woodward, Garrick entered the playhouse, and, unperceived, attended to the transaction of the scene. After waiting sometime, he stept on the stage, and cried, "Bravo, Harry! bravo! upon my soul, bravo! — Why, now this is — no, no, I can't say this is quite my idea of the thing — Yours is, after all — to be sure, rather

— ha!" — Woodward, perceiving the manager a little embarrassed, with much seeming modesty, said, "Sir, I will act the part, if you desire it, exactly according to your notion of it." — "No, no! by no means, Harry. D—n it, you have actually clenched the matter. — But why, my dear Harry, would not you communicate before."

21. REMOVAL OF STAGE SPECTATORS

In 1763, Garrick removed the spectators from the stage of Drury Lane. Although on the actors' benefit nights the spectators, who paid for the privilege of watching the performance from the stage, had not been an unpleasant sight in the eyes of the player to whom the proceeds went, on ordinary nights the players had been occasionally disturbed by the pranks of some of these stage spectators. Tate Wilkinson described the situation that prevailed prior to Garrick's reform:

The advantages I have mentioned the London theatres flourish with at present are not all confined to what I have asserted as to the theatres, dresses, scenery, and many accommodations; but there is no alteration better, than the stage in these days not being infested with persons behind the scenes in common, but particularly on benefit nights. — As a proof of the force of absurdity I have often wondered, and so have others, why new stage boxes (placed where the useful stage doors used to be) were frequented; but, in short, there are persons always who would prefer such a box, were it much higher on the stage, so few want really to see the piece attentively: — Witness ladies of fashion in London, thirty years ago, sitting at the very backs of the performers. — When I had the honour at York to wait upon his Royal Highness the late Duke of York, he said, "Wilkinson! where am I to sit?" — I replied, "In the stage box." — At which he smiled, and said, "So because I am the Duke of York I must sit in the worst box in the theatre for seeing the play!"

The theatres formerly were not large enough on such occasions, as frequently, on the benefit of a Woodward, a Mrs. Cibber, a Shuter, and others, was the case; therefore the following advertisement appeared at the bottom of each playbill on any benefit of consequence: — "Part of the pit will be railed into the boxes;

Spectators on the English Stage.

Hogarth's painting of a scene from Act III ("When my hero in court appears") of Gay's *The Beggar's Opera*
Engraving by Blake.

and for the better accommodation of the ladies, the stage will be formed into an amphitheatre, where servants will be allowed to keep places." When a great house was not sufficiently ascertained (as the performer judged) for the places taken and the tickets sold, at the bottom of the bill was, "*N.B.* Not any building on the stage." What was termed *building* on the stage, certainly was the greatest nuisance that ever prevailed over an entertainment for the elegant and general resort of any metropolis. . . .

But, my kind reader, suppose an audience behind the curtain up to the clouds, with persons of a menial cast on the ground, beaux and no beaux crowding the only entrance, what a play it must have been whenever Romeo was breaking open the supposed tomb, which was no more than a screen on those nights set up, and Mrs. Cibber prostrating herself on an old couch, covered with black cloth, as the tomb of the Capulets, with at least (on a great benefit night) two hundred persons behind her, which formed the back ground, as an unfrequented hallowed place of *chapless* skulls, which was to convey the idea of where the heads of all her buried ancestors were packed.

I do not think at present any allowance but peals of laughter could attend such a truly ridiculous spectacle: — Yet strange as it would now seem and insufferable, yet certain it is that I have seen occasionally many plays acted with great applause to such mummery, as to general appearance and conception: A strange proof, and the strongest I think that can be given, how far a mind may be led by attention, custom, and a willingness to be pleased without the least aid of probability; its chief and sole object certainly tended only to create laughter and disgust. Nay, the stage, which was not thirty years ago near so wide as at present, also the stage-doors, (which must be well remembered) and the stage-boxes, before which there were false canvas, inclosed fronts on each side of two or three seats, on to the lamps, for ladies of distinction, which rendered it next to impossible for those ladies in the stage-boxes to see at all; but still it was the fashion, and therefore of course charming and delightful. — And whenever a Don Choleric in the Fop's Fortune, or Sir Amorous Vainwit, in Woman's a Riddle, or Charles in the Busy Body, tried to find out secrets or plot an escape from a balcony, they always bowed and thrust themselves into the boxes over the stage-door amidst the company, who were greatly disturbed, and obliged to give up their seats.

The stage spectators were not content with piling on raised seats, till their heads reached the theatrical cloudings; which seats were closed in with dirty worn out scenery, to inclose the painted round from the first wing, the main *entrance* being up steps from the middle of the *back scene,* but when that amphitheatre was filled, there would be a group of ill-dressed lads and persons sitting on the stage in front, three or four rows deep, otherwise those who sat behind could not have seen, and a riot would have ensued: So in fact a performer on a popular night could not step his foot with safety, least he either should thereby hurt or offend, or be thrown down amongst scores of idle tipsey apprentices.

The first time Holland acted Hamlet it was for his own benefit, when the stage was in the situation here described. On seeing the Ghost he was much frightened, and felt the sensation and terror usual on that thrilling occasion, and his hat flew *a-la-mode* off his head. An inoffensive woman in a red cloak, (a friend of Holland's) hearing Hamlet complain the air bit shrewdly, and was very cold, with infinite composure crossed the stage, took up the hat, and with the greatest care placed it fast on Hamlet's head, who on the occasion was as much alarmed in *reality* as he had just then been feigning. But the audience burst out into such incessant peals of laughter, that the Ghost moved off without any ceremony, and Hamlet, scorning to be outdone in courtesy, immediately followed with roars of applause: The poor woman stood astonished, which increased the roar, &c. It was some time before the laughter subsided; and they could not resist a repetition (that merry tragedy night) on the re-appearance of the Ghost and Hamlet.

Mr. Quin, aged sixty-five, with the heavy dress of Falstaff, (notwithstanding the impatience of the audience to see their old acquaintance) was several minutes before he could pass through the numbers that wedged and hemmed him in, he was so cruelly encompassed around. — What must the reader suppose at so barbarous and general a custom being not only yielded to, but approved by the performers — Mrs. Cibber arrayed for Juliet

in a full white satin dress, with the then indispensable large
hoop, in all her pomp of woe, thus shaken and taken prisoner
as it were by foes sarcastic and barbarous!

22. DRURY LANE ENLARGED

GARRICK's banishment of the stage spectators would not have been
popular with the actors had he not first, in 1762, enlarged the auditorium
and in this way made certain that the actors' benefit income would not
be reduced. Davies left a record of the innovation:

To the disgrace of common apprehension we have often
seen likewise in our theatres two audiences, one on the stage,
and another before the curtain; more especially at the actors'
benefits, when a large amphitheatre has covered almost the whole
stage; and the battle of Bosworth Field has been fought in a
less space than that which is commonly allotted to a cock-match.

Mr. Garrick was fully sensible of all the incoherence arising
from this glaring offence against what the painters call the costume, but knew not how to bring about a reformation. He was
reminded that Mr. Sheridan, by his spirited behaviour, had
conquered the refractory tempers of the Irish gentlemen, by
shutting his stage door against them; and, after suffering many
vexations and much opposition, had supported his right with the
sanction of legal authority.

Mr. Garrick indeed must have called to mind a very ridiculous circumstance that happened on the Dublin theatre when
he acted the part of King Lear. When the old King was recovering
from his delirium, and sleeping with his head on Cordelia's lap,
a gentleman stepped at that instant from behind the scenes, upon
the stage, and threw his arms round Mrs. Woffington, who acted
that character; nor did I hear that the audience resented, as
they ought, so gross an affront offered to them, and to common
decency; so long had they been accustomed to riotous and illib-
eral behaviour in the theatre.

The comedians, by waving the advantage of an amphitheatre
on a benefit night, would be considerable losers; and, to remedy
that evil, Mr. Garrick very judiciously observed, that the plan
of reformation must be preceded by a considerable enlargement

of the playhouse; and if it could be so contrived, that the space before the curtain might contain as many persons as had formerly filled the pit, boxes, galleries, and the stage, nobody could have any pretence to murmur.

Mr. Lacy was of the same opinion, and he concurred with his partner in the prosecution of his scheme; and having a taste for architecture, he took upon himself the enlarging of the theatre, which was completely finished in the year 1762. From that time scarcely any but the performers were permitted to visit the scenes of the playhouse.

23.   MRS. BELLAMY ON COSTUMING

In her apologetic memoirs, for which she turned over the largely amorous material to a ghost writer a few years before her death in 1788, Mrs. George Anne Bellamy has little to offer which could be of interest to the theater historian. A few pages, however, where explosive costume matters enter the record, are of a certain value, as they illuminate the prevailing casualness with which theatrical costume was treated on the English stage. Mrs. Bellamy thought that conditions during the first half of the eighteenth century were rather disgusting:

The dress of the gentlemen, both of the sock and buskin, was full as absurd as that of the ladies. Whilst the empresses and queens appeared in black velvet, and, upon extraordinary occasions, with the additional finery of an embroidered or tissue petticoat; and the younger part of the females, in cast gowns of persons of quality, or altered habits rather soiled; the male part of the dramatis personae strutted in tarnished laced coats and waistcoats, full bottom or tye wigs, and black worsted stockings.

24.   MORE COSTUME PROBLEMS FOR MRS. BELLAMY

While "stage brides and virgins" may have had to be satisfied with soiled dresses, Mrs. Bellamy always saw to it that her own costumes outshone those of any other actress on the stage with her. This got her into trouble at least twice when she attempted to draw inspiration from the "brilliancy of her ornaments." The fresh and becoming look of Mrs.

Bellamy's dresses marked a distinct advance, though we cannot fail to note from her remarks that she would wear the same costume whether she portrayed a Persian Princess or a Roman Empress, just as her rival, when playing a Roman matron, would don a costume meant to adorn the Queen of Egypt:

Early in the season, the tragedy of "All for Love, or the World well Lost," was revived [at the Dublin Theatre under Thomas Sheridan's management]; in which Barry and Sheridan stood unrivalled in the characters of Antony and Ventidius. The getting it up produced the following extraordinary incidents. The manager, in an excursion he had made during the summer to London, had purchased a superb suit of clothes that had belonged to the Princess of Wales, and had been only worn by her on the birth-day. This was made into a dress for me to play the Character of Cleopatra; and as the ground of it was silver tissue, my mother thought that by turning the body of it in, it would be a no unbecoming addition to my waiste, which was remarkably small. My maid-servant was accordingly sent to the theatre to assist the dresser and mantua-maker in preparing it; and also in sewing on a number of diamonds, my patroness not only having furnished me with her own, but borrowed several others of her acquaintance for me. When the women had finished the work, they all went out of the room, and left the door of it indiscreetly open.

Mrs. Furnival (who owed me a grudge, on account of my eclipsing her, as the more favourable reception I met with from the public, gave her room to conclude I did; and likewise for the stir which had been made last season about the character of Constance) accidently passed by the door of my dressing room in the way to her own, as it stood open. Seeing my rich dress thus lying exposed, and observing no person by to prevent her, she stepped in and carried off the Queen of Egypt's paraphernalia, to adorn herself in the character of Octavia, the Roman matron, which she was to perform. By remarking from time to time my dress, which was very different from the generality of heroines, Mrs. Furnival had just acquired taste enough to despise the black velvet in which those ladies were usually habited. And without considering the impropriety of enrobing a Roman matron in the habiliments of the Egyptian Queen; or perhaps not knowing that there was any impropriety in it, she determined for once in her lifetime, to be as fine as myself, and that at my expence. She accordingly set to work to let out the cloaths, which through my mother's oeconomical advice, had been taken in.

When my servant returned to the room, and found the valuable dress, that had been committed to her charge, missing, her fright and agitation were beyond expression. She ran like a mad creature about the theatre, enquiring of every one whether they had seen any thing of it. At length she was informed that Mrs. Furnival had got possession of it. When running to that lady's dressing-room, she was nearly petrified at beholding the work, which had cost her so much pains, undone. My damsel's veins, unfortunately for Mrs. Furnival, were rich with the blood of the O'Bryens. And though she had not been blest with so polished an education as such a name was entitled to, she inherited at least the *spirit* of the Kings of Ulster. Thus qualified for carrying on an attack even of a more important nature, she at first demanded the dress with tolerable civility; but meeting with a peremptory refusal, the blood of her great forefathers boiled within her veins, and without any more ado, she fell tooth and nail upon poor Mrs. Furnival. So violent was the assault, that had not assistance arrived in time to rescue her from the fangs of the enraged Hibernian nymph, my theatrical rival would probably have never had an opportunity of appearing once in her life adorned with *real* jewels.

When I came to the theatre, I found my servant dissolved in tears at the sad disaster; for notwithstanding her heroic exertions, she had not been able to bring off the cause of the contest. But so far was I from partaking of her grief, that I could not help being highly diverted at the absurdity of the incident. Nothing concerning a theatre could at that time affect my temper. And I acknowledge I enjoyed a secret pleasure in the expectation of what the result would be. I sent indeed for the jewels; but the lady, rendered courageous by Nantz, and the presence of her paramour, Morgan, who was not yet dead, condescended to send me word, that I should have them after the play.

In this situation I had no other resource than to reverse the dresses, and appear as plain in the character of the luxurious

Queen of Egypt, as Antony's good wife, although the sister of Caesar, ought to have been. In the room of precious stones, with which my head should have been decorated, I substituted pearls; and of all my finery I retained only my diadem, that indispensable mark of royalty.

Every transaction that takes place in the theatre, and every circumstance relative to it, are as well known in Dublin as they would be in a country town. The report of the richness and elegance of my dress had been universally the subject of conversation, for some time before the night of performance; when, to the surprise of the audience, I appeared in white sattin. My kind patroness, who sat in the stage-box, seemed not to be able to account for such an unexpected circumstance. And not seeing me adorned with the jewels she had lent me, she naturally supposed I had reserved my regalia till the scene in which I was to meet my Antony.

When I had first entered the green-room, the manager, who expected to see me splendidly dressed, as it was natural to suppose the enchanting Cleopatra would have been upon such an occasion, expressed with some warmth his surprise at a disappointment, which he could only impute to caprice. Without being in the least discomposed by his warmth, I coolly told him, "that I had taken the advice Ventidius had sent me by Alexis, and had parted with both my clothes and jewels to Antony's wife." Mr. Sheridan could not conceive my meaning; but as it was now too late to make any alteration, he said no more upon the subject. He was not however long at a loss for an explanation; for going to introduce Octavia to the Emperor, he discovered the jay in all her borrowed plumes. An apparition could not have more astonished him. He was so confounded, that it was some time before he could go on with his part. At the same instant Mrs. Butler exclaimed aloud, "Good Heaven, the woman has got on my diamonds!" The gentlemen in the pit concluded that Mrs. Butler had been robbed of them by Mrs. Furnival; and the general consternation, occasioned by so extraordinary a scene, is not to be described. But the house observing Mr. Sheridan to smile, they supposed there was some mystery in the affair, which induced them to wait with patience till the conclusion of the act. As soon as it was finished, they bestowed their applause upon Antony and his faithful veteran; but as if they had all been animated by the same mind, they cried out, "No more Furnival! No more Furnival!" The fine dressed lady, disappointed of the acclamations she expected to receive on account of the grandeur of her habiliments, and thus hooted for the impropriety of her conduct, very prudently called fits to her aid, which incapacitated her from appearing again. And the audience had the good nature to wait patiently till Mrs. Elmy, whom curiosity had led to the theatre, had dressed to finish the part. . . .

Mr. Rich [Covent Garden, January 1756] had been advised to revive Lee's tragedy of "Alexander;" as the character of that hero would suit the powers, and show the person of Barry to singular advantage. The parts of the rival queens he judged would be likewise well filled by Mrs. Woffington and myself. The animosity this lady had long borne me had not experienced any decrease. On the contrary, my late additional finery in my jewels, &c. had augmented it to something very near hatred. I had during the summer given Madam Montête, wife of the hair dresser of the time, who was going to Paris, a commission to bring me from thence two tragedy dresses, the most elegant she could purchase. I have already observed that the proprietor allowed me a certain sum to find my own habiliments.

My *chargée d'affaire* opened her credentials at Madam Bonfoy's, principal *marchand du mode* in that metropolis. I had requested this lady to consult Brilliant, who would consult Du Menil. She was likewise to take the point opinion of all the people of taste there, upon an affair of such momentous consequence. The revival of "Alexander," furnished me with an opportunity of showing all my elegance in the character of the Persian Princess.

My royal robes in which I represented the Empress Fulvia, in Doctor Francis's "Constantine," to the great loss of the public, had not been seen by them. They were showy and proper for the character. But in these *robes de cours*, taste and elegance were never so happily blended. Particularly in one of them, the ground of which was deep yellow. Mr. Rich had purchased a suit of her royal highness's the Princess Dowager of Wales for Mrs. Woffington to appear in Roxana. It was not in the least soiled, and looked very beautiful by day-light; but being a straw colour, it seemed to be a dirty white, by candle-light; especially when my splendid yellow was by it. To this yellow dress I had added a purple robe; and a mixture so happy, made it appear, if possible, to greater advantage.

Thus accoutred in all my magnificence, I made my *entrée* into the Green Room, as the Persian Princess. But how shall I describe the feelings of my inveterate rival! The sight of my pompous attire created more real envy in the heart of the actress, than it was possible the real Roxana could feel for the loss of the Macedonian hero. As soon as she saw me, almost bursting with rage, she drew herself up, and thus, with a haughty air, addressed me, "I desire, Madam, you will never more, upon any account, wear those cloaths in the piece we perform to night."

You are too well acquainted with my disposition, and so I dare say are my readers by this time, to suppose this envious lady took the proper way to have her request granted.

I replied, "I know not, Madam, by what right you take upon you to dictate to me what I shall wear. And I assure you, Madam, you must ask it in a very different manner, before you obtain my compliance." She now found it necessary to solicit in a softer strain. And I readily gave my assent. The piece consequently went through, without any more murmuring on her part, whatever might be her sensations.

However, the next night I sported my other suit; which was much more splendid than the former. This rekindled Mrs. Woffington's rage, so that it nearly bordered on madness. When, oh! dire to tell! she drove me off the carpet, and gave me the *coup de grace* almost behind the scenes. The audience, who I believe preferred hearing my last dying speech, to seeing her beauty and fine attitude, could not avoid perceiving her violence, and testified their displeasure at it.

Though I despise revenge, I do not dislike retaliation. I therefore put on my yellow and purple once more. As soon as I appeared in the Green Room, her fury could not be kept within bounds; notwithstanding one of the *corps diplomatique* was then paying homage to her beauty, and, for the moment, made her imagine she had the power of controul equal to a real queen. She imperiously questioned me, how I dared to dress again, in the manner she had so strictly prohibited? The only return I made to this insolent interrogation, was by a smile of contempt.

It was not long before I had my plenipo likewise; the never-failing Comte de Haslang; to whom I told the reason of my changing my attire, which was meant *par oblique* to her. Upon hearing which, she immediately sent for Mr. Rich; but that gentleman prudently declined attending her summons.

Being now ready to burst with the contending passions which agitated her bosom, she told me it was well for me that I had a *minister* to supply my extravagance with jewels and such parapharnelia. Struck with so unmerited and cruel a reproach, my asperity became more predominant than my good nature; and I replied, I was sorry that *even half the town* could not furnish a supply equal to the minister she so illiberally hinted at. Finding I had got myself into a disagreeable predicament . . . I made as quick an exit as possible, notwithstanding I wore the regalia of a Queen. But I was obliged in some measure to the Comte for my safety; as his Excellency covered my retreat, and stopped my enraged rival's pursuit: I should otherwise have stood a chance of appearing in the next scene with black eyes, instead of the blue ones which nature had given me.

25. INFERIOR COSTUMES

TATE WILKINSON, the actor-manager, when writing his *Memoirs* (1790), remembered very well the costume situation about mid-century:

The expence for the necessary profusion of stage-dresses is enormous, but there is nothing real: Taste may be discerned. That this is the period for taste in dress will be readily admitted; but the money expended, and all the true value, rests in the word _taste_. I know this myself perfectly, by having had, about twenty years ago, an old wardrobe I found in the ruins of my theatrical Herculaneum, and which was of great antiquity, and had appertained to Roman emperors, kings, &c. when not a performer, lady or gentleman of the London theatres, but would have involuntarily laughed at the old broad seams of gold and silver lace, and have cast piteous and contemptuous looks on the country performers thus loaded with trumpery: Yet those despicable clothes had, at different periods of time, bedecked real lords and dukes, and were bought at much less price than now; and would produce, by one day's labour of stripping merely the old materials, forty or fifty pounds to provide a supper if the stomach required. And I can assert and prove, that my present wardrobe is far superior to any out of London, without excepting Dublin or Edinburgh, and has been attended with considerable expence, far beyond the bounds of prudence or common-sense. It is true, as a purchaser of the theatre, the wardrobe is of great cost and value, and would shew a play without fear or disgrace to any audience whatever, as numbers can testify; but would not, in a state of bankruptcy, pay intrinsically, as the old despised King Lear's suit almost singly would have done; as all now consists of foil, spangles, beads, interwoven fast embroidery, silks, satins, &c. which soon wear: An old petticoat, made for a large hoop of the Duchess of Northumberland, thirty years ago, would have served a queen in the theatre several years, then descended to a duchess of Suffolk, afterwards made two handsome tragedy shapes for an old rich Spaniard, and ten years after that burn and produce money to purchase thirty yards of lustring for a modern stage lady. Thirty years ago not a Templar, or decent-dressed young man, but wore a rich gold laced hat, and scarlet waistcoat with a broad gold lace; — as the miser says, "he carried an estate upon his back;" — also laced frocks for morning dress. I have now worn, occasionally, by comedians (for old characters of wealth) a suit of purple cloth, with gold vellum holes, that I frequently wore when a young man as a fashionable dress, and spoke the prologue to the Author, gave Tea, &c. on the London stage, and after that used it as my common dress to parade the streets at noon: But I must justly coincide with the point of truth, and declare, the characteristic dressing of plays forty years ago was very inferior indeed to what is seen in these riper years, particularly the comedians. At that time, no more than two or three principal characters, (at Covent Garden in particular) were well dressed, and those not with any variety as now. Mrs. Woffington's wardrobe had only the increase of one tragedy-suit, in the course of the season, in addition to the clothes allotted to her, unless she indulged herself; and she had a new suit for Sir Harry Wildair, in which character Mrs. Woffington looked the man of fashion; and Mrs. Jordan sports now in Sir Harry one of the best legs in the kingdom. Sir Joshua Reynolds is a judge of legs, and has, like Paris with his apple, given his decree on that said leg.

But the gentlemen and ladies in modern-dressed tragedies, forty years ago, at Covent Garden theatre, wore the old laced clothes which had done many years service at Lincoln's-Inn-Fields, besides having graced the original wearers; and the ladies were in large hoops, and the velvet petticoats, heavily embossed, proved extremely inconvenient and troublesome, and always a page behind to hear the lover's secrets, and keep the train in graceful decorum. If two princesses met on the stage, with the frequent stage-crossing, then practised, it would now seem truly entertaining to behold a page dangling at the tail of each heroine; and I have seen a young lady, not of the most delicate form, who sustained that office frequently — a Miss Mullart; — they are now dismissed, as judged unnecessary and superfluous — but luckily they were pages of honour, and as truly to be depended upon as Edinburgh caddies, as I have never heard of any misdemeanor brought into court by their impeachment: — Yet theatrical kings and queens, like their brethren mortals, sometimes have been frail; but they were family secrets, and ought not to be mentioned again. I have seen Mrs. Woffington dressed in high taste for Mrs. Phillis, for then all ladies' companions or gentlewomens' gentlewomen, actually appeared in that style of dress; nay, even the comical Clive dressed her Chambermaids, Lappet, Lettice, &c. in the same manner, authorised from what custom had warranted when they were in their younger days; and in my remembrance, not a first servant maid, or unfortunate female, that usurped a right of Strand walk, which she termed her own trodden ground, from St. Mary-le-Strand to Exeter Change, but what swaggered in her large banging hoop, to the terror of any young novice who dared usurp a footing of those territories: — In short, a large hoop was a requisite and indispensable mode of dress. Strict propriety of habiliment not any manager has yet arrived at, even in London; and though it is so highly improved these last twenty years, yet the achievement not even money will ever be able to obtain, that is, while the stage is honoured with pretty women, as I sincerely hope it ever will be; — for common sense, reason, persuasion, nor intreaty, will ever persuade handsome women to appear in a farmer's daughter, or a witch, or a servant maid, but with the head dressed in full fashion, and the feet decked in satin shoes; yet I think they would be gainers by trying dear variety: For what will attract more than the simple Quaker, or the truly neat chambermaid? and it is not every man that wishes for a duchess: besides what an advantage to be seen in a gaudy attire one night, and another arrayed in pure simplicity, and be viewed with propriety in a green stuff gown, &c. and not as Madge in *Love in a Village*, or Betsy Blossom, with a French head, white silk stockings, and white satin shoes; by such contradictions Nature is as distant from the stage now as she was an hundred years ago; and stuff shoes and clean cotton stockings would look not only as well, but better, by the preservation of character: — Nay, the plain woman (if such there be) would not be behind hand, as she would, I fear, keep equal pace in absurdity, and relinquish all pretensions to propriety, by being as fantastical as the most beautiful young one. And these contradictions of dress and manner of behaviour are often beheld off the stage by chance observers, and are very properly introduced and ridiculed on, and receive the rod of correction from the comic Muse, as proper objects for the poet's satire and the public mirth. Not any plays throughout were ever dressed as they are now — there the public enjoy a splendor indeed superior to their forefathers.

26.   AARON HILL'S COSTUME DIRECTIVES

THE FIRST ENGLISH DRAMATIST, who insisted on realistic propriety in costuming and, at the same time, had an eye for the artistic qualifications of stage dress, was Aaron Hill (1685 - 1750). When Hill's play, *The Generous Traitor, or Aethelwold* was about to be staged in 1731, the author sent a letter, accompanied by costume sketches, to Wilks, one of the Drury Lane managers, giving detailed instructions as to how the old Saxon costumes could be executed with both propriety and grace:

LEOLYN, because a *Briton*, ought not to have his habit *Saxon* all; the rest gave the authority of *Verstegan's Antiquities*, for the ground-work of their appearance; only I need not observe to you, that some *Heightenings* were necessary, because *beauty* must be join'd to *propriety*, where the decoration of the stage, is the purpose to be provided for.

For this reason, too, I had regard to a *contrast* of colours, in the several parts of each person's dress; and in those of the whole number, with respect to their appearance, together. These are little things, but I have often observed that their effect is *not little*.

To say nothing, as to *impropriety*, in the custom of dressing characters *so far back, in time*, after the common fashions of our days, it weakens *probability*, and cuts off, in great measure, what *most strikes* an audience; for it relaxes the pomp of Tragedy, and the generality, being led, by the *eye*, can conceive nothing extraordinary, where they *see* nothing uncommon. It is, also, worth notice, that a fine, natural *shape*, receives great *advantage*, from a well-imagined turn of *habit*, and an aukward, unnatural one has an *air*, that *burlesques* dignity without it.

THE *Furrs*, which you will observe pretty frequent, in the *figures*, are a prime *distinction*, in the *old Saxon* habits; and will have something of a *grandeur*, not without *beauty*: but they need not be *real* furrs — many cheap *imitations* will have the same effect, at the distance, they will be seen from. Most other parts of the dresses may be compleated, by giving *new* uses, to the *old* reserves of your wardrobe; for if I do not mistake, it is rather *fancy*, than *expence*, that does the business in these cases.

As to the *coronets*, it was the custom of those times, for persons of *high rank*, to wear them, upon *common*, as well as extraordinary occasions; but they must be distinguished, more than they are in the papers [the letter was accompanied by some sketches], to point out the different degrees; and worn in a more becoming position, higher off from the forehead, and a little leaning to one side. There is an advantage will attend the use of their long *single feather*, beyond *that* of the *plume* — It will be light, and may be worn, throughout five acts, without warmth or inconvenience.

27. "SO MUCH SHABBINESS AND MAJESTY"

DURING 1734-1736, Aaron Hill published a theatrical paper, *The Prompter*, where, in the number of January 24, 1735, he attacked the current practice of chance costuming:

I have been greatly offended at the ridiculous Dresses, in which our inferior Sons of the Buskin generally make their Appearance. — I have frequently seen a Duke, in a Coat half a yard too long for him; and a Lord High-Chamberlain, that had shed most of his Buttons. — I have seen Men of Proud Hearts submitting, unnaturally, to strut in tarnish'd Lace; and there is a Certain Knight of the Garter, who condescends to tye back his Wig, with a Packthread. — When a King of England has honour'd the Stage, with his whole Court, in full Splendor, about him, I'd have undertaken to purchase the Cloathes of all his Nobility, for the value of five Pounds. — It exceeds (as my Brother Satirist has it) all Power of Face to be serious, at the sight of so much Shabbiness and Majesty!

The Reason of This, I am inform'd, is that the Habits do not become Perquisites of Earls and Barons, till they have been worn out, by the Emperors of the Theatre; but, whether This is always the Case, or, whether those Noble Personages are not sometimes obliged to travel toward Monmouth street for their Equipment, I will not take upon me to determine.

The Bounds of Probability, in the Mean Time, may be as openly transgress'd, in the Appearance of an Actor, as in the Sentiments which he utters. — And the Dress therefore shou'd always be suited to the Person who takes it upon him. — An old Roman cou'd never with any Propriety, be made to look like a Modern Frenchman; nor a Dutch Burgo-master's Wife, like a Queen of Great Britain. — When, therefore, Persons of Rank and Figure are introduc'd upon the stage, they shou'd be cloath'd so as to represent Themselves, and not the Patchwork Inconsistencies of their Management.

They will say in their Excuse, that some of these Actors' own Cloathes, are as shabby, as those they wear in the Theatre; no matter for that. . . . I am sensible, it wou'd be more Expensive, to cloath Every Actor with Propriety . . . so it would, to qualify Managers with Judgment. Yet, Both the One, and the Other, are what the Publick have a right to expect.

28. "CONFORMITY TO NATURE"

AARON HILL's crusade may have prompted Macklin to adopt a red hat when appearing as Shylock in 1741. He explained to Pope that Jews in Venice wore hats of that color. After Aaron Hill's death, John Hill, quack doctor, actor, and pupil of Macklin, stepped forward with the plea for a stage cleared of spectators, for greater realism in costume, and complete stage illusion. In 1750, he wrote in his treatise, *The Actor*:

It cannot but be acknowledg'd it wou'd be much more reasonable that the scenery should always represent at least the place where the action represented is said to be perform'd, than that it should be left at random in this point: And above all things it is absurd and monstrous to admit a part of the audience upon the stage and behind the scenes. This is a piece of folly that had its rise in France, and that has been often attempted to be introduced among us, but always with that ill success it deserves. Tho' the avarice of our managers seems very well dispos'd to suffer the stage to be fill'd as well as the boxes in this manner, the indignation of the generality of the audience has never fail'd to express itself too severely against the people who place themselves there, to encourage them to make a practice of doing so.

We readily pardon the abuses of this kind in the particular instance of the benefit nights of favorite players; paying them the compliment of sacrificing to their interest the appearance of reality, which the play might have without this, but which can never be given it under such circumstances: it might however be wish'd, that even on these occasions, some care were taken in the distribution of these people, and some decency observ'd in the fault: as, that the stage were never crowded till every other part of the house were full; that even then the people were so dispos'd on it, as to give free passage to the performers in their coming on and going off the stage, and a space sufficient left for the representation; scarce any one of which particulars is now ever comply'd with.

The dresses of the actors is another particular that we are usually as careless about as the scenery in our plays. We shou'd indeed be offended if we saw a person who perform'd the part of a man of rank and quality, act in a plain suit; but we are very unconcern'd to see an actress, whose part is that of a chambermaid, enter upon the stage in a habit that in real life might be worn by a Dutchess. We forget the necessary plainness, that a person of the character and station represented to us ought to appear in, and only say upon the occasion, that Mrs. Clive has a great many very good cloaths. The general taste which we have for extravagance in dress, makes us forget the interest we have in the truth of the representation.

This is another folly which we have imported from France, where it is carry'd to so much a greater height than with us, that it is as common for a stranger at first sight to mistake the waiting gentlewoman for the sister of the lady she belongs to, as it is for him to hear the gentlemen in the pit call out to those on the stage, to entreat they will favour them so far as not to stand between them and the performers.

We are no more to expect that the generality of players will ever be brought of their own choice to prefer the dress under which they may best and most naturally affect the heart, to that by which they may charm the eyes, and make the audience believe them to be genteel and clever people, than that the master of the house will of his own motion deny himself the crowns that offer at the stage door, for the sake of representing the play the more naturally to us. Let us at least however desire that the manager will draw his magick circle in each of the openings of the scenes, beyond which the persons admitted behind them may not advance; that they may be kept, in as great a measure as may be, out of our sight; and let us entreat of the players, that they wou'd regulate, as well as they can, their vanity and love of finery, by the nature of the part they are to perform, and not by their native pride make it impossible for us to know what character it is they are playing, unless we are inform'd of it before hand.

One great source of these abuses in the parts of the waiting maids is, that the authors of our farces in general have made persons of that rank the principal characters of the piece, while their mistresses have been little better than cyphers. But we are apt to believe that the authors of those pieces, intended that the superiority of character in the servant, shou'd be discovered in the course of performance, not by the habit; and that the whole wou'd have somewhat more the air of nature, if when they are both to appear often together upon the stage, the maid were at least not better dress'd than the mistress. We are not without instances where the footman is made the hero of a farce, and his master a mighty insignificant person in it; yet we have never found the absurdity carry'd so high among the men, as to see the Lying Valet better dress'd than his master, tho' there wou'd be a peculiar contradiction in it in this character, that wou'd never have fail'd of spiriting up an actress to have shewed her judgment by doing it. The men, tho' in general much less blameable than the women on this occasion, yet are not without their errors in it, and those such as greatly hurt the air of probability in the representation. We wou'd entreat of them in general to remember that their parts concern them not only in what we see of them on the stage, but in every thing which we hear passes without, in which they are concern'd. We wou'd not desire things to be carry'd so far indeed on this occasion, as to expect a beau to enter in dirty boots, because he is to mention his having come a journey; but then we wou'd not have an Orestes return from the temple, where at the instigation of Hermione, he has been causing Pyrrhus to be assassinated, without one curl of his peruke out of order. Let the look of reality be kept up; and when the actor tells us of some dreadful bustle he has been in, we wou'd have him shew some marks of it by the disorder of his person.

The first time that Mr. Garrick play'd Macbeth, he took occasion in one of his scenes of greatest confusion, to enter upon the stage with his coat and waistcoat both unbutton'd, and with some other discomposures in his dress, that added greatly to the resemblance of nature in that part of his character. He did this however only the first night, and lost, by the omitting it afterwards, all the merit of having done it at all. We are apt to believe that some of his friends who assume to themselves the character of criticks on stage performances, advis'd him to omit this striking particular, in the following representations: we have no objection to that gentleman's using the friendship of these people hereafter, but hope he will not any more follow their advice.

We are very sensible of the merit that some of our modern players claim to themselves from their judgment in dressing their characters; and we allow it to be a merit of a higher kind on these occasions, than the world in general are willing to think it. But some late instances on one of the theatres make it necessary that we shou'd remind the people who are so fond of their talents in this way, that the habits of characters on the stage shou'd be proper as well as pretty; and that the actors are not only to dress so as not to offend probability, but they are to be ty'd down as much as painters to the general customs of the world. Alexander the great, or Julius Caesar, wou'd appear as monstrous to us in bag wigs on the stage as in a picture. . . .

We have in a former part of this treatise, occasionally mention'd the general and vague resemblance, which there ought always to be between the original and the copy of it on the stage; but we here enter on the subject of a much more particular and more determinate similarity.

We remember very lately, an excellent actress Mrs. Pritchard, playing the part of Jane Shore: She spoke it, as she does every thing else, at least as well as any body cou'd; but we were shock'd in the first scenes, at the face and figure of this actress, under the representation of all those charms that are so lavishly ascrib'd by the poet to that unfortunate heroine; and in the conclusion, nothing cou'd be so unnatural as to see that plump and rosy figure endeavouring to present us with a view of the utmost want, and starving. . . .

If the player wou'd have the representation carry with it an entire air of truth, he must be cautious not only to conduct his action and recitation with a strict regard to nature; but he must never select a character to appear in, which is remarkable for any particular striking singularity which is not in himself. He cannot too frequently remember that the representation of a play is a sort of painting, which owes all its beauty to a close imitation of nature, and that its touches are expected to be even vastly more expressive than those of the pencil: That the more advantages the stage has for the making the illusion perfect, the more perfection we expect to find in it there; and that it is not enough that the fictions it exposes to our view, seem to bear a resemblance to the events which they are intended to figure to us, but that we expect that resemblance to be so perfect, that we shall be able to persuade ourselves that what is in reality but a copy, is an original, and that the very events themselves, and the very persons concern'd in them, are really and truly present before our eyes.

29. MACKLIN'S SCOTTISH MACBETH

IN 1773, when Macklin was in his seventies, he attempted the character of Macbeth at Covent Garden. He abandoned the traditional gold-braided scarlet suit and appeared dressed in Scottish attire, while Lady Macbeth was still decked with the robes of contemporary fashion. John Taylor looked upon the experiment with favor:

> The character of Macbeth had been hitherto performed in the attire of an English general; but Macklin was the first who performed it in the old Scottish garb. His appearance was previously announced by the Coldstream March. . . . When Macklin appeared on the bridge, he was received with shouts of applause, which were repeated throughout the performance. I was seated in the pit, and so near the orchestra that I had a full opportunity of seeing him to advantage. Garrick's representation of the character was before my time; Macklin's was certainly not marked by studied grace of deportment, but he seemed to be more in earnest in the character than any actor I have subsequently seen.

30. PRAISE FOR THE INNOVATION

WILLIAM COOKE, Macklin's biographer, commented on the innovation:

> Previously to this period, Macbeth used to be dressed in a suit of scarlet and gold, a tail wig, etc., in every respect like a modern military officer. Garrick always played it in this manner. . . . Macklin, however, whose eye and mind were ever intent on his profession, saw the absurdity of exhibiting a Scotch character, existing many years before the Norman Conquest, in this manner, and therefore very properly abandoned it for the old Caledonian habit. He shewed the same attention to the subordinate characters as well as to the scenes, decorations, music, and other incidental parts of the performance.

31. LOUTHERBOURG'S ILLUSIONISM

PHILIPPE JACQUES DE LOUTHERBOURG (1740 - 1812), an Alsatian, received his training as a painter of battle scenes and romantic landscapes in Paris. In 1771, Garrick engaged him as a scene designer for

Drury Lane. Even though Loutherbourg wasted his talents on trifling pantomimes and "dramatic entertainments," only rarely entering the field of legitimate drama, he must be regarded as a pioneer designer under whose guidance the conventional wing-and-border stage lost its aridity, and illusionistic realistic scenery made its entrance on the English stage. Loutherbourg broke up the scene by means of practicable set pieces. His backdrops were marvels of picturesque perspective painting. He used cloud effects and transparent scenery and gave flexibility to the wing and border lights by using filters of colored silk. Loutherbourg was chiefly interested in presenting geographical accuracy in romantic picturesqueness. He studied the topography of Derbyshire on the spot, and, from sketches made there, designed the scenery for *The Wonders of Derbyshire* (January 1779). In 1785, when O'Keeffe's pantomime *Omai* was produced at Covent Garden, Loutherbourg made use of the sketches which John Webber had painted in the South Seas while accompanying Captain Cook on his last voyage. In his *Recollections*, O'Keeffe paid tribute to Loutherbourg's ingenuity, and the critic of *The London Magazine* watched with fascination Loutherbourg's sets for the afterpieces of Drury Lane:

At Barnes I composed a grand spectacle for Covent Garden, called *Omai*; the incidents, characters, &c. appropriate to the newly-discovered islands in the southern hemisphere, and closing with the apotheosis of Captain Cook. The effect of this piece was most happy. Shield's melodies were beautifully wild, as suiting his romantic theme; and the dresses and scenery were done from drawings of Mr. Webber, the artist, who had made the voyages with Captain Cook. . . . Loutherbourg planned the scenery. He had previously invented transparent scenery — moonshine, sunshine, fire, volcanoes, &c. as also breaking the scene into several pieces by the laws of perspective, showing miles and miles distance. Before his time, the back was one broad flat, the whole breadth and height of the stage. *Omai* was acted forty nights the first season. Loutherbourg had £100 for his designs, and I another £100 for the composition of the piece, besides the sale of my songs, which brought me about £40.

✦ ✦ ✦

This piece [*The Maid of the Oaks*] is said to have been written by General [John] Burgoyne, and seems entirely calculated for a vehicle to introduce the music and scenery: the latter of which, it must be allowed, is equal, if not superior, to any theatrical exhibition we have ever seen. . . .

Wings and Backdrop Designed by De Loutherbourg for John O'Keefe's Spectacle, *Omai*, Covent Garden, 1785.

The most remarkable scenes were Mr. Oldworth's mansion, which we are informed is taken from a view of Lord Stanley's house and improvements: the portico is an imitation of the temporary building at the late celebrated *Fête Champêtre*; the magnificent scene of the saloon is also similar to that nobleman's grand apartment, which changes to one of the most beautiful scenes ever exhibited, representing a celestial garden, terminated by a prospect of the Temple of Love, in which the statue of the Cyprian goddess appears in the attitude of the Venus of Medicis. The back ground is illuminated by the rays of the sun, which have a most splendid and astonishing effect. . . .

The attention which Mr. Garrick has shewn to the decorations of this piece, is a convincing proof that he never spares either labour or expence, where there is a likelihood of promoting the pleasure of the public. It is said that the scenery only, which has been painted on purpose for the *Maid of the Oaks*, cost £1500. This is a prodigious sum; yet it will not appear in the least extravagant to any body who sees it. The landscapes of Claud are scarcely equal to some of the views exhibited; and if nothing beyond the bare merit of the paintings was held forth to attract the town, we should not be surprised at its bringing twenty crouded audiences. Mr. Garrick's care however has not been confined to the scenery; it has extended to the minutest object that could encrease either the beauty or the magnificence of the entertainment. The number of singers and dancers who are pastorally habited on the occasion, is incredible, and the engagement of *Slingsby* and *Hidou*, the two greatest performers in their stile perhaps on earth, is a circumstance that deserves the highest approbation.

✓   ✓   ✓

A new pantomime was introduced, called, *The Wonders of Derbyshire*, or *Harlequin in the Peak*.

This subject was judiciously chosen for the display of Mr. Loutherbourgh's abilities; but he should have been accompanied into Derbyshire by a man of some dramatick genius; or at least of talents for the invention of a pantomime.

The wonders of the *Peak* is the emphatic phrase in Derbyshire, of which the Peak is a division, and they are, we believe, seven in number. The common tour of curiosity in that country takes them all in; and if Mr. Loutherbourgh had given them in the order in which they are usually observed, and there had been just so much dialogue with the inhabitants as to mark them, the pantomime would not only have been a matter of wonder, but of delight and pleasure.

The view of Castleton, under the hills of which are those astonishing caverns, which are named after the most dishonourable parts of the devil's person, is given with great truth and taste; that of the entrance is too much beautified and illumined; and we suppose the caverns themselves cannot be presented. Indeed Castleton is among the few wonders which may be described and painted, and after all exceed the traveller's expectation.

If the short view of the road between the rocks was designed for Middleton Dale, it was an imperfect one: and it was injudicious to direct the fooleries of harlequin and his pursuers without the dale, when they might have been within it. This dale is in the fracture of a large rock; and a perspective of it would have been a curious and pleasing object.

Harlequin's travels conclude at and near Buxton. The view of the wells, and of that wonderful cavern called Poole's Hole, is taken with great exactness. This *Hole,* of which the inhabitants and guides tell a thousand stories, and which owes its name to the residence of a famous robber in it, called Poole, Mr. Loutherbourgh has made the residence of the genius who protects harlequin. The only advantage arising from this to a man of taste is the pretence, by his ascending, of introducing such a quantity of light, as to show the manner in which Mr. Loutherbourgh has imitated nature in the very process of *petrefaction.*

The view of Chatsworth is a fine landscape, and properly introduced, as it is one of the reputed wonders, and is the residence of the principal owner of all the other wonders.

32. PROMINENCE OF THE DESIGNER

A PASSAGE IN O'Keeffe's *Recollections* indicates that by 1780, perhaps due to Loutherbourg's influence, the scene designer had achieved a prominent place within the theatrical organism:

The mode of the theatre is this: a copy of the drama is put into the hands of the artist who is to plan the scenes (Richards, an R. A. highly distinguished, had the office at this time); he considers upon it, makes models in card-paper, and gives his orders to the painters. The author is often brought into the scene-room to give his opinion on the progress of their work. The wardrobe-keepers, having also their copy of the play, produce the dresses of each character to the author. After this, the several performers when dressed, before the curtain goes up on the first night, make their appearance before the author, to obtain his approbation.

33. ALTERATIONS AT COVENT GARDEN

COVENT GARDEN, opened by John Rich in 1732, was altered in 1784, and six years later, George Saunders, in the course of an examination of the principal European theaters, described its interior:

This theatre is 86 feet long from the stage-opening to the opposite wall at the end of the gallery, and 56 feet wide between the walls; 31 feet 6 inches high from the stage-floor to the ceiling, which slopes upwards to make room for the upper gallery. The form of the area between the box and gallery fronts is an oblong, 36 feet 6 inches from the front of the stage-floor, and 56 feet from the scene to the opposite boxes, and 38 feet 6 inches wide between the boxes. The front boxes are 18 feet deep from the front to the back, the first gallery 30 feet 6 inches, and the second gallery 21 feet 6 inches. I will first take notice of the inconveniences theatres are subjected to, when built of this form, and then examine the present one in particular.

If the sides of a square be ill adapted for viewing . . . the sides of an oblong must be proportionably worse: it is impossible to view the actor from the distant end of the side boxes without great pain, and even then he must be seen very imperfectly, and those seated behind cannot see at all. But the distance occasioned by this form is not the only defect; a considerable one arises from the great depth of the front boxes and two galleries over them. The fronts being low, necessarily obstruct the sound: the little that enters is presently attracted and absorbed by the persons, clothes, &c. of the spectators in the foremost rows (this observation I have often made in the first gallery, where the difference of hearing before the upper gallery and under it was very apparent); the continual respiration of so great a concourse of people in this confined situation, together with the lights, soon renders the air unfit for the purpose of conveying sound; the air losing it's elastic property becomes extremely unwholesome and any remedy applied to those particular parts by the partial introduction of cold air would be productive of bad consequences. If it be necessary to have apertures to renew the air, they should be general; or where one only is used it ought to be situated so as equally to affect the whole theatre.

Persons of rank and private parties are obliged to resort to the side boxes in order to avoid being incommoded by the much complained of admission of all characters into the front boxes; but here they lose the advantage of sight, besides being obliged to a distortion of the body in turning towards the actor; or if, to avoid these inconveniences, they make choice of the stage-box, the line of lamps before their eyes is equally offensive. I believe it is universally agreed that the pit is the only good situation in our present theatres.

Covent Garden theatre has been built about 60 years; during which time it has not undergone any material alteration, except in the decorations, till the year 1784, when it was judiciously widened under the direction of Mr. Richards, who was confined to the present walls, and therefore could not extend it as he wished. This therefore with respect to it's form remains with all the defects usual in English theatres.

Mr. Richards would have acted judiciously had he introduced more painted ornaments in lieu of projecting ones, which as a scenepainter I am rather surprised he did not. For example, the parapets of the gallery-fronts and upper boxes, which afforded opportunities for plain surfaces, are filled in with solid balusters; the others are divided into panels and tablets, with carved ornaments in the friezes; pilasters are placed at the sides of the gallery without the least apparent necessity, and the like all round the lower range of boxes, with decorative arches over; and all the partitions are lined with paper, and festoons of drapery hang in front (this I imagine to have been done to hide an architectural defect, the floor of the upper ranges being below the architrave of the under range); than which nothing can be more injurious to the progress of sound.

The public should not submit to be crowded into such narrow seats: 1 foot 9 inches is the whole space here allowed for seat and void; though a moderate-sized person cannot conveniently sit in a less space than that of 1 foot 10 inches from back to front, nor comfortably in less than that of 2 feet.

The frontispiece is such an one as no architect would have applied. Were a painted frame to be proposed for a picture, how would a connoisseur exclaim! The scene is the picture, and the frontispiece, or in other words the frame, should contrast the picture, and thereby add to the illusion. The great advance of the stage-floor was made with a view to obviate the great difficulty of hearing in this theatre. . . . The stage is very much confined, and therefore subjected to those inconveniences so ably set forth by Monsieur Noverre in his "Observations sur la Construction d'une nouvelle Salle de l'Opéra."

The original form of this theatre was similar to the present theatre in Drury-lane.

34. MORE CHANGES

In 1791, Covent Garden was altered once again. Boaden throws light on the resultant treatment of the spectators in the galleries:

Mr. Harris thought that the rise of prices, which had become absolutely necessary, would be at all events better justified by an obvious and recent expense. He therefore determined to make his innovation in his new building; and Mr. Holland had constructed, in the recess, a theatre in the lyral form, rather solid than light in its appearance, and of which the fronts of the boxes bulged something in the curve of a ship's side. The effect was grand and imposing, as to the tiers and number of the boxes; but the gallery called the first, or two shilling gallery, had been hoisted up to the mansions of the gods; and those turbulent deities were indiscreetly banished [from] the house altogether. The solitary shilling, however splendid, was disdained in the new establishment. This plan insulted two classes of frequenters. The *gout de comparaison* leads people to be tolerably content with their own position, while they see another worse. But when the persons who used to inhabit the first gallery, coming down as it did upon the roof of the lower boxes, saw themselves hoisted over three tiers, and scarcely able to see the actors, or what alone was of much moment, their faces; when they saw, too, no misery beyond their own; they could not but feel, that their modest quota had subjected them to contempt; and that they were to be worse treated than they had been, simply because their pockets had been spared. Thus the very humble man was denied his amusement altogether; and the next class was put into a worse situation, where every thing but his own condition seemed improved. As I cannot report the confusion of Babel, I shall say little as to the riot on the first night — the cat-call, the legitimate pipe of displeasure, . . . was triumphant in the strife, and the actors played unheard.

35. THE SHILLING-GALLERY RESTORED

IN 1794, Mr. Harris had to give in and restore the one-shilling gallery. According to Boaden, the interior was modified considerably:

Now, however, by cutting away a painted gallery, the shilling was permitted to see the stage; indeed, the whole ceiling was new. The frontispiece also a new one. The former column became a pilaster. The general character of the house was a fawn colour, with green and gold pannels. The cappings of the boxes were of green morocco leather; the seats stuffed of the same colour. The seats through the whole house were raised. Behind the curtains some red borders were soberly changed for green, and the machinist . . . obtained more room for his operations.

36. TREND TOWARD LARGER THEATERS

DRURY LANE, which had been built in 1672 from plans of Christopher Wren, was condemned in 1793 and torn down. A new Drury Lane rose on the same site. During Garrick's time the theater had accommodated 2,000 spectators, but as Sheridan, the new manager, was in financial difficulties, the audience capacity was increased to 3,611. Boaden and Cumberland, among others, bewailed the passing of theatrical intimacy when they compared the larger houses of the Sheridan-Kemble era with the playhouses in Garrick's time:

Our present theatres differ materially from that of Garrick. The gallery formed more of his plan, than it does of ours. It came down upon the lower circle of boxes, and its visitors were not seldom exceedingly intelligent persons and passionate admirers of the drama: they sat in a very favorable position for the enjoyment of a play, and seconded the pit in the just distribution of censure and praise. The boxes did not contain anything like the number of persons now nightly visitors of the theatre, but certainly more real fashion. The necessities of proprietors had not then multiplied new renters upon old renters, nor opened their doors to a free list extending beyond authors and newspapers, to nearly every review and magazine, which takes any sort of cognizance of theatrical amusements. Their private boxes, too, were few — what there was showed itself fairly as audience. Upon great occasions seven or eight rows of the pit were laid into the boxes, and then the old Drury exhibited, two months before it closed, £412 as the total taken at the door for the first benefit of Mrs. Siddons, after her return. London, however, was rapidly increasing, and it was conceived that larger theatres were demanded. All the articles of consumption, too, were upon the rise; among these were the salaries of performers; and the patentees thought that they needed not only more spectators, but greater prices. Both of these objects, they now determined to carry, on what they thought sure, because reasonable grounds.

(Cumberland)

Since the stages of Drury Lane and Covent Garden have been so enlarged in their dimensions as to be henceforward theatres for spectators rather than playhouses for hearers, it is hardly to be wondered at if their managers and directors encourage those representations, to which their structure is best adapted. The splendor of the scenes, the ingenuity of the machinist and the rich display of dresses, aided by the captivating charms of music, now in a great degree supercede the labours of the poet. There can be nothing very gratifying in watching the movements of an actor's lips, when we cannot hear the words that proceed from them; but when the animating march strikes up, and the stage lays open its recesses to the depth of a hundred feet for the procession to advance, even the most distant spectator can enjoy his shilling's-worth of show. What then is the poet's chance? Exactly what the parson's would be, if the mountebank was in the market-place, when the bells were chiming for church.

On the stage of old Drury in the days of Garrick the moving brow and penetrating eye of that matchless actor came home to the spectator. As the passions shifted, and were by turns reflected from the mirror of his expressive countenance, nothing was lost; upon the scale of modern Drury many of the finest touches of his art would of necessity fall short. The distant auditor might chance to catch the text, but would not see the comment, that was wont so exquisitely to elucidate the poet's meaning, and impress it on the hearer's heart.

37.   NEW DRURY LANE

THE NEW Drury Lane was opened in 1794 under the management of John Philip Kemble (1757 - 1823). Oulton's first continuation of Victor's *Theatres of London* affords some data on the new building:

The accommodations for the stage are upon a much larger scale than those of any other theatre in Europe. The opening for the scenery is 43 feet wide, and 38 high; after which the painter and machine contriver will have a large space 85 feet in width, 92 in length, and 110 in height, for the exertion of their respective abilities. In the roof of the theatre are contained, besides the

Interior of the Old Intimate Drury Lane Theatre in 1792.
Print Engraved by Hewlet after a Drawing by Capon.

Henry Holland's Enlarged Drury Lane in 1794.
Destroyed by Fire in 1809.
Engraving after a Drawing by John Winston.

The Enlarged Covent Garden in 1794.
Destroyed by Fire in 1808.

barrel-loft, ample room for the scene-painters, and four very large reservoirs, from which water is distributed over every part of the house for the purpose of instantly extinguishing fire. . . . Besides other precautions, an iron curtain has been contrived, which, on any such occasion, would completely prevent all communications between the audience and stage. . . . The audience part of the theatre is formed nearly on a semicircular plan. It contains a pit, eight boxes on each side [of] the pit, two rows of boxes above them, and two galleries, which command a full view of every part of the stage. On each side of the galleries are two more rows of boxes, rising to a cove, which is so contrived as to form the ceiling into a complete circle. The proscenium, or that part of the stage which is contained between the curtain and orchestra, is fitted up with boxes, but without any stage door or the usual addition of large columns.

38.   VISIT TO CAPON'S WORKSHOP

THE LARGER STAGE of Drury Lane required new settings, and Kemble engaged William Capon (1757-1827) to provide them. Capon shared with Kemble a taste for architectural accuracy. His chief interest was architecture of the Gothic type, and, along with this predilection, went an antiquarian's inclination for historical scenes in general. Capon designed the sets for Kemble's new *Macbeth* (April 21, 1794). He painted a view of the Tower of London for *Richard III*, and a replica of the Council Chamber of Crosby House for Nicholas Rowe's *Jane Shore*. The Westminster Palace and English street scenes were further additions to Kemble's loft. When Kemble opened Covent Garden in 1809, he relied once more on Capon who furnished the scenery for his Shakespearean revivals. With Boaden's help we can visit Capon's workshop:

As the dimensions of the new theatre were calculated for an audience, the price of whose admission would amount, even at 6*s.* in the boxes, to more than £700, it was quite clear that for all grand occasions they would want scenery of greater height and width than had been exhibited at old Drury; and that in fact but little of the old stock could be used at all. On this occasion it gives me sincere pleasure to mention the very great acquisition Mr. Kemble had met with in an old friend of mine, who really seemed expressly fashioned, as a scene-painter, to carry into effect the true and perfect decorations which he meditated for the plays of Shakspeare: the artist to whom I allude is Mr. William Capon, who has the honour of being draughtsman to H. R. H. the Duke of York. Mr. Capon, like his old acquaintance, the late John Carter, was cast in the mould of antiquity; and his passion was, and is, the ancient architecture of this country. With all the zeal of an antiquary, therefore, the painter worked as if he had been upon oath; and as all that he painted for the new theatre perished in the miserable conflagration of it a few years after, I indulge myself in some description of the scenery, which so much interested Mr. Kemble. The artist had a private painting room, and Mr. Kemble used to walk me out with him to inspect the progress of these works, which were to be records as well as decorations, and present with every other merit, that for which Kemble was born, — truth.

A chapel of the pointed architecture, which occupied the whole stage, for the performance of the Oratorios, with which the new theatre opened in 1794.

Six chamber wings, of the same order, for general use in our old English plays — very elaborately studied from actual remains.

A view of New Palace Yard, Westminster, as it was in 1793. — 41 feet wide, with corresponding wings.

The ancient palace of Westminster, as it was about 300 years back; from partial remains, and authentic sources of information — put together with the greatest diligence and accuracy — the point of view the S. W. corner of Old Palace Yard. About 42 feet wide and 34 feet to the top of the scene.

Two very large wings, containing portions of the old palace, which the artist made out from an ancient draught met with in looking over some records of the augmentation office in Westminster. It was but a pen and ink sketch originally, but though injured by time, exhibited what was true.

Six wings representing ancient English streets; combinations of genuine remains, selected on account of their picturesque beauty.

The tower of London, restored to its earlier state, for the play of King Richard III.

39. KEMBLE STAGES *MACBETH*

THE FIRST PLAY offered in the enlarged Drury Lane was *Macbeth* (March 1794). Kemble dispensed with the services of Banquo's ghost, but bestowed great care upon the staging of the Witches' scenes:

The scenes were all new, and the witches no longer wore mittens, plaited caps, laced aprons, red stomachers, ruffs, &c, (which was the dress of those weird sisters, when Mess. Beard, Champness, &c. represented them with Garrick's Macbeth) or any human garb, but appeared as preternatural beings, distinguishable only by the fellness of their purposes, and the fatality of their delusions. Hecate's companion spirit descended on the cloud and rose again with him. In the Cauldron-scene, new groups were introduced to personify the black spirits and white, blue spirits and grey. The evil spirits had serpents writhing round them, which had a striking effect.

It has been observed that these imaginary beings have been sometimes dressed above their rank, and as often beneath it: they were elevated into majestic Sibylls by the late Mr. Colman, and by Mr. Garrick sunk down into beggarly Gammers, though intended by Shakespeare as terrific hags. . . . The present attempt of the managers of Drury-lane was to strike the eye with a picture of supernatural power, by such appropriate vestures, as marked neither mortal grandeur nor earthly insignificance; and likewise to avoid all buffoonery in those parts, that *Macbeth* might no longer be deemed a Tragi-Comedy.

40. KEMBLE'S HAMLET

JOHN PHILIP KEMBLE made his London debut as Hamlet (September 30, 1783, Drury Lane). His first biographer, Boaden, pointed out that Kemble's Dane was decidedly original, even with regard to costume:

He had seen no great actor whom he could have copied. His style was formed by his own taste or judgment, or rather grew out of the peculiar properties of his person and his intellectual habits. He was of a solemn and deliberate temperament — his walk was always slow, and his expression of countenance contemplative — his utterance rather tardy for the most part, but always finely articulate, and in common parlance seemed to proceed rather from organization than voice. . . .

We have for so many years been accustomed to see Hamlet dressed in the Vandyke costume, that it may be material to state, that Mr. Kemble played the part in a modern court dress of rich black velvet, with a star on the breast, the garter and pendant ribband of an order — mourning sword and buckles, with deep ruffles: the hair in powder; which, in the scenes of feigned distraction, flowed dishevelled in front and over the shoulders.

As to the expression of the face, perhaps the powdered hair, from contrast, had a superior effect to the short curled wig at present worn. The eyes seemed to possess more brilliancy. With regard to costume, correctness in either case is out of the question, only that the Vandyke habit is preferable, as it removes a positive anachronism and inconsistency.

41.   KEMBLE'S PRODUCTION BOOKS

THE ATTENTION paid to the visual elements of production was but one aspect of Kemble's Shakespearean revivals; his labor started with the preparation of new stage versions, and, before rehearsals began, a detailed production book was made available:

The inexhaustible stores of Shakspeare presented to Mr. Kemble a highly tempting monodram, in the play of King Henry V. . . . He therefore set himself seriously to prepare the play for representation. Now this, in Mr. Kemble's notion of the business, was, not to order the prompter to write out the parts from some old mutilated prompt copy lingering on his shelves; but himself to consider it attentively in the author's genuine book: then to examine what corrections could be properly admitted into his text; and, finally, what could be cut out in the representation, not as disputing the judgment of the author, but as suiting the time of the representation to the habits of his audience, or a little favouring the powers of his actors, in order that the performance might be as uniformly good as it was practicable to make it. The stage arrangements throughout the play were all distinctly marked by him in his own clear exact penmanship, and when he had done his work, his theatre received, in that perfected copy, a principle of exactness, which was of itself sufficient to keep its stage unrivalled for truth of scenic exhibition.

42. THE SIDDONIAN DIGNITY

IN 1789 - 1790, Mrs. Sarah Kemble Siddons (1755 - 1831) developed a taste for Greek sculpture. A sculptress friend, Mrs. Damer, may have helped to stimulate her interest in Greek statues from which the actress tried to recapture the simplicity of attire and the severity of attitude. As Boaden put it: "It soon became apparent that Mrs. Siddons was conversant with drapery more dignified than the shifting robes of fashion; and in truth, her action also occasionally reminded the spectator of classic models." Elsewhere in his biography of the actress, Boaden made this comment on her predilection for the classic costume:

So few English performers are ever perfectly at their ease upon the stage, that the springing off with a glance at the pit, if it were not thought energetic, would be chosen from nervous impatience at supporting the gaze of thousands, while the performer merely walks away. All the rhymed couplets, to carry them off with effect, attest the misery of departure; and the speaking a few words as entering, also shew the desire to come into as speedy a commerce with the audience as can possibly be achieved.

The amazing self-possession of Mrs. Siddons rendered distance only the means of displaying a system of graceful and considerate dignity, or weighty and lingering affliction, as the case might demand. In the hurry of distraction, she could stop, and in some frenzied attitude speak wonders to the eye, till a second rush forward brought her to the proper ground on which her utterance might be trusted. I will not be so ungallant as to ascribe the composure of this grand woman to any vain complacency in her majestic form. By thinking so, I should ill repay that artist-like admiration with which I always beheld it. No: I believe she thought at such moments only of the character, and the support it demanded from her of every kind. When Mrs. Siddons quitted her dressing-room, I believe she left there the last thought about herself. Never did I see her eye wander from the business of the scene — no recognizance of the most noble of her friends exchanged the character for the individual. In this duty her brother would frequently fail; and he seemed to take a delight in shewing how absolute a mastery he possessed — that he could make a sign and sometimes speak to a friend near him, and yet seem to carry on the action and the look of the character. I never saw this in his sister — no, not for a moment. . . .

Conspiring with the larger stage to produce some change in her style, was her delight in statuary, which directed her attention to the antique, and made a remarkable impression upon her, as to simplicity of attire and severity of attitude. The actress had formerly complied with fashion, and deemed the prevalent becoming; she now saw that tragedy was debased by the flutter of light materials, and that the head, and all its powerful action from the shoulder, should never be encumbered by the monstrous inventions of the hair-dresser and the milliner. She was now, therefore, prepared to introduce a mode of stage decoration, and of deportment, parting from one common principle, itself originating with a people qualified to legislate even in taste itself What, however, began in good sense, deciding among the forms of grace and beauty, was, by political mania in the rival nation, carried into the excess of shameless indecency. France soon sent us over her amazons to burlesque all classical costume, and her models were received among us with unaffected disgust. What Mrs. Siddons had chosen remains in a great degree the standard of female costume to the present hour; and any little excesses by degrees dropt off, and left our ladies the heirs of her taste and its inseparable modesty. I have said that her deportment now varied considerably; and I have no doubt of the fact. In a small space the turns are quick and short. Where the area is considerable the step is wider, the figure more erect, and the whole progress more grand and powerful, the action is more from the shoulder; and we now first began to hear of the perfect form of Mrs. Siddons's arm. Her walk has never been attempted by any other actress; and in deliberate dignity was as much alone, as the expression of her countenance.

43.   SIR JOSHUA'S COUNSEL

Mrs. Siddons was encouraged in her reform of stage costume by Sir Joshua Reynolds, who paid frequent visits to her dressing room and, after she had dismissed the curls and lappets, praised "the round apple form" which she had given to her head. In Mrs. Siddons' own words:

Sir Joshua often honoured me by his presence at the theatre. He approved very much of my costumes, and of my hair without powder, which at that time was used in great profusion, with a reddish-brown tint, and a great quantity of pomatum, which, well kneaded together, modelled the fair ladies' tresses into large curls like demi-cannon. My locks were generally braided into a small compass, so as to ascertain the size and shape of my head, which, to a painter's eye, was of course an agreeable departure from the mode. My short waist, too, was to him a pleasing contrast to the long stiff stays and hoop petticoats, which were then the fashion, even on the stage, and it obtained his unqualified approbation.

44. TWO FAMOUS ROLES OF MRS. SIDDONS

Two of Mrs. Siddons' famous roles were Mrs. Beverley in Edward Moore's *The Gamester* and Lady Randolph in John Home's *Douglas*. In 1811 - 1812, William Charles Macready, then a budding actor, played Mr. Beverley and Norval to Mrs. Siddons' respective heroines. In his *Reminiscences* Macready left an emotional account of her acting:

I will not presume to catalogue the merits of this unrivalled artist, but may point out, as a guide to others, one great excellence that distinguished all her personations. This was the unity of design, the just relation of all parts to the whole, that made us forget the actress in the character she assumed. Throughout the tragedy of 'The Gamester' devotion to her husband stood out as the mainspring of her actions, the ruling passion of her being; apparent when reduced to poverty in her graceful and cheerful submission to the lot to which his vice has subjected her, in her fond excuses of his ruinous weakness, in her conciliating expostulations with his angry impatience, in her indignant repulse of Stukeley's advances, when in the awful dignity of outraged virtue she imprecates the vengeance of Heaven upon his guilty head. The climax to her sorrows and sufferings was in the dungeon, when on her knees, holding her dying husband, he dropped lifeless from her arms. Her glaring eyes were fixed in stony blankness on his face; the powers of life seemed suspended in her; her sister and Lewson gently raised her, and slowly led her unre-

sisting from the body, her gaze never for an instant averted from
it; when they reached the prison door she stopped, as if awakened
from a trance, uttered a shriek of agony that would have pierced
the hardest heart, and, rushing from them, flung herself, as if
for union in death, on the prostrate form before her. . . .

In the part of Mrs. Beverley the image of conjugal devotion
was set off with every charm of grace and winning softness. In
Lady Randolph the sorrows of widowhood and the maternal
fondness of the chieftain's daughter assumed a loftier demeanour,
but still the mother's heart showed itself above all power of re-
pression by conventional control. In her first interview with Norval, presented as Lord Randolph's defender from the assassins,
the mournful admiration of her look, as she fixed her gaze upon
him, plainly told that the tear which Randolph observed to start
in her eye was nature's parental instinct in the presence of her
son. The violence of her agitation while listening to old Norval's
narration of the perils of her infant seemed beyond her power
longer to endure, and the words, faintly articulated, as if the
last effort of a mortal agony, "Was he alive?" sent an electric
thrill through the audience. In disclosing the secret of his birth
to Norval, and acknowledging herself his mother, how exquisite
was the tenderness with which she gave loose to the indulgence
of her affection! As he knelt before her she wreathed her fingers
in his hair, parted it from his brow, in silence looking into his
features to trace there the resemblance of the husband of her
love, then dropping on her knees, and throwing her arms around
him, she showered kisses on him, and again fastened her eyes on
his, repeating the lines,

> "Image of Douglas! Fruit of fatal love!
> All that I owe thy sire I pay to thee!"

Her parting instructions, under the influence of her fears for
her son's safety, were most affectingly delivered. When he had
fallen under the treacherous stab of Glenalvon, she had sunk in
a state of insensibility on his body. On the approach of Randolph
and Anna she began to recover recollection. To Randolph's excuses her short and rapid reply, "Of thee I think not!" spoke
her indifference, and disregard of every worldly thing beyond the

beloved object stretched in death before her. Leaning over him, and gazing with despairing fondness on his face, she spoke out in heartrending tones —

> "My son! — My son!
> My beautiful, my brave! — How proud was I
> Of thee, and of thy valour; my fond heart
> O'erflowed this day with transport when I thought
> Of growing old amidst a race of thine!"

The anguish of her soul seemed at length to have struck her brain. The silence of her fixed and vacant stare was terrible, broken at last by a loud and frantic laugh that made the hearers shudder. She then sprang up, and, with a few self-questioning words indicating her purpose of self-destruction, hurried in the wild madness of desperation from the scene.

45. WANTED: A DISCIPLINARIAN

AT THE TIME when England's classical repertoire was eclipsed by melodrama and the child actor, Betty, stole the thunder from the Kembles, Thomas Holcroft, in his *Theatrical Recorder* of 1805, subjected the acting of the period to an analysis which manifested the lack of a central artistic authority on the stages of both Theatres Royal:

Among performers, who are favorites with the public in particular, it is far from uncommon to see them so totally forget decency, the respect due to an audience, and the contempt which they bring upon themselves, as to look about them, into the boxes and the pit, in order either to discover who they know, or even, at some times, impudently to make slight nods, signs, or grins: a fault so very insolent, and so totally forgetful, not merely of public respect, but of the whole tenor of the business in which they are engaged, that it would be scarcely too severe a punishment if an audience were unanimously to rise, and insist on the performer, who thus transgresses, not daring to appear again for a month, and if they were, during that space of time, to lose their emoluments. . . .

Performers are not unfrequently seen to read a letter on the stage, and, perhaps from accident, perhaps from fright, or some passion which the scene is supposed to inspire, they will suffer the letter to drop, and never condescend to pick it up again.

It is needless to detail the many reasons that render such conduct ridiculous, absurd, and unnatural. It is a fault for which no excuse can be offered.

Of the same nature is that of the stage hero, who, being about to tilt with another, puts himself into an attitude, but first carefully, but with a flourish, throws away his hat; and after battle, walks away bare-headed to cool himself: no doubt wishing it to be supposed he is either too important a person, or has too feverish a brain, at such a time, for him to walk with a hat on; and therefore the stage keepers are sent, in the face of the audience, to take it away. . . .

Swords are frequently seen left, with the same unaccountable carelessness, when the owners hear their cues for leaving the stage.

In short, the neglectful and ridiculous incidents, of this nature, of which performers are very frequently guilty, do but denote a laxity of discipline, and prove, what we well know, that there is no person whose nightly duty it is to superintend the whole conduct of a piece, and exact a rigid but a just decorum. The want of such a censor, such a disciplinarian, is much greater than is imagined.

Going off at a wrong door, or rather where there is not supposed to be any door, nor any aperture, is another of these strange but still more familiar absurdities. It is true that, when a play is first put into rehearsal, great care is taken on this head; but the neglect, that nightly increases, becomes at length truly disgusting. The actors are not aware how much they offend common sense, and the people whose esteem they ought most carefully to court, when their slovenliness becomes so very reprehensible.

In the mode of entering and retiring from the stage, a judicious actor cannot too carefully consider what is the tone of feeling, which he himself is supposed to have in combination with that of other performers, or rather of the scene itself. Offence is sometimes given, to a discriminating judge, by the performer's neglect of this consideration, at entering; but more frequently at forgetting as it were to give intimation, either by a restless look, an attitude, an approach to the door, or some other mode of intending soon to depart. Unless in particular cases, departure should never appear to be unexpected, and abrupt; for then it is not only spiritless, but often improbable, and certainly unmeaning. To enter and retire perfectly in unison with the tone, or passion, of the scene, is what may be called a delicate branch of the art of acting; which, though it does not require deep study, demands great attention.

To tragedians and the performers of gentlemen, a short step is peculiarly destructive of dignity; while in characters of low breeding but of animation, it is no less a true mark of such persons. To step with measured affectation, like an opera dancer to a march, is no less laughable; it destroys reality: for a spectator cannot but imagine he sees a foolish actor, instead of the character he ought to personify.

The short step excites risibility at first, and at length contempt and weariness, when it is accompanied, as is seen in some actors, by a mechanical and uninterruptedly alternate habit of first stepping forward and then stepping back. Among country actors this is no uncommon fault; and in London it is seen, but, in a less glaring manner.

The action of the arms ought to be carefully modest and restrained. There are performers who, at the first sentence with their right hand, and the second with their left, continue an alternate through each speech. They must have taken peculiar pains to have acquired such a puppet-show mode of disposing of themselves.

There are many who have a seesaw eternally monotonous motion, which, were nothing else seen or heard, would soon lull every patient spectator to sleep.

There are others who continually shake a little finger; some two fingers; some the whole hand; but the shaking must continue, while they continue speaking.

A frequent clenching of the fist is a favorite mode, which several actors have, of endeavouring to make the audience believe how much they are in earnest; especially in the characters of tyrants.

The arms akimbo is also often thought the attitude of grandeur, instead of, as it really is, the certain sign of vulgar and inflated imbecility. . . .

One habitual error, very injurious to the piece and the performer, ought carefully to be noticed; which is, that there scarcely can be an occasion when an actor ought to speak with his profile, much less with half his back, turned to the audience; for then, not only his voice, but, his features, are without effect. Yet, there are many performers who will continue, through a whole scene, with the profile, a little more or a little less, toward the audience. This is an unpardonable fault. If possible, the face should front the stage, yet the eye remain totally unconscious of the presence of an audience; and, when the nature of the scene absolutely requires the actor to look directly at the person with whom he is speaking, he still should keep a three-quarter face to the audience.

Chapter XI

Weimar Classicism

1. THE WEIMAR AUDIENCE

In 1775, Johann Wolfgang Goethe (1749 - 1832) accepted the invitation of Duke Karl August to make Weimar his permanent residence. In 1791, he assumed the management of the new Ducal Court Theater, a post which he held for twenty-six years. The Weimar theater audience had a good reputation even prior to Goethe's appointment. The conditions on which he could continue to build are described in a Berlin journal of 1785:

> The drama is included among the manifold pleasures which one can enjoy in Weimar and which give this small city an advantage over so many larger ones in Germany. Here more than anywhere else is the drama loved and the theater very well attended. Since the time of Koch, Weimar had a good theater, and this explains why, in respect to the stage as well as in respect to various other things, the more cultured part of the population had developed a really good and solid taste, which gradually spread to the lower classes. Consequently, a very poor company could achieve success nowhere less than here. For although it would be assured against the danger of being hooted off the stage — since such license was never allowed here — yet in a very short time the attendance would fall off considerably. Nowhere, however, can a better company develop from a poor one in a shorter period than in Weimar. For, aside from the fact that every actor must of necessity exert all his powers while playing before a crowd of people who have seen the best in Germany, he has also to fear the criticism of the experts whose opinions carry great weight with the public in Weimar, as well as with that in all Germany.

2. GOETHE'S MANAGEMENT

GOETHE'S WEIMAR THEATER appealed to a cultural elite, a well-balanced fusion of middle-class and aristocratic elements, and thus closely resembled the audience coalition of French classicism, *la court et la ville*. In Weimar, this hybrid of courtly residence and country village, where there were ten thousand poets and just a few inhabitants, there could not be, as Goethe pointed out to Eckermann, much talk of the common people. The management was pleased that it did not have to deal with the rabble. Goethe found himself face to face with his ideal audience during the summer seasons in Lauchstädt. In the autumn, his company would return to Weimar and play for a more general audience: nobility in the boxes, prosperous and highly cultured middle-class people and students in the pit, and servants and young craftsmen in the gallery. Since Goethe was in a position to offer plays which would please only an elite, he could, with a clear conscience, put on others more suited to a general taste. He tried to develop versatility in his actors and considered such adaptability equally desirable for the audience. When Eckermann once praised Goethe's management of the Ducal Theater, Goethe stated some of the principles that had guided him:

I did not look to magnificent scenery, and a brilliant wardrobe, but I looked to good pieces. From tragedy to farce, every species was welcome; but a piece was obliged to have something in it to find favor. It was necessary that it should be great and clever, cheerful and graceful, and, at all events, healthy and containing some pith. All that was morbid, weak, lachrymose, and sentimental, as well as all that was frightful, horrible and offensive to decorum, was utterly excluded; I should have feared, by such expedients, to spoil both actors and audience.

By means of good pieces I educated the actors; for the study of excellence, and the perpetual practice of excellence, must necessarily make something of a man whom nature has not left ungifted. I was, also, constantly in personal contact with the actors. I attended the readings of plays, and explained to every one his part; I was present at the chief rehearsals, and talked with the actors as to any improvements that might be made; I was never absent from a performance, and pointed out the next day anything which did not appear to me to be right. By these means I advanced them in their art. But I also sought to raise the whole class in the esteem of society by introducing the best and most promising into my own circle, and thus showing to the world that I considered them worthy of social intercourse with myself. The result of this was that the rest of the higher society in Weimar did not remain behind me, and that actors and actresses gained soon an honorable admission into the best circles. By all this they acquired a great personal as well as external culture. My pupil Wolff, in Berlin, and our Durand are people of the finest tact in society. Oels and Graff have enough of the higher order of culture to do honor to the best circles.

Schiller proceeded in the same spirit as myself. He had a great deal of intercourse with actors and actresses. He, like me, was present at every rehearsal; and after every successful performance of one of his pieces, it was his custom to invite the actors, and to spend a merry day with them. All rejoiced together at that which had succeeded, and discussed how anything might be done better next time. But even when Schiller joined us, he found both actors and the public already cultivated to a high degree; and it is not to be denied that this conduced to the rapid success of his pieces.

3. SELECTION OF PLAYERS

ON ANOTHER OCCASION, Eckermann asked Goethe how he had chosen his actors:

"I can scarcely say," returned Goethe; "I had various modes of proceeding. If a striking reputation preceded the new actor, I let him act, and saw how he suited the others; whether his style and manner disturbed our ensemble, or whether he would supply a deficiency. If, however, he was a young man who had never trodden a stage before, I first considered his personal qualities; whether he had about him anything prepossessing or attractive, and, above all things, whether he had control over himself. For an actor who possesses no self-possession, and who cannot appear before a stranger in his most favorable light, has, generally speaking, little talent. His whole profession requires continual self-denial, and a continual existence in a foreign mask.

"If his appearance and his deportment pleased me, I made him read, in order to test the power and extent of his voice, as well as the capabilities of his mind. I gave him some sublime passage from a great poet, to see whether he was capable of feeling and expressing what was really great; then something passionate and wild, to prove his power. I then went to something marked by sense and smartness, something ironical and witty, to see how he treated such things, and whether he possessed sufficient freedom. Then I gave him something in which was represented the pain of a wounded heart, the suffering of a great soul, that I might learn whether he had it in his power to express pathos.

"If he satisfied me in all these numerous particulars, I had a well-grounded hope of making him a very important actor. If he appeared more capable in some particulars than in others, I remarked the line to which he was most adapted. I also now knew his weak points, and, above all, endeavored to work upon him so that he might strengthen and cultivate himself here. If I remarked faults of dialect, and what are called provincialisms, I urged him to lay them aside, and recommended to him social intercourse and friendly practice with some member of the stage who was entirely free from them. I then asked him whether he could dance and fence; and if this were not the case, I would hand him over for some time to the dancing and fencing masters.

"If he were now sufficiently advanced to make his appearance, I gave him at first such parts as suited his individuality, and I desired nothing but that he should represent himself. If he now appeared to me of too fiery a nature, I gave him phlegmatic characters; if too calm and tedious, I gave him fiery and hasty characters; that he might thus learn to lay aside himself and assume a foreign individuality."

4.   THE "RULES FOR ACTORS"

EVERY DIRECTION which Goethe gave during rehearsals was designed to have a specific effect upon the spectator whom he regarded as the chief personage in the theater. He impressed upon his players that there was no Fourth Wall to the Weimar stage, and that the actor had to bear in mind that he was definitely acting for an audience. The maxims of Goethe's system of directing have survived in the so-called *Rules for Actors*. In 1803, Goethe coached two Weimar actors, Pius Alexander Wolff and Karl Franz Grüner, who kept a record of Goethe's instructions. In 1824, Eckermann brought order to these notes and published them with Goethe's consent as a sort of primer of acting. The basic principle that stood behind these rules emerged in one of Goethe's conversations with Eckermann, when Goethe said: "An actor should properly go to school to a sculptor and a painter; for, in order to represent a Greek hero, it is necessary for him to study carefully the antique sculptures which have come down to us, and to impress on his mind the natural grace of their sitting, standing, and walking. But the merely bodily is not enough. He must also, by diligent study of the best ancient and modern authors, give a great cultivation to his mind. This will not only assist him to understand his part, but will also give a higher tone to his whole being and his whole deportment."

The sections which Goethe devoted to the subject of purity of speech may safely be omitted here, but his instructions, concerning bodily stage movement, must be considered as a valiant attempt to stem the tide of realism and to defend the sacred precinct of poetic drama:

35. First of all, the player must consider that he should not only imitate nature but also portray it ideally, thereby, in his presentation, uniting the true with the beautiful.

36. Therefore the actor must have complete control over each part of his body so that he may be able to use each limb freely, harmonically, and gracefully, in accord with the expression called for.

37. The body should be carried in the following manner: the chest up, the upper half of the arms to the elbows somewhat close to the torso, the head slightly turned toward the person to whom one is speaking. But this should be done only slightly so that three quarters of the face is always turned to the audience.

38. For the actor must always remember that he is on the stage for the sake of the audience.

39. Nor should actors play to each other as if no third person were present. This would be a case of misunderstood naturalness. They should never act in profile nor turn their backs to the spectators. If it is done in the interest of the characterization or out of necessity, then let it be done with discernment and grace.

40. One should also take care never to speak in an upstage direction, but always toward the audience. For the actor must always be conscious of two elements, namely, of the person with whom he is engaged in conversation, and of the spectators. Rather than turn the head completely, the eyes should be moved.

41. It is an important point that when two are acting together, the speaker should always move upstage, while the one who has stopped speaking should move slightly downstage. If this advantageous shifting is carried out with skill — and through practice it can be done with great ease — then the best effect is achieved for the eye as well as for the intelligibility of the declamation. An actor who masters this will produce a very beautiful effect when acting with others who are equally trained. He will have a great advantage over those who do not observe this rule.

42. If two persons speak with each other, the one who stands

on the left should be careful not to approach too closely the one on the right. The person of higher social scale (women, elders, noblemen) always occupies the right side. Even in everyday life a certain distance is kept from a person who is respected. The opposite betrays a lack of education. The actor should show himself to be an educated person and therefore very closely observe this rule. Whoever stands at the right should insist on his prerogative and not allow himself to be driven toward the wings; rather should he stand still, signalling with the left hand to the obtrusive person to move away.

43. A beautiful contemplative pose (for a young man for instance): the chest and the entire body erect and up, the feet in the fourth dance position, the head somewhat inclined to one side, the eyes fixed to the ground, with both arms hanging loosely.

44. The actor should never carry a cane, for the free motion of the hands and arms must be assured.

45. To be avoided: the newfangled fashion of hiding one hand behind the lapel of the coat.

46. It is very improper to have one hand on top of the other or have them resting on the stomach, or to stick one or even both into the vest.

47. The hand itself should never form a fist, nor should it be pressed flat against the thigh (as soldiers do). Some of the fingers should be a little bent, others straight; under no circumstance should they be kept stiff.

48. The two middle fingers should always stay together; the thumb, index and little finger should be somewhat bent. In this manner the hand is in its proper position and ready for any movement.

49. The upper half of the arm should always be somewhat close to the torso; it should move to a much lesser degree than the lower half which should have the greatest agility. For, if I raise my arms just slightly when the talk concerns common things only, then much more effect is produced if I raise it on high. If I do not conform my gestures to the weaker accents of my speech, then I shall not have sufficient strength for the stronger accents, thereby losing all gradation of effect.

50. Nor should the hands return to their rest position prior to the conclusion of the speech, and then only gradually, just as the speech is being concluded.

51. The movement of the arms should be done in sequence. First the hand should be moved, then the elbow, and finally the entire arm. It should never be lifted suddenly, for any movement in disregard of the sequence would result in ugly stiffness.

52. It is of great advantage for the beginner to keep his elbows close to his torso so that he may thereby gain control over this part of the body. Even in his daily life the beginning actor should exercise by consistently holding his arms bent back and even bound back when he is alone. While walking or in moments of leisure, the player should keep his fingers constantly in motion.

53. Descriptive gestures with the hand should be made but sparingly, though they cannot be omitted altogether. . . .

55. Descriptive gestures cannot be avoided, but they must be made in an unpremeditated manner. . . .

57. One should be very careful not to cover the face or body while moving the hands.

58. If I must extend the hand, and the right is not expressly prescribed, I can extend the left hand as well, for there is no right or left on the stage. One must always try not to destroy the pictorial composition by an awkward position. If I am forced, however, to extend the right hand, and I am so placed that I have to pass my hand across my body, then I should rather step back a little and extend it so that I show my entire front to the audience.

59. The player should consider on which side of the stage he is standing so that he can adapt his gestures accordingly.

60. Whoever stands on the right side should act with his left hand, and vice versa, so that the chest be covered as little as possible.

61. Even in emotional scenes, when both hands are in action, consideration has to be given to the preceding paragraphs.

62. For this very purpose and that the chest be in full view of the spectator, it is advisable that the actor on the right side places his left foot forward, while the actor on the left has his right foot forward. . . .

65. In order to acquire pantomimic skill and to make his arms supple, the beginner will draw great advantage from trying to convey his role to another person purely by means of pantomime and without words; for this will force him to choose the most suitable gestures.

66. In order to acquire an easy and appropriate movement of the feet, boots should never be worn during rehearsals.

67. The actor, especially the one who has to play lovers and other light parts, should keep a pair of slippers on stage in which to rehearse, and he will soon notice the good results.

68. In rehearsal nothing should be tolerated that could not also occur in performance.

69. The actresses should lay aside their small purses.

70. No actor should rehearse in his overcoat, but have the hands and arms free, as in the play. For the coat not only prevents him from making the appropriate gestures, but forces him to assume wrong ones which he will mechanically repeat in performance.

71. In rehearsal the actor should make no movement that is not appropriate to the part.

72. He who sticks his hand in his bosom during the rehearsal of a tragic part is in danger of reaching for an opening in his armor during the performance.

73. A very coarse blunder to be avoided: if the seated actor, raising himself slightly, pulls his chair forward after he has seized it by passing his hands between the thighs. This is an offense not only against the ideal of beauty, but still more against propriety.

74. The actor should not produce a handkerchief on the stage, nor blow his nose or spit. It is terrible, within the sphere of a work of art, to be reminded of such physical necessities. To take care of an emergency, one should always carry a small handkerchief, which is now in fashion anyway. . . .

82. The stage and the auditorium, the actors and the spectators, together represent the theatrical entity.

83. The stage is to be regarded as a figureless tableau for which the actor supplies the figure.

84. Hence, one should never act too close to the wings.

85. Nor should one step under the proscenium arch. This is the greatest fault, for the figure leaves the very space in which it makes a composite whole with the scenery and the other players.

86. An actor standing alone on the stage should remember that he is called to fill out the stage with his presence, and this so much the more when the attention is focused solely upon him.

87. As the augurs with their staffs divided the heavens into various areas, the actor, in his mind, can divide the stage into various spaces which for experiment can be represented on paper by rhombic areas. The stage floor then becomes a sort of checkerboard. The actor can determine which square he will enter on. He can note these on paper and is then certain that, in emotional scenes, he will not inartistically rush back and forth, but will join the beautiful with the meaningful.

88. Whoever makes his entrance for a soliloquy from an upstage wing does well to move diagonally so that he reaches the opposite side of the proscenium. Diagonal movements are in general very pleasing.

89. He who comes downstage from the rearmost wing to join a person already standing on the stage, should not walk parallel with the wings, but should move slightly toward the prompter.

5.   A MALE HOSTESS OF THE INN

As a manager, Goethe welcomed plays that served to remind the spectator "that the whole essence of the theater is play, and that he must stand above it, without enjoying it any less on that account, if he is to be benefited aesthetically or, indeed, morally." It was in Italy that Goethe recognized the theater as an institution dedicated to sensualism. In Rome, at a performance of Goldoni's *La Locandiera*, he was surprised to see men acting women's parts. After the initial strangeness had disappeared, Goethe experienced the unique aesthetic pleasure which Elizabethan playgoers must have felt when they watched boys playing Juliet and Cressida:

I visited the Roman comedies not without prejudice, but I soon found myself unconsciously reconciled. I found a pleasure to which I had hitherto been a stranger, and observed that many others shared it with me. I reflected on the cause of it, and came to the conclusion that, in the particular kind of representation we witnessed, the idea of imitation, the thought of art was called forth vividly, and that, on the other hand, with all the skilful playing, only a kind of self-conscious illusion was produced.

We Germans remember how the parts of old men were represented to the point of deception by an able young man, and how that actor afforded us a double pleasure. In the same way, we experience a double charm from the fact that these people are not women, but play the part of women. We see a youth who has studied the idiosyncrasies of the female sex in their character and behavior; he has learned to know them, and reproduces them as artist; he plays not himself, but a third, and, in truth, a foreign nature. We come to understand the female sex so much the better because some one has observed and meditated on their ways, and not the process itself, but the result of the process, is presented to us.

All art being, under the light of this consideration, especially distinguished from simple imitation, it follows that, with respect to the peculiar kind of representation in question, we should experience a peculiar kind of pleasure, and overlook many an imperfection in the execution of the whole. Of course, it is understood, as was above touched upon, that the pieces chosen ought to be suitable for this kind of representation.

The public could not refuse giving universal applause to the *Locandiera* of Goldoni. The young man who took the part of hostess of an inn expressed as happily as possible the different shades of such a character — the composed coldness of a maiden who looks after her business, who is polite, friendly, and obliging to every one, but neither loves nor wishes to be loved, still less will give ear to the passionate suits of her distinguished guests; the secret tender coquetries by which she contrives to captivate anew her male guests; her offended pride when one of them meets her in a harsh, unfriendly way; the many dainty blandishments by which she allures him, and, finally, her triumph in having got the better of him also.

I am convinced, and have indeed personally seen, that a skilful and intelligent female actress may acquire for herself much praise in this part, but the concluding scenes, represented by a lady, will always give offense. The expression of that invincible coldness, of that sweet feeling of revenge, of that arrogant, spiteful pleasure, will, when manifested before us in immediate reality, excite our indignation. Finally, when she gives her hand to the footman, in order to have only a servant-man in the house — such a lame conclusion of the piece would give little satisfaction. In the Roman theater, on the other hand, it was not lack-love coldness or female arrogance itself we observed; the representation only reminded us of that. People consoled themselves by the reflection that this time at least it was not true; people clapped their hands in merry spirits to the young man, rejoicing that he knew so well the dangerous qualities of the loved sex, and that by a happy imitation of their behavior he revenged us, as it were, on the fair ones for all the ills of that kind we had suffered at their hands.

6. THE IDEALITY OF THE STAGE

Upon his return from Italy (1788), Goethe looked with disgust at the crude realism that had invaded the German stage. The idea of the box set had been imported from France, where Diderot and Beaumarchais threatened the ideality of the stage, something which the French had attained only after great effort. Goethe rejected the box set which, in his eyes, could give pleasure only to the uneducated, who confused a work of art with a work of nature:

The highest problem of any art is to produce by appearance the illusion of a higher reality. But it is a false endeavor to realize the appearance until at last only something commonly real remains. As an ideal locality, the stage, by the application of the laws of perspective to wings ranged one behind the other, had attained the greatest advantage; and this very gain they now wished wantonly to abandon, by shutting up the sides of the theater and forming real room walls. With such an arrangement of the stage, the play itself, the actors' mode of playing, in a word, everything was to coincide, and thus an entirely new theater was to arise.

7. AESTHETIC EDUCATION OF A PLAYGOER

Goethe's artistic credo concerning matters theatrical can best be deduced from the truly Platonic dialogue which the poet published in 1798, in *Die Propyläen*:

In a certain German theatre there was represented a sort of oval amphitheatrical structure, with boxes filled with painted spectators, seemingly occupied with what was being transacted below. Many of the real spectators in the pit and boxes were dissatisfied with this, and took it amiss that anything so untrue and improbable was put upon them. Whereupon the conversation took place of which we here give the general purport.

The Agent of the Artist. Let us see if we cannot by some means agree more nearly.

The Spectator. I do not see how such a representation can be defended.

Agent. Tell me, when you go into a theatre, do you not expect all you see to be true and real?

Spectator. By no means! I only ask that what I see shall appear true and real.

Agent. Pardon me if I contradict even your inmost conviction and maintain this is by no means the thing you demand.

Spectator. This is singular! If I did not require this, why should the scene painter take so much pains to draw each line in the most perfect manner, according to the rules of perspective, and represent every object according to its own peculiar perfection? Why waste so much study on the costume? Why spend so much time to insure its truth, so that I may be carried back into those times? Why is that player most highly praised who most truly expresses the sentiment, who in speech, gesture, delivery, comes nearest the truth, who persuades me that I behold not an imitation, but the thing itself?

Agent. You express your feeling admirably well, but it is harder than you may think to have a right comprehension of our feelings. What would you say if I reply that theatrical representations by no means seem really true to you, but rather to have only an appearance of truth?

Spectator. I should say that you have advanced a subtlety that is little more than a play upon words.

Agent. And I maintain that when we are speaking of the operations of the soul, no words can be delicate and subtle enough; and that this sort of play upon words indicates a need of the soul, which, not being able adequately to express what passes within us, seeks to work by way of antithesis, to give an answer to each side of the question, and thus, as it were, to find the mean between them.

Spectator. Very good. Only explain yourself more fully, and, if you will oblige me, by examples.

Agent. I shall be glad to avail myself of them. For instance, when you are at an opera, do you not experience a lively and complete satisfaction?

Spectator. Yes, when everything is in harmony, one of the most complete I know.

Agent. But when the good people there meet and compliment each other with a song, sing from billets that they hold in their hands, sing you their love, their hatred, and all their passions, fight singing, and die singing, can you say that the whole representation, or even any part of it, is true? or, I may say, has even an appearance of truth?

Spectator. In fact, when I consider, I could not say it had. None of these things seems true.

Agent. And yet you are completely pleased and satisfied with the exhibition?

Spectator. Beyond question. I still remember how the opera used to be ridiculed on account of this gross improbability, and how I always received the greatest satisfaction from it, in spite of this, and find more and more pleasure the richer and more complete it becomes.

Agent. And you do not then at the opera experience a complete deception.

Spectator. Deception, that is not the proper word, — and yet, yes! — But no —

Agent. Here you are in a complete contradiction, which is far worse than a quibble.

Spectator. Let us proceed quietly; we shall soon see light.

Agent. As soon as we come into the light, we shall agree. Having reached this point, will you allow me to ask you some questions?

Spectator. It is your duty, having questioned me into this dilemma, to question me out again.

Agent. The feeling you have at the exhibition of an opera cannot be rightly called deception?

Spectator. I agree. Still it is a sort of deception; something nearly allied to it.

Agent. Tell me, do you not almost forget yourself?

Spectator. Not almost, but quite, when the whole or some part is excellent.

Agent. Are you enchanted?

Spectator. It has happened more than once.

Agent. Can you explain under what circumstances?

Spectator. Under so many, it would be hard to tell.

Agent. Yet you have already told when it is most apt to happen, namely, when all is in harmony.

Spectator. Undoubtedly.

Agent. Did this complete representation harmonize with itself or some other natural product?

Spectator. With itself, certainly.

Agent. We have denied to the opera the possession of a certain sort of truth. We have maintained that it is by no means faithful to what it professes to represent. But can we deny to it a certain interior truth, which arises from its completeness as a work of art?

Spectator. When the opera is good, it creates a little world of its own, in which all proceeds according to fixed laws, which must be judged by its own laws, felt according to its own spirit.

Agent. Does it not follow from this, that truth of nature and truth of art are two distinct things, and that the artist neither should nor may endeavor to give his work the air of a work of nature?

Spectator. But yet it has so often the air of a work of nature.

Agent. That I cannot deny. But may I on the other hand be equally frank?

Spectator. Why not? our business is not now with compliments.

Agent. I will then venture to affirm, that a work of art can seem to be a work of nature only to a wholly uncultivated spectator; such a one the artist appreciates and values indeed, though he stands on the lowest step. But, unfortunately, he can only be satisfied when the artist descends to his level; he will never rise with him, when, prompted by his genius, the true artist must take wing in order to complete the whole circle of his work.

Spectator. Your remark is curious; but proceed.

Agent. You would not let it pass unless you had yourself attained a higher step.

Spectator. Let me now make trial, and take the place of questioner, in order to arrange and advance our subject.

Agent. I shall like that better still.

Spectator. You say that a work of art could appear as a work of nature only to an uncultivated person?

Agent. Certainly. You remember the birds that tried to eat the painted cherries of the great master?

Spectator. Now does not that show that the cherries were admirably painted?

Agent. By no means. It rather convinces me that these connoisseurs were true sparrows.

Spectator. I cannot, however, for this reason concede that this work could have been other than excellent.

Agent. Shall I tell you a more modern story?

Spectator. I would rather listen to stories than arguments.

Agent. A certain great naturalist, among other domesticated animals, possessed an ape, which he missed one day, and found after a long search in the library. There sat the beast on the ground, with the plates of an unbound work of Natural History scattered about him. Astonished at this zealous fit of study on the part of his familiar, the gentleman approached, and found, to his wonder and vexation, that the dainty ape had been making his dinner of the beetles that were pictured in various places.

Spectator. It is a droll story.

Agent. And seasonable, I hope. You would not compare these colored copperplates with the work of so great an artist?

Spectator. No, indeed.

Agent. But you would reckon the ape among the uncultivated amateurs?

Spectator. Yes, and among the greedy ones! You awaken in me a singular idea. Does not the uncultivated amateur, just in the same way, desire a work to be natural, that he may be able to enjoy it in a natural, which is often a vulgar and common way?

Agent. I am entirely of that opinion.

Spectator. And you maintain, therefore, that an artist lowers himself when he tries to produce this effect?

Agent. Such is my firm conviction.

Spectator. But here again I feel a contradiction. You did me just now the honor to number me, at least, among the half-cultivated spectators.

Agent. Among those who are on the way to become true connoisseurs.

Spectator. Then explain to me, Why does a perfect work of art appear like a work of nature to me also?

Agent. Because it harmonizes with your better nature. Because it is above natural, yet not unnatural. A perfect work of art is a work of the human soul, and in this sense, also, a work of nature. But because it collects together the scattered objects, of which it displays even the most minute in all their significance and value, it is above nature. It is comprehensible only by a mind that is harmoniously formed and developed, and such an one discovers that what is perfect and complete in itself is also in harmony with himself. The common spectator, on the contrary, has no idea of it; he treats a work of art as he would any object he meets with in the market. But the true connoisseur sees not only the truth of the imitation, but also the excellence of the selection, the refinement of the composition, the superiority of the little world of art; he feels that he must rise to the level of the artist, in order to enjoy his work; he feels that he must collect himself out of his scattered life, must live with the work of art, see it again and again, and through it receive a higher existence.

Spectator. Well said, my friend. I have often made similar reflections upon pictures, the drama, and other species of poetry, and had an instinct of those things you require. I will in future give more heed both to myself and to works of art. But if I am not mistaken, we have left the subject of our dispute quite behind. You wished to persuade me that the painted spectators at our opera are admissible, and I do not yet see, though we have come to an agreement, by what arguments you mean to support this license, and under what rubric I am to admit these painted lookers-on.

Agent. Fortunately, the opera is repeated to-night; I trust you will not miss it.

Spectator. On no account.

Agent. And the painted men?

Spectator. Shall not drive me away, for I think myself something more than a sparrow.

Agent. I hope that a mutual interest may soon bring us together again.

Friedrich Beuther's Set for Mozart's *Titus* in Weimar.

8.   NEOCLASSIC SCENE DESIGN

IN 1797, on his way to Switzerland, Goethe stopped in Frankfort, where he visited the studio of the Italian scene designer, Giorgio Fuentes (1756-1822), whose neoclassic sets he admired. Unable to persuade the Milanese artist to come to Weimar, Goethe later (1815) succeeded in acquiring the services of a Fuentes student, Friedrich Beuther (1777-1834), for the Ducal Theater. In 1817, he commented on this appointment in his *Annals*:

In this epoch it might well be said that the Weimar theater, in respect to pure recitation, powerful declamation, natural and, at the same time, artistic representation, had attained a considerable height of excellence. In outward respects, too, it gradually improved; the wardrobe, for example, through emulation first of the ladies, then of the gentlemen. Exactly at the right time we gained an excellent artist in the decorator Beuther, who was trained in the school of Fuentes, and who, by means of perspective, was able to enlarge our small spaces endlessly; by characteristic architecture, to multiply them; and, by taste and ornament, to render them highly agreeable. Every kind of style he subjected to his perspective skill. In the Weimar library he studied the Egyptian as well as the old German architecture, and thereby gave to the pieces requiring such illustration new attraction and peculiar splendor.

9.   SCENIC COLOR SCHEMES

GOETHE outlined his ideas on the use of color in stage costumes in one of his conversations with Eckermann:

Generally, the scenes should have a tone favorable to every color of the dresses, like Beuther's scenery, which has more or less of a brownish tinge, and brings out the color of the dresses with perfect freshness. If, however, the scene-painter is obliged to depart from so favorable an undecided tone, and to represent a red or yellow chamber, a white tent or a green garden, the actors should be clever enough to avoid similar colors in their dresses. If an actor in a red uniform and green breeches enters a red room, the upper part of his body vanishes, and only his legs are seen; if, with the same dress, he enters a green garden, his legs vanish, and the upper part of his body is conspicuous. Thus I saw an actor in a white uniform and dark breeches, the upper part of whose body completely vanished in a white tent, while the legs disappeared against a dark background.

10.   THE FUNCTION OF THE CHORUS

IN HIS CAMPAIGN against realism Goethe had the help of Friedrich Schiller (1759 - 1805), who, influenced by his reading of Kant's *Kritik der Urteilskraft* and of Mendelssohn's *Briefe über die Empfindungen*, had abandoned his youthful confusion of the stage with the pulpit. Under Goethe's influence, Schiller took the last step toward a purified concept of theatrical art. In Schiller's preface to *Die Braut von Messina* (1803) can be found his esthetic testament. In it the poet established the theater as a symbolic institution. Theatrical illusion, as Diderot understood it, was to Schiller nothing but "a miserable juggler's

Goethe-Nationalmuseum, Weimar

Schiller's *The Bride of Messina* in Weimar (1803).

deception." He rejected the request that the action on the boards be real, when, after all, the daylight in the theater can only be artificial and the architecture symbolic. To dismiss any notion of an ordinary imitation of nature in a work of dramatic art, Schiller decided to introduce the ancient chorus, which would serve as a living wall, built by tragedy around itself, so as to shut itself off from the world of reality:

The mind of the spectator ought to maintain its freedom through the most impassioned scenes; it should not be the mere prey of impressions, but calmly and severely detach itself from the emotions which it suffers. The commonplace objection made to the chorus, that it disturbs the illusion, and blunts the edge of the feelings, is what constitutes its highest recommendation; for it is this blind force of the affections which the true artist deprecates — this illusion is what he disdains to excite. If the strokes which tragedy inflicts on our bosoms followed without respite, the passion would overpower the action. We should mix ourselves up with the subject-matter, and no longer stand above it. It is by holding asunder the different parts, and stepping between the passions with its composing views, that the chorus restores to us our freedom, which would else be lost in the tempest. The characters of the drama need this intermission in order to collect themselves; for they are no real beings who obey the impulse of the moment, and merely represent individuals — but ideal persons and representatives of their species, who enunciate the deep things of humanity.

Chapter XII

Nineteenth-Century England

Edmund Kean as Richard III. Painting by John James Halls (abt. 1815).

1. COVENT GARDEN REBUILT

ON SEPTEMBER 20, 1808, Covent Garden was destroyed by fire. The company found a temporary home at the Haymarket Theatre, while Covent Garden was being rebuilt in a pretentious classical style by the architect, Robert Smirke, jr., at a cost of £150,000. In 1809, when Covent Garden reopened under Kemble's management, more than sixty nights of rioting ensued. These so-called O.P. (Old Price) riots, the fiercest in London's theatrical history, were organized by playgoers who resented the sixpence advance in the admission price to the pit and the introduction of private boxes. James Boaden had little good to say about the architecture of the new structure, but he did praise the stage, which had a proscenium width of 42 ft. and measured 68 ft. from the footlights to the rear wall:

There is, externally, not a particle of taste — a heavy portico of four doric columns, the largest in any modern building, astonishes by its ponderous inutility; the columns are 5 feet 6 inches in diameter. The doric, it should be observed, was the earliest of the three orders properly Grecian; the enormous thickness of the column diminished with the refinement of art, and the accomplished Corinthian consummated the invention of the Greeks.

The halls and stair-cases of this theatre, its lobbies and saloons, are really wretched, when compared with the contrivances of Wyatt at Drury-Lane; and to allow such a clownish exhibition as the long unmeaning figure, called Shakspeare, to remain where it stands a single night, proves nothing, but that the managers of the house must pass always by it as rapidly as the people do.

In speaking of it as a play-house, its highest excellence was the stage itself, constructed by Mr. Saul; certainly the most perfect with which I am acquainted. In the audience part of the building some positive improvements claim to be stated.

The boxes were calculated to hold as many people as they did in the former theatre; only, from the encroachment of the private circle, now occupying the whole of the third tier, 140 persons were accommodated in the lower circles. Six feet six inches were now the average depth of the three rows, which had been only six feet three inches in the old theatre, and but six feet in Drury Lane.

The pit had still its former twenty seats, but the declivity, instead of being, as formerly, only three feet, was now four feet nine inches.

In the two-shilling gallery of Drury Lane a person seated in the back row was one hundred feet from the stage-door; in the old Covent Garden he was eighty-eight feet, and in the present only eighty-six. In the upper gallery these relative distances were one hundred and four feet, ninety-three feet, and eighty-five feet.

The house was lighted by glass chandeliers in front of each circle — 270 wax-candles was the nightly supply: 300 patent lamps lighted the stage and its scenery. The prevailing colour of the house was white; the ornament, gold upon a light pink ground; the box doors were all of solid mahogany.

The first and second circles of the boxes were appropriated to the public. From the third circle they were entirely excluded — the boxes here were let annually, and each of them had a small anti-room about six feet wide, opening outwards into a general saloon, appropriated to these renters, as that below was to the public. To these boxes the entrances were private.

2. NEW DRURY LANE

On February 24, 1809, Drury Lane, too, was consumed by flames. The new theater, built by Benjamin Wyatt after the pattern of the theater in Bordeaux, was opened on October 10, 1812. While the just proportion and noble dignity of the edifice was generally admired, Boaden objected to the vastness of the stage on which the actor was "lost in an immense space, and the scenery which should have borne upon his performance, and given a locality to the character, was a diminutive picture, hung behind him at a distance. You might set a wood, for instance, in the back-ground, but the persons of the play, however simply attired, were wandering about under gorgeous vaultings, illuminated by massy tripods in the forms of venerable antiquity." Oulton's impressions as a playgoer were more favorable:

From a limited subscription fund, the architect, Mr. Benjamin Wyatt, was commissioned to build a theatre of a certain magnitude: he had no opportunity for external magnificence, and could aim at little more than convenience and utility.

The grand entrance is in Brydges-street, through a spacious

hall, leading to the boxes and pit. This hall is supported by fine Doric columns, and illuminated by two large brass lamps: three large doors lead from this hall into the house, and into a rotunda of great beauty and elegance. On each side of the rotunda are passages to the great stairs, which are peculiarly grand and spacious; over them is an ornamented ceiling, with a turret light. The body of the theatre presents nearly three-fourths of a circle from the stage. This circular appearance is partly an optical deception, and has the effect of making the spectator imagine himself nearly close upon the stage, though seated in the centre box. The colour of the interior is gold upon green, and the relief of the boxes is by a rich crimson.

There are three circles of boxes, each containing 24 boxes, with four rows of seats, and sufficient room between each; there are seven slip boxes on each side, ranging with the first gallery, and the like number of private boxes nearly on a level with the pit. The boxes will hold 2100 individuals; the pit about 850; the lower gallery 820; and the upper gallery 480; in all, 2810 persons may be accommodated. The entrance to all the boxes and pit is easy and secure. The theatre is indebted to Colonel Congreve for an excellent contrivance, which promises effectually to secure the building from fire. — The appearance of the house is brilliant without being gaudy, and elegant without affectation. — The fronts of the boxes have all diversified ornaments, which are neatly gilt, and give a variety and relief to the general aspect. — We must not omit the just praise which is due to the architect for those arrangements, which exclude the interruption caused by indecent persons, and, by necessary attractions, draw off the noisy and frivolous part of the audience from the grave and sober hearers.

The grand saloon is 86 feet long, circular at each extremity, and separated from the box corridors by the rotunda and grand staircase. It has a richly gilt stove at each corner, over which are finely imitated black and yellow-veined marble slabs as pedestals in the niches. The ceiling is arched, and the general effect of two massy Corinthian columns of verd antique at each end, with ten corresponding pilasters on each side, is grand and pleasing. The rooms for coffee and refreshments at the ends of the saloon, though small, are very neat; they consist of recesses, Corinthian pilasters, four circular arches supporting domes with sky-lights, from which glass lamps are suspended. On the north side of the theatre is the wardrobe. The retiring rooms for the stage boxes are decorated with rich crimson carpets, and with deep crimson embossed paper. The private boxes have no ante-chambers.

In the pit are seventeen rows of seats with four short ones, in consequence of the orchestra making two projections into it. The orchestra is about eight feet wide, and extends nearly the whole width of the pit. The stage is about 33 feet wide, the proscenium 19½, and the whole constructed so as to render the circular appearance of the theatre nearly complete. The part usually appropriated to stage doors, were occupied by two very fine large lamps, with tripods on triangular pedestals, each lamp containing a circle of small burners with lights. As these drew the attention of the audience from the performers, they were afterwards removed, and the stage doors restored. On each side are two stage boxes, forming an acute angle with the stage, and above them are niches with statues. The space over the side boxes, and ranging with the upper gallery is left entirely open; hence the more perfect transmission of sound to the remotest parts of the house, where the lowest whisper may be distinctly heard. Between the pedestal lamps and the curtain on each side is a massy Corinthian column of verd antique, with the gilt capital supporting the arch over the stage, in the circle of which are the arms of his majesty. Corresponding with these columns are three pilasters, ornamented with connected rigs entwined with grapes and vine leaves, all richly gilt.

3. THEATRICAL DIMENSIONS

THE CAPACITY FIGURES, given by Wyatt himself in his *Observations on the Design for the Theatre Royal, Drury Lane,* differ from those in Oulton's account, and the architect's comparison of the dimensions of the new theater with those of older theaters is highly informative:

Drury-lane Theatre, consisting of three-fourths of a circle, with a Proscenium limiting the Stage-opening to 33 feet, contains, in four different heights, 80 Boxes, holding 1098 persons; with four Boxes — of larger size than the rest — next to the Stage, on each side of the Theatre, capable of containing 188 Spectators in addition to the 1098 before mentioned; amounting in an aggregate to 1286 persons. A Pit capable of containing 920 persons, a Two-Shilling Gallery for 550 persons, a One-Shilling Gallery for 350 persons, exclusive of four Private Boxes in the Proscenium, and 14 in the Basement of the Theatre, immediately under the Dress Boxes. . . . I confined the distance from the front of the Stage to the back wall of the Boxes, facing the Stage, to 53 Feet 9 inches . . . 38 feet 6 inches laterally. — I have already stated, that the extreme distance from the front line of the Stage to the back wall of the Boxes, facing the Stage, according to my Plan, is 53 feet 9 inches; in the late Theatre in Drury Lane it was 74 feet, or 20 feet 3 inches more than at present; in the Old Theatre in Covent Garden (I mean as it was built about the year 1730), the distance between the front of the Stage, and the back wall of the front Boxes, was 54 feet 6 inches, or 1 foot 3 inches more than in my design. In the Old Opera House, built by Sir John Vanbrugh, in the Haymarket, it was 66 feet, or 12 feet 3 inches more than in my design. . . . In the present Theatre at Covent Garden it is 69 feet 8 inches, or fifteen feet eleven inches more.

4. MAJESTIC KEMBLE

ON OCTOBER 25, 1816, shortly before John Kemble retired, William Charles Macready saw him act Cato at Covent Garden. By then, the vogue of the classical style had passed. A new generation of actors, led by the romantic Edmund Kean, was about to invade the theater. Both the grandeur and the shortcomings of Kemble's style revealed themselves to Macready's discerning eyes:

But there was Kemble! As he sat majestically in his curule chair, imagination could not supply a grander or more noble presence. In face and form he realised the most perfect ideal that ever enriched the sculptor's or the painter's fancy, and his deportment was in accord with all of outward dignity and grace that history attributes to the *patres conscripti* [the Roman Senate]. In one particular, however, I was greatly disappointed: having heard much of his scholarly correctness, I expected in his costume to see a model of the *gens togata* [Roman people]; but the cumbrous drapery in which he was enveloped bore no resemblance, in any one fold or peculiarity, to the garment that distinguished the Roman as one of the *rerum dominos* [master race]. The *ensemble* was nevertheless remarkably striking, and the applause that greeted him proved the benches to be occupied by very devoted admirers. The tragedy, five acts of declamatory, unimpassioned verse, the monotony of which, correct as his emphasis and reading was, Kemble's husky voice and laboured articulation did not tend to dissipate or enliven, was a tax upon the patience of the hearers. The frequently-recurring sentiments on patriotism and liberty, awakening no response were listened to with respectful, almost drowsy attention. But, like an eruptive volcano from some level expanse, there was one burst that electrified the house. When Portius entered with an exclamation, —

> "Misfortune on misfortune! grief on grief!
> My brother Marcius," —

Kemble with a start of unwonted animation rushed across the stage to him, huddling questions one upon the other with extraordinary volubility of utterance —

> "Ha! what has he done? —
> Has he forsook his post? Has he given way?
> Did he look tamely on and let them pass?"

Then listening with intense eagerness to the relation of Portius, — how

> "Long at the head of his few faithful friends
> He stood the shock of a whole host of foes,
> Till, obstinately brave, and bent on death,
> Oppress'd with multitudes, he greatly fell" —

as he caught the last word he gasped out convulsively, as if suddenly relieved from an agony of doubt, "I am satisfied!" and the theatre rang with applause most heartedly and deservedly bestowed. This was his great effect — indeed his single effect; and great and refreshing as it was, it was not enough so to compensate for a whole evening of merely sensible cold declamation. I watched him intently throughout — not a look or a tone was lost by me; his attitudes were stately and picturesque but evidently prepared; even the care he took in the disposition of his mantle was distinctly observable. If meant to present a picture of Stoicism, the success might be considered unequivocal, but unbroken except by the grand effect above described; though it might satisfy the classic antiquary, the want of variety and relief rendered it uninteresting, and often indeed tedious.

5. THE FLASHES OF LIGHTNING

IN JANUARY 1814, Edmund Kean (1787 - 1833) made his London debut as Shylock at Drury Lane; the Kean, of whom Coleridge said that to see him "was to read Shakespeare by flashes of lightning." This was the romantic way to read Shakespeare, in contrast to the classical reading of Kemble. Leigh Hunt, in *The Tatler* of 1831, drew a judicious comparison between the two acting styles:

We believe it was the opinion of a great many besides ourselves that Kean did extinguish Kemble: at all events, we hold it for certain that Kean hastened his going out; and we are greatly mistaken if Kemble did not intimate as much to his friends, putting the case as Quin did on a like occasion respecting Garrick, — that new notions had come up in acting, and that if those were true, it was time for the teachers of the old ones to be gone. Garrick's nature displaced Quin's formalism: and in precisely the same way did Kean displace Kemble. The opinion is no new one on our parts, nor on those of many others. We expressed it at the time. We always said that John Kemble's acting was not the true thing; and the moment we heard what sort of an actor Kean was (for circumstances prevented our seeing him at the moment) we said that he would carry all before him. It was as sure a thing as Nature against Art, or tears against cheeks of stone.

We do not deny a certain merit of taste and what is called "classicality" to John Kemble. He had one idea about tragedy, and it was a good one; namely, that a certain elevation of treatment was due to it, that there was a dignity, and a perception of something superior to common life, which should justly be regarded as one of its constituent portions; and furthermore, that in exhibiting the heroes of the Roman world, it was not amiss to invest them with the additional dignity they had received from the length of their renown and the enthusiasm of scholarship. These ideas were good: and as he had a fine person, a Roman cast of countenance, and equal faith in the dignity of his originals and

his own, he obtained, in the absence of any greater and more
natural actor, a whole generation for his admirers, many of whom
could not bear to give him up when the greater came. This is
the whole secret of the fondness entertained for his memory. It
is a mere habit and a prejudice, though a respectable one; and
we should be the last to quarrel with it were nature let alone.
It is observable that Mr. Kemble's admirers never enter into any
details of criticism or comparison. They content themselves with
a fine assumption or two, like his own — a stately or sovereign
metaphor — and a reference to his *gentility*. Now Mr. Kemble
had a solemnity of manner off the stage, analogous to what he
had on it, and we believe he kept "good company," in the ordinary
sense of that phrase; but that he was more of a gentleman than
Mr. Kean, either in his strongest or weakest moments, we have
yet to learn. Allusions are frequently made to a habit in Mr.
Kean, which his predecessor certainly shared with him, though
with comparative harmlessness to his less sensitive temperament.
On the other hand (for we never saw him in private) Mr. Kean,
we believe, is as much of a gentleman in ordinary as Kemble was;
and we have heard accounts of his behaviour to his brother actors
and inferiors, which argue an inner gentility — a breeding of the
heart — which at all events we never *did* hear of the other. In
the *power* of appreciating moral and intellectual refinement, we
should say that there could be no sort of comparison between the
man who can act Othello as Kean does, and the dry, tearless,
systematical, despotical style of all Mr. Kemble's personations.
Everything with Kemble was literally a *personation* — it was a
mask and a sounding-pipe. It was all external and artificial. There
was elegance, majesty, preparation: it was Gracchus with his
pitch-pipe, going to begin — but nothing came of it. It was not
the man, but his mask; a trophy, a consul's robe, a statue; or if
you please, a rhetorician. It was Addison's "Cato," or an actor's
schoolmaster, which you will; but neither Shakspeare nor genuine acting.

The distinction between Kean and Kemble may be briefly
stated to be this: that Kemble knew there was a difference between tragedy and common life, but did not know in what it
consisted, except in *manner,* which he consequently carried to
excess, losing sight of the passion. Kean knows the real thing,
which is the height of the *passion,* manner following it as a matter

of course, *and grace being developed from it in proportion to the truth of the sensation,* as the flower issues from the entireness of the plant, or from all that is necessary to produce it. Kemble began with the flower, and he made it accordingly. He had no notion of so inelegant a thing as a root, or as the common earth, or of all the precious elements that make a heart and a life in the plant, and crown their success with beauty. Grace exalts the person of Kean. In Kemble's handsomer figure it came to nothing, because it found nothing inside to welcome it. It received but "cold comfort." Kean's face is full of light and shade, his tones vary, his voice trembles, his eye glistens, sometimes with withering scorn, sometimes with a tear: at least he can speak as if there were tears in his eyes, and he brings tears into those of other people. We will not affirm that Kemble never did so, for it would be hard to say what Shakspeare might not have done in spite of him; but as far as our own experience goes we never recollect him to have moved us except in one solitary instance, and that was in *King Lear,* where there is the fine passage about children's ingratitude and the tooth of a serpent. Now Kean we never see without being moved, and moved too in fifty ways — by his sarcasm, his sweetness, his pathos, his exceeding grace, his gallant levity, his measureless dignity: for his little person absolutely becomes tall, and rises to the height of moral grandeur, in such characters as that of Othello. We have seen him with three or four persons round him, all taller than he, but himself so graceful, so tranquil, so superior, so nobly self-possessed, in the midst, that the mind of the spectator rose above them by his means, and so gave him a moral stature that confounded itself with the personal.

6.   EDMUND KEAN'S RICHARD III

WILLIAM HAZLITT, brought up in the Kemble religion, became one of Kean's first admirers. Though he was frequently awed by the depth of feeling, the anarchy of passions, the cyclonic energy, that poured forth from this fiery soul in a diminutive body, Hazlitt could not fail to censure some of Kean's mannerisms. In 1814, Hazlitt saw Kean's Richard three times, twice in February and a third in October. In the intervening months the actor had made some alterations in his mode of acting. Excerpts from the Hazlitt reviews on all three occasions follow:

If Mr. KEAN does not completely succeed in concentrating all the lines of the character, as drawn by SHAKESPEAR, he gives an animation, vigour, and relief to the part, which we have never seen surpassed. He is more refined than COOKE; more bold, varied, and original than KEMBLE, in the same character. In some parts, however, we thought him deficient in dignity; and particularly in the scenes of state business, there was not a sufficient air of artificial authority. The fine assumption of condescending superiority, after he is made king — "Stand all apart — Cousin of Buckingham," &c. was not given with the effect which it might have received. There was also at times, a sort of tip-toe elevation, an enthusiastic rapture in his expectations of obtaining the crown, instead of a gloating expression of sullen delight, as if he already clutched the bauble, and held it within his grasp. This was the precise expression which Mr. KEAN gave with so much effect to the part where he says, that he already feels

"The golden rigol bind his brows."

In one who *dares* so much, there is little indeed to blame. The only two things which appeared to us decidedly objectionable, were the sudden letting down of his voice when he says of Hastings, "chop off his head," and the action of putting his hands behind him, in listening to Buckingham's account of his reception by the citizens. His courtship scene with Lady Anne was an admirable exhibition of smooth and smiling villany. The progress of wily adulation, of encroaching humility, was finely marked throughout by the action, voice, and eye. He seemed, like the first tempter, to approach his prey, certain of the event, and as if success had smoothed the way before him. We remember Mr. COOKE's manner of representing this scene was more violent, hurried, and full of anxious uncertainty. This, though more natural in general, was, we think, less in character. Richard should woo not as a lover, but as an actor — to shew his mental superiority, and power to make others the playthings of his will. Mr. KEAN's attitude in leaning against the side of the stage before he comes forward in this scene, was one of the most graceful and striking we remember to have seen. It would have done for Titian to paint. The opening scene in which Richard descants on his own deformity, was conceived with perfect truth and character, and delivered in a fine and varied tone of natural recitation. Mr. KEAN did equal justice to the beautiful description of the camps the night before the battle, though, in consequence of his hoarseness, he was obliged to repeat the whole passage in an under-key. (The defects in the upper tones of Mr. KEAN's voice were hardly perceptible in his performance of Shylock, and were at first attributed to hoarseness.) His manner of bidding his friends good night, and his pausing with the point of his sword, drawn slowly backward and forward on the ground, before he retires to his tent, received shouts of applause. He gave to all the busy scenes of the play the greatest animation and effect. He filled every part of the stage. The concluding scene, in which he is killed by Richmond, was the most brilliant. He fought like one drunk with wounds: and the attitude in which he stands with his hands stretched out, after his sword is taken from him, had a preternatural and terrific grandeur, as if his will could not be disarmed, and the very phantoms of his despair had a withering power.

⚡ ⚡ ⚡

. . . the research, the ingenuity, and the invention manifested throughout the character are endless. We have said before, and we still think so, that there is even too much effect given, too many significant hints, too much appearance of study. There is a tone in acting, as well as in painting, which is the chief and master excellence. Our highest conception of an actor is, that he shall assume the character once for all, and be it throughout, and trust to this conscious sympathy for the effect produced. Mr. KEAN's manner of acting is, on the contrary, rather a perpetual assumption of his part, always brilliant and successful, almost always true and natural, but yet always a distinct effort in every new situation, so that the actor does not seem entirely to forget himself, or to be identified with the character. The extreme elaboration of the parts injures the broad and massy effect; the general impulse of the machine is retarded by the variety and intricacy of the movements.

⚡ ⚡ ⚡

His pauses are twice as long as they were, and the rapidity with which he hurries over other parts of the dialogue is twice as great as it was. In both these points, his style of acting always bordered on the very verge of extravagance; and we suspect it has at present passed the line. There are, no doubt, passages in which the pauses can hardly be too long, or too marked; — these must be, however, of rare occurrence, and it is in the finding out these exceptions to the general rule, and in daring to give them all the effect, that the genius of an actor discovers itself. But the most common-place drawling monotony is not more mechanical or more offensive, than the converting these exceptions into a general rule, and making every sentence an alternation of dead pauses and rapid transitions. It is not in extremes that dramatic genius is shewn, any more than skill in music consists in passing continually from the highest to the lowest note. The quickness of familiar utterance with which Mr. KEAN pronounced the anticipated doom of Stanley, "chop off his head," was quite ludicrous. Again, the manner in which, after his nephew said, "I fear no uncles dead," he suddenly turned around, and answered, "And I hope none living, sir," was, we thought, quite out of character. The motion was performed, and the sound uttered, in the smallest possible time in which a puppet could be made to mimic or gabble the part. For this we see not the least reason; and can only account for it, from a desire to give excessive effect by a display of the utmost dexterity of execution. . . .

The part which was least varied was the scene with Lady Anne. This is, indeed, nearly a perfect piece of acting. In leaning against the pillar at the commencement of the scene, Mr. KEAN did not go through exactly the same regular evolution of graceful attitudes, and we regretted the omission. He frequently varied the execution of many of his most striking conceptions, and the attempt in general failed, as it naturally must do. We refer particularly to his manner of resting on the point of his sword before he retires to his tent, to his treatment of the letter sent to Norfolk, and to his dying scene with Richmond.

Mr. KEAN's *bye-play* is certainly one of his greatest excellences, and it might be said, that if SHAKESPEAR had written marginal directions to the players, in the manner of the German dramatists, he would often have directed them to do what Mr. KEAN does. Such additions to the text are, however, to be considered as lucky hits, and it is not to be supposed that an actor is to provide an endless variety of these running accompaniments, which he is not in strictness bound to provide at all. In general, we think it a rule, that an actor ought to vary his part as little as possible, unless he is convinced that his former mode of playing it is erroneous. He should make up his mind as to the best mode of representing the part, and come as near to this standard as he can, in every successive exhibition. It is absurd to object to this mechanical uniformity as studied and artificial. An actor is no more called upon to vary his gestures or articulation at every new rehearsal of the character, than an author can be required to furnish various readings to every copy of his work. To a new audience it is quite unnecessary; to those who have seen him before in the same part, it is worse than useless. They may at least be presumed to have come to a second representation, because they approved of the first, and will be sure to be disappointed in almost every alteration. The attempt is endless, and can only produce perplexity and indecision in the actor himself. He must either return perpetually in the same narrow round, or if he is determined to be always new, he may at last fancy that he ought to perform the part standing on his head instead of his feet. Besides, Mr. KEAN's style of acting is not in the least of the unpremeditated, *improvisatori* kind: it is throughout elaborate and systematic, instead of being loose, off-hand, and accidental. He comes upon the stage as little unprepared as any actor we know. We object particularly to his varying the original action in the dying scene. He at first held out his hands in a way which can only be conceived by those who saw him — in motionless despair, — or as if there were some preternatural power in the mere manifestation of his will: — he now actually fights with his doubled fists, after his sword is taken from him, like some helpless infant. . . .

To conclude our hypercritical remarks: we really think that Mr. KEAN was, in a great many instances, either too familiar, too emphatical, or too energetic. In the latter scenes, perhaps his energy could not be too great; but he gave the energy of action alone. He merely gesticulated, or at best vociferated the part. His articulation totally failed him. We doubt, if a single person in the house, not acquainted with the play, understood a single sentence that he uttered. It was "inexplicable dumb show and noise."

7. AUTHENTIC COSTUMES

In November 1823, Charles Kemble (1775 - 1854) revived *King John* at Covent Garden. All the emphasis was placed on the historical accuracy of the costumes; the playbills listing the "indisputable" authorities for the "precise habits of the period," such as illuminated manuscripts, monumental effigies, painted glass windows, etc., attesting to the truthfulness of the statement that an attention "never equalled on the English stage" had been bestowed upon the costumes. James Robinson Planché, in his *Recollections and Reflections,* proudly assumed full responsibility for this innovation:

In 1823, a casual conversation with Mr. Kemble respecting the play of "King John," which he was about to revive for [Charles Mayne] Young, who had returned to Covent Garden, led to a step, the consequences of which have been of immense importance to the English stage. . . . I complained to Mr. Kemble that a thousand pounds were frequently lavished on a Christmas pantomime or an Easter spectacle, while the plays of Shakespeare were put upon the stage with make-shift scenery, and, at the best, a new dress or two for the principal characters; that although his brother John, whose classical mind revolted from the barbarisms which even a Garrick had tolerated, had abolished the bag-wig of *Brutus* and the gold-laced suit of *Macbeth,* the alterations made in the costumes of the plays founded upon English history in particular, while they rendered them more picturesque, added but little to their propriety; the whole series, *King Lear* included, being dressed in habits of the Elizabethan era, the third reign after its termination with Henry VIII, and, strictly speaking, very inaccurately representing the costume even of that period.

At that time I had turned my attention but little to the subject of costume, which afterwards became my most absorbing study; but the slightest reflection was sufficient to convince any one that some change of fashion must have taken place in the civil and military habits of the people of England during several hundred years. . . . Mr. Kemble admitted the fact, and perceived the pecuniary advantage that might result from the experiment. It was decided that I should make the necessary researches, design the dresses, and superintend the production of "King John," *gratuitously,* I beg leave to say; solely and purely for that love of the Stage, which has ever induced me to sacrifice all personal considerations to what I sincerely believed would tend to elevate as well as adorn it. Fortunately I obtained, through a mutual friend, an introduction to Doctor, afterwards Sir Samuel Meyrick, who had just published his elaborate and valuable work, "A Critical Inquiry into Ancient Arms and Armour," and was forming that magnificent and instructive collection now exhibiting at South Kensington. He entered most warmly and kindly into my views, pointed out to me the best authorities, and gave me a letter of introduction to Mr. Francis Douce, the eminent antiquary, from whom also I met with the most cordial reception.

This gentleman had assisted Mr. John Kemble when he introduced several alterations in the costume of Shakespeare's plays, particularly those founded on Roman history; for which latter, however, he drew his materials from the columns and arches of the Emperors, and not from contemporaneous republican authorities. When urged to do so, and to "reform it altogether," he exclaimed to Mr. Douce, in a tone almost of horror, "Why, if I did, sir, they would call me an antiquary." "And this to me, sir!" said the dear old man, when he told me of this circumstance, "to *me*, who flattered myself I *was* an antiquary." Mr. Douce . . . most liberally placed the whole of his invaluable collection of illuminated MSS. (now in the Bodleian Library, to which he bequeathed them) at my disposal. He paid me also the great compliment of lending me his fine copy of Strutt's "Dress and Habits of the People of England," coloured expressly for him by its author. . . . In the theatre, however, my innovations were regarded with distrust and jealousy. Mr. Fawcett, the stage-manager, considered his dignity offended by the production of the play being placed under my direction. He did not speak to me, except when obliged by business, for, I think, nearly three years; but I lived it down, and remained very good friends with that excellent actor to the day of his death. Mr. Farley — dear old Charles Farley — also took huff. He was the recognised purveyor and director of spectacle, and dreaded "the dimming of his shining star." The expenditure of a few hundred pounds on any drama, except an Easter piece or a Christmas pantomine, was not to be tolerated. "Besides," he piteously exclaimed, "if Shakspeare is to be produced with such splendour and attention to costume, what am I to do for the holidays?" . . . Never shall

I forget the dismay of some of the performers when they looked upon the flat-topped *chapeaux de fer* (*fer blanc*, I confess) of the twelfth century, which they irreverently stigmatized as *stewpans*! Nothing but the fact that the classical features of a Kemble were to be surmounted by a precisely similar abomination would, I think, have induced one of the rebellious barons to have appeared in it. They had no faith in me, and sulkily assumed their new and strange habiliments, in the full belief that they should be roared at by the audience. They *were* roared at; but in a much more agreeable way than they had contemplated. When the curtain rose, and discovered King John dressed as his effigy appears in Worcester Cathedral, surrounded by his barons sheathed in mail, with cylindrical helmets and correct armorial shields, and his courtiers in the long tunics and mantles of the thirteenth century, there was a roar of approbation, accompanied by four distinct rounds of applause, so general and so hearty, that the actors were astonished; and I felt amply rewarded for all the trouble, anxiety, and annoyance I had experienced during my labours. Receipts of from £400 to £600 nightly soon reimbursed the management for the expense of the production, and a complete reformation of dramatic costume became from that moment inevitable upon the English stage.

8.   TRIBUTE TO MADAME VESTRIS

MME. VESTRIS (Eliza Lucy Bartolozzi, 1797-1856), having started her theatrical career as a dancer and opera singer, decided in 1830 to enter the field of theatrical management. This extraordinary woman opened one of London's "minor" theaters, the Olympic, and completely revolutionized the current staging practices. J. R. Planché summed up her innovations when he paid her the following tribute:

In a time of unexampled peril to the best interests of the Drama — whilst theatrical property was at the lowest ebb, the larger theatres changing hands continually, and the ruin of their lessees involving that of hundreds of their unfortunate dependents — the little Olympic, the most despised nook in the dramatic world, became not only one of the most popular and fashionable theatres London ever saw, but served as a life-boat to the respectability of the stage, which was fast sinking in the general wreck. Your [Mme. Vestris'] *success* is a matter of notoriety; not so, however, the principal *causes* of your success; which also constitute the claims you have upon the good wishes of all who regard the true interests of the English Stage. To those causes thousands are blind, and none perhaps so blind as the very persons who are most concerned in clearly perceiving and reflecting on them; I allude to the majority of Theatrical Managers, Provincial as well as Metropolitan.

In the first place, you have never allowed a temporary decline of attraction to scare you into the destructive system of filling your Boxes with orders.

Secondly — You have never suffered your Play-bill to be disgraced by a puff, but rigidly restricted it to the simple announcement of the Performances.

Thirdly — In the production of every Drama, without regard to its comparative importance, the most scrupulous attention has been paid to all those accessories which form the peculiar charm of Theatrical Representation, by perfecting the illusion of the scene, and consequently at the same time every possible chance of success has been afforded to the author.

Fourthly — That if, notwithstanding such aid, a Drama has occasionally failed, it has been as soon as possible withdrawn in deference to the opinion of the public.

Fifthly — That the advantage of early hours was first perceived by the audiences of the Olympic, the performances having been generally so regulated as to enable families to reach their homes before midnight.

It is to these few "Golden Rules" which you have had the good taste and sound policy to adopt and persevere in, more even than to your deserved popularity as an Actress, that you owe your unequalled success, and when by the adoption of similar measures, similar prosperity shall attend other Theatrical Speculations, and the benefit of that prosperity be felt throughout the various branches of the Dramatic Profession, I trust it will not be forgotten that the laudable experiment was first made by Madame Vestris.

9.   OLYMPIC DRAWING ROOMS

IN HIS AUTOBIOGRAPHY, Charles Mathews (1803 - 1878) explained why he had been attracted to the Olympic whose manageress he later married:

The lighter phase of comedy, representing the more natural and less laboured school of modern life, and holding the mirror up to nature without regard to the conventionalities of the theatre, was the aim I had in view. The Olympic was then the only house where this could be achieved, and to the Olympic I at once attached myself. There was introduced for the first time in England that reform in all theatrical matters which has since been adopted in every theatre in the kingdom. Drawing-rooms were fitted up like drawing-rooms, and furnished with care and taste. Two chairs no longer indicated that two persons were to be seated, the two chairs being removed indicating that the two persons were not to be seated. A claret-coloured coat, salmon-coloured trowsers with a broad black stripe, a sky-blue neckcloth with a large paste brooch, and a cut-steel eye-glass with a pink ribbon no longer marked the "light comedy gentleman," and the public at once recognised and appreciated the change.

10.   MACREADY'S *CORIOLANUS*

As a manager, first at Covent Garden (1837 - 1839) and later at Drury Lane (1841 - 1843), William Charles Macready (1793 - 1873) continued along the path of Shakespearean production which the Kembles had opened. He gave even more attention to the proprieties of scenery and costume, and his revivals of *Coriolanus*, *The Tempest*, and *Henry V* were spectacles of elaborate magnificence, mating the scholarly with the picturesque. For many of his settings Macready relied on the scene painter and diorama specialist, Clarkson Stanfield, who, in *Henry V*, used moving dioramas to accompany the descriptive poetry of the Chorus, thus marring a great poetic convention with the gaudy trimmings of a Christmas pantomime. Kemble had played *Coriolanus* against a setting of Imperial Rome, while Macready's sets were pedantically suggestive of the Republic. With the aid of *John Bull* (1838) we can recapture the spirit of scenic display that permeated the Macready revival:

A play more difficult of production . . . could not have been fixed upon. In the first place, the intent of the author had to be reverentially adhered to; in the second, every occasion was to be seized which could be made subservient to our more correct notions on the early ages of the Eternal City. The opening scene then has, with admirable judgment, been selected by Mr. Macready, as a vantage ground on which he could reconcile these two *desiderata*. And on this he has built up a scenic illusion that for reality, power, and masterly effect beggars all that we have ever witnessed in our own theatres, and shames even the most splendid efforts of that temple of display, the Opera at Paris; equals it, to the utmost of its magnificence, and shames it even in its strongest and least vulnerable point, historic faithfulness and antiquarian minutiae.

And what is this first scene? A very simple one as regards the painting, which is yet as an index to the time, a very vivid one as regards the tide of human existence poured upon the stage by the presence of the *dramatis personae*. The scene represents early Rome, seen from the south-west side of the Tyber, which forms part of the foreground; beyond the river rises the steep height of the southern summit of the Capitoline hill, crowned with its *Arx* and temples; underneath, to the right, are seen the *Cloaca Maxima*, and the Temple of Vesta; whilst the remainder of the picture is occupied by the Palatine, crested with a few larger mansions, but its shelving side, up which a rude street winds its way, densely crowded with the thatch-covered huts — "*tecta pauperis Evandri*," which, at a much later date even, contrasted with the *aurea tecta* of a more modern though still ancient Rome. We are thus directly transported to the stronghold of Patrician power; for be it remembered that the Lay of *Coriolanus* has its date in aristocratic, not republican Rome; and when the stage becomes animated with a seemingly countless mob of barbarians, armed with staves, mattocks, hatchets, pickaxes, and their wrongs, we become sensible that it is not a mere coward crowd before us, but the onward and increasing wave, the *decumanus fluctu*, of men who have spied their way to equal franchises, and are determined to fight their way to the goal. There is no mistaking the struggle for power that has begun. It is not noble against serf, but against freeman. The illusion is still further maintained by their dress. They are no longer the mere *tunicatus popellus*, who have hitherto caricatured the Roman commonalty. In many there is an approximation to the toga; and the squalor, at least only distinctive of the slave, is altogether done away with. The suggestions of the scene are thus fraught with a true sense of antiquity. Rome is there rough-hewn, and her sons breathe her own rude majesty. . . .

But it is not with the acting of one or two parts that we

now have to do. A whole people are summoned up, and a drama instinct with their life rolls its changes o'er the scene. The multitudes crowd round their Tribunes; the Patricians defy or deprecate both; and all walk, contend, harangue, stand singly, or are grouped together seemingly without reference to the spectators. Not for an instant is the illusion suffered to be broken. We are present at the popular assemblies, and wild turbulence of infant Rome. The spell begun in the first scene, is woven deftly to the last. The rude magnificence of the Capitol is ever in contrast with the turbulent commotion of the Forum.

We have described the opening scene. This is succeeded by the *atrium* of *Coriolanus's* house, lighted through its *compluvium*, and adorned by the tesselated floor, and shining brick-work of the period. The square lintelled-doors; the one candelabrum; and the extreme simplicity of the compartment are in excellent taste. The war before Corioli is seized as an opportunity for presenting the well-known form of the Roman camp, with its *vallum* and fosse. On the hero's return, crowned with the oaken garland, the stage gives a marvellous picture of a Roman holyday. It is filled with crowds of all classes, with laurel boughs in their upraised hands; the walls and battlements are lined with spectators; and the massy gate through which the procession moves, framed of alternate brick, with large blocks of *peperino*, bespeaks at once the walls of Servius. To take the scenes in order, and to do them full justice, would double the tediousness of this long article. But we must not pass over the Senate, held in the temple of Capitoline Jove, with its assembled fathers seated in triple rows on their benches of stone, the lighted altar in the midst, the Consul on his curule chair, backed by the bronze wolf to whom Rome owed her founders, with no other ornament than its simple columns, and the vaulted heavens seen through its open roof. Or the two views of the busy Forum, the one displaying the Tribunal and the warning statue of Marsyas in front, whilst high above tower the *Arx,* the Tarpeian rock, and the fane of Jupiter Capitolinus, which rises in Doric majesty and stretches with its hundred pillars, and massy porticos, half across the scene; the other showing the Forum lengthwise, looking towards the Temple of Vesta, which is seen through a centre arch, and the whole harmonised to the severe antiquity that reigns throughout by the lowly huts and mean *tabernae* that rest against its pillars. The view of the port and mole of Antium, with its *pharos,* seen by night, is in rich poetic feeling with the circumstance — its deadliest enemy, who "made its widows," gliding into it, like a lone spectre; and the next scene is in accordant grace, the *aula* of *Tullus's* mansion, lit by the glimmering brazier on the hearth, *Coriolanus* sitting, shrouded in his mantle on the sacred spot, which is flanked on one side by a lofty trophy, on the other by the ancestral image; the solemn beauty of the whole picture carrying us back to the most touching of all classical associations — the inviolability of the hearth, the seat of the family worship the shrine of the *Lares,* the prompter of high and endearing recollections, which nerved the arm to heroic deeds *pro aris et focis.* The last scene mocks description. The city frowns in the distance, begirt with the lofty and turreted walls of *Servius,* and encircled (the view is from the Appianway) by its wide moat. The Volscian army literally fills the stage with its dense files, and when the mourning Roman matrons pierce through them in long array, we breathlessly acknowledge the majesty of the historic fact, and feel that at length *Roma moribus antiquis stat.*

The costume of the piece is strictly realised. Even to the *tuba palmata* of the triumpher, and the eagle-crowned sceptres of the consuls, all is correct; and the brass covered legionaries are strictly those of antique Rome. We might raise objections; wish the toga to wear its natural colour of the wool, in order to make the candidate's gown — a leading point — more conspicuous; the *fasces* to be without their axes whilst borne in the city; the *rostra* away from the tribunal, where they were placed a century after; in the contentions of the Forum, a larger train of clients to support the Senators, and counterbalance the Plebeians. Yet these would be captious exceptions, which are as a mote to a beam, when compared with the high classical fidelity sustained throughout.

11.   REHEARSAL DISCIPLINE

APPALLED by the slipshod fashion with which plays were customarily mounted, Macready insisted on stern rehearsal discipline. In his *Reminiscences,* the actor-manager dwelled on the advance of the director's art toward which Garrick and the Kembles had made only sporadic contributions:

It was the custom of the London actors, especially the leading ones, to do little more at rehearsals than read or repeat the words of their parts, marking on them their entrances and exits, as settled by the stage-manager, and their respective places on the stage. To make any display of passion or energy would be to expose oneself to the ridicule or sneers of the green-room, and few could be more morbidly sensitive to this than myself. But the difficulty of attaining before an audience perfect self-possession, which only practice can give, made me resolve to rehearse with the same earnestness as I would act; reasoning with myself that if practice was of the value attributed to it, this would be a mode of multiplying its opportunities, of proving the effect of my performance, and of putting myself so much at ease in all I might intend to do that the customary nervousness of a first night would fail to disturb or prevent the full development of my conceptions. Upon making the experiment I may quote Dryden's line, "'Tis easy said, but oh! how hardly tried!" I found it much more difficult to force myself to act in the morning with the cold responses and composed looks of Miss O'Neill, Young, and the rest, than at night before the most crowded auditory. Frequently in after-years when I have given certain directions to actors rehearsing, the answer has been, "Sir, I never can act at rehearsal, but I will do it at night." To which I had only one reply, "Sir, if you cannot do it in the morning, you cannot do it at night; you must then do something because you must go on, but what you cannot do now, or cannot learn to do, you will not be more able to do then." The task I found a very hard one, but I fought successfully against my *mauvaise honte*, and went doggedly to it. By this means I acquired more ease in passing through the varieties of passion, confirming myself in the habit of acting to the scene alone, and, as it were, ignoring the presence of an audience, and thus came to wield at will what force or pathos I was master of.

12.   MACREADY ON TALMA

As AN ACTOR Macready may be classed with the romantic school, though, by introducing elements of commonplace and domesticity, he actually paved the way for melodramatic acting. Aside from Kean's influence, François Joseph Talma's (1763 - 1826) art seems to have made the most lasting impression upon him. In 1822, when on a continental tour, Macready watched with fascination the French tragedian's business and delivery:

I visited of course the theatres, and at the Français witnessed with delight the performances of the charming Mdlle. Mars. Her voice was music, and the words issuing from her lips suggested to the listener the clear distinctness of a beautiful type upon a rich vellum page. It was a luxury to the ear to drink in the "dulcet and harmonious breath" that her utterance of the poet gave forth. Nor was her voice her only charm: in person she was most lovely, and in grace and elegance of deportment and action unapproached by any of her contemporaries. Potier was the favourite comedian of the day, and in genuine humour was unrivalled either on the French or English stage. Mdlle. Duchesnois and Lafond, in Voltaire's tragedy of 'Alzire,' furnished the best examples of the declamatory style of the French school of acting; but the genius of Talma (whom I saw at a subsequent period) rose above all the conventionality of schools. Every turn and movement as he trod the stage might have given a model for the sculptor's art, and yet all was effected with such apparent absence of preparation as made him seem utterly unconscious of the dignified and graceful attitudes he presented. His voice was flexible and powerful, and his delivery articulate to the finest point without a trace of pedantry. There was an ease and freedom, whether in familiar colloquy, in lofty declamation, or burst of passion, that gave an air of unpremeditation to every sentence, one of the highest achievements of the histrionic art. It is a custom with many actors purposely to reach their dressing-rooms in just sufficient time to go on the stage, in order to avoid the nervousness which waiting for their entrance occasions. But Talma would dress some time before, and make the peculiarities of his costume familiar to him; at the same time that he thereby possessed himself more with the feeling of his character. I thought the practice so good, that I, frequently adopted it, and derived great benefit from it. His object was not to dazzle or surprise by isolated effects: the character was his aim; he put on the man, and was attentive to every minutest trait that might distinguish him. To my judgment he was the most finished artist of his time, not below Kean in his most energetic displays, and

Talma as Titus in Voltaire's
Brutus.

Macready as Macbeth in
Act I, Scene iii
"Two truths are told."
From an Engraving by Sherratt
after a Painting by Tracey.

fa: above him in the refinement of his taste and extent of his research, equalling Kemble in dignity, unfettered by his stiffness and formality.

13. MACBETH WITHOUT POETRY

WILLIAM HAZLITT and Leigh Hunt deplored the drawing-room familiarity to which Macready subjected the great roles of the classical repertory. Hunt's observations on this subject, written in 1831, are especially revealing:

Macbeth was performed here [Drury Lane] last night — the principal character by Mr. Macready; Lady Macbeth by Miss Huddart. We are loth to find fault with one who gives us so much pleasure as Mr. Macready; but his Macbeth is not one of his most effective performances. It wants the poetry of the original; that is to say, it wants in its general style and aspect that grace and exaltation which is to the character what the poetry is to the language; which, in fact *is* the poetry of the tragedy; and which, without depriving it of its nature, enables the tragic criminal to move fitly in the supernatural sphere of his error. In other words, the passion of Mr. Macready's Macbeth wants imagination. There is the same defect in it, but in a greater degree, as was observable in his King John. It wants the Royal warrant. We do not mean the mouthing and strut of the ordinary stage King; which are things that Mr. Macready is above; but that habitual consciousness of ascendency, and disposition to throw an ideal grace over its reflections, whether pleasurable or painful, which enables the character to present itself to us as an object of intellectual and moral contemplation, with whatsoever infirmities it may be accompanied. Now the Macbeth of Mr. Macready, before he commits the murder, is (so to speak) *nothing* but a misgiving anticipator of crime; and after it, nothing but the misgiving or despairing perpetrator. He has no golden thoughts in him, before or after; no morning hopes, nor sad beams of evening: — not a leaf is gilded by a ray. Whereas, however weak and unhappy a character Macbeth is, he cannot talk as he does, and vent the poetical images with which his mind is graced, without showing that there is a divinity within him, though an en-

feebled one, and though at once ashamed, and angered, and over-
awed by the intrusion of some monstrous stranger. The very first
words Macbeth utters, when he comes on the stage, show the
natural vivacity of his character, and its tendency to be divided
in its feelings; and the way in which these were spoken by Mr.
Macready did not augur well for his performance.

"So foul and fair a day I have not seen,"

says the good-humoured conquering general, looking cheerily up
at the sky, and playing, as it were, with the harmless struggle of
the elements. Mr. Macready delivered the words like a mere commonplace. So when he says, in the third act (in that beautiful
picturesque passage)

"Light thickens; and the crow
Makes wing to the rooky wood,"

he spoke these words, as merely intimating a fact — a note of
time — pointing with his hand as he did it, and as he might have
pointed to a clock, to convince his witness of the truth of what he
was saying. And again, in what follows,

"Good things of day begin to droop and drowse,
While night's black agents to their prey do rouse."

This was spoken with too much rapidity and indifference, as a
fact, and not with the solemnity required by the reflection of a
man in a melancholy state of mind, at once aggravating and
exalting his melancholy by it. Mr. Macready seems afraid of the
poetry of some of his greatest parts, as if it would hurt the effect
of his naturalness and his more familiar passages: but such a
fear is not a help towards nature; it is only an impulse towards
avoiding a difficulty. The highest union of the imaginative with
the passive is the highest triumph of acting, as it is of writing.
It is this which has made Mr. Kean so surpassing an actor. He
always gives you the grace and the nature too — the ideal with
the common — the charm of the thought with the energy of the
passion. Mr. Macready, who is a fine actor when he is at his
best, is most graceful and ideal when he is moved by domestic
tenderness. He is best in the pain which seems to have a right
to take pity on itself; which may complain justly, and shed

honourable tears, and has a right to combine manliness and softness. He cannot so well fetch out "the soul of goodness in things evil." Violent or criminal pains he makes simply violent and criminal. Nothing remains to him, if his self-respect, in the ordinary sense of the word, is lost. In the rest, he is often admirable.

14. IN PRAISE OF MACREADY'S MACBETH

YET HUNT'S CRITICISM must be balanced by holding against it the praise which Prince Pückler-Muskau, a German visitor to England in 1826 - 1829, lavished upon the "Eminent Tragedian":

This evening, for the first time since my residence here, I saw Macbeth, — perhaps the most sublime and perfect of Shakspeare's tragedies. Macready, who has lately returned from America, played the part admirably. The passages in which he appeared to me peculiarly true and powerful, were, first, the night-scene in which he comes on the stage after the murder of Duncan, with the bloody dagger, and tells his wife that he has done the deed. He carried on the whole conversation in a low voice, as the nature of the incident requires; — like a whisper in the dark, — yet so distinctly, and with such a fearful expression, that all the terrors of night and crime pass with the sound into the hearer's very soul. Not less excellent was the difficult part with Banquo's ghost. The fine passage — "What man dare, I dare". . . . with great judgment he began with all the vehemence of desperation; then, overcome by terror, dropped his voice lower and lower, till the last words were tremulous and inarticulate. Then, uttering a subdued cry of mortal horror, he suddenly cast his mantle over his face and sank back half-lifeless on his seat. He thus produced the most appalling effect. As man, you felt tremblingly with him, that our most daring courage can oppose nothing to the terrors of another world; — you saw no trace of the stage-hero, who troubles himself little about nature; and, playing only to produce effect on the galleries, seeks his highest triumph in an ascending scale of noise and fury. Macready was admirable, too, in the last act; in which conscience and fear are equally deadened and exhausted, and rigid apathy has taken the place of both; when the last judgment breaks over the head of the sinner in three rapidly succeeding strokes, — the death of the Queen, the fulfilment of the delusive predictions of the witches, and Macduff's terrific declaration that he is not born of woman.

What had previously tortured Macbeth's spirit — had made him murmur at his condition, or struggle against the goadings of his conscience, — can now only strike him with momentary terror, like a lightning flash. He is weary of himself and of existence; and fighting, as he says in bitter scorn, 'bear-like,' · he falls at length, a great criminal — but withal a king and a hero.

Equally masterly was the combat with Macduff, in which inferior actors commonly fail; — nothing hurried, yet all the fire, nay, all the horror, of *the end,* — of the final rage and despair.

I shall never forget the ludicrous effect of this scene at the first performance of Spiker's translation at Berlin. Macbeth and his antagonist set upon each other in such a manner, that, without intending it, they got behind the scenes before their dialogue was at an end; whence the words "Hold — enough!" (what went before them being inaudible,) sounded as if Macbeth was run down, and had cried, (holding out his sword and deprecating any further fighting,) "Leave off — hold — enough!"

Many of the stage arrangements were very praiseworthy. For instance, the two murderers whom Macbeth hires to murder Banquo, are not, as on our stage, ragged ruffians, — by the side of whom the King, in his regal ornaments and the immediate vicinity of his Court, exhibits a ridiculous contrast, and who could never find access to a palace in such a dress; but of decent appearance and behaviour, — villains, but not beggars.

The old Scottish costume is thoroughly handsome, and is probably more true to the times, certainly more picturesque, than with us. The apparition of Banquo, as well as the whole disposition of the table, was infinitely better. In this the Berlin manager made a ludicrous 'bévue.' When the King questions the murderers concerning Banquo's death, one of them answers, "My lord, his throat is cut." This was taken so literally, that a most disgusting pasteboard figure appears at table with the throat cut from ear to ear. The ascent and descent of this monster is so near akin to a puppet-show, that, with all the good-will in the world to keep one's countenance, one can hardly manage it. Here the entrance of the ghost is so cleverly concealed by the bustle of the guests taking their seats at several tables, that it is not till the King prepares to sit down that the dreadful form seated in his place, is suddenly visible to him and to the audience. Two bloody wounds deface his pale countenance (of course it is the actor himself who played Banquo), without rendering it ludicrous by nearly severing the head from the body; and when he looks up fixedly at the King from the festive tables, surrounded by the busy tumult of the guests, then nods to him, and slowly sinks into the earth, the illusion is as perfect as the effect is fearful and thrilling.

But, to be just, I must mention one ridiculous thing that occurred here. After the murder of the King, when there is a knocking at the door, Lady Macbeth says to her husband —

> ". . . Hark, more knocking!
> Get on your nightgown, lest occasion call us,
> And show us to be watchers."

Now 'nightgown' does indeed mean dressing-gown; but yet I could scarcely believe my eyes, when Macready entered in a fashionable flowered chintz dressing-gown, perhaps the one he usually wears, loosely thrown over his steel armour, which was seen glittering at every movement of his body, and in this curious costume drew his sword to kill the chamberlains who were sleeping near the King.

I did not observe that this struck anybody; indeed the interest was generally so slight, the noise and mischief so incessant, that it is difficult to understand how such distinguished artists can form themselves, with so brutal, indifferent, and ignorant an audience as they have almost always before them. As I told you, the English theatre is not fashionable, and is scarcely ever visited by what is called 'good company.' The only advantage in this state of things is, that actors are not spoiled by that indulgence which is so ruinous to them in Germany.

15.   TURBULENT AUDIENCES

PRINCE Pückler-Muskau, who referred to the absence of polite society in English playhouses, is more explicit, elsewhere in his *Tour*, on the subject of London audiences in 1826:

The most striking thing to a foreigner in English theatres is the unheard-of coarseness and brutality of the audiences. The consequence of this is that the higher and more civilized classes go only to the Italian Opera, and very rarely visit their national theatre. Whether this be unfavourable or otherwise to the stage, I leave others to determine.

English freedom here degenerates into the rudest license, and it is not uncommon in the midst of the most affecting part of a tragedy, or the most charming 'cadenza' of a singer, to hear some coarse expression shouted from the galleries in stentor voice. This is followed, according to the taste of the bystanders, either by loud laughter and approbation, or by the castigation and expulsion of the offender.

Whichever turn the thing takes, you can hear no more of what is passing on the stage, where actors and singers, according to ancient usage, do not suffer themselves to be interrupted by such occurrences, but declaim or warble away, 'comme si rien n'était.' And such things happen not once, but sometimes twenty times, in the course of a performance, and amuse many of the audience more than that does. It is also no rarity for some one to throw the fragments of his 'gouté, which do not always consist of orange-peels alone, without the smallest ceremony on the heads of the people in the pit, or to shail them with singular dexterity into the boxes; while others hang their coats and waistcoats over the railing of the gallery, and sit in shirt-sleeves. . . .

Another cause for the absence of respectable families is the resort of hundreds of those unhappy women with whom London swarms. They are to be seen of every degree, from the lady who spends a splendid income, and has her own box, to the wretched beings who wander houseless in the streets. Between the acts they fill the large and handsome 'foyers,' and exhibit their boundless effrontery in the most revolting manner.

It is most strange that in no country on earth is this afflicting and humiliating spectacle so openly exhibited as in the religious and decorous England. The evil goes to such an extent, that in the theatres it is often difficult to keep off these repulsive beings, especially when they are drunk, which is not seldom the case. They beg in the most shameless manner, and a pretty, elegantly dressed girl does not disdain to take a shilling or a sixpence, which she instantly spends in a glass of rum, like the meanest beggar. And these are the scenes, I repeat, which are exhibited in the national theatre of England, where the highest dramatic talent of the country should be developed; where immortal artists like Garrick, Mrs. Siddons, Miss O'Neil, have enraptured the public by their genius, and where such actors as Kean, Kemble, and Young still adorn the stage.

Is not this — to say nothing of the immorality — in the highest degree low and undignified? It is wholly inconsistent with any real love of art, or conception of its office and dignity. The turbulent scenes I have described above scarcely ever arise out of anything connected with the performance, but have almost always some source quite foreign to it, and no way relating to the stage.

16. PHELPS AT SADLER'S WELLS

SADLER'S WELLS, the home of water melodramas and tank spectacles in the unfashionable Islington district of northern London, was transformed into a legitimate playhouse by Samuel Phelps, who for eighteen years (1844 - 1862) maintained it as a temple of Shakespearean worship. The idealism which animated Phelps is clearly expressed in a public address in which the management stated that "a theatre ought to be a place for justly representing the works of our great dramatic poets. . . . Each separate division of our immense metropolis, with its 2,000,000 of inhabitants, may have its own well-conducted theatre within a reasonable distance of the homes of its patrons." The critic, Henry Morley, explained the success of the Phelps venture when he wrote:

A main cause of the success of Mr. Phelps in his Shakespearean revivals is, that he shows in his author above all things the poet. Shakespeare's plays are always poems, as performed at SADLER'S WELLS. The scenery is always beautiful, but it is not allowed to draw attention from the poet, with whose whole conception it is made to blend in the most perfect harmony. The actors are content also to be subordinated to the play, learn doubtless at rehearsals how to subdue excesses of expression that by giving undue force to one part would destroy the balance of the whole, and blend their work in such a way as to produce everywhere the right emphasis. If Mr. Phelps takes upon himself the character which needs the most elaborate development, however carefully and perfectly he may produce his own impression of his part, he never by his acting drags it out of its place in the drama. He takes heed that every part, even the meanest, shall have in the acting as much prominence as Shakespeare gave it in his plan, and it is for this reason that with actors, many of whom are anything but "stars," the result most to be desired is really obtained. Shakespeare appears in his integrity, and his plays are found to affect audiences less as dramas in a common sense than as great poems.

17. A PHELPS DREAM

PHELPS' greatest triumph was his revival of *A Midsummer Night's Dream* in 1853. Henry Morley, who three years later intensely disliked the Charles Kean version of the fairy tale, had nothing but admiration for the Phelps conception:

Mr. Phelps has never for a minute lost sight of the main idea which governs the whole play, and this is the great secret of his success in the presentation of it. He knew that he was to present merely shadows; that spectators, as Puck reminds them in the epilogue, are to think they have slumbered on their seats, and that what appeared before them have been visions. Everything has been subdued as far as possible at SADLER'S WELLS to this ruling idea. The scenery is very beautiful, but wholly free from the meretricious glitter now in favour; it is not so remarkable for costliness as for the pure taste in which it and all the stage-arrangements have been planned. There is no ordinary scene-shifting; but, as in dreams, one scene is made to glide insensibly into another. We follow the lovers and the fairies through the wood from glade to glade, now among trees, now with a broad view of the sea and Athens in the distance, carefully but not at all obtrusively set forth. And not only do the scenes melt dreamlike one into another, but over all the fairy portion of the play there is a haze thrown by a curtain of green gauze placed between the actors and the audience, and maintained there during the whole of the second, third, and fourth acts. This gauze curtain is so well spread that there are very few parts of the house from which its presence can be detected, but its influence is every-

where felt; it subdues the flesh and blood of the actors into something more nearly resembling dream-figures, and incorporates
more completely the actors with the scenes, throwing the same
green fairy tinge, and the same mist over all. A like idea has
also dictated certain contrivances of dress, especially in the case
of the fairies. Very good taste has been shown in the establishment
of a harmony between the scenery and the poem. The main feature — the Midsummer Night — was marked by one scene so
elaborated as to impress it upon all as the central picture of the
group. The moon was just so much exaggerated as to give it the
required prominence. The change, again, of this Midsummer
Night into morning, when Theseus and Hippolyta come to the
wood with horn and hound, was exquisitely presented. And in
the last scene, when the fairies, coming at night into the hall
of Theseus, "each several chamber bless," the Midsummer moon
is again seen shining on the palace as the curtains are drawn
that admit the fairy throng. Ten times as much money might
have been spent on a very much worse setting of the *Midsummer Night's Dream*. It is the poetical feeling prompting a judicious but not extravagant outlay, by aid of which Mr. Phelps
has produced a stage-spectacle more refined and intellectual, and
far more absolutely satisfactory, than anything I can remember
to have seen since Mr. Macready was a manager.

18.   PHELPS' *PERICLES*

ELSEWHERE in his *Journal of a London Playgoer* Morley refers to the
spectacular element which, though governed by pure taste, pervaded
Phelps' production of *Pericles* in October 1854:

Of the scenery, indeed, it is to be said, that so much splendour of decoration is rarely governed by so pure a taste. The
play, of which the text is instability of fortune, has its characteristic place of action on the sea. Pericles is perpetually shown
(literally as well as metaphorically) tempest-tost, or in the immediate vicinity of the treacherous waters; and this idea is most
happily enforced at SADLER'S WELLS by scene-painter and machinist. They reproduce the rolling of the billows and the whistling of
the winds when Pericles lies senseless, a wrecked man on a shore.

When he is shown on board ship in the storm during the birth of Marina, the ship tosses vigorously. When he sails at last to the temple of Diana of the Ephesians, rowers take their places on their banks, the vessel seems to glide along the coast, an admirably painted panorama slides before the eye, and the whole theatre seems to be in the course of actual transportation to the temple at Ephesus, which is the crowning scenic glory of the play. The dresses, too, are brilliant. As beseems an Eastern story, the events all pass among princes. Now the spectator has a scene presented to him occupied by characters who appear to have stepped out of a Greek vase; and presently he looks into an Assyrian palace and sees figures that have come to life and colour from the stones of Nineveh. There are noble banquets and glittering processions, and in the banquet-hall of King Simonides there is a dance which is a marvel of glitter, combinations of colour, and quaint picturesque effect. There are splendid trains of courtiers, there are shining rows of Vestal virgins, and there is Diana herself in the sky.

19. CHARLES KEAN'S ANTIQUARIAN
MACBETH

ANOTHER LONDON PLAYHOUSE that benefited from the Theatre Regulation Act referred to by Phelps was the Princess's Theatre. Its transformation had been less spectacular, however, than that of Sadler's Wells. Prior to 1843 the Princess's had been an inceptive illegitimate house, and during the first years of theatrical freedom it had successively seen such guest stars as Charlotte Cushman, Macready, E. L. Davenport, and Mrs. Mowatt. In the autumn of 1850, Charles Kean took control and for nine years staged his sumptuous Shakespeare revivals, which were characterized by an overindulgence in scholarly lavishness. Kean made a paramount issue of adhering scrupulously to historical truth in costume, architecture, and the details of stage business. *King John* (1852) was followed by a restoration of *Macbeth* (1853) on which occasion the director appended to the playbill a "fly-leaf," to prepare the audience for the scenic innovations, and naming the authorities consulted. Here are a few paragraphs from Kean's antiquarian *Macbeth* notes:

The very uncertain information . . . which we possess respecting the dress worn by the inhabitants of Scotland in the eleventh century, renders any attempt to present this tragedy

I. Days' Set for Act III, Scene iv of *Macbeth*.
Charles Kean's production at the Princess's Theatre on February 14, 1853.

attired in the costume of the period a task of very great difficulty. . . .

In the absence of any positive information handed down to us upon this point, I have borrowed materials from those nations to whom Scotland was constantly opposed in war. The continual inroads of the Norsemen, and the invasion of Canute, in 1031, who, combining in his own person the sovereignty of England, Norway, and Denmark, was the most powerful monarch of his time, may have taught, at least, the higher classes, the necessity of adopting the superior weapons and better defensive armour of their enemies; for these reasons I have introduced the tunic, mantle, cross gartering, and ringed byrne of the Danes and Anglo-Saxons, between whom it does not appear that any very material difference existed; retaining, however, the peculiarity of "the striped and chequered garb," which seems to be generally admitted as belonging to the Scotch long anterior to the history of this play; together with the eagle feather in the helmet, which, according to Gaelic tradition, was the distinguishing mark of a chieftain. Party-coloured woollens and cloths appear to have been commonly worn among the Celtic tribes from a very early period.

Diodorus Siculus and Pliny allude to this peculiarity in their account of the dress of the Belgic Gauls; Strabo, Pliny, and Xiphilin, record the dress of Boadicea, Queen of the Iceni, as being woven, chequer-wise, of many colours, comprising purple, light and dark red, violet, and blue.

There is every reason to believe, that the armour and weapons of the date of *Macbeth* were of rich workmanship.

Harold Hardrada, King of Norway, is described by Snorre as wearing in the battle with Harold II., King of England, A.D. 1066, a blue tunic, and a splendid helmet. The Norwegians not having expected a battle that day, are said to have been without their coats of mail.

This mail appears to have been composed of iron rings or bosses, sewn upon cloth or leather, like that of the Anglo-Saxons. Thorlef, a young Icelandic, or Norwegian warrior of the tenth century, is mentioned in the Eyrbiggia Saga as wearing a most beautiful dress, and it is also said that his arms and equipments were extremely splendid.

The seals and monuments of the early kings and nobles of Scotland represent them as armed and attired in a style similar to their Anglo-Norman contemporaries. Meyrick, in his celebrated work on ancient armour, gives a plate of Alexander I., who commenced his reign in 1107 (only fifty years after the death of Macbeth), and there we find him wearing a hauberk, as depicted in Saxon illuminations, over a tunic of red and blue cloth. . . .

In the Life of St. Colomba, written in Latin by Adomnan . . . in the early part of the seventh century, . . . we are told that the monks at that time were clothed in the skins of beasts, though latterly they had woollen stuffs, manufactured by themselves, and linen, probably imported from the continent. The houses were made of wicker, or wands, woven on stakes, which were afterwards plastered with clay; and even the Abbey of Iona was built of the same rude materials. . . .

In the four centuries and a half which intervened between the death of St. Colomba and the reign of Macbeth, it is reasonable to presume that considerable improvements took place among the Scotch, and that the fashion of their dress and buildings was borrowed from their more civilized neighbours. Under these considerations, the architecture, previous to the Norman conquest, has been adopted throughout the play. During the five centuries which preceded that event, the Anglo-Saxons made great advances, and erected many castles and churches of considerable importance; they excelled in iron work, and ornamented their buildings frequently with colour. On this subject I have availed myself of the valuable knowledge of George Godwin, Esq., F.R.S., of the Royal Institute of Architects, to whose suggestions I take this opportunity of acknowledging my obligation.

20. KEAN'S SHAKESPEAREAN REVIVALS

GLEANED from the glowing eulogies of J. W. Cole, Kean's official biographer, the following excerpts give a clear conception of what happened on the stage of the Princess's during Kean's revivals of *A Midsummer Night's Dream* (1856) and of *Richard II* (1857) respectively:

In the "Midsummer Night's Dream," which is almost exclusively a creation of fancy, there is scarcely any scope for that illustrative and historical accuracy, or for that classical research, so peculiarly identified with Mr. Kean's system of management, and with which his name had now become almost synonymous: nevertheless, he availed himself of the few opportunities afforded by the subject, of carrying out his favourite plan. So little is known of Greek manners and architecture in the time of Theseus, twelve hundred years before the Christian era, and so probable is it that the buildings were of the rudest form, that any attempt to represent them on the stage would have failed in the intended object of profitable instruction. Holding himself, for these reasons, "unfettered with regard to chronology," Mr. Kean presented ancient Athens to us, in the opening scene, at the culminating period of its magnificence, "as it would have appeared to one of its own inhabitants at a time when it had attained its greatest splendour in literature and art." His scholastic taste took advantage of the specified scene of action, to place before the eyes of the spectators, on the rising of the curtain, a restored view of that famous city, "standing in its pride and glory," which excited the spontaneous sympathy, and called up some of the earliest and deepest impressions of every educated mind. We saw, on the hill of the Acropolis, the far-famed Parthenon, the Erichtheum, and the statue of the tutelary goddess Minerva, or Athena; by its side the theatre of Bacchus; in advance, the temple of Jupiter Olympus, partially hiding the hall of the Museum; and on the right, the temple of Theseus.

*   *   *

All readers of Shakespeare, from their schoolboy days, are familiar with the often-quoted description of the entry of the two cousins into London, so pathetically described by their uncle *York* to his *Duchess,* in the latter portion of the play. This was declared by Dryden, a jealous critic, to be a sublime passage of dramatic poetry superior to anything in Sophocles or Euripides, and which left the moderns, without exception, at an immeasurable distance. Mr. C. Kean here seized the boldest idea, and transferred to the scene the most graphic Shakespearean illustration that ever entered into the mind of actor or manager: an illustration that gave a reality to the play it was never supposed to possess. He embodied and anticipated the description of *York,* in an episode of action, introduced between the third and fourth acts, carrying on the story, connecting the chain of events, and preparing the spectators for the solemn abdication of *Richard* which immediately follows. The contrast of feeling and position between the falling and the rising monarch is thus brought out in masterly relief. This episode was pronounced by thousands who witnessed it on repeated occasions, to be, beyond all comparison, the most marvellous scenic illusion that had ever been attempted. If a citizen of London, at 1399, could have been actually revived, and seated within the stalls of the theatre without passing through the changed external world, he would have fancied that he saw a living repetition of what he once had taken part in. There could not have been less than from five to six hundred persons on those contracted boards, all moving in trained regularity or organized disorder, according to the varying incidents. The music, the joy-bells, the dances, the crowded balconies and windows, the throngs in the streets, the civic processions, the mailed warriors, the haughty *Bolingbroke,* the heart-broken *Richard,* the maddening shouts of gratulations which attend the one, while the other is received with silence, gradually deepening into murmurs, groans, and insults, the scrupulous accuracy with which every dress and movement is portrayed; — all this completed a picture which brought back the past to the eyes of the present, and bewildered the spectators with a mingled sensation of astonishment and admiration. The scene altogether surpassed the glories of *Wolsey's* banquet and ball in "Henry the Eighth," or the maddening reality of the Dionysian pastime in the "Winter's Tale." The spell was rendered still more potent by the knowledge that we saw passing before us the resuscitation of a memorable passage from our own domestic chronicles.

21. THE SACRIFICE OF POETRY

Henry Morley did not care for Kean's Periclean Athens, nor could he ever forget the dreamlike quality with which Phelps had imbued the forest scenes three years earlier:

I do not think money ill spent upon stage-furniture, and certainly can only admire the exquisite scenery of the play now being presented at the Princess's; but there may be a defect of taste that mars the effect of the richest ornament, as can best be shown by one or two examples.

Shakespeare's direction for the opening scene of the *Midsummer Night's Dream* is: "Athens, a Room in the Palace of Theseus." For this, is read at the PRINCESS'S THEATRE: "A Terrace adjoining the Palace of Theseus, overlooking the City of Athens"; and there is presented an elaborate and undoubtedly most beautiful bird's-eye view of Athens as it was in the time of Pericles. A great scenic effect is obtained, but it is, as far as it goes, damaging to the poem. Shakespeare took for his mortals people of heroic times, Duke Theseus and Hippolyta, and it suited his romance to call them Athenians; but the feeling of the play is marred when out of this suggestion of the antique mingled with the fairy world the scene-painter finds opportunity to bring into hard and jarring contrast the Athens of Pericles and our own world of Robin Goodfellow and all the woodland elves. "A Room in the House of Theseus" left that question of the where or when of the whole story to be touched as lightly as a poet might desire; the poetry was missed entirely by the painting of the scene,

Courtesy of the Victoria and Albert Museum, London, Crown Copyright

W. Gordon's Set for Act I, Scene i of *A Midsummer Night's Dream.*
A Terrace Adjoining the Palace of Theseus.
Charles Kean's production at the Princess's Theatre on October 15, 1856.

beautiful as it is, which illustrates the first act of the *Midsummer Night's Dream* at the PRINCESS'S.

In the second act there is a dream-like moving of the wood, beautifully managed, and spoilt in effect by a trifling mistake easily corrected. Oberon stands before the scene waving his wand, as if he were exhibitor of the diorama, or a fairy conjurer causing the rocks and trees to move. Nobody, I believe, ever attributed to fairies any power of that sort. Oberon should either be off the stage or on it still as death, and it should be left for the spectators to feel the dreamy influence of wood and water slipping by their eyes unhindered and undistracted. This change leads to the disclosure of a fairy ring, a beautiful scenic effect, and what is called in large letters upon the play-bills, "Titania's Shadow Dance." Of all things in the world, a shadow dance of fairies! If anything in the way of an effect of light was especially desirable, it would have been such an arrangement as would have made the fairies appear to be dancing in a light so managed as to cast no shadow, and give them the true spiritual attribute.

Elaborately to produce and present, as an especial attraction, fairies of large size, casting shadows made as black and distinct as possible, and offering in dance to pick them up, as if even they also were solid, is as great a sacrifice of Shakespeare to the purposes of the ballet-master, as the view of Athens in its glory was a sacrifice of poetry to the scene-painter. Enough has been said to show the direction in which improvement is necessary to make the stage-ornament at the PRINCESS'S THEATRE as perfect as it is beautiful. The Puck is a pretty little girl, belted and garlanded with flowers! From the third act we miss a portion of the poem most essential to its right effect — the quarrel between Hermia and Helena; but we get, at the end, a ballet of fairies round a maypole that shoots up out of an aloe, after the way of a transformation in a pantomime, and rains down garlands. Fairies, not airy beings of the colour of the greenwood, or the sky, or robed in misty white, but glittering in the most brilliant dresses, with a crust of bullion about their legs, cause the curtain to fall on a splendid ballet; and it is evidence enough of the depraved taste of the audience to say that the ballet is encored.

I make these comments in no censorious mood. It is a pleasure to see Shakespeare enjoyed by the large number of persons who are attracted to the PRINCESS'S THEATRE by the splendours for which it is famous. I do not wish the splendour less, or its attraction less, but only ask for more heed to the securing of a perfect harmony between the conceptions of the decorator and those of the poet.

22. KEAN'S SELF-DEFENSE

IN 1859, Charles Kean retired from the Princess's Theatre. During the last season, 243 of the acting nights were dedicated to Shakespeare. *Henry VIII* was the closing play. After the final curtain, Kean came forward and delivered a farewell address in which he defended his managerial principles:

I may, perhaps, be expected, on an occasion like the present, to make some allusions to the principles of management I have invariably adopted. I have always entertained the conviction that, in illustrating the great plays of the greatest poet who ever wrote for the advantage of men, historical accuracy might be so blended with pictorial effect, that instruction and amusement would go hand in hand; and that the more completely such a system was carried out, so much the more valuable and impressive would be the lesson conveyed.

In fact, I was anxious to make the theatre a school as well as a recreation; and the reception given to the plays thus submitted to your judgment, combined with the unprecedented number of their repetitions, bear, I think, conclusive evidence that my views were not altogether erroneous.

I find it impossible to believe, as some have asserted, that because every detail is studied with an eye to truth, such a plan can in the most remote degree detract from the beauties of the poet.

My admiration of Shakespeare would never have allowed me to do that which I could possibly conceive would be detrimental to his mighty genius; nor can I suppose that this great master would have been more highly esteemed had I been less correct in the accessories by which I surrounded him.

I would venture to ask if, in the play of this evening, you have lost one jot of the dramatic interest, because in the ball-room at York Place, and at the *Queen's* trial at Blackfriars, every incident introduced is closely adopted from the historical descriptions recording those very events as they actually occurred above three hundred years ago? I would ask, I repeat, whether the fall of *Wolsey* has been thereby rendered less effective, or the death of *Katherine* less solemn and pathetic?

I would also venture to add, that I do not think you would have been more impressed with the address of *King Henry V.* to his army at Agincourt, had it been delivered to a scanty few, incorrectly attired, and totally undisciplined; instead of a well-trained mass of men, representing the picture of a real host, clothed and accoutred in the exact costume and weapons of the time.

I remember that when I produced the "Winter's Tale" as a Greek play — that is, with Greek dresses, Greek customs, and Greek architecture, — an objection was raised by some, that, although the scene was situated at Syracuse, then a Greek colony, whose King consults the celebrated oracle of Delphi, yet the play was said to be essentially English, and ought to be so presented, because allusions in various parts bore reference to this country and to the period when the author wrote.

You would, perhaps, ladies and gentlemen, have been somewhat astonished and perplexed to have seen the chest containing the answer of the Greek oracle to the Greek King, — supposed to have been delivered above two thousand years ago — borne upon the stage by the Beefeaters of Queen Elizabeth; you would, perhaps, have been equally surprised to have witnessed at this theatre, *Leontes,* as a Greek King, in the last act, attired as *Hamlet,* Prince of Denmark; and yet such an incongruity was accepted within the last twenty years.

I have been blamed for depriving *Macbeth* of a dress never worn at any period or in any place, and for providing him instead, with one resembling those used by the surrounding nations with whom the country of that chieftain was in constant intercourse.

Fault was also found with my removal of the gorgeous banquet and its gold and silver vessels, together with the massive candelabra (such as no Highlander of the eleventh century ever gazed upon), and with the substitution of the more appropriate feast of coarse fare, served upon rude tables, and lighted by simple pine torches. I was admonished that such diminution of regal pomp impaired the strength of *Macbeth's* motive for the crime of murder, the object being less dazzling and attractive. Until that hour I had never believed that the Scottish Thane had an eye to King *Duncan's* plate. I had imagined that lofty ambition, the thirst of power, and the desire of supreme command, developed themselves with equal intensity in the human heart, whether the scene of action might be the palace of a European monarch or the wigwam of an American Indian.

In the tragedy of "Macbeth" I was condemned for removing splendour that was utterly out of place, while in "Henry VIII." I was equally condemned for its introduction, where it was in place, and in perfect accordance with the time and situation.

I was told, that I might be permitted to present a true picture of ancient Assyria in Lord Byron's play of "Sardanapalus," but on no account must I attempt to be equally correct in Shakespeare's "Macbeth" — that drama must remain intact, with all its time-honoured, conventional improprieties.

What would the poet gain, and how much would the public

lose, by the perpetuation of such absurdities? Why should I present to you what I know to be wrong, when it is in my power to give what I know to be right?

If, as it is sometimes affirmed, my system is injurious to the poet, it must be equally so to the actor; and surely my most determined opponents will admit that at least I have pursued a very disinterested policy in thus incurring for many years so much labour and expense for the purpose of professional suicide.

Had I been guilty of ornamental introductions for the mere object of show and idle spectacle, I should assuredly have committed a grievous error; but, ladies and gentlemen, I may safely assert that in no single instance have I ever permitted historical truth to be sacrificed to theatrical effect.

As a case in point, let me refer to the siege of Harfleur, as presented on this stage: it was no ideal battle, no imaginary fight; it was a correct representation of what actually had taken place; the engines of war, the guns, banners, fire balls, the attack and defence, the barricades at the breach, the conflagration within the town, the assault and capitulation, were all taken from the account left to us by a priest who accompanied the army, — was an eye-witness, and whose Latin MS. is now in the British Museum.

The same may be said of the episodes in "Henry V." and "Richard II." Indeed, whatever I have done has been sanctioned by history, to which I have adhered in every minute particular.

23. TOM ROBERTSON'S THEATRICAL TYPES

BEFORE ACHIEVING SUCCESS as a playwright, Thomas William Robertson wrote for a number of London newspapers and periodicals. To the weekly *Illustrated Times* he contributed a series of articles dealing with "Theatrical Types." His sketches of the manager, stage director, scene painter, stage carpenter, and property man are a mine of information about theatrical conditions in the 1850's:

[*Varieties of Managers*]

The Actor Manager of thirty years ago was a man of totally different type to his successor of the present day. He was an intensely clever, bustling, wrong-headed, highly appreciative fellow, fond of his authors, his company, his orchestra, his sceneshifters, his supernumeraries, and all that belonged to the little world he ruled. During the rehearsal of a new piece he would swear horribly and stamp on the stage till the soles of his feet tingled again. On the night of its production, attired in his character-dress, he would be here, there and everywhere — assisting the actors in the adjustment of their wigs, finding fault with the coiffure of a soubrette, discharging the prompter, imprecating every portion of the anatomy of his stage-manager, helping a carpenter in the "setting" of a rock-piece, challenging his leading tragedian to mortal combat on the morrow, making speeches to the audience to appease them for the long delays between the acts, and conducting himself generally like a lunatic in fancy costume; but, the piece over, he would raise the prompter's salary, ask his stage-manager to join him in a bottle of champagne, treat the carpenters to beer, invite his leading tragedians to dine with him on Sunday, and thank his generous and liberal public for once more cr-r-r-owning his humble efforts with their kind approval. The first to recognise merit in an aspirant, he was the last to listen to the grumbling of a fastidious author or a tyrannical stage-manager. Beloved by all tragedians, comedians, carpenters, callboys, sceneshifters, and supernumeraries, his funeral presented a long procession of grateful and weeping mourners, who dated all the events of their lives from his death, and who said constantly, "When poor Yorick was living he would never," etc. "Alas! poor Yorick!"

Hie over the last five and twenty years to the present caterers for the public! The change is great, and, like many other changes, the reverse of an improvement. There are so many varieties of the species that our limits will only permit us to touch upon a few. . . .

The Commercial Manager is a very common type . . . and is willing to exploit opera, ballet, equestrianism, and Shakespeare. . . . He takes an entirely commercial view of all things — Ramo-Samee Indiarubber Peruvians, real water, the legitimate drama, speaking pantomime, or pantomimic tragedy — so that it bring in the ready sixpence. . . . He prides himself greatly upon his practical commonsense, distrusts manuscripts, fears authors, but places great reliance upon his costumier and property-man. His conversation is not choice, except as regards oaths, which are of a raciness and full flavour that would do discredit to an irate

cabman. Although he professes a high respect for dramatic literature, he judges of the merit of a drama like a butterman — by
its weight in paper. He is a great man for bargains, and will buy
a quantity of damaged velvets for a fabulously small sum, after
which he will search for an author to write him a piece for the
velvets. "Lovely velvets — make any piece popular them velvets
would," says the Commercial Manager. The drama found, if it
fail he despairs of the prospects of the theatre. Publics are so
fickle nowadays. "Who would have thought that with them velvets any piece could fail?" The Commercial Manager is a great
financial genius, and cuts down salaries and expenses to the very
lowest scale. He is also fertile in expedients for stopping a night's
salary from his employés, and was the original inventor and intro-
ducer of that wonderful piece of economical meanness, a Com-
plimentary Benefit, which means a benefit for the manager, on
which occasion the actors, actresses, sceneshifters, supernumeraries and all give their services gratuitously. . . .

Lastly, the C. M. is very litigious, and always involved in
lawsuits; in fact, an attorney is laid on to his establishment like
gas, and picks out holes in engagements and flaws in arrangements for his clever client's interest. The Actor Manager is a
good second or third rate sort of artist, who forces himself into
a prominent position by taking a theatre, and, by carefully stew-
ing down the abilities of the authors and actors he employs, and
mixing with his own their mental and artistic porridge, makes his
weak water-gruel talents thick and slaby. Just now the stage
is terribly plagued by various sorts of these self-sufficient entre-
preneurs. There is your Tragedian Manager, who kindly puts
Shakespeare right, and explains what that erring author really
meant; and there is your High Comedy Manager, who knows
three Lords to speak to, and once met a Countess at a ball, and
is in consequence a great authority on fashionable life; and, like
Goldsmith's bear-leader, can't abide anything that is low. These
two varieties are very fond of teaching young actors how to act,
and so successful is their tuition, that very often a promising
young comedian from the provinces has in six difficult lessons
been tamed and tortured into the ineffective and passionless delivery which forms so valuable a setting to managerial mediocrity.
Another of these peculiarities is remarkable. They seldom, if ever,
engage an actor or actress taller than themselves. An engagement

at their theatre depends more on inches than genius. No mere actor should be taller than his manager. Banquo should always be smaller than Macbeth, and the jeune premier rôle shorter than the grand premier rôle. Height, like individual talent, must be kept down to one regulation standard. In regard to their well-disguised servility to the gentlemen who notice the theatres in the daily and weekly papers, actor-managers are by no means more open to animadversion than either the commercial or the invisible ones. . . . There are many other varieties of Managers, too many for us to give a full and particular account of; many well-meaning, kind-hearted and honourable gentlemen, the sort of men who require no detailed description, for the good of all classes are alike.

[*Stage Directors*]

The Stage-Manager is the man who should direct everything behind the scenes. He should be at one and the same time a poet, an antiquarian, and a costumier; and possess sufficient authority, from ability as well as office, to advise with a tragedian as to a disputed reading, to argue with an armourer as to the shape of a shield, or to direct a wardrobe-keeper as to the cut of a mantle. He should understand the military science like a drill-sergeant, and be as capable of handling crowds and moving masses as a major-general. He should possess universal sympathies, should feel with the sublime, and have a quick perception of the ludicrous. Though unable to act himself, he should be able to teach others, and be the finger-post, guide, philosopher, and friend of every soul in a theatre, male or female, from the manager and author to the call-boy and the gasman, from the manageress and principal soprano to the back row of the extra children's ballet and the cleaners.

Above all, he should be endowed with a perfect command of his own temper, and the power of conciliating the temper of others. The art of stage management consists chiefly in a trick of manner that reconciles the collision of opposing personal vanities.

That is what he should be; what he is, is a very different affair.

Some Stage-Managers are appointed to their office for curious reasons: because they have grey hair or a fatherly-looking stomach, or because they once wrote a piece which failed, or because they know nothing of stage business, or because they know nothing *but* stage business, or because they are deferential, or because they have a large family, or because they wear a heavy gold watch and chain, or because they knew the late Charles Kemble, or any other good theatrical reason.

One man, who for many years was Stage-Manager of the patent theatres — a position for which he was totally unqualified — was appointed solely because he was well acquainted with the hours at which the coaches started from one town to another. . . .

Then there is the Cruel Stage-Manager, who hates everybody in the theatre and out of it, and who abuses his power in the largest spirit of the smallest tyranny, and, while he fawns on public favourites, is the bane of the actors of inferior parts and the terror of the ballet. If a poor girl be one minute late by the Cruel Stage-Manager's infallible chronometer, which, with the Green-room clock, he always keeps five minutes before the Horse Guards, he directs the Prompter to "fine her."

"Fine her — fine her, Brooks" and the girl who walks twenty miles a day, and, being a clever dancer, earns eighteen shillings a week, is mulcted of one shilling. . . .

The Affectionate Stage-Manager is a flint-musket of a different bore. He lives but to employ adjectives agreeable to his hearers, and is of an incompetency compared to which ordinary inability soars to genius. With him every male is his "dear boy;" every woman "his darling child;" every manager "a splendid fellow;" every actor "a first-rate man;" every actress "a charming creature;" every supernumerary "a good chap;" and the world in general a Bower of Bliss and Home of Happiness. "Whatever is is best" is his motto and his *bonhommie* is supposed by actors — an easily-persuaded and credulous race — to spring from a kind heart, whereas it is only pure, simple, unadulterated blarney. He could not live by his ability, so he ekes out his thin, weak, conventional knowledge with a mouthful of tender words.

The Traditional Stage-Manager is the man who knew Charles Kemble, and whose knowledge — dramatic, artistic, literary, and general — ends there. To the stupidity of this creature no pen could do justice; to the density of his intellectual powers lignumvitae is as a transparent soap-bubble.

The Muddle-headed Stage-Manager is a donkey of another colour. He will listen to every suggestion and understand none. In the inmost recesses of that cerebral pulp which in his skull does duty for brain, he has a confused notion that the Act of Parliament forbidding marriage with a deceased wife's sister somehow or other affects the probability of the plot of 'Hamlet.' . . . Under his auspices — and be it always remembered that the deeper his incapacity the prouder he is of his "experience" — rehearsals progress but slowly.

[*The Scene Painter*]

The Scene-painter is usually one of the pleasantest men in the theatre. King in his snug painting-room high above the stage, he recks not of the whirl of passions and vanities below. It is a great power the theatrical scene-painter holds between his pliant thumb and fingers. He copies Nature on a large scale. It must be high delight to look upon a broad, flat, white surface, and choose whether it shall be converted into an Emir's palace, all pillars, curtains, gold tassels, fringes, and polished-mirror marble floor, the hot sun shining on a fountain in the distance; or into an Alpine gorge, with blocks of snow-covered stone and funereal fir-trees, with plains of ice conducting to a frosty horizon; or into a magician's cavern, where the dark rocks, cut in fantastic forms, loom into sight in the shape of squatting demons, petrified giants, and ghostly vertebrae of huge and hideous reptiles; or into a sparkling, rippling sea, with but one white speck of sail between it and the clear dome of blue sky above it. These are great privileges. . . .

In these present days of scenic display, when even no poor ghost can walk undisturbed by scientific satellites, lime-lights, mirrors, and the like, the Scene-painter is a far more important person in a theatre than the Tragedian — not that the bearing of those gentlemen would impress a stranger with the fact; for by so much as the Tragedian is pompous, blatant, and assuming, the Scene-painter is easy, natural, and polite. Perhaps the Tragedian takes his tone from the brigand-chiefs and aspiring patriots whose characters he assumes; and the Scene-painter, with his keen eye for the glories of colour and knowledge of the combinations of natural beauty, knows how to blend himself harmoniously.

[The Stage Carpenter]

The Stage Carpenter is a singular creature. He is the victim of a delusion, by which he is bound hand, and foot, and brain. It is a belief, as deeply rooted in his mind as is his two-foot rule inserted in his trousers-pocket, that while he is in the theatre he is "at work." If he is what, in theatrical parlance, is termed a day-man, he reaches the theatre at a quarter to ten if the rehearsal be at ten, at a quarter to eleven if the rehearsal be at eleven, at a quarter to twelve if the rehearsal be at twelve, and so on. Once in the theatre, his first proceeding is to hide himself in the scene-dock, where nobody can find him; he then takes off his coat, puts on his "working" canvas-jacket, sticks a hammer in his girdle or apron pistol-wise — after the fashion of bold buccaneers in penny plates — uses his coat-sleeve as a pocket-handkerchief, sits down in a corner, and goes to sleep. And here commences his delusion. It is his firm belief that while he has on his canvas-jacket and his hammer stuck into his girdle that he is hard at work — nay, perspiring copiously. He will even carry this delusion out so far as to wake up after an hour and a half's nap and feel fatigued, so much so as to be compelled to adjourn to the nearest public-house and recruit exhausted nature with half a pint — for he is also the victim of half a pint, or, rather, the victim of a pint and a half, not to say two gallons — and in three days, when not an interval of labour, not the screwing out of an old nail from a rusty hinge, has occurred to vary the tedious monotony of slumber, he will declaim in the taproom on the wrongs of the working man and the tyranny of employers. It has been said by a popular novelist of the day that no set of men can idle as nautical men can. From this observation it is evident that the servants of a theatre have never passed under that popular novelist's eye.

The Stage Carpenter works but once a year — for the production of the pantomime, and then he works *con amore*; for during the run of the pantomime the genius of stage carpentry is properly estimated, and authors, actors, composers, musicians, and such mere idlers sink into their proper insignificance.

[*The Property Man*]

The Property Man — *i.e.*, the man who looks after the chairs and tables and things movable by hand, and who manufactures the sheep, fish, carrots, and huge chamber-candlesticks used in the pantomime — is a mysterious mechanic, whose habits are unclean, predatory, and mendacious. His complexion is a singular compound of the perspiration of the Midsummer before last with the dust of the preceding Christmas. Dust rests upon his eyelashes as moss rests on the boughs of an old tree. If ever he wash himself — which is doubtful, save on his wedding day — his ablutions are made in the glue-pot. He is so sticky that, were he to lean against a wall, portions of his garments would adhere to it when he summoned up sufficient energy to walk away. Why does this gifted getter-up of gnomes, salamanders, dragons' heads, and fairies' wings abjure cold water and ignore all crystal streams, save the pantomime fountains framed of wire, blue gauze, white Dutch metal, and spangles? Would his fingers lose their cunning if occasionally polluted by the use of soap? his tongue its power of ready excuse, or his brain its inventive faculty, if fluid touched his external man? The cause of this dramatico-mechanico-hydrophobia is inexplicable, and ever must remain a mystery, to be solved only by a treacherous member of the craft, who, converted to cleanliness by a Turkish bath, shall renounce the property-room and divulge its secrets.

The Property Man has the same peculiarity as the oldest inhabitant — he never remembers anything; nor will he, no matter how familiar the object, confess that he has ever seen a specimen, or that it is procurable, save by the expense of large quantities of money, time, difficulty, and danger.

"Grimes!" calls the Stage Manager.

Grimes is very often absent, not in mind, but in body; but an active call-boy, knowing Grimes's haunts, fetches him from the tap, where he had been rendering himself more adhesive with half a pint of treacly beer.

"Grimes," says the Stage Manager; very authoritatively if he be ignorant of his calling, but rather kindly if he have some perception of it.

"Yes, Sir!" answers Grimes, with respect or deference; for

it is part of the Property Man's instincts to be too deferential and respectful.

"We shall use the red furniture for this farce."

"Yes, Sir."

"Tables, chairs, sofas and all that, you know. And then there's breakfast things, and — and that's all. No — by-the-way, there's a cat wanted."

"A what, Sir?"

"A cat."

"A cat, Sir!" echoes Grimes, as if the word were strange to him as unicorn, phoenix, or ichthyosaurus.

"Yes. Should be a tortoiseshell."

"Taught us who, Sir?"

"Yes, tortoiseshell cat, I say."

The eyes of Grimes wander over the footlights into the empty pit, inhabited by the dust, orange-peels, mice, and fleas. After a pause he looks into the face of the Stage Manager and says,

"Where am I to get one, Sir?"

"Get what?"

"A — a cat, Sir."

"A cat! Anywhere."

"Anywhere, Sir?"

Repetition is one of the principal weapons in the Grimes armoury.

"Yes anywhere," says the Stage Manager. "Cats are plenty, are they not?"

"They may ha' been, Sir, some years ago; but *I hardly never seen one lately*," is the reply.

24.   THE MEININGER IN LONDON

IN THE SPRING of 1881, the Saxe-Meiningen Company visited London and showed their productions of *Julius Caesar, Twelfth Night, The Winter's Tale, The Robbers,* and *William Tell* on the Drury Lane stage. The London critics were not unanimously pleased, but all observers were startled by the handling of the stage crowds, the picturesqueness of the scenes, and the harmony of the *ensemble*. Here are some observations by the *Athenaeum* critic:

Seven years have elapsed since the merits of the Saxe-Meiningen company of players, which made in 1874 its first appearance in Berlin, were the subject of controversy in the *Athenaeum*, and the actors whose reputation was then first made known to the English public, with no special information, are now in our midst. Adhering to the course which has won them the distinction they enjoy, they have chosen for their first appearance Shakspeare's 'Julius Caesar' and 'Twelfth Night.' The report which preceded their coming has done the actors no more than justice. How far scenic adjuncts aid or impede the effect of a dramatic representation is a question which remains where it was. There are few intelligent English playgoers, however, who would not be thankful for the chance of seeing constantly upon our boards representations such as German actors have now brought within our reach. That any especially noteworthy instance of interpretation is afforded, or that any single performance may claim to rank upon a level higher than that which has recently been reached, cannot be maintained. Performances, however, which from the intellectual and the technical standpoint are equally valuable, have been afforded. In such respects as costume and scenic effect, the superiority of which we have heard is over the English stage of yesterday, not that of to-day. No one would dream of saying that the dresses, Roman and Italian, which are exhibited are handsomer than those to which we are accustomed at the Lyceum, or that the representation of the Forum in 'Julius Caesar' is superior to that of the Temple of Diana in 'The Cup.' It may, however, be maintained that no spectacular play of Shakspeare, such as 'Julius Caesar' may claim to be considered, has ever been put upon our stage in a fashion equally effective. As in the case of the Dutch comedians, with whom it is natural to compare the newcomers, the principal gain is in the manner in which those who are little or nothing more than supernumeraries wear the costumes of a bygone age, and take intelligent part in actions and movements of which they can have had no experience in real life. Add to this that in both companies, Rotterdam and Saxe-Meiningen, the openly manifested desire to obtain an ascendency over his fellows, which has been the disgrace of the English actor, is kept out of sight, and the cause why performances such as are now given attract is apparent.

In the case of 'Julius Caesar' the most noteworthy features

Die Gartenlaube, 1879

Shakespeare's *Julius Caesar,* Act III, Scene ii.
Meiningen Crowd Scene, after a Sketch by the Duke of Saxe-Meiningen.

consisted of the arrangement of the tableaux and the disposition of the supernumeraries when, as in the case of the oration of Antony over the body of Caesar, strong and growing emotion has to be expressed. From the picturesque standpoint these things were perfect. That they were wholly natural is less clear. No one has had experience of a tumult such as is depicted, and it is difficult to say what amount of consentaneous gesture on the part of masses of men stirred by the same words to the same emotion is conceivable. The violence of the outbreak seemed, however, out of keeping with the quasi-symmetrical arrangement of the tableaux. A like fault was evident when passengers during the early speech of Brutus and Caesar crossed the stage. The movements of these were too formal and artificial. That superbly impressive effects were more than once produced may be at once allowed. . . .

A performance, however, of 'Twelfth Night' so picturesque and so faultless has not been seen upon the modern English stage. A chief reason why 'Twelfth Night' is rarely played in England is because there is no part prominent enough to suit the vanity of a star actor. The harmony and beauty which are the chief features in the performance of 'Twelfth Night' are impossible under the conditions ordinarily prevailing in England, and can never be obtained while the vanity of the individual is allowed to override the requirements of art. One more observation is permissible. That purity of diction which is indispensable to fit an actor for the Comédie Française is not universal. Provincial pronunciation is distinguishable in one or two cases. Still the performances are creditable, and Englishmen are to blame if they do not obtain from them some lessons of which they stand in need.

✓   ✓   ✓

Everything in the performance of 'The Robbers' is praiseworthy, the balance is admirable, and all that can add vitality to mimic action and *vraisemblance* to illusion is present. Abundant horrors are, of course, supplied in the recital by Franz Moor of his dream, and the picture of his sufferings previous to his death by his own hands. . . . In *ensemble* the performance leaves little to desire. The scenery and decorations are, moreover, excellent, one view, that of the robbers' encampment on the bank of the Danube, being especially noteworthy. In the arrangement of masses admirable stage management is shown. It is doubtful, however, whether in the dresses of the robbers the costumes are not too varied, and the employment of red is not too frequent. One censure which may perhaps smack of hypercriticism is incurred: the robbers look too old.

25. PICTORIALIZED SHAKESPEARE

DURING THE SEASON 1878 - 1879, Henry Irving (1838 - 1905) assumed control of the Lyceum Theatre, which for the next two decades was regarded as London's foremost playhouse and temple of Shakespearean worship. Irving shared Charles Kean's belief that Shakespeare's plays should be "perfectly mounted." In his speech to the Garrick Club he defined his idea of perfection by pointing out that Shakespeare, were he still alive, "would try it with scenery." The London visit of the Meininger had made a lasting impression upon Irving, and, still under its spell, he mounted his productions of *Romeo and Juliet* and of *Much Ado* in 1882. *Twelfth Night* followed two years later. In 1888, Irving resumed a part he had first undertaken thirteen years earlier under the Bateman management: he revived *Macbeth*. Irving's neurotic interpretation of the title role (Macbeth as a "frightened poltroon") was still the subject of critical debate, but the reviewers were unanimous in their praise of the visual aspects the evening at the Lyceum afforded the Victorian playgoer. Hawes Craven had done the principal sets; Ellen Terry wore exquisite dresses designed by Mrs. Comyns Carr; and the rest of the cast appeared in clothes of Charles Cattermole's design. Arthur Sullivan's new music replaced the traditional Locke-Purcell strains. Sir Edward R. Russell, a stanch Irvingite, recorded his enchantment in the Liverpool *Daily Post*:

By the co-operation of costumiers and scenepainters, each scene is a very noble picture. But of all the scenes, the most effective is the court of Macbeth's castle, where he sees the air-drawn dagger, and where practically the central tragedy of the play is performed, though with great art kept out of sight of the audience. It is of irregular construction, built in the style wherein Norman architecture began to put on decoration, but fully retained its rounded masses and its rugged strength. The rude entrance-hall in the rear — sombre or bright as the outer portal is open or closed — faces the spectators. Above the passage leading to it are murky arcaded galleries. On the right is a staircase. On the left is a round tower-like structure suggestive of a spiral stairway. Against this Lady Macbeth leans her back restlessly while the murder is in progress. The passage past it is the way Macbeth is marshalled by the dagger which he sees before him. The place is comparatively dark. The revellers have settled to their slumbers. Banquo has gone through on his way to bed, and said 'Good night' to his host, and received with distant though courteous austerity his sinister overture for future co-operation. The murderous intriguer is alone. The last attendant is dismissed by Macbeth's hasty order. Mr. Irving's dagger soliloquy is most searching in its ghastly truth. His exit to commit the murder is a living embodiment of the wonderful text, which, as it were, reels and yawns and rocks, a very abyss of moral dread and sickened horror. Then enters Lady Macbeth with a firm step, making a frank and meaning confession of one source of her courage. The words 'Had he not resembled my father,' etc., are presently given, not with the old groaning pathos, but with cursory half-sensibility and entire practical freedom. When Macbeth returns, the scene merges so far as she is concerned into a cool though anxious partner's solicitude. She frets, she gesticulates with vexation as she almost dispairingly beholds her huband's dazed and demoralised condition. There is a curious commonplace practicality in the tone of her question, 'Who was it that thus cried?' when Macbeth has been maundering on with his spiritual fancy — so fine and fit in the situation — of the 'Sleep no more.' There is no blenching when she snatches the daggers from him. It is with cool and perfect sincerity that this fierce, firm woman declares that the sleeping and the dead are but as pictures. Yet Miss Terry never misses the greatness, the thrill, the suspense, the dread of the action. This is all felt unremittingly, though her keen practical perception keeps hold solely of the one great exigency of concealing the crime and, what is involved in it, the controlling of her husband's quivering self-betrayal. When she returns with bloody hands from depositing the daggers, it is clear enough that she scorns to wear a heart as white as Macbeth's; and note the curious, curdling touch of detail when she lifts by the tips of her fingers only the robe which lies fallen on the ground. The exit during the knocking at the gate is magnificently real, and the audience is left in a tumult of agitation, when the drunken porter enters to open the door tardily to Macduff and Lennox. What follows can be easily imagined. I have only to record the perfect timing and balancing of the incidents so as to consult reality at every point — the not too rapid but at last turbulent entrance of the guests from the galleries and staircase — the distant alarm-bell — Macbeth's manner before and after the revelation — the stolid plausibility of his defence of the killing of the grooms — and a splendid idea of Ellen Terry as she stands behind Banquo, nervously assenting by unconscious nods and gestures and inarticulate lip-movements to her lord's story, until her woman's strength fails her, and the cry is raised 'Look to the lady,' and she falls and is raised and carried out with her fair head thrown back over a thane's shoulder, and her red hair streaming in the torchlight. The eager exit of the coward towards the hall where the murder is to be debated brings this wonderful scene to a grand termination.

Space and time must fail to describe the play in detail. The banquet scene is very fine in the vein of a Cattermole picture, with a Burne Jones background. Light and darkness are admirably managed, the apparition rises gloomily and vaguely, and makes a part, not too strongly but strongly enough, of the picture. I cannot understand the lowering and raising of torches at the appearance and disappearance of Banquo's spirit; but the necessary effect of etherealising the vision is certainly achieved, though too mechanically. At the close, when Lady Macbeth with strong exhortations has made her guests depart, she remains listless or hopeless on the throne while her husband completes the rhapsodies of his horror. Presently she soothes him, but it is with as little hope as she showed when she drooped on the throne. The hand of spiritual Nemesis is on her. At last husband and wife leave the scene together, and the final incident is a striking one. Macbeth takes a torch from behind a pillar, but suddenly, in a paroxysm, hurls it blazing to the ground. He shrouds his face in his robe as he leans rapidly forward and rests against a pillar. The Queen as swiftly kneels behind him, and remains clinging to his skirts, with an upturned face full of tragical solicitude.

Anon we see the last of Lady Macbeth in the sleep-walking scene. Here she is comparatively fragile, but has not that deathly appearance which has usually been aimed at. Nor is there any melodrama in her tones. The chief note of the elocution is a sort of dreamy, half-asleep prolongation of the syllables. Miss Terry is here again beautifully dressed, but is now in drapery, dove-colour across white. If one were seeing the scene for the first time, its touchingness would seem infinite. There is no denying, however, that the solemn splendour of the grander Lady Macbeth lingers too impressively in the mind to give tender realism its fair chance in this scene. All that tender realism can do Miss Terry effects, and her natural way of re-enacting the incidents of the murder ought to seem more real than the older and more melodramatic manner. Old associations are strong, however. . . .

The cauldron scene is a triumph of bold invention by Mr. Craven, the cauldron being placed in a circular cavity of rock in a mountainous defile, with jagged steps on which Macbeth stands to consult the witches. This, by a happy idea, is not insisted upon in the way of length. It is made brief, and Sir Arthur Sullivan's music is all the more a beautiful feature of this revival, because its prominence is so modest and its province so artistically subordinate. It is excellent and full of fancy, not only in the song and chorus, but in the incidental music, some of which is perfectly delightful. I would instance as especially exquisite the bars which are played as King Duncan arrives at the castle. In the 'Mingle' chorus there is a curious eccentricity of time. Hecate, happily, is made little of in the new version of the tragedy. She is a difficulty, and is best 'minimised'.

The English woodland scene in which Malcolm and Macduff have their interview is a charming and Finnie-like contrast and relief to the other scenery, Mr. Craven being again the artist; and from this we advance to the well-managed military scenes which close the tragedy. I felt more than I ever did before the utility and dramatic impressiveness of that little talk in which Macbeth's enemies discuss upon rumour the condition of the tyrant. It leads up effectively to the spectacle of ruin which Macbeth affords as he roams his castle arguing himself into courage, but relaxing all the time into perfectly hopeless feebleness of will and nature, only relieved by fierce gleams of capricious irascibility. The Birnam Wood difficulty is cleverly surmounted. The forces under arms are numerous. Many details are strikingly illustrative — as, for instance, when the three soldiers stare in through the door in a peeping attitude, with fright in their eyes, while their comrade with blanched cheeks tells the King of the moving wood.

One feature of the battle-scenes had a peculiar effect upon

me. The soldiers 'off' sang as they fought. Simulated distance made it a kind of hum, but there was a distinct tune in it. Whether this is a slogan or not I am too Southron to know, but it greatly added to the irresistible reality of what seemed to be going on.

The last combat is fierce and sanguinary, and its episodes — all historic and familiar, so powerful is the impress of Shakespeare's art in his greatest moments — may be said to be lit up from instant to instant, or from incident to incident, by the wonderful expression of Mr. Irving's gaunt and wearied face as he talks and acts out the great life or death debate with Macduff. He falls face forwards, after dashing his dagger point downwards at his antagonist's feet. The soldiers execrate the prostrate tyrant in shouts, and Malcolm is raised shoulder high as the green curtain descends.

Chapter XIII

The American Theater

Early American Playgoers.
(From an engraving in Frances Trollope, *Domestic Manners of the Americans,* New York: Alfred A. Knopf, 1949.)

1. LEWIS HALLAM'S COMPANY AND REPERTORY

WILLIAM HALLAM, manager of the Goodman's Fields Theatre in London, was declared insolvent in 1750. "Under these circumstances he turned his thoughts to the New World and conceived the plan of sending a company of players to the colonies" (Dunlap). The task of shepherding the English players to America was given to Lewis Hallam, William's brother. Dunlap, basing his information on the rather hazy recollections of Lewis Hallam, jr., left a description of the organization and repertory of the English company that arrived at the Colony of Virginia in the middle of June 1752:

Lewis and his wife having consented to cross the Atlantic and seek their fortunes in what might then not improperly be called the western wilderness, the ex-manager's next step was to find suitable persons to fill up the *corps dramatiq*ue, and to induce them to join his brother and sister in this theatrical forlorn hope. He succeeded in enlisting a good and efficient company, willing to leave their country (and perhaps their creditors), and fitted to ensure success to the perilous adventure. The emigrants were next assembled at the house of William Hallam; a list of *stock plays* produced by him, with attendant farces, and the *cast* of the whole agreed upon in full assembly of the body politic: which appears to have been a well organized republic, every member of which had his part assigned to him, both private and public, behind and before the curtain. Lewis Hallam was appointed manager, chief magistrate, or king, and William, who staid at home, was to be "viceroy over him," according to Trinculo's division of offices. The brothers were to divide profits equally after deducting the expenses and *shares*. Thus William was entitled to half of such profits as projector and proprietor, and Lewis to the other half as manager and conductor.

The names of the persons who under the direction of the Hallams introduced the drama into our country, having been communicated to the writer by one of the number, he takes pleasure in recording them, and feels that although under other circumstances they would be, perhaps, suffered to float down the tide of time consigned to oblivion, their adventure and its consequences render them worthy subjects for the pen of the dramatic historian, and interesting to all who take an interest in the literature of our country. Mr. and Mrs. Hallam were first in consequence and in talents. Mr. Rigby played the first line in tragedy and comedy, and was only inferior to the leaders. Mrs. Rigby does not appear to have had high pretensions. Mr. and Mrs. Clarkson were of the class called useful. Miss Palmer, Mr. Singleton, Mr. Herbert, Mr. Winnell, or Wynel, Mr. Adcock, and Mr. Malone completed the company, and filled the *dramatis personae* of the plays that were cast at the proprietor's house.

Of the twenty-four plays and their attendant farces, *cast* and *put in study* before leaving England, we have the names of the following: — The Merchant of Venice, The Fair Penitent, The Beaux' Stratagem, Jane Shore, The Recruiting Officer, King Richard the Third, The Careless Husband, The Constant Couple, Hamlet, Othello, Theodosius (a great favourite everywhere, added our informant), Provoked Husband, Tamerlane, The Inconstant, Woman's a Riddle, The Suspicious Husband, The Conscious Lovers, George Barnwell, The Committee, and The Twin Rivals. We cannot record the names of these twenty plays without interest. They were doubtless the favourites of the metropolis of Great Britain at that time, and stood paramount wherever the stage spoke the English tongue. How many of them now hold possession of the scene? At most, six. And of the six, four are Shakspeare's, the only four from his pen in the twenty. All Farquhar's comedies, whose dialogue for wit was unrivalled but by Shakspeare's, are laid on the shelf, or occasionally revived at a benefit, *cut down* to afterpieces. Colley Cibber's Careless Husband, pronounced by Pope the best comedy in the language, cannot be tolerated; and even Bishop Hoadley's Suspicious Husband exhibits licentiousness that we turn from as unfit for representation. The farces cast and studied for the common stock were, Lethe, The Lying Valet, Miss in her Teens, The Mock Doctor, The Devil to Pay, Hob in the Well, Damon and Philida, and The Anatomist. . . .

Of pantomimes, the company had but one for many years, which was called Harlequin Collector, or the Miller Deceived.

We will remark of these eight farces, that three were Garrick's, and two of the three are still played.

Lewis Hallam, junior, known by those who remember him by the familiar appellation of old Hallam (the son of the Lewis Hallam who led these adventurers as manager and first low comedian), from whom this account of the adventure and its origin is derived, was at the time a boy of twelve years of age, and at a grammar school at Cambridge. The choice was given him of remaining at his school, or going with his parents, and he had no hesitation in preferring the latter. A younger son, Adam, and a daughter, soon introduced on the stage as Miss Hallam, made a part of the company of emigrants, and eventually of the company of players.

A daughter, still younger, being then six years of age, was left with her uncle William, and became afterward famous in dramatic history as Mrs. Mattocks.

We have said that the profits of the adventure were to be equally divided between the original proprietor and projector, and his brother the conductor and manager. These profits were to be the residue and remainder, after deducting the shares, for this was what is known among players as a sharing company or scheme, and so continued until some time after our revolution. In such *schemes* the manager has one or more shares as reward for the trouble of governing; one or more shares pay him for the use, wear and tear of the property; one or more shares according to his abilities or reputation as an actor; and he generally avails himself of the power which rests with him of casting plays so as to keep up his reputation by appropriating the best or most popular parts to himself. The remaining shares, after the manager is satisfied, are divided among the members of the commonwealth according to ability, reputation in the profession, or the influence obtained by becoming favourites with the public. . . .

It is proper in the early history of the stage in this country to state many particulars which would be out of place in a record of the affairs of a more recent date. As we have the power to lay before the reader the original proportions in which the receipts of the first company were divided, with the shares assigned to each individual, we shall proceed so to do.

The number of shares was fixed at eighteen. The number of adult performers was twelve, including the manager, each being entitled to one share. Mr. Hallam had another as manager. Four shares were assigned to the property, and one share was allowed for the manager's three children. It is to be presumed that the four shares assigned for the property were to be divided between the brothers, as the profits of the partnership, otherwise it is hard to say from whence profit was to accrue.

Having despatched these preliminaries, we will attend this band of adventurers on their voyage of experiment. Early in the month of May they embarked in the "Charming Sally," Captain Lee, and after a voyage of six weeks, a short passage in those days, arrived safely at Yorktown, Virginia.

2. A VISIT TO THE NASSAU STREET THEATER

NEW YORK HAD its first theatrical season in 1750 - 1751, when a company headed by Thomas Kean and Walter Murray produced a score of plays in a converted warehouse in Nassau Street. In 1753, while Murray and Kean were touring the South, Lewis Hallam came to New York and opened his theater in Nassau Street on September 17. George C. D. Odell unearthed a letter in which Philip Schuyler tells of his visit to Hallam's playhouse on September 19. This is the only, if sketchy, eyewitness account of Hallam's early days in New York:

The schooner arrived at Ten Eyck's wharf on Wednesday, at one o'clock, and the same evening I went to the play with Phil. You know I told you before I left home that if the players should be here I should see them, for a player is a new thing under the sun in our good province. Phil's sweetheart went with us. She is a handsome brunette from Barbadoes, has an eye like that of a Mohawk beauty, and appears to possess a good understanding. Phil and I went to see the grand battery in the afternoon, and to pay my respects to the governor, whose lady spent a week with us last spring, and we bought our play tickets for eight shillings apiece, at Parker and Weyman's printing office, in Beaver Street, on our return. We had tea at five o'clock, and before sundown we were in the Theatre, for the players commenced at six. The room was quite full already. Among the company were your cousin Tom and Kitty Livingston, and also Jack Watts, Sir Peter Warren's brother-in-law. I would like to tell you about the play, but I can't now, for Billy must take this to the wharf for Captain Wynkoop in half an hour. He sails this afternoon.

A large green curtain hung before the players until they

were ready to begin, when, on the blast of a whistle, it was raised, and some of them appeared and commenced acting. The play was called The Conscious Lovers, written you know, by Sir Richard Steele, Addison's help in writing the *Spectator*. Hallam, and his wife and sister, all performed, and a sprightly young man named Hulett played the violin and danced merrily. But I said I could not tell you about the play, so I will forbear, only adding that I was no better pleased than I should have been at the club where, last year, I went with cousin Stephen, and heard many wise sayings which I hope profited me something.

3. DIFFICULT TERRITORY: PHILADELPHIA

HALLAM CONCLUDED his first New York season on March 25, 1754. Philadelphia was next to be conquered. The difficulties which the players encountered in the Quaker City are vividly set forth in Dunlap's *History*:

Already had the religious toleration wisely and benevolently established by William Penn, peopled his city with inhabitants of every sect and denomination. While Presbyterianism was intolerant and exclusive in the east, and Episcopacy in the south, Penn and Baltimore, the Quaker and the Roman Catholic, had opened Pennsylvania and Maryland as lands of refuge for liberty of conscience. The consequence was that the plain Quaker-colour made only a part of the garb of the citizens of Philadelphia even at this early period; but still *drab* was the livery of the majority. A large portion of the inhabitants, however, saw no offence to morality or religion in any of the colours which diversify and beautify the works of creation; or any of those innocent amusements which bring men together to sympathize in joys or sorrows, uniting them in the same feelings and expressions with a brotherly consciousness of the same nature and origin. Many, also, had been accustomed to the representations of the dramatists in their native land, and longed to renew the associations of their youth. Others who had only read the works of Shakspeare were anxious to experience the influence of the living personification of those thoughts and characters which had delighted them in the closet, and looked towards the sister and then secondary city of New-York with a strong desire to participate in her pleasures and

advantages. These causes produced an application to the manager
while the company were playing at New-York. Several gentlemen from Philadelphia urged Mr. Hallam to apply to Governor
Hamilton for permission to open a theatre in that city, and
pledged themselves for the success notwithstanding any opposition
from the followers of Penn. They suggested that it would be best
to make application for liberty to play for a few nights.

Hallam received these overtures with pleasure, and looked
around upon his companions for a man fitted for the task of
opening the way to so desirable an acquisition as this hitherto
hostile city would be to the cause of the Muse. Such a pioneer
and negotiator needed address and talents, and we must suppose
that Mr. Malone had evinced powers of persuasion, and possessed
engaging manners or accomplishments superior to most of his
fellows, as he was selected by the manager for the important and
difficult mission.

The nature of the reward offered to induce Malone to undertake this *long journey,* and trust himself, face to face, with these
broad-brimmed, brown-wigged Quakers in their own stronghold,
lets us into some of the secrets of the green-room. "He undertook the business," says our informant, "on condition, that if
successful, he should have for his reward the parts of *Falstaff*
in "Henry the Fourth" and "The Merry Wives," and of *Don
Lewis* in "Love makes a Man, or the Fop's Fortune."

At that period, and long since, the parts in which an actor
was cast, if the manager's decree was confirmed by the public,
became his inalienable property while in the company, and ofttimes the proprietor continued to figure as a youthful hero or
lover long after all nature's qualifications for the parts had become the prey of time the despoiler, and the wrinkles of age, and
the cracked voice changed to "childish treble" should have consigned him to the representation of the lean and slippered pantaloon. . . .

Malone willingly undertook the embassy with the hope of
attaining this brilliant accession to his theatrical property, but
he experienced such a strenuous opposition, and found the strife
with these disciples of peace so perilous, that he wrote for the
manager to come to his assistance. The cry was "Hallam to the
rescue." The manager flew, as fast as mortals could then fly, to
the assistance of his emissary. The relief was effectual, for "the

king's name is a tower of strength," or was in those good old times. The manager found the city of brotherly love and passive peace divided into two hostile factions, as violent as the green and red of Constantinople where charioteers shook the empire of the Cesars to its foundation. Here it was not one colour against its opposite, but colours against colourless: the rainbow struggling through a cloud.

The Quakers and their adherents carried a petition to the governor for the prohibition of profane stage-plays. Counter petitions were signed and presented, and finally the friends of action and passion prevailed, and the manager was favoured by Governor Hamilton with a permission to open a theatre and cause twenty-four plays with their attendant afterpieces to be performed, on condition that they "offered nothing indecent and immoral," and performed one night for the benefit of the poor of the city, — and further, that the manager gave security for all debts contracted and all contracts entered into by the company. How characteristic is all this of the time.

Such was the treaty by which the first histrionic adventurers gained a narrow and precarious footing in a new region which seemed forbidden ground. . . .

The first regular company of comedians opened their theatre, the store-house of Mr. William Plumstead, on the corner of the first alley above Pine-street, and commenced playing in April, 1754, with the tragedy of the Fair Penitent. The place has since been occupied as a sail-loft, and the remains or traces of scenic decoration were to be seen within forty years. This was called the new theatre. The word "new" seems to have applied to all the places or buildings used by this company, although there had been no previous establishment of any kind. The prices of admittance were, box 6 shillings, pit 4 shillings, gallery 2 shillings and 6 pence. The company gained money and reputation, notwithstanding a continued and vigorous opposition. Pamphlets were published and distributed gratis during the whole theatrical campaign, and every effort made to show the evils attendant upon plays and players, and play-houses; but Shakspeare and his followers prevailed. The tree was planted and could not be rooted out. The effort of the wise should be to improve its fruit by cultivation, trimming, and grafting.

4.   APPRAISAL OF THE "AMERICAN COMPANY"

UPON LEWIS HALLAM's death (1755) in Jamaica, West Indies, the actor, David Douglass, married Hallam's widow and reorganized the troupe, of which Mrs. Hallam-Douglass and Lewis Hallam, jr., aged eighteen, were the featured players. This "American Company" visited New York (Cruger's Wharf Theater), Philadelphia, Annapolis, and Newport, R. I. Captain Graydon, in his *Memoirs*, appraised the performers as follows:

A short time before the epoch of my becoming a student of law, the city [Philadelphia] was visited by the company of players, since styling themselves, The Old American Company. They had for several years been exhibiting in the islands, and now returned to the continent in the view of dividing their time and labours between Philadelphia and New York. . . . The manager was Douglas, rather a decent than shining actor, a man of sense and discretion, married to the Widow Hallam, whose son, Lewis, then in full culmination, was the Roscius of the theatre. As the dramatic heroes were all *his* without a competitor, so the heroines were the exclusive property of Miss Cheer, who was deemed an admirable performer. The singing department was supplied and supported by the voices of Woolls and Miss Wainwright, said to have been pupils of Dr. Arne; while, in the tremulous drawl of the old man, in low jest and buffoonry, Morris, thence the minion of the gallery, stood first and unrivalled. As for the Tomlinsons, the Walls, the Allens, &c. they were your Bonifaces, your Jessamys, your Mock Doctors, and what not. On the female side, Mrs. Douglas was a respectable, matron-like dame, stately or querulous as occasion required, a very good Gertrude, a truly appropriate Lady Randolph, with her white handkerchief and her weeds; but then, to applaud, it was absolutely necessary to forget, that, to touch the heart of the spectator, had any relation to her function. Mrs. Harman bore away the palm as a duenna, and Miss Wainwright as a chambermaid. Although these were among the principal performers at first, the company was from time to time essentially improved by additions. Amony these the Miss Storers, Miss Hallam, and Mr. Henry were valuable acquisitions, as was also a Mr. Goodman, who had read law in Philadelphia with Mr. Ross. This topic may be disgusting to persons of gravity; but human manners are my theme.

as well in youth as in age. Each period has its play-things; and if the strollers of Thespis have not been thought beneath the dignity of Grecian history, this notice of the old American stagers may be granted to the levity of memoirs.

Whether there be any room for comparison between these, the old American Company, and the performers of the present day, I venture not to say. . . . I can not but say, however, that in my opinion the old company acquitted themselves with most animation and glee; they were a passable set of comedians. Hallam had merit in a number of characters, and was always a pleasing performer. No one could tread the stage with more ease. Upon it, indeed, he might be said to have been cradled, and wheeled in his go-cart. In tragedy, it can not be denied, that his declamation was either mouthing or ranting; yet a thorough master of all the tricks and finesse of his trade, his manner was both graceful and impressive. . . . He once ventured to appear in Hamlet, either at Drury Lane or Covent Garden, and was endured. In the account given of his performance he is said not to have been to the taste of a London audience, though he is admitted to be a man of pleasing and interesting address. He was, however, at Philadelphia, as much the soul of the Southwark Theatre as ever Garrick was of Drury Lane; and if, as Dr. Johnson allows, popularity in matters of taste is unquestionable evidence of merit, we cannot withhold a considerable portion of it from Mr. Hallam, notwithstanding his faults.

5. INSIDE THE JOHN STREET THEATER

DOUGLASS SHOWED admirable courage in penetrating into the difficult New England territory and in building new theaters wherever he took his players. In 1767, he was again in New York, where he built the John Street Theater which opened on December 7 with *The Beaux' Stratagem*. No authentic print of the theater's interior has survived, so Dunlap's description of it is our only reliable evidence:

In the summer of 1767, the theatre in John-street, New-York, was built. . . . It was principally of wood; an unsightly object. painted red. The situation of this house was on the north side of the street, nearly opposite the present Arcade (1832). It was about 60 feet back from the street, having a covered way of rough wooden material from the pavement to the doors. There is reason to believe that at this time the dressing-rooms and green-room were under the stage, for after the revolution, Hallam and Henry added on the west side of the building a range of rooms for dressing, and a commodious room for assembling previous to being called to "*go on.*" Two rows of boxes, with a pit and gallery, could accommodate all the play-going people of that time, and yield to the sharers eight hundred dollars when full, at the usual prices. The stage was of good dimensions, as far as memory serves, equal to that of Colman's theatre in the Haymarket, London, originally Foote's.

6.   POOR SCENERY

IN 1777, the officers of the British garrison requisitioned the John Street Theater and turned it into a home for military amateur theatricals. Thus the playhouse survived the period of military occupation, and after the evacuation of the city by the enemy, conditions tended to return to normal. Lewis Hallam, jr., was now old enough to assume (in partnership with John Henry) the management of the John Street Theater. Odell discovered in the *Daily Advertiser* a reference to the sloppy staging methods of 1787:

Tho' we do not look for a theatre here conducted in so regular a manner as those in Europe, or the decorations so expensive and elegant, yet a proper respect to the audience, and decent and proper scenery, is and ought to be expected. . . . Surely the scenes should have as much the appearance of nature as possible; which those we generally behold at the theatre have not. For frequently where the author intended a handsome street or a beautiful landscape, we only see a dirty piece of canvas; what else can we call a scene in which the colours are defaced and obliterated? Nor is it uncommon to see the back of the stage represent a street, while the side scenes represent a wood, as if two of the most opposite appearances must be put together to cause a natural effect. — The musicians too instead of performing between the play and the farce, are suffered to leave the orchestra to pay a visit to the tippling houses, and the ladies in the meantime, must amuse themselves by looking at the candles and empty benches.

7. IMPROVEMENT OF SCENE PAINTING

IN THE POST-REVOLUTIONARY PERIOD there seems to have been a growing interest in scenery. This was partly due to the emphasis laid on pantomime. In 1793, Charles Ciceri, a scenic artist of considerable European experience, was brought to the John Street Theater. Dunlap commented on his appointment:

Heretofore, the scenic decorations of the American theatre had been lamentably poor. [John] Henry had not brought out with his recruits any artist to paint his scenes. Those of the old stock were originally of the lowest grade, and had become black with age. At this time [1794] Charles Ciceri painted the scenes for *Tammany* [an operatic spectacle by Mrs. Hatton]. They were gaudy and unnatural, but had a brilliancy of colouring, reds and yellows being abundant. Ciceri afterwards made himself a better painter, and proved himself an excellent machinist.

8. THE STAGE BATTLE OF BUNKER HILL

DURING THE LAST DECADE of the eighteenth century, there was an increase in illusionistic scenery, the audiences becoming accustomed to such painted sights as Mount Vernon and the Boston State House. Of considerable interest is the documentary evidence contained in a letter which John D. Burk, the author of the melodrama *Bunker Hill*, wrote to John Hodgkinson, one of the managers of the John Street Theater. In 1797, *Bunker Hill* was produced at the Haymarket in Boston, and the Irish playwright relates how it had been staged there with scenery by the French scene painter, Audin:

The hill is raised gradually by boards extended from the stage to a bench. Three men should walk abreast on it, and the side where the English march up, should for the most part be turned towards the wings; on our hill there was room for eighteen or twenty men, and they were concealed by a board painted mud colour, and having two cannon painted on it — which board was three feet and a half high. The English marched in two divisions from one extremity of the stage, where they ranged, after coming from the wings, when they come to the foot of the hill. The Americans fire — the English fire — six or seven of your men should be taught to fall — the fire should be frequent for some minutes. The English retire to the front of the stage —

second line of English advance from the wing near the hill —
firing commences — they are again beaten back — windows on
the stage should be open to let out the smoak. All the English
make the attack and mount the hill. After a brisk fire, the Americans leave works and meet them. Here is room for effect, if the
scuffle be nicely managed. Sometimes the English falling back,
sometimes the Americans — two or three Englishmen rolling
down the hill. A square piece about nine feet high and five wide,
having some houses and a meeting-house painted on fire, with
flame and smoak issuing from it, should be raised two feet distance from the horizon scene at the back of your stage, the windows and doors cut out for transparencies — in a word, it should
have the appearance of a town on fire. We had painted smoak
suspended — it is raised at the back wing, and is intended to
represent Charlestown, and is on a line with the hill, and where
it is lowest. The fire should be played skilfully behind this burning town, and the smoak to evaporate. When the curtain rises in
the fifth, the appearance of the whole is good — Charlestown on
fire, the breastwork of wood, the Americans appearing over the
works and the muzzles of their guns, the English and the American music, the attack of the hill, the falling of the English troops,
Warren's half descending the hill and animating the Americans,
the smoak and confusion, all together produce an effect scarce
credible. We had a scene of State-street — if you had one it would
not be amiss — we used it instead of the scene of Boston Neck
— it appears to me you need not be particular, but the hill and
Charlestown on fire. We had English uniforms for men and officers. You can procure the coats of some company at New-York
which dresses in red. Small cannon should be fired during the
battle, which continued with us for twelve or fifteen minutes. I
am thus prolix that you may find the less difficulty in getting it
up — it is not expensive and will always be a valuable stock piece.
I should not wonder if every person in New-York, and some
miles round it, should go to see it represented.

9. AUDIENCE EDUCATION

In January 1795, the management of the John Street Theater had to
do a bit of audience education by publishing, in the *Minerva,* the following apologetic plea:

Hallam & Hodgkinson, anxious to preserve not only the peace of the House, but perfect approbation of *every* part of their audience, respectfully acquaint the citizens and public in general, that in the future they wish to recommend, no *side Box* to be taken for a less number than 8; the Boxes to be kept locked and a screw key to them all deposited with the Box Keeper, who will shew the proprietor of any Box for the Night, to his number the moment he arrives and unlock it for him: a Bolt will also be made inside of each door, to prevent any interruption; and all those Boxes not taken, will be left entirely open for such Ladies and Gentlemen as do not take seats, or who honor the Theater casually. — The mistakes that have unfortunately happened recently, make *some* resolution necessary, that may tend to prevent the like in future. Gentlemen not perfectly acquainted with the *rules* of the Theatre, may be guilty of indecorum, not *from intention,* but want of *information.*

The Managers hope the above method will be found adequate to the removal of so disagreeable a circumstance; it is their wish to act in the most open and unbiassed manner to every one, and should it happen that the rules, peace or good order of the House should at any time be interrupted, they deem themselves *compelled* to point out such measures as shall if possible restore its tranquillity. They wish the Theater to be esteemed a moral, rational, and instructive amusement, free from the least riot or disorder. Thankful for the liberal patronage, they have this season experienced, they can only hope to merit a continuance by the strictest justice, and unceasing assiduity.

N. B. No Persons of notorious ill fame will be suffered to occupy any seat in a box where places are already taken.

Ladies and Gentlemen will please send their Servants at a quarter before 5 o'clock to keep Places.

10.   THE FIRST PARK THEATER

ON JANUARY 29, 1798, the first Park Theater was opened in New York, William Dunlap and John Hodgkinson being the joint lessees. At the end of the season Hodgkinson withdrew from the management and went to Boston, leaving Dunlap in sole control. Ireland has recorded the pertinent facts concerning the physical aspects of the New Theater, as it was originally called:

The New Theatre, as it was styled for many years — the Theatre, Park, as it was afterward designated by its managers — or the Park Theatre, as more commonly called by the public, stood in Park Row, about two hundred feet east of Ann Street, and nearly opposite the present fountain, on lots now numbered 21, 23 and 25.

It occupied a space of eighty feet front by one hundred and sixty-five feet deep, running through to Theatre Alley in the rear, where a wing was attached.

It was one of the most substantial buildings ever erected in New York, and though externally devoid of architectural pretension, was in its interior harmoniously proportioned and admirably well adapted for the purposes of sight and sound.

The plans for its construction were originally furnished by Marc Isambaud Brunel, the celebrated French engineer and builder of the Thames Tunnel, who, during the stormy days of the French Revolution, was an exile in America.

It is doubtful if they were ever carried out — that for the exterior, which included a range of fluted pilasters by way of ornament, certainly was not, and for many years the front wall remained perfectly plain and barn-like in appearance.

An engraving of the original design may be seen in the New York Directory for 1796.

The Park Theatre was first projected in the year 1795, and was intended to be ready for occupation in October, 1797. Its estimated cost was raised by a subscription of one hundred and thirteen shares of $375 each, making the sum of $42,375. Its actual cost, owing to the inexperience and mismanagement of its builders, amounted to more than $130,000. After several years' profitless ownership, the original proprietors parted with it to Messrs. Beekman and Astor, who held it until its destruction, in 1848. Its first lessees were John Hodgkinson and William Dunlap, who opened it to the public, in an unfinished state, on the 29th of January, 1798. The nights of performance at this period were Mondays, Wednesdays, Fridays and Saturdays. Mr. Hodgkinson was stage manager; Mr. Dunlap, treasurer; Mr. Falconer, box-office keeper; Mr. Hughes, prompter; Messrs. Ciceri and Audin, scene-painters; and Mr. Hewitt, leader of the orchestra.

11.   THE OPENING NIGHT

ADDITIONAL information is supplied in the *Daily Advertiser* and the *Commercial Advertiser* of January 31, 1798:

On Monday evening last, the New Theatre was opened to the most overflowing house that was ever witnessed in this city. Though the Commissioners have been constrained to open it in an unfinished state, it still gave high satisfaction.

The essential requisites of hearing and seeing have been happily attained. We do not remember to have been in any Theatre where the view of the stage is so complete from all parts of the house, or where the actors are heard with such distinctness. The house is made to contain about 2,000 persons. The audience part, though wanting in those brilliant decorations which the artists have designed for it, yet exhibited a neatness and simplicity which were highly agreeable. The stage was everything that could be wished. The scenery was executed in a most masterly style. The extensiveness of the scale upon which the scenes are executed, the correctness of the designs, and the elegance of the painting, presented the most beautiful views which the imagination can conceive. The scenery was of itself worth a visit to the theatre.

The company are known to the public, and they played with great spirit. We indeed think it the best company of comedians which has yet appeared on the boards of any Theatre in this place, and we presume they will this season receive an uncommon share of public patronage.

Great credit is due to the Messrs. Mangins, who were the architects of the house [Brunel is not even mentioned], for their skilful and commodious arrangements, and too much cannot be said for the science of Mr. Ciceri as the machinist, and for his taste as scene-painter. They are artists who would do honor to any country, and a great acquisition.

ⵣ   ⵣ   ⵣ

The audience part of the New Theater is a segment of a large circle — and of course the spectators, even in the front boxes, are brot within a very convenient distance, both for seeing and hearing. The Pit is remarkably commodious. The Boxes are disposed in three semi-circular rows, from one side to the other of the stage — and the Gallery is thrown back of the upper front boxes. The total omission of pillars as supports to the boxes, avoids a common and great obstacle (in Theaters) to the view — and when the house is filled, presents an unbroken line of spectators, which forms no uninteresting part of the *spectacle*.

The stage is remarkably commodious — and no language will give the reader an adequate idea of the scenery, which is universally spoken of as surpassing for elegance and effect, everything of the kind heretofore seen in America.

12.   DUNLAP'S BUDGET

ON APRIL 27, 1798, Dunlap became the sole manager of the Park Theater. A glance at his budget will indicate that he faced a financial loss when his weekly receipts dropped below twelve hundred dollars:

The theatre of New-York had now but one director or manager, — a circumstance which had not occurred in the United States before. An estimate of the expenses of the theatre at this time, 1798-9, will perhaps be acceptable to the general reader, and useful to those concerned in similar establishments. The salaries to actors and actresses, as follows, amount to 480 dollars weekly, viz: Mr. and Mrs. Hallam, 50; Mr. and Mrs. Johnson, 45 — the first 20, the second 25; Mrs. Oldmixon, 37; Mr. Cooper, 25; Mrs. Melmoth, 20; Mr. Tyler, 20; Mr. Jefferson, 23; Mr. Martin, 18 (and for superintending the stage and making properties, 7 more); Mr. Hallam, jun., 16; Mrs. Hogg, 14; Mr. Hogg, 13; Miss Westray, 13; Miss E. Westray, 12; Mr. Lee, 12, as performer and property-man; two message carriers (each 8), 16; Mrs. Seymour, 16; Mr. Seymour, 9; Mr. Miller, 12; Miss Hogg, 4; estimate for three others, 54; Mrs. Collins, 12; with supernumeraries, 32. To this was added a wretched prompter of the name of Hughes, at 10; and an intelligent box-office keeper, Mr. Joseph Falconer, at 14. Dressers, 20; orchestra, 140 (consisting of Mr. James Hewet, as leader, Messrs. Everdel, Nicolai, Samo, Henri, Ulshoeffer, Librecheki, Pellessier, Dupuy, Gilfert, Nicolai, jun., Adet, Hoffman, and Dangle). Other expenses were estimated thus: — Lights, 109; Labourers, 24; Doors and Constables, 50; Cleaning, 5; printing, 68; properties, 6; wardrobe, 15; fires,

15; Mr. Ciceri and his department (the scenery and painting, not including materials), 60; rent, 145; amounting to $1161, without including any remuneration for the personal services of the manager.

13. THE AUDIENCE OF THE FIRST PARK THEATER

WHAT TYPE AUDIENCE frequented the first Park Theater? In the second of Washington Irving's Jonathan Oldstyle letters for the *Morning Chronicle* of 1802, there is a wealth of information concerning the composition of this colorful crowd:

As I entered the house some time before the curtain rose, I had sufficient leisure to make some observations. I was much amused with the waggery and humour of the gallery, which, by the way, is kept in *excellent* order by the constables who are stationed there. The noise in this part of the house is somewhat similar to that which prevailed in Noah's ark; for we have an imitation of the whistles and yells of every kind of animal. This, in some measure, compensates for the want of music, as the gentlemen of our orchestra are very economic of their favours. Somehow or another, the anger of the gods seemed to be aroused all of a sudden, and they commenced a discharge of apples, nuts, and gingerbread, on the heads of the honest folks in the pit, who had no possibility of retreating from this new kind of thunderbolts. I can't say but I was a little irritated at being saluted aside of my head with a rotten pippin; and was going to shake my cane at them, but was prevented by a decent looking man behind me, who informed me that it was useless to threaten or expostulate. They are only *amusing themselves* a little at our expense, said he; sit down quietly and bend your back to it. My kind neighbour was interrupted by a hard green apple that hit him between the shoulders — he made a wry face, but knowing it was all a joke, bore the blow like a philosopher. I soon saw the wisdom of this determination; a stray thunderbolt happened to light on the head of a little sharp faced Frenchman, dressed in a white coat and small cocked hat, who sat two or three benches ahead of me, and seemed to be an irritable little animal.

Monsieur was terribly exasperated; he jumped upon his seat, shook his fist at the gallery, and swore violently in bad English. This was all nuts to his merry persecutors; their attention was wholly turned on him, and he formed their *target* for the rest of the evening.

I found the ladies in the boxes, as usual, studious to please; their charms were set off to the greatest advantage; each box was a little battery in itself, and they all seemed eager to outdo each other in the havoc they spread around. An arch glance in one box was rivalled by a smile in another, that smile by a simper in a third, and in a fourth a most bewitching languish carried all before it.

I was surprised to see some persons reconnoitring the company through spy-glasses; and was in doubt whether these machines were used to remedy deficiencies of vision, or whether this was another of the eccentricities of fashion. Jack Stylish has since informed me, that glasses were lately all *the go*; though hang it, says Jack, it is quite *out* at present; we used to mount our glasses in *great snuff,* but since so many *tough jockies* have followed the lead, the bucks have all *cut* the custom. I give you, Mr. Editor, the account in my dashing cousin's own language. It is from a vocabulary I do not well understand.

I was considerably amused by the queries of the country-man mentioned in my last, who was now making his first visit to the theatre. He kept constantly applying to me for information, and I readily communicated, as far as my own ignorance would permit.

As this honest man was casting his eye round the house, his attention was suddenly arrested. And pray, who are these? said he, pointing to a cluster of young fellows. These, I suppose, are the critics, of whom I have heard so much. They have, no doubt, got together to communicate their remarks, and compare notes; these are the persons through whom the audience exercise their judgments, and by whom they are told when they are to applaud or to hiss. Critics! ha! ha! my dear sir, they trouble themselves as little about the elements of criticism, as they do about other departments of science and belles-lettres. These are the beaux of the present day, who meet here to lounge away an idle hour, and play off their little impertinences for the entertainment of the public. They no more regard the merits of the play, nor of the actors, than my cane. They even *strive* to appear inattentive; and I have seen one of them perched on the front of the box with his back to the stage, sucking the head of his stick, and staring vacantly at the audience, insensible to the most interesting specimens of scenic representation, though the tear of sensibility was trembling in every eye around him. I have heard that some have even gone so far in search of amusement, as to propose a game of cards in the theatre, during the performance. The eyes of my neighbour sparkled at this information — his cane shook in his hand — the word *puppies* burst from his lips. Nay, says I, I don't give this for absolute fact: my cousin Jack was, I believe, *quizzing* me (as he terms it) when he gave me the information. But you seem quite indignant, said I, to the decent looking man in my rear. It was from him the exclamation came: the honest *countryman* was gazing in gaping wonder on some new attraction. Believe me, said I, if you had them daily before your eyes, you would get quite used to them. Used to them, replied he; how is it possible for people of sense to relish such conduct? Bless you, my friend, people of sense have nothing to do with it; they merely endure it in silence. These young gentlemen live in an indulgent age. When I was a young man, such tricks and follies were held in proper contempt. Here I went a little too far; for, upon better recollection, I must own that a lapse of years has produced but little alteration in this department of folly and impertinence. But do the ladies admire these manners! Truly, I am not as conversant in female circles as formerly; but I should think it a poor compliment to my fair countrywomen, to suppose them pleased with the stupid stare and cant phrases with which these votaries of fashion add affected to real ignorance.

Our conversation was here interrupted by the ringing of a bell. Now for the play, said my companion. No, said I, it is only for the musicians. These worthy gentlemen then came crawling out of their holes, and began, with very solemn and important phizzes, strumming and tuning their instruments in the usual style of discordance, to the great *entertainment* of the audience. What tune is that? asked my neighbour, covering his ears. This, said I, is no tune; it is only a pleasing *symphony* with which we are regaled, as a preparative. For my part, though I admire the effect of contrast, I think they might as well play it in their cavern under the stage. The bell rung a second time — and then

began the tune in reality; but I could not help observing, that
the countryman was more diverted with the queer grimaces and
contortions of countenance exhibited by the musicians, than their
melody. What I heard of the music, I liked very well; (though I
was told by one of my neighbours, that the same pieces have
been played every night for these three years;) but it was often
overpowered by the gentry in the gallery, who vociferated loudly
for *Moll in the Wad, Tally ho the Grinders,* and several other
airs more suited to their tastes.

I observed that every part of the house has its different
department. The good folks of the gallery have all the trouble
of ordering the music; (their directions, however, are not more
frequently followed than they deserve). The mode by which they
issue their mandates is stamping, hissing, roaring, whistling; and,
when the musicians are refractory, groaning in cadence. They
also have the privilege of demanding a *bow* from *John,* (by which
name they designate every servant at the theatre, who enters to
move a table or snuff a candle); and of detecting those cunning
dogs who peep from behind the curtain.

By the by, my honest friend was much puzzled about the
curtain itself. He wanted to know why that carpet was hung up
in the theatre? I assured him it was no carpet, but a very fine
curtain. And what, pray, may be the meaning of that gold head,
with the nose cut off, that I see in front of it? The meaning —
why, really, I can't tell exactly — though my cousin, Jack Stylish,
says there is a great deal of meaning in it. But surely you like
the *design* of the curtain? The design, — why really I can see
no design about it, unless it is to be brought down about our ears
by the weight of those gold heads, and that heavy *cornice* with
which it is garnished. I began now to be uneasy for the credit
of our curtain, and was afraid he would perceive the mistake of
the painter, in putting a *harp* in the middle of the curtain, and
calling it a *mirror*; but his attention was *happily* called away
by the *candle-grease* from the chandelier, over the centre of the
pit, dropping on his clothes This he loudly complained of, and
declared his coat was *bran-new.* Now, my friend? said I; we
must put up with a few trifling inconveniences, when in the pursuit of pleasure. True, said he; but I think I pay pretty dear for
it; — first to give six shillings at the door, and then to have my
head battered with rotten apples, and my coat spoiled by candle-

grease; by and by I shall have my other clothes dirtied by sitting down, as I perceive every body mounted on the benches. I wonder if they could not see as well if they were all to stand upon the floor.

Here I could no longer defend our customs, for I could scarcely breathe while thus surrounded by a host of strapping fellows, standing with their dirty boots on the seats of the benches. The little Frenchman, who thus found a temporary shelter from the missive compliments of his gallery friend, was the only person benefited. At last the bell again rung, and the cry of *down, down — hats off,* was the signal for the commencement of the play.

14. SPECIAL BOXES

WASHINGTON IRVING made no mention of the one group of playgoers for whom a special box section was set aside in all American theaters of the period. Dunlap had thoughts of reform on this subject:

In a former chapter we have recommended the interference of the state in the regulation of the theatre. The more we reflect upon the subject the more we are convinced of the propriety, utility, and necessity of the measure. It is a great and powerful engine for good or ill; and though its general tendency may have been favourable to civilization and morals, evils have attended, and do attend it. In Germany, where it is altogether under the direction and control of the government, one of these evils is unknown; and where it is under the supervision and partial direction of the rulers, it is in its worst form avoided; as in France. The evil we mean, and shall protest against, is that which arises from the English and American regulation of theatres, which allots a distinct portion of the proscenium to those unfortunate females who have been the victims of seduction. In Germany, the theatre is the prince's; it is directed by a literary man in his service. The director and players are paid by the government, and being chosen for talents and moral conduct, are honoured by the prince and his court. Here the theatre is the people's, as all things are. And the representatives and guardians of the people ought to prevent the misuse and perversion of it in any way. The directors ought to be controlled to their own and the public good by the official servants of the public, and in the particular abuse above mentioned, the prohibition of immoral display would remove a just stigma from the theatre, and would further the views of managers by increasing their receipts.

In France the theatres are under strict control, and some of them are supported by the government. The abominable regulation which causes this evil is there unknown, and the evil is unknown. It is not practicable to exclude the impure and the vicious from public resorts, neither is it to be wished. If the drama is such as good government ought to permit, its influence cannot be ill on the immoral auditor, and may be good. But no separate place should be set apart, to present to the gaze of the matron and virgin the unabashed votaries of vice, and to tempt the yet unsullied youth by the example of the false face which depravity assumes for the purposes of enticing to guilt. . . .

We would not propose that our countrymen should take any European mode of government for a model; or that the theatres of America should be regulated according to the usages of Germany and France; but we do hope that what is good, will be adopted from the laws and customs of every country, as far as it can be adapted to our republican institutions. In France the audience see no display of the nature we have mentioned. It is only in England and America that the nuisance exists. If a regulation was enforced, that no female should come to a theatre unattended by a protector of the other sex, except such whose standing in society is a passport to every place, the evil would be effectually remedied. The moral would not be deterred from a rational amusement, and the public and the manager would both be benefited. . . .

It is to be lamented that when the people of Massachusetts introduced the theatre in their capital, having the experience of the world before them, they had not set an example to their fellow-citizens, by purifying the dramatic establishment and abolishing this evil. They appear to have noticed it, but instead of remedying, they, if possible, made it worse. The Federal-street theatre provided a separate entrance for those who came for the express purpose of alluring to vice. The boxes displayed the same row of miserable victims, decked in smiles and borrowed finery, and the entrance could only, by its separation from those appropriated to the residue of the audience, become a screen inviting to secret guilt. The new theatre of Philadelphia gave an opportunity for reform, as did that of New-York; but these opportunities were neglected, and those who wished to support, as a mode of improvement, the representation of good dramatic works, have been driven from the boxes by the spectacle presented, not on the stage, but on seats placed opposite to them, and attracting their attention *from* the stage.

15.   LUDICROUS STAGE BUSINESS

THE MOUNTING OF PLAYS on the Park Theater stage seems to have been a rather slovenly affair. One of the Jonathan Oldstyle Letters is quite explicit on the subject. On November 24, 1802, Washington Irving attended a performance of the younger Colman's *Battle of Hexham*. The bill included the "new comic opera," *The Tripolitan Prize*:

I took my seat in the pit, and was so impatient that I could hardly attend to the music, though I found it very good. The curtain rose — out walked the Queen with great majesty; she answered my ideas — she was dressed well, she looked well, and she acted well. The Queen was followed by a pretty gentleman, who, from his winking and grinning, I took to be the court fool; I soon found out my mistake. He was a courtier *"high in trust,"* and either general, colonel, or something of *martial* dignity. They talked for some time, though I could not understand the drift of their discourse, so I amused myself with eating pea-nuts.

In one of the scenes I was diverted with the stupidity of a corporal and his men, who sung a dull song, and talked a great deal about nothing: though I found by their laughing, there was a great deal of fun in the corporal's remarks. What this scene had to do with the rest of the piece, I could not comprehend; I suspect it was a part of some other play, thrust in here *by accident*.

I was then introduced to a cavern, where there were several hard looking fellows, sitting round a table carousing. They told the audience they were banditti. Then they sung a *gallery song,* of which I could understand nothing but two lines:

The Welshman lik'd to have been chok'd by a mouse,
But he pull'd him out by the tail!

Just as they had ended this elegant song, their banquet was disturbed by the *melodious sound* of a horn, and in marched a *portly gentleman,* who, I found, was their captain. After this worthy gentleman had fumed his hour out, after he had slapped his breast and drawn his sword half a dozen times, the act ended.

In the course of the play, I learned that there had been, or was, or would be, a battle; but how, or when, or where, I could not understand. The banditti once more made their appearance, and frightened the wife of the portly gentleman, who was dressed in man's clothes, and was seeking her husband. I could not enough admire the dignity of her deportment, the sweetness of her countenance, and the unaffected gracefulness of her action; but who the captain really was, or why he ran away from his spouse, I could not understand. However, they seemed very glad to find one another again; and so at last the play ended, by the falling of the curtain.

I wish the manager would use a *drop scene* at the close of the acts; we might then always ascertain the termination of the piece by the *green* curtain. On this occasion, I was indebted to the polite bows of the actors for this pleasing information. I cannot say that I was entirely satisfied with the play, but I promised myself ample entertainment in the after-piece, which was called the *Tripolitan Prize.* Now, thought I, we shall have some *sport* for our money; we shall, no doubt, see a few of those Tripolitan scoundrels spitted like turkeys, for our amusement. Well, sir, the curtain rose — the trees waved in front of the stage, and the sea rolled in the rear — all things looked very pleasant and smiling. Presently I heard a bustling behind the scenes — here, thought I, comes a band of fierce Tripolitans, with whiskers as long as my arm. No such thing — they were only a party of village masters and misses, taking a walk for exercise, and very pretty behaved young gentry they were, I assure you; but it was cruel in the manager to dress them in *buckram,* as it deprived them entirely of the use of their limbs. They arranged themselves very orderly on each side of the stage, and sung something, doubtless very affecting, for they all looked pitiful enough. By and by came up a most tremendous storm: the lightning flashed, the thunder roared, and the rain fell in torrents: however, our pretty rustics stood gaping quietly at one another, until they must have been wet to the skin. I was surprised at their torpidity, till I found they were each one afraid to move first, for fear of being laughed at for their awkwardness. How they got off I do not recollect: but I advise the manager, in a similar case, to furnish every one with a *trap-door,* through which to make this exit. Yet this would deprive the audience of much amusement; for nothing can be more laughable than to see a body of guards with their spears, or courtiers with their long robes, *get* across the stage at our theatre.

Scene passed after scene. In vain I strained my eyes to catch a glimpse of a Mahometan phiz. I once heard a great bellowing behind the scenes, and expected to see a strapping Mussulman come bouncing in; but was miserably disappointed, on distinguishing his voice, to find out by his *swearing* that he was only a *Christian.* In he came — an American navy officer. Worsted stockings — olive velvet small clothes — scarlet vest — pea-jacket, and *gold-laced hat* — dressed quite in *character.* I soon found out, by his talk, that he was an American prize-master; that, returning through the *Mediterranean* with his Tripolitan prize, he was driven by a storm on the *coast of England.* The honest gentleman seemed, from his actions, to be rather intoxicated: which I could account for in no other way than his having drank a great deal of salt water, as he swam ashore.

Several following scenes were taken up with hallooing and huzzaing, between the captain, his crew, and the gallery, with several amusing tricks of the captain and his son, a very funny, mischievous little fellow. Then came the cream of the joke: the captain wanted to put to sea, and the young fellow, who had fallen desperately in love, to stay ashore. Here was a contest between love and honour — such piping of eyes, such blowing of noses, such slapping of pocket-holes! But *old Junk* was inflexible — What! an American tar desert his duty! (three cheers from the gallery,) impossible! American tars for ever!! True blue will never stain, &c., &c. (a continual thundering among the gods). Here was a scene of distress — here was bathos. The author seemed as much puzzled to know how to dispose of the young tar, as old Junk was. It would not do to leave an American seaman on foreign ground, nor would it do to separate him from his mistress.

Scene the last opened. — It seems that another Tripolitan

cruiser had bore down on the prize, as she lay about a mile off shore. How a Barbary corsair had got in this part of the world — whether she had been driven there by the same storm, or whether she was cruising to pick up a few English first rates, I could not learn. However, here she was. Again were we conducted to the sea-shore, where we found all the village gentry, in their buckram suits, ready assembled, to be entertained with the rare show of an American and Tripolitan engaged yard-arm and yard-arm. The battle was conducted with proper decency and decorum, and the Tripolitan very politely gave in — as it would be indecent to conquer in the face of an American audience.

16.   SHAKESPEARE AT THE PARK

CONTEMPORARY CRITICS, while praising the actors in special scenes, often pointed up instances of ridiculous business in the Shakespearean performances on the Park stage. The following reviews appeared in the *Commercial Advertiser*:

Macbeth was played last night [November 27, 1799] to a crouded house, with the afterpiece of The Romp. [Thomas Abthorpe] Cooper in the principal character exhibited occasionally marks of real genius, his conception was sometimes very just, his tones fine and attitude striking; but after all justice compels us to say, Macbeth is certainly not his Chef-d'oeuvre. He assumed the character and appearance of a murderer too early; he should remember that to *introduce* Macbeth as a villain is to destroy the moral of the piece. Mr. Hodgkinson in Macduff, was on the whole very good, but he failed in some of the finest scenes, mistaking as he sometimes does, strong vociferation for energy; When Macduff expresses his wish that Heaven would face to face set him — methinks the low strong tone of high wrought courage should not give place to the ranting style of a braggart. Mrs. Melmoth in Lady Macbeth was excellent, particularly in her sleep-walking; but she was unequal to the difficulty of trying to entertain her guests, that so she might arrest and divert their attention from the horrid and alarming situation of her husband, and at the same time of concealing the violence of her own emotions. But of all "sorry sights," ever exhibited to an audience, surely nothing has equalled that presented us by the Ghost of Duncan, "shaking his gory locks." Macbeth in a phrenzy of guilt and terror addressing the spectre, and Mr. Hallam, jun. seated with his friends at the supper table quietly and unconcernedly going on with their repast, munching their apples and smirking and drinking healths to the ladies, and the ladies to them. We hope never again to be obliged to witness such a shocking incongruity. As to the witches, 'twas pitiful, "'twas wondrous pitiful." The sublime bard never dreampt of bringing forward his supernatural personages to excite laughter.

*   *   *

Hamlet was played last evening [December 4, 1799] to a very full house. Cooper in his favorite character was much and deservedly applauded. It is perhaps not exaggerated eulogy to say he is unrivalled in Hamlet on the American stage, but he must also permit us to say that it requires much study before he can be allowed to have arrived at perfection; he ought to avoid all approach to rant, remembering that it is "the sin that most easily besets him" in common with other players of no uncommon merit. He has a method of endeavoring to ally sense to sound indiscriminately; in pronouncing the line "Or that the Everlasting had not fixed his *canon* 'gainst self-slaughter!" he stops with all the strength of his voice and with an improper inflexion on the word "canon," but that word has no antithesis either expressed or implied, and is therefore unemphatical, and so in many other instances which we cannot now remember sufficiently to particularize, but we submit the observation to his own good sense to profit by in future. In the scene of the interment of Ophelia, at the time when the body was letting down into the grave, and Laertes ranting over it, we were shocked to see him carelessly surveying the boxes and recognizing his acquaintance, we will not say gazing at particular ladies. It was an indecency which we hope never again to witness. But of all the particular instances in which he excelled, nothing is equal to his attitude and his eye when the ghost appears to him in the chamber scene with his mother; we do not think it going too far to say it cannot be excelled and it serves to show to what a superior degree of excellence Mr. Cooper may with attention attain. In the grave digging scene he was totally defective both in conception and execution. We were pleased to hear him restore the vowel *y* to its proper sound in defiance of

Courtesy of the Harvard Theatre Collection

Screen Scene from Sheridan's *The School for Scandal* at the First Park Theater.
From a Painting by William Dunlap.

Joseph Jefferson as Sir Peter Teazle, John Hodgkinson as Charles, Mrs. Whitlock as Lady Teazle, Joseph Tyler as Joseph Surface.

the theatric affection of softening it invariably to *e,* thereby injuring essentially the pronunciation and emasculating the language.

Mrs. Hodgkinson, in Ophelia, delighted the audience. In the mad scene, she is without competitor — whenever she sings, she charms — in the sweetness of her voice, and the distinctness of her articulation, she is unquestionably peerless. Mr. Hallam, in the ghost, was correct and excellent; but the word swear, pronounced from under the stage in a drawling nasal tone, was faulty and excited laughter. It should have been low, strong and guttheral. Claudius was played by Crosby, to the annoyance as well as surprise of the audience.

We beg permission to observe to the Manager, *whoever he is,* that it is rather too much to be obliged to hear a long part of any play twice over the same evening, once from the prompter, and once again from the player; we hope he will not put our good nature to so severe a trial again.

17. THE FIRST PARK THEATER REBUILT

In 1807, the interior of the Park Theater was remodeled by the English architect, J. J. Holland. A 2,700-capacity is probably a newspaper exaggeration, but otherwise we may trust the following account:

Previous to this opening, the theatre had been taken to pieces, except the walls and the stage, and rebuilt under the direction of Mr. J. J. Holland. It was to appearance (within) a new house, and the whole proscenium was in fact new. We copy the following:

"NEW YORK THEATRE. — This theatre has lately undergone considerable alterations, which have materially added to the comfort and convenience of the spectators. The audience part, which is entirely rebuilt, now consists of four rows of boxes; in the lower lobby, there is a handsome colonnade, with mirrors, and fireplaces at each end, the whole lighted by glass lamps between the columns. In every part of the theatre, the spectator may both hear and see the performance. The box-fronts, instead of being, as usual, perpendicular, fall in at top, and thus give room to the knees, which is considered an improvement upon the plan of all former theatres. There are several coffee-rooms, one of which is fitted in an elegant style for the accommodation of the ladies, where they may be supplied with every kind of fruit, confections, tea, coffee, &c. &c. This room is spacious, the furniture in the newest fashion, and is lighted by three elegant chandeliers suspended from the ceiling. In case of fire, there are three communications from the boxes with the street, and two from the pit. The boxes will accommodate upwards of 1600 persons, and the pit and gallery about 1100. The ceiling painted as a dome, with panels of a light purple, and gold mouldings; the centre a balustrade and sky. The box-fronts (except the fourth row) are divided into panels, blue ground, with white and gold ornaments; a crimson festoon drapery over each box. The lower boxes are lighted by ten glass chandeliers, projecting from the front, and suspended from gilt iron brackets, and the whole house is extremely well lighted. There are four private boxes, with rooms to retire to on the stage. A beautiful effect is produced by a large oval mirror at the end of the stage boxes, which reflects the whole of the audience on the first row.

"The whole of the alterations and improvements were completed under the superintendence of Mr. Holland, in the short space of three months, and the whole amount of expenditure (a circumstance which rarely happens) is less than the estimate, by five thousand dollars."

As the Park theatre was originally constructed, and as it remained until the proscenium was remodelled by Mr. Holland, there were no pillars as props to the upper boxes: they were supported by timbers projecting from the walls, and appeared, with their tenons, self-balanced. Of course, there were no obstructions in front of the boxes, as is commonly the case; and however ornamental pillars so placed may be, that they impede the view of the spectator, and prevent his seeing more or less of the stage, is undeniable.

Another peculiarity belonged to the boxes of this theatre, as first erected. There was a large box occupying the front of the second tier, and directly in front of the stage, capable of containing between two and three hundred persons, which was called "The Shakspeare," and was the resort of the critics, as the pit of the English theatres had been in former times.

The remodelled building had none of the above peculiarities. It was a more splendid and more commodious theatre than that which it superseded.

18. THE SECOND PARK THEATER

In 1820, the first Park Theater was destroyed by fire, and on the same site the second was built, which opened its doors to the public on September 1, 1821. Ireland is once more our guide:

The New Park Theatre was so far completed as to be ready for performance on the 1st of September, 1821.

Its dimensions were, in front, on Park Row, eighty feet in width and fifty-five in height, with a depth of one hundred and sixty-five feet, running through to Theatre Alley, where a large wing was attached, containing the green-room, dressing-rooms, &c. The audience entered by seven arched doorways, the central five of which were reached by a low flight of steps, and opened into an extensive vestibule communicating with the corridor of the first row of boxes; and the other two, on a level with the street and on either side of the steps, from which they were separated by a heavy abutment, afforded an easy access to the pit and gallery. The doors to these entrances all opened outward, the well-remembered and terrible catastrophe at Richmond rendering such an arrangement to all public buildings indispensable to safety. Six large arched windows surmounted the doorways, besides a blank one in the centre, which was afterward converted into a niche, wherein was ensconced a well-carved figure of Shakespeare.

Another row of smaller square windows was above these, and the whole front, though plain in its appearance and destitute of architectural beauty, was inoffensive and respectable. Its interior was neatly and conveniently fitted up, with as much regard to elegance and taste as the limited time between its erection and opening allowed. In the audience part of the house, which was calculated to hold 2,500 persons, there was a pleasant pit, with a gradual rise in each succeeding row of seats. Surrounding those rose three tiers, of fourteen boxes each, supported by small columns of burnished gold, six feet and six inches in height, and above was a commodious gallery, entirely disconnected from the boxes, and used principally for colored persons.

The front of the first circle of boxes was a Grecian balustrade, relieved by a crimson ground. On the second were *basso-relievos* on a fawn-colored ground, representing boys supporting

Interior of the Second Park Theater, New York (1834).

medallion portraits of poets and dramatists, with the figures of Tragedy and Comedy for a central group. The third circle was a Doric cornice with enrichments, which continued round the proscenium, the arch of which was supported by four Doric columns of yellow marble with white caps. The ceiling was flat, painted to imitate a cone, and divided into eight panels. The whole was lighted by patent oil-lamps, hung in three chandeliers of thirty-five lights each — gas not yet having been introduced into the city.

The drop-scene represented a crimson damask curtain, drawn into festoons of gold cord and tassels, — in the centre, a porch of mosaic workmanship with balustrade, and beyond, an equestrian statue of Washington.

The width of the stage at the drop-curtain was forty-five feet, and its depth seventy feet.

The architect of the building was Hugh Reinagle, and the scenery and decorative paintings were executed by Messrs. Robbins, Reinagle, Evers and Henry Isherwood. The latter is the present well-known artist, who was at that time acquiring the rudiments of his profession. Robbins had been scene-painter for nearly thirty years [he was engaged as scene painter and "occasional singer" in 1793], and in his department was always effective. Reinagle and Evers are too highly distinguished in the history of American art to need encomium here.

The stage and machinery were constructed by Mr. George Conklin, long connected with the establishment, and the lamps, glasses, hangings, &c., were all of American manufacture.

19. AN EARLY AMERICAN REHEARSAL

ON MARCH 24, 1845, Mrs. Mowatt's *Fashion*, America's first social comedy, had its première at the Park Theater. In her *Autobiography* Mrs. Mowatt has a sketch of an early American rehearsal:

There were no attempts in *Fashion* at fine writing. I designed the play wholly as an *acting* comedy. A *dramatic*, not a literary, success was what I desired to achieve. Caution suggested my not aiming at both at once.

Fashion was offered to the Park Theatre. In the usual course of events, its fate would have been to gather dust amongst an

ever-increasing pile of manuscripts on Mr. Simpson's table —
heaps of rejected plays, heaps of plays, the merits of which were
never even investigated. It generally takes several months to induce a manager to read a new play — several months more before
he consents to its production. Making an exception to prove this
rule, Mr. Simpson read *Fashion* at once. He liked it, and handed
the manuscript to his stage manager, Mr. Barry, who also approved it, and pronounced that the play would make a hit.

A few more days, and I received official information that
Fashion was accepted by the Park Theatre — that it would be
produced without delay, and in a style of great magnificence —
also, that I would receive an author's benefit on the third night,
and a certain percentage of the nightly receipts of the theatre for
every performance of the play after it had run a stipulated number of nights.

On listening to this intelligence, I very quietly asked myself
whether I was awake. It took some time, and needed some practical experiments upon my own sensibilities, before I could feel
assured that I was not enjoying a pleasant dream. I was almost
too much surprised to be elated.

It was necessary that I should call on Mr. Barry, to hear
his suggestions concerning the casting of the play and certain
slight alterations. I did so, and listened with seeming attention
to his laying down of dramatic law; but I was in a state of
agreeable bewilderment through the whole interview. When I
rose to leave, and received his very patronizing congratulations
on having written a "remarkable play," I could not help fancying
that he was saying to himself, "What a silly little soul it is!"
Indeed, I half expected that he was going to pat me on the head
and commend me for my "smartness." The impression I left upon
his mind was certainly not that I was a very formidable or a very
brilliant character.

The play was at once announced and put in rehearsal. The
day before its representation I became anxious to witness one of
these rehearsals, that I might form some idea of the chances of
success. It is an author's privilege to attend the rehearsals of his
own production, his acknowledged seat being at the manager's
table, upon the stage. He is also at liberty to make suggestions
to the actors explanatory of his ideas — though, as a general rule,
he finds they understand what he intended much better than he

does himself; at least, they politely assure him that such is the case. Of these customs, I was too uncertain of success to avail myself. I preferred to overlook the mysterious doings from a private box, unseen by the actors.

Rehearsal was just commencing, when Mr. Mowatt and myself were introduced by Mr. Blake (for many years boxkeeper of the Park Theatre) into the theatre. The whole front of the building was so dark that we had to feel our way, stumbling over benches and chairs, until we succeeded in gaining our seats.

The stage was lighted by a single branch of gas, shooting up to the height of several feet in the centre light, that gave a phantom-like appearance to surrounding objects. On the right of the stage was the prompter's table — on the left, the manager's table. Beneath the ghastly light sat a palefaced prompter, with the manuscript of *Fashion* in his hand. At his side stood the "call boy," a child of about ten years of age. He held a long strip of paper, somewhat resembling the tailors' bills of young spendthrifts, as they are represented on the stage. This was the "call" for the actors, and directed him which to summon from the greenroom.

The rehearsal of *Fashion* had begun. It was singular to see these kings and queens of the stage, whom I had been accustomed to behold decked in gold-embroidered robes and jewelled crowns, glittering in the full blaze of the footlights — now moving about in this "visible darkness," some of the men in "shocking bad hats" and rough overcoats, and the ladies in modern bonnets in place of tiaras or wreaths of flowers, and mantles and warm cloaks instead of peasant petticoats or brocade trains. I found it difficult to recognize the romantic heroes and injured heroines in whose sufferings I had so often sympathized.

Every actor held his part, to which he constantly referred. It gave me an odd sensation to hear my own language uttered in all varieties of tones, and often conveying a meaning of which I did not suppose it to be susceptible. But I soon discovered that a rehearsal was a very serious affair. There was no laughing, except now and then at the situations of the play, — at which, by the by, I was particularly flattered, — no talking except in reference to the business of the scene, and now and then a remark from some critical malcontent, which was never intended for the author's ears. There are two dances in the fourth act of *Fashion,* and these were gone through with a business-like gravity that was alarming. While witnessing this solemn rehearsal, I began to fancy I had made a mistake, and unconsciously written a tragedy. Rehearsal lasted several hours. At its close, when we stumbled through the dark passage into the box office, and stood once more in the light of day, it seemed to me again as though I had been dreaming. But the dream was a very sober one, and while it lasted I received a lesson upon the "vanity of human wishes." Of the probable success of the play I could not form the faintest idea.

20.   THE DEGRADING STAR SYSTEM

WILLIAM B. WOOD (1779 - 1861), who, in association with William Warren, had managed theaters in Philadelphia (Chestnut Street), Baltimore, and Washington for sixteen years, retired from theatrical life (1826) before the star system entrenched itself on the American stage in the 1830's. But he lived long enough to study the pernicious influence of the new system and also the resurrection of the stock companies. In his autobiography (1855), Wood enumerated some of the sociological reasons why the star system had invaded the American continent at that particular time:

The breaking up of the great English theatres — a season of general inflation and excitement in all things, (brought about, I suppose, by a commercial season of great excess, and, as was then supposed, of high prosperity) — a spirit of locomotiveness hitherto unexampled, and incident, I suppose, to our feeling, as we then first fairly did, that we could annihilate time and space by the use of steam vessels across the Atlantic, and railroads over our continent — the total break up with Warren of the old management and of its system, in short a spirit of change — of exhilaration — of excitement, incident to an end of an old order of things, and the advent of some new and undefined ones — all these, with some other causes, had now made the system of stars the order of 1835. That system was now in its height; the regular actors no longer forming a joint stock company, but being reduced to the condition of mere ministers or servants upon some principal performer, whose attractions it was now their sole and chief duty to increase, illustrate, or set off. This system is one into which the theatre is likely from time to time to fall. The bankruptcy of the manager, and the degradation of the stage will always be the end of it; and having gone through the experience, the drama will revive again, as it is now reviving, on the true principle of stock companies.

21. FORREST AS GLADIATOR

THE FIRST ENGLISH ACTOR imported to be starred in an American performance was George Frederick Cooke (1755 - 1812). He was 55 when he arrived in New York in 1810 to play some of his most famous roles (Richard III, Shylock, Sir Giles Overreach) at the Park Theater. Edmund Kean, Charles Mathews, Junius Brutus Booth, James H. Hackett, William Charles Macready, Charles and Fanny Kemble were the most conspicuous among the English stars that followed the Cooke trail. In the meantime, the first great American tragedian, Edwin Forrest (1806 - 1872), had come of age. Having acquired technique and fame in provincial theaters, he finally appeared at the Park Theater in 1829. Aside from such Shakespearean parts as Lear, Othello, and Macbeth, Forrest triumphed in roles that were fashioned for him by the American playwrights, John A. Stone (*Metamora*) and Robert M. Bird (*The Gladiator*). In 1846, Walt Whitman, writing in the *Brooklyn Eagle,* described Forrest's romantic-melodramatic acting and warned lesser talents of its inherent dangers:

From footlights to lobby doors — from floor to dome — were packed crowds of people last night at the Park Theatre, New York, to see Mr. Forrest in *The Gladiator.* . . . This play is as full of "Abolitionism" as an egg is of meat. It is founded on that passage of Roman history where the slaves — Gallic, Spanish, Thracian and African — rose against their masters, and formed themselves into a military organization, and for a time successfully resisted the forces sent to quell them. Running o'er with sentiments of liberty — with eloquent disclaimers of the right of the Romans to hold human beings in bondage — it is a play, this *Gladiator,* calculated to make the hearts of the masses swell responsively to all those nobler manlier aspirations in behalf of mortal freedom! — The speech of Spartacus, in which he attributes the grandeur and the wealth of Rome, to her devastation of other countries, is fine; and Mr. Forrest delivered it passing well. Indeed, in the first part of the play, this favorite actor, with his

Courtesy of the Theatre Collection, New York Public Library
Edwin Forrest as Spartacus in Bird's Melodrama,
The Gladiator.

herculean proportions, was evidently i' the vein — but the later
parts were not so well gone through with. . . . We do not intend
the following reflections — which started during the view of Mr.
Forrest's performances — to bear directly on that actor. Mr. F.
is a deserved favorite with the public — and has high talent
in his profession. But the danger is, that as he has to a measure
become identified with a sort of American style of acting, the
crowd of vapid imitators may spread quite all the faults of that
style, with none of its excellencies. Indeed, too, in candor, all persons of thought will confess to no great fondness for acting which
particularly seeks to "tickle the ears of the groundlings." We allude to the loud mouthed ranting style — the tearing of every
thing to shivers — which is so much the ambition of some of our
players, particularly the younger ones. It does in such cases truly
seem as if some of Nature's journeymen had made men, and not

made them well — they imitate humanity so abominably. They take every occasion, in season and out of season, to try the extremist strength of their lungs. They never let a part of their dialogue which falls in the imperative mood — the mood for exhorting, commanding, or permitting — pass by without the loudest exhibition of sound, and the most distorted gesture. If they have to enact passion, they do so by all kinds of unnatural and violent jerks, swings, screwing of the nerves of the face, rolling of the eyes, and so on. To men of taste, all this is exceedingly ridiculous. And even among the inferior portion of the audience it does not always pass safely. We have frequently seen rough boys in the pit, with an expression of sovereign contempt at performances of this sort. — For there is something in real nature which comes home to the "business and bosoms" of all men. — Who ever saw love made as it is generally made upon the stage? How often have we heard spontaneous bursts of approbation from inferior audiences, toward acting of the most unpretending kind, merely because it was simple, truthful, and natural! . . . If we thought these remarks would meet the eye of any young theatrical artist, we would like through him to beg all — for we cannot call to mind any who are not more or less tainted with this vice — to take such hints as the foregoing, to their hearts — aye, to their heart of hearts. It is a common fallacy to think that an exaggerated, noisy, and inflated style of acting — and no other — will produce the desired effect upon a promiscuous audience. But those who have observed things, theatres, and human nature, know better. Where is there a good, truthful player that is not appreciated? Who, during the past season, has dared compare the quiet polish of Mrs. [Charles] Kean with the lofty pretensions of the general run of tragedy queens?

22. THE FORREST-MACREADY CONTROVERSY

In 1836, Forrest went to England for the first time. In 1845, he paid a second visit and was hissed while acting Macbeth. Forrest assumed that his rival, Macready, was responsible for this hostile reception, and when, shortly afterward, Macready played Hamlet in Edinburgh, Forrest, in a box, returned the hiss. Coleman gives an eyewitness account of this incident, which was to lead to the bloody Astor Place Riot on May 10, 1849 when Forrest's American partisans clashed with Macready's admirers, the National Guard, and the New York police:

The house was crowded in all parts by an eager and excited audience. When the scene drew off, Macready was discovered amidst a tempest of applause. I could not realize why on earth the people applauded him. With the modesty of youth, I mentally ejaculated, "What an antiquated guy!"

He wore a dress the waist of which nearly reached his arms; a hat with a sable plume big enough to cover a hearse; a pair of black silk gloves, much too large for him; a ballet shirt of straw-coloured satin, which looked simply dirty; and, what with his gaunt, awkward, angular figure, his grizzled hair, his dark beard close shaven to his square jaws, yet unsoftened by a trace of pigment, his irregular features, his queer, extraordinary nose — unlike anything else in the shape of a nose I have ever seen — and his long skinny neck, he appeared positively hideous. But, after all, "mind is the brightness of the body," and, O ye gods! when he spoke, how he brightened, illumined, irradiated the atmosphere; his *gaucherie*, his ugliness, disappeared, and he became transformed into the very *beau-ideal* of the most poetic, subtle, intellectual, dramatic, and truly human Prince of Denmark I have ever seen. But although he lifted you to heaven one moment, he brought you to earth the next with some weird eccentricity. For example, in the Play scene, he strutted from side to side, waving his handkerchief above his head, in the most extravagant manner. As he uttered the words, "Of the chameleon's dish, I eat the air, promise-crammed, you cannot feed capons so!" a mighty hiss arose in front — a hiss like that of a steam-engine. At the sound, he trembled and turned pale; then he became livid, and convulsed with passion, absolutely hysterical with rage. Turning to the quarter whence the sibilation proceeded, he bowed derisively, then staggered back and sank into a chair.

Looking to the upper side boxes, on the right, I saw the American tragedian. A conspicuous figure at all times, Forrest was now more conspicuous than ever. At this moment, from the Students' Gallery (which was separated from the upper boxes only by some interfoliated iron-work) a cry arose of "Turn him out!" I can see him now. The square brow, the noble majestic head, the dark eyes flashing fire, the pallor of the white face enhanced by his blue-black beard, which contrasted strangely with his turned-down white collar (an unusual mode of wearing the collar at that time), his jaw set like a bull-dog's, his arms folded

Courtesy of the Theatre Collection, New York Public Library

The Astor Place Riot (1849)
From an engraving in *The Illustrated London News,* June 2, 1849.

on his broad chest. As he rose and faced his would-be assailants, he looked exactly as he used to look in "The Gladiator," when he said, "Let them come; we are prepared."

The people on the other side of the screen absolutely recoiled, as if they expected some king of the forest to leap from his iron den amongst them; they then concluded to let the American alone. On the stage the actors were at a standstill; in the auditorium the multitude were awed into silence. After a short pause, I suppose the man's better nature prevailed, for Edwin Forrest slowly turned away, and left the house.

Then Macready, like a man possessed, leaped into the breach, and took the house by storm. Surely he must have been inspired by the ordeal through which he had passed. Such a delirium of excitement for actors and audience as followed that Play scene and the Closet scene I have rarely, if ever, witnessed.

23. W. B. WOOD'S DIAGNOSIS OF THE ILLS OF THE AMERICAN STAGE

AFTER A QUARTER of a century of irregular and disastrous management, things began to look bright again when J. W. Wallack purchased the Lyceum Theater in New York (1852) and decided to run it on a sound stock company principle. W. B. Wood, who just then was working on his memoirs, was filled with hope for the future. In his *Personal Recollections* he summed up the lessons he had drawn from periods of true and false management—a summary which still has validity:

The perfect representation of dramatic pieces is a matter requiring great time and practice. It is an immense business — pieces, casts, rehearsals, stage-business, stage-scenery, stage effect, final performance, and with all this the regulation of a band of people in their nature somewhat unsettled, exposed to great temptations, and every way impatient of control. When the actors are a permanent body, and the manager a permanent person, everything can be pre-arranged. I have already stated how admirably Warren used to project his season. It was one secret of our success. We knew what our power and resources were, and we knew also wherein we were weak or deficient, and we arranged things accordingly. But when a season is made up of a rapid succession of numerous stars, the first effect is that nothing can be arranged ahead. The star is the light of everything; the centre about which all must move. He has his own times, his own pieces, his own plan of business, and his own preferences of every sort. One star is very tall, and will play with no person of diminutive stature. The company must be changed to suit him. The next is very short, and will play with no one of ordinary height. Everything has again to be unsettled. One star brings half a company with him, and the stock actors thus displaced, retire in disappointment. The next looks to us for all his support, and the manager must get them all back in the best way he can. The result is that when the star does come everything is to be done *impromptu*. What the effect of this is in many departments, let the reader a little while consider; and first, for example, its effect on

The Important Matter of Rehearsal

A star arrives from England with some new pieces of his own, manuscripts perhaps, and written probably for himself alone. No one of the company with which he is to play has even seen them. The star begins his transit. The piece is to be performed at once. But how is it possible for the principal actors to study, each of them, a long part, and then to rehearse it with the star in time for the performance. The star will probably not come at all till the very afternoon of the day on which he is to perform. The rehearsal is impossible, and therefore is not attempted.

It has not been unfrequently the case of late that an actor has been expected to learn from three to five hundred lines (sometimes much more) within twenty-four hours, during which he must also appear in the play for the evening. This was a subversion of all former requirement. For a number of years our actors were not bound to study more than eighty-four lines of tragedy, or one hundred and sixty-eight of comedy within twenty-four hours, then acting only three or four times a week. While in London, Mr. Pope was entitled to a month for the study of Mordent, in the "Deserted Daughter," a very long and difficult part no doubt; and he was a very busy actor. Time, therefore, is not, or when I left the stage was not, given even to learn so much as the language of the author. Even where the words were caught for the hour, yet being learned in haste, confusion and anxiety, with no reference at all to its meaning or effect, the memory cannot retain them, and an effort nearly equal to the former is required every time the piece is performed. It is a fact well known to me, that during the reign of the star system many pieces which in London occupied the study and labor of the best and most practised actors for weeks, have been produced here after a study of as many days, and sometimes of no more than as many hours. As for the meaning, to say nothing of refinement and shades of meaning, the matter was not once thought of. An audience would scarcely credit the fact, that many pieces (manuscripts chiefly) were acted which the performers who played in them never had a chance of even hearing read, nor any means of knowing the drift or object of the story, beyond the scene in which their own parts lay. It was by no means an uncommon thing when I left the theatre, to hear an actor inquire of another during the performance, "What is this play about?"

The rehearsals, therefore, so indispensable towards the production of entertainments worthy of an audience, became the strangest exhibitions that can well be conceived. Instead of a quiet and orderly exercise of memory and judgment, and a careful observation of the effects, trial of power, situations and machinery, preparatory to the performance of the piece, it was not uncommon to hear even the principal parts *read* for the first time on the very day of performance, amid the noise of supernumeraries and other idle inferiors, lounging about and picking up what they chose or could for their duties in the evening. The star of the night, if present at all, sitting at the prompter's table, either writing or affecting to write letters of vast importance, or gossipping with some visitor, to the utter destruction of silence and discipline. Of course when the piece came to be performed, blunders and delays marked it from the beginning to the end of the performance, and the result was that on the first representation — the representation always formerly considered the most attractive — no audience could be got together at all. In regard to those actors who by extraordinary exertions learned their parts, the thing was still unfair and cruel. . . .

I need not, I think, endeavor, by further remarks, to show how injuriously in this respect the star system operates, not only on the reputation of both the author and body of actors in the piece, but how it necessarily tends to destroy the effect of the whole representation, and so to destroy the drama itself. Let the reader next consider how unavoidably the system must lead to the destructive result of

Bad Casting

In stock companies settled from year to year, improved by additions as wanted, regulated in their composition and changes by the necessities of the play, and the general character of the public taste, a bad cast of a piece is a matter which certainly need occur but seldom. Indeed, with a good manager it will hardly occur at all. The reason is that these pre-arrangements can be made. Almost every contingency can be foreseen and provided for. The manager knows his company's ability, tempers, tastes and distastes, fancies, aversions, dependability, and everything about them. He can cast the performer to the part for which he is especially qualified. If his company cannot perform a piece well, or will not perform it willingly, he will not perform it at all, or perform it, perhaps, but seldom. But the star comes, and must perform in a particular piece — which has never been produced at this theatre before — or he can perform in nothing. He is no star when seen by any light but his own. Even if it is a piece well known, there may be reasons in the structure of the immediate company why it is not in the list. The result is that everything is a matter of experiment. Casts have to be made with very imperfect regard to the capacity of the actor to perform the parts, often in plain defiance of that capacity. One person is not able to represent the part. But it is a long one: he has a great memory, and can learn the words, which a person of more genius and capability, (if he had time,) to play the part, could not do in the short space of twenty-four hours, which is all the time that can be allotted. There can be no delay. The purpose of the star is to exhibit *himself*. *He* is as well prepared as he cares to be; and the piece is played at once, regardless of the cast of it at all. Unless the drama is a monologue the effect is obvious.

Among the minor results of this system we must count the gross disregard often seen of late in

The Scenic Department

I am far from meaning to uphold the propriety of excessive attention to mere scenic effect. On the contrary, I shall speak directly of the outlays of money on this department as one of the great mistakes of modern management. Put a company of good actors into a barn, and of poor ones on the most gorgeous stage that money can construct in a theatre, and it will soon be seen where the drama is. Still, scenic arrangement is a very important thing. If good, it adds greatly to illusion and effect; if bad, it is worse than none. I need hardly say that this is a matter which must all be arranged. It never can be when, as under the system of stars, the order of things is unknown, uncertain, shifting, or changed. The result has been that the scenic department has received no attention until the matter became so glaring as to cause too much attention to it, and to cause stage decoration to be mistaken for the drama itself. The contempt of all propriety in the scenic department was so frequent as to cause no surprise in the audience, when even Virginius was arraigned on Ludgate Hill, and that spot presented to them night after night as the well-known residence of Brabantio, the Venetian, of Damon, the Syracusian, and of all the foreigners of every nation and ages whom the drama ever had occasion to make known to them.

On a late representation of *Virginius*, the Roman Centurion received his friends, Dentatius and Icilius, in a chamber, the walls of which were ornamented with pictures of various events in the history of England, and among the rest with an excellent copy of Charles Leslie's well-known "Murder of Young Rutland." All this was originally the result of haste. It afterwards became a chronic affair. The audience allowed it, and the manager having troubles enough of other kinds, gave himself no uneasiness about it.

These were some of the primary effects of the system. The matter of scenic absurdity I mention, of course, only incidentally, and as a very small affair.

True and False Stars

In immediate result from the effects I have mentioned, and from the labors and positions into which the regular members of the stock companies were thrown by the advent of numerous stars, came certain secondary consequences vastly more obvious to the public, and which ended in the total prostration and ruin of the drama. When the performance of great leading parts were claimed by Cooke or Kean as stars, the regulars never, in my experience, showed dissatisfaction. In taking a place above all the actors around them, such men seemed to be asserting nothing more than their natural position in the drama. They were such real masters too of their profession that they understood the necessities of it in all departments; and though starring entirely, such was the order and adjustment of all they did, and so well was it known what they would do, that no practical loss was produced. I have often spoken of Cooper. He was in truth a star, but his starring was so regular, so dependable, and so long continued, that it was reduced to all the advantages of stock acting. He was in truth in many aspects of the case a stock actor; a stock actor attached to several companies; permanently, in fact, to all of them, though not in form and in their structure to any. His relation with all was a perfect illustration of the extent to which starring is not only allowable, but absolutely beneficial and almost indispensable, by enriching the season with variety. The same remark is true of John Kemble's starring, and also of Forrest's in the United States. But when with the break up of the London theatres at the termination of their monopolies . . . we had cast upon us, as stars, the whole body of London actors of all grades, the case became widely different. The companies here found, night after night, some new person they had never before heard of, announced in big letters — all their own plans deranged, themselves forced into extraordinary and severe study, and their whole time absorbed, and their powers over-worked — merely that they might act as subsidiaries, or, perhaps, as foils to some foreign adventurer, who possessed no merit half so great as their own; while he took away in one night twice as much as they could earn as their whole weekly wages. Of course such a state of things would not be endured by them long, and accordingly men who, up to this time, had been perfectly contented with their wages, and with their home reputation of clever stock actors, which they really deserved, now abandoned that safe position for the attractive honors of the star. The example being propagated downward, the necessary effect was a corps or body no longer, but was disintegrated, and all its members converted into stars. Abandoning the path of systematic labor and quiet study, and persuading themselves that an imitation of some eminent actor would not fail to charm an audience, the young men of the theatre begin where they should be proud to find themselves at the end of seven years, and make their debut in possession of leading characters. Under the delusion that they will, thus reach real eminence, they have wasted the first few years of their professional lives in a silly dream of success, and until the audience are provoked into an expression of discontent, or entirely abandon them, flatter themselves that they have obtained, by a sort of magic, that which actors of the greatest natural genius required years of intense study and labor to achieve. Such men would, by proper effort and by time, have made most useful, respectable, and often eminent actors in a proper position, and by good habits and economy in a regular company, have secured the means of comfortably living as respectable members of a settled community. And this is reputation and success enough for them or for most men. As it is, they have ended in some public exposure, and in many grievous private experiences of their miserable mistake. In all this, let me say, however, the young actor is less to blame than the manager and the system. There was no proper place for him reputably to occupy.

I need not, of course, now ask what sort of a theatre that will be from which every actor, capable of doing anything above the humblest part, has been splintered off, exploded, or expulsed in the office of a star. It contains, of course, and can contain no stock company at all. There is nobody to support the star. Pieces are performed by him, such as he is, alone. All the minor parts are given of necessity to performers wholly incapable and totally uneducated, who think, of course, if they think at all, that stage directions, manner, deportment, dressing, and even the first rules of grammar concern no one but the performer. The messenger or guard dashes unbonneted into the presence of his king with the freedom of an equal; he bawls out that he done this, seen that, and come as soon as called; and even if the merits of the star were of the highest kind, the violations of all propriety in the underparts would destroy the effect of them, and dissipate all illusion. When the theatre arrives at such a condition that it has no stock company at all, of course the drama is at an end.

In immediate connection with the conversion of all the actors into stars follows another evil, itself productive of further injury; I mean the

Excessive Number of Benefits

Under the management of Wignell and his immediate successors, and indeed in all managements everywhere till those of the star ascendancy, it was usual to allow those stock actors who were of good talents, industrious habits; and of fair character, and who had earned some title to one by a faithful and satisfactory discharge of all their duties throughout a season, the privilege, towards its close, of a benefit night. It was a custom both useful and graceful. It was a merited tribute of respect and encouragement given both by the public, the managers, and his fellow actors to a performer whose merits all were acquainted with, without any special blazoning of them when the night arrived. The performances were much the same as on ordinary occasions, and neither previous nor subsequent nights were allowed by the manager to be sacrificed to them. The same privilege was allowed to the very few performers who appeared as stars. Being really eminent, or at least very well known performers, the tribute was always deserved. The public knew perfectly well that the performance, like all the others of that person, would be interesting; and the announcement of the benefit was all that was needed to attract the auditors. At all times, however, the matter of benefits was one held with a pretty tight hand. They were not allowed to be very frequent. The stars had them of course. But this made but few benefits; and as regarded stock actors, they were never allowed to obscure actors, to irregular ones, or to those who from other causes deserved no such privilege. When, however, all the stock actors were converted into stars, then the case became different. The immense number of stars, and the want of attractiveness in most of them from anything but novelty, necessarily makes short engagements. And when each star has a benefit, and the season is composed of nothing but a rapid succession of stars, the effect at once is to convert every night or two into a benefit night. The star, of course, has no concern in the permanent interests of the season, nor in the interests of the management at all, further than as concerns his own engagements. On his benefit night he takes, perhaps, a clear benefit, or the whole gross receipts, while on other nights he takes but a portion of them. The result is it is expected that he will hold back his best efforts till his benefit night. Then his friends, if he has any, and the public, if they go at all, will certainly turn out. The night is forced as much as possible, and the manager's nights, before and after, are reduced to empty boxes. Of course, when the manager is thus ruined, the stars must follow him, and the very star system itself is broken up, not by an immediate restoration of stock companies, but primarily by the entire prostration of the drama itself. Thus it is, in one way, as I have said, that the star system has destroyed itself, and so been working a revival of the drama. Another consequence, destructive of the drama, of this system, by which every actor is made a star, is the

Newspaper and Bill Puffing and Lying

and every other possible sort of vaunting, swaggering, and imposition which it necessarily engenders. Of course when nearly all the members of the theatrical profession are seeking a livelihood as stars, the largest portion of those stars cannot possibly possess any high degree of merit. They are therefore obscure, though they are stars. They have never gained, nor indeed have sought to gain, a reputation founded on time, study, and labor, and an exhibition of their talents. Such a reputation, even where high merit exists, is necessarily slow in every profession. In the theatrical profession, even where great dramatic genius is found, there is so much of an actor's duty which can be acquired by practice alone, that the greater opportunities which, in comparison with other professions, he has for showing his merits, is counter-

balanced, perhaps, by the greater necessity of practical experience. How then, they naturally get to thinking, are the public to
be attracted? In no way, they think, but through the press and
by the hand-bills. Every species of lie is resorted to. Hand-bills,
flaming in every color of paper and type, and proclaiming the
name of the star in display letters a foot or a yard long, epithets
of every kind — "distinguished," "popular," "unrivalled," "unparalleled," "immensely successful," "the great American," "the
great English," "the wonder of two hemispheres" — are set forth
with profuse and lying ostentation. A regular system of newspaper puffing is supposed indispensable to any success, and a
connection with the press is the first object now sought. With
the editors — a body too honorable and too politic thus to be used
— an intercourse is not easy. The resort is to the underlings of the
press; and the effort is by suppers, dinners, tickets, loans of
money never returned, a contingent interest in the result of the
night, and every sort of poor bribe, to engage this humble and
amiable class. Services of plates, cups, books, rings, and all sorts
of things are presented, and all sorts of fooleries gone through
(at the actor's own cost,) simply that a grand account may appear of them in the morning's paper. Vast quantities of tickets
are undersold, that it may be reported that the house was full.
A correspondence, offering dinners and benefits, or entreating the
actor's portrait, is got up, not with a view of having any dinner,
or by paying anything for a benefit or a portrait, but simply with
a view of having the correspondence published. And what does
all this come to? For a little while it did very well. People had
not as yet got used to such things. But they found out, of course,
very soon that it was a system of imposture merely, and therefore
gave no more heed to the report of all that was written, said or
done, than they did to anything else that they knew to be a paid
for puff, or to speak in plainer English, a paid for lie. Nobody
could be puffed into the house. If this had ended with the immediate actor concerned, it would have been comparatively un-
important. What I am speaking of more particularly was or is
its effects on the theatre or drama in general. Managers and actors come to be regarded as no better than showmen, quacks,
swaggerers and imposters. The public believe that they can give
no credit to anything announced. The whole pursuit and connec-

tion is disgraced, and if such practices belong to it, is rightly disgraced. . . .

Another way in which, without any of this gross fraud, the star system is injurious to the drama, will readily present itself to the reader's mind in

The Inability to Afford Variety

There are few general actors — I mean by this term "general," actors capable of acting many and various parts, and in performing both tragic, comic, and melo-dramatic pieces. There are no general stars. The system is at variance with general acting. It must be the great tragedian or the great comedian, and which ever line they adopt they confine themselves to a few characters in it. The result is, that there is a want of that constant though regulated variety in the performances which every manager knows is necessary to sustain the public interest. Even with Mr. Cooke and Mr. Kean to perform them, the public would grow weary of an eternal succession of this same dozen pieces night after night without relief. Yet this is exactly what the star system engenders and brings upon us, with this exception only, that the pieces, instead of being performed by Mr. Cooke and Mr. Kean, are done by all sorts of adventurers, usually English ones (secondary performers) from minor theatres, and without talent, manners, education, or a single requisite for the part in which they audaciously assume to exhibit themselves before the American public.

Particularly conditions of society, the great overtradings of 1834 '5 '6, and the bankruptcy of the trading classes which took place in 1837, the stagnation of affairs for some years afterwards, and especially in 1841, '2, and thereabouts, had something to do with the ruin about the latter time of the drama; but it was the star system which really broke it down, and that system will break it down just as often as ever the system itself gets the ascendant. It is that which has upon it "the primal eldest curse." With the prostration of managers and the repulsion of auditors, it has come, or, I hope, for the sake of the drama, it is coming to an end itself. Not, however, until it does come to an end entirely, shall we ever see the drama reputably revived.

24. NEW MANAGERS

WHILE WOOD WAS MAKING his brilliant diagnosis, the manager, James William Wallack (1795 - 1864), was planning to introduce a number of reforms designed to eliminate the shortcomings of the star system. The elder Wallack, English born and trained, made his first attempt at artistic integrity in 1837 while managing the National Theater in New York. During two successful seasons he challenged the supremacy of the Park Theater. In 1839, the National Theater was destroyed by fire, and it was not till 1852 that Wallack returned to the managerial field by opening Brougham's Lyceum as Wallack's Lyceum. The elder Wallack believed in a well-disciplined stock company and in ensemble acting. On his stage the greatest attention was paid to minute details in scenery and costume. The tradition established by the elder Wallack was carried on by his son, Lester, and by Laura Keene, the English-born actress, who made her American debut at Wallack's in 1852 and who was soon to become a powerful force in the theatrical world. She entered the field of management not only in New York but also in Baltimore, Philadelphia, and San Francisco. While conducting rehearsals she was such an absolute ruler that the company referred to her simply as "The Duchess." Intensive rehearsals under centralized authority—this was the secret behind her finished productions, a secret she had learned from Madame Vestris. In 1869, Laura Keene opened the remodelled Chestnut Street Theater in Philadelphia. Here is the *Evening Bulletin*'s account of the opening night:

If the success of the first performance in the Chestnut Street Theatre, under Miss Laura Keene's management, is a true indication of the future, the theatre will be blessed as it never has been before with prosperity and popularity. The house was literally full, and there was in the street a large crowd of persons, who, unable to enter, contented themselves with gazing through the doors into the vestibule. Many of those present were attracted, of course, by curiosity to see the improved building, and they were completely satisfied. There has been an entire transformation of the interior, and now this theatre, once the ugliest, most uncomfortable in town, with smells reeking up from kitchens in the cellar, seats which gave visitors the back-ache, and a hundred other defects, has been made the prettiest, brightest, snuggest, most picturesque theatre we have ever had. Its good qualities, in detail, are: the most comfortable seats of any place of amusement in Philadelphia, the most convenient boxes, the best effects of contrast in the decorations and hangings, the visibility of every portion of the stage from any place in the house; a perfect system of ventilation, which poured in upon the warm audience, last night, a constant stream of cool, fresh air; an absence of anything like gaudiness; novel and beautiful ornaments in the shape of hangings, baskets of flowers and graceful plants, and altogether a brilliant, striking and very rich general effect, which pleases the eye and gives to the place an art character which is very gratifying.

25. REHEARSALS UNDER DALY

THE WALLACK-KEENE tradition was continued by Augustin Daly (1838 - 1899). First at the various Fifth Avenue theaters, then at Daly's, he instituted an autocratic regime. But once a player had submitted to Daly's stern discipline, he could not but admire the unfailing instinct that guided the stage director in all decisions. Let us watch a Daly rehearsal through the eyes of Clara Morris:

Before I came under the management of Mr. Daly, I may say I never really knew what stage-management meant. He was a young man then; he had had, I believe, his own theatre but one season before I joined his forces, yet his judgment was as ripe, his decisions were as swift and sure, his eye for effect was as true, his dramatic instinct as keen as well could be.

We never exchanged so much as a frown, let alone a hasty word, over work. I realized that he had the entire play before his "mind's eye," and when he told me to do a thing, I should have done it, even had I not understood why he wished it done. But he always gave a reason for things, and that made it easy to work under him.

His attention to tiny details amazed me. One morning, after Mr. Crisp had joined the company, he had to play a love-scene with me, and the "business" of the scene required him to hold me some time in his embrace. But Mr. Crisp's embrace did not suit Mr. Daly — no more did mine. Out he went, in front, and looked at us.

"Oh," he cried, "confound it! Miss Morris, relax — relax! lean on him — he won't break! That's better — but lean more! lean as if you needed support! What? Yes, I know you don't need it — but you're in love, don't you see? and you're not

a lady by a mile or two! For God's sake, Crisp, don't be so stiff
and inflexible! Here, let me show you!"

Up Mr. Daly rushed on to the stage, and taking Crisp's place,
convulsed the company with his effort at acting the lover. Then
back again to the front, ordering us to try that embrace again.

"That's better!" he cried; "but hold her hand closer, tighter!
not quite so high — oh, that's too low! Don't poke your arm out,
you're not going to waltz. What in — are you scratching her back
for?"

It was too much; in spite of the awe in which Mr. Daly was
held, everyone, Crisp included, screamed with laughter, while
Mr. Daly fumed and fretted over the time that was being wasted.

One of my early experiences of his way of directing a rehearsal made a deep impression upon me. In the play of "Jezebel"
I had the title part. There were a number of characters on in the
scene, and Mr. Daly wanted to get me across the stage, so that
I should be out of hearing distance of two of the gentlemen. Now,
in the old days, the stage-director would simply have said: "Cross
to the Right," and you would have crossed because he told you
to; but in Mr. Daly's day you had to have a *reason* for crossing
the drawing-room, and so getting out of the two gentlemen's way
— and a reason could not be found.

Here are a few of the many rejected ideas: There was no
guest for me to cross to in welcoming pantomime; no piano on
that side of the room for me to cross to and play on softly; ah,
the fireplace! and the pretty warming of one foot? But no, it was
summer-time, that would not do. The ancient fancy-work, perhaps? No, she was a human panther, utterly incapable of so
domestic an occupation. The fan forgotten on the mantel-piece?
Ah, yes, that was it! you cross the room for that — and then
suddenly I reminded Mr. Daly that he had, but a moment before,
made a point of having me strike a gentleman sharply on the
cheek with my fan.

"Oh, confound it, yes!" he answered, "and that's got to stand
— that blow is good!"

The old, old device of attendance upon the lamp was suggested; but the hour of the day was plainly given by one of
the characters as three o'clock in the afternoon.

These six are but few of the many rejected reasons for that
one cross of the stage; still Mr. Daly would not permit a mo-

tiveless action, and we came to a momentary standstill. Very doubtfully, I remarked: "I suppose a smelling-bottle would not be important enough to cross the room for?"

He brightened quickly — clouded over even more quickly: "Y-e-e-s! N-o-o! at least, not if it had never appeared before. But let me see — Miss Morris, you must carry that smelling-bottle in the preceding scene, and — and, yes, I'll just put in a line in your part, making you ask some one to hand it to you — that will nail attention to it, you see! Then in this scene, when you leave these people and cross the room to get your smelling-bottle from the mantel, it will be a perfectly natural action on your part, and will give the men their chance of explanation and warning." And at last we were free to move on to other things.

Above all was he eager to have his stage present a home-like interior. Never shall I forget my amazement when I first saw a piece of furniture occupying the very centre of the stage, while I with others were reduced to acting in any scrap of room we could "scrooge" into, as children say.

Long trains were fashionable then, and it was no uncommon sight to see the lover standing with both feet firmly planted upon his lady's train while he implored her to fly with him — the poor man had to stand somewhere! Miss Davenport, in one of her comedy scenes, having to move about a good deal on the crowded stage, finally wound her trailing skirts so completely about a chair that, at her exit, the chair went with her, causing a great laugh.

One night a male character, having to say boastfully to me: "I have my hand upon a fortune!" I added in an undertone: "And both feet upon my white satin dress!" at which he lost his grip (as the boys say) and laughed aloud — said laugh costing him a forfeit of fifty cents, which really should have been paid by me, as I was the guilty cause of that disastrous effect. But the gentleman was not only gallant but well used to being forfeited, and unconcernedly paid the penalty exacted.

But really it was very distressing trying to make your way between pieces of furniture — stopping to release your skirts from first one thing and then another, and often destroying all the effect of your words by such action. One evening I petulantly observed to Mr. Daly: "I see now why one is only *woolly* in the

West — in the East one gets the wool all rubbed off on unnecessary pedestals and centre-divans."

He laughed first, then pulled up sharply, saying: "Perhaps
you did not notice that your comment contained a criticism of
my judgment, Miss Morris? If I think the furniture necessary,
that is sufficient," and I gave him a military salute and ran down-
stairs. At the foot Mr. George Brown and one of the pretty young
women stood. She was saying: "Now if any of *us* had said there
was too much crowding from that rubbishy old furniture, he would
have made us pay a nice forfeit for it, but Miss Morris gets off
scot-free!"

"Yes, I know," said Mr. Brown, "but then she amused him
first with the idea of rubbing the Western wool off here, and you
can't very well laugh and then turn around and forfeit the person
who made you do it."

And so I learned that if no detail was too small for Mr. Daly
to consider carefully in his preparation of a play, so no detail
of daily life in his theatre was too small for notice, consideration,
and comment, and I resolved to try hard to curb my careless
speech, lest it get me into trouble.

26.   THE ACTOR EDWIN BOOTH

EDWIN BOOTH (1833 - 1893) served his apprenticeship under his father,
Junius Brutus Booth. After engagements along the Pacific Coast and in
the South, he conquered New York in 1857, quickly establishing himself as Forrest's heir and the foremost American tragedian. There is no
finer pen-portrait of Booth than the one drawn by William Winter:

The personality of Booth was greater than his achievement.
By birth and heredity he possessed faculties and qualities that
most actors pass laborious lives in the fruitless effort to emulate
— the faculties and qualities, namely, of genius and personal
charm, that constitute distinction and lead directly to conquest.
His face, his voice, his person, his demeanour, and his brilliant,
indomitable spirit — those were his authentic preordination to
empire and renown. As a young man his beauty was extraordinary.
His dark eyes flashed with superb fire, not alone of physical
vitality, but of imagination, emotion, and exaltation of the soul.
In mature years the same nobility of presence continued to sub-

sist, but it was softened and hallowed by experience and grief. Alike in youth and age, in bloom and in decline, he was exceptional and rare, a striking product of nature, and as such a puissant and predominant force. He needed not to seek after novelties; he was himself a novelty. The old plays were adequate for his purpose, because, in his inspired expression of their thought and feeling, character and action, he made them ever new. His success was that of a great personality, — specially shown in the equilibrium of his intellectual life and its freedom from fret and fume. All his mistakes and most of his troubles resulted from the amiable weakness with which he sometimes permitted himself to become entangled with paltry, scheming, unworthy people. By himself, — isolated, introspective, strange, wayward, variable, moody, yet noble, gentle, affectionate, generous, — he was incarnate victory.

The salient attributes of Booth's art were imagination, insight, grace, intense emotion, and melancholy refinement. In Hamlet, Richelieu, Othello, Iago, King Lear, Bertuccio, and Lucius Brutus they were conspicuously manifest. But the controlling attribute, — that which imparted individual character, colour, and fascination to his acting, — was the thoughtful, introspective habit of a stately mind, abstracted from passion and suffused with mournful dreaminess of temperament. The moment that charm began to work, his victory was complete. It was that which made him the true image of Shakespeare's thought, in the glittering halls of Elsinore, on its midnight battlements, and in its lonely, wind-beaten place of graves.

Under the discipline of sorrow, and through "years that bring the philosophic mind," Booth drifted further and further away from things dark and terrible, whether in the possibilities of human life or in the world of imagination. That is the direction of true growth. In all characters that evoked his essential spirit — in characters which rest on spiritualised intellect, or on sensibility to fragile loveliness, the joy that is unattainable, the glory that fades, and the beauty that perishes — he was peerless. Hamlet, Richelieu, Faust, Manfred, Jacques, Esmond, Sydney Carton, and Sir Edward Mortimer are all, in different ways, suggestive of the personality that Booth was fitted to illustrate. It is the loftiest type that human nature affords, because it is the embodied supremacy of the soul, and because therein it denotes the only possible escape from the cares and vanities of a transitory world.

27.   THE BOOTH THEATER IN NEW YORK

ON FEBRUARY 3, 1869, Booth opened the Booth Theater at the corner of Sixth Avenue and Twenty-third Street. The new playhouse was the finest in New York. Laura Keene called it a temple, and Joseph Jefferson compared it to a "church behind the curtain and a countinghouse in front of it." The church part was never questioned, but the counting-house got into disorder, and when Booth retired from the management (1873), bankruptcy was just around the corner. But we are concerned here with the temple only. William Winter gives all the information on the technical aspects of Booth's playhouse:

Booth's theatre was made of granite. The front of the structure, in Twenty-third street, was one hundred and eighty-four
feet in length — the theatre front measuring one hundred and
fifty feet. The other thirty-four feet was the width of a wing
of the main building, abutting on its west end, with a frontage
of seventy-six feet in Sixth avenue. This wing was devoted to
shops, studios, and miscellaneous rooms. The theatre was one
hundred feet deep, from north to south, and one hundred and
twenty feet in height. The main entrance was in Twenty-third
street, but there was another door in Sixth avenue. In the north
front was a great door to the stage, corresponding in size and
style with the main entrance to the auditorium. Between these
were three smaller doors, used as means of exit. Three large
panels surmounted those doors, made to contain sculpture. All the
doors were arched. Higher, and placed equidistant along the
front of the theatre, were three large niches, with Ionic pillars, to
contain statues. There were four large windows level with those
alcoves. Above was a beautiful cornice, and above that was a
mansard roof, surmounted by three short towers. In each tower
was an oval window. A flagstaff rose from the centre of the flat
roof. The summit of each tower was girdled by an ornamental
iron trellis, and the lightning-rods which trailed over the towers
and roof were adorned with gilded stars and crescents. Entering
at the principal door the visitor stood in a commodious vestibule,
paved with Italian marble tiles and lined with Italian marble

Interior of the Booth Theater in New York (1869).
Water Color by Charles W. Witham.

cement — the ceiling being frescoed. The vestibule extended in a semi-circle along the rear of the auditorium, to which entrance was afforded by three arched doors. The lower floor of the theatre comprised the divisions of parquet and orchestra. A spacious stone staircase, at the south end of the vestibule, led to the balcony. Midway on the staircase rested Gould's noble bust of the elder Booth. Above the balcony was a second gallery, and above that the amphitheatre, reached by a stone staircase from the Sixth avenue entrance. There were three proscenium boxes on each side of the stage, and the house contained seats for seventeen hundred and fifty persons, and standing room for three hundred more. In shape the auditorium followed the horseshoe model. From every part of the theatre the stage could be distinctly seen. Bright frescos shone upon the ceilings. A chandelier depended from the centre of the roof, and all the gas-jets in the building were ignited by electricity. Marble pillars, adorned with statues, arose on either side of the boxes. In the centre of the proscenium arch stood a statue of Shakespeare, the work of Signor G. Turini, an Italian artist, representing the poet meditating and in act to write. Other statues and emblematic devices surrounded that figure, and completed the decoration of the arch. There was a neatly designed pit for the band, sunk below the front of the stage, and below the level of the main floor. Sitting in the amphitheatre the spectator could contemplate, upon the wall above the proscenium arch, portrait busts of Garrick, Talma, Edmund Kean, George Frederick Cooke, and Betterton. Those were in white ovals, relieved against a dark background. Overhead, in an ascending perspective, was an elaborate painting of Apollo, the Muses and the Graces. On the walls immediately beneath the ceiling were painted various symbolic figures and devices. One panel represented Venus in her chariot. Another depicted the march of Cupid. On the right were figures of Lear and Hamlet; on the left, figures of Othello and Macbeth; while above the proscenium arch, and under the statue of Shakespeare, was painted the Shakespeare coat-of-arms. Those decorations, following the style of Raphael, were planned and furnished by Signor G. G. Gariboldi; the paintings were chiefly from the hand of Signor C. Brumidi. The stage was large and well proportioned. The distance from the footlights to the rear wall was fifty-five feet, and the arch was seventy-six feet wide. Beneath was a pit, thirty-two feet deep, blasted out of the solid rock. That useful chasm was paved with brick. A scene could be sunk into it, out of sight. On the stage, as in every other part of the theatre, double floors were laid, and were secured by screws. In each of the rear corners of the stage was a spiral staircase, leading to the four fly galleries, two on each side, up beneath the roof. The flats were raised and lowered by hydraulic rams, under the stage. At the south side of the stage was the scene-room, stocked with scenery. Above this was the paint-room, fifty-seven feet by sixteen feet, in which a flat thirty feet high could be stretched and painted. At the south side of the theatre were five stories of rooms, approached by a convenient staircase, including the green-room, a fireproof room for the wardrobe of the theatre, the star apartments, and about thirty dressing-rooms, comfortably appointed. The greenroom was a parlour, on the second floor, the walls of which were adorned with theatrical engravings. From the vaults beneath the stage ran passages leading into the vaults beneath the auditorium and also into those beneath the sidewalks. Here was seen the foundation, of solid rock. Here were the supports — stone pillars nearly three feet square. The front wall was nearly five feet thick, and the other walls upward of two feet. Under the sidewalk in Twenty-third street was the carpenters' shop of the theatre, in a large, dry vault, together with the boiler-room, in which were two large boilers, to supply steam for an engine, and for hot-air pipes by which the theatre was heated. There were tanks of water at the top of the building.

28. BELASCO'S DIRECTION

DAVID BELASCO (1859 - 1931) gave the American theater the external brilliance of pictorial impressionism from which it has not yet recovered, though Hollywood has since drawn off some of the deadening literalness from the Broadway stage. Belasco left us a step-by-step description of his methods in mounting one of his switchboard-melodramas:

Let us now assume that a play has been brought into acceptable form in its manuscript and I have made up my mind to produce it. My first step in the practical work of production is to study out the scenes, which must be constructed as carefully as the play itself, for a skilfully devised scene is always of vital assistance to an episode. In this preliminary work I seldom follow the stage directions on the printed page, either of my own plays or those of other dramatists. I prefer to plan the scenes myself with reference to stage values.

I consider where a window or door, a balcony or a fireplace will be most effective. The feeling of the scene is always a great factor in determining its arrangement, for symbolism to a certain extent enters the production of every play. For instance, sunlit scenes imply happiness, moonlit scenes give a suggestion of romance, while tragedy or sorrow should be played in gloom. It is never advisable to stage comedy scenes, which depend for their interest upon the wittiness of the dialogue, in exterior settings, for the surroundings suggest too great an expanse; if acted in an interior setting the lines become immeasurably more effective.

Such details as these must be carefully thought out, and as I become more familiar with the lines and episodes the scenes gradually form themselves. Then I make a rough sketch, taking into account the necessary arrangement of furniture or other properties and considering how the characters can be maneuvered to best advantage.

When I have settled these matters approximately, I send for my scenic artist. With him seated in front, I take the empty stage and, as far as possible, try to act the whole play, making every entrance and exit and indicating my ideas of the groupings of the characters and their surroundings. This process, which would probably seem farcical to a casual onlooker, will consume perhaps four or five evenings, for not one detail can be left to chance or put aside until I am satisfied that it cannot be improved. . . .

Having explained in detail my ideas and turned over a manuscript to him, the scenic artist proceeds to make a drawing of the scenes, following my crude sketches, and thus we reach a definite starting-point. In due course of time — it may be a week or a month — the scenic artist will have constructed the actual scene models which are set up in the perfectly equipped miniature theatre of my studio. But changes are always suggesting themselves, and often these models, which are about four feet long, have to be taken apart and reconstructed several times.

It is time now to begin to consider what to me is the all-important factor in a dramatic production — the lighting of the scenes. With my electrician I again go over the play in detail, very much according to the method I have previously followed with my scenic artist. When he has thoroughly grasped my ideas and become quite familiar with the play itself, we begin our experiments, using the miniature theatre and evolving our colors by transmitting white light through gelatin or silk of various hues. Night after night we experiment together to obtain color or atmospheric effects, aiming always to make them aid the interpretation of the scenes.

Lights are to drama what music is to the lyrics of a song. No other factor that enters into the production of a play is so effective in conveying its moods and feeling. They are as essential to every work of dramatic art as blood is to life. The greatest part of my success in the theatre I attribute to my feeling for colors, translated into effects of light. Sometimes these effects have been imitated by other producers with considerable success, but I do not fear such encroachments. It may be possible for others to copy my colors, but no one can get my feeling for them.

The lighting effects on my stages have been secured only after years of experiment and at an expense which many other producers would consider ridiculous. Sometimes I have spent five thousand dollars attempting to reproduce the delicate hues of a sunset and then have thrown the scene away altogether. I recall that when I produced "The Girl of the Golden West," I experimented three months to secure exactly the soft, changing colors of a Californian sunset over the Sierra Nevadas, and then turned to another method. It was a good sunset, but it was not Californian. Afterward I sold it to the producers of "Salomy Jane," and it proved very effective and perfectly adjusted to the needs of that play.

These experiments have always been the most interesting part of my work as a producer, although they have also been the most perplexing and sometimes the most baffling. It is no easy matter, for instance, to indicate the difference between the moon and stars of a Japanese night and the fanciful moon and stars of fairyland. But there is, nevertheless, a difference which an audience must be made to feel, without detecting the mechanism, just as one is conscious of heat, yet does not see it, on entering a warm room.

Belasco's Production of *The Rose of the Rancho* (1906)

The problem of lighting was especially difficult in my production of "The Return of Peter Grimm," since in that play it was necessary to indicate the contrast between life and death. Doing away with footlights helped me considerably, but it took five months of experiments to accomplish the results I sought. I invented special reflectors to produce the ashen hue of death, but something always seemed lacking. I kept David Warfield in New York all summer, standing alone on the stage for hours at a stretch, while I threw various lights upon him. Then it occurred to me that the trouble lay in the kind of clothes he wore. I sent for fifty bolts of cloth and wrapped him in the different fabrics and colors, until I found one which made him look mysterious and far away. Even then his appearance was not quite right. When other characters came on the stage things went wrong. Finally I tried the expedient of casting a cold gray light upon his features from above, while, at the same time, I illuminated the faces of the other characters in the play with a faint rosy glow. It was necessary to have many of these lights of differing quality which, one after the other, "picked up" the people as they moved from place to place on the stage. The effect was exactly what I desired, and it proved to be one of the most important factors in the success of the play.

In my production of "The Darling of the Gods" in 1902 it was comparatively easy to indicate by lights the tragic feeling of the scene in which the band of Samurai commit suicide by hari-kari. I set the stage in the picture by a gaunt bamboo forest, behind which was a great blood-red setting sun to symbolize ebbing life. In the shadows Kara's followers could be faintly seen and the audience could hear the clatter of their lacquered armor as they went to their self-inflicted deaths.

But when it came to the scene of the River of Souls, in which the dead were to swim to the lower depths, or purgatory, in preparation to entering the celestial hereafter, a most troublesome problem arose. I had built the translucent scene of the river at a cost of $6,500 and had devised a kind of harness in which fifteen girls were suspended to represent the passage of the souls. When I tested the scene with manikins in my miniature theatre, it invariably worked perfectly; but when I tried it on the regular stage something was sure to go wrong. Some of the girls swam well, while others swam badly, and almost always one or two got tangled in their harness. Such accidents in a perform-ance before an audience would have caused laughter, which would have been fatal to a production that had cost $80,000.

For two days and two nights, barring short recesses, we worked over that stubborn scene, and at last I decided to give it up. Blanche Bates, who was to play the character of the heroine, Yo-San, was almost in despair. George Arliss lay asleep on a lounge at the side of the stage, and every one else was vexed, discouraged, and completely fagged out. The opening performance had already been twice postponed, but reluctantly I made up my mind to put it off again.

I ordered the scene "struck," and my carpenters hoisted all the opaque setting which had been made at great cost, leaving a single gauze curtain suspended in irregular folds at the front of the stage. Just at this moment one of the workmen happened to pass between the curtain and a light at the back. Seen through the folds of the curtain his movements were almost ghostly. I saw at once that the effect for which I had been striving had come to me ready-made. Each of the fifteen girls was told to count ten and then cross the stage, using her arms to suggest a kind of swimming motion. The effect was remarkable, for the number of figures seemed increased a thousand-fold. Having already thrown away $6,500, I built the scene in a day for $90 and it is being imitated yet.

In "Du Barry" one of the problems which arose was how to change from a brilliantly lighted scene to a dark scene without abruptly turning out the lights, and also how to invent an ex-cuse for the ensuing darkness. I thought of midnight bathing and other pastimes of the court of Louis XV, but I could not put them on the stage. While looking over some books on the customs of the period, I ran across descriptions of the lighted balls which were tossed about by the courtiers and ladies in court games. Thus I not only found the excuse I needed for turning out my stage lights, but the brilliantly illuminated balls did away with the abruptness of the change, while the novelty of it appealed strongly to the audience at a point in the play where a surprise was needed to stimulate its interest.

The scene models having been approved and the very im-portant matter of the lighting being well under way, it is time now to begin the building of the actual scenes. I turn my carpenters over to my scenic artist, who furnishes to them the plans. They then construct the scenery in my own shops, for I never have such work done by contract. I will allow nothing to be built out of canvas stretched on frames. Everything must be real. I have seen plays in which thrones creaked on which monarchs sat, and palace walls flapped when persons touched them. Nothing so destructive to illusion or so ludicrous can happen on my stage.

Chapter XIV

European Naturalism

A Set for Antoine's Production of Hauptmann's *The Weavers.*

Stanislavsky's Production of Gorky's *The Lower Depths.*
Moscow Art Theater.

1. INSIDE THE THEATRE-LIBRE

THE BEGINNINGS of the Théâtre-Libre were very modest, and yet, this theater in a wooden shack in the Passage de l'Élisée des Beaux Arts, where, on March 30, 1887, André Antoine (1858-1943) presented the first production of his experimental theater, was soon to become a battle cry and symbol for the progressive forces of the age. Antoine — by profession still a clerk in the Gas Company, by avocation an actor, stage director, and dreamer — succeeded from the start in sponsoring dramatic literature of which a critic like Zola was not ashamed; but, on the tiny stage of his first theater, Antoine was not able to carry out the basic principles of naturalistic production. The amateur actors and the 343 spectators were like one great family; there was no Fourth Wall and no objectivity of scenic environment in this intimate theater. Lemaître describes a visit to the original Théâtre-Libre:

Toward half-past eight in the evening, you might have seen some shadows gliding along the booths of the street-fair of Montmartre, and carefully avoiding the puddles of water on the pavements of the Place Pigalle, scrutinizing through their *lorgnettes* the nameplates at the corners of the streets; no passage, no theatre! We finally make for the light of a wineshop, and we enter a steep and winding alley, dimly lighted. A line of cabs is slowly climbing up. We follow them; on each side, shadowy buildings in ruins, and dirty walls, at the far end an obscure flight of steps. We looked like magi in topcoats, seeking a hidden and glorious manger. Is it the cradle where will be reborn the drama, that decrepit and doting old man? I can't answer for that yet. All that I know is that we passed a very amusing evening at the Théâtre-Libre.

The hall is very small and rather naïvely decorated; it resembles the concert hall of a county-seat. One might stretch out one's hand to the actors over the footlights and put one's legs on the prompter's box. The stage is so narrow that only the most elementary scenery can be used on it, and it is so near us that scenic illusion is impossible.

2. ANTOINE AND THE MEININGEN CROWD
SCENES

IN JULY OF 1888, André Antoine saw some performances of the Meiningen troupe in Brussels. In a letter to Françisque Sarcey he evaluated the strength and weakness of this company:

Their stage crowds are not, as with us, composed of elements gathered at random from artisans, engaged only for dress rehearsals, badly dressed, and little practised in wearing bizarre or awkward costumes, especially when they are accurate. Nearly always, we recommend immobility to our actors, whereas, over there, the supernumeraries of the Meiningen Company must play their parts in pantomime. Do not think that they thereby overact, and so divert attention from the principals; no, the tableau is held in check, so that, wherever one's eye looks, it always catches a detail of situation or character. At times, this gives the illusion an incomparable power.

The Meiningen Company consists of some sixty-six artists of both sexes. All those who do not play a speaking part are required to appear nightly as supernumeraries in the play. If twenty players are cast for essential roles, the remaining fifty must, without exception, appear on the stage in ensemble scenes. In this manner, even those who are leading actors in their particular field are each placed in charge of a group of supernumeraries whom they direct and supervise as long as the group is on stage. This obligation is so binding that when Hans von Bülow's wife, one of the leading actresses of the troupe, refused to meet it, saying she found it unworthy of her talents, she was dismissed, even though her husband was conductor for the Duke of Saxe-Weimar. The incident provoked such a quarrel that Bülow himself left the ducal court.

In this way the Meininger achieve ensemble scenes that are extraordinarily lifelike. But think of applying this practice to *our* theaters; think of requiring even a fifth-rate player to serve as a supernumerary in the drawing room of the Princess de Bouillon! So we are forced to use simple fellows who hardly know why they are there, let alone what they should do. I know all that: I was once a supernumerary at the Français with Mévisto; we wished to see close up the actors who had enraptured us in the auditorium. . . .

There you have the secret of their crowd scenes, which are absolutely superior to ours. And I well believe that if you had seen the arrest of William Tell and the incident of the apple, you would have been as enchanted as I.

This production of [Schiller's] *William Tell* contained another superb touch: the murder of Gessler. On a practicable ledge that formed a narrow passage at least eight meters from the footlights, Gessler's way was blocked by a beggar and his two children who played a long scene of supplication with their backs to the audience, while Tell looked on. Seeing this, you would have agreed that fitting use of full-back positions contributes greatly to the actor's conviction and the spectator's illusion.

Why could not these things — simple, logical, and by no means costly — replace those insupportable conventions which we must all submit to here without reason? . . .

The mechanics of stage groupings is capitally perfected in the Meiningen crowd scenes, that's all.

The only objection I have to their technique is this: in *William Tell,* for example, Schiller having written a part for the crowd, all the supernumeraries recited the same phrase in unison. The result was heavy and artificial. Could not the cues of the crowd be handled by means of a cleverly conducted uproar?

If, for instance, we are having them cry out: "Long live Gambetta!" — do you know what I would do? I would divide my two hundred supernumeraries into ten or twelve groups, if you like: peasant women, children, commoners, etc. I would start the commoners off with *Long.* . . . The peasant women, increasing the rhythm, would begin when the first group reached *live,* and I would bring in the urchins five seconds after all the others. In short, I would be conducting a choir. I am very sure that the hall would ring with a loud outcry: *"Long live Gambetta!"* And if, as the Meiningen Company does it, the postures, gestures, and groupings were diversified with equal care, there is no doubt but that a large and lifelike effect would result.

In ensemble scenes, the protagonist dominating the action can command complete silence with a gesture, a word, a movement. And if the crowd hears and sees the actor, instead of looking into the auditorium or, as at the Comédie-Française, of gazing at the shareholders with a silent, but obvious, deference, you will find that it can hear easily and that two hundred persons can fall silent together, intent on hearing a person who interests everyone.

I know nothing of music, but I have heard that Wagner has, in certain operas, divided the chorus into several groups, each of which represents a distinct element of the crowd, achieving a perfect ensemble. Why, on the spoken stage, should we not do likewise? Émile Zola wanted to do it for *Germinal*, but could not for budgetary reasons — or so the managers asserted. His purpose was to rehearse the crowds at length under the leadership of supernumerary actors. That is, you see, the practice of the Meiningen Troupe.

Observe that I am not at all, so to speak, carried away by them. Their discordant settings, oddly erected, are infinitely less well painted than ours. They overdo the use of practicables, putting them everywhere. The costumes, splendid and ridiculously rich when they are strictly historical, are almost always in bad taste when, there being no documentary evidence, imagination and originality must be employed.

Their lighting effects are very successful, but too often they are regulated without art. For instance, instead of moving gradually, a very beautiful ray from the setting sun that shone on the noble head of an old man dying in his armchair, all of a sudden passed across a stained-glass window at the exact moment that the good man died, with the sole purpose of providing a tableau.

Also, after an extraordinary torrential rain, obtained by means of projections, I was disturbed to see the water stop abruptly, instead of letting up slowly.

The Meiningen performances were full of such things. The same stage carpet served for every act; there were squeaking floorboards among the mountains. . . .

The actors were adequate, that's all. Several wore their costumes badly. All the mountaineers had white hands and spotless knees, clean as if they were at the Opéra-Comique.

3.   ANTOINE'S AUDIENCES

ANTOINE BEGAN WITH ONE-ACT PLAYS (*tranches de vie* and *rosseries*), but as his ambition grew, he ventured productions of *The Power of Darkness*, *Ghosts*, and *The Wild Duck*. In the meantime, the Théâtre-Libre had moved into new quarters on the Boulevard Strasbourg, where, on the stage of the Menus-Plaisirs, Antoine could come closer to his naturalistic conception of staging. Moreover, he had learned several lessons from the Saxe-Meiningen Troupe. Though his most trusted advisers warned him that Ibsen would be rejected by Latin minds, Antoine brushed the objections aside. The reactions to the foreign dish were varied. We have an interesting account from a German spectator who witnessed the production of *The Wild Duck* in 1891:

Like all offerings of the Théâtre-Libre, *The Wild Duck* was performed on three successive evenings, and on each of the three evenings it took effect in a different manner. On the first, at the dress rehearsal, where only writers and artists invited by the management were present, a devout solemnity prevailed, in which sympathy soon overcame surprise, and comprehension conquered doubt. On the following evening, with a very fashionable public of stock jobbers, club cretins, and drawing-room esthetes, many found the everlasting wild duck quite as funny as M. Sarcey had. But only twenty-four hours later, the second group of sub-scribers put this element in its place, when they indignantly hissed down two very timid attempts at humor on the part of very isolated rowdies, in order that they might follow the events on the stage with obviously increasing absorption.

4. STRINDBERG'S NATURALISM

When Strindberg's *Miss Julia* had its first performance at the Théâtre-Libre (January 1893), the spectators received a French translation of the author's Preface, which is perhaps the most articulate manifesto of naturalistic stagecraft:

As far as the scenery is concerned, I have borrowed from impressionistic painting its asymmetry, its quality of abruptness, and have thereby in my opinion strengthened the illusion. Because the whole room and all its contents are not shown, there is a chance to guess at things — that is, our imagination is stirred into complementing our vision. I have made a further gain in getting rid of those tiresome exits by means of doors, especially as stage doors are made of canvas and swing back and forth at the lightest touch. They are not even capable of expressing the anger of an irate *pater familias* who, on leaving his home after a poor dinner, slams the door behind him "so that it shakes the whole house." (On the stage the house sways.) I have also contented myself with a single setting, and for the double purpose of making the figures become parts of their surroundings, and of breaking with the tendency toward luxurious scenery. But having only a single setting, one may demand to have it real. Yet nothing is more difficult than to get a room that looks something like a room, although the painter can easily enough produce waterfalls and flaming volcanoes. Let it go at canvas for the walls, but we might be done with the painting of shelves and kitchen utensils on the canvas. We have so much else on the stage that is conventional, and in which we are asked to believe, that we might at least be spared the too great effort of believing in painted pans and kettles.

I have placed the rear wall and the table diagonally across the stage in order to make the actors show full face and half profile to the audience when they sit opposite each other at the table. In the opera "Aida" I noticed an oblique background, which led the eye out into unseen prospects. And it did not appear to be the result of any reaction against the fatiguing right angle.

Another novelty well needed would be the abolition of the footlights. The light from below is said to have for its purpose to make the faces of the actors look fatter. But I cannot help asking: why must all actors be fat in the face? Does not this light from below tend to wipe out the subtler lineaments in the lower part of the face, and especially around the jaws? Does it not give a false appearance to the nose and cast shadows upward over the eyes? If this be not so, another thing is certain: namely, that the eyes of the actors suffer from the light, so that the effective play of their glances is precluded. Coming from below, the light strikes the retina in places generally protected (except in sailors, who have to see the sun reflected in the water), and for this reason one observes hardly anything but a vulgar rolling of the eyes, either sideways or upwards, toward the galleries, so that nothing but the white of the eye shows. Perhaps the same cause may account for the tedious blinking of which especially the actresses are guilty. And when anybody on the stage wants to use his eyes to speak with, no other way is left him but the poor one of staring straight at the public, with whom he or she then gets into direct communication outside of the frame provided by the setting. This vicious habit has, rightly or wrongly, been named "to meet friends." Would it not be possible by means of strong side-lights (obtained by the employment of reflectors, for instance) to add to the resources already possessed by the actor? Could not his mimicry be still further strengthened by use of the greatest asset possessed by the face: the play of the eyes?

Of course, I have no illusions about getting the actors to play *for* the public and not *at* it, although such a change would be highly desirable. I dare not even dream of beholding the actor's back throughout an important scene, but I wish with all my heart that crucial scenes might not be played in the centre of the pro-scenium, like duets meant to bring forth applause. Instead, I should like to have them laid in the place indicated by the situation. Thus I ask for no revolutions, but only for a few minor modifications. To make a real room of the stage, with the fourth wall missing, and a part of the furniture placed back toward the audience, would probably produce a disturbing effect at present.

In wishing to speak of the facial make-up, I have no hope that the ladies will listen to me, as they would rather look beauti-ful than lifelike. But the actor might consider whether it be to his advantage to paint his face so that it shows some abstract type which covers it like a mask. Suppose that a man puts a markedly choleric line between the eyes, and imagine further that some re-mark demands a smile of this face fixed in a state of continuous wrath. What a horrible grimace will be the result? And how can the wrathful old man produce a frown on his false forehead, which is smooth as a billiard ball?

In modern psychological dramas, where the subtlest move-ments of the soul are to be reflected on the face rather than by gestures and noise, it would probably be well to experiment with strong sidelight on a small stage, and with unpainted faces, or at least with a minimum of make-up.

If, in addition, we might escape the visible orchestra, with its disturbing lamps and its faces turned toward the public; if we could have the seats on the main floor (the orchestra or the pit) raised so that the eyes of the spectators would be above the knees of the actors; if we could get rid of the boxes with their tittering parties of diners; if we could also have the auditorium completely darkened during the performance; and if, first and last, we could have a small stage and a small house: then a new dramatic art might rise, and the theatre might at least become an institution for the entertainment of people with culture.

5. *SEAGULL* REHEARSALS

AT THE TIME WHEN Konstantin Stanislavsky and Vladimir Ivanovich Nemirovich-Danchenko had their legendary eighteen-hour conversation at the Slavyansky Bazaar (June 21, 1897) and decided on the founding of the Moscow Art Theater, there was no playhouse in Russia where adequate performances of the plays of Chekhov and the other naturalistic playwrights could be given. In 1898, the Moscow Art Theater began to revolutionize the Russian repertoire and staging methods. When Stanislavsky directed *Czar Fedor Ivanovich,* he could get along with what he had learned from the antiquarian zeal and pictorial realism of the Saxe-Meiningen Company, but when he tackled the first Chekhov play, a period of errors and trials and — triumphs began. In the course of his Chekhovian endeavors, Stanislavsky evolved his personal technique of psychological realism through which the Chekhov plays came to life for the first time. In his autobiography, the Russian director has given us fascinating glimpses of his workshop agonies. *The Seagull* (1898) was his first Chekhovian attempt:

I have already said that after my first acquaintance with Chekhov's "Seagull" I did not understand the essence, the aroma, the beauty of his play. I wrote the *mise en scène,* and still I did not understand, although, unknown to myself, I had apparently felt its substance. When I directed the play I still did not understand it. But some of the inner threads of the play attracted me, although I did not notice the evolution that had taken place in me. . . .

Nemirovich-Danchenko and I approached the hidden riches each in his own way, Vladimir Ivanovich by the literary road and I by the road of the actor, the road of images. Vladimir Ivanovich spoke of the feeling which he sought or foresaw in the play and the roles. I could not speak of them and preferred to illustrate them. When I entered into a debate of words I was not understood and I was not persuasive. When I mounted the stage and showed what I was talking about, I became understandable and eloquent. True, often these varied approaches to the play interfered with the work and the rehearsals and caused long discussions which passed from debates of a detail to debates about principles, from the role to the play, from the play to art, from art to its fundamentals. There were even quarrels, but these quarrels were always of artistic origin and they were more useful than dangerous. They taught us that very essence which we seemed to foreknow in its general outlines, but not in concrete, systematic and clear rules. We seemed to be digging tunnels from two opposite sides towards one central point. Little by little we approached each other; now only a thin wall separated us; now the wall was broken and we could easily pass from the literary to the artistic and unite them for the general procession of the actors along the way that we had found. Once we found that inner line of the play, which we could not define in words at that time, everything became comprehensible of itself not only to the actors and the stage directors, but to the artist and the electrician and the *costumier* and all the other co-creators of the production. Along this line of inner action, which Chekhov has in a greater degree than any other dramatist, although until this time only actors are aware of it, there was formed a natural force of gravity towards the play itself, which pulled all of us in one direction. Much was correctly guessed by the interpreter of the play, Nemirovich-Danchenko, much by the stage directors, the *mise en scène*, the interpreters of the roles (with the exception of myself), the scenic artist, and the properties.

6. STILL WRESTLING WITH CHEKHOV

THE PROBLEMS to be solved were still formidable when the Moscow Art Theater did *The Three Sisters* in 1901. There were new frustrations, as we gather from the director's frank confessions:

The work of stage direction began. As was the custom I wrote a detailed *mise en scène,* — who must cross to where and why, what he must feel, what he must do, how he must look, — things that are considered strange, superfluous and harmful at the present time, but which were unavoidable and necessary at that time because of the immaturity of the actors and the swiftness of production.

We worked with spirit. We rehearsed the play, everything was clear, comprehensive, true, but the play did not live; it was hollow, it seemed tiresome and long. There was something missing. How torturing it is to seek this something without knowing what it is. All was ready, it was necessary to advertise the production, but if it were to be allowed on the stage in the form in which it had congealed, we were faced with certain failure. And then what would happen to Anton Pavlovich? And what would happen to the Theatre? Yet, nevertheless, we felt that there were elements that augured great success, that everything with the exception of that little something was present. But we could not guess what that something was. We met daily, we rehearsed to a point of despair, we parted company, and next day we would meet again and reach despair once more.

"Friends, this all happens because we are trying to be smart," some one suddenly pronounced judgment. "We are dragging the thing out, we are playing bores on the stage. We must lift the tone and play in quick tempo, as in vaudeville, without any foolishness."

We began to play quickly, that is, we tried to speak and move swiftly, and this forced us to crumple up the action, to lose the text of our speeches and to pronounce our sentences meaninglessly. The result was that the play became worse, more tiresome, from the general disorder, hurry and flying about of actors on the stage. It was hard to understand what was taking place on the stage and of what the actors were talking. The prevalent mistake of beginning stage directors and actors is that they think that the heightening of tone is the quickening of tempo; that playing in full tone is loud and quick talking and strained action. But the expressions the "heightening of tone," "full tone," "quickening of tempo" have nothing to do with the actor and all with the spectator. To heighten tone means to heighten the mood of the audience, to strengthen the interest of the spectator in the performance; to quicken tempo means to live more strongly and intensively and to live over all that one says and does on the stage. And in talking and acting so that the spectator does not understand either the words or the problems of the actors, all that the actor really accomplishes is the letting down and lowering of the interest of the spectator in the performance and the general tone of his spiritual state of being.

At one of our torturing rehearsals the actors stopped in the middle of the play, ceased to act, seeing no sense in their work and feeling that we were standing in one place and not moving forward. At such times the distrust of the actors in the stage director and in each other reaches its greatest height and threatens to cause demoralization and the disappearance of energy. This took place late at night. Two or three electric lights burned dimly. We sat in the corners, hardly able to restrain our tears, silent, in the semigloom. Our hearts beat with anxiety and the helplessness of our position. Some one was nervously scratching the bench on which he sat with his finger nails. The sound was like that of a mouse. Now again there happened to me something incomprehensible, something that had remained a secret to me ever since an analogous happening during the rehearsals of "The Snow Maiden." Apparently the sound of a scratching mouse, which must have had some meaning for me at an early period of my life, in conjunction with the darkness and the condition and the mood of the entire night, together with the helplessness and depression, reminded me of something important, deep and bright that I had experienced somewhere and at some time. A spiritual spring was touched and I at last understood the nature of the something that was missing. I had known it before also, but I had known it with my mind and not my emotions.

The men of Chekhov do not bathe, as we did at that time, in their own sorrow. Just the opposite; they, like Chekhov himself, seek life, joy, laughter, courage. The men and women of Chekhov want to live and not to die. They are active and surge to overcome the hard and unbearable impasses into which life has plunged them. It is not their fault that Russian life kills initiative and the best of beginnings and interferes with the free action and life of men and women.

ACKNOWLEDGMENTS

It is with appreciation that I wish to acknowledge the kindness of those who have granted me permission to include passages from published material:

C. W. Beaumont — Jean Georges Noverre, *Letters on Dancing and Ballet*;

G. Bell and Sons, Ltd. — *Autobiography of Goethe together with His Annals, Conversations of Goethe with Eckermann and Soret,* and *Goethe's Travels in Italy*;

Cambridge University Press — Enid Welsford, *The Court Masque*;

Chatto & Windus — Denis Diderot, *The Paradox of Acting*;

The Clarendon Press, Oxford — *The Works of Lucian of Samosata,* Apuleius, *The Metamorphoses or Golden Ass,* E. K. Chambers, *The Medieval Stage* and *The Elizabethan Stage,* Alfred W. Pollard, *English Miracle Plays, Moralities and Interludes,* M. L. Mare and W. H. Quarrell, *Lichtenberg's Visits to England,* Charles H. Herford and Percy Simpson, *Ben Jonson,* and Gerald E. Bentley, *The Jacobean and Caroline Stage*;

Columbia University Press — George C. D. Odell, *Annals of the New York Stage* and Talma, *Reflexions on the Actor's Art*;

E. P. Dutton & Co. — Giorgio Vasari, *The Lives of the Painters, Sculptors and Architects*;

Samuel French — James Robinson Planché, *Extravaganzas*;

Harcourt, Brace and Co. — J. E. Spingarn, *Goethe's Literary Essays*;

Harvard University Press — Translations in the Loeb Classical Library (*Livy, Quintilian, Cicero, Athenaeus*), Samuel M. Waxman, *Antoine and the Théâtre-Libre,* Vitruvius, *The Ten Books on Architecture,* and Leslie Hotson, *The Commonwealth and Restoration Stage*;

The Johns Hopkins Press — E. N. Hooker, *The Critical Works of John Dennis*;

The Macmillan Company — William Charles Macready, *Reminiscences* and William Winter, *Life and Art of Edwin Booth*;

The Hispanic Society of America — Hugo Albert Rennert, *The Spanish Stage in the Time of Lope de Vega*;

Houghton Mifflin Company — Joseph Quincy Adams, *Shakespearean Playhouses* and ed. *Hamlet*;

Princeton University Press — Staring B. Wells, *A Comparison between the Two Stages*;

Public Record Office, Great Britain — A. B. Hinds, *Calendar of State Papers, Venice*;

Random House, Inc. — Plutarch, *The Lives of the Noble Grecians and Romans* and George E. Duckworth, *The Complete Roman Drama*;

Routledge and Kegan Paul, Ltd. — Henry Morley, *Journal of a London Playgoer*;

Charles Scribner's Sons — Preface to August Strindberg's *Miss Julia* and George C. D. Odell, *Shakespeare from Betterton to Irving*;

Theatre Arts Books — Constantin Stanislavsky, *My Life in Art*;

University of Washington Press — Professor Edward Noble Stone's translation of the *Adam Play*;

Yale University Press — Roswell Gray Ham, *Otway and Lee*.

I also wish to thank Mr. Henry Loverich for permission to reprint some pages from David Belasco's *The Theater through Its Stage Door*. Moreover, thanks are due to the British Museum and to Mrs. Margaret McNaught for permission to include the Covent Garden Inventory originally published in H. S. Wyndham's *The Annals of Covent Garden*; to Mr. Howard C. Stone for permitting me to use the late Professor Noble Stone's translation of the *Adam* stage directions; to the editors of *The New Statesman and Nation* for giving their consent to the inclusion of some *Athenaeum* reviews; to Mr. James R. Spencer for permission to reprint the review of Henry Irving's *Macbeth* from the *Liverpool Daily Post*; and to the Philadelphia *Evening Bulletin* and the *Brooklyn Eagle*.

I am indebted to the following museums, libraries, collections, and publishing houses for permission to reproduce pictorial material: The Art Institute of Chicago, the Victoria and Albert Museum in London, the Landesmuseum in Hanover, the Stadtverwaltung of Cologne, the Theatermuseum in Munich, the Goethe-Nationalmuseum in Weimar, the Nationalmuseum in Stockholm, and the Museum of Modern Art in New York; the Oesterreichische Nationalbibliothek in Vienna, the Biblioteca Palatina in Parma, the Stadtbibliothek Vadiana in St. Gall, and the Bibliothèque et Musée le l'Opéra in Paris; the Theatre Collection of the New York Public Library where Mrs. Elizabeth P. Barrett was especially helpful in locating prints, the Yale Theatrical Prints Collection, the Harvard Theatre Collection, the New York Historical Society, the William Seymour Theatre Collection of Princeton University, the Trustees of the Chatsworth Settlement, and the Gabinetto disegni e stampe degli Uffizi in Florence; publishers Alfred A. Knopf, Inc., New York, W. Kohlhammer, Stuttgart, and the Presses Universitaires de France in Paris.

And finally I wish to thank Dr. John Cranford Adams of Hofstra College, Professor Erwin Goodenough of Yale University, and Mr. M. Logothetis, who kindly gave me permission to reproduce photographs in their possesion.

REFERENCES

I. ANTIQUITY

1. Plutarch, *The Lives of the Noble Grecians and Romans*, trans. John Dryden and Arthur Hugh Clough (New York: Random House, n.d.), p. 115.
2. "Bios Aischylou," trans. John J. Walsh, S.J., from *Aeschyli Tragoediae*, ed. Ulrich von Wilamowitz-Moellendorff (Berlin, 1914), Secs. 2-16.
3. *Athenaeus, The Deipnosophists*, trans. Charles Barton Gulick (Cambridge, Mass.: Harvard University Press, 1927), I (The Loeb Classical Library), 93-97.
4. *Ibid.*, p. 91.
5. Plutarch, "De Audiendo," in *Plutarch's Miscellanies and Essays*, ed. William W. Goodwin (Boston: Little, Brown and Co., 1889), I, 458.
6. Iulius Pollux, "Extracts Concerning the Greek Theatre and Masks," in *Aristotle's Poetics; or, Discourses Concerning Tragic and Epic Imitation* (London, 1775) pp. 7-29 (Appendix).
7. *The Works of Lucian of Samosata*, trans. H. W. Fowler and F. G. Fowler (Oxford: The Clarendon Press, 1905), II, 247-248.
8. *Livy*, trans. B. O. Foster (Cambridge, Mass.: Harvard University Press, 1924), III (The Loeb Classical Library), 359-365.
9. *Quintilian, The Institutio Oratoria*, trans. H. E. Butler (Cambridge, Mass.: Harvard University Press, 1936), IV (The Loeb Classical Library), 345-347.
10. Prologue to Plautus' *Poenulus*, trans. George E. Duckworth, in *The Complete Roman Drama* (New York: Random House, 1942), I, 727-728.
11. Gaius Plinius Secundus, *Naturalis Historia*, Bk. XXXVI, Chap. 24.
12. *Ibid.*
13. Vitruvius, *The Ten Books on Architecture*, trans. Morris Hicky Morgan (Cambridge, Mass.: Harvard University Press, 1926), pp. 146-150.
14. *Cicero, the Letters to His Friends*, trans. W. Glynn Williams (Cambridge, Mass.: Harvard University Press, 1928), II (The Loeb Classical Library), 5-7.
15. *The Works of Lucian of Samosata*, ed. cit., III, 249-263.
16. Apuleius of Madaura, *The Metamorphoses or Golden Ass*, trans. H. E. Butler (Oxford: The Clarendon Press, 1910), II, 119-123.

II. THE MIDDLE AGES

1. Translated from the original Latin in E. K. Chambers, *The Medieval Stage* (Oxford: The Clarendon Press, 1903), II, 14-15.
2. Giorgio Vasari, *The Lives of the Painters, Sculptors and Architects*, trans. A. B. Hinds (New York: E. P. Dutton & Co., 1927), I (Everyman's Library No. 784), 295-297.
3. *Ibid.*, II (Everyman's Library No. 785), 56-57.

4. Edward Noble Stone, trans., *Adam, a Religious Play of the Twelfth Century,* University of Washington Publications in Language and Literature, IV (Seattle, 1926). 159, 169, 170, 176, 178-179.
5. H. d'Outreman, *Histoire de la ville et comté de Valenciennes* (Douai, 1639), p. 396.
6. Alfred W. Pollard, ed., *English Miracle Plays, Moralities and Interludes* (Oxford: The Clarendon Press, 1890), pp. xxv-xxvi.
7. Richard Carew, *Survey of Cornwall* (London, 1811), p. 192.

III. THE GOLDEN AGE OF SPAIN

1. Quoted and translated by Hugo Albert Rennert, *The Spanish Stage in the Time of Lope de Vega* (New York: The Hispanic Society of America, 1909), pp. 151-154.
2. Quoted *ibid.,*, pp. 336-338.
3. Quoted *ibid.,* pp. 334-336.
4. Quoted in A. F. von Schack, *Geschichte der dramatischen Literatur und Kunst in Spanien* (Frankfort, 1854), II, 542-543.
5. Countess d'Aulnoy, *The Lady's Travels into Spain* (London, 1808), II, 20-21.
6. *Ibid.,* II, 52-55.
7. Madame de Motteville, *Memoirs for the History of Anne of Austria* (London, 1725), V, 42-43.

IV. ITALIAN RENAISSANCE

1. Quoted in Alessandro d'Ancona, *Origini del teatro italiano* (Torino, 1891), II, 102-103.
2. Giorgio Vasari, *The Lives of the Painters, Sculptors and Architects,* trans. A. B. Hinds (New York: E. P. Dutton & Co., 1927), II (Everyman's Library No. 785), 297.
3. *Ibid.,* III (Everyman's Library No. 786), 296-297.
4. Sebastian Serly (Serlio), *The First Book of Architecture . . .* (London, 1611), Bk. II, Chap. 3, Fol. 25-26.
5. *Due lettere descrittive l'una dell' ingresso a Vicenza della Imperatrice Maria d'Austria nell' anno MDLXXXI l'altra della recita nel Teatro Olimpico dell' Edippo di Sofocle nel MDLXXXV* (Padua, 1830), pp. 25-31.
6. With the exception of the chapters on lighting, which are in the First Book, the chapters have been selected and translated from the Second Book of Nicola Sabbattini, *Pratica di fabricar scene e machine ne' teatri* (Ravenna, 1638).
7. MS. Biblioteca Palatina, Parma (1556 ?), Fol. 69-70, 71-74, 76-79, 90-95, trans. Salvatore J. Castiglione.

V. TUDOR AND STUART PERIODS

1. Quoted in Edmund K. Chambers, *The Elizabethan Stage* (Oxford: The Clarendon Press, 1923), IV, 316-317.
2. Quoted *ibid.,* IV, 322.
3. Translated from the original Latin in Joseph Quincy Adams, *Shakespearean Playhouses* (Boston: Houghton Mifflin Co., 1917), pp. 167-168.
4. Translated from the German original in Chambers, *op. cit.,* II, 365.
5. Quoted *ibid.,* II, 436-437.
6. M. W. Sampson has drawn attention to this passage in *Modern Language Notes,* June, 1915.
7. Henry Wotton, *Reliquiae Wottonianae* (London, 1671), p. 425.
8. a) *Hamlet,* III, ii, 1-47. Quoted after Joseph Quincy Adams, ed., *Hamlet* (Boston: Houghton Mifflin Co., 1929), pp. 81-83.

b) Thomas Heywood, *An Apology for Actors*, Shakespeare Society Publications, No. III (London, 1841), pp. 28-30.

c) *Ibid.*, pp. 43-44.

d) John Webster (?), quoted in Chambers, *op. cit.*, IV, 257-258.

e) Edmund Gayton, *Pleasant Notes upon Don Quichote* (London, 1654), p. 144.

f) "Epitaph on Burbage" (1619), quoted in Chambers, *op cit.*, II, 309.

g) Richard Flecknoe, *A Short Discourse of the English Stage* (1664), quoted *ibid.*, IV, 370.

9. a) Phillip Stubbes, *The Anatomie of Abuses* (1583), quoted *ibid.*, IV, 223-224.

b) Stephen Gosson, *The School of Abuse* (1579), ed. E. Arber (London, 1868), English Reprints, III, 35.

c) Stephen Gosson, *Playes Confuted in fiue Actions* (1582), in William C. Hazlitt, ed., *The English Drama and Stage* (London, 1869), p. 215.

d) Henry Chettle, *Kind-Harts Dreame* (1592), in Clement M. Ingleby, ed., *Shakspere Allusion-Books* (London, 1874), New Shakspere Society Publications, Ser. IV, No. 1, Part I, 65-66.

e) Gayton, *op. cit.*, pp. 271-272.

10. Great Britain, Public Record Office, *Calendar of State Papers, Venice and Northern Italy*, ed. A. B. Hinds (London, 1909), XV, 67-68.

11. Thomas Dekker, *The Guls Horne-Booke* (1609), Chap. VI, as quoted in Chambers, *op cit.*, IV, 365-369.

12. Henry Fitzgeffrey, *Certain Elegies, Done by Sundrie Excellent Wits* (London, 1620). The stanzas are taken from "The Third Booke of Humours: Intituled Notes from Black-Friars."

13. Quoted in Enid Welsford, *The Court Masque* (Cambridge, Eng.: Cambridge University Press, 1927), pp. 250-251.

14. Charles H. Herford and Percy Simpson, eds., *Ben Jonson* (Oxford: The Clarendon Press, 1925-1947), VII, 169-172.

15. *Ibid.*, VII, 229-232.

16. Quoted in Welsford, *op. cit.*, p. 179.

17. Great Britain, Public Record Office, *op. cit.*, XV, 110-112.

18. *Ibid.*, XV, 112-114.

19. Quoted in Welsford, *op. cit.*, pp. 251-253.

20. Francis Kirkman, *The Wits, or Sport upon Sport* (1672), quoted in Leslie Hotson, *The Commonwealth and Restoration Stage* (Cambridge, Mass.: Harvard University Press, 1928), p. 48.

21. Reprinted in J. P. Collier, *The Works of Shakespeare* (London, 1844), I, ccxli.

22. [James Wright], *Historia Histrionica* (London, 1699) as reprinted in Gerald Eades Bentley, *The Jacobean and Caroline Stage* (Oxford: The Clarendon Press, 1941), II, 691-696.

VI. THE AGE OF LOUIS XIV

1. The French description (Rouen, 1650) of the *Andromède* settings is available in S. Wilma Holsboer, *L'histoire de la mise en scène dans le théâtre français de 1600 à 1657* (Paris, 1933), pp. 151-154.

2. F. H. d'Aubignac, *The Whole Art of the Stage* (London, 1657), Bk. III, pp. 93-99.

3. *Ibid.*, Bk. IV, pp. 166-176.

4. Samuel Chappuzeau, *Le théâtre français* (1674, reprint Brussels, 1867), pp. 54-61 (with omissions).

5. *Ibid.*, pp. 61-62.

6. *Ibid.*, pp. 114-115.

7. *Ibid.*, pp. 118-121.

8. C. F. Ménestrier, *Des représentations en musique anciennes et modernes* (Paris, 1684), pp. 171-173.

9. C. F. Ménestrier *Des ballets anciens et modernes* (Paris, 1682), pp. 250-257. This passage trans. by John J. Walsh, S.J.
10. *The Works of Molière* (London, 1755), III, 291-293.
11. *Ibid.*, VIII, 191-195.
12. Donneau de Visé, *Zélinde, ou La veritable critique de l'eschole des femmes*, reprinted by the bibliophile, Jacob, Collection Molièresque (Genève, 1868), p. 7.
13. *The Works of Molière, ed. cit.*, III, 355-357, 363-373.

VII. THE RESTORATION THEATER

1. François Brunet, *Voyage d'Angleterre* (1676), quoted in the original French in Leslie Hotson, *The Commonwealth and Restoration Stage* (Cambridge, Mass.: Harvard University Press, 1928), pp. 234-235.
2. Pepys, *Diary,* May 8, 1663.
3. *Ibid.,* March 19, 1666.
4. *Travels of Cosmo the Third Grand Duke of Tuscany through England* (1669), trans. from the Italian Manuscript in the Laurentian Library at Florence (London, 1821), pp. 190-191.
5. Quoted in George C. D. Odell, *Shakespeare from Betterton to Irving* (New York: Charles Scribner's Sons, 1920), I, 10.
6. *An Apology for the Life of Mr. Colley Cibber* (London, 1740), pp. 81-82.
7. *Ibid.,* pp. 339-340.
8. *Misson's Memoirs and Observations in His Travels over England* (London, 1719), pp. 219-220.
9. Pepys, *op. cit.,* December 21, 1668.
10. *Ibid.,* February 1, 1664.
11. *Ibid.,* February 18, 1667.
12. Cibber, *op. cit.,* p. 219.
13. In the Quarto of *Sir Courtly Nice* (1685), quoted in Montague Summers, *The Restoration Theatre* (London: Kegan Paul, Trench, Trubner & Co., 1934), p. 89.
14. Quoted *ibid.,* pp. 88-89.
15. Thomas Shadwell, *A True Widow* (Dorset Garden, 1678), IV, i.
16. Sam Vincent, *The Young Gallant's Academy* (1674), Chap. V, as quoted in Summers, *op. cit.,* pp. 322-323.
17. Anthony Aston, *A Brief Supplement to Colley Cibber, Esq; His Lives of the Late Famous Actors and Actresses* (London, 1748), pp. 75-77.
18. Cibber, *op. cit.,* pp. 84-92.
19. a) *The Tatler,* No. 167 (May 4, 1710).
    b) Anonymous, *The Laureat or, the Right Side of Colley Cibber, Esq.* (London, 1740).
20. Thomas Betterton [William Oldys], *The History of the English Stage* (London, 1741), pp. 74-94.
21. a) Cibber, *op. cit.,* pp. 131-134.
    b) Aston, *op. cit.,* pp. 78-80.
22. a) Cibber, *op. cit.,* pp. 141-143.
    b) Aston, *op. cit.,* pp. 81-82.
23. Staring B. Wells, ed., *A Comparison between the Two Stages* (Princeton: Princeton University Press, 1942), pp. 7-10.
24. Quoted in Hotson, *op. cit.,* pp. 303-304.
25. a) Cibber, *op. cit.,* pp. 254-255.
    b) *A Comparison . . . , ed. cit.,* pp. 27-29.
26. Cibber, *op. cit.,* pp. 185-187.
27. John Downes, *Roscius Anglicanus, or An Historical Review of the Stage* (London, 1708), pp. 22, 24, 27-28, 29, 33.
28. Betterton-Oldys, *op. cit.,* pp. 21-22.

29. Anonymous satire, *The Playhouse*, quoted in Roswell Gray Ham, *Otway and Lee* (New Haven: Yale University Press, 1931), pp. 30-31.
30. *The Spectator*, No. 42 (April 18, 1711).
31. Cibber, *op. cit.*, pp. 257-260.
32. Tom Brown, "Amusements Serious and Comical, Calculated for the Meridian of London," in *Works* (London, 1709), III, 40-45.
33. John Dennis, "A Large Account of the Taste in Poetry, and the Causes of the Degeneracy of It," as a preface to *The Comical Gallant*, in *The Critical Works*, ed. E. N. Hooker (Baltimore: The Johns Hopkins Press, 1939), I, 290-294.

VIII. VENETIAN COMEDY

1. Italian original of Peruzzi's treatise in Enzo Petraccone, ed., *La commedia dell' arte, storia, tecnica, scenari* (Napoli, 1927), pp. 190, 193-196, trans. Salvatore J. Castiglione.
2. *Coryat's Crudities, Reprinted from the Edition of 1611* (London, 1776), II, 16-18.
3. *Ibid.*, II, 50-54 (with omissions).
4. A. T. Limojon de St. Didier, *The City and Republick of Venice* (London, 1699), Part III, pp. 55-67 (with omissions).
5. Edward Wright, *Some Observations Made in Travelling through France, Italy, etc.* (London, 1730), I, 84-85.
6. Lewis (Luigi) Riccoboni, *An Historical and Critical Account of the Theatres in Europe* (London, 1741), pp. 55-58.
7. *Ibid.*, pp. 75-77 (with omissions).
8. *Mercure Galant*, March 1683, pp. 251-255.
9. Carlo Goldoni, *Memoirs*, trans. John Black (London, 1814), II, 53-57.
10. *Ibid.*, I, 271-275.
11. *Ibid.*, I, 280-281.
12. *Ibid.*, I, 291-292.
13. *Ibid.*, II, 94-95.

IX. EIGHTEENTH-CENTURY FRANCE

1. Lewis (Luigi) Riccoboni, *An Historical and Critical Account of the Theatres in Europe* (London, 1741), pp. 144-149.
2. Charles Collé, *Journal et Mémoires* (Paris, 1868), I, 139-140 (March, 1750).
3. *Ibid.*, p. 140.
4. "Portrait de Mlle. Dumesnil," in *Mémoires de Mlle. Clairon* (Paris, 1822), pp. 288-291.
5. Collé, *op. cit.*, I, 141.
6. *Ibid.*, I, 142.
7. Jean François Marmontel, *Memoirs, Written by Himself* (London, 1805), II, 43-49.
8. "The Several Revolutions Which Have Happened in the Tragic Art," in *The Works of M. de Voltaire* (London, 1770), XXV, 168-169.
9. Denis Diderot, *The Paradox of Acting*, trans. Walter Herries Pollock (London: Chatto & Windus, 1883), pp. 9-12 (with omissions).
10. Abraham Fleury, *The French Stage and the French People*, ed. Th. Hook (London, 1841), I, 59-65.
11. "De la poésie dramatique," in *Diderot's Writings on the Theatre*, ed. F. C. Green (Cambridge, Eng.: Cambridge University Press, 1936), pp. 191-192.
12. *Mémoires de Mlle. Clairon*, pp. 261-263.
13. Hippolyte Clairon, *Memoirs* (London, 1800), I, 88-96.

14. C. S. Favart, *Mémoires et correspondance littéraires, dramatiques et anec-dotiques* (Paris, 1808), I, lxxvii-lxxviii.
15. Marmontel, *op. cit.*, I, 394-396.
16. *Mémoires de Mlle. Clairon*, pp. 242-245.
17. François Joseph Talma, *Reflexions on the Actor's Art* (New York: Publications of the Dramatic Museum of Columbia University, 1915), Ser. II, Paper 4, 28-34.
18. Francesco Algarotti, *An Essay on the Opera* (London, 1767), pp. 72-76.
19. *Mercure de France*, March 1728, pp. 568-569.
20. *Ibid.*, January 1730, pp. 147-150.
21. Algarotti, *op. cit.*, p. 86.
22. *l'Avant-Coureur*, April 21, 1760.
23. Collé, *op. cit.*, II, 33-34.
24. "Lettre de Lekain à M. de - - - ," (January 10, 1750) in *Mémoires de Lekain, précédés de réflexions sur cet acteur et sur l'art théâtral par M. Talma* (Paris, 1825), pp. 380-382.
25. Fleury, *op. cit.*, I, 16-19.
26. Favart, *op. cit.*, I, 122-123.
27. *The Works of M. de Voltaire*, ed. *cit.*, XIII, 28-29.
28. Diderot, "De la poésie dramatique," in *ed. cit.*, pp. 188-191.
29. Pierre Augustin Caron de Beaumarchais, *Eugénie*, pantomimic interludes introducing Acts II - V.
30. Jean Georges Noverre, *Letters on Dancing and Ballets*, trans. Cyril W. Beaumont (London: C. W. Beaumont, 1930), pp. 29-30.
31. *Ibid.*, pp. 72-76.
32. "Réponse à la lettre de Mme. Riccoboni," in *Diderot's Writings on the Theatre*, ed. *cit.*, p. 216.
33. L. S. Mercier, *Tableaux de Paris* (Amsterdam, 1783), VII, 95.
34. *Ibid.*, II, 302-306.
35. Fleury, *op. cit.*, I, 291-294.

X. EIGHTEENTH-CENTURY ENGLAND

1. *An Apology for the Life of Mr. Colley Cibber* (London, 1740), pp. 441-442.
2. *Ibid.*, pp. 361-362.
3. Thomas Davies, *Memoirs of the Life of David Garrick* (London, 1808), I, 128-131.
4. John Jackson, *The History of the Scottish Stage* (Edinburgh, 1793), pp. 365-368.
5. John Thurmond, *Harlequin Doctor Faustus: with the Masque of the Deities* (London, 1724), reprinted in Arthur Diebler, "Faust- und Wagnerpantomimen in England," *Anglia*, VII, 341-354.
6. Tate Wilkinson, *Memoirs of His Own Life* (York, 1790), IV, 91-92.
7. Henry Saxe Wyndham, *The Annals of Covent Garden Theatre* (London: Chatto & Windus, 1906), II, 309-313. The manuscript of the Inventory is in the British Museum, Addl.MS. 12,201, F. 30.
8. The Smollett passage is quoted in Edward Abbott Parry, *Charles Macklin* (London: Kegan Paul, Trench, Trubner & Co., 1891), pp. 42-43.
9. *The Dramatic Censor*, quoted *ibid.*, p. 67.
10. *Lichtenberg's Visits to England as Described in His Letters and Diaries*, trans. Margaret L. Mare and W. H. Quarrell (Oxford: The Clarendon Press, 1938), p. 40.
11. a) [John Hill], *The Actor* (London, 1750), pp. 194-195.
    b) [John Hill], *The Actor* (London, 1755), pp. 239-240.
12. Davies, *op. cit.*, I, 39-41.
13. Richard Cumberland, *Memoirs* (London, 1806), pp. 59-60.

14. *Lichtenberg's Visits . . . , ed. cit.,* pp. 6-7.
15. *Ibid.,* pp. 9-11.
16. *Ibid.,* pp. 25-27, 17-19.
17. James Boaden, *Memoirs of the Life of John Philip Kemble* (London, 1825), I, 440-443.
18. Davies, *op. cit.,* I, 144-145.
19. *Ibid.,* I, 148-149.
20. Thomas Davies, *Dramatic Miscellanies* (London, 1783), II, 64-69.
21. Wilkinson, *op. cit.,* IV, 108-116.
22. Davies, *Memoirs . . . Garrick,* I, 375-378.
23. *An Apology for the Life of George Anne Bellamy* (London, 1785), VI, 21.
24. *Ibid.,* I, 130-136 and II, 205-209.
25. Wilkinson, *op. cit.,* IV, 86-91.
26. *The Works of the Late Aaron Hill* (London, 1753), I, 89-91 (Letter dated October 28, 1731).
27. *The Prompter,* January 24, 1735.
28. [John Hill], *The Actor* (London, 1750), pp. 222-229.
29. Quoted in Parry, *op. cit.,* p. 161.
30. William Cooke, *Memoirs of Charles Macklin* (London, 1806), pp. 283-284.
31. a) *Recollections of the Life of John O'Keeffe* (London, 1826), II, 113-114.
    b) *The London Magazine,* November 1774, pp. 518-519; January 1779, p. 31.
32. *Recollections of . . . O'Keeffe,* II, 39.
33. George Saunders, *A Treatise on Theatres* (London, 1790), pp. 81-84.
34. Boaden, *op. cit.,* II, 68-70.
35. *Ibid.,* II, 132.
36. a) *Ibid.,* II, 41-42.
    b) Cumberland, *op. cit.,* pp. 57-58 (Supplement).
37. W. C. Oulton, *The History of the Theatres of London* (London, 1796), II, 136-137.
38. Boaden, *op. cit.,* II, 101-103.
39. Oulton, *op. cit.,* II, 139-140.
40. Boaden, *op. cit.,* I, 92, 104.
41. *Ibid.,* II, 2-3.
42. James Boaden, *Memoirs of Mrs. Siddons* (London, 1827), II, 288-292.
43. Thomas Campbell, *Life of Mrs. Siddons* (London, 1834), I, 244-245.
44. William Charles Macready, *Reminiscences,* ed. Sir Frederick Pollock (New York: Macmillan Co., 1875), pp. 42-44.
45. Thomas Holcroft in *The Theatrical Recorder,* I (1805), 345-349.

XI. WEIMAR CLASSICISM

1. *Ephemeriden der Litteratur und des Theaters,* Berlin, I (1785), 20, 316-318.
2. Goethe to Eckermann, March 22, 1825. The quotations from Goethe's conversations with Eckermann are given in the John Oxenford translation, *Conversations of Goethe with Eckermann and Soret* (London: George Bell and Sons, 1874).
3. Goethe to Eckermann, April 14, 1825.
4. "Regeln für Schauspieler" in *Goethes sämtliche Werke* (Stuttgart and Berlin, n.d.), XXXVI, 205-214.
5. "Women's Parts Played by Men in the Roman Theatre" in *Goethe's Travels in Italy,* trans. Charles Nisbeth (London: George Bell and Sons, 1883), pp. 569-570.
6. Goethe, *Autobiography,* trans. John Oxenford, in *Autobiography of Goethe together with His Annals* (London: George Bell and Sons, 1894), I, 422.
7. "On Truth and Probability in Works of Art" in *Goethe's Literary Essays,* ed. J. E. Spingarn (New York: Harcourt, Brace & Co., 1921), pp. 51-58.

8. Goethe's *Annals,* trans. Charles Nisbeth, in *ed. cit.,* II, 422-423.
9. Goethe to Eckermann, February 17, 1830.
10. "On the Use of the Chorus in Tragedy," trans. A. Lodge, in *The Works of Frederick Schiller* (London: Bell & Daldy, 1871), III, 443.

XII.   NINETEENTH-CENTURY ENGLAND

1. James Boaden, *Memoirs of the Life of John Philip Kemble* (London, 1825), II, 488-489.
2. W. C. Oulton, *A History of the Theatres of London* (London, 1818), I, 228-231.
3. Quoted in George C. D. Odell, *Shakespeare from Betterton to Irving* (New York: Charles Scribner's Sons, 1920), II, 12-13.
4. William Charles Macready, *Reminiscences,* ed. Sir Frederick Pollock (New York: Macmillan Co., 1875), pp. 101-102.
5. Leigh Hunt in *The Tatler,* No. 278 (July 25, 1831).
6. William Hazlitt, *A View of the English Stage* (London, 1818), pp. 7-9, 11-12, 51-56.
7. James Robinson Planché, *Recollections and Reflections* (London: Sampson Low, Marston & Co., 1901), pp. 35-39.
8. *The Extravaganzas of J. R. Planché* (London: S. French, 1879), I, 286-288.
9. Charles Dickens, ed., *The Life of Charles James Mathews Chiefly Autobiographical* (London: Macmillan & Co., 1879), II, 76.
10. *John Bull,* March 19, 1838.
11. Macready, *op. cit.,* pp. 109-110.
12. *Ibid.,* p. 180.
13. Leigh Hunt in *The Tatler,* No. 165 (March 15, 1831).
14. Hermann Pückler-Muskau, *Tour in England, Ireland, and France, in the Years 1826, 1827, 1828, and 1829* (Philadelphia, 1833), pp. 249-253.
15. *Ibid.,* pp. 51-52.
16. Henry Morley, *Journal of a London Playgoer* (London: George Routledge & Sons, 1891), pp. 129-130.
17. *Ibid.,* pp. 57-58.
18. *Ibid.,* pp. 83-84.
19. *Shakespeare's Tragedy of Macbeth, . . . Arranged for Representation at the Princess's Theatre, with Historical and Explanatory Notes by Charles Kean* (London, n. d. [1853]), Preface, pp. v-ix.
20. John William Cole, *The Life and Theatrical Times of Charles Kean* (London: Richard Bentley, 1860), II, 197-198, 209-210.
21. Morley, *op. cit.,* pp. 133-135.
22. Cole, *op. cit.,* II, 379-382.
23. T. W. Robertson, "Theatrical Types" in *Illustrated Times,* London, January 9, June 4, August 6, 1864.
24. *The Athenaeum,* No. 2797 (June 4, 1881), p. 762, No. 2798 (June 11, 1881), p. 796, No. 2799 (June 18, 1881), p. 826.
25. *Daily Post,* Liverpool, December 31, 1888.

XIII.   THE AMERICAN THEATER

1. William Dunlap, *History of the American Theatre* (New York, 1832), pp. 4-6.
2. Quoted in George C. D. Odell, *Annals of the New York Stage* (New York: Columbia University Press, 1927), I, 58-59.
3. Dunlap, *op. cit.,* pp. 15-17.
4. Alexander Graydon, *Memoirs of a Life Chiefly Passed in Pennsylvania* (Edinburgh, 1822), pp. 82-84.
5. Dunlap, *op. cit..* p. 28.

6. *The Daily Advertiser,* April 4, 1787, quoted in Odell, *op. cit.,* I, 254.
7. Dunlap, *op. cit.,* p. 346.
8. Quoted *ibid.,* pp. 162-163.
9. *Minerva,* January 20, 1795, quoted in Odell, *op. cit.,* I, 380-381.
10. Joseph N. Ireland, *Records of the New York Stage from 1750 to 1860* (New York, 1866), I, 172-173.
11. *The Daily Advertiser,* January 31, 1798; *Commercial Advertiser,* January 31, 1798, quoted in Odell, *op. cit.,* II, 7.
12. Dunlap, *op. cit.,* p. 248.
13. Washington Irving, *Letters of Jonathan Oldstyle,* No. IV (December 3, 1802).
14. Dunlap, *op. cit.,* pp. 210-211.
15. Irving, *op. cit.,* No. III (December 1, 1802).
16. *Commercial Advertiser,* November 18, December 3, 1799, quoted in Odell, *op. cit.,* II, 73-75.
17. Dunlap, *op. cit.,* pp. 343-344.
18. Ireland, *op. cit.,* I, 380-382.
19. Anna Cora Mowatt, *Autobiography of an Actress* (Boston, 1854), pp. 203-206.
20. William B. Wood, *Personal Recollections of the Stage* (Philadelphia, 1855), pp. 391-392.
21. *Brooklyn Eagle,* December 26, 1846.
22. John Coleman, *Players and Playwrights I Have Known* (Philadelphia: Gebbie & Co., 1890), I, 31-33.
23. Wood, *op. cit.,* pp. 440-456.
24. *Evening Bulletin,* Philadelphia, September 21, 1869.
25. Clara Morris, *Life on the Stage* (New York: McClure, Phillips & Co., 1902), pp. 326-329.
26. William Winter, *Life and Art of Edwin Booth* (New York: Macmillan Co., 1893), pp. 151-153.
27. *Ibid.,* pp. 48-51.
28. David Belasco, *The Theatre through Its Stage Door* (New York: Harper & Brothers, 1919), pp. 53-61.

XIV. EUROPEAN NATURALISM

1 Quoted in Samuel M. Waxman, *Antoine and the Théâtre-Libre* (Cambridge, Mass.: Harvard University Press, 1926), pp. 72-73.
2. Quoted in Adolphe Thalasso, *Le Théâtre-Libre* (Paris, 1909), pp. 165-168.
3. S. Feldmann in *Freie Bühne für modernes Leben* (Berlin, 1891), II, 477.
4. Preface to *Miss Julia,* trans. Edwin Björkmann, in *Plays by August Strindberg* (New York: Charles Scribner's Sons, 1912), pp. 23-26.
5. Constantin Stanislavsky, *My Life in Art,* trans. J. J. Robbins (New York: Theatre Arts Books, 1948. Copyright 1924 by Little, Brown & Co. Copyright 1948 by Elizabeth Reynolds Hapgood for the Stanislavsky Estate), pp. 352-353.
6. *Ibid.,* pp. 371-374.

INDEX

A CATALOG OF SELECTED DOVER
BOOKS IN ALL FIELDS OF INTEREST

DRAWINGS OF REMBRANDT, edited by Seymour Slive. Updated Lippmann, Hofstede de Groot edition, with definitive scholarly apparatus. All portraits, biblical sketches, landscapes, nudes. Oriental figures, classical studies, together with selection of work by followers. 550 illustrations. Total of 630pp. 9⅛ × 12¼.
21485-0, 21486-9 Pa., Two-vol. set $25.00

GHOST AND HORROR STORIES OF AMBROSE BIERCE, Ambrose Bierce. 24 tales vividly imagined, strangely prophetic, and decades ahead of their time in technical skill: "The Damned Thing," "An Inhabitant of Carcosa," "The Eyes of the Panther," "Moxon's Master," and 20 more. 199pp. 5⅜ × 8½. 20767-6 Pa. $3.95

ETHICAL WRITINGS OF MAIMONIDES, Maimonides. Most significant ethical works of great medieval sage, newly translated for utmost precision, readability. Laws Concerning Character Traits, Eight Chapters, more. 192pp. 5⅜ × 8½.
24522-5 Pa. $4.50

THE EXPLORATION OF THE COLORADO RIVER AND ITS CANYONS, J. W. Powell. Full text of Powell's 1,000-mile expedition down the fabled Colorado in 1869. Superb account of terrain, geology, vegetation, Indians, famine, mutiny, treacherous rapids, mighty canyons, during exploration of last unknown part of continental U.S. 400pp. 5⅜ × 8½. 20094-9 Pa. $6.95

HISTORY OF PHILOSOPHY, Julián Marías. Clearest one-volume history on the market. Every major philosopher and dozens of others, to Existentialism and later. 505pp. 5⅜ × 8½. 21739-6 Pa. $8.50

ALL ABOUT LIGHTNING, Martin A. Uman. Highly readable non-technical survey of nature and causes of lightning, thunderstorms, ball lightning, St. Elmo's Fire, much more. Illustrated. 192pp. 5⅜ × 8½. 25237-X Pa. $5.95

SAILING ALONE AROUND THE WORLD, Captain Joshua Slocum. First man to sail around the world, alone, in small boat. One of great feats of seamanship told in delightful manner. 67 illustrations. 294pp. 5⅜ × 8½. 20326-3 Pa. $4.95

LETTERS AND NOTES ON THE MANNERS, CUSTOMS AND CONDI-TIONS OF THE NORTH AMERICAN INDIANS, George Catlin. Classic account of life among Plains Indians: ceremonies, hunt, warfare, etc. 312 plates. 572pp. of text. 6⅛ × 9¼. 22118-0, 22119-9 Pa. Two-vol. set $15.90

ALASKA: The Harriman Expedition, 1899, John Burroughs, John Muir, et al. Informative, engrossing accounts of two-month, 9,000-mile expedition. Native peoples, wildlife, forests, geography, salmon industry, glaciers, more. Profusely illustrated. 240 black-and-white line drawings. 124 black-and-white photographs. 3 maps. Index. 576pp. 5⅜ × 8½. 25109-8 Pa. $11.95

THE BOOK OF BEASTS: Being a Translation from a Latin Bestiary of the Twelfth Century, T. H. White. Wonderful catalog real and fanciful beasts: manticore, griffin, phoenix, amphivius, jaculus, many more. White's witty erudite commentary on scientific, historical aspects. Fascinating glimpse of medieval mind. Illustrated. 296pp. 5⅜ × 8¼. (Available in U.S. only) 24609-4 Pa. $5.95

FRANK LLOYD WRIGHT: ARCHITECTURE AND NATURE With 160 Illustrations, Donald Hoffmann. Profusely illustrated study of influence of nature—especially prairie—on Wright's designs for Fallingwater, Robie House, Guggenheim Museum, other masterpieces. 96pp. 9¼ × 10¾. 25098-9 Pa. $7.95

FRANK LLOYD WRIGHT'S FALLINGWATER, Donald Hoffmann. Wright's famous waterfall house: planning and construction of organic idea. History of site, owners, Wright's personal involvement. Photographs of various stages of building. Preface by Edgar Kaufmann, Jr. 100 illustrations. 112pp. 9¼ × 10. 23671-4 Pa. $7.95

YEARS WITH FRANK LLOYD WRIGHT: Apprentice to Genius, Edgar Tafel. Insightful memoir by a former apprentice presents a revealing portrait of Wright the man, the inspired teacher, the greatest American architect. 372 black-and-white illustrations. Preface. Index. vi + 228pp. 8¼ × 11. 24801-1 Pa. $9.95

THE STORY OF KING ARTHUR AND HIS KNIGHTS, Howard Pyle. Enchanting version of King Arthur fable has delighted generations with imaginative narratives of exciting adventures and unforgettable illustrations by the author. 41 illustrations. xviii + 313pp. 6⅛ × 9¼. 21445-1 Pa. $5.95

THE GODS OF THE EGYPTIANS, E. A. Wallis Budge. Thorough coverage of numerous gods of ancient Egypt by foremost Egyptologist. Information on evolution of cults, rites and gods; the cult of Osiris; the Book of the Dead and its rites; the sacred animals and birds; Heaven and Hell; and more. 956pp. 6⅛ × 9¼. 22055-9, 22056-7 Pa., Two-vol. set $21.90

A THEOLOGICO-POLITICAL TREATISE, Benedict Spinoza. Also contains unfinished *Political Treatise*. Great classic on religious liberty, theory of government on common consent. R. Elwes translation. Total of 421pp. 5⅜ × 8½. 20249-6 Pa. $6.95

INCIDENTS OF TRAVEL IN CENTRAL AMERICA, CHIAPAS, AND YUCATAN, John L. Stephens. Almost single-handed discovery of Maya culture; exploration of ruined cities, monuments, temples; customs of Indians. 115 drawings. 892pp. 5⅜ × 8½. 22404-X, 22405-8 Pa., Two-vol. set $15.90

LOS CAPRICHOS, Francisco Goya. 80 plates of wild, grotesque monsters and caricatures. Prado manuscript included. 183pp. 6⅝ × 9⅝. 22384-1 Pa. $4.95

AUTOBIOGRAPHY: The Story of My Experiments with Truth, Mohandas K. Gandhi. Not hagiography, but Gandhi in his own words. Boyhood, legal studies, purification, the growth of the Satyagraha (nonviolent protest) movement. Critical, inspiring work of the man who freed India. 480pp. 5⅜ × 8½. (Available in U.S. only) 24593-4 Pa. $6.95

ILLUSTRATED DICTIONARY OF HISTORIC ARCHITECTURE, edited by Cyril M. Harris. Extraordinary compendium of clear, concise definitions for over 5,000 important architectural terms complemented by over 2,000 line drawings. Covers full spectrum of architecture from ancient ruins to 20th-century Modernism. Preface. 592pp. 7½ × 9⅝. 24444-X Pa. $14.95

THE NIGHT BEFORE CHRISTMAS, Clement Moore. Full text, and woodcuts from original 1848 book. Also critical, historical material. 19 illustrations. 40pp. 4⅝ × 6. 22797-9 Pa. $2.50

THE LESSON OF JAPANESE ARCHITECTURE: 165 Photographs, Jiro Harada. Memorable gallery of 165 photographs taken in the 1930's of exquisite Japanese homes of the well-to-do and historic buildings. 13 line diagrams. 192pp. 8⅜ × 11¼. 24778-3 Pa. $8.95

THE AUTOBIOGRAPHY OF CHARLES DARWIN AND SELECTED LETTERS, edited by Francis Darwin. The fascinating life of eccentric genius composed of an intimate memoir by Darwin (intended for his children); commentary by his son, Francis; hundreds of fragments from notebooks, journals, papers; and letters to and from Lyell, Hooker, Huxley, Wallace and Henslow. xi + 365pp. 5⅜ × 8. 20479-0 Pa. $5.95

WONDERS OF THE SKY: Observing Rainbows, Comets, Eclipses, the Stars and Other Phenomena, Fred Schaaf. Charming, easy-to-read poetic guide to all manner of celestial events visible to the naked eye. Mock suns, glories, Belt of Venus, more. Illustrated. 299pp. 5¼ × 8¼. 24402-4 Pa. $7.95

BURNHAM'S CELESTIAL HANDBOOK, Robert Burnham, Jr. Thorough guide to the stars beyond our solar system. Exhaustive treatment. Alphabetical by constellation: Andromeda to Cetus in Vol. 1; Chamaeleon to Orion in Vol. 2; and Pavo to Vulpecula in Vol. 3. Hundreds of illustrations. Index in Vol. 3. 2,000pp. 6⅛ × 9¼. 23567-X, 23568-8, 23673-0 Pa., Three-vol. set $37.85

STAR NAMES: Their Lore and Meaning, Richard Hinckley Allen. Fascinating history of names various cultures have given to constellations and literary and folkloristic uses that have been made of stars. Indexes to subjects. Arabic and Greek names. Biblical references. Bibliography. 563pp. 5⅜ × 8½. 21079-0 Pa. $7.95

THIRTY YEARS THAT SHOOK PHYSICS: The Story of Quantum Theory, George Gamow. Lucid, accessible introduction to influential theory of energy and matter. Careful explanations of Dirac's anti-particles, Bohr's model of the atom, much more. 12 plates. Numerous drawings. 240pp. 5⅜ × 8½. 24895-X Pa. $4.95

CHINESE DOMESTIC FURNITURE IN PHOTOGRAPHS AND MEASURED DRAWINGS, Gustav Ecke. A rare volume, now affordably priced for antique collectors, furniture buffs and art historians. Detailed review of styles ranging from early Shang to late Ming. Unabridged republication. 161 black-and-white drawings, photos. Total of 224pp. 8⅜ × 11¼. (Available in U.S. only) 25171-3 Pa. $12.95

VINCENT VAN GOGH: A Biography, Julius Meier-Graefe. Dynamic, penetrating study of artist's life, relationship with brother, Theo, painting techniques, travels, more. Readable, engrossing. 160pp. 5⅜ × 8½. (Available in U.S. only) 25253-1 Pa. $3.95

HOW TO WRITE, Gertrude Stein. Gertrude Stein claimed anyone could understand her unconventional writing—here are clues to help. Fascinating improvisations, language experiments, explanations illuminate Stein's craft and the art of writing. Total of 414pp. 4⅝ × 6⅜. 23144-5 Pa. $5.95

ADVENTURES AT SEA IN THE GREAT AGE OF SAIL: Five Firsthand Narratives, edited by Elliot Snow. Rare true accounts of exploration, whaling, shipwreck, fierce natives, trade, shipboard life, more. 33 illustrations. Introduction. 353pp. 5⅜ × 8½. 25177-2 Pa. $7.95

THE HERBAL OR GENERAL HISTORY OF PLANTS, John Gerard. Classic descriptions of about 2,850 plants—with over 2,700 illustrations—includes Latin and English names, physical descriptions, varieties, time and place of growth, more. 2,706 illustrations. xlv + 1,678pp. 8½ × 12¼. 23147-X Cloth. $75.00

DOROTHY AND THE WIZARD IN OZ, L. Frank Baum. Dorothy and the Wizard visit the center of the Earth, where people are vegetables, glass houses grow and Oz characters reappear. Classic sequel to *Wizard of Oz*. 256pp. 5⅝ × 8.
24714-7 Pa. $4.95

SONGS OF EXPERIENCE: Facsimile Reproduction with 26 Plates in Full Color, William Blake. This facsimile of Blake's original "Illuminated Book" reproduces 26 full-color plates from a rare 1826 edition. Includes "The Tyger," "London," "Holy Thursday," and other immortal poems. 26 color plates. Printed text of poems. 48pp. 5¼ × 7. 24636-1 Pa. $3.50

SONGS OF INNOCENCE, William Blake. The first and most popular of Blake's famous "Illuminated Books," in a facsimile edition reproducing all 31 brightly colored plates. Additional printed text of each poem. 64pp. 5¼ × 7.
22764-2 Pa. $3.50

PRECIOUS STONES, Max Bauer. Classic, thorough study of diamonds, rubies, emeralds, garnets, etc.: physical character, occurrence, properties, use, similar topics. 20 plates, 8 in color. 94 figures. 659pp. 6⅛ × 9¼.
21910-0, 21911-9 Pa., Two-vol. set $15.90

ENCYCLOPEDIA OF VICTORIAN NEEDLEWORK, S. F. A. Caulfeild and Blanche Saward. Full, precise descriptions of stitches, techniques for dozens of needlecrafts—most exhaustive reference of its kind. Over 800 figures. Total of 679pp. 8⅛ × 11. Two volumes. Vol. 1 22800-2 Pa. $11.95
Vol. 2 22801-0 Pa. $11.95

THE MARVELOUS LAND OF OZ, L. Frank Baum. Second Oz book, the Scarecrow and Tin Woodman are back with hero named Tip, Oz magic. 136 illustrations. 287pp. 5⅝ × 8½. 20692-0 Pa. $5.95

WILD FOWL DECOYS, Joel Barber. Basic book on the subject, by foremost authority and collector. Reveals history of decoy making and rigging, place in American culture, different kinds of decoys, how to make them, and how to use them. 140 plates. 156pp. 7⅞ × 10¾. 20011-6 Pa. $8.95

HISTORY OF LACE, Mrs. Bury Palliser. Definitive, profusely illustrated chronicle of lace from earliest times to late 19th century. Laces of Italy, Greece, England, France, Belgium, etc. Landmark of needlework scholarship. 266 illustrations. 672pp. 6⅛ × 9¼. 24742-2 Pa. $14.95

ILLUSTRATED GUIDE TO SHAKER FURNITURE, Robert Meader. All furniture and appurtenances, with much on unknown local styles. 235 photos. 146pp. 9 × 12. 22819-3 Pa. $7.95

WHALE SHIPS AND WHALING: A Pictorial Survey, George Francis Dow. Over 200 vintage engravings, drawings, photographs of barks, brigs, cutters, other vessels. Also harpoons, lances, whaling guns, many other artifacts. Comprehensive text by foremost authority. 207 black-and-white illustrations. 288pp. 6 × 9. 24808-9 Pa. $8.95

THE BERTRAMS, Anthony Trollope. Powerful portrayal of blind self-will and thwarted ambition includes one of Trollope's most heartrending love stories. 497pp. 5⅜ × 8½. 25119-5 Pa. $8.95

ADVENTURES WITH A HAND LENS, Richard Headstrom. Clearly written guide to observing and studying flowers and grasses, fish scales, moth and insect wings, egg cases, buds, feathers, seeds, leaf scars, moss, molds, ferns, common crystals, etc.—all with an ordinary, inexpensive magnifying glass. 209 exact line drawings aid in your discoveries. 220pp. 5⅜ × 8½. 23330-8 Pa. $4.50

RODIN ON ART AND ARTISTS, Auguste Rodin. Great sculptor's candid, wide-ranging comments on meaning of art; great artists; relation of sculpture to poetry, painting, music; philosophy of life, more. 76 superb black-and-white illustrations of Rodin's sculpture, drawings and prints. 119pp. 8⅜ × 11¼. 24487-3 Pa. $6.95

FIFTY CLASSIC FRENCH FILMS, 1912–1982: A Pictorial Record, Anthony Slide. Memorable stills from Grand Illusion, Beauty and the Beast, Hiroshima, Mon Amour, many more. Credits, plot synopses, reviews, etc. 160pp. 8¼ × 11. 25256-6 Pa. $11.95

THE PRINCIPLES OF PSYCHOLOGY, William James. Famous long course complete, unabridged. Stream of thought, time perception, memory, experimental methods; great work decades ahead of its time. 94 figures. 1,391pp. 5⅜ × 8½. 20381-6, 20382-4 Pa., Two-vol. set $19.90

BODIES IN A BOOKSHOP, R. T. Campbell. Challenging mystery of blackmail and murder with ingenious plot and superbly drawn characters. In the best tradition of British suspense fiction. 192pp. 5⅜ × 8½. 24720-1 Pa. $3.95

CALLAS: PORTRAIT OF A PRIMA DONNA, George Jellinek. Renowned commentator on the musical scene chronicles incredible career and life of the most controversial, fascinating, influential operatic personality of our time. 64 black-and-white photographs. 416pp. 5⅜ × 8¼. 25047-4 Pa. $7.95

GEOMETRY, RELATIVITY AND THE FOURTH DIMENSION, Rudolph Rucker. Exposition of fourth dimension, concepts of relativity as Flatland characters continue adventures. Popular, easily followed yet accurate, profound. 141 illustrations. 133pp. 5⅜ × 8½. 23400-2 Pa. $3.50

HOUSEHOLD STORIES BY THE BROTHERS GRIMM, with pictures by Walter Crane. 53 classic stories—Rumpelstiltskin, Rapunzel, Hansel and Gretel, the Fisherman and his Wife, Snow White, Tom Thumb, Sleeping Beauty, Cinderella, and so much more—lavishly illustrated with original 19th century drawings. 114 illustrations. x + 269pp. 5⅜ × 8½. 21080-4 Pa. $4.50

SUNDIALS, Albert Waugh. Far and away the best, most thorough coverage of ideas, mathematics concerned, types, construction, adjusting anywhere. Over 100 illustrations. 230pp. 5⅜ × 8½. 22947-5 Pa. $4.50

PICTURE HISTORY OF THE NORMANDIE: With 190 Illustrations, Frank O. Braynard. Full story of legendary French ocean liner: Art Deco interiors, design innovations, furnishings, celebrities, maiden voyage, tragic fire, much more. Extensive text. 144pp. 8⅞ × 11¾. 25257-4 Pa. $9.95

THE FIRST AMERICAN COOKBOOK: A Facsimile of "American Cookery," 1796, Amelia Simmons. Facsimile of the first American-written cookbook published in the United States contains authentic recipes for colonial favorites— pumpkin pudding, winter squash pudding, spruce beer, Indian slapjacks, and more. Introductory Essay and Glossary of colonial cooking terms. 80pp. 5⅜ × 8½. 24710-4 Pa. $3.50

101 PUZZLES IN THOUGHT AND LOGIC, C. R. Wylie, Jr. Solve murders and robberies, find out which fishermen are liars, how a blind man could possibly identify a color—purely by your own reasoning! 107pp. 5⅜ × 8½. 20367-0 Pa. $2.50

THE BOOK OF WORLD-FAMOUS MUSIC—CLASSICAL, POPULAR AND FOLK, James J. Fuld. Revised and enlarged republication of landmark work in musico-bibliography. Full information about nearly 1,000 songs and compositions including first lines of music and lyrics. New supplement. Index. 800pp. 5⅜ × 8¼. 24857-7 Pa. $14.95

ANTHROPOLOGY AND MODERN LIFE, Franz Boas. Great anthropologist's classic treatise on race and culture. Introduction by Ruth Bunzel. Only inexpensive paperback edition. 255pp. 5⅜ × 8½. 25245-0 Pa. $5.95

THE TALE OF PETER RABBIT, Beatrix Potter. The inimitable Peter's terrifying adventure in Mr. McGregor's garden, with all 27 wonderful, full-color Potter illustrations. 55pp. 4¼ × 5½. (Available in U.S. only) 22827-4 Pa. $1.75

THREE PROPHETIC SCIENCE FICTION NOVELS, H. G. Wells. *When the Sleeper Wakes, A Story of the Days to Come* and *The Time Machine* (full version). 335pp. 5⅜ × 8½. (Available in U.S. only) 20605-X Pa. $5.95

APICIUS COOKERY AND DINING IN IMPERIAL ROME, edited and translated by Joseph Dommers Vehling. Oldest known cookbook in existence offers readers a clear picture of what foods Romans ate, how they prepared them, etc. 49 illustrations. 301pp. 6⅛ × 9¼. 23563-7 Pa. $6.50

SHAKESPEARE LEXICON AND QUOTATION DICTIONARY, Alexander Schmidt. Full definitions, locations, shades of meaning of every word in plays and poems. More than 50,000 exact quotations. 1,485pp. 6½ × 9¼. 22726-X, 22727-8 Pa., Two-vol. set $27.90

THE WORLD'S GREAT SPEECHES, edited by Lewis Copeland and Lawrence W. Lamm. Vast collection of 278 speeches from Greeks to 1970. Powerful and effective models; unique look at history. 842pp. 5⅜ × 8½. 20468-5 Pa. $11.95

THE BLUE FAIRY BOOK, Andrew Lang. The first, most famous collection, with many familiar tales: Little Red Riding Hood, Aladdin and the Wonderful Lamp, Puss in Boots, Sleeping Beauty, Hansel and Gretel, Rumpelstiltskin; 37 in all. 138 illustrations. 390pp. 5⅜ × 8½.   21437-0 Pa. $5.95

THE STORY OF THE CHAMPIONS OF THE ROUND TABLE, Howard Pyle. Sir Launcelot, Sir Tristram and Sir Percival in spirited adventures of love and triumph retold in Pyle's inimitable style. 50 drawings, 31 full-page. xviii + 329pp. 6½ × 9¼.   21883-X Pa. $6.95

AUDUBON AND HIS JOURNALS, Maria Audubon. Unmatched two-volume portrait of the great artist, naturalist and author contains his journals, an excellent biography by his granddaughter, expert annotations by the noted ornithologist, Dr. Elliott Coues, and 37 superb illustrations. Total of 1,200pp. 5⅜ × 8.
Vol. I 25143-8 Pa. $8.95
Vol. II 25144-6 Pa. $8.95

GREAT DINOSAUR HUNTERS AND THEIR DISCOVERIES, Edwin H. Colbert. Fascinating, lavishly illustrated chronicle of dinosaur research, 1820's to 1960. Achievements of Cope, Marsh, Brown, Buckland, Mantell, Huxley, many others. 384pp. 5¼ × 8¼.   24701-5 Pa. $6.95

THE TASTEMAKERS, Russell Lynes. Informal, illustrated social history of American taste 1850's-1950's. First popularized categories Highbrow, Lowbrow, Middlebrow. 129 illustrations. New (1979) afterword. 384pp. 6 × 9.
23993-4 Pa. $6.95

DOUBLE CROSS PURPOSES, Ronald A. Knox. A treasure hunt in the Scottish Highlands, an old map, unidentified corpse, surprise discoveries keep reader guessing in this cleverly intricate tale of financial skullduggery. 2 black-and-white maps. 320pp. 5⅜ × 8½. (Available in U.S. only)   25032-6 Pa. $5.95

AUTHENTIC VICTORIAN DECORATION AND ORNAMENTATION IN FULL COLOR: 46 Plates from "Studies in Design," Christopher Dresser. Superb full-color lithographs reproduced from rare original portfolio of a major Victorian designer. 48pp. 9¼ × 12¼.   25083-0 Pa. $7.95

PRIMITIVE ART, Franz Boas. Remains the best text ever prepared on subject, thoroughly discussing Indian, African, Asian, Australian, and, especially, Northern American primitive art. Over 950 illustrations show ceramics, masks, totem poles, weapons, textiles, paintings, much more. 376pp. 5⅜ × 8.   20025-6 Pa. $6.95

SIDELIGHTS ON RELATIVITY, Albert Einstein. Unabridged republication of two lectures delivered by the great physicist in 1920-21. *Ether and Relativity* and *Geometry and Experience*. Elegant ideas in non-mathematical form, accessible to intelligent layman. vi + 56pp. 5⅜ × 8½.   24511-X Pa. $2.95

THE WIT AND HUMOR OF OSCAR WILDE, edited by Alvin Redman. More than 1,000 ripostes, paradoxes, wisecracks: Work is the curse of the drinking classes, I can resist everything except temptation, etc. 258pp. 5⅜ × 8½.   20602-5 Pa. $4.50

ADVENTURES WITH A MICROSCOPE, Richard Headstrom. 59 adventures with clothing fibers, protozoa, ferns and lichens, roots and leaves, much more. 142 illustrations. 232pp. 5⅜ × 8½.   23471-1 Pa. $3.95

PLANTS OF THE BIBLE, Harold N. Moldenke and Alma L. Moldenke. Standard reference to all 230 plants mentioned in Scriptures. Latin name, biblical reference, uses, modern identity, much more. Unsurpassed encyclopedic resource for scholars, botanists, nature lovers, students of Bible. Bibliography. Indexes. 123 black-and-white illustrations. 384pp. 6 × 9. 25069-5 Pa. $8.95

FAMOUS AMERICAN WOMEN: A Biographical Dictionary from Colonial Times to the Present, Robert McHenry, ed. From Pocahontas to Rosa Parks, 1,035 distinguished American women documented in separate biographical entries. Accurate, up-to-date data, numerous categories, spans 400 years. Indices. 493pp. 6½ × 9¼. 24523-3 Pa. $9.95

THE FABULOUS INTERIORS OF THE GREAT OCEAN LINERS IN HISTORIC PHOTOGRAPHS, William H. Miller, Jr. Some 200 superb photographs capture exquisite interiors of world's great "floating palaces"—1890's to 1980's: *Titanic, Ile de France, Queen Elizabeth, United States, Europa,* more. Approx. 200 black-and-white photographs. Captions. Text. Introduction. 160pp. 8⅞ × 11¾. 24756-2 Pa. $9.95

THE GREAT LUXURY LINERS, 1927–1954: A Photographic Record, William H. Miller, Jr. Nostalgic tribute to heyday of ocean liners. 186 photos of Ile de France, Normandie, Leviathan, Queen Elizabeth, United States, many others. Interior and exterior views. Introduction. Captions. 160pp. 9 × 12. 24056-8 Pa. $9.95

A NATURAL HISTORY OF THE DUCKS, John Charles Phillips. Great landmark of ornithology offers complete detailed coverage of nearly 200 species and subspecies of ducks: gadwall, sheldrake, merganser, pintail, many more. 74 full-color plates, 102 black-and-white. Bibliography. Total of 1,920pp. 8⅝ × 11¼. 25141-1, 25142-X Cloth. Two-vol. set $100.00

THE SEAWEED HANDBOOK: An Illustrated Guide to Seaweeds from North Carolina to Canada, Thomas F. Lee. Concise reference covers 78 species. Scientific and common names, habitat, distribution, more. Finding keys for easy identification. 224pp. 5⅜ × 8½. 25215-9 Pa. $5.95

THE TEN BOOKS OF ARCHITECTURE: The 1755 Leoni Edition, Leon Battista Alberti. Rare classic helped introduce the glories of ancient architecture to the Renaissance. 68 black-and-white plates. 336pp. 8⅜ × 11¼. 25239-6 Pa. $14.95

MISS MACKENZIE, Anthony Trollope. Minor masterpieces by Victorian master unmasks many truths about life in 19th-century England. First inexpensive edition in years. 392pp. 5⅜ × 8½. 25201-9 Pa. $7.95

THE RIME OF THE ANCIENT MARINER, Gustave Doré, Samuel Taylor Coleridge. Dramatic engravings considered by many to be his greatest work. The terrifying space of the open sea, the storms and whirlpools of an unknown ocean, the ice of Antarctica, more—all rendered in a powerful, chilling manner. Full text. 38 plates. 77pp. 9¼ × 12. 22305-1 Pa. $4.95

THE EXPEDITIONS OF ZEBULON MONTGOMERY PIKE, Zebulon Montgomery Pike. Fascinating first-hand accounts (1805–6) of exploration of Mississippi River, Indian wars, capture by Spanish dragoons, much more. 1,088pp. 5⅜ × 8½. 25254-X, 25255-8 Pa. Two-vol. set $23.90

A CONCISE HISTORY OF PHOTOGRAPHY: Third Revised Edition, Helmut Gernsheim. Best one-volume history—camera obscura, photochemistry, daguerreotypes, evolution of cameras, film, more. Also artistic aspects—landscape, portraits, fine art, etc. 281 black-and-white photographs. 26 in color. 176pp. 8⅜ × 11¼. 25128-4 Pa. $12.95

THE DORÉ BIBLE ILLUSTRATIONS, Gustave Doré. 241 detailed plates from the Bible: the Creation scenes, Adam and Eve, Flood, Babylon, battle sequences, life of Jesus, etc. Each plate is accompanied by the verses from the King James version of the Bible. 241pp. 9 × 12. 23004-X Pa. $8.95

HUGGER-MUGGER IN THE LOUVRE, Elliot Paul. Second Homer Evans mystery-comedy. Theft at the Louvre involves sleuth in hilarious, madcap caper. "A knockout."—Books. 336pp. 5⅜ × 8½. 25185-3 Pa. $5.95

FLATLAND, E. A. Abbott. Intriguing and enormously popular science-fiction classic explores the complexities of trying to survive as a two-dimensional being in a three-dimensional world. Amusingly illustrated by the author. 16 illustrations. 103pp. 5⅜ × 8½. 20001-9 Pa. $2.25

THE HISTORY OF THE LEWIS AND CLARK EXPEDITION, Meriwether Lewis and William Clark, edited by Elliott Coues. Classic edition of Lewis and Clark's day-by-day journals that later became the basis for U.S. claims to Oregon and the West. Accurate and invaluable geographical, botanical, biological, meteorological and anthropological material. Total of 1,508pp. 5⅜ × 8½. 21268-8, 21269-6, 21270-X Pa. Three-vol. set $25.50

LANGUAGE, TRUTH AND LOGIC, Alfred J. Ayer. Famous, clear introduction to Vienna, Cambridge schools of Logical Positivism. Role of philosophy, elimination of metaphysics, nature of analysis, etc. 160pp. 5⅜ × 8½. (Available in U.S. and Canada only) 20010-8 Pa. $2.95

MATHEMATICS FOR THE NONMATHEMATICIAN, Morris Kline. Detailed, college-level treatment of mathematics in cultural and historical context, with numerous exercises. For liberal arts students. Preface. Recommended Reading Lists. Tables. Index. Numerous black-and-white figures. xvi + 641pp. 5⅜ × 8½. 24823-2 Pa. $11.95

28 SCIENCE FICTION STORIES, H. G. Wells. Novels, *Star Begotten* and *Men Like Gods,* plus 26 short stories: "Empire of the Ants," "A Story of the Stone Age," "The Stolen Bacillus," "In the Abyss," etc. 915pp. 5⅜ × 8½. (Available in U.S. only) 20265-8 Cloth. $10.95

HANDBOOK OF PICTORIAL SYMBOLS, Rudolph Modley. 3,250 signs and symbols, many systems in full; official or heavy commercial use. Arranged by subject. Most in Pictorial Archive series. 143pp. 8⅛ × 11. 23357-X Pa. $5.95

INCIDENTS OF TRAVEL IN YUCATAN, John L. Stephens. Classic (1843) exploration of jungles of Yucatan, looking for evidences of Maya civilization. Travel adventures, Mexican and Indian culture, etc. Total of 669pp. 5⅜ × 8½. 20926-1, 20927-X Pa., Two-vol. set $9.90

DEGAS: An Intimate Portrait, Ambroise Vollard. Charming, anecdotal memoir by famous art dealer of one of the greatest 19th-century French painters. 14 black-and-white illustrations. Introduction by Harold L. Van Doren. 96pp. 5⅜ × 8½.
25131-4 Pa. $3.95

PERSONAL NARRATIVE OF A PILGRIMAGE TO ALMANDINAH AND MECCAH, Richard Burton. Great travel classic by remarkably colorful personality. Burton, disguised as a Moroccan, visited sacred shrines of Islam, narrowly escaping death. 47 illustrations. 959pp. 5⅜ × 8½. 21217-3, 21218-1 Pa., Two-vol. set $17.90

PHRASE AND WORD ORIGINS, A. H. Holt. Entertaining, reliable, modern study of more than 1,200 colorful words, phrases, origins and histories. Much unexpected information. 254pp. 5⅜ × 8½. 20758-7 Pa. $5.95

THE RED THUMB MARK, R. Austin Freeman. In this first Dr. Thorndyke case, the great scientific detective draws fascinating conclusions from the nature of a single fingerprint. Exciting story, authentic science. 320pp. 5⅜ × 8½. (Available in U.S. only) 25210-8 Pa. $5.95

AN EGYPTIAN HIEROGLYPHIC DICTIONARY, E. A. Wallis Budge. Monumental work containing about 25,000 words or terms that occur in texts ranging from 3000 B.C. to 600 A.D. Each entry consists of a transliteration of the word, the word in hieroglyphs, and the meaning in English. 1,314pp. 6⅞ × 10.
23615-3, 23616-1 Pa., Two-vol. set $27.90

THE COMPLEAT STRATEGYST: Being a Primer on the Theory of Games of Strategy, J. D. Williams. Highly entertaining classic describes, with many illustrated examples, how to select best strategies in conflict situations. Prefaces. Appendices. xvi + 268pp. 5⅜ × 8½. 25101-2 Pa. $5.95

THE ROAD TO OZ, L. Frank Baum. Dorothy meets the Shaggy Man, little Button-Bright and the Rainbow's beautiful daughter in this delightful trip to the magical Land of Oz. 272pp. 5⅜ × 8. 25208-6 Pa. $4.95

POINT AND LINE TO PLANE, Wassily Kandinsky. Seminal exposition of role of point, line, other elements in non-objective painting. Essential to understanding 20th-century art. 127 illustrations. 192pp. 6½ × 9¼. 23808-3 Pa. $4.50

LADY ANNA, Anthony Trollope. Moving chronicle of Countess Lovel's bitter struggle to win for herself and daughter Anna their rightful rank and fortune—perhaps at cost of sanity itself. 384pp. 5⅜ × 8½. 24669-8 Pa. $6.95

EGYPTIAN MAGIC, E. A. Wallis Budge. Sums up all that is known about magic in Ancient Egypt: the role of magic in controlling the gods, powerful amulets that warded off evil spirits, scarabs of immortality, use of wax images, formulas and spells, the secret name, much more. 253pp. 5⅜ × 8½. 22681-6 Pa. $4.50

THE DANCE OF SIVA, Ananda Coomaraswamy. Preeminent authority unfolds the vast metaphysic of India: the revelation of her art, conception of the universe, social organization, etc. 27 reproductions of art masterpieces. 192pp. 5⅜ × 8½.
24817-8 Pa. $5.95

CHRISTMAS CUSTOMS AND TRADITIONS, Clement A. Miles. Origin, evolution, significance of religious, secular practices. Caroling, gifts, yule logs, much more. Full, scholarly yet fascinating; non-sectarian. 400pp. 5⅜ × 8½.
23354-5 Pa. $6.50

THE HUMAN FIGURE IN MOTION, Eadweard Muybridge. More than 4,500 stopped-action photos, in action series, showing undraped men, women, children jumping, lying down, throwing, sitting, wrestling, carrying, etc. 390pp. 7⅞ × 10⅝.
20204-6 Cloth. $19.95

THE MAN WHO WAS THURSDAY, Gilbert Keith Chesterton. Witty, fast-paced novel about a club of anarchists in turn-of-the-century London. Brilliant social, religious, philosophical speculations. 128pp. 5⅜ × 8½.
25121-7 Pa. $3.95

A CEZANNE SKETCHBOOK: Figures, Portraits, Landscapes and Still Lifes, Paul Cezanne. Great artist experiments with tonal effects, light, mass, other qualities in over 100 drawings. A revealing view of developing master painter, precursor of Cubism. 102 black-and-white illustrations. 144pp. 8¾ × 6⅝.
24790-2 Pa. $5.95

AN ENCYCLOPEDIA OF BATTLES: Accounts of Over 1,560 Battles from 1479 B.C. to the Present, David Eggenberger. Presents essential details of every major battle in recorded history, from the first battle of Megiddo in 1479 B.C. to Grenada in 1984. List of Battle Maps. New Appendix covering the years 1967–1984. Index. 99 illustrations. 544pp. 6½ × 9¼.
24913-1 Pa. $14.95

AN ETYMOLOGICAL DICTIONARY OF MODERN ENGLISH, Ernest Weekley. Richest, fullest work, by foremost British lexicographer. Detailed word histories. Inexhaustible. Total of 856pp. 6½ × 9¼.
21873-2, 21874-0 Pa., Two-vol. set $17.00

WEBSTER'S AMERICAN MILITARY BIOGRAPHIES, edited by Robert McHenry. Over 1,000 figures who shaped 3 centuries of American military history. Detailed biographies of Nathan Hale, Douglas MacArthur, Mary Hallaren, others. Chronologies of engagements, more. Introduction. Addenda. 1,033 entries in alphabetical order. xi + 548pp. 6½ × 9¼. (Available in U.S. only)
24758-9 Pa. $11.95

LIFE IN ANCIENT EGYPT, Adolf Erman. Detailed older account, with much not in more recent books: domestic life, religion, magic, medicine, commerce, and whatever else needed for complete picture. Many illustrations. 597pp. 5⅜ × 8½.
22632-8 Pa. $8.95

HISTORIC COSTUME IN PICTURES, Braun & Schneider. Over 1,450 costumed figures shown, covering a wide variety of peoples: kings, emperors, nobles, priests, servants, soldiers, scholars, townsfolk, peasants, merchants, courtiers, cavaliers, and more. 256pp. 8⅜ × 11¼.
23150-X Pa. $7.95

THE NOTEBOOKS OF LEONARDO DA VINCI, edited by J. P. Richter. Extracts from manuscripts reveal great genius; on painting, sculpture, anatomy, sciences, geography, etc. Both Italian and English. 186 ms. pages reproduced, plus 500 additional drawings, including studies for *Last Supper, Sforza* monument, etc. 860pp. 7⅞ × 10⅝. (Available in U.S. only) 22572-0, 22573-9 Pa., Two-vol. set $25.90

THE ART NOUVEAU STYLE BOOK OF ALPHONSE MUCHA: All 72 Plates from "Documents Decoratifs" in Original Color, Alphonse Mucha. Rare copyright-free design portfolio by high priest of Art Nouveau. Jewelry, wallpaper, stained glass, furniture, figure studies, plant and animal motifs, etc. Only complete one-volume edition. 80pp. 9⅜ × 12¼. 24044-4 Pa. $8.95

ANIMALS: 1,419 COPYRIGHT-FREE ILLUSTRATIONS OF MAMMALS, BIRDS, FISH, INSECTS, ETC., edited by Jim Harter. Clear wood engravings present, in extremely lifelike poses, over 1,000 species of animals. One of the most extensive pictorial sourcebooks of its kind. Captions. Index. 284pp. 9 × 12. 23766-4 Pa. $9.95

OBELISTS FLY HIGH, C. Daly King. Masterpiece of American detective fiction, long out of print, involves murder on a 1935 transcontinental flight—"a very thrilling story"—NY Times. Unabridged and unaltered republication of the edition published by William Collins Sons & Co. Ltd., London, 1935. 288pp. 5⅜ × 8½. (Available in U.S. only) 25036-9 Pa. $4.95

VICTORIAN AND EDWARDIAN FASHION: A Photographic Survey, Alison Gernsheim. First fashion history completely illustrated by contemporary photographs. Full text plus 235 photos, 1840–1914, in which many celebrities appear. 240pp. 6½ × 9¼. 24205-6 Pa. $6.00

THE ART OF THE FRENCH ILLUSTRATED BOOK, 1700–1914, Gordon N. Ray. Over 630 superb book illustrations by Fragonard, Delacroix, Daumier, Doré, Grandville, Manet, Mucha, Steinlen, Toulouse-Lautrec and many others. Preface. Introduction. 633 halftones. Indices of artists, authors & titles, binders and provenances. Appendices. Bibliography. 608pp. 8⅜ × 11¼. 25086-5 Pa. $24.95

THE WONDERFUL WIZARD OF OZ, L. Frank Baum. Facsimile in full color of America's finest children's classic. 143 illustrations by W. W. Denslow. 267pp. 5⅜ × 8½. 20691-2 Pa. $5.95

FRONTIERS OF MODERN PHYSICS: New Perspectives on Cosmology, Relativity, Black Holes and Extraterrestrial Intelligence, Tony Rothman, et al. For the intelligent layman. Subjects include: cosmological models of the universe; black holes; the neutrino; the search for extraterrestrial intelligence. Introduction. 46 black-and-white illustrations. 192pp. 5⅜ × 8½. 24587-X Pa. $6.95

THE FRIENDLY STARS, Martha Evans Martin & Donald Howard Menzel. Classic text marshalls the stars together in an engaging, non-technical survey, presenting them as sources of beauty in night sky. 23 illustrations. Foreword. 2 star charts. Index. 147pp. 5⅜ × 8½. 21099-5 Pa. $3.50

FADS AND FALLACIES IN THE NAME OF SCIENCE, Martin Gardner. Fair, witty appraisal of cranks, quacks, and quackeries of science and pseudoscience: hollow earth, Velikovsky, orgone energy, Dianetics, flying saucers, Bridey Murphy, food and medical fads, etc. Revised, expanded In the Name of Science. "A very able and even-tempered presentation."—The New Yorker. 363pp. 5⅜ × 8. 20394-8 Pa. $6.50

ANCIENT EGYPT: ITS CULTURE AND HISTORY, J. E Manchip White. From pre-dynastics through Ptolemies: society, history, political structure, religion, daily life, literature, cultural heritage. 48 plates. 217pp. 5⅜ × 8½. 22548-8 Pa. $4.95

SIR HARRY HOTSPUR OF HUMBLETHWAITE, Anthony Trollope. Incisive, unconventional psychological study of a conflict between a wealthy baronet, his idealistic daughter, and their scapegrace cousin. The 1870 novel in its first inexpensive edition in years. 250pp. 5⅜ × 8½. 24953-0 Pa. $5.95

LASERS AND HOLOGRAPHY, Winston E. Kock. Sound introduction to burgeoning field, expanded (1981) for second edition. Wave patterns, coherence, lasers, diffraction, zone plates, properties of holograms, recent advances. 84 illustrations. 160pp. 5⅜ × 8¼. (Except in United Kingdom) 24041-X Pa. $3.50

INTRODUCTION TO ARTIFICIAL INTELLIGENCE: SECOND, EN-LARGED EDITION, Philip C. Jackson, Jr. Comprehensive survey of artificial intelligence—the study of how machines (computers) can be made to act intelligently. Includes introductory and advanced material. Extensive notes updating the main text. 132 black-and-white illustrations. 512pp. 5⅜ × 8½. 24864-X Pa. $8.95

HISTORY OF INDIAN AND INDONESIAN ART, Ananda K. Coomaraswamy. Over 400 illustrations illuminate classic study of Indian art from earliest Harappa finds to early 20th century. Provides philosophical, religious and social insights. 304pp. 6⅜ × 9⅜. 25005-9 Pa. $8.95

THE GOLEM, Gustav Meyrink. Most famous supernatural novel in modern European literature, set in Ghetto of Old Prague around 1890. Compelling story of mystical experiences, strange transformations, profound terror. 13 black-and-white illustrations. 224pp. 5⅜ × 8½. (Available in U.S. only) 25025-3 Pa. $5.95

ARMADALE, Wilkie Collins. Third great mystery novel by the author of *The Woman in White* and *The Moonstone*. Original magazine version with 40 illustrations. 597pp. 5⅜ × 8½. 23429-0 Pa. $9.95

PICTORIAL ENCYCLOPEDIA OF HISTORIC ARCHITECTURAL PLANS, DETAILS AND ELEMENTS: With 1,880 Line Drawings of Arches, Domes, Doorways, Facades, Gables, Windows, etc., John Theodore Haneman. Sourcebook of inspiration for architects, designers, others. Bibliography. Captions. 141pp. 9 × 12. 24605-1 Pa. $6.95

BENCHLEY LOST AND FOUND, Robert Benchley. Finest humor from early 30's, about pet peeves, child psychologists, post office and others. Mostly unavailable elsewhere. 73 illustrations by Peter Arno and others. 183pp. 5⅜ × 8½. 22410-4 Pa. $3.95

ERTÉ GRAPHICS, Erté. Collection of striking color graphics: *Seasons, Alphabet, Numerals, Aces* and *Precious Stones*. 50 plates, including 4 on covers. 48pp. 9⅜ × 12¼. 23580-7 Pa. $6.95

THE JOURNAL OF HENRY D. THOREAU, edited by Bradford Torrey, F. H. Allen. Complete reprinting of 14 volumes, 1837–61, over two million words; the sourcebooks for *Walden*, etc. Definitive. All original sketches, plus 75 photographs. 1,804pp. 8½ × 12¼. 20312-3, 20313-1 Cloth., Two-vol. set $80.00

CASTLES: THEIR CONSTRUCTION AND HISTORY, Sidney Toy. Traces castle development from ancient roots. Nearly 200 photographs and drawings illustrate moats, keeps, baileys, many other features. Caernarvon, Dover Castles, Hadrian's Wall, Tower of London, dozens more. 256pp. 5⅜ × 8¼. 24898-4 Pa. $5.95

CATALOG OF DOVER BOOKS

AMERICAN CLIPPER SHIPS: 1833–1858, Octavius T. Howe & Frederick C. Matthews. Fully-illustrated, encyclopedic review of 352 clipper ships from the period of America's greatest maritime supremacy. Introduction. 109 halftones. 5 black-and-white line illustrations. Index. Total of 928pp. 5⅜ × 8½.
25115-2, 25116-0 Pa., Two-vol. set $17.90

TOWARDS A NEW ARCHITECTURE, Le Corbusier. Pioneering manifesto by great architect, near legendary founder of "International School." Technical and aesthetic theories, views on industry, economics, relation of form to function, "mass-production spirit," much more. Profusely illustrated. Unabridged translation of 13th French edition. Introduction by Frederick Etchells. 320pp. 6⅛ × 9¼. (Available in U.S. only)
25023-7 Pa. $8.95

THE BOOK OF KELLS, edited by Blanche Cirker. Inexpensive collection of 32 full-color, full-page plates from the greatest illuminated manuscript of the Middle Ages, painstakingly reproduced from rare facsimile edition. Publisher's Note. Captions. 32pp. 9⅜ × 12¼.
24345-1 Pa. $4.95

BEST SCIENCE FICTION STORIES OF H. G. WELLS, H. G. Wells. Full novel *The Invisible Man,* plus 17 short stories: "The Crystal Egg," "Aepyornis Island," "The Strange Orchid," etc. 303pp. 5⅜ × 8½. (Available in U.S. only)
21531-8 Pa. $4.95

AMERICAN SAILING SHIPS: Their Plans and History, Charles G. Davis. Photos, construction details of schooners, frigates, clippers, other sailcraft of 18th to early 20th centuries—plus entertaining discourse on design, rigging, nautical lore, much more. 137 black-and-white illustrations. 240pp. 6⅛ × 9¼.
24658-2 Pa. $5.95

ENTERTAINING MATHEMATICAL PUZZLES, Martin Gardner. Selection of author's favorite conundrums involving arithmetic, money, speed, etc., with lively commentary. Complete solutions. 112pp. 5⅜ × 8½.
25211-6 Pa. $2.95

THE WILL TO BELIEVE, HUMAN IMMORTALITY, William James. Two books bound together. Effect of irrational on logical, and arguments for human immortality. 402pp. 5⅜ × 8½.
20291-7 Pa. $7.50

THE HAUNTED MONASTERY and THE CHINESE MAZE MURDERS, Robert Van Gulik. 2 full novels by Van Gulik continue adventures of Judge Dee and his companions. An evil Taoist monastery, seemingly supernatural events; overgrown topiary maze that hides strange crimes. Set in 7th-century China. 27 illustrations. 328pp. 5⅜ × 8½.
23502-5 Pa. $5.95

CELEBRATED CASES OF JUDGE DEE (DEE GOONG AN), translated by Robert Van Gulik. Authentic 18th-century Chinese detective novel; Dee and associates solve three interlocked cases. Led to Van Gulik's own stories with same characters. Extensive introduction. 9 illustrations. 237pp. 5⅜ × 8½.
23337-5 Pa. $4.95

Prices subject to change without notice.

Available at your book dealer or write for free catalog to Dept. GI, Dover Publications, Inc., 31 East 2nd St., Mineola, N.Y. 11501. Dover publishes more than 175 books each year on science, elementary and advanced mathematics, biology, music, art, literary history, social sciences and other areas.